This book is to be returned on
or before the date stamped below

COPING WITH HOMELESSNESS: ISSUES TO BE TACKLED AND BEST PRACTICES IN EUROPE

Coping with Homelessness: Issues to be Tackled and Best Practices in Europe

Edited by
DRAGANA AVRAMOV

Ashgate

Aldershot • Brookfield USA • Singapore • Sydney

Published by
Ashgate Publishing Ltd
Gower House
Croft Road
Aldershot
Hants GU11 3HR
England

Ashgate Publishing Company
Old Post Road
Brookfield
Vermont 05036
USA

British Library Cataloguing in Publication Data
Coping with homelessness : issues to be tackled and best
    practices in Europe
    1. Homelessness - Europe 2. Homelessness - Law and
    legislation - Europe 3. Homeless persons - Services for -
    Europe
    I. Avramov, Dragana
    362.5'5'094

Library of Congress Cataloging-in-Publication Data
Coping with homelessness : issues to be tackled and best practices in
    Europe / edited by Dragana Avramov.
        p.   cm.
        "FEANTSA--ICCR--SFI--DST--STAKES--KIVOTOS."
        ISBN 1-84014-909-4 (hb)
        1. Homelessness--Europe. 2. Homelessness--Government policy-
    -Europe. 3. Homeless persons--Services for--Europe. I. Avramov,
    D. (Dragana) II. FEANTSA (Organization)
    HV4544.A4C66 1999
    362.5'8'094--dc21
                                                                98-46597
                                                                CIP

ISBN 1 84014 909 4

Printed in Great Britain by Galliards, Great Yarmouth

Contents

PART 2: THE RESEARCH OF HOMELESSNESS: DATA AND METHODOLOGY   143

List of Figures

List of Tables

Foreword

To enrich the experience of those who are working everyday to tackle homelessness, and to support the analysis of decision-makers, by means of academic research on a European scale. This was the ambition of FEANTSA – the European Federation of National Organisations Working with the Homeless – in proposing the EUROHOME research project to the European Commission (DG XII – Science, Research and Development) in 1995 as part of the important Targeted Socio-Economic Research (TSER) Programme.

FEANTSA was able to draw upon the experience gained since 1991 through its work in running the European Observatory on Homelessness, which each year produces 15 national reports and one transnational report, with the participation of a network of research institutes across the 15 Member States and the valuable support of the European Commission (DG V – Employment and Social Affairs). A group of five research institutes, already involved in the work of the Observatory, were brought together by FEANTSA to form the 'EUROHOME' partnership: the Interdisciplinary Centre for Comparative Research in Social Sciences (ICCR) in Austria; the Danish National Institute of Social Research (SFI); the Department of Territorial Studies (DST) at Milan Polytechnic in Italy; the National Research and Development Centre for Welfare and Health (STAKES) in Finland; and the Kivotos Scientific Research Institute in Greece. Dr. Dragana Avramov – who was then Coordinator of the Observatory – was asked to supervise the scientific content of the EUROHOME project.

This publication – *Coping with Homelessness* – brings together the results of the work done by more than 20 experienced researchers over a period of two years. As a collection of separate articles, it does not presume to suggest that there is only one correct set of answers. The various contributions can only be considered to reflect the personal views of the individual authors concerned, and it is therefore understood that those who work with homeless people will not necessarily agree with all of the contents.

Leaving aside the debates about the definition of concepts and the causes of homelessness, and without being able to fully share all of the judgements made in relation to the evaluation of various practices, FEANTSA must surely endorse the central idea that solutions based solely on financial resources and social rights are inadequate unless there are also means of providing individuals with appropriate social support.

This collection of articles represents an important step forward in terms of our knowledge and understanding of homelessness. For this I would like to thank the Project Coordinator, Dragana Avramov, the members of the Editorial Board and all of the contributors, as well as the European Commission (DG XII) for entrusting FEANTSA and its academic partners to complete this ambitious research project.

Michel Mercadié
President of FEANTSA

Preface

In this preface I want to provide information about the set-up of the project under which this volume was produced and to set the stage for the reading of the book.

This volume presents the collected set of papers solicited under the project EUROHOME – *Emergency and Transitory Housing for Homeless People: Needs and Best Practices.* The project brought together experts in the study of social protection, social exclusion, family and population sociology, housing and homelessness to review the body of knowledge in the field, analyse recent trends and discuss prospects for the improvement of the prevention and public response to housing exclusion in Europe. The project was organised around four major questions: What is known about homelessness? What are the key risk factors of social exclusion and homelessness? Are social services adequately dealing with the needs of homeless people? Can we identify models of good practice in integrated policies of social protection and complementary services for homeless people?

EUROHOME was funded by the European Commission, Directorate General XII, Science, Research and Development under the Targeted Socio-Economic Research programme, Area III Research Into Social Exclusion and Social Integration in Europe. The consortium which implemented the project was composed of four contractors and two associated contractors: The European Federation of National Organizations Working with the Homeless (FEANTSA) Brussels, Belgium (coordination); the Interdisciplinary Centre for Comparative Research in the Social Sciences (ICCR) Vienna, Austria; the Danish National Institute of Social Research (SFI), Copenhagen, Denmark; Polytechnic of Milan, Department of Territorial Sciences (DTS), Milan, Italy; the National Research and Development Centre for Welfare and Health (STAKES), Helsinki, Finland; the Research Institute Kivotos, Athens, Greece.

The implementation of the project was carried out by means of workshops focused on four research topics: data, services, risks and models of best practice.

The workshop *Data Available on Homelessness, Data Needed for the Analysis and Recommendations to Official Statistical Offices* addressed the key research problems related to the evaluation of existing data sources on homelessness and assessment of needs for the future methodologically well-founded research. This first project workshop was held in Vienna from 11–13 July 1996. It was organized and hosted by the Interdisciplinary Centre for Comparative Research in the Social Sciences (ICCR), Austria.

The workshop *Urgent and Transitory Accommodation – Needs and Provisions* dealt with the crisis intervention, temporary housing, support and assistance provided within the service sector. It addressed the controversy between immediate and long-term needs of homeless people and ways their needs are met within the institutional framework of services. A preliminary evaluation was made of the capability of the existing system of urgent and temporary assistance to deal effectively with multiple problems of homeless people. The workshop was held in Athens on 4 and 5 October 1996. It was organized jointly by FEANTSA and the Research Institute Kivotos, Greece.

The workshop *Vulnerable Groups and Social Safety Nets Against Homelessness* focused on the debate about the relationship and interdependence between poverty and social exclusion with the aim of understanding how various processes and factors of vulnerability are relevant for the production of homelessness. It provided a framework for understanding the role that policies play in the protection against vulnerability and homelessness. The workshop was held in Milan on 23 and 24 May 1997. It was organized and hosted by the Polytechnic of Milan, Department of Territorial Sciences (DTS), Italy.

The workshop *Models of Best Practice: Integrated Approach v. Complementary Services* dealt with the relationship between welfare policy, values and norms and the consequences for homelessness. The workshop addressed the issues of solidarity and its limits, the meaning of work and integration, and the importance of preventing and minimizing effects of homelessness. The role of housing policy and of the service sector was extensively examined. The meeting was held in Copenhagen on 12 and 13 October 1997. It was organized and hosted by the Danish National Institute of Social Research (SFI).

Two types of papers were prepared under the project: academic papers giving the state-of-the-art research and case studies presented by the local authorities, service providers and activists as illustrations of field experience and practical problems encountered. Workshops and their outputs were part of the working process under the project EUROHOME.

Preparation of this volume was a team work of 20 contributors supervised by the editorial board composed of Dr Ronald Pohoryles, Ms Inger Koch-

Nielsen, Professor Antonio Tosi, Ms Sirkka Liisa Kärkkäinen, Dr Aris Sapounakis, Mr Volker Busch-Geertsema, Ms Maryse Marpsat, Professor Marc-Henry Soulet, Dr Dragana Avramov (editor-in-chief). The book is a systematic set of research findings organised into meaningful groupings. Only workshop papers meeting the academic requirements were selected and 10 additional contributions were solicited specifically for this volume.

The Introduction gives an overview of the main lessons learned from the research about homelessness and ways to tackle housing deprivation and exclusion in Europe. The research perspective, concepts, causes, prevalence of homelessness, trends at the European level and the policy options are addressed by the editor in order to set stage for the reading of this book.

Part 1 provides a broad research perspective on poverty, social exclusion and homelessness. It highlights how various concepts differ from each other – sometimes in their underlying fundamental philosophical assumptions and sometimes in the dilemmas as to the usefulness of their use for research and policy. Paugam, Duffy, Soulet and Tosi address the key dilemmas emerging in a dynamic and expanding research of various aspects of deprivation in advance market economies with developed social protection and welfare assistance.

Part 2 deals with data on homelessness and research methodology. The first contribution gives an overview of primary and secondary data available in Europe and a critical analysis of the 'usability' of existing sources for scientifically sound comparative research at the European level (Avramov). Pertinent national surveys a description of the methodology applied in Finland (Kärkkäinen) and the Netherlands (de Feijter), the cities of Vienna (Kofler), Paris (Marpsat and Firdion) and Plymouth (Williams) provide insight into best methods to be used according to the target population and research and policy aims. In terms of the development of the state-of-the-art methodology lessons learned from the United States (Burt) provide further sound grounds for an informed debate about research options and the choice of best tools.

Part 3 deals with values underlying policies which have an indirect or direct impact on homelessness. Different regimes of social policy (Daly) and different approaches to homelessness (Vranken) set the framework for understanding models of policies and patterning of homelessness. Case studies for Denmark (Kristensen) and Finland (Kärkkäinen) are examples of what may currently be considered as best practice in Europe in integrated policy approaches to homelessness.

Part 4 addresses the role of crisis intervention and emergency needs of people who find themselves homeless. The role of emergency is analysed by

Soulet and the heterogeneity of homelessness and the consequences for service provision are examined by Koch-Nielsen and Børner Stax. Three examples of approaches to temporary and emergency accommodation are given: Germany (Busch-Geertsema) with focus on needs of immigrants and asylum seekers, Greece (Sapounakis) with focus on the newly emerging phenomena of homelessness in that country and Denmark (Brandt) where homelessness may be seen as something other than lack of housing .

Part 5 provides an overview of what we have learned from the EUROHOME research project and sets the stage for our future research (Avramov).

The authors are addressing a diverse audience: academics, teachers and students, public authorities at the European, national and local levels, social workers and other service providers, interest groups and lobbyists. We are aware that expectations of various readers of this book are diverse. Thus, in order to meet academic standards we provide in each chapter empirical facts, guidance for the development and testing of hypothesis which organise the research findings and enable tentative generalisations and we assess prospects for the future. In order to facilitate the interpretation of diverse research findings we conclude each chapter with a summary of facts and ideas and propose a direction for feasible policy action. An informed interpretation of policy implications of research about homelessness with which each chapter is concluded is an expression of personal views of authors. Conclusions and policy recommendations for Parts 1, 2, 3 and 4 are drafted by Tosi, Kofler, Koch-Nielsen and Kärkkäinen. Reflections about needs for future research are formulated by Avramov. The debates about implications of our research for the development of future policies and measures to prevent and tackle homelessness were a constant activity of out network throughout the work on this volume. The conclusions provided here are based on research, but the interpretation of policy implications of research and proposed recommendations reflect also our views as citizens as to what kind of society we wish to live in today and what kind of tomorrow we see for the future generations.

Grateful acknowledgement is made to the European Commission for the financial support provided to the project and the production and publication of this book.

Dr Dragana Avramov
Project director and editor

The State-of-the-art Research of Homelessness and Provision of Services in Europe

DRAGANA AVRAMOV

Introductory Comments

The European policy discourse on housing exclusion in the 1990s reflects an awareness that homelessness can persist as a serious social problem in prosperous economies on the one hand, and by dissent about the nature of social processes which generate or are conducive to housing exclusion on the other hand. The political debate tends to disassociate situations of housing exclusion from social processes at work. The social perception of homelessness as a marginal situation which affects a small number of people largely determines the scope of the political action, perception of social responsibility and allocation of public resources for tackling housing deprivation. In the few European countries in which legislation or administrative practice address homelessness as an issue of public responsibility, there are marked differences in the perception of living and housing conditions which fall in the homeless category. A comparative overview of legislation and administrative practice reveals that the term *homeless* is used to cover quite diverse living conditions of socially deprived individuals or households (see Avramov, 1995a and 1996). There are marked differences in the criteria for the identification of homeless populations who are eligible for housing assistance and those homeless who may expect only humanitarian assistance.

The European research discourse has largely been influenced by the policy context under which homelessness emerged as a social construction in Europe. The early studies were simple counts of literally homeless people sleeping in night shelters and on the streets. At the time of the growing visibility of homeless people in the second half of the 1980s there was hardly any credible primary research in Europe about paths into and out of homelessness. Small scale research about needs and problems of homeless people was limited to

1

situations of no abode or to night shelter users. Throughout the 1980s the major research efforts to count, describe and identify problems of homeless populations were made in the United States. Findings from the United States were frequently extrapolated to the homeless populations in developed market economies in general. The conceptual field of European research of homelessness in the early 1990s has evolved along two mainstream approaches: homelessness as a housing problem and homelessness as a problem of social *'fragilisation'*. The analysis of processes which are conducive to homelessness went in two directions: system inadequacy and personal deficiency.

It is only in most recent years that the homelessness research agenda at the European level is taking into due account the organisation and functioning of society and in particular its social policies and services. The role which public provisions play in the protection against vulnerability in the European context is increasingly being acknowledged. Research questions which are opening the Pandora's box regarding the future of social and welfare protection in Europe, namely 'What would Europe look like without social protection and welfare safety-nets?' and 'How can we make social protection and welfare assistance more effective and efficient from the point of view of the public, service providers and users?' – are a challenge also for research on the housing dimension of social vulnerability, exclusion and integration.

After initial stock taking and *'cataloguing'* situations of homelessness in the early 1990s there is now a clear cognitive and policy need to relocate the realm of homelessness from the periphery of research to the core of the new policy context of social exclusion research. That is why in this contribution I will first broaden the perspective by addressing homelessness in the framework of social exclusion and social integration processes. Then I will look at the levels of causality which need to be addressed in research of housing deprivation and homelessness and finally will report on what is known about levels and trends in homelessness and policy responses.

I intend to show that the weaknesses of early research efforts and lack of empirical documentation to support many of our research hypotheses do not originate from the biased or underdeveloped social theories but rather from a lack of resources to implement targeted primary research in which all levels of causality could be addressed. I argue in this contribution that pragmatic obstacles can explain the scientific reductionism which prevailed in the early 1990s and which served as fertile ground for the quick-fix policy and lobbying platforms throughout the 1990s.

Lessons Learned from Research

Social Exclusion and Homelessness: Broadening of Perspective

Research about poverty in Europe has evolved, over the past two decades or so, towards a wider debate, measurement and analysis of deprivation in both distributional and relational terms and the broadening of perspective towards issues of social exclusion. Research about homelessness has lagged behind. It suffered from both a too narrow a perspective and too much generic judgment.

It is only in recent years that research is gradually moving away from the focus on individual deficiencies towards the analysis of social processes which are conducive to different degrees and forms of housing exclusion. As long as research of homelessness was limited to the phenomenological level and focused only on the literally homeless it constituted a legitimate, albeit a narrow research domain. But, in order to break the deadlock of a static approach homelessness research needed to broaden its perspective. The enlargement of the research domain posed new challenges. In its initial phases it tended to blur the perception of its main subject – housing deprivation and homelessness – and it opened ground for misinterpretation. Some social activists and lobbyists (mis)took the broadening of the research perspective as an identification of the phenomenon of homelessness with other phenomena such as poverty, social marginalisation and social exclusion. It is only in recent years that it has been effectively argued by researchers that the interpretation of the process of production of homelessness as being identical to the production of poverty turns a blind eye to the specificity of paths into and out of homelessness. Housing deprivation is perhaps the most obvious indicator of material deprivation in Europe today. Homeless people are a small albeit the most visible fraction of the socially excluded. This, however, does not mean that we can automatically regard as identical paths in and out of poverty and various situations of social exclusion with paths into and out of homelessness. Homelessness as a specific form of extreme social exclusion and social detachment of individuals cannot be understood and tackled effectively from the perspective of generic debates about unmet housing needs, unemployment and material deprivation which '*ultimately and inevitably*' lead to homelessness.

Resources, opportunity and ability to make use of social institutions – namely family and informal networks and public provisions – are the supporting pillars of social integration in contemporary societies. The erosion of one or more of these pillars, be it through lack of access to material resources, social barriers to access meaningful activity or lack of access to care and support, is conducive to marginalisation and different forms of social exclusion. Social exclusion entails an accumulation of deprivation in several of the most important domains of human activity: labour, education, consumption of public services and care, family and informal networks, communication, political participation, leisure and recreation. Its material dimension includes poverty in terms of the lack of resources at the disposal of an individual or a household and its relational aspects include inadequate social participation, lack of social integration and lack of power (Room, 1995; Duffy, Paugam, Soulet and Vranken in this volume). Exclusion is associated with social stigmatisation and isolation, low self-esteem, the feeling of not belonging and never having been given a chance to be included in the society.

The underlying common denominators of social and housing exclusion are lack of material resources and weakening of social ties. Material poverty may be said to be a dependent variable of homelessness in developed market economies. It operates in conjunction with other risks. A broader look at the society and vulnerable groups shows unequivocally that only a small proportion of very poor people become homeless. But when we limit the perspective to homeless people only then poverty seems to be a common denominator of homelessness. All homeless people are poor. Homeless people experience material deprivation as the overwhelming majority depend on welfare, day labour, casual work and/or begging. The impact of the lack of material resources refracts through the limited ability of poor families to provide assistance to the vulnerable or non-earning adults. Poor families may be able to provide support and care for young adults only as long as they remain in the parental household. For those in pursuit of independent living arrangements, or for conflict-burdened families the home leaving of one of its members often implies cessation of transfers of resources and services and weakening of bonds. Informal networks of socially weak families tend to be limited to the neighbourhood and networks generally have a low capacity to transfer material and non-material resources to those who move away to another region or town. Research indicates that the majority of people unable to fend for themselves end up on the street or in an emergency shelter after relatives and friends are no longer able or willing to provide accommodation. However, not all homeless people originate from poor families.

Small-scale research illustrates difficulties which homeless people have to establish and maintain family and informal networks and to make use of other social institutions. These difficulties seem to be partly inherent to social structures and ways our societies operate and partly to personality features of people affected. Indeed, social ties are built through most important domains of human activity which bind housing with family life, work, health and culture. The majority of those who become roofless and end up on the street or in an emergency shelter for homeless people are poor, have no stable work, have weak health, can no longer rely on family and friends for help and are not well equipped to take part in or make use of the mainstream culture.

In order to look at homelessness as a social process rather then just as a condition of '*non-housing*', the research community needed to address risk factors, risk groups and ways risks materialise for particular individuals and families belonging to risk groups. Initially this brought considerable confusion about the habitual use of the concept of *risk*. In social research methodology the notion of risk is understood as the probability of an event occurring. The risk period is conceptualised as the duration of the non-occurrence of a given event (Yamaguchi, 1991). People under eviction proceedings are at risk of becoming homeless but the event has not occurred yet and may never occur. In the cost-benefit analysis conceptualised and widely used by economists it is postulated that success comes when opportunities exceed risks. By analogy some social scientists interpret the notion of being at risks as having poor opportunities or few options. In market economies, it is argued, one can more easily take risks when one has multiple opportunities. Changing a job may be opportunity-enhancing for highly skilled people. But, moving from welfare to casual jobs may be too risky for low-skilled individuals. Duffy (1997a) argues that for the poor and disadvantaged groups 'flexibility is both more risky and more difficult to achieve'.

First research hypotheses in the domain of homelessness analysis emerged around the notion of risks as a consequence of social '*fragilisation*' due to the increasing burden of housing costs. Indeed, contextual research confirms that difficulties in maintaining housing may be considered to be conducive to social exclusion both in its material and relational dimensions. Low income people may suffer serious deprivation because they are overburdened by housing costs. The issue is not only what percentage of household income is spent on rent and related housing costs but what amount of disposable income remains for other needs after housing costs are paid. Research points in the direction of a conclusion that housing costs are causing deprivation and may be contributing to the '*ghettoisation*' more particularly of the urban poor. Rent and housing related costs are permanent costs. In most European market economies they are the second highest expenditure of an average household. As a proportion of household income housing follows immediately the expenditure on food. Research has shown that socially vulnerable people have to make serious savings on nutrition, medication, education, communication, culture and leisure in order to keep up with market rents. Containing telephone costs to a minimum, not being able to buy or having to give up a car and to cut down on public transportation costs may lead to social isolation. Housing costs may be said to be one of the key causes of general deprivation of the unemployed, those with casual or low paid jobs, and people dependent on welfare transfers or low pensions. While the causal relationship between poverty, poor housing conditions and deprivation due to high housing costs can be documented, the relationship between housing costs and homelessness is less obvious and under-researched.

The broadening of perspective is necessary to include in the analysis of housing exclusion not only those literally homeless using night shelters, soup kitchens or people living on the street but also people living under conditions of severe housing stress in dilapidated housing estates, in crime-ridden neighbourhoods, conflict burdened households and overcrowded apartments. The broadening of perspective is necessary so that we can address the process of exclusion and paths into and out of deprivation and vulnerability. But broadening of the perspective requires conceptual rigor and research discipline (see Soulet and Tosi in this volume). The conceptualisation and development of assumptions as to why and how risks do or do not materialise for particular individuals belonging to risk groups, analysis of the risk period and rates of occurrence of the event during the risk period, relationship between transition rates and explanatory variables require scrupulous research and use of advance methods.

Risk Factors and Causes of Homelessness

The first step towards understanding homelessness is the acknowledgement of the complexity of paths into homelessness. The second step is imminently analytical. It entails separating or breaking the complex deterministic system into its component parts and regrouping into meaningful systems the indicators, explanatory variables and causes. In a simplified way it may be said that the *decomposition* of the complex reality is necessary so that we can analyse, measure and connect the variables; *reconstruction* is necessary so that we can interpret, assess prospects for the future and explain *why* and *how* things happen the way they do.

Research about homelessness has made sufficient progress so that we can make informed assumptions about macro or structural causes, meso or intermediate causes, and micro or proximate causes (often referred to as personal causes) as components of the deterministic system. The structural, intermediate and proximate causes of homelessness are different levels of causation and not independent variables of homelessness. The combination and the feedback between background, intermediate and personal factors causes homelessness.

My personal research has led me to identify the following components of the three levels of causation which are specific to the housing dimension of social exclusion. They are relevant for the accumulation and organisation of research findings and the connection and interpretation of the phenomena of housing exclusion and homelessness.

The key structural factors of housing exclusion may be identified as:

- lack of affordable housing;
- lack of adequate social protection;
- lack of adequate assistance and care for individuals with mental disability or personality disorders;
- juridical and social segregation of particular individuals or classes of individuals.

The way these macro social factors operate may be summarised in the following way:

- lack of affordable housing entails a severe competition at the bottom level of the rental market. Individuals who have a social, physical or mental disability are weak competitors and are at risk of being excluded from the regular housing market;
- lack of adequate social protection of people who do not have enough income to live in a way compatible with human dignity ghettoises people in severely substandard housing and run down neighbourhoods;
- lack of community-based mental health care for individuals suffering mental and personality disorders is one of the key determinant of homelessness for those belonging to the risk group. People who do not need to be institutionalised but need care and support in order to be able to live in independent housing are at risk of becoming homeless if not assisted by the community;
- legislation which restricts movement, access to land or housing for particular groups or classes of individuals (e.g. travellers and Gypsies, ethnic minorities, non-nationals, migrants, ex-offenders, mentally or

physically handicapped) is one of the key structural cause of homelessness. Even when legislation does not sanction segregation, the social practice may still operate as a strong factor of housing exclusion. Research shows that particular ethnic groups, individuals who cannot produce a secure employment record and those with a visible physical or mental disability are discriminated against in the private rental market.

The missing link in research of housing exclusion and homelessness remains the identification and analysis of intermediate causes and better understanding of ways they operate. While we can advance hypotheses about the importance of structures and functions of:

- family;
- friends;
- informal networks;
- neighbourhood;
- peer groups;
- street-gangs and other subcultural groups;

we still know little about ways they operate. We have no reliable research which could highlight how networks may be preventing or exacerbating housing exclusion and homelessness.

The proximate or personal causes of homelessness are a set of factors associated with a personal history and personality features of individuals. These may be conducive to social isolation and homelessness. Proximate causes of dislocation from regular housing may be identified as:

- history of inadequate institutions (orphanage, succession of youth care institutions and foster families, mental hospitals, prisons, etc.);
- troubles in the family;
- dropping out of school;
- substance abuse;
- mental disability or personality disorder.

When risks materialise they may result in temporary living conditions which exacerbate fragility and produce new proximate causes. Sleeping rough, in an emergency shelter, squatting, and, becoming estranged from the family may be associated with minor criminal activity and identification with the counter culture on the street. If social intervention does not occur in these initial phases of the process of detachment the condition of homelessness may lead to:

- prostitution;
- major criminal activity;
- heavy substance abuse;
- severe mental disability.

The experience of life on the street and in emergency shelters where individuals encounter abuse, crime and self-abuse may become a determinant of long-term and lifelong rupture of social ties and detachment from the values of the mainstream culture.

In a somewhat simplified way it may be said that the identification of structural factors which tell us how the society is organised helps us to identify the general risk factors of homelessness. The identification of intermediate or meso level causes, through which background factors operate, tell us which specific population subgroups are most exposed to risks of homelessness. The micro or personal causes help us to perceive which particular individuals in a specific society are running the highest risk of homelessness.

The notion of risks implies a possibility, threat, hazard, chance of loss or peril. It can be measured as the probability of an event occurring. The size and the composition of groups for whom risks materialise and who find themselves homelessness depends ultimately on the effectiveness of the system of family and social protection. In all societies only a small proportion of individuals belonging to groups at risk of homelessness fall through all the existing social safety nets. Some of those who encounter the world of homelessness are able to develop personal coping strategies and build their own paths out of homelessness. Some are effectively assisted by the public authorities. Others just drift and rely on daily survival. A universal rule for every exposure to deprivation and hazard which affects those belonging to the risk groups and those who become actually homelessness is: the longer the struggle – the higher the casualties (Avramov, 1997).

The organisation and functioning of society and in particular its social services illustrate how risks materialise or how they are buffered in different European countries. Although there is a general shortage of affordable housing, the unemployment rate is high, and the divorce rates are among the highest in Europe, there are almost no homeless families in Finland. Those families who found themselves homeless are accommodated in temporary apartments for a few weeks before they are provided permanent accommodation. In 1996

360 household composed of two or more persons (many of them Ingrian returnees awaiting permanent accommodation) were reported to have been temporarily homeless. In the United Kingdom, by contrast, the overwhelming majority of those officially recognised as homeless are families. They may find themselves as homeless on waiting lists for housing for several years.

Excluded from Housing = Excluded from Official Statistics

The first practical obstacle to a comprehensive analysis of housing exclusion is the lack of reliable data organised into meaningful groupings which would document the living conditions of people suffering housing stress and those who find themselves homeless. Generally, contextual data can be used as indicators of the key structural causes and small scale research of actually homeless people may give information about proximate causes of homelessness. The meso level causes are least researched. The *connection* between poverty, social marginalisation, social exclusion, housing stress, the nature and strength of networks of socially vulnerable groups and individuals, personality features, individual handicaps and homelessness remains largely an unexplored territory.

Data collected in household surveys provide an abundance of information about housing conditions of people who have a home. But they tell us nothing about homeless people and their living conditions. Technically, the absence of homeless people from household surveys from which data on housing conditions of the population are drawn are easy to explain. The sampling method for household and family budget surveys is based on a selection of respondents from a pool of people who have a home. A private household is generally defined as a unit composed of people who share a dwelling and housing-related costs. In some countries the definition of a household will focus on the sharing of accommodation and income (e.g. Ireland). In others, it will focus on whether members share accommodation and meals (e.g. Spain), or household chores or the use of a living room (e.g. UK). Although the meaning of living together and sharing may vary between countries, everywhere a household implies an address, a dwelling. The majority of homeless people do not have an address in a conventional dwelling. They do not live in private households. They do not have a principal residence.

Population censuses in Europe do not follow the same sampling technique as housing and household budget surveys. Homeless people are not intentionally left out of the count. But, so far, no specific effort has been made to ensure a comprehensive coverage of this population subgroup. No effort has been made to process and tabulate data in a way which would make it possible to identify homeless people as an aggregate. Even if we assume that homeless people are included in a statistically significant manner in the general population count it is difficult to imagine how this population could be identified as a specific group on the basis of census data. Namely, no country has developed an official definition of the conditions of homelessness for census purposes. In any case, one should not expect to obtain from a population census data which can be better gathered in targeted surveys. Indeed, population censuses are a massive counting exercise which is too bulky a tool and too expensive an enterprise to be used for collecting data about homelessness and housing deprivation which affect a small proportion of the total population.

Technical aspects explain how homeless people remain beyond official statistics. They do not provide an explanation why in a value-knowledge society in which services are planned and resources allocated on the basis of inform-ation, we have no reliable data about homelessness and the housing dimension of deprivation. The conspicuous absence of data on living conditions of home-less people in EUROSTAT's *Social Portrait of Europe* (1996) and the absence of comprehensive survey of homelessness at the European level confirm that authorities are willing to measure social progress only in terms of the improvement of housing conditions of well-housed people (Avramov, 1997).

What Have we Learned about the Extent of Homelessness and Housing Deprivation?

One of many reasons for the lack of data about the prevalence of homelessness is a lack of agreement about what homelessness is. In order to distinguish homeless people as a separate category we need a specific definition. It comes as no surprise that only countries in which there is a statutory obligation to assist the homeless or a high degree of political commitment to house the homeless there is an administrative definition of homelessness in official use.

In the United Kingdom positive law (Housing Act, 1985) imposes a statutory obligation on local authorities to provide housing to homeless people found to be in priority need. People are homeless if they do not have access to housing or if they do have housing but access to it is denied. The criteria for the identification of people eligible for accommodation are developed in the guidelines for the implementation of the legislation. They are: that the applicant is homeless or threatened by homelessness, that she/he is not homeless or potentially homeless intentionally, that she/he has a priority need.

The legislative definition in Ireland is enshrined in the 1988 Housing Act. Under the Act someone is homeless if, in the opinion of the authority, there is no accommodation available which he/she can reasonably occupy or remain in occupation of, and, if a person is living in a hospital, country home, night shelter or other such institutions because they are unable to provide reasonable accommodation from his/her own resources.

The Housing Fund of Finland which conducts an annual survey on homelessness uses an operational definition which enumerates a series of situations of homelessness which affect persons living outdoors or in temporary shelters, in night shelters or other shelters for the homeless, in institutions or institutional homes either temporarily or permanently due to lack of housing, prisoners soon to be released who have no housing, persons living temporarily with relatives or acquaintances due to lack of housing, families who have split up and are in temporary accommodation due to housing (see Kärkkäinen in this volume).

If we resort to administrative definitions the population which is included in the homeless category will obviously vary from one country to another. Furthermore the opinions of public authorities as to who should and who should not be considered to be homeless and entitled to assistance may vary from year to year in the function of resources allocated rather than in the function of the level of needs.

A group of experts who prepared a report on homelessness for the Council of Europe proposed the following definition of homeless people 'individuals or families socially excluded from lasting occupancy of a suitable dwelling' (Council of Europe, 1993 p. 23). The authors operationalise the definition by identifying situations of homelessness which range from rooflessness to unacceptable housing conditions. Similarly Daly defines homelessness as 'a continuum of condition and need' (1993, p. 16) and identifies circumstances which can be combined to form a definition of homelessness and which range from rooflessness, houselessness and insecure accommodation to inferior or substandard housing.

While descriptive definitions provide a useful nomenclature, a combination of descriptive and normative elements of above definitions has left too much space for freehanded interpretations of concepts such as 'unacceptable', 'insecure' or 'inferior'. Outside the research community such definitions give grounds to the 'game of numbers' in which figures are blown up to imply that tens of millions of people in Europe are homeless. What the sum of figures stands for is in fact is a small proportion of literally homeless people and an overwhelming majority of housed albeit badly housed people – those living in old housing, substandard accommodation and overcrowded dwellings.

My personal research has convinced me about the usefulness of a casual approach in defining homelessness. The housing dimension of deprivation is characterised by the absence of a personal, permanent, adequate dwelling. Difficulties and obstacles in accessing and maintaining a home are seen as defining criteria of homelessness. A social condition is thus defined through social mechanisms and processes which induce it. Homeless people are those who are unable to access a personal, permanent, adequate dwelling or to maintain such a dwelling *due to* financial constraints and other social barriers, and those people who are unable to access and maintain such a dwelling *because* they are unable to lead a fully independent life and need care and support but not institutionalisation.

Concepts such as personal, private and adequate which I refer to have been extensively elaborated by the United Nations (see for example 1992). The proposed casual definition, nevertheless, has its share of shortcomings. Namely, at present we are not able to identify with precision the 'weight' of clusters of causes (associated with financial constraints, social barriers and need for care) and their interrelationship. However, the key assumptions incorporated in these definitions are based on reliable research across Europe and in my view contribute to a better understanding of what is specific to homelessness.

Exclusion from housing is a process marked by the accumulation of problems associated with poverty, breakdown of family and social networks, personality disorders, isolation and social detachment of individuals. Homelessness is neither a group characteristic nor is it a static condition. For the overwhelming majority of people who find themselves homeless it is not a lifelong condition. The majority of those affected experience only an episode of literal homelessness.

A socially correct way to assess the level of needs for housing and assistance and care for people unable to access and maintain a home from their own resources would be to ensure a statutory obligation to provide and monitor the demand over time. In practice, however, what is usually monitored is the level of provision by a variety of institutions which range from soup kitchens run by charities to social housing provided from public funds. Thus what is currently on the market of services is (wrongly) identified with the level of needs and by analogy a wrong assumption is made that the number of service users stands for the number of homeless people.

Homeless People as Users of Services and Groups at Risk of Housing Stress and Deprivation

Services for homeless people are often the only source of information concerning the tip of the iceberg of housing deprivation. In many European countries the number of current users of services depends on the supply rather than on the demand for accommodation assistance and care. Thus, countries with a weak institutional framework of assistance will record a small number of homeless people together with countries with strong preventive policies and measures

The number of people dependent on services for homeless people cannot be explained by macro economic parameters. Indeed, less prosperous European countries do not register a higher number of service users than countries with the higher GDP per inhabitant. The number of people estimated to be homeless in Greece, a country with no minimum income scheme, is lower than in the Netherlands, the forerunner country in social protection. The number of people officially recognised as homeless or threatened by homelessness in the UK is 40 times higher than the estimated number of homeless users of services in Spain. In the UK local authorities have a statutory obligation to house homeless people found to be in priority need. Spanish authorities make no such commitment. Figures provided by public and voluntary services for homeless people tell us more about housing standards and the level of development of services than about the extent of housing exclusion.

The interpretation of the prevalence of homelessness and exclusion from adequate housing in an international comparative perspective needs to take into account national housing standards and environmental factors, infrastructure, climate and general habitat. People living in shacks, tents, containers and caravans are not considered to be homeless in Portugal. Public authorities cannot be held responsible for providing proper housing. In Sweden, by contract, a caravan is not considered to provide adequate housing. Local authorities can expect to receive a court order to provide proper housing if they fail to offer accommodation to the needy which corresponds to the housing standards compatible with the Swedish standard of human dignity. In the United Kingdom guidelines for the implementation of the homelessness legislation have in practice become guidelines for the attribution of social housing. Authorities argue that the number of people accepted for housing under the homeless legislation is much higher then the number of homeless. Thus, comparing figures about service users in Portugal, Sweden and the United Kingdom requires great rigour.

In order to understand homelessness in a comparative perspective we need to take into account the social context within which risks of homelessness materialise. Comparing only numbers of users of services for homeless people and social, demographic and medical profiles of those who are considered to be homeless in different countries can be misleading. Currently available information about service users is a useful indicator (not a measurement) of needs which are met. The number of users of services is furthermore useful information for service providers – in market economies it justifies their existence.

Homelessness is a residual of public, family and informal protection. The composition of the homeless population ultimately depends on the efficacy with which these networks operate. It is generally known that people who are at risk of homelessness have a combination of two or more handicaps and have experienced multiple severely stressful life experiences. Low income or no regular income, low educational attainment, poor qualification, a history of mental health problems, chronic illness, alcohol and drug abuse, experience of institutionalisation (psychiatric hospitalisation, jail, orphanage, foster care), traumatic events in the family of origin, sexual abuse and domestic violence constitute a web of handicaps and traumatic events which may be conducive to homelessness.

The stronger the public and/or family support is, the stronger and more serious are handicaps which lead a person into homelessness. Typically, families at risk of homelessness are better protected then single persons; women are better protected then men. If a women falls through all social support safety-nets and ends up sleeping rough she is more likely than a man to have a history of mental health problems which precede the experience of homelessness. Research in the USA and Spain (Koegel, 1996; Vazquez and Muñoz, 1996) confirm that among people sleeping rough and those using soup kitchens, temporary shelters and other emergency services for the homeless, women more often then men will have had severe mental disorders before and during their transition to homelessness. Mental disorders are a risk factor of homelessness which does not operate independently from other social and personal handicaps. Risks can be reduced or reinforced by the system of social support. The nature and the targeting of the system of protection will determine *which* personal handicaps will be conducive to homelessness.

The number of service users is the measure of the emergency housing demand which is met. This indicator does not tell us about the level of unmet needs for emergency accommodation and other services for homeless people nor about people in housing need in general. What do we know about living conditions of people who are not covered by housing surveys because they do not live in houses and flats, because they do not live in a private household, because they do not have a principal usual residence, because they rotate between a street, squat, transitional accommodation, marginal, often illegal lettings? How many people depend on night shelters and soup kitchens? How many people rent a single occupancy room on short term basis (while they hold a casual job or the week in which they receive a welfare benefit) and double up with acquaintances and relatives or squat when they run out of meagre resources? What coping strategies are developed by households living under conditions of severe housing stress? Although answers cannot be found in official statistical publications general indicators of housing exclusion can be identified from a variety of sources.

Although no systematic count of people in housing need has even been attempted by the statistical offices, it is possible to use the available data for an initial estimation of the number of people who are living under conditions of severe housing stress due to bad housing, overcrowding and tenure insecurity. Estimates about the prevalence of housing deprivation are possible only for some European countries. On the basis of available data from public and non-for profit service providers, primary research, population censuses and secondary sources I have estimated the prevalence of housing deprivation for the 15 European Union countries.

People living in economic hardship form the core of risk groups which are threatened by housing stress and housing deprivation. In the European Union those at highest risk of housing deprivation emerge from the lowest income tranche which encompasses:

- 57 million people living below the poverty threshold;
- 31 million people dependent on welfare;
- 18 million unemployed dependent on unemployment benefits or family transfers.

In terms of bad housing conditions it can be estimated that in the European Union at least:

- 15 million people live in severely substandard and/or overcrowded dwellings;
- 2.4 million people live in 'unconventional dwellings' which are mobile, semipermanent or not built for human habitation.

In terms of housing insecurity and housing stress in the 15 European Union countries it may be estimated that:

- 1.6 million people are under eviction procedures;
- 400,000 people are evicted each year.

It may be estimated that homelessness affects each year:

- 2.7 million homeless people who rotate between friends and relatives, furnished rooms rented on a short term basis and services for homeless people;
- 1.8 million people dependent on public and voluntary services for homeless people.

All of the above conditions may overlap and therefore it is not possible to add any of the given numbers in order to estimate the prevalence of housing exclusion. The above figures may be considered only as a preliminary indicator of the housing dimension of deprivation in the most prosperous European countries.

What Have We Learned about Recent Trends in Homelessness and Housing Deprivation?

The 1980s mark a decade of accelerated improvement of housing standards and housing conditions in general. The 1980s are also a decade of growing visibility of homelessness. In the 1980s and early 1990s a visible presence of people sleeping rough in European cities coincides with an invisible pressure on services for homeless people. Fragmented research and information gathered by service providers enables us to describe a trend in the late 1980s and early 1990s. It may be summarised as follows. A growing number of people who could not afford a home from their own resources were turning to services for homeless people. The duration of stay in shelters and transitional dwellings funded by public and voluntary organisations was increasing. A growing number of women with and without children were being provided temporary accommodation in shelters for homeless people. The fastest growing population of users of services for the homeless seem to have been women and young adults in the 18–25 age group.

However, in the second half of the 1990s there are indicators that trends may have reversed in some West European countries. Information from

Finland, Denmark, Sweden, Belgium, the United Kingdom and West Germany seem to indicate that the number of homeless people users of services has been decreasing.

Recent figures which are documenting a decline in the number of users of services for homeless people in several countries put before researchers a number of important questions to be answered. The same type of data from service providers which now indicate a decline in numbers have been used by the research community, social workers, service providers and their lobbyists to argue that there was an increase in homelessness throughout the 1980s and early 1990s. Can we then conclude that the most recent figures announce the reversal of the trend in homelessness? If that is the case how can the decline in homelessness be explained? The mid-1990s coincide with an increase in structural risks of homelessness (unemployment, decline in the provision of publicly funded housing for rent, rent increases and cuts in social benefits) and yet the number of people for whom risks materialise is decreasing. The question as to why and how under conditions which are exposing more and more people to risks of homelessness the number of people who have become homeless seems to have declined can at best be addressed through a number of hypotheses (see Avramov, 1998).

It is not possible to quantify trends in homelessness in a consistent, statistically relevant manner for all the European countries. Emergency, basic need services are typically provided by charities, non-profit organisations and voluntary associations. They neither have the means nor the know-how to engage in data gathering and analysis. In fact, the humanitarian nature of services provided by voluntary organisations may exclude asking of questions about the origin or the nature of problems of their clients. Data on trends are generally available only when public authorities have a statutory obligation to provide housing for the homeless and/or when emergency services are funded by the public authorities. We generally have to resort to indicators using a variety of sources to tentatively identify trends.

The first countries to react to the growing homelessness by developing and implementing integrated preventive policies and complementary services for homeless people were the northern European countries. Finland is a country with an outstanding record in containing housing deprivation and reducing homelessness: between 1987 and 1994 the number of homeless people has been reduced by half. The number of people who found themselves homeless has continued to decline throughout the second half of the 1990s (see Kärkkäinen in this volume). The number of users of services for homeless people seems to have decreased in recent years also in Sweden, West Germany and Belgium while the supply of services has remained stable or has even increased. The decline in the number of people accepted on waiting lists for housing under the homeless legislation in the United Kingdom has also declined but it is not yet clear whether this is due to a fall in demand or in supply.

In most southern European countries a relatively large stock of substandard housing and single-occupancy rooms accessible to low-income people have traditionally been a buffer against a rise in the number of those literally roofless. Several hundreds of thousands of people live on the borderline of homelessness in shacks, tents, containers, caravans, staircases, caves or premises not actually designed for human habitation. They are generally not recognised by the public authorities as homeless but are classified as people living in 'unconventional dwellings'.

In Eastern and Central European countries homelessness has become visible only in the 1990s and is generally associated with the difficulties of transition to market economy. It is often argued that the present upsurge of homelessness is largely a legacy of the former establishment but researchers in some countries also acknowledge that the recent closings down of worker's hostels and even orphanages have pushed some of the most vulnerable adults and children onto the streets. Nothing is known about their number. Preliminary research points in the direction of the conclusion that the burden of housing costs has increased substantially for the whole population, that the security of tenure has decreased for socially vulnerable groups, that the population at risk of homelessness is increasing and that people who find themselves homeless live in extreme misery (Avramov, 1995b; Duffy, 1997b). What differs currently between European developed market economies and countries in transition from planned economy are not so much paths into homelessness but chances of receiving public support and assistance when homeless and prospects for getting out of homelessness.

The visible homeless, those sleeping rough or in night shelters, are only the tip of the iceberg of people experiencing housing deprivation. The hidden homeless – those living in forced cohabitation under conditions of severe family conflicts, domestic abuse or overcrowding – and people at the borderline of homelessness living in dilapidated accommodation unfit for human habitation, form the overwhelming majority of those experiencing deprivation. But we have no data to document recent trends in hidden homelessness, housing stress or housing deprivation.

Lessons Learned about Tackling Homelessness

What Have We Learned about Preventive Policies and Services for Homeless People?

There has been no comprehensive analysis in Europe about the impact of current direct and indirect policies on housing deprivation and homelessness. Conclusions about the effects of policies are generally drawn from contextual data, macro economic parameters and the creative reading of political statements of intention. Lack of resources and policy interest in a scientifically sound analysis of whether policies work and what unintended effects they may produce has been a major issue of concern within the EUROHOME network of researchers. In this volume Daly discusses different regimes of social policy and concludes that there is no immediate cross-national patterning between welfare regimes and the extent of homelessness.

Comparative overviews of policy options and practice in various European countries indicates that the strong political will and an effective commitment in terms of (material and non-material) resources are the key variables to be analysed (Avramov, 1995a, 1996). Policy choices translated into practice in advanced welfare states show that anti-poverty and social integration measures are more effective when income protection is accompanied by a comprehensive system of housing supply, and, housing subsidies, benefits, allowances. The Nordic countries Denmark, Finland and Sweden have been successful in progressively removing obstacles to housing for low-income groups. They also implement a generous system of income transfers which enable people to maintain a home (see Kristensen, Koch-Nielsen, Kärkkäinen in this volume). They have all managed to contain the effects of structural causes of housing deprivation and to reduce homelessness over past 10 years or so.

In countries which focused their anti-poverty measures on minimum subsistence means and emergency assistance for the homeless but pursued throughout the 1980s the policy of disengagement from the public funding of permanent housing for socially vulnerable groups – risks of homelessness persisted (see Busch-Geertsema in this volume). In many countries the lack of adequate housing assistance to low-income groups has been a serious deficiency in the system of social protection. In countries with a weaker public system of welfare protection lack of adequate housing support to low-income and non-earning groups has been an additional stumbling point in the development of a comprehensive system of protection from poverty (see Tosi, Sapounakis in this volume). Lack of guaranteed minimum subsistence means and a new market housing strategy which does not foresee efficient safety nets for the poor are increasing risks of poverty and housing stress in southern European countries as well as in countries in transition to market economies. In southern Europe the absence of effective public policies and measures, the family support has been so far the most effective (and often only) buffer against homelessness. Housing deprivation in terms of substandard housing and overcrowding remained however widespread. In many countries family solidarity has traditionally played a significant role in preventing homelessness of adults with no income. However, changing family structures and culture are affecting the functional basis of direct family support. These changes have not, so far, been accompanied by new welfare models. Transition to market economies in eastern and central Europe has not been accompanied in the 1990s by effective social protection and welfare and housing assistance to those who are too young or too old, too weak or too slow to profit from the new economic opportunities.

In order to go beyond just informed assumptions in addressing the impact of policies on housing deprivation and homelessness there is an urgent need to evaluate how well are current social policies, welfare benefits and housing allowances reinforcing housing security of individuals and families. There is a cognitive and policy need to analyse whether and how policies, measures and services are reinforcing social cohesion at the European, national and regional levels. There is need to develop housing impact methodology (lessons can be learned from family impact studies) and to evaluate the efficacy and efficiency of policies which are aimed at helping people to maintain housing and measures and services set in place for people who find themselves outside the housing system.

The consolidation of European Union requites reforms of welfare protection on different levels. It also requires that the system ensures sustainable living conditions and that people are treated fairly in their daily life. Innovative institutional changes which take into account competition, globalisation and sustainability have to be based on an informed dialogue. Informed choices are needed in order to alleviate existing social tensions, to deal with various forms of spatial dimensions of social exclusion and to promote social integration. Change and dialogue is needed to achieve gradual harmonisation of sustainable policies of welfare protection and measures of social integration. A pre-requirement for informed choices is sound knowledge about the impact of past and present social, welfare and housing policies and targeted measures.

Within the scope of the EUROHOME project we could not develop and implement a policy impact approach – due to financial constraints and time limitation – however I consider the recommendation to pursue this research road as one of the key research challenges for our network in the future (see Avramov in Part 5).

As for responsive policy measures they have traditionally been influenced by the way homeless people are perceived. Social detachment of homeless people has often been interpreted to imply that homelessness is a lifestyle choice. Homeless people were seen as consumers and abusers of public services and resources. This perception of homelessness leads to assertions that the greater the number of services provided the higher the number of 'free loaders'. By analogy it was assumed that people will intentionally make themselves homeless in order to profit from the public handouts. The Finnish example extensively discussed by Kärkkäinen in this volume testifies to the fault in reasoning in advancing the 'free loader-hypothesis'. Our research unambiguously shows that the higher the number of effectively assisted and cared for people – the lower the number of those who become homeless and remain a heavy burden for public expenditures.

The Nordic countries which can be quoted as an example of best practice in integrated policy approach to homelessness show that tackling difficulties associated with homelessness requires complementation between preventive and responsive measures and a well thought approach to services. In the late 1990s models of best practice are those schemes which extend services far beyond temporary emergency assistance. They acknowledge that homelessness is not only a housing condition (see Koch-Nielsen and Børner Stax, Koch-Nielsen, Brandt, Kärkkäinen in this volume). They operate under the assumption that housing the homeless is indispensable but that it is not a sufficient tool for social reintegration of homeless people. They provide for people in need of housing and social support and their aim is to resettle homeless people into independent housing and to provide sufficient support and care so that they are able to stay in individual housing. Depending on the set of specific needs of individuals, the integrated approach implies that in addition to personal housing (as opposed to placement in institutions) formerly homeless people may expect to receive: individual guidance; counselling on how to manage their financial resources; how to reconstitute family and social ties; professional training; access to employment; psychological and medical support. This approach also questions the validity and usefulness of the assumption that all homeless people *can-ought to-will-be* integrated in the labour market.

Although there is evidence that effective preventive and responsive policy measures can reduce homelessness, many European countries seem to be giving way to pressures to reduce the public involvement. The new policy climate seems to be characterised by a shift away from comprehensive preventive measures and a move towards responsive measure of mainly short-term nature and lip-service to innovation and new forms of partnerships between public, private and voluntary sectors. More and more public resources are being channelled towards emergency provisions which include temporary accommodation. This is often done without examining whether these provisions are actually determined by client needs. The effectiveness and efficacy of services is not monitored from the point of view of providers, other institutions and clients. There is an urgent need to develop performance measurements of services and to develop standards of service provision. We have found no evidence that voluntary services are more effective, less expensive and more client-friendly than publicly funded and publicly run chains of services. Unless more focus is put on the control of quality and material and non-material costs and benefits of services in general and crisis intervention in particular the result could be that the short-term funding of exploratory pilot projects may turn out to be a policy flirtation with innovation rather than a commitment to a pursuit of flexible but efficient and stable chains of services.

In the 1990s initiatives have been launched by numerous institutions in Europe with the aim to describe innovative projects and to collect information about pilot projects and new partnerships. But, there has been no coordinated effort to evaluate the impact and to measure the real outcomes in terms of material and non-material costs and benefits of such projects. There is no project which brings together at the European level experts to develop adequate methodology for performance measurements which could be implemented at the local, national and European levels. Paradoxically, at the time of budgetary constraints which impose reforms in the welfare systems in Europe there are currently no scientifically sound tools to evaluate the effectiveness, efficacy and long-term outcomes of past and current homelessness policies, outcomes of crisis intervention and supported housing services for socially deprived individuals and families.

The deadlock of the mainstream policy debate about services and the role of different partners in the resettlement-rehabilitation-reintegration programmes highlights the need for a U-turn in rethinking services. As researchers we can reiterate the importance of acknowledging different levels of causation of housing deprivation and homelessness. The importance of the analysis of the interaction and the feedback between different levels of causation is not a matter of academic pedantry. To ignore or to deny the underlying structural causes, just as to ignore or deny the impact of personal histories and personality features, is disruptive for an effective action. In the public debate about homelessness the policy makers typically tend to ignore or underestimate the impact of structural causes; the lobbyists tend to ignore or underestimate the impact of personal factors. An uninformed debate about homelessness is often translated into costly ad hoc programmes and services which fail to address the real needs of homeless people. Services for homeless people are increasingly becoming a market-driven sub-sector driven by an economic cost-benefit rhetoric and (re)production of clients. What we have learned from our research is that services for homeless people are expensive. Costs to the public may be as high as ECU 1,809 per month for one place in an institution for homeless people (Hanover, Germany) and ECU 940 per month for long term housing provision in flats combined with social support for single homeless persons (IMPACT, 1998). These costs to the public are one more in the chain of reasons why services need to be made more accountable to the general public and to their clients.

There are indicators that services are mushrooming across Europe and may be providing more 'care' than the clients actually need (IMPACT, 1998). Under these circumstances reducing the debate about tackling homelessness to a debate about '*models of best practice*' resembles an attempt to reduce the issue to a mere technical task of '*writing-out recipes*' just because a product looks appealing – rather then *looking for remedies* which require more rigour and are less marketable. A thread connecting all the parts of this book is the ultimate conclusion that there is no quick-fix solution to homelessness. Action is needed at the level of integrated policies which bind social protection, welfare assistance, housing policies, housing support with complementary services providing material and non-material support and care to people with specific multiple needs. The composition of the population that becomes homeless varies between countries and over time. Services for homeless people need to be systematically monitored in terms of the quality of assistance and care and material and non-material benefits for the public and clients. This volume does not prescribe services. Authors identify best research methodologies and highlight models of best policy choices in tackling homelessness.

Bibliography

Avramov, D. (1991), 'Present Demographic Trends and Lifestyles in Europe', *General Introductory Statement, Seminar Proceedings*, Strasbourg, Council of Europe Press.

Avramov, D. (1995a), *Homelessness in the European Union, Social and Legal Context of Housing Exclusion in the 1990s*, Brussels, FEANTSA.

Avramov, D. (1995b), 'Homelessness in market economies and in countries in transition: similarities and differences' in Avramov, D. (ed.), *Housing Exclusion in Central and Eastern Europe*, Brussels, FEANTSA.

Avramov, D. (1996), *The Invisible Hand of the Housing Market, A Study of Effects of Changes in the Housing Market on Homelessness in the European Union*, Brussels, FEANTSA.

Avramov, D. (1997), 'Western Europe thematic housing report' in *The Human Dignity and Social Exclusion Initiative*, Strasbourg, Council of Europe Press.

Avramov, D. (ed.) (1998), *Youth Homelessness in the European Union*, Brussels, FEANTSA.

Blau, J. (1992), *The Visible Poor*, New York, Oxford University Press.

Bourdru, F. (1992), *Une première approche européenne des politiques spécifiques et des actions en faveur des sans-abri*, first report of the European Observatory on Homelessness, Brussels, FEANTSA.

Cecodhas (1995/96), *Les européens et leur logement*, Paris, L'Observatoire Européen du Logement Social.

Commission of the European Communities (1993), *Living in Europe, How we live in Europe and how we feel on the subject*, Brussels, Commission of the European Communities, DG V.

Commission of the European Communities (1993), *Social Protection in Europe*, Luxembourg, Office for Official Publications of the European Communities.

Commission of the European Communities (1993), *Housing statistics in the European Union*, Brussels, Directorate-General V Employment, Industrial relations and Social Affairs.

Council of Europe (1993), *Homelessness*, Strasbourg, Steering Committee on Social Policy (CDPS) Council of Europe Press.

Daly, M. (1992), *Homeless People in Europe – The Rising Tide*, Brussels, FEANTSA.

Department of Environment (1993), *The English House Condition Survey*, London, HMSO.

Duffy, K. (1997a), 'Opportunity and risk: Broad perspective arising from the result of HDSE Phase 1 (1996–1997)', colloquy *Towards a better social cohesion in Europe: today and tomorrow*, 16–17 September, Bratislava. Social, Health and Family Affairs Committee, Parliamentary Assembly, Council of Europe

Duffy, K. (1997b), 'Opportunity and risk: A report on the risks of social exclusion in countries of central and eastern Europe' in *The Human Dignity and Social Exclusion Initiative*, Strasbourg, The Council of Europe.

European Commission (1995), *Employment in Europe*, Brussels, Directorate-General V Employment, Industrial relations and Social Affairs.

EUROSTAT (various years), *Database on housing*, Luxembourg.

EUROSTAT (1990), *La pauvreté en chiffres. L'Europe au début des années '80*, Bruxelles.

EUROSTAT (1991), *Population and Social Conditions*, Rapid Reports, 1991/4.

EUROSTAT (1992), *Europe in Figures*, Luxembourg, Office for Official Publications of the European Communities.

EUROSTAT (1996), *Social Portrait of Europe*, Luxembourg, Office for Official Publications of the European Communities.

IMPACT (1997), 'Project proposal under the European Commission TSER call', prepared by the Consortium: Interdisciplinary Centre for Comparative Research in the Social Sciences, Austria; Danish National Institute of Social Research, Denmark; Department of Territorial Studies Polytechnic Milan, Italy; Population and Social Policy Consultants, Belgium; National Research and Development Centre for Welfare and Health, Finland; Association for Innovative Social Research and Social Planning, Germany; Chair of Social Work, University of Fribourg, Switzerland; Homeless Initiative, Ireland

Koegel, P. (1996), 'Homeless people in the United States', paper presented at the seminar *Personas sin hogar y exclusion social en la Union Europea: Factores economicos y psicosociales*, El Escorial, 5–9 August.

MISSOC (1993), *Social Protection in the Member States of the Community, Situation on July 1st 1993 and Evolution*, Brussels, Commission of the European Communities, DG V.

Room, G. (1995), *Beyond the Threshold. The Measurement and Analysis of Social Exclusion*, Bristol, The Policy Press.

United Nations (1992), 'The right to adequate housing', working paper submitted by Rajindar Sachar to the Commission on Human Rights, E/CN 4/Sub./1995/15.

Vazquez, C. and Muñoz, M. (1996), 'Homelessness in Spain' in Helvie, C.O. and Kunstmann, W. (eds), *Homelessness in International Perspective*, forthcoming.

Yamaguchi, K. (1991), *Event History Analysis*, Applied Social Research Methods Series, Volume 28, Newbury Park, London, New Delhi, Sage Publications.

PART 1
POVERTY, SOCIAL EXCLUSION AND HOMELESSNESS

1 Weakening and Breaking of Social Ties: Analysis of Explanatory Factors

SERGE PAUGAM

Introduction

In any society that perceives poverty as intolerable and unacceptable on a personal level, the social status of 'poverty' becomes a stigma. Those members of society who are 'poor' are consequently forced to lead their lives in a state of isolation. They try to cover up their inferiority to those who surround them and maintain distant relations with others who would, under different circumstances, be close to them. The humiliating nature of their situation leads them to consider themselves as not belonging to any definable social class. The social category to which all poor people could be said to belong is extremely varied, which increases the risk of its individual members becoming isolated. At the beginning of this century Georg Simmel had already noticed that in modern society the social category of 'the poor' constituted a 'unique sociological synthesis'.

> Concerning its place in society as a whole the group is extremely homogeneous, but the individuals that make up the group are extremely heterogeneous. It is the common end of a great variety of paths, a sea in which lives that come from all social classes float side by side. Every social change or development however radical or lenient adds a certain number of members to the ranks of the poor. The worst aspect of poverty is that it covers a group of people whose only identifiable social status is the fact that they are poor (Simmel, 1908).

This analysis of poverty as a heterogeneous social phenomenon is verified by present analysis. Studies conducted in France and other European countries concerning those who receive RMI (Income Support) (see Paugam, 1993) have lead to similar conclusions. The dependence upon social welfare within a social structure that is increasingly marked by unemployment has lead to the social group that we classify as poor becoming more and more varied. Often the process of social disqualification can be identified by an exclusion from professional activity and hence an increasing dependence on others and associations with other poor people with very different backgrounds.

Social Disqualification Concept

In 1986/87 when I first undertook a social study of this nature at Saint-Brieuc (80 years after Simmel's text was published) one thing struck me immediately – the large and rapid increase in the number of people who were dependent upon the various services provided by the welfare state. It therefore seemed appropriate to analyse the phenomenon of poverty through its relation to welfare state dependence, particularly so considering the social structure with which we are dealing at the present time.

Both the statistics resulting from the study and my own consideration of the problem on a theoretical basis led me to the view that poverty today is better defined as an ongoing process rather than as a fixed state. No definition of social poverty as static can account for the heterogeneous nature of its individual members. Any such definition also avoids the central issue that faces us: the progressive accumulation of difficulties from their origins to their final effects, whether we are considering individuals or whole families. In order to develop a better understanding of the phenomenon as a whole I developed the concept of 'social disqualification'. 'Social disqualification' takes into account the increasingly common phenomenon of long-term lack of regular work, for whatever reason. 'Social disqualification' also examines the different stages through which the poor have passed and the way in which they have been affected by their contact with the social welfare structure. The notion of 'social disqualification' therefore places an emphasis upon the varying and changing nature of poverty. There are three main elements.

First is what might be called the branding or labelling of those who receive welfare assistance. The mere fact of accepting assistance marks 'poor' people apart, changing all the relations they have and even their perception of those that are finished – receiving assistance changes the identity of the recipient. In a society where most of the members spend a large part of their lives and their energy in order to avoid becoming poor, the label of poor can only be a pejorative one. Consequently anyone to whom the label 'poor' is attached is almost forced into a state isolation. Resistance to the effects of branding vary of course from case to case depending upon the relations maintained with the social welfare institutions and also the possibility of active work being undertaken.

The second element of 'social disqualification' concerns the particular methods used to reintegrate the poor. Owing to the fact that the 'poor' are dependant upon the rest of the community, they are often defined as 'useless' or as form of 'social residue'. This pejorative imagery and labelling are often internalised by those to whom it is applied. The logical deduction that comes from such thinking is that if there were not a class of 'the poor' who do nothing but drain the well-earned resources of the rest of society, then the whole social structure would be in a more positive state, and would be able to put to a positive use those resources used to support a minority of its members. Such a social conception takes no account whatsoever of the important role of social welfare as a form of regulator of the social system as a whole. Even if 'the poor' are prevented by the fact of their accepting 'social aid' from playing an active role in society, that does not necessarily imply that they are to be excluded. Although their positions on the rung are lower, they are still members of society. This is an important difference between 'disqualification' and 'exclusion'. The notion of 'disqualification' allows us to analyse social situations that might otherwise be called partial exclusion. In addition to this difference, notice that the concept itself is derived from the relations between parts of the social structure that are interdependent. The concept of 'disqualification' allows us not only to study those who are on the edges of society and the reasons for their being so placed; it also allows us to examine what links the edges of society to the social centre and hence how the society as a whole is to be defined and understood.

The third element of 'social disqualification' can be divided into several distinct parts. In order to take account of the varied nature of those who benefit from the help of social action I have defined three groups according to the type of relations that they develop with such services: fragile (those who are only occasionally in contact with welfare services), assisted (regular or contractual relations), marginal (substandard relations). Within these three groups I have distinguished the members according to their past history: 'internalised fragility', 'negotiated fragility', 'deferred assistance', 'established assistance', 'claimed assistance', 'warded-off marginality', 'organised marginality'. Such a method of categorising 'the poor' takes account not only of the partially institutionalised analyses effectuated by the different social services, but also of the way in which the subjects of assistance gave a sense to their own need for assistance. Each organism of assistance defines its role in regard to its work in relation to one or more of the categories of 'the poor'.

If I was asked to qualify or update *La disqualification sociale*, which was first published in 1991, one thing I would certainly insist more upon would be the direct correspondence between the three main groups of the population and three distinguishable phases in the development of poverty.[1] In order to underline the importance of the process and to reduce misconceptions that are widespread concerning the categorisation that takes place, I would alter some of the key vocabulary. Instead of 'fragile persons' I would use 'fragility'. Instead of 'assisted persons' I would use 'dependence'. Instead of 'marginals' I would use the idea of 'social ties breaking or rupture'. Of course the type of categorisation established was not statistically based upon fixed social strata; its basic principle implied the possibility of passing from one phase to another. The analysis of seven types of experience took account both of social transformations that had taken place and of previous social identity. The very circumstances in which the monograph on Saint-Brieuc was published dictated that it was undertaken with certain caution. The question of passing from one phase to another could only be supported by material from a limited number of interviews during which the subjects were able to give information about their own past history as well as analyse their own development. Such an analysis, of course, depends upon the subject's being conscious of the development of his own relations with the institutions of assistance – this was certainly not always the case. The material was too limited to develop any satisfactory line of investigation. It was also impossible to prove that Saint-Brieuc was exactly representative of the whole of France in terms of poverty and its classification. The work that has been completed subsequently has allowed me to reinforce the approach I took then and also to develop the notion of 'social disqualification'.

It will be my hypothesis that the weakening and breaking of social links play a fundamental part in the process of the development of poverty.

The Weakening of Social Links

Recent studies completed in France, in particular the multidimensional study effected by INSEE, concerning the living conditions of households that are termed 'disadvantaged situations' (i.e. *situations défavorisées*) clearly show a correlation between instability in professional life and weakness of social links. The unemployed often maintain distant relations with family members outside their immediate household. The greater the professional instability, the greater probability of no family relation at all being maintained. Men are more sensitive than are women to this phenomenon of isolation and internalisation. The age range of 30–50 is most highly affected; professional instability is hardest to bear during that period which is normally considered as the most active of a working person's life. Possibilities of help either from close relations or from social relations diminish directly in relation to the degree of instability experienced.[2]

It can be concluded that the risk of a weakening of social links is directly proportional to the difficulties that an individual encounters in obtaining regular work. This clearly explains the current and widespread phenomenon of the decay of the social fabric and uneasiness in communities that suffer a high rate of unemployment. That is not to say that every working class community has become a social vacuum, but if we make a comparison between the current situation and the descriptions of sociologists and ethnologists during the 1950s and 1960s, it is clear that there has been a weakening of community life in these areas. Community life has undergone transformations as a result of social differentiations that have developed in the working class: certain groups have left the areas as a result of their increasing affluence; others have been constrained to immobility. More and more families have no choice but to live in the unfavourable areas of a city. One of the widespread results is the development of a negative image of themselves and a wish to distance themselves from their immediate neighbours. Knowing how family reputations are created, the main objective for many is to hide their everyday problems and worries in the hope that future re-employment will allow them to move away into better area.

The weakening of social links takes place essentially during the first two places of the process of 'social disqualification': fragility and dependence. By analysing the experiences that subjects have undergone we can formulate an understanding of the process itself. Both dismissal, which is often interpreted as professional failure, and the failure to obtain a first job are causes of an increasing consciousness of the distance between the individual subject and the large majority of the population. An overbidding sense of all-too-visible failure develops which leads to the thought that everyday behaviour and habits will necessarily be interpreted, by those who are in a position to observe, as clear indication of social ineptness or inferiority; in extreme cases as a social handicap. The unemployed often feel that they are perceived as carriers of a 'social plague' when they try to explain their problems openly in public. Many who live in underprivileged areas or areas with a bad reputation prefer to conceal their address in order to avoid the humiliation of being associated with the socially unacceptable. In the case where social assistance becomes an absolute necessity, often the shame which this stigma invokes is extremely difficult to accept. They prefer to maintain a clear distance between themselves and social workers. 'Opening the door' to welfare assistance is often thought of as the first stage in the loss or resignation of any real social status and its accompanying self-respect and dignity.

People in such a position do not give up all hope of re-employment. They search actively for work both in the newspapers and at the work exchange, ANPE (French employment agency). When they are the beneficiaries of RMI (Income Support) they normally wish to become independent again as soon as possible. RMI is seen as a transitional compensation for unemployment, which also creates the risk of becoming more and more dependent upon assistance while social integration is dependent upon a professional activity. They are fully aware of the danger of becoming habitually inactive, with the final consequence of the loss of all professional identity whatsoever. These beneficiaries of RMI have fully understood the moral judgments that are aimed at those who are considered to be simply taking advantage of the welfare system. They see no use in strengthening their links with the institution of social assistance by signing an 'insertion contract' that would simply make them more dependent on a world they wish escape (see Paugam, 1993).

As a result of the experience of this first phase and its accompanying uneasiness, someone who is unemployed will tend to focus his attention upon his close family relations. Many subjects feel discouraged to the point of giving up, and direction of all attention onto the family helps to avoid the criticism or supposed criticism of others. Both fear and guilt force many to live within the four walls of their own home, either with hobbies or else in front of the television. At Saint-Brieuc the unemployed who inhabited *la Cité du Point du Jour* admitted that they often entered their own houses through the cellar in order to avoid contact with the other inhabitants either in the courtyard or at the windows. They positively avoided their neighbours and took no part in communal life.

The process of losing your position in society can be humiliating, and it changes relations with others and leads to a self-imposed isolation. Even close family relations can suffer owing to the fact that a subject no longer appears to be capable of fulfilling the role he wished to play for his family. Many of the unemployed speak of a direct link between their loss of employment and the development of marital difficulties that led to separation or divorce. Hence the loss of a professional situation incites a loosening of family ties and the deepening of sense of guilt. Examining the study 'disadvantaged situations' (i.e. *situations défavorisées*) it is possible to see a correlation, without the support of a direct causal line, between the difficulty of finding employment in a given community and the difficulty of establishing a stable conjugal relationship, particularly in the case of men. The risk of separation or divorce is also increased (see Paugam, Zoyem and Charbonnnel, 1993, particularly chapter II, 'Famille et vie conjugale'). In such a situation a victim of unemployment very quickly loses his sense of position socially, and often enters a personal identity crisis. The continuation of such a situation can lead to the development of a state of dependence upon the social services.

'Fragility' can lead to the stage of 'dependence' when professional instability leads to a reduction in income and a lowering of living conditions, which can be alleviated by the help of social welfare. Dependence can be considered as the phase where the social services play a regular role in alleviating the difficulties that a subject encounters. Most subjects in this phase have given up regular employment. Excluding cases of the physically and mentally handicapped, this is always the result of a period, short or long, of continued discouragement and fatigue in the face of the lack of employment. After such a period those who have no longer any clear role turn to the social services for assistance. The acceptance of being dependent upon such services for a regular and fixed income is the result of its being impossible for them to do otherwise. Those who maintain their ambition of finding employment also maintain a distance between themselves and the social services. However, after different training programmes and many varied efforts to gain re-employment have all proved unsuccessful, they give up hope that they will ever be able to find regular work. Several subjects receiving RMI who were in the stage of 'fragility' at the beginning of the above-mentioned study declared a year later that they had health problems which prevented them from working. This type of health problem, which also serves as a justification for numerous other difficulties, signifies the beginning of the stage of 'dependence'. Many subjects in such circumstances made contact themselves with the social services in order to sign insertion contracts. Their only obligation in such a situation is to accept the obligation and constraints imposed by the contract. The signing of the contract is the beginning of another phase that is usually accompanied by a rapid character transformation. They are taught a new social role which corresponds to the expectations of the social workers. This is the starting point of the justification and rationalisation of the assistance that they receive. Parents sometimes explain their decision to seek assistance in terms of their children rather than themselves. In such cases the acceptance of help corresponds to a form of maternal devotion or self-sacrifice for the ultimate good of the offspring. Another common explanation invokes the bad state of the economy, which allows assistance to be seen as a permanent social obligation or social right, even if in reality some forms of assistance are temporary and subject to specific conditions.

This form of integration allows social links to be kept going. Those who undertake the route of 'dependence' are often looking for a form of compensation for their previous failures by placing greater value on their role as parents and people of use in the immediate community by doing odd jobs and helping out in various ways. Pleasant and positive relations are often maintained with social workers, who can come to play the role of 'confidante' -- someone to whom the dependent person turns to for a solution to some of their problems. The income thus generated is almost always insufficient to keep up regular payments of rent, bills and maintenance, as well as the expense of children. Such households are often in debt.[3]

The Breaking of Social Links

Dependence is followed by a third phase – that of the severing of social ties. This is brought about in cases where the social aid comes to an end and the dependants are left facing a number of significant handicaps. Such cases risk no longer being included in the catchment zone of the social security system and hence falling into a form of misery and degradation that might be called desocialisation. Those who go through the phase of social rupture often face a number of problems; declining health, estrangement from family and reduced possibilities of work. This is the most extreme stage, which is the result of an accumulation of failures. Those in such cases no longer nurture any hope of regaining a stable situation and live with the underlying thought that they are useless to society. They have lost all sense of *raison d'être* (reason for living). Consolation is often sought in alcohol and heavy drinking. Those social workers responsible for the reinsertion of such cases often state the largest problem to be that of alcohol or drugs.

This segment of the poor population is made up not only of certain subjects who have experienced a brutal fall during the period that should have been the heart of their professional life, but also of young people in a state of physical and moral distress. Some of them have passed directly from the state of fragility to the final stage of the process without ever being regularly dependent upon social welfare. The most common explanation for this extreme development is the lack of stable family relations. For many who have problems finding a first job, the lack of strong family support leaves them with very little or no help at all.

In cases where not only employment but also housing is lost, we can talk not of weakening of social contacts but of social rupture. Two studies completed in France by a survey institute, the CSA,[4] of a representative selection of homeless people allow us to develop a fuller understanding of the problem and also to support the qualitative comments made above. Hence we can better understand the original circumstances that have led to social rupture. In answer to the question 'What has been missing in your life?' asked in 1994 it is very noticeable that two factors are mentioned in a far greater number than any others; firstly problems concerning work (46 per cent), secondly family problems (55 per cent); bad relations with parents (29 per cent); bad relations with spouse (26 per cent). The homeless often talk about a lack of chance or luck, but they also talk about their lack of any family life and the corresponding love and confidence that it cultivates.

The studies also allow us to analyse the effects of the duration of homelessness upon the experiences of the subjects and the development of their attitudes (Table 1.1). There is a far greater likelihood of social rupture in the case of a subject losing all form of residence, and it increases with the duration of this situation. Several questions put to the homeless verify this correlation. In 1994, 50 per cent of people homeless for three months confided in their families as opposed to 27 per cent of those homeless for a period of three years. The difference is less striking in 1997 but the trend is similar; family links dissolve with the lengthening of the period of homelessness. There are two main reasons: families obviously feel a growing sense of shame concerning one of their number who appears to be drifting further and further away from mainstream social life. To break family lines is a form of disownership. It is also the case that many of the homeless, particularly the young, leave their homes of their own will in the wake of cumulating conflicts and difficulties of a personal nature. The subjects also look upon themselves as in some way unworthy of contact with their families as long as they are unable to fulfil what they see as expected of them. Isolation is preferable to humiliation in such cases. Only when confidence is regained and their situation improved do the homeless re-establish contact with their families.[5]

Contact between the homeless and the police – which is another index of social integration – is higher during the first few months of homelessness. In 1997, 41 per cent of the homeless for less than three months, diminishing to 23 per cent for the three years bracket, make contact with the police. Many of the homeless, particularly those who sleep in the open, avoid contact with the police in order to keep their own individual freedom in a public area. It is well

Table 1.1   Experience and attitudes of the homeless according to the length of the period of homelessness

	< 3 months	3–6 months	7–12 months	12–36 months	> 36 months	Total > 12 months	*in %* Together
1	50	50	49	42	27	34	44
2	44	39	39	37	35	36	39
3	32	29	30	28	26	27	29
4	41	37	31	25	23	24	31
5	6	6	17	12	20	16	12
6	43	42	33	39	26	32	37
7	45	57	30	30	28	29	38
8	12	8	6	8	13	11	12
9	11	13	14	14	20	18	15
10	12	8	11	18	19	18	14
11	12	13	19	22	23	13	18
12	23	20	23	23	34	30	25
13	11	15	15	16	26	22	17
14	10	20	22	22	24	22	19
15	36	26	23	25	19	22	26
16	59	43	36	54	24	37	43
17	61	61	33	38	32	35	45

1   Has confidence in family, 1994.
2   Has confidence in family, 1997.
3   Has confidence in the police, 1994.
4   Has confidence in the police, 1997.
5   Consider themselves as marginal, 1994.
6   Consider themselves to be well received in social centres, 1994.
7   Consider themselves to be well received in social centres, 1997.
8   Suffer from dirt and filth, 1994.
9   Suffer from dirt and filth, 1997.
10 Suffer from cold, 1994.
11 Suffer from cold, 1997.
12 Main daily priority is to find someone to speak to, 1997.
13 Consider that the best way to avoid depression is to keep a domestic animal, 1997.
14 Consider the most common reaction of general public to be that of scorn, 1997.
15 Consider the most common reaction of general public to be that of solidarity, 1997.
16 Think that their personal situation will be better within one or two years, 1994.
17 Think that their personal situation will be better within one or two years, 1997.

Coverage: national representative sample of 503 homeless in November 1994 and 515 in January 1997.

Source: CSA Institute, 1994, 1997.

know that the forces of law and order perform the task of shepherding the homeless to centres, where they are maltreated or highly constrained. Particularly striking is the reaction of the homeless to such centres, of lodging or for health. Those who have been homeless for a relatively short period of time consider themselves to be well treated; such an appreciation diminishes directly in relation to the length of the period of homelessness. When they are not yet prepared to face the hardships that confront them living in the open, the centres provide urgent and necessary help. Women are more receptive to the work of the centres than men; it is easier for them to suffer the constraints imposed because they have little or no chance of surviving in the street where insecurity and violence reign. Those who have recently known the misfortune of homelessness often look for help; in contrast those who have already been homeless for a period of years tend to place no confidence at all in the social welfare institutions.

Those homeless for more than three years consider themselves to be marginal more frequently than do others. They also suffer more frequently from cold and from dirt and filthiness. Thirty-four per cent declare that their most important daily priority is to find someone to speak to, which is a very telling comment upon the radical nature of social rupture. Dogs are often a source of constant company. The 1997 study showed that the proportion who placed their friendship with a domestic animal rose with those who longer suffered homelessness for longer. More than a quarter of homeless for more than three years chose this answer out of a possible 10, while only 11 per cent did so among the 'less than three months' category. The company of a dog acts both as cause and effect of their marginal situation; a dog gives company when there are no humans forthcoming but conversely it makes much harder their being accepted into a social centre where contact with other humans would be regular.

The 'over three years' are also the most numerous category to find themselves the object of scorn; 24 per cent against 10 per cent for the 'less than three months'. Thirty-six per cent of the 'less than three months' find others show solidarity with their position: the figure decreases progressively with the time passed without a regular home, a decrease that is similar for the question of whether a subject hopes his situation will improve in one or two years: 60 per cent of the 'less than three months', 24 per cent in 1994 and 32 per cent in 1997 for the 'over three years'.

The results of the study provide a very coherent picture of social rupture as the result of a process. After a number of months or years the life of the homeless resembles a hopeless lunge into the future. Many of them have nothing left to lose; they have internalised all the consequences of their situation and occupied essentially with their immediate needs.

European Variations

While both the weakening and the breaking of social links are fundamental to the process of social disqualification, it must be stated that major differences exist in different parts of Europe. Multidimensional studies undertake by Eurostat in 1994, equivalent to those of 'defavorised situations' (i.e. *situations défavorisées*) for INSEE allows us to develop a clear picture of both the similarities and differences between countries.[6] Certain similarities are easily predictable: the link between professional instability and low income and poor housing. In all countries the probability of marital separation or of living alone is higher for those people without regular work. Unemployment also increases the risk of health problems and dependence upon the social services. The most striking difference for country-to-country is at the level of the strength of the social links. In not all countries is the lack of stable work directly related to a weakening of family relations or of sources of private help. In Spain and the Netherlands the unemployed have equally strong relations with their family as the employed; in Italy the relations can be even stronger. In these countries the support from personal sources is sometimes strong even for people with an accumulation of difficulties.[7] At the opposite end, England, France and Germany are three examples of countries in which social relations decline with professional instability. This leads us to the hypothesis that in such countries the process of social disqualification is more radical in its effects than in other European countries.

The first instance of European-wide survey of households allows us both to verify these results and to go further in our deduction. Four questions were posed concerning social links in 1994, two of which concern distance and social relations: How often do you talk to any of your neighbours? How often do you meet friends and relatives who are not living with you? Another question deals with the reception of basic support: Did you personally receive in 1993 any financial support or maintenance from relatives, friends or other persons outside your household? The final question deals with relations with associations or clubs: Are you a member of any club or organisation, such as sport or entertainment club, a local of neighbourhood group, a party, etc.? Immediately obvious is the fact that, taken by themselves, the questions are not sufficient to study the nature of social links. Such questions can only indicate a general direction of inquiry and must be complemented by other sources, particularly more qualitative and descriptive ones. However, the questions can be asked in the same form in every European country and hence can serve as the basis of a comparison at the macro-sociological level.[8]

For each one of the questions a logical process of reasoning was undertaken in order to calculate the link between the strength of the relation to regular work and the strength of social links. Five separate cases appeared: stable job, insecure job, precarious job, unemployment for less than one year, unemployment for more than one year (cf. Appendix).[9]

An important question that emerges is the following: does the social life which centres around neighbour's friends and relations decrease in strength with a decrease in the regularity of work? Looking at the results concerning neighbours this would not seem to be the case (Appendix Table I.2). Several countries show the opposite tendency, particularly for those unemployed for more than a year. In the Netherlands, Belgium, Spain, Portugal and Italy the unemployed speak more often to their neighbours than the regularly employed. The relation is significantly negative only in France. However in several countries – France, Greece, Italy and Spain – there exists a negative correlation for those in a precarious job, although we are presently unable to explain this phenomenon fully. Greater detail about the nature of the habitation (communal or individual) and the size of the community is necessary before we can further establish the reasons for such coefficients.

The relations between neighbours are very different in the country from in a large city, for example. In further analyses we would expect to see a greater divergence between the countries. The results concerning friends and relations show a greater contrast (Appendix Table II.2). In France the coefficient is sufficiently negative for the categories of precarious job and unemployment of more than one year; in Ireland, for precarious job and the two lengths of unemployment; in Greece the same, as well as insecure job; and in Great Britain, though less significantly, for insecure job and precarious job. In Spain, Portugal and Denmark the coefficient is positive for the unemployed over one year, which signifies that they have more contact with parents and friends than those who have a stable job. Italy shows no clearly-defined trend. The conclusion of these figures is that the unemployed are significantly more isolated in some countries than others.

This tendency is confirmed when we look at fundamental solidarity (Cf. Appendix Table III.2). The results are extremely different concerning the category of the long-term unemployed because it is well known that they are the least well-off among the active population, for the reason that the resources of the unemployed are reduced progressively with the length of unemployment. Hence examining the help given by family and friends is a way of measuring the strength of the social links that exist. In southern Europe – Italy, Spain, Portugal and Greece – the coefficient is significantly positive, whereas it is weaker in Belgium and most important of all in France, Denmark, Great Britain and Ireland. The same division between northern and southern Europe reappears more obviously than in the previous Eurostat survey. The case of the Netherlands provides particular points of interest; the coefficient is higher than in the countries in the South of Europe, which is surprising, as social welfare help is higher than in the south. It would be natural to assume that the overall efficiency of the social welfare system would reduce the need for private help or at least restrict it to areas of fundamental need. This result confirms what we have already discovered through a different source (see Paugam, 1996a) namely that the social links are unusually strong in the Netherlands which, more than other northern European countries, presents an anthropological profile of a more socially-constructed community. Wout Ultee, a Dutch specialist on behaviour concerning work habits, also confirms the particularity of the Netherlands. The unemployed remain close to their families and often fixed, geographically speaking.

Finally, by taking note of the relations with clubs and associations we notice that there are differences between the countries. There is a significant weakness in the link between the unemployed and clubs or associations for the unemployed, compared to the club life of regularly employed people in Denmark, France, Belgium and Ireland. The result is slightly less significant in the Netherlands and not at all significant in other countries (cf. Appendix Table IV.2). The results are similar for all the countries in the southern part of Europe, where the unemployed are as active as the fully-employed in this area of social life. In these countries we have established that unemployment is less of a stigma than it can be in some of the northern countries, which explains the fact that the unemployed continue to play their previous role in social life. An example of particular note is Great Britain. Previous studies have shown that in Great Britain the unemployed remain socially integrated with groups of unemployed people or clubs of their own social class, even if their participation is not always as regular as it had been previously. This is probably similar to the situation in the southern part of Europe. It must also be noted that association with clubs is weaker for the southern countries not for the unemployed, but for those with an insecure job (Italy) or for those with a precarious job (Spain and Portugal); there is no similar trend in other countries. This can be explained by the fact that, in such countries, precarious employment is very widespread and habitual for many: those individuals finding themselves in such a situation devote all their energies to their professional work. Social activities are of secondary or no importance.

Conclusion

The differences that emerge between the European countries have several theoretical implications. From the position that the strength and the nature of the social links are different from country to country we can deduce that 'social disqualification' is not equally probable in the different countries. Private networks of help afford varying degrees of support in the struggle for work and financial stability to prevent the process starting and to prevent the passage from one phase to another. This does not necessarily imply, however, that the social logic of the process itself is different from one national context to another. We can confidently put forward the hypothesis that the progressive phases of the process are almost identical in all of the countries under consideration and that the weakening of social links and social rupture are universally essential elements. The homeless in the southern part of Europe are confronted with similar problems – this must of course be checked – to the homeless in other countries as well as a similar development and set of experiences as the period of homelessness lengthens. The initial risk of becoming homeless, however, varies from country to country, as does the risk of becoming socially isolated. Often, stress is placed upon the low level of homelessness in southern Europe.

Any analysis of the process of 'social disqualification' must take account of the differences of scale – the qualitative differences – without isolating them from the social structures of which they are a product. A similarity of appearances in the behaviour of similar groups in the populations of similar countries does not imply that the phenomenon in question has the same social meaning and importance, nor that groups that represent the phenomenon are necessarily the same. These first results open the way to further investigations not only of the social links concerning the underprivileged populations, but also of the wider issue of the regulation and fluctuation of social links in European societies, taking into account economic development, the role of the state help and also of non-institutionalised help. The combination of these three elements might explain both the relations that each society develops with that segment of its population that it labels as poor and also the national characteristics of the process and overall experience of poverty. The studies that are presently being undertaken at CREST (Centre for Research in

Economics and Statistics) in conjunction with several European research teams,[10] with particular notice being paid to European data, have the verification of these hypotheses as their aim.

This perspective leads naturally to a study of what I have called 'the elementary forms of poverty' which correspond to the type of relations of interdependence which are developed between a segment of the population labelled as poor, by its relations with social services, and the rest of the population.[11] Such a definition is radically different from one that depends upon a straightforward substantialist view of the poor or the excluded. It implies that poverty has a distinct place of its own in the structure of a society as a regulatory instrument which acts through the channels of social assistance or social welfare upon the society as a whole. An elementary form of poverty shows firstly the relation that a society has with those it considers to be on its edge, but is at the same time obliged to support, and secondly the relation of the edges of the society to the centre. The living conditions and experiences of 'the poor' must be analysed in this light of interdependence, which varies throughout history and in different sociocultural contexts.

Notes

1   A full explanation of this point is given in the introduction to the third edition of *La disqualification sociale* published in 1994.
2   Active participation in the life of clubs and associations is twice as high among regularly-employed people as among the unemployed. See Paugam, Zoyem and Charbonnel (1993), particularly chapter V, 'Sociabilité', the results of which confirm the analyses of Paul Lazarsfeld and his team (1931) concerning the effects of unemployment in a small Austrian village at the beginning of the 1930s.
3   The amount of the RMI (Income Support) was fixed not in relation to any fundamental financial needs for a household but in relation to the minimum wage. In order to prevent the RMI from becoming a discouraging factor in the search for employment it was thought that it must be lower than the minimum wage. This principle was agreed unanimously in the National Assembly. The status of being the subject of social welfare help is socially degrading and only allows extreme poverty and misery to be avoided.
4   Studies made by CSA Institute in 1995 and 1997, each one taking a sample of 500 homeless people.
5   Among those recipients of the RMI who had had no close relation with their family for a long time it was noticeable that some renewed contact with their children or parents when they began to receive a regular income. See Euvrard and Paugam (1991).
6   This research was undertaken on the subject of the non-monetary indexes that contribute to the state of poverty following a demand made by Eurostat with the support of the European Community. Several national teams were involved in the work which was coordinated by the Research Centre of Income and Costs (*Centre d'Etude des Revenus et des Coûts*). The

main results are set out in an article summarising the research: see Paugam, 1996a.

7   Denmark could also be added to the list, if the size of the social network was taken as an index of importance: it was the only index available for the research in Denmark. This, however, is less precise and different from the indexes used in analysing the situation in other countries.

8   No Europanel information is available concerning Germany.

9   The different levels of job stability were established by a question concerning the satisfaction of the employed with the stability of their work. Those who were satisfied were put into the 'stable job' category. Those not satisfied but who had held their job for more than a year were classed as 'insecure job'. Those not satisfied and who had held their job for less than a year were classified as 'precarious'.

10 The research (EPUSE, Employment Precarity, Unemployment and Social Exclusion) demanded by the European Commission.

11 I have already presented a more detailed approach to these questions in two symposia: 'Poverty and Social Exclusion : Sociological View', Florence, 5–6 October 1995, symposium on *A New Social Contract?*, organised by the Institut Universitaire Européen et le Centre Robert Schuman (Working paper no. 96/37 de European University Institute) and 'Elements of a comparative research perspective on poverty in European societies', Blarney, 26–30 March 1996, Communication for European Science Foundation Conference on *Social Exclusion and Social Integration in Europe: Theoretical and Policy Perspectives on Poverty and Inequalities*. See also Paugam, 1996b.

Bibliography

Anderson, N. (1923), *The Hobo. The Sociology of Homeless Man*, Chicago, University of Chicago Press (trad. en français, Paris, Nathan, 1993).

Damon, J. and Firdion, J.-M. (1996), 'Vivre dans la rue : la question SDF' in Paugam, S. (ed.), *L'exclusion, l'état des savoirs*, Paris, La Découverte, coll. 'Textes à l'appui', 1996, pp. 374–86.

Lazarsfeld, P., Jahoda, M. and Zeisel, H. (1981), *Les chômeurs de Marienthal*, Paris, Editions de Minuit, (1ère édition en allemand, 1931).

Paugam, S. (1991), *La disqualification sociale. Essai sur la nouvelle pauvreté*, Paris, Presses Universitaires de France, coll. 'Sociologies', 4ème édition mise à jour 1997.

Paugam, S. (1993), *La société française et ses pauvres. L'expérience du revenu minimum d'insertion*, Paris, Presses Universitaires de France, Coll. 'Recherches politiques', 2ème édition mise à jour 1995.

Paugam, S. (1995), 'The Spiral of Precariousness: a Multidimensional Approach to the Process of Social Disqaulification in France' in Room, G. (ed.), *Beyond the Threshold. The Measurement and Analysis of Social Exclusion*, Bristol, The Policy Press, pp. 49–79.

Paugam, S. (1996a), 'Poverty and Social Disqualification. A Comparative Analysis of Cumulative Social Disadvantage in Europe', *Journal of European Social Policy*, 6 (4), pp. 287–303.

Paugam, S. (ed.) (1996b), *L'exclusion, l'état des savoirs*, Paris, La Découverte, coll. 'Textes à l'appui'.

Paugam, S., Zoyem, J.-P. and Charbonnnel, J.-M. (1993), *Précarité et risque d'exclusion en France*, Paris, La Documentation Française, coll. 'Documents du CERC', no. 109.

Room, G. (éd.) (1995), *Beyond the Threshold. The Measurement and Analysis of Social Exclusion*, Bristol, The Policy Press.

Rossi, P. (1989), *Down and out in America. The Origin of Homelessness*, Chicago, The University of Chicago Press.

Simmel, G. (1908), 'Der Arme' in *Soziologie. Untersuchungen über die Formen der Vergesellschaftung*, Leipzig, Duncker-Humboldt, (trad. en français, *Les pauvres*, Paris, Presses Universitaires de France, coll. 'Quadrige', 1997).

Snow, D. and Anderson, L. (1993), *Down on Their Luck. A Study of Homeless Street People*, Los Angeles, University of California Press.

Appendix

Tables on dynamics of social networks in Europe (using questions of Europanel, wave 1, 1994)

Table I.1   How often do you talk to any of your neighbours?

	0	1	2	3	4	Total
Denmark	4.6	9.6	13.6	37.3	34.9	100
France*	–	23.5	31.6	44.9	–	100
Great Britain	3.1	3.4	10.7	34.5	48.3	100
Belgium	5.0	7.6	15.2	39.4	32.8	100
Ireland	1.6	2.1	6.4	28.2	61.6	100
Netherlands	13.8	6.6	14.8	41.3	23.5	100
Italy	7.4	5.9	8.6	25.9	52.2	100
Spain	3.0	3.5	6.5	22.6	64.4	100
Portugal	2.3	3.7	8.1	25.7	60.2	100
Greece	1.3	1.9	3.3	16.7	76.8	100

0   Never
1   Less often than once a month
2   Once or twice a month
3   Once or twice a week
4   On most days
*1   Rarely, 2: sometimes, 3: often

Source: Europanel, 1994, wave 1, Coverage: population 18–65 years of age.

Table I.2   Logistic regression on relations with neighbours

	Denmark coeff. sig	France coeff. sig	Great Britain coeff. sig	Belgium coeff. sig	Ireland coeff. sig
Stable job	Const.	Const.	Const.	Const.	Const.
Insecure job	- 0.08 ns	- 0.16 ***	0.07 ns	0.04 ns	- 0.21 ***
Precarious job	- 0.01 ns	- 0.26 ***	0.08 ns	0.12 ns	0.11 ns
Unempl. <1	0.12 ns	- 0.09 ns	0.44 ***	0.23 ns	0.24 ns
Unempl. >1	0.14 ns	- 0.20 **	- 0.07 ns	0.58 ****	0.33 ***
Inactive	0.37 ****	0.03 ns	0.40 ****	0.46 ****	0.25 ***

Table I.2 (cont'd)

	Netherlands coeff. sig	Italy coeff. sig	Spain coeff. sig	Portugal coeff. sig	Greece coeff. sig
Stable job	Const.	Const.	Const.	Const.	Const.
Insecure job	- 0.43 ns	- 0.01 ns	- 0.08 ns	- 0.10 ns	- 0.14 *
Precarious job	0.09 ns	- 0.29 ***	- 0.14 *	0.08 ns	- 0.33 ***
Unempl. <1	0.75 ****	0.37 **	0.51 ***	0.20 ns	0.15 ns
Unempl. >1	0.40 ***	0.26 *	0.33 ****	0.48 ***	0.13 ns
Inactive	0.40 ****	0.47 ****	0.25 ****	- 0.19 **	- 0.08 ns

* = P < .1, ** = P < .0.5, *** = P < .0.1, **** = P < .001
Reference: stable job, woman, aged 40–54, with partner and children, primary education or less, low income.

Source: Europanel, 1994, wave 1, Coverage: population 18–65 years of age.

Table II.1   How often do you meet friends and relatives who are not living with you?

	0	1	2	3	4	Total
Denmark	0.0	2.6	16.8	52.9	27.7	100
France*	–	9.7	28.2	62.1	–	100
Great Britain	0.3	2.9	12.1	46.4	38.3	100
Belgium	0.9	8.1	18.4	39.5	33.1	100
Ireland	0.2 .	1.1	3.7	25.1	69.9	100
Netherlands	0.7	2.3	15.0	59.3	22.7	100
Italy	5.2	7.7	13.1	30.6	43.4	100
Spain	0.3	2.1	5.0	24.7	67.9	100
Portugal	3.2	9.4	15.2	33.0	39.2	100
Greece	0.9	4.5	9.3	27.6	57.7	100

0 Never
1 Less often than once a month
2 Once or twice a month
3 Once or twice a week
4 On most days
*1 Rarely, 2: sometimes, 3: often

Source: Europanel, 1994, wave 1, Coverage: population 18–65 years of age.

Table II.2   Logistic regression on relations with friends and relatives

	Denmark coeff. sig		France coeff. sig		Great Britain coeff. sig		Belgium coeff. sig		Ireland coeff. sig	
Stable job	Const.		Const.		Const.		Const.		Const.	
Insecure job	- 0.16	*	- 0.02	ns	- 0.10	*	0.35	ns	- 0.04	ns
Precarious Job	- 0.01	ns	- 0.26	***	- 0.18	*	- 0.09	ns	- 0.36	***
Unempl. <1	0.25	*	- 0.15	ns	- 0.17	ns	0.39	ns	- 0.35	**
Unempl. >1	0.45	***	- 0.34	***	- 0.17	ns	0.01	*	- 0.37	***
Inactive	0.31	***	- 0.21	***	0.11	*	0.16	*	- 0.31	***

	Netherlands coeff. sig		Italy coeff. sig		Spain coeff. sig		Portugal coeff. sig		Greece coeff. sig	
Stable job	Const.		Const.		Const.		Const.		Const.	
Insecure job	- 0.11	ns	-0.08	ns	- 0.10	*	0.12	**	- 0.19	***
Precarious job	- 0.22	ns	0.20	*	- 0.10	ns	0.00	ns	- 0.23	**
Unempl. <1	0.33	*	0.23	ns	0.39	****	0.01	ns	- 0.02	ns
Unempl. >1	0.12	ns	0.12	ns	0.20	**	0.49	***	- 0.34	**
Inactive	0.36	****	0.02	ns	0.12	*	- 0.20	**	- 0.12	ns

* = P < .1, ** = P < .0.5, *** = P < .0.1, **** = P < .001
Reference: stable job, woman, aged 40–54, with partner and children, primary education or less, low income.

Source: Europanel, 1994, wave 1, Coverage: population 18–65 years of age.

Table III.1   Did you personnally receive in 1993 any financial support or maintenance from relatives, friends or other persons outside your household?

	Yes	No	Total
Denmark	8.7	91.3	100
France	3.4	96.6	100
Great Britain	6.0	94.0	100
Belgium	6.1	93.9	100
Ireland	0.7	99.3	100
Netherlands	2.3	97.7	100
Italy	3.5	96.5	100
Spain	2.6	97.4	100
Portugal	1.2	98.8	100
Greece	5.5	94.5	100

Coverage: population 18–65 years of age

Source: Europanel, 1994, wave 1, Coverage: population 18–65 years of age.

Table III.2   Logistic regression on financial support

	Denmark coeff. sig	France coeff. sig	Great Britain coeff. sig	Belgium coeff. sig	Ireland coeff. sig
Stable job	Const.	Const.	Const.	Const.	Const.
Insecure job	- 0.02 ns	0.03 ns	- 0.25 ns	0.06 ns	- 0.27 ns
Precarious job	0.21 ns	0.46 **	0.62 ****	0.47 ns	1.17 **
Unempl. <1	0.02 ns	0.47 **	- 0.12 ns	- 0.10 ns	1.50 **
Unempl. >1	- 0.19 ns	0.14 ns	0.22 ns	0.64 ***	0.59 ns
Inactive	0.47 ***	0.86 ****	0.40 ***	0.59 ***	1.82 ****

	Netherlands coeff. sig	Italy coeff. sig	Spain coeff. sig	Portugal coeff. sig	Greece coeff. sig
Stable job	Const.	Const.	Const.	Const.	Const.
Insecure job	- 0.29 ns	0.08 ns	0.24 ns	0.31 ns	0.13 ns
Precarious job	1.31 ***	0.51 **	0.64 ***	- 0.58 ns	0.84 ****
Unempl. <1	- 0.24 ns	0.27 ns	0.30 ns	0.87 *	0.20 ns
Unempl. >1	2.15 ****	1.46 ****	1.04 ****	1.60 ****	1.72 ****
Inactive	2.11 ****	1.58 ****	1.39 ****	0.68 **	1.93 ****

$* = P < .1, ** = P < .0.5, *** = P < .0.1, **** = P < .001$
Reference: stable job, woman, aged 40–54, with partner and children, primary education or less, low income.

Source: Europanel, 1994, wave 1, Coverage: population 18–65 years of age.

Table IV.1   Are you member of any club or organisation, such as sport or entertainment club, a local or neighbourhood group, a party, etc?

	Yes	No	Total
Denmark	42.5	57.5	100
France	28.0	72.0	100
Great Britain	45.4	54.6	100
Belgium	34.5	65.5	100
Ireland	44.7	55.3	100
Netherlands	47.8	52.2	100
Italy	17.1	82.9	100
Spain	27.4	72.6	100
Portugal	15.3	84.7	100
Greece	11.3	88.7	100

Source: Europanel, 1994, wave 1, Coverage: population 18–65 years of age.

Table IV.2   Logistic regression on social participation

	Denmark coeff. sig	France coeff. sig	Great Britain coeff. sig	Belgium coeff. sig	Ireland coeff. sig
Stable job	Const.	Const.	Const.	Const.	Const.
Insecure job	- 0.09 ns	- 0.05 ns	0.61 ns	- 0.17 *	0.01 ns
Precarious job	- 0.16 ns	- 0.02 ns	- 0.14 ns	- 0.41 *	- 0.11 ns
Unempl. <1	- 0.58 ****	- 0.29 **	- 0.09 ns	- 0.22 ns	- 0.31 ns
Unempl. >1	- 0.44 ***	- 0.26 **	- 0.18 ns	- 0.41 ***	- 0.63 ****
Inactive	- 0.10 ns	0.05 ns	- 0.03 ns	0.03 ns	- 0.26 ***

	Netherlands coeff. sig	Italy coeff. sig	Spain coeff. sig	Portugal coeff. sig	Greece coeff. sig
Stable job	Const.	Const.	Const.	Const.	Const.
Insecure job	- 0.02 ns	- 0.19 ***	- 0.05 ns	- 0.10 ns	- 0.02 ns
Precarious job	- 0.23 ns	- 0.27 ns	- 0.20 **	- 0.54 ***	- 0.02 ns
Unempl. <1	- 0.31 *	0.12 ns	- 0.05 ns	0.09 ns	- 0.03 ns
Unempl. >1	- 0.09 ns	0.08 ns	- 0.10 ns	0.10 ns	0.30 ns
Inactive	0.06 ns	0.29 ***	0.06 ns	- 0.15 ns	0.00 ns

* = P < .1, ** = P < .0.5, *** = P < .0.1, **** = P < .001
Reference: stable job, woman, aged 40–54, with partner and children, primary education or less, low income.

Source: Europanel, 1994, wave 1, Coverage: population 18–65 years of age.

2 Free Markets, Poverty and Social Exclusion

KATHERINE DUFFY

Introduction

This chapter does not seek to make an exhaustive taxonomy of social exclusion. It focuses on social exclusion as a political concept (Murard, 1997), and aims to typify some possible relationships between poverty and social exclusion. In so doing, it identifies two divergent perspectives on the processes causing social exclusion. The chapter concludes by suggesting that a neo-liberal perspective is increasingly dominant at the level of the European Union, and that this perspective both neglects the interaction between the three dimensions of integration and increases the risks of poverty for the least advantaged.

The Concept of Poverty

The core concept of poverty is well understood. It refers to inadequate financial or material resources. Two categories of poverty are generally accepted, absolute and relative, where the latter is related to a measure of central tendency in the distribution of income and the former is not. Measurement of these is more problematic. Absolute measures are caught in the debate about nutrition adequacy and are not able in practice to surmount cultural frameworks of adequacy. Relative measures get caught in arguments about the arbitrariness of objective income-band choices, and the debate about the cultural incompatibility of subjectively-derived measures for cross-national research.

Townsend (1979) and others have broadened the concept of poverty to that of relative deprivation, and this is widely accepted. However, while Article 2 of the Council Decision of December 1984 on specific Community action to combat poverty defined poverty more widely than monetary resources, it refers to a minimum threshold, namely as 'material, cultural and social resources which are so limited as to exclude people from a minimally

52

acceptable way of life'.[1]

Nevertheless, the European Union measure of poverty remains financial and relative: half or less of average household (or personal) income or expenditure in the member state. Few European countries have an 'official' definition of poverty, and many use an administrative low-income measure based on threshold incomes for payment of social assistance. However, many also refer to this relative measure. The question of the validity of relative or absolute concepts for discussing poverty remains unresolved, but may be one reason why the focus of the European 'Poverty' model action programmes shifted from a focus on poverty to a focus on exclusion and integration (Select Committee of the European Communities, 1994). Council of Ministers of the European Union referred to social exclusion for the first time in 1989 in a resolution that emphasised

> that social exclusion is not simply a matter of inadequate means, and that combating exclusion also involves access by individuals and families to decent living conditions by means of measures for social integration and integration into the labour market.[2]

The Distinction Between Poverty and Social Exclusion

The distinction between poverty and social exclusion is discussed in a number of previous documents from the author (Duffy, 1995, 1996). Generally, the distinction made is between a focus on inadequate or unequal material resources, vis-à-vis inadequate or unequal participation in social life (Room, 1996, p. 5). Further, social exclusion is often seen as a way to breathe new life into poverty research, by focusing on processes and dynamics.

However, it is not clear that there is a consistent perspective on what is the relationship between poverty and exclusion. For example, the 1994 Eurobarometer survey of public opinion indicated that the public perception was that societies are more divided, that more people are 'becoming' poor who were not 'born poor' and that there is a hard core who are not able to get out of poverty (1995, tables 2.16–2.22, pp. 54–9). More of the people interviewed who were in financially poorer groups believed poverty had increased and so had the gap between rich and poor (ibid., table 2.13, p. 50). Similarly more of the poorer groups stressed the importance of the fight against poverty. However, the link between socioeconomic variables and social exclusion was much less clear (ibid., tables 2.26 and 2.27, pp. 62–3). Poorer groups were those most likely to say that they did not know about the concept of social exclusion, or not to respond to the question. (ibid., p. 63).

Nevertheless, the Eurobarometer survey did indicate that the public perceived a relationship between poverty and social exclusion. However, social exclusion was felt to encompass non-financial barriers to social participation, such as discrimination, as well as social problems such as marital breakdown and substance abuse, that may or may not be connected to low material resources.

In the early 1990s, academics were no clearer than was the public. For example, for France, Bouget and Nogues (1993) listed 22 terms describing the phenomena of exclusion, and in its report on least advantaged groups, the General Report on Poverty in Belgium considered the term social exclusion 'too imprecise' and chose to utilise the notion of 'extreme poverty' (Fondation Roi Badouin, 1994; Council of Europe, 1995a).

Nevertheless, following Xiberras (1993) and Lambert (1995) exclusion has the meaning of being expelled from a place where you stood before, and of being kept outside by denial of access. Disadvantage concerns not only disparity between the top and bottom of the income scale, but between those comfortable within society and those on the margins or excluded. The most commonly shared perspective on social exclusion can be summarised as that of a segmented society, tiered through the labour market and through state policies. The key relationship is 'in' or 'out' rather than 'up' or 'down' (Touraine, 1991,1992; Castel, 1995).

Vranken (1995) and Martin (1996) have categorised three dimensions of exclusion; in terms of rights, in terms of marginalisation from production and in terms of weakened social networks which at the extreme result in catastrophic break-off from the rest of society (Pieretti, 1994). This extreme exclusion is often identified with residents of particular urban spaces. These three dimensions of the concept of exclusion will be considered in turn, before presenting a model of social integration, and considering the effect of the European Union's approach to combating to social exclusion.

The Link to Social Rights

Early reports from the International Institute for Labour Studies' (IILS) project on social exclusion in 10 non-European countries confirm at least two of Vranken's categories. For example, Rodgers (1994) suggested that social exclusion was more evident where social rights (including property rights) were weak. The report concluded that while social exclusion 'appears to occur within all economies' (1994, p. 19), there are key differences between industrialised and 'non-industrialised countries'. In the 'non-industrialised countries', there are issues of market formation and provision of political and civic as well as social rights. Reflecting the views of the European public and the intergovernmental organisations, in industrialised countries, long-term unemployment and loss of acquired rights are key issues. For example, over 94 per cent of respondents in the 1994 Eurobarometer survey agreed that there should be basic rights to housing, schooling and medical care. While for 81 per cent of respondents unemployment is the top priority in the fight against poverty and social exclusion (1995, table 3.2, p. 68), the 'right to work' ranked fifth in terms of rights, but supported by 87 per cent of respondents (ibid., table 3.3, p. 69). Forty-five per cent of respondents thought that the right to a guaranteed minimum income should be granted, but with conditions attached concerning housing, training and work (ibid., table 3.6, p. 74).

The intergovernmental steering committee on social policy of the Council of Europe also recognised a link between poverty and rights. Thus, 'poverty by definition is the consequence of a failure to adequately secure economic and social rights' but the committee doubted 'whether states would be prepared to add to their existing obligations in this sphere' (Council of Europe, 1992a, p. 75).

Funded by the European Commission, the Observatory on Social Exclusion, now in abeyance, was amongst the first to take a social rights approach to making the concept of social exclusion operational: 'social exclusion can be analysed in terms of the denial – or non-realisation – of social rights ...' (Robbins, 1993, p. 14). The support of DG V of the European Commission for an expert group on rights (Vogel-Polsky 1993), for the Comité des Sages (de Foucauld, 1996) and for the European Social Policy Forum (including the participation of the Platform of Social NGOs) is evidence of a concern for social rights, both as a means of combating social exclusion, and to give meaning to European citizenship. In its Opinion to the Intergovernmental Conference ('Reinforcing Political Union and Preparing for Enlargement') the Commission stated that 'above all there has to be a common base of social rights for all'.[3] However, the Amsterdam Treaty[4] outcome constituted a minimum agenda in this respect. In a step forward from the Maastricht Treaty specific provisions on employment were written into the Amsterdam Treaty (Title XIII), but the goal of a high level of employment is without prejudice to the 'monetarist' economic policy evident in the earlier Titles, and in particular the role of the European Central Bank.

Further, despite the concern for 'proper' social protection in Article 136, poverty is referred to in the Amsterdam Treaty only once (Article 177 on development cooperation with less-developed countries). Thus, despite the strength of public support for the right to work and for the provision of income maintenance without conditions, the climate of opinion in national governments, as represented in the Amsterdam Treaty, is concerned to roll back social rights and replace them with labour market opportunities and self-reliance. In this climate, the risks of poverty are likely to increase.

Sachs's (1996) structural analysis of the impact of globalisation provides a plausible explanation for the resistance to social rights as a means of combating poverty and social exclusion. Globalisation results in the 'sterilisation of capital', a slowdown in the real economy, and an austerity policy response by governments and international economic agencies. At the same time, new thinking on choice and autonomy legitimates this reaction, criticising the over-protectiveness of welfare and arguing that the rise of individualism marks the minimisation of state responsibility for social functions. There is exclusion of the useless who cannot or will not sell their labour and these useless individuals are localised in specific places and regions. A weak interpretation of 'empowerment' locates it in families and communities rather than in rights guaranteed by the state, and the 'commodification of social services' undermines the welfare state.

The European Commission's Communication on modernising social protection[5] is indicative of this strengthening neo-liberal perspective. In its section on 'social protection as a productive factor', it refers to the Florence Economic Council's call for the restructuring of public expenditure to promote employment. It raises the question of access to the labour market as a 'prerequisite for all the measures that put more responsibility on the individual through cuts in social security protection' (1997, p. 5). However, whereas there may be weakening support for the right to income maintenance as a means to combat poverty, other rights are not weakening. A later section of the Communication, on the subject of adapting social protection to maximise women's labour market participation, is subtitled 'towards an individualisation of rights' (1997, p. 15). The emphasis on equality between men and women, rather than other forms of inequality, reflects the content of the Treaty of Rome to which all other Treaties are essentially revisions. However, the downgrading of equality in relation to resources fits well with contemporary attitudes. In her discussion of the changing welfare paradigm, Ferge has referred to the 'individualization of the social' (1997, p. 23), to the weakening of the rights of the poor, and acknowledgement of group and minority rights, in particular those of women. She suggests this trend is related to the rejection of the 'modern' categories of class and social determinism, and adoption of the post-modern recognition of 'the right to differ' (1997, p. 27).

The Centrality of the Labour Market

One can see that the importance of the labour market as a means of integration, rather than 'passive' income maintenance, is central to the distinction between poverty and exclusion. Primarily, poverty has implied exclusion from goods and services and, more recently, consequent inability to participate in social life. Social exclusion goes beyond membership of society through consumption, to encompass exclusion from a place in society, thus the emphasis on the 'productive', and on the social role of employment. Thus also the concern with the 'moral hazard' of unemployment, and the fear that long-term absence from the labour market corrupts the family and community values which support labour market and social integration.

However, while work is central to the concept of exclusion, there is of course more than one perspective on the processes leading to worklessness. The following sections argue that the academic debate in France has not much influenced thinking elsewhere, and, at the level of the European Union, the term is becoming part of a neo-liberal economic and social agenda. This development is likely to reinforce the strength of the neo-liberal perspective in all Member States.

Segmentation and Social Exclusion

Like the concept of poverty, the concept of social exclusion seems to encompass both 'relative' and 'absolute' dimensions (Duffy, 1995). Social exclusion contains both a relative but porous risk of location in a less advantaged segment (group, area, market) and the absolute of the 'complete biographical break-off' from which there is no route back (Pieretti, 1994).

Castel's work (1995), which has been influential in France, is illustrative of a broad concern with unemployment and labour market segmentation, and with structural and regulatory processes causing poverty and exclusion. Paugam's model of 'social disqualification' characterises three situations of increasing exclusion for individuals: labour market precarity, social welfare dependency and lack of social networks (1993a, 1994). However, it is not clear whether Paugam's three stages are steps on a path taken by particular individuals, or, if they are what may be considered 'niches', occupied most frequently by particular groups in society (perhaps due to lack of social rights or discrimination). For example, labour market precarity may be a more-or-less permanent condition experienced by migrants and refugees, but may be a temporary phenomenon for many young people in their 'entry job' or 'McJob'. Orthodox economists have long concluded (for Anglo-Saxon countries) that there is limited evidence for labour market segmentation and that low human capital rather than dead-end jobs or exploitative wages, explain the primary distribution of income (Cain, 1976). Studies of 'turnover' out of poverty (Callan, Nolan and Whelan, 1993; Bruckner, 1995) certainly suggest that most individual life-courses are more fluid and reversible than notions such as a 'downward escalator' might imply. However, such evidence might also be used to suggest that a permanent 'culture of dependency' is not widespread, since when the opportunities are there, most people seem able to take them. Nevertheless, it may be the case that many individuals and households remain clustered close to any poverty line, whether in terms of the European Union measure, or social assistance thresholds, and never get a secure foothold in the comfortable 'two-thirds' society (Heady, 1997).

Recent common use of the term social exclusion in France has been concerned not only with segmentation, but with precariousness arising from the high levels of unemployment (over 12 per cent) in the context of a 'solidarity' model of social inclusion (Silver, 1994). There is a mass risk of slipping into a less favourable segment of the labour market. The recent French parliamentary initiative concerning a possible law on social exclusion referred to part-time, government-subsidised non-permanent contracts for 'socially useful work', a strategy of marginal insertion. The risk, given the employment security of tenured public sector employees, is that a two-tier labour market will be reinforced (Meurs and Prelis, 1997).

A definition of precarity developed by the French-origin NGO, ATD Quart Monde, is presented below. This definition has been influential at government level. So also has this organisation's emphasis on the link between social exclusion, loss of human dignity and denial of social rights.

> Precarity is the absence of one or more of the forms of security, notably employment which enable individuals and families to meet professional, family and social obligations, and enjoy fundamental rights. The resulting insecurity may be more or less extensive and have more or less serious and permanent consequences. It leads to extreme poverty when it affects several areas of existence, becomes persistent and jeopardises a person's chances of reassuming

his responsibilities and regaining his rights by himself in the foreseeable future (Economic and Social Council, '"Extreme Poverty and Economic and Social Precarity" Journal Officiel de la République Française, 1987' in Council of Europe, March 1993, p. 9).

This broad condition of precarity is evident in the view of the former president of the European Commission. In a speech at the European Social Forum in March 1993 in Copenhagen, he declared that social exclusion contained poverty, but poverty did not necessarily contain social exclusion. However, it also contains a narrower category of severe poverty, or 'great poverty' which has been the particular concern of Catholic NGOs, and is evident in the reports to the French Economic and Social Committee (Wresinski, 1994) and the Report of the Roi Badouin Foundation discussed earlier.

The concept of social exclusion as it is developing in Britain is narrow, and approaches the concept of an underclass. This narrow perspective is reflected both in the speeches of government ministers, and in the approach of a number of British academics (for example Walker, 1995). From this perspective the excluded are a subset of the poor, with aberrant behaviour or particular characteristics that prevent them from sharing in the high turnover out of low income or poverty, that characterises the experience of the majority of poor people. However, the remedy proposed does not share the solidaristic concerns for social rights that infuse the social and liberal-Catholic perspective. The following section discusses the impact of the welfare regime.

The Impact of Differing Welfare Regimes on the Approach to Poverty and Social Exclusion

The results of the IILS' project on social exclusion in 10 non-European countries (Rodgers et al., 1995) tend to suggest that it is not possible to be excluded when you were never included, and that the concept of social exclusion relates most appropriately to advanced industrial societies with highly developed welfare states. The 'crisis' in the welfare state and the crisis in the form of the social, social retreat and the search for individual alternatives, are two strands that have informed thinking about social exclusion.

Those countries with welfare regimes which are more universal and redistributive, in particular in Scandinavia, are less likely to focus on a long list of 'excluded' groups, and have been more concerned to focus on the conditions generating poverty. Ritakallio (1994) has referred to the preventative nature of the Finnish welfare regime, so that the existence of poverty constitutes a policy failure. Integration into society is secured by the ability to live the Scandinavian lifestyle, and therefore there is a stronger concern with resource equality. An emphasis on labour market participation and high replacement incomes are key elements of social integration. The Scandinavian concept of social exclusion as it is perceived for their own countries is close to a notion of multiple deprivation and sometimes-social pathology. In Scandinavia, the 'socially excluded' are taken to be a subset of poverty, the 'poorest of the poor' (Abrahamson and Hansen, 1996, p. 9). Scandinavian countries identify groups such as substance abusers, in particular isolated single men, for whom a lack of networks and associative life is a more pressing problem than resources (the question of social networks is considered later in the chapter).

The 'northern' or Anglo-Saxon sense of social exclusion is of small groups with severe problems of social integration. There is some debate as to whether there is a separate 'southern' model of welfare (Ferrera, 1996; Katrougalis, 1996) but nevertheless, the central analysis has concerned the causes and consequences of the underdevelopment of capitalism and of the welfare state, the role of the 'welfare society' (family and religious organisations) and the underdevelopment of secular civil society. These concerns are evident in Greece, the poorest member of the European Union. The debate on poverty and insecurity in employment was moderated by rapid increases in income and wealth until recent years, but there has been a low degree of development of a 'universalist' culture. Petmesidou (1996, pp. 327–8) has argued that this is a consequence of a shift to a 'post-Fordist' economy before industrialisation had deepened collective solidarities and social citizenship. The result is a high degree of statism, familialism and clientalism (ibid., p. 330). However, the *terminology* used in 'southern' countries, in government and academic circles, has been influenced by their position as net recipients of European Union Structural Funds for cohesion of the territories, and for labour market and social integration programmes. While Greek spending on the able-bodied unemployed is relatively low (whether for unemployment benefit, vocational training or other measures), Petmesidou noted the increase following receipt of Structural Funds, and the establishment, over a few years, of one million non-profit organisations concerned with training and what she refers to as 'a machinery of "fake" vocational training programmes' established by public-private agencies and politicians (ibid., p. 342).

Clearly, the welfare regime, both at the level of the nation-state and supra-nationally, are important influences on the way social exclusion is understood in society. This can be illustrated by the case of the UK, outlined below.

The Centrality of 'Employability'

For France, Murard (1997, p. 26–7) notes the origins of the term social exclusion within the state sector, both within the Socialist Party, and amongst liberal-Catholic civil servants. Paradoxically, whereas the earliest use of the term 'exclusion' in France concerned the problem of the exclusion of the *mal adapté* from social protection (Lenoir 1974),[6] current UK political usage is the reverse. In a speech to the General Assembly of the European Anti-Poverty Network held in Belfast in 1997, the UK Minister for Social Security, Harriet Harman, stated that the socially excluded are 'trapped in dependency', they 'inhabit a parallel world where income is derived from benefits, not work' (*Network News*, 1997, p. 4). For the young unemployed 'a life on benefits is not an option' (ibid., p. 5). It is likely that this perspective (shared to some extent by Scandinavian countries such as Denmark) reflects the long existence of universal minimum incomes in these countries, and therefore a view that the excluded are a 'residual' category for whom money is not the solution. The characteristic which so far distinguishes the UK from the Scandinavian countries is the developing perspective that the function of the welfare system is to provide subsistence prevention of severe poverty; welfare as a social safety net, rather than as a social cohesion instrument (wherein welfare systems would tackle inequality in incomes and other resources). This perspective on the role of the welfare system is indicative of the welfare regime of a liberal 'exchange' society as opposed to the solidaristic perspective ascribed to France by Silver (op. cit.) (though as Rustin and Rix point out, the 'ideal' and real in any country may be very different (1997, p. 13)). From the liberal perspective the emphasis is on behavioural self-exclusion which can be combated through programmes of 'job-readiness' so that the excluded are always 'imminent' workers, sharing the virtues of the working majority, and escaping poverty through waged work (Jones, 1996).

Relative to the two strands of French concern, with globalisation and consequent concern with segmentation of labour markets, and with the rupture of social ties, the emerging 'Blairite' British perspective perhaps underplays both structural barriers and bridges. The solution offered does not reflect segmented labour market theory, with its emphasis on 'bad jobs' (Doeringer and Piore, 1971), neither does it reflect a solidarity model of society. Rather, it reflects the assumptions of neoclassical economic models, in proposing an opportunity to access the personal and portable – general human capital (education and training). For example, the UK Secretary of State for Social Security, in her speech to the 1997 General Assembly of the European Anti-

Poverty Network, stated that 'work is central to the government's attack on social exclusion', that 'employability will tackle the root cause of social exclusion and poverty – worklessness' (*Network News*, 1997, p. 4), and that 'those who propose that higher benefits should be the first priority of government ... have failed to learn from the past' (ibid., p. 5).

This chapter suggests that the Anglo-Saxon 'solution' to social exclusion is emerging as the dominant perspective at the level of the European Union. Given the constraints of the legal framework of conditions for economic and monetary union, it is likely that Member States' policies to combat social exclusion will increasingly converge.

Throughout the European Union, unemployment is seen as the key social problem, most recently expressed in the Amsterdam Resolution on Growth and Employment.[7] For example, the new Title VIII of the Amsterdam Treaty discusses employment, and Title XI on social policy discusses vocational training.[8] The solution to unemployment is envisaged to be active labour market policies and integration 'contracts' For example, the European Commission's paper on the modernisation of social protection refers to minimum income schemes as 'a kind of exclusion compensation' and argues that there is 'a growing consensus on the necessity of moving from the traditional social assistance approach'.[9]

The European Union's Green Paper on the organisation of work takes a rather Anglo-Saxon approach, concerned with a more flexible legal framework for employment, to match the 'flexible firm' required to respond to globalisation. The chapter discusses the 'centrality' of 'questions concerning the balance of regulatory powers' and 'in particular the possibility of derogating from legislation by collective agreements and the scope for individual contracts versus collective agreements'.[10] Redistribution, in addition to insertion policies, is a weakening concern even in Nordic countries. Many governments are constrained in the short term by preparation for European Monetary Union.

It seems, then, that whereas the European Commission in principle supports social rights for all (op. cit.), the liberal perspective on the operation of free markets (that they provide the optimum welfare solution), takes precedence. The internal market and EMU are the perceived routes to growth and stability (Agenda 2000, p. 3). Free trade will guarantee optimum output and therefore full employment demand, and 'supply-side' education and training will guarantee fair opportunities to access them (ibid., pp. 8, 13). However, the 'decommodification' of workers is reduced, by weakening of labour market regulation and of the rights conferred by systems of social protection. This must increase the risks of poverty for those least able to access opportunities.

The Link Between the Labour Market and Social Networks

Policy-makers have been concerned to emphasise the role of self-help and of communities in supporting economic and social integration (for example Harman, 1997, p. 4). However, in the context of urban disadvantage and urban policy, Colenutt and Cutten (1994) have argued that government is 'localising and internalising these problems firmly within the context of the community' so that 'it rids central government of responsibility for them' (Colenutt and Cutten, 1994, p. 239). Further, in a review of the French debate on social exclusion, Martin argues that globalisation has created a process of marginalisation 'inherent in society itself and in its mode of production' (1996, p. 382). In addition to labour market precarity, Martin identified 'relational vulnerability' as a risk factors for social exclusion, resulting in lack of 'social' or 'network' capital. Loss of social capital and networks reinforces vulnerability on the labour market. The outcome is labour-market-related 'new' poverty and the threat to social reproduction inherent in long-term unemployment (ibid., p. 384).

One may raise the question of what are the necessary conditions for 'communitarianism', for example, of the sort proposed by Etzioni (1995), in which civil society reclaims more of the responsibility for integration? In contemporary urban areas there are unlikely to be many communities which correspond to the classic notion of a common bond between inhabitants sharing the same territory, in which the spiritual bond is one of friendship and is expressed by the frequent interaction of the guilds and crafts (Tonnies, 1955). Keating (1995, p. 128) notes that this model of urban society is generally considered to be in decline; a key determinant of this decline is unemployment (Adamson, 1995). Hence the experience of work is essential to the existence of precisely those 'ideal' communities which are really expected to shoulder more of the burden of reintegration. Unemployment blocks the bond of friendship that is nurtured through frequent social interaction. It necessitates greater mobility, as those who are able to will move elsewhere to seek work. Further, unemployment also affects those with jobs as employment is less certain in an increasingly volatile job market, and the impact of unemployment means that the basis for generalised reciprocity is gone.

Crouch (1995) has referred to Massey's definition of communities as 'nets of social relations'. Frazer (1995) has described the gay community and the black community as new communities. These 'communities of interest' and their new forms of sociability, are based neither on proximity (territory, work, blood), nor contract; Maffessoli (1996) has referred to the neo-tribes, or 'tribus' whose bond is 'being together'. In this context, exclusion also concerns lack of communication and a failure to negotiate group membership (Lambert, 1995).

In comparison with women, the relative lack of participation in community activities other than paid work by many men and young single people has been frequently noted. Joye (1995) explained this in terms of the importance of life cycle and the presence of children in social integration and involvement in neighbourhood affairs. If male affiliation to community has been mainly invested in paid work, in the interaction of life through crafts and trade, then loss of work will impact on the bonds holding them to community to a greater extent than women, who may still have more emotional and other resources invested in kinship. The likely weakness of the social networks of some unemployed men may impact upon the efficacy of active labour market policies and urban intervention (Duffy and Hutchinson, 1997).

Thus, changes in economic and social structures are weakening the role of the labour market, both as a source of primary distribution of income for many, and as a mechanism of inclusion. The ability of families to undertake either redistribution, or to sustain the social integration of family members without a place in the formal labour market, has diminished. Equally, the same forces have weakened the cohesiveness of traditional local geographic communities, particularly in urban areas and in rural areas undergoing rapid transformation. These forces must increase the risk that it will be more difficult in the future than in the past to find a 'route back' from unemployment or other risk situations. The current concentration on reform of the presumed perverse effects of the welfare state, which yet supports the society of strangers, fails to capture the impact of labour market processes on the family, community and the state, and the interactions between them.

Nevertheless, many states now place greater reliance on the organisations of civil society than in the past, and, more so, on market mechanisms, as means of inclusion. This trend may be characterised as a shift from the state as guarantor of social security to the state as promoter of economic opportunity, implemented through the markets and civil society organisations. The European Union and Commission documents described earlier, illustrate the strengthening neo-liberal perspective. Long evident in clearly economic policy areas (for example the Single Market) it has grown more prominent in social policy since the Delors Presidency. Common influences on the risks of social exclusion may be effecting a convergence in Member States' experience and their policy orientation. One transmission mechanism is the process of European integration (for example see Spicker, 1997, on the impact of federalism in the European Union, and Greve, 1997, on the convergent trends influenced by the European Union's role in agenda-setting, common standards, spillover effects from the internal market, and social dialogue). Thus, this chapter suggests that the 'Blairite' perspective on social exclusion is increasingly reflected elsewhere in the Union. The United Kingdom was instrumental in framing the Single Market legislation, which has given the push to this deepening neo-liberal convergence. Under the Blair presidency of the European Union, the United Kingdom may be instrumental in promoting further the subservience of social policy to the requirements of the free market.

Note that, given such an approach, policy to combat social exclusion will not tackle poverty; indeed, pressure on social rights and levels of social protection may exacerbate poverty. On the other hand, the 'Delors' approach to combating social exclusion would have included combating poverty, seen as a specific form of social exclusion.

In a model of social exclusion which is neither 'Blairite' nor 'Delorsian', there is no causal relationship between poverty and social exclusion, but there will be some correlation (if the same forces affect both), and one might posit that this correlation may be closer to the extent that communication networks, or status hierarchies, are 'commodified', or 're-commodified' in the sense of Esping-Anderson (1990) so that people must 'buy their way into society'. It may be argued by governments that in market-based societies with highly unequal income distributions, relative poverty is by definition more prevalent, but is not poverty in any absolute or policy-relevant sense, given the wealth of the countries concerned, and is a price worth paying for rapid growth. However, even were the underlying economic analysis correct, low material resources are more likely to exclude people from social integration than is the case in relatively equal but low-income traditional societies or state-socialist countries. A lack of social integration may adversely affect possibilities of economic integration. Finally, in fast-paced societies, the risk of social exclusion is likely to be greater for the poor and the disadvantaged groups (see below) than for others. For those without liquid assets, flexibility is both more risky and more difficult to achieve.

Drawing on the debate outlined earlier in the chapter, it seems that social exclusion concerns the failure of one or more of the mechanisms that integrate people into society. These are the family and personal networks, including the local community; markets, including the labour market; and state entitlements to income and services. It is distinct from discrimination (which relates to equal opportunity issues) and poverty (which relates to wealth and income distribution), although these are risk factors for social exclusion. In this version of the 'welfare triangle' (Evers, 1988; Duffy, 1997), risks and opportunities are related to the strength of a person's relationships with all three dimensions necessary for integration. Individuals at greater risk of exclusion and risk groups are those with a weak relationship to at least one of the dimensions of integration. Individuals in severe poverty or exclusion are those with a weak/absent relationship in two or three of these dimensions.

Examples of groups with a weak relationship to the state would be those with illegal or irregular status, those considered by the authorities to be somewhat 'at fault' in their situation (young single mothers, substance abusers, ex-offenders ...). Those with a weak relationship to the labour market might be the less skilled, those facing discrimination, those facing other barrier to labour market participation (caring responsibilities, ill health or disability). Those with a weak relationship to family and personal networks might be elderly and isolated, some rural-dwellers, substance abusers such as alcoholics, and those who have been in the care of the state such as orphans, children and adults with psychosocial problems, prisoners. It would be necessary, in a fuller analysis, to distinguish between 'entry' and 'exit' risk. For example, both the entry and exit to youth unemployment may be high, and to roofless homelessness, low, and the constellation of policies must take account of this.

Given this framework, a perspective on social exclusion that focuses solely on labour market status is not likely to generate adequate policies to combat exclusion. But more so, 'targeting' as a substitute, rather than complement, to universal income support and health and social services, is likely, not only to increase the risk of poverty an exclusion for under-identified groups, but also to exacerbate the politics of difference. The impact at the urban level, as an unintended consequence of urban intervention, has been discussed in Duffy and Hutchinson (op. cit.). The bureaucracy and difficulties of categorical-based extensions of insurance schemes are one of the drawbacks of occupation-based social protection systems, although they have in northern Europe provided better benefits for those included (workers in the 'primary' as opposed to 'secondary' labour markets) than the tax-financed universal income and health systems in the UK. Nevertheless, in many countries, whether tax-financed or otherwise, 'new risks' such as long-term unemployment or care of elderly dependants are excluded from the core benefit systems, and marginalised into means-tested assistance, underlying which is a subsistence concept of poverty.

There remains considerable diversity in Member States' approaches and experience, because the precise constellation of influences will vary between different localities, regions and countries, as will Members States' perspectives and responses. Nevertheless, the documents from the European Commission and the European Union referred to in this chapter are evidence that there has been a shift, to varying degrees, in the perspective of governments. That is, a shift from the provision of collective security, supported by the state, the 'downside' of which has been suggested to be 'passivity' of persons ('dependency culture'), to a culture of individual opportunity. Increasingly, resources are targeted on fitting people for opportunities, thus, for example, active labour market policy. The 'downside' of this 'opportunity society' is that an opportunity is not a right. There is an increased risk of poverty and social exclusion for those not able to grasp opportunities, whatever the source of the barrier (personal, environmental, economic, and social). Another consequence is the increasing demand for, and creation of, intermediate organisations, which operate between the individual and the state or the market. Examples are local public-private partnerships, social entrepreneurial agencies, etc. However, Petmesidou (op. cit.) has noted that this flourishing must not be accepted uncritically. Further, accession of countries from central Europe may also raise the question of the strength of civil society (Duffy, 1996b). The lobbying activities of the Platform of Social NGOs, and in particular the European Anti-Poverty Network, indicate that at least one part of the civil society looks to the Member States and to the Union for a framework of social rights to protect against social risks, even if they see also opportunities in more plural approaches to integration. This dissonance between the expectations placed on civil society (including the family and personal networks as well as NGOs), their capacity to meet these expectations, and their own expectations of their rights, as opposed to their responsibilities, is likely to create tension between state and civil society, and may increase the risks of social exclusion. In the meantime, processes in the labour markets are unquestioned. Supply-side policy focuses on persons rather than structures, and demand-side policy is constrained by an ideological commitment to monetarist economics, enshrined in the Amsterdam Treaty, and in the commitments to multilateral organisations such as the World Trade Organisation.

In conclusion, the concept of social exclusion has two main versions, both centred around exclusion from the labour market; the primary causal mechanism is either behavioural (related to the perverse effects of the welfare state or the rupture of social ties) or structural (related to globalisation). Despite these differing views of the processes, everywhere, active labour market policies and 'employment-friendly social protection' are the main solution. The effectiveness of active labour market policies in combating exclusion from some of these sources has been questioned. Further, whatever the causal mechanisms proposed, there is little concern with inequality in the distribution of resources. Consequently, policies to reduce exclusion from the labour market may not only have no impact on poverty, but may exacerbate it, when insertion per se is more important than the terms of insertion, and in a climate where social rights, distributed by the state, are weakening and losing legitimacy.

Notes

1   Council Decision (85/8/EEC) 19.12.1984.
2   Official Journal No. C221, 28.8.1989.
3   COM (96) 90 final, Brussels 28. 02.1996, p. 4.
4   Consolidated Version of the Treaty Establishing the European Community (Treaty of Amsterdam 1997), Europa.
5   Social Protection in the European Union: Modernisation and Improvement (COM (97) 102) CEC, Brussels.
6   Universal minimum income has been established in France only since 1989.
7   Consolidated Version of the Treaty Establishing the European Community (Treaty of Amsterdam 1997).
8   The language of the Treaty gives a much lower priority to other dimensions of disadvantage. As indicated above, poverty is referred to only once. Further, inequality is discussed solely in relation to men and women, racism not at all (discrimination is only explicitly prohibited on grounds of nationality), exclusion only once (Article 137, which refers to exclusion from the labour market) and fundamental social rights only once (Article 136).
9   Social Protection in the European Union: Modernisation and Improvement (COM (97) 102 of 12.3. 97) CEC, Brussels, pp. 8–9.
10   Green Paper: Partnership for a New Organisation of Work, Com(97) 128 final, adopted 16 April 1997, p. 14.

Bibliography

Abrahamson, P. and Hansen, F-K. (1996), *Poverty in the European Union: Report for the European Parliament*, Denmark, Centre for Alternative Social Analysis, Roskilde University.

Adamson, D. (1995), 'The spatial organisation of difference and exclusion in a working class community', paper delivered to the *Ideas of Community* conference, University of Bristol, 13–14 September.

Bouget, D. and Nogues, H. (1993), *Évaluation des politiques de lutte contre les exclusions sociales*, Review française des Affaires sociales, Centre d'économie des besoins sociaux (CEBS), Faculté des Sciences économiques de Nantes.

Bruckner, H. (1995), 'Research on the dynamics of poverty in Germany', *Journal of European Social Policy*, 5 (4), pp. 317–22.

Cain, G. (1976), 'The Challenge of Segmented Labor Market Theories to Orthodox Theory: A Survey', *Journal of Economic Literature*, 14, pp. 1215–57.

Callan, T., Nolan, B. and Whelan, C. (1993), 'Resources Deprivation and the Measurement of Poverty', *Journal of Social Policy*, 22, 2, pp. 141–72.

Castel, R. (1995), *Les metamorphoses de la Question Sociale en Europe, une Chronique du Salariat*, Paris, Fayard.

Chamberlayne, P. (1997), 'Social Exclusion: Sociological Tradition and National Contexts' in *Social Exclusion in Comparative Perspective*, London, Social Strategies in Risk Societies, Sostris Working Paper 1, University of East London.

Colenutt, B. and Cutten, A. (1994), 'Community Empowerment in Vogue or Vain?', *Local Economy*, 9, pp. 236–50.

Commission of the European Communities (1992), *Treaty on European Union, Including the Protocols and Final Act with Declarations Maastricht*, 7 February, Brussels.

Commission of the European Communities (1995), *Eurobarometer: Perception of Poverty in Europe*, Brussels, Commission of the European Communities Directorate-General.

Commission of the European Communities (1997), *A Stronger and Wider Union* (Agenda 2000) Volume 1, Doc. 97/6 Commission of the European Communities, Strasbourg, http://europa.eu.int/comm/dg1a/agenda2000/en/agenda.htm.

Commission of the European Communities (1997), *Green Paper: Partnership for a New Organisation of Work*, Com(97) 128 final, adopted 16 April 1997, Brussels, Commission of the European Communities.

Council of Europe (1992a), *Steering Committee on Social Policy 9th Meeting Strasbourg 2–5 Nov.*, PS-EV (92) 8, Strasbourg, Council of Europe.

Council of Europe (1992b), *Europe 1992–2000: European Municipalities and Democracy: The Exclusion of Poverty Through Citizenship*, Charleroi 5–7 February, Strasbourg, Council of Local and Regional Authorities of Europe, Council of Europe.

Council of Europe (1994a), *In or Out: Social Exclusion and Human Dignity: The Right to Self-Respect*, Strasbourg, Council of Europe.

Council of Europe (1994b), *Texts Drawn Up by the Council of Europe in the Field of Poverty and Social Exclusion: Resolutions and Recommendations of the Committee of Ministers*, CDPS III.5 (94) 4, Strasbourg, Council of Europe Press.

Council of Europe (1995a), '*Network of Cities. Citizenship and Extreme Poverty: The Charleroi Declaration, Belgium. General Report on Poverty*', CG/GT/Pauv (1) 5, Strasbourg,Congress of Local and Regional Authorities of Europe, Council of Europe.

Council of Europe (1995b), *Social Cohesion: the Causes and Manifestations of Exclusion; Ways of Combating It*, BI ONG/ No. Sp. 1 (1995), Strasbourg, Council of Europe Press.

Crouch, D. (1995), 'Remaking communities: place and geographical knowledge', paper delivered to the *Ideas of Community* conference, University of Bristol, 13–14 September.

de Foucauld, J-B. (rapporteur) (1996), *For a Europe of Civic and Social Rights: Report by the Comité des Sages chaired by Maria Lourdes Pintasilgo, Brussels, October 1995–February 1996*, Brussels, European Commission, DG V.

Doeringer, P. B. and Piore, M. J. (1971), *Internal Labor Markets and Manpower Analysis*, Lexington, Mass., Heath.

Duffy, K. (1995), *Social Exclusion and Human Dignity: Background Report for the Proposed Initiative by the Council of Europe*, CDPS (95) 1 Rev., Steering Committee on Social Policy (CDPS) Activity II 1b on human dignity and social exclusion, Strasbourg, Council of Europe.

Duffy, K. (1996a), *Project Human Dignity and Social Exclusion: Work Programme*, HDSE (96) 3. rev. April 10, Strasbourg, Council of Europe.

70   *Coping with Homelessness*

Duffy, K. (1996b), 'Putting Right Social Wrongs – the Scope for European Social Rights', *Poverty: Journal of the Child Poverty Action Group*, Spring, no. 93, pp. 13–6.

Duffy, K. (1997), 'Opportunity and Risk: Broad Perspectives Arising from the Results of HDSE Phase 1 (1996–1997)', paper presented to the Colloquy *Towards a Better Social Cohesion in Europe: Today and Tomorrow* (16–17 September, Bratislava), Social, Health and Family Affairs Committee of the Parliamentary Assembly of the Council of Europe, AS/soc/bratis (1997) 3, Strasbourg.

Duffy, K. and Hutchinson, J. (1997), 'Urban Policy and the Turn to Community', *Town Planning Review*, July, pp. 347–62.

Esping-Andersen, G. (1990), *The Three Worlds of Welfare Capitalism*, Cambridge, Polity Press.

Esping-Andersen, G. (ed.) (1996), *Welfare States in Transition: National Adaptations in Global Economies*, London, Sage.

Etzioni, A. (1995), *The Spirit of Community*, London, Fontana.

Evans, M., Paugam, S. and Prélis, J. (1995), *Chunnel Vision: Poverty, Social Exclusion and the Debate on in France and Britain*, Discussion Paper WSP/115, London School of Economics, *Social Welfare*, London, October.

Evers, A. and Wintersberger, H. (eds.) (1988), *Shifts in the Welfare Mix: Their Impact on Work, Social Services and Welfare Policies*, Vienna, Eurosocial.

Ferge, Z. (1997), 'The Changed Welfare Paradigm: The Individualization of the Social', *Social Policy & Administration*, 31 (1), pp. 20–44.

Ferrera, M. (1996), 'The Southern Model of Welfare in Social Europe', *Journal of European Social Policy*, 6 (1), pp. 17–37.

Fondation Roi Badouin (1994), *Rapport General sur la Pauvreté. Realise a la demande du Ministre de l'Integration Sociale*, Brussels, Charleroi: Fondation Roi Badouin en Collaboration avec ATD Quart Monde Belgique et Union des Villes et Communes Belges, Section CPAS.

Frazer, L. (1995), 'Communitarians and Feminists', paper delivered to the *Ideas of Community* conference, University of Bristol, 13–14 September.

Greve, B. (1996), 'Indications of Social Policy in Europe', *Social Policy & Administration*, 30 (4), pp. 348–67.

Heady, C. (1997), 'Labour Market Transitions and Social Exclusion', *Journal of European Social Policy*, 7 (2), pp. 119–28.

Join-Lambert, M. (1995), *Exclusion, Equality Before the Law and Non-Discrimination*: introductory report, seminar organised by the Secretariat General Council of Europe in cooperation with the 'Intercenter' of Messina (Italy), Taormina-Mare (Italy), 29 September–1 October 1994, Council of Europe, Strasbourg.

Jones, M. (1996), 'Full Steam Ahead to a Workfare State?', *Policy and Politics*, 24 (2), pp. 137–58.

Joye, M. (1995), *Council for Cultural Co-operation*, Strasbourg, Council of Europe.

Katrougalis, G. (1996), 'The South European Welfare Model: the Greek Welfare State, in Search of an Identity', *Journal of European Social Policy*, 6 (1), pp. 39–60.

Keating, M. (1995), 'Size, Efficiency and Democracy: Consolidation, Fragmentation and Public Choice' in Judge, D., Stoker, G. and Wolman, H. (eds) (1995), *Theories of Urban Politics*, London, Sage.

Lenoir, R. (1974), *Les Exclus*, Paris, SEUIL.

Levitas, R. (1996), 'The Concept of Social Exclusion and the New Durkheimian Hegemony', *Critical Social Policy*, 46, vol. 16, pp. 5–20.

Maffesoli, M. (1996), *The Times of the Tribes*, London, Sage.

Martin, C. (1996), 'French Review Article: the Debate in France over "Social Exclusion"', *Social Policy & Administration*, 30 (4), pp. 328–92.

Meurs, D. and Prelis, J. (1997), *Western Europe Thematic Employment Report, Report to the Human Dignity and Social Exclusion Initiative*, Strasbourg, Council of Europe.

Ministry of Social Affairs (1993), *Social Policy in Denmark*, Copenhagen, The Ministry of Social Affairs.

Murard, N. (1997), 'The Economy is Destroying Society: Social Exclusion in France' in *Social Exclusion in Comparative Perspective*, London, Social Strategies in Risk Societies, Sostris Working Paper 1, University of East London.

Network News (1997), newsletter of the European Anti-Poverty Network.

Paugam, S. (1992), 'Les Allocataires du RMI. Face a Leur Difficultes' in Castel, R. and Lae, J.-F., *Le Revenu Minimum d'Insertion. Un Dette Social*, Paris, Logiques Sociales, L'Harmattan.

Paugam, S. (1993a), 'La Dynamique de la Disqualification Social', *Science Humaines*, Paris, May.

Paugam, S. (1993b), *La Societe Francaise et ses Pauvres. L'experience du Revenu Minimum d'Insertion*, Paris, Presses Universitaires de France.

Paugam, S. (1994), 'Precarite et Risque d'Exclusion en Europe', *Understanding Social Exclusion in Europe*, a conference supported by the Commission of the European Communities, Organised by PSI, London 24–26 November.

Petmesidou, M. (1996), 'Social Protection in Greece: A Brief Glimpse of a Welfare State', *Social Policy & Administration*, 30 (4), pp. 324–47.

Pieretti, G. (1994), 'Extreme Urban Poverty as a Salient Phenomenon', *Understanding Social Exclusion in Europe*, a conference supported by the Commission of the European Communities, Organised by PSI, London 24–26 November.

Rhodes, M. (1996), 'Globalization and West European Welfare States: A Critical Review of Recent Debates', *Journal of European Social Policy*, 6 (4), pp. 305–27.

Ritakallio, V. (1994), *Finnish Poverty: A Cross-National Comparison*, unpublished paper, University of Turku, Turku.

Robbins, D. et al. (1994), *Observatory on National Policies to Combat Social Exclusion, Third Annual Report*, Brussels, Commission of the European Communities, DG V.

Rodgers, G. (1994), *Overcoming exclusion: Livelihood and Rights in Economic and Social Development*, International Labour Organisation.

Rodgers, G., Gore, C. and Figueredo, J.B (eds.) (1995*), Social Exclusion: Rhetoric, Reality, Responses*, Geneva, International Institute for Labour Studies/United Nations Development Programme.

Room, G. (1995), 'Poverty in Europe; Competing Paradigms of Analysis', *Policy and Politics*, April.

Rosanvallon, P., (1995), *La Nouvelle Question Sociale*, Paris, Seuil.

Rustin, M. and Rix, V. (1997), 'Anglo-Saxon Individualism and its Vicissitudes: Social Exclusion in Britain' in *Social Exclusion in Comparative Perspective*, Social Strategies in Risk Societies, Sostris Working Paper 1, University of East London, London.

Select Committee of the European Communities (1994), *The Poverty Programme with Evidence* 9th Report HL Paper 51, London, HMSO.

Silver, H. (1994), 'Social Exclusion and Social Solidarity: Three Paradigms', *International Labour Review'*, 133, 5–6, pp. 531–78.

Spicker, P. (1996), 'Social Policy in a Federal Europe', *Social Policy & Administration*, 30 (4), pp. 293–304.

Tonnies, F. (1955), *Community and Association*, tr. C. P. Loomis, London, Routledge and Kegan Paul.

Touraine, A. (1991), *Face a l'Exclusion, Citoyennete et Urbanite. Ouvrage Collectif*, Paris, Esprit.

Touraine A. (1992), 'Inegalities de la Societe Industrielle, Exclusion Du Marche' in Affichard, J. and de Foucauld, J.-B. (eds), *Justice Sociale et Inegalites*, Paris, Esprit.

Townsend, P. (1979), *Poverty in the United Kingdom: a Survey of Household Resources and Standards of Living*, London, Allen Lane.

Vogel-Polsky, E. (1993), *Terms of Reference for the Paper Presenting the Work of the Rights/ Exclusion Group on Asserting the Rights of the Most Underprivileged in the EEC*, paper (unpublished) presented by the Expert Committee on Social Rights, Commission of the European Communities DG V, Brussels.

Vranken, J. (1995) 'Poverty and Social Exclusion in Modern Western Societies: Some Elements for a Model', paper submitted to a meeting of experts, Directorate-General XII, 5 May.

Walker, R. (1995), 'The Dynamics of Poverty and social Exclusion' in Room, G. (ed.), *Beyond the Threshold: The Management and Analysis of Social Exclusion*, Bristol, Policy Press.

Wresinski, J. (1994), *Chronic Poverty and Lack of Basic Security*, Paris, Economic and Social Council of France.

Xiberras, M. (1993), *Theories de L'exclusion Sociale*, Paris, Meridiens Klincksieck.

3 Theoretical Uses and Misuses of the Notion of Exclusion

MARC-HENRY SOULET

For over a decade, exclusion has been a crucial issue. It has held the social discourse in thrall; it has pervaded political discussions and has taken over the media. It has replaced former notions of marginality and even of poverty, thus implying that the older vocabulary no longer fits this new social reality. The scientific field has also succumbed to its appeal; publications on the subject have multiplied:[1] conferences, workshops and speeches echo each other mutually. In short, exclusion is incontestably a central phenomenon as the century draws to an end.

Such imperialism of a notion that has become a category of representation of the social and a category of action upon it does nevertheless raise some questions, if not some tempers.[2] 'Is it not a risk to allow analyses in terms of exclusion and the excluded to develop?' (Chopart and Roy, 1995, p. 5). In other words, would it not be more appropriate to look closely at this term and to ask if it designates a singular phenomenon, unedited in a way, which is being enacted right under our noses, or if it contributes to concealing more fundamental questions. Is it a conceptual tool appropriate for understanding contemporary transformations that affect our developed societies?[3]

Or, is it on the contrary an artefact which blurs our comprehension of these mutations by virtue of the fact that it provides an interpretation of reality through a prism which deforms the urgency and the suffering? Or is it simply a catchword for sociologists to rally around, having been dispossessed of poverty by the economists?[4]

This contribution would like to partake of this movement and question the notion of exclusion. On the basis of the evidence marshalled, it will single out the difficulties of using the term. In other words, it will endeavour to determine under what conditions the term can be used and to what degree it is possible to use it as an operative concept, especially to clarify the extreme forms, which this notion can be applied to in reality, such as homelessness. The difficulties that the analyst is often confronted with are often attributed to the vagueness of the notion of exclusion. But no matter how pertinent these explications of vagueness and of its all-pervasive use may be, they nonetheless seem inadequate to lay bare the difficulties which the notion of exclusion presents for the sociology of the social. Therefore, I wish to propose complementary explanations which extend beyond one single notion of exclusion by re-inscribing the enquiry; on the one hand, at the heart of the social signification of poverty and on the interior of the representations which form the basis of the necessity for intervening socially in the context of exclusion, on the other hand, in the logic of putting in motion of a continuum of social positions which underlies the analysis of exclusion as a process.

The Vagueness of the Notion of Exclusion

The proliferation of more or less scientific publications and the abundance of new designations (relegation, exile, disqualification, disinsertion, disintegration, vulnerability, disaffiliation ...) convey at least as much the sense of urgency to act, an obligation to do something, as much as a real difficulty to think what exclusion could cover and all connected notions, to theorise the phenomenon of social marginalisation which is agitating our societies. In a previous contribution (Soulet, 1994) I singled out some of the characteristics of exclusion as a conceptual tool. I set out five types of explanation to account for this difficulty which I now wish to take up again and complete by referring to recently published analyses.

First, insofar as exclusion harbours a great evocative power and a strong mobilising potential today, it is used widely ideologically, which, whilst enabling a bigger rallying, increases its semantic imprecision.[5] The latter authorises an uncontrolled use with almost a total absence of construction and of theoretical reasoning. Twenty years ago Elliot Jacques (1997, p. 2) stressed that with regard to the term 'marginality', the obstacle to its theoretical application constituted by the intensive social use of a notion was that

> in spite of current usage, the notion and its theoretical content remain very vague. Besides, its daily use, the use of the label marginal makes us think of social facts which it designates (situations and behaviour) on the basis of generalisations which it operates and hasty interpretations which it suggests.

The inevitably resultant obscuring of the analysis stems from the fact that recourse to this notion is simply a substitute for an explanation. Shirley Roy (1995, p. 74) came to a similar conclusion when she pointed out the almost total absence of a definition of what is meant by term 'exclusion'.

> In fact, in public declarations as well as in more 'academic' texts, this expression is generally used in a synthetic manner to designate the less well provided for, the poor people in difficulty, no more. Here the use of this term is a substitute for an explanation.

The second critique comes from the very complexity of the phenomena which the notion of exclusion purports to account for. It attempts to cover multiple situations and phenomena and the reduction that underlies the work of theorisation does not exhaust its multidimensionality. Thus, the variety of the modalities and the extent of exclusion do not enable a totalisation of those who experience it in a group whose coherency makes it possible to single out the distinct and unequivocal criteria of definition of a homogenous status, to the degree that one could say

> exclusion regroups an ensemble of persons who have been ejected from a standard situation: having a stable full-time job, a family life or a satisfying relationship, a comfortable home, a level of education commensurate with one's ambitions, easy access to health-care and adequate resources ... (Mazel, 1996, p. 69).

Exclusion can thus be reduced to living an existence defined by a lack: lack of work, of family, of a home, of education, of social relations, of access to institutions, of participation in society.[6] Is there not a risk (in all respects comparable to the claim of a definition of poverty as an accumulation of handicaps) of finding oneself faced with a variable geometrical concept which fluctuates according to representations and preoccupations? The heterogeneity of these usages is therefore not surprising.

> It names numerous different situations by erasing the specificity of each one. In other words, exclusion is not an analytical notion. It does not lead to precise investigations of the contents which it claims to cover (Castel, 1995b, p. 13).

The third explanation is on the level of shifting realities and contexts. An example illustrates this clearly. The experience of exclusion made by the immigrant populations at the height of the years of prosperity during the *Golden Sixties* and that experienced more recently by the third generation are not only incomparable but take on an opposing significance. In the first context, the immigrant workers were socially integrated through their work but culturally non-integrated, remaining foreigners in terms of the values and norms of the host society in which they found themselves. In the second context, the descendants of those immigrant workers are assimilated culturally – they have much in common with young people from the same social background, bear like-minded aspirations and are moved by similar cultural attitudes – but they are excluded from work. The twin concepts of cultural assimilation and marginalisation can be considered as substitutes for integration through work and cultural difference.

The fourth explanation set out refers to the limitation of the explanatory capacity of exclusion. This notion cannot be separated from the pair inclusion and integration. There are no such clear-cut situations. In other words, it is difficult to imagine someone who is totally excluded. Someone excluded is still included, no matter how little. 'No doubt there are nowadays *ins* and *outs* but they do not inhabit a separate universe, strictly speaking, there are never extra-social situations' (ibid., p. 15). In fact, it is exclusion from the sphere of the social activity of employment that very often determines our interpretation of reality. This, in turn, leads to total social exclusion and to misrecognising other forms of inclusion. This extension of one sphere to cover all others is a frequent deformation which leads to a simplification of the social reality of the persons involved.

Finally, exclusion is used to designate two distinct levels of reality. It is in fact underpinned alternatively by a social and by an individual interpretation. In the one case, a macro-social level proposes an analysis of the factors of integration against the background of dwindling social, public and family protection, which produces widespread insecurity and a crisis of citizenship. In the other case, it involves a micro-social level which attempts to trace the individual social history and development which led to the exclusion of particular individuals, by reconstituting how the persons excluded act as subjects, participating in the situation they are living through on the basis of a competence often denied them.[7] The oscillation between these two analytical poles of exclusion is the sign of a lack of integrated theories able to comprehend the social mechanisms of exclusion and the process of individual exclusion.

Other critical analyses of exclusion have recently been developed. Among these, two made a point of doing so systematically and called for a limitation of the use of the former, that is of the notion of exclusion. The first, that of Shirley Roy, insists on two new elements. On the one hand, she takes up the argument of the heterogeneity of the situations encompassed by the notion of exclusion and adds to it the implications on the stigmatising and discriminating effect of grouping together realities which are very different from one another. This generic usage leads to 'starting off a process of social indistinction which reinforces the negative images associated with these groups' and 'to stressing the social distance between the groups called excluded and included' (Roy, 1995, p. 74). On the other hand, she considers that part of the confusion caused by recourse to this notion comes from the reference to an implicit model which presupposes an idealised relationship to the social.

> This reversal of exclusion is based on an autonomous subject who has a rewarding and identifying professional activity, an adequate network of social relations, considerable potential of consumption ... Yet, not only does this model occur less and less frequently in reality, but its non-reproduction would amount to 'crossing the barrier between insertion and exclusion'.[8]

Thus it is that Shirley Roy logically comes to the conclusion that only through a limited and structured use can the notion retain any of its analytical pertinence. Such a restriction of the extension of the field to be covered by this notion means reserving its usage for the more extreme forms and for actually becoming marginalised. In other words, she recommends refraining from using it to describe either the first stages of dropping out from society or the first upheaval after one or several ruptures, but to keep its force for naming the phenomena that characterise being on the verge of social disinsertion. Therefore, instead of characterising those who are experiencing one form or another of social rupture

> exclusion marks the downfall of those who accumulate social and individual handicaps reuniting thus the objective and subjective conditions of those for whom remedial mechanisms no longer function, of those put in a position of no longer acting or reacting for want of being able to take control of their life following repeated failures (ibid., p. 76).

It is in this sense that itinerancy is, in her eyes, an exemplary form of this exclusion to be reserved for special usage.

Robert Castel has undertaken to lay bare the current widespread use of exclusion in order to emphasise the limits as well as the dangers. His well-researched critique rests primarily on the contention that recourse to exclusion plays a part in making marginal situations autonomous by disassociating them from the processes which produced them and gives them meaning. To consider them as extreme and intolerable states leads in turn to isolating them from the transformations which occur in society, at the least to disjoin them from the analysis at the precise moment when the sociological work consists of analysing the previous phenomena of exclusion and especially the way the elements which ensure inclusion in the society are themselves modified in the same way as those who support the integrating capacity of the society. This is precisely why, stresses Robert Castel, the growing attention given to exclusion functions like a trap at two levels, namely on the cognitive and political level. By obstructing the interrogation of the social mechanisms of the system responsible for the current ruptures, one produces sectarian analyses accounting for 'states of dispossession', which thus lead to misrecognising the very social features of so-called excluded persons, i.e. that they had been invalidated by the economic situation, that they are 'outnumbered' 'normal useless people'. 'Their predicament is', he tells us,

> that the new demands of competitiveness and rivalry, the reduction of employment opportunities, mean that henceforth there is *no longer room* for everyone in the society which we must resign to living in (Castel, 1995b, pp. 16–17).

This analytical reduction results in a misrecognition of what exclusion entails, 'a general dynamism of precariousness which defeats assured status', and refers to policies of a remedial nature aimed at a particular public. This explains the successive array of measures whose main feature is to intervene time after time to patch up the social net which has been ravaged. In this sense the political popularity of exclusion has to do with the savings allowed by the level and extent of the measures taken.

> It seems more and more realistic to deploy interventionism for treating the most visible forms of malfunctioning rather than to control the process which sets it off because dealing with its effects can be carried out in a *technical* manner whereas coming to grips with the process itself demands *political* action (ibid.).

But Robert Castel goes further in his critique by showing, in an analysis of what should be a rigorous use of the notion of exclusion, how these same measures which aim at dealing with exclusion run the risk of literally producing the conditions of exclusion in the strict sense of the term. What should one logically mean by exclusion? Should its legitimate use be reserved for describing the result of official procedures that result in a status which is virtually negative in its discrimination. In this sense, exclusion denotes either the forms of actually being pushed out of society and of being banished, as history has illustrated in innumerable examples; or, it is used to characterise the formation of enclaves within society like ghettos, here too history is a powerful source of reference; or it allows the declaration of a special status which authorises the coexistence of individuals characterised by different social states in the same society, but which 'deprives them of certain rights and of participation in certain social activities' (ibid., p. 18). Yet, if it can be considered that in our democratic societies the first two forms of exclusion in the strict sense do not threaten us – let us hope so at least – the third form is indeed to be feared because of the paradox entailed in the policies of positive discrimination which constitute the basis of the policies designed to deal with exclusion. Do not the specific measures aimed at people in great difficulty play a role - slowly but surely, even if they fight against it – in officially bringing about a special status of second class citizen?

However, no matter how pertinent may be these explanations of the conceptual vagueness of exclusion as a term and its all-pervasive use, they fail to lay bare the actual difficulties which the notion of exclusion represents for sociologists of the social. Therefore, I wish to propose two complementary explanations which overlap with the notion of exclusion by re-inscribing the enquiry, on the one hand, at the heart of social phenomena of poverty, and on the other hand, within the representations which form the basis for the necessity of social intervention related to exclusion.

The Loss of the Sense of Exclusion

It has been a long time since sociological analysis of poverty gave up a perspective in terms of the state, be it the sum of economic, social and cultural disadvantages or as a specific culture, to promote an interpretation in terms of social relations. However, the explanations of the phenomenon of poverty, even using only the latter perspective, have of course varied depending on how society thought of itself and how it represented the issues at stake and the problems affecting it.

A *Reality Without* Raison d'être

Briefly, it can be said that the result of these explanations was mainly to give a meaning to poverty, in a double sense. On the one hand, it invested poverty with a *raison d'être* in the sociopolitical and socioeconomic configuration in question. On the other hand, it gave a sense of direction to deal with the poverty, at least to combat efficiently its effects. Yet, like many authors, I put forward the hypothesis that we have reached a point where the explanation is bereft of meaning: it is known how poverty comes about but not why it exists.

In other words, if there is a logical explanation for the existence of poverty in terms of exclusion as experienced in modern societies, this explanation fails to specify a reason per se for this kind of poverty which is socially meaningful and acceptable. To put it bluntly, it does not provide poverty with a social utility value, utility which is, of course, not meant as a functional malfunctioning, but in a symbolic sense of that which links it to the logic of the social system and which allows social identities to go beyond individual trials. Neither does it, as opposed to the previous topics, constitute the epicentre of the social question.

To understand fully what the absence of a foundation related to exclusion means, I have attempted, at the risk of being reductionist, to draw up a schema of what would seem to constitute the three principal configurations of the meaning of poverty. Table 3.1 visualises the three topics, which I subjected to the scrutiny of different criteria. How is poverty seen figuratively by the rest of society? What social relations qualify poverty? What meaning is attributed to it? What status do the poor inherit? What impact on society and on their own destiny are they capable of? What priorities does society give to counteracting the effects of poverty?

I shall not comment on each of these topics at length; they represent a synthesis of aspects already sufficiently known. It will suffice to sketch an outline and I shall go into the last topic, namely that of exclusion, in more detail.

	Exploitation	Transition	Exclusion
Symbolisation	UP DOWN	CENTRE MARGIN	IN OUT
Social relations	Domination		Disinsertion
Sense	Profit	Inadaptation	Without sense
Social status of the 'poor'	Working classes	Progress Delayed fractions	Outnumbered/ useless for the world
Capacity for action of the poor	Organised struggle/ workers' movement	Passive resistance or individual catching up	Struggle for places/ resignation
Policy of struggle against impoverishment	Assurance policy for covering individual risks and generalisation of wage-earning	Reduction of inequalities by a policy of general access to mass consumption and promotion by education	Minimum revenue for all citizens Interior humanitarian aid

Figure 3.1   The topics of poverty

The topic of exploitation is greatly indebted to the Marxist analysis of industrial capitalism. It characterises at best the relations of society and poverty in the countries that experienced the industrial revolution. Poverty and nascent wage-earning were on a par in this movement, which drew large parts of the population into industrial work. The impoverishment of the workers as an ensemble that constituted the social question of the greater part of the nineteenth century was founded on the logic of the economic and political system. This produced, in turn, collective identifications and generated potential forces of mobilisation and action. In a way, the exploitation of the working classes by the owning classes, which characterised a relation of dominance at the centre of a hierarchical society (the Anglo-Saxon terms *upper* and *lower* classes illustrate this clearly), while presenting an explicit *raison d'être*, namely that of profit, gave sense and interest to a collective organisation, the workers' movement, whose obvious aim was the transformation of this relationship.

This purports to be a mere brief outline. However, what is of particular interest here is that in this configuration of social relations, each one occupied a meaningful place which was at the same time interdependent, thus giving each one the opportunity to lean on the latter, that is to say on the meaningful place – for some with a view to a radical transformation of the social structure, for others it was to perpetuate it at the expense of some concessions of a social nature. Thus, as Robert Castel reminds us

> the labourer or the skilled worker, the skilled worker of the last big struggles of the workers, exploited no doubt, was no less indispensable. Put differently, he continued to be involved with social exchanges. Although he was in the last row, according to the Durkheimian model, he belonged to society as one of a number of interdependent elements. The result was that his subordination could be conceived in terms of the problem of integration, that is in his 'reformist', in terms of levelling out inequalities, of income policies, of climbing the social ladder and of cultural participation, or in his 'revolutionary' version, in terms of a complete upheaval of the social structure to ensure true equal conditions for everyone (Castel, 1995a, p. 20).

The second topic, that of transition, refers us to a different theoretical-historical context, that of the 30-year period generally referred to as the years of economic recovery following the second world war. Here too the situation is well-known; in a period of strong growth, the concept of society rested on the idea of an ongoing movement towards liberation from constraint. Thanks to technical progress, the economic and therefore social development was assured; the improvement of living conditions was illustrated objectively day after day. But the working classes got caught up in this consumer society in the making. Some pockets of poverty did indeed exist, but these were swept aside by the general movement of progress. They owed their existence to the fact that society was at a turning point, a moment of transition between two kinds of society. With time, as Durkheim said with regard to anomic forms of the division of social work due to the change from mechanical and organic solidarity, self-regulation would operate, enabling the full deployment of modernity.

Poverty could therefore only describe the situation of those who found themselves on the margin of this movement. It involved only fractions of the population who had not or could not jump on the bandwagon of progress – those who had lagged behind or those who were maladjusted – and so could not fully partake of modernity. Henceforth, one of the main issues was either to set up a general remedial programme for the more adaptable among this population and to focus on the next generation by working on the human capital policies (development of education for everyone, of training and of readjustment) which promoted access to the consumer society, the symbol of progress as well as a wall of protection for economic growth; or, to await the end, the natural death as it were, of this fraction of the population sacrificed on the altar of progress. Obviously, in the latter case, this was no matter to rejoice about, offering them as it were only passive resistance to change, which remained profoundly foreign to them. However, here again meaningful places with regard to the logic of the economic and social system had been assigned to this segment of the population and this enabled them to situate themselves socially and symbolically, if uncomfortably, in such a world.

The last topic, exclusion, seeks to account for contemporary society. Exclusion has become such a crucial topic that it appears to be *the* social question at the end of the century. It has become the point of crystallisation of discussions about the social, the fragmentation of present day society – just as it was with the exploitation of the labour force so it is with industrial society – the dichotomy insiders/outsiders has replaced the traditional opposition/complementarity between capital and work (Touraine, 1992). This sectioning between insiders and outsiders constitutes a new kind of social conflict: the logic at work is difficult to grasp in its entirety. As François Dubet (1987) points out, the principle at stake in the outbursts of the youth who are idle, is the feeling of domination without meaning, of being pushed out for no apparent reason, it must also be admitted that this exclusion seems unfounded, without meaning when seen within the logic of the same social system.

To speak of being pushed out without reason amounts to admitting socially that this exclusion is not consubstantial to a concept of the social order able to account for the basic elements of the situation experienced, as one was able to do for the working-class conscience of the exploitation of the labour force.

> Our society organised itself essentially to deal with the problems of exploitation: the trade unions, the collective negotiations developed within companies so as to establish counter-powers, to lay down the rules of the game, to codify the relations and to avoid blatant imbalances. The phenomenon of exploitation is characterised by the fact that it is based on social relationship, a more or less balanced relationship, but at any rate present. The most obvious characteristic of exclusion is that there is no social relationship. An unemployed person is someone who has no social relations; he is isolated, he is alone, his base is not his workplace and he can exert no pressure: whom can he strike against? He cannot go on strike. He is opposed to all of society (de Foucauld, 1994, p. 156).

Consequently, it is impossible for those excluded to identify themselves with a homogenous status – because, perhaps, they do not consider themselves as constituting a group per se, as a social actor moved by a collective action concerning his own group situation or as a driving force of a project for the transformation of social relations. And this is so because, without any doubt, what they represent socially does not exist; it has no unity, no coherence. This is not to say that what is meant by exclusion is merely an idea, rather that the social status of what is involved is precisely that of being nothing; not class, nor body, nor group, nor social movement, nor nation. *To be nothing socially* is the sociopolitical definition of exclusion in the current state of affairs. How can something exist which has neither interests to promote nor rights to defend, or which cannot add them up or only does so in terms of lack? How can something exist socially which has no social utility, since the exploitation of the unemployable or superfluous population is no longer necessary for the working of the economic machine and for the collective acquisition of wealth?

Metaphorically, the struggle of the classes has given way to the struggle of places (de Gaulejac and Taboada-Leonetti, 1994) among the outnumbered. These no longer have the 'luck' of being exploited, for to be eligible one must possess a socially convertible value.

> Solidarity which formerly was an expression of interest must become disinterested, and this is not something which can be taken for granted. This new situation is dramatic for it is not auto-corrective. When the rich needed the poor, they took care of them. Exploitation implied a kind of solidarity. The outcome was indeed an imperfect world, but human. Now that the poor are in the minority and useless (for the rich) who cares about them? (Prud'homme, 1994, p. 7).

These individuals are no longer regarded as social actors, nor even as an army of reserves, but as a 'social non-force', as 'useless normal human beings' (Donzelot and Estèbe, 1994) despite being very much present, and that is where the problem resides, in society.

If exclusion forms the essence of a new social conflict, it is a hollow one that is emerging. It is not composed of actors opposed to each other on different social projects in an endeavour to gain control of the normative and cultural directions of society. Conversely, the former – that is exclusion – only mobilises society when it comes to a lack; it is only through a lack that one of the parties in power transforms itself into a social actor. The risk of fracture, which, as a consequence, the excluded subjects the whole of society to, forces the latter to redefine itself and to work towards reinforcing its integrity particularly with regard to the relationship between citizenship and invalidation.

But from then on exclusion appears as a paradox object. Cumbersome on the one hand, it calls for a focusing of attention because of the urgency of the situations experienced and the intolerable social system which it shows up. Without a sense of the other, it implies a transfer of the analysis, compelling an examination of the social utility of the outnumbered for economic production and for the social functioning as well as of the question of the meaningful places in the overall functioning of the social system. In other words, one is faced with an alternative. Either the social question is shifted from the centre to the periphery, to take up Robert Castel's expression again, and an analytical reduction is carried out which focuses on the most visible effects of a more general movement, and thus deprives itself of an in-depth understanding of the destabilisation of society. Or the issue of exclusion is reintegrated at the heart of the social question, i.e. the representation society has of itself, of its mechanisms of solidarity and of the workplace in the formation of individual and social identities. However, in doing so exclusion becomes a secondary object and is diluted as a notion; it was no more than an indicator launching the reflection which itself does not constitute the focus of the reflection, nor the conceptual cornerstone of the analysis.

A Blind Oscillation Between Pity and Social Fracture

Another difficulty involved in fully grasping the notion of exclusion for purposes of a sociological analysis comes from the balancing between or the superimposition of two forms of social treatment of exclusion or rather from the assumptions of what constitutes the basis of intervention intending to resolve the social problem. Before making any such commitment one must

first consider that, as Saül Karz observed, poverty 'is not *per se* a social problem
…' it 'is nothing but the necessary condition – only – of the social problem of
poverty' (Karz, 1992, p. 143). For example, the new poor only showed up in
the sociopolitical reality when they were publicised as social products; this
does not mean that these individuals were not actually going through a
problematic personal situation – merely that up to that point there did not
exist any transversalisation of these individual situations, nor had it been
brought into relation with the issue of regulation. Pertinent distinctions were
made by Wright Mills (1967, p. 10) between 'personal trials' and 'collective
stakes of the social structure', the former calling for individual commitment
to alleviate the visible suffering of a real person, the latter assuming the
deployment of a collective action intended to eradicate a social ill.

The underlying framework of the representations of social problems,
particularly of exclusion, within contemporary society – and which is the
source of legitimisation of actions aimed at eradication, or at least alleviation
– reveals three distinct aspects: 1) compassion based on the proximity of
unhappy existences and suffering bodies; 2) emergency backed by the necessity
to react and to come up with immediate results and allowing no delay as the
time given has run out; 3) risk inherent in the alarming dimension of extreme
situations which intertwine the obligation to provide assistance to a person in
danger and the necessity of protecting the security of society at large against
the danger such persons can represent. Therefore, social intervention is in
this sense founded on a basis not so much of reason but more on a basis of
emotion.

However, it would appear possible on the same premise to draw up two
different symbols of society's self-intervention: a frame of reference based
on the social evidence of this social work, obviously in the professional sense
of the term, in order to sustain social unity and cohesion on the one hand, and
a frame of reference based on the moral evidence of an action aimed at
improving the conditions of human beings and the affirmation of their rights
to live in dignity, on the other hand. I have drawn up a synthesis (Figure 3.1)
which brings together both the symbolic and political configurations in a
schema by using various indicators to retrace the passage through personal
trials in terms of social issues and to describe the political rise of these
categories.

I would call the first frame of reference, using by extrapolation an
expression of Hannah Arendt (1967), a policy of pity, i.e. a generic category
subsuming compassion and emergency. But what is this introduction of the
model of pity as a policy?

	Fracture	Pity
Nature of issue	Social problem	Moral problem
Nature of explanation	Breakdown of traditional regulations	Normative difference
Nature of process	Difficult social production	Spectacular treatment of the suffering
Nature of the mediation	Political representation	Dramatic representation
Nature of disposition	Risk of social dualisation or explosion of society	Feeling of indignation
Nature of action	Social intervention	Humanitarian action

Figure 3.2   Synthesis of symbolic and political configurations

Firstly, it characterises the transfer of a religious category, charity, a selfish way of attaining salvation on earth as alms-giving obliterates sin, towards a category of laity, humanist altruism and its law of minimum oppression: 'Therefore, one single but ferocious rule: to attend to minorities and the oppressed. Without any illusions, however, for these minorities can become oppressive themselves' (Battati and Kouchner, 1982, p. 21). But in this transfer, the frame remains identical; it is woven in moral terms. It is based on representation of a normative discrepancy between what one is and what one thinks one is. It is based on a crack in the given order of things conceived as normal and desirable for human beings. It is based on a violation of what society perceives to be good and right. In short, it is based on a consciousness of the intolerable and, therefore, plays alternatively on a spectrum of feelings and on a register of indignation. But for this moral apprehension of the world to function, a condition is presupposed, namely what Emile Durkheim had already realised when he addressed his critique of the amorality of charity, amoral because it is essentially non universal. 'So that a charity can be practised, some must accept not to do it or not to be in a position to do it' (Durkheim, 1976, p. 50). Hannah Arendt was even more explicit half a century later when – in assessing the French Revolution which had, in her opinion, abandoned the question of liberty for that of a policy of pity – she affirmed, that to deploy pity it is important to identify two entities of men unequal in terms of happiness and unhappiness.

Secondly, a cleavage, be it unfortunate/not-unfortunate, does not however suffice for the creation of a policy.

These two classes should have, on the other hand, enough contact with each other so as that the happy people can observe, directly or indirectly, the misery of the unhappy, but from a certain distance or detachment so that their experiences and their actions can remain separate (Boltanski, 1993, p. 18).

The passage from personal trials to social issues rests on the spectacularisation of suffering, in the etymological sense of what speaks to the eyes, of what draws attention and of what plays on the imagination. This necessary aspect of seeing without direct experience is not to be understood as charity entertainment as when the television turns into a fairy godmother by putting misery and unhappiness into the limelight. Rather it is to be conceived as a condition of political action, beyond a generality of a spiritual order, that is to say as a unification of individual expressions of suffering which overcomes their dispersion and their fundamental irreducibility by making them equivalent in space and time. But so that the performance can enable the expression 'acting words', to use an expression by Luc Boltanski, that is to say, so that the chain of pity can be upheld in spite of the distance and ensure for the spectator continuity of the responsibility in the situation of suffering of the other, dramatisation is resorted to. All depends on the quality of enacting it/ making its presence felt at a distance. A policy of pity in this sense is based mainly on categories of eloquence/convincing and on exemplary putting on view, which are nevertheless indifferent to the singularity of the suffering or miserable persons thus exposed.

The second figure, that of a social fracture, is based on an imagining of social rupture, of its duality or its explosion.[9] The problem is not moral but social. But this distinction is not simply a matter of numbers. It presupposes social work, in the sense of work operated by social agents (who by all means can be social workers) (Tachon, 1985). The modalities of this process rest on political work of representation (Bourdieu, 1981), which consists of that which hitherto had remained unspoken, to name that which previously was not or could not be, to objectivise by the discourse that which beforehand belonged to the realm of subjective behaviour and experience as essentially individual. It is in this sense possible to speak of social problems only when a problem situation presents itself which cannot be an object of primary regulation and which calls for explicit and voluntary intervention in terms of social relations in order to preserve the social balance. Therefore, a social problem can be said to exist from the moment when society can no longer use self-regulation in an informal manner to solve certain problems and when such a situation calls for special intervention. In short, a social problem is a product of a construction, leaning of course on a minimum of objective conditions, presupposing a working process whose two phases are, on the one hand, public and identical recognition of the problem, and on the other hand, its political legitimisation and institutionalisation (Lenoir, 1989).

But oscillation between two symbols of the problematisation of exclusion, pity and fracture should not mask the essentials by misleading us into thinking that there is an alternative. This dichotomy is real in the forms of social treatment implemented, but by producing its terms it blurs what is to be understood by exclusion. In fact, the extreme cases, the social expression of suffering, of emergency and of danger saturate apprehension about social problems by the media effect of the intolerable social and by the obligation to intervene which are the result. Moreover, whenever there is a use of reasoning based on moral or social evidence of the humanitarian interference or of the struggle against the social fracture in the name of a logic of compassion, of emergency, and/or the risk, differences inevitably emerge as to the understanding of the fundamental problems, as Zaki Laïdi reminds us when he calls for an intellectual *tour de force* to 'combat emergency not so much as a category of action, but as a central category in the representation of our societies, of their problems and of their future' (Laïdi, 1995). Subsequently, it is clear that besides a theoretical reduction, there prevails an epistemological obstacle that does not take account of the extreme and alarming dimensions of social problems – if one wishes to comprehend them in their essence and seize the forms of social regulation they call for.

The Counterproductive Effects of Putting in Motion a Continuum of Positions

A second difficulty emerges in the introduction inherent in the initiation of the concept of exclusion to substitute that of poverty, of the reference to a process, to a course instead of a state. Previously, poverty was an accumulation of inequalities. Henceforth, exclusion signifies an accumulation of deficiencies, the result of ruptures producing a continual falling down the ladder of social integration. It takes into account particularly 'the essential question of the process of progressive accumulation of the difficulties of individuals and households' (Paugam, 1998, p. 2). And, in this important shift, the notion of exclusion induces that of a continuum going from more to less.

Dominique Schnapper, having structured the ulterior analyses in an article, was one of the first to make such a logic operational, by suggesting a hierarchy of social status based on a distance to employment codified with reference to a contract of undetermined duration (Schnapper, 1989). It distinguishes between: 1) a job with status; 2) a job without status; and 3) status derived from jobs related to past employment (unemployment, retirement, ...); 4) status related to social protection as defined by the rights independent of the job; 5) those without status.

But that which was a continuum of positions allowing one to think in terms of work relations, a central value upon which is based integration, has become a practical commodity for the representation of an individual trajectory, a measure of the social collapse that is in the forefront of everyone's mind, as illustrates, among others, this scale of five degrees of exclusion (Gros-Jean and Padieu, 1995), which enables fragile populations to situate themselves and to scan an individual course on the decline: 1) *the risk* regrouping predisposing factors and designating social precariousness; 2) *the threat* marking a context creating strong individual vulnerability; 3) *the destabilisation* indicating how the shock was experienced; 4) *the sinking* identifying the nonexistence of social bond and the entry into social assistance; 5) *the general exclusion* cumulating the rupture of the three basic social bonds which are employment, accommodation and family.

In a certain way, the continuum is not only important for reasons of classification, as it refers back at the same time to the process of an ideal type of interpreting the process of being put out, i.e. from the world of work or ordinary society. It is an easy step to take – and the temptation to do so is great – between establishing hierarchical social categories in virtue of one factor or another and the focusing on the passage from one to another, then the clarifying of the explanatory factors of this passage.

Serge Paugam illustrates clearly this putting in motion of a continuum (largely due to the dominant position he occupies in the debate on exclusion; largely, too, because he has explicitly signified this shift). In his first work (Paugam, 1991) he set out a typology of the beneficiaries of social action which distinguishes: 1) *the fragile* situated on the upper end of the mechanism for picking up people in difficulty; 2) *the assisted* at the heart of the mechanism; 3) *the marginalised* on the lower end of the mechanism. In a later publication he, as it were, corrected his analysis, indicating that in his work the typology was based on an ensemble of states, and stressed that it would be better to reason in terms of a process marked by three successive phases.

> If today I had to rewrite the social disqualification ..., I would state more clearly that the three types of population studied corresponded to three different phases of this process [of social disqualification]. Therefore, to convey this idea of process more clearly and to remove any misunderstanding which arose with

regard to typologies, which unfortunately many did not distinguish from empirical categories, I would speak of fragilities instead of those who are fragile, of dependence on social workers instead of those who are assisted and of rupture of the social bond instead of the marginalised (Paugam, 1998, p. 4).

What is the basic idea of this putting in motion of a continuum? In a certain way, it appears to be a tautology. Let us take the example of exclusion. Even if the latter is an umbrella notion, it can be minimally defined by a double dimension, as Katherine Duffy has suggested in her synthesis for the Council of Europe of studies related to the apprehension of this phenomenon: 1) it refers back to the loss of a job and to utility; 2) it focuses on a relational deficit, on the weakening of social bonds (Duffy, 1995). And on the basis of the overlapping of these two dimensions one can logically construct a series of different states resembling a topological typology (Queloz, 1994, p. 158). This modelling has a strong heuristic virtue: it accounts for the states of being marginalised which can be empirically described while presenting at the same time the principles of being marginalised for theoretical purposes.

However, such a model would seem to conceal certain construction defects: the same factors are at one and the same time cause and result, principle and state, analyst and analysis: the weakness of social bonds and the loss of utility. Such a state is not in itself dramatic; it is simply a matter of a redundancy which can be seen as a validation. This, however, becomes problematic when this typology becomes sequential, when the principle of transition becomes the describer. In this case, what is the motor of the passage from one state to another? What element can explain this process? Yet again, they are the same variables: the weakening of the social bonds and dwindling social utility. Serge Paugam expresses this very clearly: 'I would like to attempt to show that the weakening and the rupture of the social bonds constitute an essential dimension of this process' (Paugam, op. cit.)

Thus, logically, for a sequential model of states to function like a process, one must introduce a different variable than those that allowed the construction of different phases. The idea of a career is thus often used to explain the mobility from one position to another. It refers to objective facts coming from the social structure and simultaneously to the subjective facts connected to the motivations and to the wishes of the individuals. Vincent de Gaulejac and his colleagues (de Gaulejac and Taboada-Leonetti) have tried to associate these two orders of facts in order to understand the process which links the different phases of the social disinsertion by distinguishing:

- *four stages*: 1) the existence of a rupture which is impossible to face; 2) a series of ruptures leading to the loss of control over one's own life; 3) a steady loss of autonomy and growing dependence on institutional services to live; 4) dropping-out and entry into the world of the marginalised;
- *three principles of sequential action* that explain the role of the people involved in disinsertion: 1) resistance; 2) adaptation; 3) settlement.

This model explains clearly the process leading to being excluded and the participation of the excluded people themselves in this process. Besides a strong propensity to individualising the analysis, this model, by pushing to its limits the logic of the process which scans the passages, still leaves a number of questions unanswered.

Primo, if one follows Howard Becker himself so that the notion of career is really explicatory after a series of stages, the passage from one stage to another must be explained logically each time by the different variables. In his justification of 'a model which takes into account the fact that the different kinds of behaviour develop in a sequential order', it is essential, he says, that 'each phase requires an explanation' and, he adds, 'a cause of one of the phases of the sequence can exert a negligible influence during another phase' (Becker, 1985, p. 46). The singular and specific explanation of each phase constitutes an explanatory element of the final behaviour. Always to use the same principle – resistance/adaptation/installation – is indeed economical, but to what extent is it heuristic and, particularly, is it efficient to understand how the bottom end of the continuum is at all possible and what, in fact, makes it different from the other parts of the continuum?

Secundo, the notion of continuum just as that of career, postulates logically the idea of a superior term, or rather, a common point of departure. This normal state is also normative. Chantal Guérin recalls that this point 'is in fact confused with a norm which continues to impose itself and which is no other than that of the obligation of adults to live in an autonomous way. But from what point of view is this norm a norm?' (Guérin, 1997, p. 47). From the point of view of those who themselves have access to this norm, one could reply that this normal state at the other end of the continuum is insertion. One can also consider that part of the confusion produced by recourse to the notion of exclusion comes from the reference to an implicit model which presupposes an idealised relation to the social context (Roy, 1995). This other side of exclusion is based on the autonomous subject who has a professional activity, which is rewarding and a source of identity, and who has an adequate network of social relations and purchasing power. However, this model is in fact less and less frequent because of the dwindling social protection, the destabilisation of those who are stable (Castel, 1995a), and, in a more general way, the emergence of an insecure society (Gauchet, 1991). Without stable, clear and real support, insofar as this can be imagined to exist at all, how can any pertinence be attached to this idea of a continuum in motion?

Tertio, thinking in terms of continuum implies moreover that the poorest of the poor exist at the end of the process, the most unemployable of the unemployable, those who have known a virtual and total break-off. But by doing so, one is condemned to see at the end of the continuum the terminal point of a trajectory as a kind of rupture, and not of a degree of greater intensity. One also shatters the continuity of the idea of a continuum if one says, as does Jan Vranken in an emblematic way that 'between those without a fixed abode and the others, there is a divide and that those concerned are incapable of reducing by themselves' (Vranken, 1998), or as Giovanna Procacci puts it 'there would exist forms of marginalisation which the excluded would have gone well beyond' (Procacci, 1998).

Besides, the space between the two terms of continuum would constitute the world of the partially included, that of those who are not fully included, which characterises the unavoidable passage on the way to becoming excluded. From then on, would one not have to reserve the use of the notion of social exclusion for the last stage of the process of being socially marginalised, as Shirley Roy invites us to do when she exhorts us not to use exclusion to designate the first stages of social disconnection, the first setbacks following one or several ruptures, but to conserve its strength to name the phenomenon which characterises the fact of having reached the furthest point of social disinsertion? Instead, therefore, of characterising those who experience one form or another of social rupture,

> exclusion would mark the point of dropping-out of those who have accumulated social handicaps and individuals, combining thus objective and subjective conditions of those for whom remedial mechanisms no longer function, of those who are in a position of not acting or reacting for want of not being able to get a grip on their lives following repeated failures (Roy, 1995, p. 76).

The itinerants would thus be placed on a point at a maximum distance from the pole of total social insertion. Lower on the scale of social bonds would be those who socially no longer exist, such as the unemployed who are no longer entitled to unemployment benefits and who have nothing left professionally, who statutorily are no longer linked to the world of work.

This contention, which not only detracts interest from the intermediary states of the continuum, but is also based on a fallacious absolutism, namely, that of the point of dropping out. The itinerants, poor as they may be, still continue to develop social bonds and to be involved in social relations just as the unemployed are not deprived of their practical or technical skills when they are no longer entitled to unemployment benefits. The latter can no longer avail themselves of social bonds with regard to a certain form of organisation of the labour market and a certain form of qualification to it. The excluded share a way of life and similar values, perhaps even the same. When one considers this world of supposedly total absence of participation and of social bonds – when one considers it per se and no longer in its relativity – one discovers that there exists a social life inhabited by social relations, one that even has its own particular structure of the latter. Jean-François Laé and Numa Murard have contributed to clarifying this through their work on exclusion and particularly on the single person who comes and goes from the street to woman-mother, from the street to sister, from the street to wife, from the street to girlfriend (Laé and Murard, 1995). By reasoning in terms of continuum, does not one participate in isolating a final stage as a space in itself, autonomous and specific, in which, by definition, as it were, there is nothing and in which everything is lacking, while this same entity can be a complex ensemble, as Ricardo Lucchini – in his work on street children – speaks of a street system to qualify the experience of the children whose condition is represented as one of total deprivation, a system founded on the alternation of places, the plurality of belonging, the complexity of situations (Lucchini, 1993)? Is not the simplicity produced by the putting in motion of a continuum for explanatory purposes a misleading form of simplicity? In fact, it obscures just as much as it explains. And, in a certain manner, it leads us into an impasse, be it by faulty reasoning (mixing cause and result) or by an analytical turnabout by pointing to precisely that which it claimed to be absent.

Moreover, the logic of the activated continuum – that it would be possible to show how much it reflects the current reasoning on exclusion or of the unemployed at the end of their benefits – despite some welcome critique from here and there, engenders a certain number of implications on the level of social policy as well as on the representation of problematic situations. It is more on the identification with such situations rather than on an in-depth development of these that I now wish to focus towards the end of this chapter.

First Implication: The Putting into Motion of a Continuum Produces an Individualisation of the Social

The logic of an activated continuum leads implicitly but logically to an individualisation in the understanding of the problems and in their social treatment. This individualisation is not done a priori in the form of damning the unemployed at the end of their benefits or by social discrimination of the excluded. This individualisation is done a posteriori by the identification of deficiencies, of inadequacies, of the fragilities that the long descent of the continuum revealed. And, *in fine*, these individuals who by a mobilisation of their willpower and of their resources, who by working on themselves and on their environment can get out of this, can get beyond this condition of being excluded, become, paradoxically, if they remain at the end of the continuum, responsible for this state of affairs, as Françoise Schafter and Fabrice Plomb stress when speaking about the unemployed at the end of their benefits:

> The individualisation of unemployment, the corollary of breaking down the problems, consists of an attitude which identifies the problem of each person and which wants to change or to adapt these to the demands of the market. According to this perspective, one is partaking in a shifting of the attribution of responsibility. When one tells a person that they lack the right qualifications, that they are not mobile enough, that they are unstable or that their expectations are too high, when in order to get out of this situation, the unemployed person is told to find out about his/her rights him/herself, attend courses, commute, adjust oneself to the market conditions, then one tends to say implicitly that the responsibility for the non-integration in the labour market rests on the person himself and not on exterior factors (Schafter and Plomb, 1997, p. 64).

The logic of the continuum in motion is to a large extent the producer of the unemployability and of the unintegrability by legitimising the idea of the objective individual traits of their unemployability and their unintegrability incorporated by the unemployed at the end of their rights or by the excluded. Through this objectivisation it favours the endogenous or intrinsic factors of the individual by privileging as a motor of reinsertion, the norm of internality, dear to social cognitive psychologists (Le Poultier, 1986), which concretises the project. But 'to say that the project is a condition of insertion, is paramount to saying that the person in that situation, because he is lacking something which normal people possess' (Coquelle, 1994). The individualisation of these measures which symbolise the project leads to identifying the handicaps and the problems of the individuals, and this attribution of the personal causality revealed by the course on the way down the continuum ends up producing a prophetic self-realisation effect when the individuals interiorise then accept their deficiencies and these fragilities as characteristics of their state. Thus, in a number of professional situations, being given one's notice is at one and the same time an invalidation. It is because it is inexplicable (Fitoussi and Rosanvallon, 1996). For those of equal skills and seniority, redundancy in the context of a social plan following restructuralisation is often arbitrary for the person who has been let go. The person feels he has been discarded and thus unacknowledged, for to consider someone as an object for whom this ejection does not fit into any explicable pattern which would enable him to act instead of leaving him nothing but resignation and guilt. Xavier Gaullier shows how this individualising logic leads to a designation/interiorisation of unemployability when he analyses the procedures of mass redundancies. To increase the shareholders' return it becomes necessary at a given moment to pinpoint the unproductive costs and very often to reduce the overall costs, particularly salaries. Calculations are made based on the number of redundancies necessary to produce a minimum profit and then the formal criteria of employability are set out before matching these with concrete individuals but not without having had to make the necessary adjustments in order to keep the social compromise in the firm (Gaullier, 1996).

Paradoxically, the logic of activation of the continuum amounts to the melting in a primary sense of process and state, then of actors and deficits. Isabelle Astier's analysis of the increase in the majority of cases of individual situations by the transformation of a private case-study to a civil one shows that when this movement is reversed, this logic of individualisation is none the less true. She makes a point of stressing the important effect individual experiences have in tracing a path of reinsertion even if they have to be pulled up by joining them to general categories and to generic principles (Astier, 1997). The excluded become in this sense separated not only from society and from other categories, those of the partially integrated, but also separate from the processes, of which exclusion is the effect, by the simple act of turning inwardly on their own situation and on their own deficiencies, an inward turning validated by the course itself of the continuum. As Jacques Donzelot says, as naively as cynically, 'unemployment reveals to individuals the handicaps they ignore, but also gives them a goal – that of overcoming them – by digging into the potential of their capacities' (Donzelot, 1984, p. 236)

But this situation involving the displacement of the responsibility onto the person excluded who then becomes the privileged object of social work of reinsertion, is troubling in itself. First of all for the analyst, by 'passing the buck', as it were, but mainly for the excluded or the long-term unemployed person himself insofar as he is the generator of social suffering whose origin lies in a formal contradiction inherent in this logic itself, since he is asked implicitly – or, as the case may be, explicitly in the framework of a contractual procedure – to come to terms with his situation by a strong teleological conscience and by a strong sense of identity, even though he is in a state of devastation and of fragility as a result of being pushed aside. Robert Castel has pinpointed the trouble with this negative individualism, 'the more this individuality is fragile and threatening to fall apart, the more it is overexposed and placed right in the foreground' (Castel, 1995a). This paradoxical situation is irrational and frustrating for an excluded individual, since he must continuously prove his intention of belonging to an entity to which he did at one time belong and which he cannot leave but which declares him off limits (Mainsondieu, 1997). The excluded must, as it were, prove that he is a good citizen just as the unemployed person at the end of his benefits must prove that he is still an acceptable worker.

Second Implication: The Putting into Motion of a Continuum is Based on a Rhetoric of Scale

But at the same time this sense of an activated common political science of continuum infers a preceding incontestable obligation to act on the field in the direction of those who find themselves at the other end of the chain; this focus produces a paradigm of emergency which paradoxically is now juxtaposed with a paradigm of progress. If one can in fact say that emergency exercises a tyranny of constraint by over-emphasising the present, it must be admitted that the rhetoric of emergency cannot be reduced to the mere provision of basic necessities, creating an endless spiral of emergency situations. Humanitarian action on the interior level serves as a means of survival but, it leans on the above-mentioned logic of continuum for its inception and to be conceived as an element of integrated services. Emergency help can only be justified on a sociopolitical level as part of long-term solutions and as a response on a continuum of prescribed responses. Thus the social SAMU conceives of its action only as a moment in a chain: collect the homeless roaming in the night and provide shelter for them, then offer them the benefit of the experience of a social worker the next morning in order to take the first step towards integration (de Gouy, 1998). If this results in setting up what can be called the rhetoric of a ladder which could be climbed step by step, it would make it possible, at the expense of specific efforts, to climb the rungs of social integration.

Insertion can be considered as a master word of this rhetoric of a ladder. By its very existence, it designates the fact that access of the unemployed to work has become difficult, at least for the majority of them, even if only indirectly. Insertion presumes the passage by intermediary status reified and supported by specific measures and implies guiding the unemployed through management and activation of their employability. From placing the unemployed, the logic slips progressively towards holding on to employability, then towards maintaining work skills and finally towards supporting the mere social capacity of workers at the end of their course.

> One way or another, one has to take stock of the personal deficiencies in order to prepare the way for paths more or less long and thorny, from the anticipated passage from beneficiary and employment, going from social adaptation, going from training to access to work ... Insertion is conceived of as a level: social adaptation first, preliminary training and then qualifying training, then access to work when the cycle of restarting has been achieved (Boismenu and Dufour, 1996, p. 122).

One can speak of a rhetoric of a staircase as these different steps are expected to be taken one by one, perhaps not lightly but surely. Social insertion is thus thought of as a preliminary stage to professional insertion.

Having accomplished this, professional and social insertion imply a distinction of categories, if not to say natural, between the ordinary unemployed who fall into the logic of employment and the applicants for insertion defined as little or not capable of holding down a job, a posteriori rather than a priori. Thus these applicants for insertion find themselves on the edge of the labour market without, however, being really inactive. They find themselves hovering in an intermediary zone which has no clear demarcation 'irreducible to placement like assistance' (Demazière, 1995, p. 76).

But insertion just as both individual trajectories and paths of getting restarted tend to take a long time, if not drag on indefinitely. From a process they become a state, to take Robert Castel's formulation. From being a provisional accompaniment they become a permanent situation, 'a long lasting transitory state' (Autès, 1995), enabling survival on the periphery of a salaried society. The staircase is cumbersome and many get stuck on the steps. But the rhetoric of the whole remains. One cannot but ask if insertion in this sense is not a socially and politically correct form of exclusion.

Nevertheless, in the same way, one can be doubtful about the existence of a continuum between the emergency service and ordinary social services (Sassier, 1997). Doubtful, for is this not a well-meaning utopia, since how many homeless picked up in the night by the humanitarian rescue service have really managed to get up all the steps of the staircase? How many followed the advice and the promotional accompaniment of the social worker in whose hands they had been put the day after?

Doubtful, for what is this continuum based on and according to what logic does it function? How does one understand that what has not been efficient in stopping the descent of the staircase can be precisely that which helps one to get up this same staircase? For social workers are anything but unknown for the excluded and the homeless. If the latter are where they are, it is precisely because they have evaded the social workers who had taken charge of them; they have shown themselves to be recalcitrant or impervious to the logic of internalisation and to the mobilisation which is dear to social work. During the long descent down the staircase, they were accompanied and followed up by social workers but they nevertheless ended up at the very bottom. By what miracle, when going up, in the opposite direction, would precisely that which did obviously not work on the way down, have become efficient?

Doubtful, for what is the pertinence of this idea of continuum between the emergency service and the ordinary social services if one admits that the extreme category at the bottom of the ladder has been marked by a virtual break off virtually disjointing it from the other categories placed on the ladder of social disintegration; if one admits that it is a discrete category, in the mathematical sense; if the homeless, in a similar way to the long-term unemployed, have been stamped in such a way as to individualise their unemployability, and if this was that of their unintegrability? Therefore, in this case what does the idea of a continuum of services mean?

It is indeed difficult to believe that this wonderful novel which claims that an unbroken chain of social intervention can lead those without a fixed abode from the streets to emergency lodgings, then from service to service – in a maelstrom of integration – to the gates of integrated society. But the fundament of action towards the destitute, from the moment when one considers them to be inferior on the continuum of inclusion, can only take root within the idea of an integrated network of responses which intertwines the radically distinct registers a priori and even justifies its efficacy by virtue of this. Otherwise the symbol of intervention, that which feeds its *raison d'être*, would collapse in face of the image of the management of stocks stacked at different levels and sealed off from each other.

Does this mean that one must throw the notion of exclusion overboard? By no means: exclusion is not a conceptual mirage; it enables a description, though somewhat confused and reductory, a segment of the reality of modern societies.[10] If this notion did not exist, another term would have to be coined and there is no indication that it would be better or more useful. For the problem of exclusion is not so much one of imperfect semantics but one of an analytical deviation. Disinsertion or non-integration, disqualification or disaffiliation, relegation or vulnerability, precariousness or exclusion certainly render it difficult to conceptualise the marginalisation of a growing number of individuals from social and economic life, but none of them, no more than the next to be born, imposes itself by greater explanatory or expressive qualities of the reality in question. They all share the same apparent defect of running the risk of blindness caused by an excess of light. Through a mechanism of tyranny of constraint, the dazzlement thus produced restricts us from seeing anything more than this problematic reality and so cuts us off from an understanding of the more global social mechanisms from which they themselves stem. It is, therefore, probable that the difficulties of handling exclusion in a scientific analysis come more from this blinding due to decentring than from an inherent inadequacy of the notion itself, which, it seems, can only be escaped by a transversalisation of the problematic.

Notes

1   Cf. an excellent review of literature on this subject in a recent edition of *Lien social et Politiques* (Chopart, 1995).

2   Cf. such as the workshops organised by Saül Karsz and the association Pratiques Sociales in December 1995: 'L'exclusion: Définir pour en finir. Quelles analyses, quelles pratiques, quels enjeux pour en finir avec l'exclusion?'.

3   As Serge Paugam states (1994, p. 53), 'Exclusion refers to the structures of our society. If this expression has been a big media success, this is so largely because it simultaneously revealed the economic disfunctions and the flaws of the system of social protection.'

4   'It might be equally said that poverty has been colonised by economists, who have reduced it to a concern about counting the poor, and social exclusion has become a portemanteau term for sociologists, concerned with accounting for the disadvantaged' (Duffy, 1997). This is similar to what Philippe Besnard (1987) said about the concept of anomie becoming a sign of professional demarcation: ' the password which opened the door of the sociological community'.

5   Katherine Duffy(1995) recalls that in the report of the Council of Europe '[t]here is as yet no standard definition of social exclusion either in terms of the concept, or operationally'.

6   In this sense, exclusion is a qualifier which is essentially negative by obscuring 'the necessity to analyse positively what the lack is composed of' (Castel, 1995b, p. 14).

7   Lockwood (1964) had already made this distinction with regard to the integration of the notions of social integration and system integration. This distinction is taken up by Riccardo Lucchini (1977, p. 39) and applied to marginality: 'If one poses the problem in terms of integration in society (that is, of an individual or a group which does not integrate itself in society), the main focus of the research is put on the individuals or the groups that cannot integrate … If, on the other hand, the problem of marginality is posed in terms of integration of society, the analysis must be shifted. Individuals or marginal groups no longer constitute the object of research, but the structures of the whole society'.

8   For my part (Soulet, 1994) when I proposed to give preference to the term of non-integration over that of exclusion, it was precisely to stress the necessity of not isolating one of the terms of social relations and to think of all forms of marginalisation in terms of the production procedures of the social tie. The reflection on the integration of such-and-such an individual or such-and-such a group cannot be approached from outside the transformations of society as a whole. To take a classic example, integration *into* society cannot be disassociated from integration *of* society. That, it seems to me, is the particular interest of the twin concepts *déliance/reliance* promoted by Marcel Bolle de Bal, as I tried to illustrate in a collective contribution dedicated to these notions (Soulet, 1996).

9   The political-mediatic use, particularly remarkable during Jacques Chirac's electoral campaign in the French presidential elections, is the counterpart, on a different level, of the spectacularisation of the suffering of the figure of pity. The explosion of society, or its euphemised form, the dualisation, acts as a foil imposing evidence of an action of society on itself.

10 This is why Serge Paugam invites one, following Claude Lévi-Strauss and Dominique Schnapper, to consider exclusion as a 'concept-horizon' constituting 'at once a fundamental question of the functioning of the whole of society and an intrinsic limit on the object itself' (Paugam, 1996, p. 566).

Bibliography

Arendt, H. (1967), *Essai sur la révolution*, Paris, Gallimard.

Astier, I. (1997), *Revenu minimum et souci d'insertion*, Paris, Desclée de Brouwer.

Autès, M. (1995), 'Genèse d'une nouvelle question sociale: l'exclusion', *Lien social et Politiques*, no. 34.

Battati, M. and Kouchner, Bm (1982), *Le Devoir d'ingérence*, Paris, Denoël.

Becker, H. (1985), *Outsiders. Etudes de sociologie de la déviance*, Paris, éditions Métailié.

Bergier, B. (1996), *Les Affranchis. Parcours de réinsertion*, Paris, Desclée de Brouwer.

Besnard, P. (1987), *L'Anomie*, Paris, PUF.

Boismenu, G. and Dufour, P. (1996), 'Régulation technicienne des sans emploi: vecteur de diffusion d'une normativité et d'une éthique sociale' in Giroux G. (ed.), *La Pratique sociale de l'éthique*, Montréal, Bellarmin.

Boltanski, L. (1993), *La Souffrance à distance*, Paris, éditions A.M. Métailié.

Bourdieu, P. (1981), 'Décrire et prescrire, note sur les conditions de possibilité et les limites de l'efficacité politique' in *Actes de la recherche en sciences sociales*, March, 38.

Castel, R. (1995a), *La Métamorphose de la question sociale. Une chronique du salariat*, Paris, Fayard.

Castel, R. (1995b), 'Les pièges de l'exclusion' in *Lien social et Politiques*, 'Y-a-t-il vraiment des exclus? L'exclusion en débat', 34.

Chopart, J.-N. (1995), 'Evolution des travaux et des problématiques concernant la pauvreté et l'exclusion en France' in *Lien social et Politiques*, 'Y a-t-il vraiment des exclus? L'exclusion en débat', 34.

Chopart, J.-N. and Roy, S. (1995), 'Editorial' in *Lien social et Politiques*, 'Y a-t-il vraiment des exclus? L'exclusion en débat', 34.

Coquelle, C. (1994), 'Attention Projet!', *Formation emploi*, no. 45.

de Foucauld, J.-B. (1994), 'Huit pistes pour développer le secteur associatif', *Panoramiques*, 'Le spectre de la déchirure sociale et politique' 13, 1st quarter.

de Gaulejac, V. and Taboada-Leonetti, I. (1994), *La Lutte des places*, Marseille, Hommes et perspectives.

de Gouy, A. (1998), 'Social Emergency in France', workshop of groups facing risks of homelessness, Milan, May.

Demazière, D. (1995), *Sociologie du chômage*, Paris, La Découverte.

Donzelot, J. (1984), *L'invention du social*, Paris, Fayard.

Donzelot, J. and Estèbe, P. (1994), *L'Etat animateur*, Paris, éditions Esprit.

Dubet, F. (1987), *La galère: jeunes en survie*, Paris, Fayard.

Duffy, K. (1995), *Social Exclusion and Human Dignity: Background report for the Proposed Initiative by the Council of Europe*, Strasbourg, Council of Europe.

Duffy, K. (1997), 'The concept of social exclusion: the approach of the Council of Europe initiative on human dignity and social exclusion', workshop of groups facing risks of homelessness, Milan, May.

Durkheim, E. (1976), *L'Education morale*, Paris, PUF.

Fitoussi, J.-P. and Rosanvallon, P. (1996), *Les nouvelles inégalités*, Paris, Seuil.

Gauchet, M. (1991), 'La société d'insécurité' in Donzelot J. (ed.), *Face à l'exclusion, le modèle français*, Paris, éditions Esprit.

Gaullier, X. (1996), 'La machine à exclure', coll. *Etat-providence; arguments pour une réforme*, Paris, Gallimard.

Gros-Jean, C.and Padieu, C. (1995), 'Les exclus', *Revue Française des Affaires Sociales*, 2–3, April–September.

Guérin, C. (1997), 'L'exclusion et son contraire' in Gauthier A. (ed.), *Aux frontières du social: l'exclu*, Paris, L'Harmattan.

Jacques, E. (1977), 'Marginalité et rapport social', *Service social dans le monde*, 4.

Karsz, S. (1992), 'Le social entre généalogie et histoire' in Karsz, S. (ed), *Déconstruire le social*, Paris, l'Harmattan.

Laé, J.-F. and Murard, N. (1995), *Les récits du malheur*, Paris, Descartes and cie.

Laïdi, Z. (1995), 'Les problêmes de fond s'enlisent dans l'urgence', *Libération*, 24 March.

Le Poultier, F. (1986), *Travail social, inadaptation sociale et processus cognitifs*, Paris, CTNERHI.

Lenoir, R. (1989), 'Objet sociologique et problême social' in Champagne, P. et al., *Initiation à la pratique sociologique*, Paris, Dunod.

Lockwood, D. (1964), 'Social Integration and System Integration' in Zollchan, G.K and Hirsch, W. (eds), *Explorations in Social Change*, London, Sage.

Lucchini, R. (1977), 'Aspects théoriques de la marginalité sociale', *Revue Suisse de Sociologie*, 3.

Lucchini, R. (1993), *Les Enfants de la rue*, Genève, Droz.

Maisondieu, J. (1997), *La Fabrique des exclus*, Paris, Fayard.

Mazel, O. (1996), *L'Exclusion, le social à la dérive*, Paris, Le Monde éditions.

Paugam, S. (1994), 'Les désillusions du RMI. Avancée sociale ou assistance aux pauvres', *Panoramiques* 'Le spectre de la déchirure sociale et politique', 13, 1st quarter.

Paugam, S. (1991), *La disqualification sociale*, Paris, PUF.

Paugam, S. (1996), 'Les sciences sociales face à l'exclusion' in Paugam, S. (ed.), *L'Exclusion: l'état des savoirs*, Paris, La Découverte.

Paugam, S.(1998) (see chapter 1 of this book).

Procacci, G. (1998), 'Citoyenneté sociale et crise du Welfare' in Soulet, M.H. (ed.), *Misère, souffrance, urgence: lutte humanitaire ou politique sociale*, Fribourg, éditions universitaires.

Prud'homme, R. (1994), 'Les nantis n'ont plus besoin des pauvres', *Le Monde*, Opinions, 5 November.

Queloz, N. (1994), 'La non-intégration, un concept qui renvoie fondamentalement à la question de la cohésion et de l'ordre sociaux' in Soulet, M.H. (ed.), *De la non-intégration; Essais de définition théorique d'un problème social contemporain*, fribourg, Editions universitaires.

Roy, S. (1995), 'L'itinérance: forme exemplaire de l'exclusion sociale?', *Lien social et politiques* 'Y-a-t-il vraiment des exclus? L'exclusion en débat', 34.

Sassier, M. (1997), 'Action sociale et action humanitaire; les contours d'une liaison dangereuse', in De Ridder, G. (ed.), *Les nouvelles frontières du social*, Paris, l'Harmattan.

Schafter, F. and Plomb, F. (1997), *Chômeurs de longue durée et en fin de droit. Enquête dans le canton du Jura*, Neuchâtel, Cahiers de l'ISSP, 20.

Schnapper, D. (1989), 'Rapport à l'emploi, protection sociale et statuts sociaux', *Revue française de Sociologie*, 1.

Soulet, M.-H. (ed.) (1994), *De la non-intégration. Essais de définition théorique d'un problème contemporain*, Fribourg, éditions universitaires.

Soulet, M.-H. (1996), 'Déliance et reliance: analyse critique de leur contribution – une sociologie des problèmes sociaux' in Bolle de Bal, M. (ed.), *Voyage au coeur des sciences humaines*, Paris, L'Harmattan.

Tachon, M. (1985), 'Travail social et gestion des problèmes sociaux' in Bailleau, F., Léomant, C. and Lefaucheur, N. (eds), *Lectures sociologiques du travail social*, Paris, Editions ouvrières.

Touraine, A. (1992), 'Inégalités de la société industrielle, exclusion du marché' in Affichard ,J. and de Foucauld, J.B. (eds), *Justice sociale et inégalités*, Paris, éditions Esprit.

Vranken, J. (1998) (see chapter 15 of this book).

Wright Mills (1967), *L'imagination sociologique*, Paris, Maspéro.

4 Homelessness and the Housing Factor: Learning from the Debate on Homelessness and Poverty

ANTONIO TOSI

To some extent the insistence on the housing aspect of homelessness seems a sort of misunderstanding: the fact that we are considering people 'with no home' invites one to think of the problem as essentially a problem of housing and determined by housing factors – that is where the causes are to be sought in the fluctuations of housing markets and policies. The risk of confusing causes with effects, the indicators with the causes, the courses the process takes with its determinants, is obvious.

If the matter were reduced to this, there would be little to add. In reality there are many reasons to continue the discussion. First of all the incongruities and simplifications in the role played by housing factors reveal unsolved points in the debate and research on homelessness. They also show that it is essential to consider the connection between the research and the construction of the problem and policies in order to be able to discuss it. Finally, there is the genuine importance of housing factors, which needs to be better defined.

Two Different Fields

The best point to start with is the well-known conceptual and terminological uncertainties and ambiguities that characterise the debate on homelessness. Of those principles that 'order' the multiplicity of notions of homelessness, the most obvious is the polarisation around two principal meanings: on the one hand the lack of a space – a 'shelter' – and on the other the absence of social relations or ties which in turn would reveal situations of social exclusion or marginalisation. Obviously the two conditions are not at all identical: many with no home have normal social relations and there are people with relational problems who live in houses.

The two poles make reference with equal relevance to two fundamental meanings of 'home'. 'Home entails both a "there" and a "they"' (Stone, 1994). The two meanings, however, coexist in the debate without their relationships really being elaborated on. The ambiguity that results from this is handled by means of various expedients.

Classification by type is the main one. The relation between the two dimensions is often taken as a criterion to distinguish between different types of homelessness. The plurality of terms (homeless, houseless, etc.) comes to the aid of this operation.

The plurality can also be used to marginalise one of the things referred to. On the one hand terms like homeless can be used – adhering undoubtedly to the most commonly accepted meaning of the term – to refer to situations of extreme poverty and marginalisation.

> The term homeless might actually best be defined as including those who are excluded from the discursively beneficially constructed terms, e.g. family, job, soberness, education etc. (Børner, 1997, p. 5).

> Homelessness can be defined as a severe condition of social, personal, and relational vulnerability, whereby functional or compassionate relationships within customary social context become virtual or entirely impossible (cited by de Feijter, 1997, p. 1).

In many cases these definitions do not even make any reference to actual housing problems – often pointing out that one can be homeless while one is at home. On the other hand homeless is 'identified' as a question of housing (need) and reference to other meanings is criticised as the effect of a misunderstanding.

> Until recently a multitude of concepts, not to say a confusion of ideas characterised the field of 'homelessness' and housing poverty (*Wohnungsnot*) in Germany .... It was only in 1987, that the Standing Conference of German Municipalities by conceiving a new (political) definition took an important step to overcome this confusing situation. The definition started from the concept of '*Wohnungsnot fall*' (case of housing need) and thus underlined the decisive characteristic that problem groups, which up to then had been differently defined, have in common, i.e. the lack or insufficiency of provision of accommodation, which is the basis of the problem of 'homelessness', loss of home and

unacceptable housing conditions .... Today we differentiate between three subgroups within the 'cases of housing need': persons/households presently affected by houselessness (*Wohnungslosigkeit*); persons/households threatened by houselessness; persons/households living in unacceptable housing conditions (*unsumutbaren Wohnverhaltnissen*). To make things easier for non-German readers, the definition 'houseless' is applied to a large part of such groups traditionally described in English as 'homeless' (Specht-Kittler, 1994, pp. 2–3).

Finally, resort can be made to copulative or disjunctive definitions of the type 'and', 'or', 'also'.

A person is homeless if she/he does not have a home that can be regarded as stable or permanent and meets one's demands to a reasonable standard of dwelling. He/she is furthermore incapable of using the different relations and institutions offered by society – e.g. family, network, and private and public institutions of every kind etc. (cited by Børner, 1997, p. 5).

(Homeless is limited to mean) 'a rootless person without a dwelling, a specific life circle or ties' (cited by Kärkkäinen, see ch. 7).

With these approaches there is a risk of missing a fundamental point which is that of analysing the relations between the two meanings and between the two conditions described by the different terms.

We may assume that the polarisation of the two meanings is constitutive of the problem homelessness. This means to acknowledge that the discourse on the homeless speaks of two different questions, and that in order to construct the field we need to admit this difference and at the same time to keep the two questions co-present in the field.

Denominating the two questions is difficult because all the available terms have already been 'used up', being employed in different ways. One area takes the more common meaning of the term homelessness as its point of reference, the socially marginalised or desocialised homeless, usually identified by terms such as 'of no (fixed) abode', *sans domicile (fixe)*, *senza dimora* etc., and the other consists of 'not having a house'. An appropriate term for the latter may be 'housing exclusion', provided it is used in a reasonably restricted sense (without extending it to bad housing conditions).

Terms such as 'no abode', etc. try to hit on relational problems or elements of vulnerability or severe hardship which are suggested by the term 'homeless' in its more restricted or more conventional sense. Terms such as 'exclusion from housing' identify the problem on the basis of the type of (non-) accommodation adopted.

Clearly the 'no abode' represent just one of the categories populating the housing exclusion field and their problems cannot be understood exclusively in terms of housing exclusion. The 'no abode' is a specific case of social exclusion, characterised by multiple deprivation and traits of social disinsertion. For the no abode the lack of housing constitutes one aspect of a wider syndrome of social exclusion. Social isolation is a crucial aspect of the syndrome. In many cases we find here those extreme outcomes of social exclusion that have been signalled by the debate as 'disaffiliation' (Castel, 1991), loss of the capabilities necessary to perform elementary functions of everyday life (Sen, 1992), etc.

The two types of notions identify two different research areas – two different research objects that are to a certain extent independent and must be kept theoretically distinct. Once their relative independence is recognized, a basic point for the construction of the field homelessness is that of analysing the relations between the two conditions described by the different terms.

The two notions raise different questions: on the one hand the general problems of the connections between poverty and housing (such as the housing factors that contribute to cause poverty and vice versa), and on the other the question of those types and processes of social exclusion or marginalisation that are 'qualified' by the privation or loss of housing. Both questions are related to (extreme) poverty, which is the general point of reference for discussing homelessness, and both are able to make essential contributions to the understanding of poverty and social exclusion – but in different ways, examining the difficult relationships between the systems of poverty and housing differently.

One shared principle of the research on homelessness is that the analytical approach must extend beyond the phenomenon of the strictly homeless or the homeless in the literal sense. The two notions provide two different criteria for this extension: the problems of poverty/social exclusion and the problems of housing exclusion. Both directions are appropriate. In the latter sense a continuity is assumed between housing exclusion and the various degrees of bad housing. In the first sense extension is to all that which is able to explain poverty. In this framework, housing factors become one of the possible explanatory dimensions together with others indicated in studies on poverty.

The relationships between the two areas can be defined in inclusive terms – marginalised homeless as cases of housing exclusion; and in excluding terms – different phenomena to be treated in different frameworks.

The difficulty in finding the relationships between the two systems in play derives from the complexity of both terms: consequently multiple relationships are possible between the different dimensions of poverty (poverty, extreme poverty, marginalisation, social exclusion ...) and the different dimensions of the housing experience (Imi, 1992; Wodon, 1992).

All combinations are possible. It is obviously possible to be marginalised and have housing, but also to be without housing without being marginalised, to be without housing but not of no abode and even to be homeless with housing. Clearly the meaning of 'housing' may change for these different cases.

If we wish to avoid nominalistic conclusions, we must recognise that the opposition between homelessness as lack of shelter and homelessness as exclusion from the relations implied by the term home correspond to two different paradigms. They identify different social representations which correspond to different interpretations on an analytical level and different solutions to problems on a practical level (Tosi, 1996). This means that different interpretative frameworks are operating in attempts to understand the same phenomenon.

The History and New 'Frames'

It is not possible to proceed further unless the problem of homelessness is set in the historical context in which it arose: the reappearance in the 1970s and 1980s of poverty and housing poverty on a large scale – as a reality and subject of discussion – in all industrialised countries. However, while the relationships between (extreme) poverty and housing hardship are more easily ascertainable, those between housing hardship, new tension on the housing markets and homelessness are more difficult.

There is nevertheless some symptomatic data that justifies attention to housing factors in an analysis of homelessness. The extremely poor seem to have severe housing problems, perhaps worse today than in the past ('what has changed is not so much the people with problems, but the fact that people with those problems are today without housing' (Marcuse, 1988, p. 654, with reference to the US)). Something similar can also be said of the homeless: their housing problems may have worsened. Whatever their social profiles, the paths to and causes of homelessness, the difficulty with which the homeless manage to find a place to live or to sleep are in any case more evident than they were in the past.

The lack of shelter as a characterisation of homelessness may constitute something new. Peter Rossi states it explicitly for the USA and also links a transformation of the notion and images of homelessness to this historical change.

The meaning of homelessness was not at the time (1950s and 1960s) centred on lack of shelter. Indeed, most were not shelterless but slept at night in the cheap accommodations available on Skid Row. Few slept out of doors or in public places. To be homeless in that period meant primarily living without the social relations that are implied in the meaning of home, namely, living alone without spouses, parents, or children (Rossi, 1994, p. 343).

This raises the question of whether a more difficult general housing situation may have made the housing problems of the homeless even more serious and the role of housing factors more important than in the past. What is clearer, however, is that at the same time the images of homelessness have changed. This brings us to the social construction of the problem. It is interesting to see how the relationships between poverty, housing and homelessness are being redefined in the context of the re-emerging poverty.

Differently in different countries. In the USA homelessness is a basic category for identifying poverty. Poverty is widely perceived through homelessness (with the risk of 'reducing' poverty to homelessness or of separating the problems of the homeless from the question of poverty (Marcuse, 1988)).

In Europe (on the continent) things have gone differently. On the one hand the (relative) persistence of welfare systems may have attenuated the extreme forms of housing deprivation which manifest in explicit homelessness. On the other hand the themes discussed are different. Serge Paugam underlines that in France the recent re-emergence of the *sans abrisme* theme brings with it a significant difference with respect to the '30 glorious years'.

In those thirty years of economic and social progress extreme forms of poverty (were) perceived, analysed and treated through the filter of housing. Persons designated as poor (were) above all, in the 50's and 60's, those who were roofless or housed in very poor conditions in hovels or 'cité de transit'.

During the employment crisis of the 80's, the problem of accommodation started to be brought up again. It was put, however, in very different terms. It is no longer in fact the insufficiency of suitable accommodation that explains the appearance of the 'new poor'. The new types of poverty are connected to different structural developments that have occurred simultaneously. The first is the worsening of the labour market and the growth of long term unemployment ... The second is the weakening of social ties ... These developments have, for fifteen years now, affected persons who mostly come from the working classes, but, as opposed to the lumpenproletariat of the hovels and bidonvilles, have not been socialised in conditions of absolute poverty. In the 80's then, poverty was no longer exclusively caught by the housing filter. It is present each time the effects of the crisis are evoked (Paugam, 1993, pp. 29, 50–51).

In other words, the 'frames' (cf. Schon, 1983) in which the housing poverty problem is constructed – as a social problem and as a subject for reflection – have changed. The new frame is given in Europe by the new conditions that produce poverty and by the new paradigm indicated by the term social exclusion. This paradigm is a designation of the problems of social cohesion as configured by the 'crisis' in progress in industrialised countries. At the same time it is a theoretical and value construct that provides a model for analysis and policy making.

The citation above suggests some consequences for discussing homelessness and the role of housing factors. In the new frame, it is no longer the insufficiency of suitable accommodation that explains the appearance of the 'new poor'; the new types of poverty are connected to different structural developments, to be essentially identified in the employment crisis and the various processes that make social ties more fragile. The precarisation processes occurring constitute widespread risk situations, involving persons who have not been socialised in conditions of absolute poverty.

Exclusion: A Process

In this frame the task to be tackled is – rather than the search for a 'determining' factor – that of seeing how the housing factor relates to the overall complex of factors involved in the production of social exclusion. This operation must be carried out at a macrostructural and at a micro-biographical level – a distinction that is also current in studies on the homeless. At the macro level it is a question of understanding how housing factors intervene among those 'underlying factors' usually considered in the analysis of poverty and social exclusion: the factors that are inherent in the unemployment crisis, in the crisis of relationship systems and in the crisis of welfare policies. At the micro-biographical level, the problem is how different types and degrees of housing deprivation intervenes in the various paths to social exclusion.

This problem can only be dealt with if the 'process' character of poverty, which is a fundamental point of the paradigm of exclusion, is taken seriously.

Poverty today is better defined as an ongoing process rather than as a fixed state. No definition of social poverty as static can account for the heterogeneous nature of its individual members. Any such definition also avoid the central issue that faces us: the progressive accumulation of difficulties from their origin to their final effects whether we are considering individuals or whole families (Paugam, 1997, p. 3).

An 'analysis of the processes that can lead from precariousness to exclusion in the sense of an accumulation of handicaps and the progressive breaking of social ties' is therefore of interest. 'It is not a question of designating one or various groups characterised by de facto exclusion, but above all of underlining the existence of processes that can lead to these extreme situations' (Paugam, 1993, p. 14).

From this viewpoint, our problem becomes how the privation or loss of housing is related to different types and stages of poverty and how they intervene in the passage from one stage to another. That is why it is not enough to record the availability or not of accommodation by itself or at a determined moment in time. The 'process' framework is applicable literally to the homeless too. 'The situation of sans-abri corresponds not so much to a state as to a point in time of a process and to a transitory situation in a career' (Damon and Firdion, 1996).

Paugam provides various indications on the subject. In his research on the users of RMI he documents the variety of housing problems that may accompany the process at different stages and that constitute risk factors on the road to exclusion. When advanced stages in the process of the weakening of social ties are reached, housing difficulties take on considerable importance, including explanatory importance. Among the many handicaps that characterise these situations, housing deprivation has a strong – cause and effect – relationship with the desocialisation in progress. 'The absence of accommodation that guarantees security and an equilibrium to daily living is simultaneously the cause and the consequence of the weakness and instability of social ties' (Paugam, 1993, p. 175).

In the research practice the accent is more often placed on the lack or the loss of housing as a feature of processes of disaffiliation and on the function of these factors in the drift towards extreme marginalisation. The role they play in social exclusion processes is seen from the extreme outcomes of such processes and non-housing situations are associated with these extreme situations. The prevalent focus of attention on these situations in some ways reflects the logic of the theoretical frameworks of exclusion, which invite one to see the process of exclusion as a progression towards extreme outcomes or as a process that is given meaning by its extreme outcomes. In reality the very meaning of the notion of process should oblige us to extend this type of analysis to the entire process of exclusion; it should invite a dynamic analysis in which the different types and degrees of housing deprivation are connected with different types and stages of social exclusion processes. Such an analysis would show that: (a) housing exclusion is a problem that as a rule may affect all types and stages of social exclusion processes; (b) being without housing may be part of different life courses: it is not necessarily an element in a drift towards marginalisation, but may be a temporary condition – and even a stage in an emancipating/improving process, or in a process of social integration. This is the case, for instance, for many foreign immigrants (Pollo, 1995).

This type of analysis would provide additional elements in support of the proposed distinction between the two notions. There is no reason for identifying housing exclusion and extreme marginalisation or desocialisation. The type of the homeless marginalised and desocialised is only one possible combination of factors. In this case, the lack of housing constitutes one aspect of a wider syndrome of social exclusion. However, there are people who are simply excluded from housing, without that involving marginalisation, and even less so disinsertion, disaffiliation or personal disabilities similar to what happens to street homeless or to the no abode. These situations are widespread. In Italy for instance many poor people find themselves in housing situations assimilable to 'non-housing', essentially because they are too poor to afford market housing or because they are excluded from social housing. Housing exclusion without serious marginalisation may even occur for some of those who resort to emergency shelters.

The phenomenon is not limited to regions hit by widespread poverty. There are cases in almost all countries for which being homeless is a frequent occurrence – even in the literal sense – without this involving marginalisation, e.g. many foreign immigrants. (Naturally the question arises, for those on the streets, of whether or for how long such situations can last without implying a process of marginalisation.) The debate on homelessness abounds with references to this type of housing exclusion as important components of the 'new' homelessness.

> Increasingly amidst the homeless are average families which do not suffer from specific social problems. The members of these families are often, but not always, unemployed: [there is an] increasing numbers of 'working poor', who remain nevertheless under the poverty line, combined with the increase of precarious, underpaid jobs throughout the EU (Parmentier, 1997, p. 3).

The identification of the two problems – as much as the focus on the situations of housing exclusion linked to extreme outcomes of the exclusion process – has been backed by the theoretical logics of many current approach to social exclusion, which 'invite' one to see exclusion as a process that is given meaning by its extreme outcomes.

There is an extremely strong insistence, in the ideology of recent research into poverty, on the multidimensional nature of the phenomenon and on the cumulative character of the processes at work. This risks hiding essential elements of the question.

There are relative deprivations, sectorial poverties and poverties that do not involve problems of marginalisation – and less so of desocialisation or disinsertion – also in the conditions of society in which the new processes of poverty work. As Serge Paugam clearly stated, different combinations of poverty and exclusion are possible and different forms of 'integrated poverty' are still present in various national and regional realities (Paugam, 1996). Furthermore the notion of accumulation does not imply 'a linear process that would lead individuals from a situation of vulnerability to one of social disaffiliation'. 'The appearing of the first difficulties does not mean for all the individuals that they will enter a cumulative process necessarily leading to more and more serious problems' (Paugam, 1993, pp. 164, 168). The cumulativeness is quite simply a description of the process, seen in its most extreme final states and the multiplicity of handicaps is the experience that characterises situations of unmistakable marginalisation or 'social disqualification'.

On the possibility that the different precariousness and poverty factors are (relatively) unconnected, particularly with regard to the weakness of social ties with respect to other factors, Paugam bases the differences between different European countries, that can basically be brought down to different correlations between the intensity of social ties and other factors. According to Paugam, however, the basic logic of the process is the same in the different national contexts.

> Private networks of help are varying degree of support in the struggle for work and financial stability to prevent the process starting and to prevent the passage from one phase to another. This does not necessarily imply however that the social logic of the process itself is different from one national context to another. We can confidently put forward the hypothesis that the progressive phases of the process are almost identical in all of the countries (under consideration) and that the weakening of social links and social rupture are universally essential elements. The homeless in the southern parts of Europe are confronted with similar problems ... to the homeless in other countries as well as similar developments and set of experiences as the period of homelessness lengthens.

The initial risk of becoming homeless however varies from country to country just as risk of becoming socially isolated. Often stress is placed upon the low level of homelessness in southern Europe (see ch. 1).

For the marginalised homeless, stress on the connection between factors is appropriate. Here a multiplicity of handicaps is 'normal', and the experience of the breaking of social ties is likely to have strong similarities in different contexts. These situations, which occur at the conclusion of processes of exclusion, are normally the result of cumulative processes.

In terms of accommodation, the marginalised homeless are characterised by the recurrent, permanent or long-term privation of a 'home'. The distinction/ opposition between the temporary or occasional homeless and the permanent homeless is a common one among researchers. Many insist on the fact that most of the homeless are not long-term homeless (Avramov, 1995, p. 79): a fact which has important practical consequences (for instance: 'to consider what services might be relevant for someone who just needs a little help to leave homelessness, as well as for someone who needs a lot of help' (Burt, see ch. 12)).

Being permanently without housing involves a qualitative difference among 'homeless'; it indicates a multiplicity of 'social problems' and chronicisation of hardship which characterise strong marginalisation. It also bears witness to a social uprooting, which manifests as geographical uprooting. The latter designation is easily correlated with some of the connotations of the terms used to indicate the strictly homeless: not having a 'fixed' abode; vagrancy; not having a place of 'one's own' (having control of a place, 'belonging' to a place etc.); estrangement from the territory/community in which one lives (Berzano, 1992), etc.

This falls in line with the well-known criteria for identifying the homeless: that it is impossible to say who is homeless on the basis of a given moment in time. But identification is also impossible on the basis of type of accommodation: not only do certain types of 'housing' arrangement involve precariousness, but there are also – for example – certain shelters for the homeless that involve a certain degree of permanence (Marpsat and Firdion, ch. 10).

The distinction between the marginalised homeless and those 'simply' excluded from housing is important because housing exclusion without marginalisation is a widespread phenomenon and because it represents an important area for policies, an area in which the policy principles for dealing with marginalisation (for instance, social reintegration programmes) do not apply. This area has been pushed to the margins of policies by the insistence on the 'socially excluded'. This is clear in the French example.

> Since it is a question of producing housing for disadvantaged persons, two categories of families are continually confused. This confusion tends to lump together in a single group families whose only difficulty is that of financial resources and whose only problem is of affordability with those who, having accumulated various handicaps, are in need of full social support. The case of the latter ... seems to be gradually becoming much better understood and treated, while families with no social integration problems but who have poor financial resources are more likely to remain with no solution to their problems (Haut Comité, 1997).

The Housing Factor

The predominant argument when the importance of housing factors in the production of homelessness is emphasised concerns the relationship between the decrease in affordable housing – or the increase in housing costs – and the decrease in incomes for various sectors of the population.

(We will leave aside here the fact that the grounds on which both these statements are based can be disputed: the fact is that the problem is set in different terms according to the contexts, also because it reflects the different housing and social policies directly: see for instance Jencks, 1994.)

In reality, credible explorations of this relationship use multi-factor explanatory approaches, analogously to that which occurs for studies on poverty. This means a virtual reduction in the importance of the housing factor. This path is the right one to take both methodologically and from an interpretative point of view, because it brings the argument back to the problem of poverty. However, it leaves the questions with which we started out unanswered: whether and why the extremely poor have such housing problems today and whether there is something in the specific development of housing systems and policy that helps us to explain homelessness as well as phenomena of bad housing.

The cost-income argument gives a more probable explanation to the phenomena of bad housing. As far as the homeless are concerned, the argument may account for one of the preconditions, or one of the paths, to homelessness, but it cannot be valid for the homeless as a whole. A little more could perhaps be explained if housing factors other than cost were added (e.g. difficulty in access to social housing for some of the poor). The fact remains that if it is true that bad housing conditions can 'translate' into homelessness, this occurs in the presence of other factors of fragility. There is at least a partial discontinuity between the two phenomena, and they require partly different explanations.

In reality the effects that market and policy developments have had on the production of homelessness constitute an extremely difficult point: the relationships vary according to the contexts and for the most part remain to be studied.

Certainly many analyses indicate that the evolution of housing systems may have played an important role in increasing homelessness, but they do this claiming a selective role for it, once again as a result of the combination of these and other factors. Jencks (1994), considering the USA, does not accept the explanation of homelessness in terms of income and cost trends, but admits that it may have validity for certain categories, such as single mothers (which brings social policies into the question). In answer to the question, 'Why is it that only some of the extremely poor become homeless?' Peter Rossi (1994) cites housing factors for newly-formed families and ethnic discrimination on housing markets among the selective factors.

The point – still more than the disagreement on the importance of housing factors – is that practically none of the arguments concerning the role played by housing factors in the production of homelessness appears to be shared. This is clear in the debate in the USA (see Quigley, 1996, pp. 1937–8). In order to proceed, a theory of the housing market capable of integrating the problem of homelessness would be needed. For the time being we have only a few first attempts and the results, to judge by the work of O' Flaherty (who, however, addresses processes highly specific to the USA) can be surprising: 'the one major change during this period which could have caused the rise in homelessness (has been) the substantial decline in housing demand by the middle class' (Quigley, 1996, pp. 1938–9).

It is not surprising, then, that the debate on the homeless abounds with references to housing variables that have dubious relationships to homelessness. There is also all the uncertainty and ambiguity of the analyses at a structural level. For housing factors too, the concepts of 'risk' and of 'context factors' are often used as a substitute for facing the difficulty of defining the relationships, for suggesting 'possible' (causal) relationships in conditions of uncertainty.

On the other hand, there are some structural factors of the housing type that seem to have more probable, strong and direct relationships with the production of homelessness. The development most frequently cited in this respect is the contraction of marginal housing markets or the reduction in traditional low cost market segments, the destruction of the SRO (single room occupancy) hotels in the American cities and the drastic contraction of what in France is called 'de facto social housing' stock, etc. (Hoch and Slayton, 1989; Jencks, 1994 etc.).

The possibility of relating the housing trends with homelessness relies to a large extent on the difficult question of the filtering mechanisms in housing markets. In fact, this is probably the main way in which general trends in housing may have influenced the production of homelessness. It is important however to consider that the role of filtration mechanisms for the low/marginal segments of the market has often been questioned. Moreover, today the possibility of gaining access to particularly low cost housing through filtering processes has been reduced, and the 'sense' of these processes is in some way reversing.

> It is not clear that this process is typical or reliable now, if it ever was. The phenomenon of gentrification and the rapid increase in the number of affluent nonfamily households and childless couples in the 1970s raised the demand for older urban housing. Rather than passing to households with lower incomes, it has become common for housing to filter up to higher-income groups. The flow of older units to low-income people seems to have been short-circuited. To the extent that this reverse filtering of housing is occurring, it could help to explain an increase in homelessness (Carliner, 1987, pp. 121–2).

One obvious comment could be that for homelessness to be understood, the suitable housing category is not 'lack of houses', but rather lack of appropriate housing circumstances. The point would deserve more analytical discussion. In one sense appropriate housing means a supply that meets particular requirements of affordability, those of very low incomes. In another sense, it means a supply that is consistent with the conditions of the socially excluded and the extremely poor and designed to cope with precariousness, to prevent homelessness and to favour recovery from homelessness. In many cases, this requires a multidimensional approach dealing with the various aspects of exclusion. The marginal markets met the first criteria and often the second. The criteria of consistency requires a series of conditions that are not necessarily associated with low cost and neither are they guaranteed by conventional social housing: suitable in type, in suitable places, providing integration between accommodation and other areas of living, etc. There is one criteria, made popular in the housing debate in recent years, which clearly states what appropriateness consists of from this point of view: 'the important thing about housing is not what it is but what it does in the lives of its inhabitants' (Ward, 1985).

The recent debate on poverty indicates the main critical factors for dealing with causality in this field. An initial factor is the impossibility of identifying a single underlying cause at the heart of the phenomenon of poverty or homelessness. The explanation must be sought in the interrelations between the different factors at each level (Jencks, 1994) and in the mechanisms connecting the different level. 'It is the combination and the feedback between the complexity of background and proximate factors which induces [homelessness]' (Avramov, 1995, p. 118).

So it is not even possible to claim any 'regular pattern' in the chains of events that produce poverty and homelessness. The 'causes' vary according to the groups (one important distinction here should be between homeless single persons and homeless families) and the places. 'Studies of homelessness in Europe and North America show how the relative importance of different underlying causes varies considerably from country to country and city to city' (Unchs, 1997, p. 233). Despite the insistence on the heterogeneity of homelessness, this simple fact is often overlooked.

One last criterion is to consider that the causal dynamics, and the notion of cause/factor itself, change according to the level of analysis. The conceptualisations in use are based on the distinction between the far reaching transformations which lie behind extreme poverty (above all job insecurity and crisis in primary relationship ties) and the way in which extreme poverty in individuals develops. This distinction – which tends to find its origin in a macro/micro opposition – is widely made in studies on homelessness in the guise of different terms: immediate or precipitating vs. underlying factors (Unchs 1997); background factors vs. proximate determinants (Avramov 1996), etc.

When applied to the discussion on housing factors, these criteria suggest a dual distinction between the cited levels of analysis on the one hand and the two constellations of problems/situations embraced by the notion of homelessness on the other hand.

If the question is that of the non-marginalised homeless, then the cost/income argument – which insists on the importance in the production of homelessness of the relationships between the decrease in affordable housing (or the increase in housing costs) and the decrease in incomes for various sectors of the population – has an importance that can be generalised. Also, if we remain at a macro/structural level, this argument is of unquestionable importance. ('Most homelessness is the result of people unable to find adequately paid work and it is often exacerbated by housing markets where adequate accommodation is beyond the means of those with low incomes' (Unchs, 1997, p. 232)).

At the micro/biographical level, however, attention shifts to the different role that the housing factor may play in the paths and processes that produce homelessness. There are many roads to homelessness and the privation of housing acts and operates in different ways and at different times (Negri and Saraceno, 1996; Pollo, 1995). This is also true for those paths in which homelessness means social marginalisation. In this light, housing appears as one of the factors and in many cases not the decisive factor in the genesis of social exclusion and homelessness.

At the same time micro analyses show the importance that being without a house or losing a house has in individual paths to social exclusion and marginalisation, an importance that can be claimed independently of causal considerations. Examples are seen in formulations such as the following. 'There is a greater likelihood of social rupture on the case of a subject losing all form or residence and it increases with the duration of this situation' (Paugam, ch. 1); 'The loss of housing marks a non-return point in the path to marginalisation', or 'it is the beginning of "wandering"' (Moreau and Guillou, 1995); 'Being without housing rapidly produces chronic deprivation' (Negri and Saraceno, 1996), etc.

The housing factor has a definite importance, therefore, which may be assessed quite apart from any hypotheses concerning its 'primary' causal meaning. As regards the variety of roles that the housing factor may play, this is partly an obvious implication of the heterogeneity of the phenomenon of homelessness. Moreover, micro analyses reflect a series of methodological constraints that have been cleared up with regard to the use of individual case histories in studies on poverty. 'The events studied in individual case histories are not connected to each other according to any single causal tie or typical sequence.' 'Given these assumptions, the concept of INUS causes was introduced, taking the INUS conditions model meaning: the "insufficient but necessary part of a condition which is itself unnecessary but sufficient"' (Mackie, 1974). These are designed to show the dynamics of processes that lead to poverty when applied to individual case histories. Thus the loss of a job does not necessarily translate into the loss of housing unless other conditions occur at the same time such as the lack of a network of support and other events (Terracina, 1996, p. 40).

It is not therefore legitimate to seek the causes of poverty, but it is legitimate to seek the INUS causes of individual downdrift processes. But if then an individual

INUS-cause recurs in more than one minimum sufficient conditions, in more than one of the possible sequences that lead individual destinies to a certain type of poverty, then it will happen frequently when crisis conditions exist and will be a reliable indicator of the presence of a state of crisis. While there is no 'integral cause' for complex phenomena like poverty, it is nevertheless possible to draw up – for each type of poverty – a list of INUS-causes in rank order which are 'more probable than others', and therefore a category of 'predictors more reliable than others (Micheli and Laffi, cited by Terracina, 1996).

The prevailing model in the research on homeless today is founded on the idea that structural factors define the risk, but personal biographical case histories must be looked at in order to understand who will actually become homeless.

While structural factors are determinants of family homelessness, there is also substantial evidence that individual characteristics operate as selection factors in deciding which poor families end up homeless (Gulati, 1994, p. 2).

The puzzling question arises as to why some people become homeless when other who appear equally vulnerable from a structural standpoint do not. To answer that question, we consider the biographic factors associated with homelessness (Snow and Anderson, 1993, p. 253).

[There are] two different narratives. The first narrative is a macro one and focuses on all the risk of impoverishment indicators ... This narrative does not focus on the 'poor' ... but rather on 'poverty', that is, a broad social area where the potential for malign circuits to become activated is high. It is only through the second narrative, focusing on the life histories and social processes involving the behaviour and chain of events affecting the individuals and households for which the malign circuits are effectively activated, that we can develop our understanding of the poor and establish an effective connection between, on one side, factors and conditions and, on the other, behaviour (Mingione, 1996, pp. 11–2).

This point of view involves various problems. In effect the uncertainties over the housing factors derive from more general difficulties as is quite clear from the bad practice of relating the micro to the macro that abounds in this field of research: reductions to one level or another, the impossible ideological oppositions between the two levels, etc.

On the one hand there is the well-known theoretical 'heterogeneity' between the two levels that makes it difficult – or impossible – to 'connect them'.

The two narratives cannot be connected either logically (the first operates with potential and quantitative correlations while the second deals with effective phenomena and qualitative processes) or technically (the quantitative data produced by the first cannot be corroborated with precision in the second, as what matters here is the typology of processes rather than numbers that cannot be representative). This has the effect of leaving the debate open (Mingione, 1996, p. 12).

We lack a coherent set of methods for bridging the gap between the micro/ individual and the macro/structural. The levels-of-analysis problem is particularly acute in research on homelessness. Most researchers understand at least implicitly that the homelessness of any given subset of people is the product of factors on different levels, from the individual psychological to the global economic. But we have nothing, on a purely metatheoretical level, equivalent to the computers models in population biology that capture both the structures of risk and incentive and the contours of individual vulnerability, revealing in simulation the nonobvious consequences of the interactions between the individual and the ecological (Blasi, 1994, p. 581).

On the other hand the differences that appear in terms of levels bring up the great divides of the social sciences, as suggested by Deborah Stone in her comparison of Jencks' way of studying the homeless and that of Liebow. 'They represent the great divide in contemporary social science, a divide that recapitulates the split between science and art described decades ago by C. P. Snow as "two cultures"' (Stone, 1994, p. 30). Moreover,

the two books illustrate another aspect of the great divide in contemporary social science. On one side are those who think there is a more or less universal rationality in the human psyche. We can explain and predict people's behavior by comparing their decisions to a universal standard of rationality, and we can find that standard by looking inside ourselves and how we think. On the other side are those who believe that power structures shape whether, and to what degree, people conceive of their lives in terms of decisions, and who believe that to understand anyone's internal thought processes, we need to look inside their particular situations (ibid.).

The Social Construction of Homelessness and Housing Policies

One last step to take in understanding the debate on housing factors is to set it in the social construction of 'new' homelessness. Which themes are being constructed with what political consequences and what is at stake? The oppositions between personal and social, between social and housing in the extreme forms that have accompanied the debate on homelessness make sense within this game of constructions. The diffusion of images which appear non-credible on the level of empirical verification can only be explained by the practical functions of the oppositions identified – to be appraised with reference to the political and public communication processes (Tosi and Cremaschi, 1989).

The homeless category itself has been abundantly criticised from this point of view. The criticisms are centred on two main arguments that proceed from the reifying character of the category. On the one hand a strongly heterogeneous category is reduced to uniformity with consequences that have little credibility such as, for example, the idea of solving the entire problem with housing measures or alternatively, at the other extreme, to provide re-insertion or social reintegration programmes in all cases. Another aspect is that a 'reduction' of the problem and the policies would occur. Homeless would be 'cut off' with respect to other wider questions: poverty, the lack of affordable housing, etc. The consequence would yet again be inappropriate solutions, which do not bring the different dimensions of poverty into play, which are focused on cure rather than prevention, etc. (Avramov, 1995).

Similar arguments have been used in the USA to criticise resort to the housing category. The idea that homelessness is a housing or a right to housing problem would also constitute a 'cut down' of the problem with respect to the wider problem of poverty. On the other hand, however, the categorisation in terms of housing has actually been defended for its extensive or inclusive character because it would be opposed to the separation between the problems of homelessness and wider housing problems that is made by the category of homelessness and because, like all the approaches that accentuate the importance of structural factors, this category opens up to the requirements of preventive policies. The critical point is in any case clear: with this category the 'non-housing' dimensions of the problem are handled badly.

The difference between these opposing arguments centres essentially on the degree of inclusiveness it is wished to achieve and the relationships of continuity/discontinuity it is wished to claim with respect to the wider problems of poverty and housing poverty, and therefore on the meaning that should be given to targeted policies. This confirms that the great determinant of the political game is the conflict over the redefinition of social policies after the crisis of welfare systems.

The extension of homelessness has also caused policies to be questioned yet again, and very radically, with regard to their traditional shortcomings. One issue is the polarisation or a split in the tradition of welfare housing policies between normal and special housing. The treatment of housing problems for the poor is dealt with by a 'reduced' system kept apart from the system for housing the population as a whole (Specht-Kittler; 1994, Tosi, 1994).

The accent on the housing nature of the problem contains a rejection of this dualism, as is clear from subjects such as pointing to the problems that special groups thinking causes for the majority of the homeless; the indication that the homeless should be offered normal houses and neither 'bottom end' nor temporary housing (Kärkkäinen, 1996); the demand that programmes for the homeless should not be separate from housing programmes (Specht-Kittler, 1994), etc.

A more general criticism of social housing policies has concerned their effectiveness with regard to the poor(est). These kinds of limits can be ascertained in two directions: on the one hand there are the obstacles met by the poorest sectors of society in gaining access to housing, even social housing and on the other, the incongruity between conventional social provision and the specific needs of the poor(est). In the latter direction, a clear policy demand is the integration of housing measures and social measures – social support – to manage the situations of multiple deficit that characterise the marginalised homeless particularly seriously. Clearly if one is to meet this demand, the traditional division between housing and social welfare measures must be overcome and that could modify the nature of housing policies. The supporters of the housing view of homelessness risk to underestimate this problem. On the other side, they rightly claim a space for a housing policy for (all) the excluded from housing, which the emphasis on multidimensional approaches risks to overshadow.

This leads to question a common idea – often taken for granted by the homeless advocates – that good solutions to the problem homelessness must be essentially looked for in good housing policies, and that provision of cheap housing would be the main road to the solution.

The debate suggests instead a dual policy direction. For the homeless with no social integration problems, a specific affordability policy, aimed at providing very cheap accommodation. For the marginalised homeless, a provision of integrated packages in which accommodation is accompanied by other, social support services. This seems to prevent any simple identification of policies aimed at the homeless with (conventional) housing policies for low-income groups.

The multidimensional character of social exclusion and of the solutions does not necessarily mean reducing the importance of affordable housing provision. In fact, the emphasis on homelessness as social exclusion risks to underestimate the importance of the housing dimensions. On one hand, the objections to the 'housing thesis' do not imply that a substantial supply of cheap housing is insignificant for the homeless – even for the extremely marginalised homeless. Rather the point raise the difficult question of the filtering mechanisms in housing markets, and on whether/how these mechanisms work for these segments of market. As we have seen, the role of housing factors in the production of homelessness is an uncertain and still under-investigated research issue.

On the other hand no homology may be assumed between the (casual) chains and paths to homelessness on one side and the role assigned to housing in the solutions on the other. The importance that a home has in terms of solutions may be supported whatever interpretation is made of the factors.

> The fact that many homeless people need further help and support does not speak against this approach. For the great majority of homeless a dwelling is essential for any other support, therapies etc. ... In most cases the provision of housing is a precondition that further support can be provided effectively (Busch-Geertsema, 1996).

> Independently of why people are on the street, giving them a place which offers a minimum of privacy and of stability is usually the most important thing that we can do to improve their lives. Without stable housing nothing else can improve easily (Jencks, 1994, p. 107).

For instance, availability of appropriate housing is an important precondition for 'integrated approaches' aimed at social re-insertion of marginalised homeless (Sapounakis, 1997).

Legislative innovations in recent years have tried to take responsibility for the dual demand (access and appropriateness) and to closely integrate housing and 'social' measures. (For instance, this was the intention of the 'more social' policies proposed by the Besson Law in France.) The task, however, is difficult and challenging, because it implies strong discontinuity with respect to conventional policies and because it poses problems of compatibility with constraints given by the prevalent strategies for reform of the Welfare State.

The multidimensional character of social exclusion obliges a discontinuity in housing policies and makes it impossible to adapt previous policies, above all where they are based around cost/income dimensions (to which the idea of access continues to be linked, taking as basic model the anti-poverty strategies of the postwar years) (Brink, 1994).

The argument that good housing policies solve the problem of homelessness is only valid if it is assumed that the housing policies incorporate 'social' objectives from the two viewpoints mentioned. This also includes the integration of non-housing measures in housing policies – which is what is (partly) happening in most European countries. Taking responsibility for social exclusion may in the final analysis involve changing the whole statute of housing policies and this is another problem that risks going unacknowledged by insisting on the housing nature of homelessness.

> It is a question of a great change, which many authors have analysed as inscribing housing policies inside the field of social policies. It is no longer a question of facilitating access to decent housing for the badly housed, but of taking responsibility in the housing field for the effects of the extension of the phenomena of poverty, precariousness and exclusion (R. Ballain).

Bibliography

Avramov, D. (1995), *Homelessness in the European Union. Social and Legal Context of Housing Exclusion in the 1990s*, Bruxelles, FEANTSA.

Avramov, D. (1996), *The Invisible Hand of the Housing Market*, Bruxelles, FEANTSA.

Ballain, R. (1995), 'La politique de logement à l'épreuve de la prècarité' in Ballain, R. (ed), *Loger les personnes défavorisés*, Paris, La Documentation Française.

Berzano, L. (1992), *Aree di devianza*, Torino, Il Segnalibro.

Blasi, G. (1994), 'And We are Not Seen: Ideological and Political Barriers to Understanding Homelessness', *American Behavioral Scientist*, 37 (4), pp. 553–85.

Børner, T. (1997), *Youth Homelessness in Denmark*, Bruxelles, FEANTSA.

Brink, S. (1994), 'Housing and the Under Class', International Research Conference *Housing: Global Challenge, Local Challenges*, Beijing, 21–24 September.

Burt, M. (1996) (see chapter 12 in this book).

Busch-Geertsema, V. (1996), *Discussion on Kärkkäinen*, communication at the Eurohome Workshop 2, Athens.

Carliner, M.S. (1987), 'Homelessness. A Housing Problem?' in Bingham, R.D., Green, R.E., White, S.B. (eds), *The Homeless in Contemporary Society*, Newbury Park, Sage.

Castel, R. (1991), *De l'indigence à l'exclusion, la désaffiliation. Précarité du travail et vulnérabilité relationnelle* in Donzelot J. (ed.), *Face à l'exclusion. Le modèle français*, Paris, Editions Esprit.

Damon, J. and Firdion, J.-M. (1996), *Vivre dans la rue, la question SDF* in Paugam, S. (ed.), *L'exclusion. L'état des savoirs*, Paris, Ed. La Découverte.

De Feijter, H. (1997), *Youth Homelessness in the Netherlands: Nature, Policy, Good Practices*, Bruxelles, FEANTSA.

Donzelot, J. (ed.) (1991), *Face à l'exclusion. Le modèle français*, Paris, Editions Esprit.

Gulati, P. (1994), *Re-conceptualizing Public Housing: An Alternative Solution to Family Homelessness*, XIII World Congress of Sociology, Bielefeld, 18–23 July.

Hartmann, H. (1997), 'Effective Local Strategies to Combat Homelessness', paper for *Eurohome Workshop 3*, Milan.

Haut Comité pour le Logement des Personnes Défavorisées (1997), *Lever les obstacles au logement des personnes défavorisées*, 4ème Rapport, Paris, Juillet.

Hoch, C. and Slayton, R.A. (1989), *New Homeless and Old. Community and the Skid Row Hotel*, Philadelphia, Temple University Press.

IMI (1992), *La exclusiòn social y la vivienda*, Madrid, Ingreso Madrileno de Integraciòn.

Jencks, C. (1994), *The Homeless*, Cambridge, Mass. and London, Harvard University Press.

Kärkkäinen, S.-L. (1998) (see chapter 17 in this book).

Marcuse, P. (1988), 'Perspectives on Homelessness', *Urban Affairs Quarterly*, June, pp. 647–56.

Marpsat, M. and Firdion, J.-M. (1998) (see chapter 10 in this book).

Mingione, E. (1996), 'Urban Poverty in the Advanced Industrial World: Concepts, Analysis and Debates' in Mingione, E. (ed.) *Urban Poverty and the Underclass*, Oxford, Blackwell.

Moreau de Bellaing and Guillou, J. (1995), *Les sans domicile fixe. Un phénomène d'errance*, Paris, L'Harmattan.

Negri, N. and Saraceno, C. (1996), *Le politiche contro la povertà in Italia*, Bologna, Il Mulino.

Parmentier, C. (1997), 'Main results and orientations for the future' in *Third International FEANTSA Congress*, Bruxelles, FEANTSA, 1–22.

Paugam, S. (1993), *La société française et ses pauvres*, Paris, PUF.

Paugam, S. (1996b), *L'exclusion. L'état des savoirs*, Paris, Ed. La Découverte.

Paugam, S. (1998) (see chapter 1 in this book)..

Pollo, M. (1995), 'I senza fissa dimora in Italia' in Pochettino, G. (ed.), *I senza fissa dimora*, PIEMME, Casale M.

Quigley, J.M. (1996), 'The Homeless', *Journal of Economic Literature*, December, pp. 1935–41.

Rossi, P.H. (1994), 'Troubling Families: Family Homelessness in America', *American Behavioral Scientist*, 37, 3, pp. 342–95.

Sapounakis, A. (1997), 'Innovative Services for the Homeless in the Greek Context', *Annual Report on Homelessness in Greece – 1997*, Bruxelles, FEANTSA.

Schon, D.A. (1983), *The Reflective Practitioner*, New York, Basic Books.

Sen, A. (1992), *Inequalities Re-examined*, Harvard University Press, Cambridge Mass.

Snow, D.A. and Anderson, L. (1993), *Down on Their Luck. A Study of Homeless Street People*, University of California Press, Berkeley.

Specht-Kittler (1994), *Housing Poverty in a Rich Society: Houselessness and Unacceptable Housing Conditions in Germany. A New Perspective on Homelessness*, Bruxelles, FEANTSA.

Stone, D. (1994), *Helter Shelter*, 'The New Republic', 27 June, pp. 29–34.

Terracina, S. (1996), 'Persone senza dimora: percorsi di povertà e servizi sociali. Analisi del dormitorio di Milano e dei suoi utenti', dissertation thesis, University of Milan.

Tosi, A. (1994a), *Abitanti. Le nuove strategie dell'azione abitativa*, Bologna, Il Mulino.

Tosi, A. (1996), 'The Excluded and the Homeless: the Social Construction of the Fight against Poverty in Europe' in Mingione, E. (ed.) *Urban Poverty and the Underclass*, Oxford, Blackwell.

Tosi, A. and Cremaschi, M. (1989), *Poverty, social marginality and housing in Italy*, XXIX International Congress, International Institute of Sociology, Rome, June.

Tosi, A. and Ranci, C. (1994), *Italy. Report for the European Observatory on Homelessness*, Bruxelles, FEANTSA.

Touraine, A. (1991), 'Face à l'exclusion', *Esprit*, 169.

UNCHS (Habitat) (1996), *An Urbanising World. A Global Report on Human Settlements 1996*, Oxford, Oxford University Press.

Vranken, J. (1997) (see chapter 15 in this book).

Ward, C. (1985), *When We Build Again*, London, Pluto Press.

Wodon, Q. (1992), *Logement. Le droit des exclus*, Paris, Les Edition Ouvrières.

5   Conclusions and Policy Implications

ANTONIO TOSI

Constructing the Theoretical Field of Homelessness

The fragility of the conceptual field indicated by the term 'homelessness' has been focused on repeatedly in the debate on this subject. It has often been claimed that homelessness, above all when it is intended in the strictly literal sense, does not constitute a substantial and consistent theoretical category and also that it is not politically useful. The considerable incongruity of the definitions is underlined in confirmation of this and also the fact that dissent over the processes implied by homelessness extends even to fundamental aspects.

Common sense and commonplaces strongly influence the social construction of the question. To some extent, the weakness of the research (see Part 2) is a consequence of this. The situation reflects the strong political determination of the subject homelessness. In the case of homelessness, the 'natural' interrelationships between social theory and research on the one hand and social and political constructions on the other are so closely woven as to represent an extreme case. (It has frequently been claimed that the very subject of homelessness is determined by its political value, that it was in fact the need to deal with its socially alarming aspects – or to control its visibility – that 'invented' the field of homelessness.)

There is great dissent over what homelessness is, its nature and the processes that constitute it and it is a dissent – confirming the relationships between research and social/political construction of the subject – that is essentially implicit and not the result of debate. The various definitions and points of view are taken for granted on the basis of commonsense notions – which may be in any case incompatible with each other – and their apparent obviousness makes any comparison and discussion superfluous.

How to find theoretical consistency and methodological rigour is the great challenge for the research on homelessness. The analytical and policy 'usefulness' of the category homelessness will depend on the possibility of strengthening the conceptual field in this sense. (In fact, the very fragility of the conceptual field may support an alternative conclusion: that homelessness is not an appropriate category – that this category is analytically and politically useless or even misleading. This viewpoint may be supported with good reasons, as the chapters in this part show.).

One essential condition is to place the theme in the debate on poverty and the theoretical framework developed by this debate, and to clarify the relationships between homelessness and poverty. This will provide the necessarily wider context in which the social production of homelessness may be investigated.

This has also been the historical movement followed by the debate on homelessness during the past decade. In some ways the broadening of perspective – from studies focused on homeless individuals and their 'disabilities' to comprehensive studies concerned with macrostructural factors; from search for single factor explanations to consideration of the complexity of forces at work etc. – has implied a convergence with studies on poverty and social exclusion.

The consequences on the consistency of the field, however, have been contradictory. On the one hand the extension has had very positive effects: it has involved the refusal of stereotypes – homelessness as a question of personal disabilities, as just a question of affordable housing, etc. – that have proved to be scarcely productive in terms of research, misleading in terms of advocacy, and dangerous in terms of social construction of the question homelessness. On the other hand there has been the risk for the question of homelessness to dissolve in the big sea of the research on poverty without even raising the question of whether specific factors should be taken into consideration.

A basic point is therefore to make clear the relationships – of both continuity and discontinuity – between homelessness on one side and poverty, social exclusion and housing deprivation on the other side. Locating the question of homelessness in the wider conceptual frame of research on poverty should imply a rigorous and systematic effort to understand what is specific to homelessness. Is it a particular form of poverty or social exclusion? Or does it represent an/the extreme degree of it? And are characterising features such as the absence of a home, vagrancy etc. essential for a definition or can we consider them as chance factors? In what direction are significant elements to be sought: in the absence of housing or in the absence of social relations or in the breaking of social ties?

In fact, the effects of the growth of socially vulnerable areas on the production of homelessness are uncertain. While it is true that all factors at work in impoverishment/exclusion processes are virtually relevant for homelessness, it is somehow obvious that homelessness involves risk factors and chains of cause and effect with specific characteristics, which do not necessarily coincide with those of poverty, nor even with those of social marginalisation.

The Polarisation of Meanings

Two different things are spoken in the debate on homelessness: social marginalisation – in its most extreme forms: desocialisation, disaffiliation, breaking of social ties, …; and housing exclusion – the lack, to a lesser or greater literal extent, of a home. Both problems are expressions of the 'reappearance' of poverty in developed countries.

The simultaneous presence of the two themes in the debate creates a duplicity in the terms of reference – held together by the polysemous nature of the word 'home' – which is the main source of inconsistency in the field of homeless. In the debate, this duplicity is taken for granted and the coexistence of the two themes is afforded little attention and is rarely elaborated on, thus avoiding the knotty problem of the relationships between them.

Naturally the two conditions are likely to be associated (at least in one of the two senses: while it is easy to be socially marginalised living in houses, it is less probable that remaining without housing for a long time will not be accompanied by marginalisation). Nevertheless these are conditions and processes that are different and a rigorous construction of the field of homelessness must start with frank recognition of this difference.

This polarisation takes place around two meanings of 'home': on the one hand the lack of a space – a 'shelter' – and on the other the absence of social relations or ties which in turn would reveal situations of social exclusion or marginalisation. The more common image of homelessness – the socially marginalised homeless (often identified by terms such as 'of no abode', *sans domicile fixe, senza dimora,* etc.) – corresponds to the latter reference. The other pole is given by 'not having a house': an appropriate term may be 'housing exclusion', provided it is used in a reasonably restricted sense, without extending it to all the situations of housing deprivation.

The different views are given different emphasis in the various national debates: which means that they also reflect 'objective' differences between the various national frameworks. The opposition between the two notions, however, is a general feature of the debate, and may be observed within any national debate. In fact, this opposition represents the great unsolved point of dissent in the debate on homelessness. The two notions identify two different research 'objects', that are to a certain extent independent. They also raise different questions, differently linked to the 'reappearance' of poverty in our societies: on the one hand the general problems of the connections between poverty and housing deprivation, and on the other the question of those types and processes of social exclusion or marginalisation that are qualified by the privation or loss of housing. In the debate on homelessness, this latter question is commonly identified – therefore exacerbating the difference between the two notions – with the marginalised single homeless, characterised by multiple deprivation and traits of social 'disinsertion'. Often reference is made to those extreme outcomes of the processes of social exclusion that are signalled in the debate as 'disaffiliation' (Robert Castel),[1] loss of the capabilities necessary to perform the elementary functions of everyday life (Amartya Sen), etc.

We may assume that this polarisation is constitutive of the field of homelessness. This means that a sound theoretical construction of the field must/should at the same time admit/recognise the difference between the two questions, and keep the two notions/questions co-present in the field, in order to see where they intersect.

The transfer of interpretative schemes from one 'object' to the other may appear manifestly untenable – for instance the extension to all the situations of housing exclusion of interpretations which apply to the 'no abode'. The transfers, however, are understandable if we admit that around the two basic notions two different, alternative paradigms are constructed. The two types of deprivation are taken as the bases for two different definitions that move in opposing directions. The two notions identify different interpretations on an analytical level and different solutions to problems on a practical level.

The Framework: Poverty and Social Exclusion

We may take up the new debate on poverty, particularly in those versions that resort to the notion of social exclusion. This debate pays particular attention to various factors that are also fundamental to the debate on homelessness.

The papers presented in this part give a very full picture of the subjects of the debate and of why a new frame for the analysis of poverty had been formed:

- the notion of poverty as a process. 'Poverty today is better defined as an ongoing process rather than as a fixed state ... The progressive

accumulation of difficulties from their origins to their final effects (means) a 'social disqualification' (process that) takes into account the increasingly common phenomenon of long term lack of regular work' (Paugam);
- precariousness in employment and the weakening of social ties as the two (variously interlinked) sets of factors on which social exclusion develops;
- the breaking of social ties as the extreme outcome of the process;
- the growth in the risk of exclusion resulting from an increase in social vulnerability, which occurs as the effect of the employment crisis and of the various processes that make social ties more fragile. The latter have their roots in the transformation of family structures and models and in the decay of previous forms of sociality;
- the contribution made by new trends in social policies, new orientations of governments and new policy models to increase (the risk of) exclusion (Duffy). The reduction of public intervention may create additional inequalities and protection gaps.

The notion and the debate on social exclusion furnish two essential elements required for an understanding of homelessness, two elements that in fact have been fully incorporated in the debate on the homeless: the idea of a breaking of social ties as the outcome of possible personal histories of precariousness and the idea that the situations of vulnerability at the basis of exclusion processes are on the increase.

The notion of social exclusion is, however, also part of a more general change that has occurred in the study of poverty: a new paradigm has taken shape, that narrates what is 'new' in poverty. The methodological indications of this paradigm are fundamental for an understanding of homelessness:

- the importance of the problems of deprivation that do not just involve economic poverty or lack of material resources, but also inadequate participation in social life, which in its most severe forms of drifting becomes moral and social disintegration, uprooting, etc. The accent on these dimensions raises the complicated question of just what the relationships are between material poverty and social exclusion and between poverty and homelessness (Duffy);
- the discontinuity with respect to previous pictures and phenomenology of poverty: the intervention of new factors leading to disaffiliation, as has been said, but also a modification of the systemic relations of social inequality ('the passage from a vertical society, a class society with people high-up and people low-down, to a horizontal society where the problem

is not to be up or down but to be in or out' (Touraine)), and the constitution, in this way, of a 'supernumerary' population, a population nobody knows what to do with, an 'unusable underclass' etc.;

• the relationships between the new frames of poverty/social exclusion and the restructuring of social policies – as *factors* of exclusion, and as a stake of the political game: the notion of exclusion may represent both a demand for new, more effective policies and at the same time a point of reference for the reduction of social policies with respect to universalist welfare models. This confirms the wisdom of recognising – in the use of the notion of exclusion – its social construction character. This is particularly evident for the homeless.

The new theoretical and conceptual frames of poverty have brought renewed reflection to match the new processes of poverty/social exclusion. Nevertheless congruent use of the debate would not be possible if we did not relate critically to objections that have been raised over the notion of social exclusion, pointing out its limits and risks from both an analytic view point and that of the policies implied. These objections are of immediate interest also for an analysis of homelessness.

On the one hand the notion of exclusion brings up an 'objective' change: the increase in the risk of breaks on a personal level (break of social ties, disaffiliation ...) and the threat to social cohesion that these represent or denounce (risk of 'social fracture' ...). On the other hand, and at the same time, it may represent a designation of 'reductive' policies.

In this sense, the shift of attention from processes and from the social (systemic) production of poverty to a focus on its acute and more visible forms is crucial. The social exclusion frame becomes a 'paradox object', which clearly represents the dislocation of the social question currently in progress.

> Either the social question is shifted from the centre to the periphery and an analytical reduction is carried out which focuses on the most visible effects of a more general movement, and thus deprives itself of an in-depth understanding of the destabilisation of society. Or the issue of exclusion is reintegrated at the hearth of the social question. However, in doing so exclusion becomes a secondary object and is diluted as a notion; it was no more than an indicator launching the reflection which itself does not constitute the focus of the reflection, nor the conceptual cornerstone of the analysis (Soulet).

The dislocation of the question is closely interconnected with the political turning-point, characterised by the effort to redefine social policies. As observed by Robert Castel, recourse to exclusion may dissociate marginal situations from the processes which produced them and give them meaning, therefore obstructing the interrogation of the social mechanisms of the system responsible for the current ruptures. This analytical reduction results in a misrecognition of what exclusion entails, 'a general dynamism of precariousness which defeats assured status', and refers to policies of a remedial nature aimed at a particular public.

> This explains the successive array of measures whose main feature is to intervene time after time to patch up the social net which has been ravaged. In this sense the political popularity of exclusion has to do with the savings allowed by the level and extent of the measures taken (Soulet).

> It seems more and more realistic to deploy interventionism for treating the most visible forms of malfunctioning rather than to control the process which sets it off because dealing with its effects can be carried out in a technical manner whereas coming to grips with the process itself demands political action (Castel).

A proposal on this basis was made to consider exclusion as a 'concept-horizon', constituting 'at once a fundamental question of the functioning of the whole of society and an intrinsic limit on the object itself, which must be rejected as forcefully as possible to find other tools of analysis'. 'For research workers, the notion of exclusion is not of interest in itself, because it does not correspond to a category of scientific thought. But at the same time it inspires reflection and helps to structure many research studies' (Paugam).

The notion of exclusion also has analytic limits. The very vagueness of the notion, which follows from its eminently practical character, reveals its conceptual uncertainty and its poor analytic capacity. Its ideological use increases its semantic imprecision, and this authorises an uncontrolled use. Here the use of this term as a substitute for an explanation. There is a risk of a variable geometrical concepts which fluctuates according to representations and preoccupations (Soulet). 'It names numerous different situations by erasing the specificity of each one. In other words, exclusion is not an analytical notion. It does not lead to precise investigations of the contents which it claims to cover' (Castel).

Its fundamental limits concern the way of understanding the relationship with society, the character of weakened/broken social ties that constitute social exclusion or non-integration:

- a negative definition, which does not take account of the characteristics of the relationships of exclusion and of their specificities and variance. 'Exclusion can be reduced to living an existence defined by a lack: lack of work, of family, of a home, of education, of social relations, of access to institutions, of participation in society' (Soulet). Exclusion is a qualifier which is essentially negative by obscuring 'the necessity to analyse positively what the lack is composed of'. 'It names numerous different situations by erasing the specificity of each one' (Castel);

- an unrealistic assumption of total exclusion, that does not recognise the elements of relationship/integration that are found even in exclusion situations. 'It is difficult to imagine someone who is totally excluded. Someone excluded is still included no matter how little' (Soulet). 'No doubt there are nowadays ins and outs but they do not inhabit a separate universe, strictly speaking, there are never extra-social situations' (Castel). In fact, it is exclusion from the sphere of social activity of employment which very often determines our interpretation of reality. This, in turn, leads to misrecognising other forms of inclusion;

- an idealised vision of the relationship with society, which is not probable any more and which risks not taking account of the diffusion of situations of precariousness, of new models of integration, etc. of not recognising, that is, the new factors which actually gave rise to the debate on social exclusion.

> Part of the confusion caused by recourse to this notion comes from the reference to an implicit model which presupposes an idealised relationship to the social. This reversal of exclusion is based on an autonomous subject who has a rewarding and identifying professional activity, and adequate network of social relations, considerable potential of consumption ... Yet, not only does this model occur less and less frequently in reality, but its non-reproduction would amount to crossing the barrier between insertion and exclusion (Shirley Roy).

Finally, a certain use of the notion of 'process' in the research on social exclusion may be criticised. The insistence on the cumulativeness, the sequential character of the process, the reasoning in terms of 'phases', may lend support to the idea of automatic mechanisms in the path along the process of exclusion. In some way the logical working of the idea of exclusion seems to suggest the normality – or the inexorability – of a cumulative process that would normally lead from situations of precariousness to final radical exclusion outcomes.

From Poverty to Homelessness

One idea of homeless corresponds to the idea of disaffiliation or desocialisation and can essentially be described in terms of the weakening/break of social ties that constitute social exclusion. The terms used to qualify the advanced stages, or outcomes, of the processes of exclusion correspond to those with which the homeless are defined in the conventional sense – the 'no abode', the marginalised homeless, social relationship deficit, loss of capabilities, uprooting, etc.

From this point of view, not only do the schemes for the analysis of social exclusion function to explain homelessness (understood as such), but the 'no abode' can be taken as the paradigm of exclusion: itinerancy, vagrancy, desocialisation are representative of those extreme forms of disinsertion for which some propose that the term exclusion should be reserved.

This representation does not nevertheless exhaust the definition of homelessness. It may represent an important aspect, or a specific type of homelessness, but it is obvious that the lack of a home must be considered as a fundamental element in the representation of the problem. The conceptual field of homelessness is given by the crossing of the two sets of problems. In fact both types of deprivation – housing and social or relationship deprivation – occur in the current definitions of homelessness. Analysing the loss of a home as a simple ingredient – or additional ingredient – in a process of may not be sufficient if one's objective is to constitute a theoretical field of the homeless. After all, 'the lack of a home is the rationale for having a separate social category called "homelessness"' (Jan Vranken).

The relationship between the two deprivations raises essential questions for the definition of the field of homelessness. In opposition to the idea of homelessness as social marginalisation, there is the representation of homelessness as a housing problem. As already seen, this implies a polarisation of meanings and frames which is essential in the constitution of the field of homelessness.

The introduction of the housing dimension brings up a set of specific questions: where is housing deprivation to be placed in the processes of exclusion and marginalisation? How is the privation or loss of housing related to different types and stages of poverty?

In the analysis of individual paths to social exclusion, the accent is more often placed on the lack or the loss of housing as a feature of processes of disaffiliation and on the function of these factors in the drift towards marginalisation. The prevalent focus of attention on extreme situations in some ways reflects the logic of the theoretical frameworks of exclusion, which invites one to see the process of exclusion as a progression towards extreme outcomes or as a process that is given meaning by its extreme outcomes. In reality the notion of process should oblige us to extend this type of analysis to the entire process of exclusion; it should invite a dynamic analysis in which the different types and degrees of housing deprivation are connected with different types and stages of social exclusion processes. Such an analysis would show that being without housing may be part of different life courses and have different 'evolutive' meanings: a stage in a process of marginalisation, but also a temporary condition, and even a stage in an 'upward' process, or in a process of social integration (this is the case, for example, for many foreign immigrants).

Between social exclusion and lack of a home, all combinations are possible. The type of the homeless marginalised and desocialised which is so common in the debate on homelessness is only one possible combination. In this case the lack of housing constitutes one aspect of a wider syndrome of social exclusion. Housing exclusion, however, may occur without that involving marginalisation and even less so disaffiliation or personal disabilities. There are people who are 'simply' excluded from housing: they may be just too poor to afford housing offered on the market, or they may lack (formal or de facto) qualification for access to social housing etc.

Housing exclusion without marginalisation is a widespread phenomenon and represents an important area for policies, an area in which the policy principles for dealing with marginalisation (e.g. social reintegration programmes) do not apply and which has been pushed to the margins of policies by the insistence on the 'socially excluded'. Here too some theoretical attitudes that are current in the analysis of poverty may have played a negative influence. The insistence on the multidimensional nature of the phenomenon and on the cumulative character of the processes at work risks hiding that there are relative deprivations, sectorial poverties and poverties that do not involve problems of marginalisation – also in the conditions of society in which the new processes of poverty work.

Given the different mix of factors, housing dimensions may assume different meanings and play different roles in the exclusion processes. After all, this is one consequence of the commonly held idea that homelessness is a diversified, heterogeneous phenomenon. Careful analyses are needed that make clear the different exclusion paths, the different interplay of social exclusion and housing exclusion, the different risk patterns.

The 'housing thesis' has the merit of setting the problem in the historical circumstances in which the 'new homelessness' appeared. The lack of shelter as a characterisation of homelessness may constitute something new. Peter Rossi states it explicitly for the USA.

> The meaning of homelessness was not (in the 1950s and 1960s) centred on lack of shelter .... To be homeless in that period meant primarily living without the social relations that are implied in the meaning of home, namely, living alone without spouses, parents, or children.

In other words, a more difficult general housing situation may have made the housing problems of the homeless even more serious and perhaps also have made the role of housing factors more important than in the past. The housing thesis – by embracing all the situations of housing exclusion in one single frame – raises precisely the question of why 'people with problems are today without housing' (Peter Marcuse), and how changes in housing markets and policies may have contributed to this.

The Causes of Homelessness

A highly controversial issue in the debate regards the 'causes' or the 'factors' of homelessness. On this aspect the research activity has often been characterised by questionable practices. There has sometimes been an elusive use of categories as vulnerability and risk: often a way for claiming possible relationships between homelessness and structural 'background' factors, when we lack sound schemes and data for verifying the relationships. And too simple causal relations have been/are often hypothesised between homelessness and poverty/social exclusion.

The recent debate on poverty indicates the main critical factors for dealing with causality in this field. An initial criterion is the distinction between the different levels of analysis, specifically as regards the macro/micro opposition: the causal dynamics, and the notion of factor itself, change according to the level of analysis. Secondly, there is the impossibility of identifying a single underlying cause at the heart of the phenomenon of poverty or homelessness. The explanation must be sought in the interrelations between the different factors at each level and in the mechanisms connecting the different level (Avramov). So it is not even possible to claim any 'regular pattern' in the chains of events that produce poverty and homelessness. The causes vary according to the groups (one important distinction from this viewpoint is between single homeless persons and homeless families) and according to the places. Moreover the factors involved are likely to be different in the case of the marginalised homeless as compared with the simply excluded from housing. Despite the insistence on the heterogeneity of homelessness, this simple fact is often overlooked.

These criteria – that are of great importance for the discussion of the role of the housing factor – are theoretically recognised in studies on homelessness. It would be a question now of making their application in actual research practice more rigorous and systematic. A challenging task however, because it runs into a number of general theoretical difficulties, which are particularly acute in research on poverty.

One particularly serious difficulty regards the links between the different levels of analysis. The prevailing model in research on homelessness today is founded on the idea that structural factors define the risk, and personal biographical case histories must be looked at in order to understand who will actually become homeless. This point of view, however, involves the well-known theoretical 'heterogeneity' between macro and micro levels that make it difficult – or impossible – to connect them. We lack a coherent set of methods for bridging the gap between the micro/individual and the macro/structural.

Policy Implications

Placing the problem of homelessness in the debate on social exclusion obviously implies a point of view on policies: that effective policies for homelessness are policies against exclusion, or that policies that are effective against exclusion are also effective against homelessness.

We may assume, first of all, that the problems at the origin of (new) policies against exclusion are pertinent:

a) the whole range of policies for fighting poverty and ensuring social protection is important;

b) but the policies are not sufficient: the 'normal' protection is not sufficient, as is shown by the actual existence of homeless even in systems with widespread protection (a definition of homelessness typical of countries with powerful social protection systems, identifies them as those that fall through the safety net);

c) the fight against social exclusion must work on both the failings implied by the notion of exclusion, not only the lack of fundamental resources, but also the inability to fully participate in one's own society;

d) the idea of exclusion involves additional requirements for policies that touch on the system of motivations implied in exclusion. Neither the offering of resources nor the granting of rights is sufficient to avoid social exclusion if the capabilities and functionings of the individuals are not addressed.

The problem remains of what importance the specific nature of homelessness has in the construction of effective policies, or whether policies aimed at homelessness should be virtually identified with policies against exclusion. Evidently the persisting uncertainty at the analytical level on the specific nature of homelessness translates into uncertainty over policies: the question remains open. (The idea that policies against homelessness should be conceptualised as mere adaptation of the general welfare housing and anti-poverty policies may be supported with good reasons.)

It is possible, however, to define the general lines connecting the various interests in a policy system. Jan Vranken for example proposes

> an integrated concept in which general policies, poverty policies (included social exclusion) and specific homelessness policies are integrated. The general policies must provide the general context, poverty policies can reduce direct processes leading to homelessness and homelessness policies are rather apt at combating the specific problems related with it and not taken into account by general and poverty policies.

Another set-up (Helmut Hartmann) sees social policies as a general frame, with respect to which policies aimed at homelessness appear as specific actions taken essentially at a local level.

One specific point regards the need for articulated policies and the need that they relate 'positively' to different situations.

On one side, the plurality of policies is implied by the fact that action may start from various points in the chains of factors which may produce homelessness.

On the other side, the heterogeneity of homelessness needs to be taken into account. While heterogeneity is recognised theoretically, the label homelessness tends to reduce solutions to uniformity.

One important aspect of this articulation derives directly from taking social exclusion as a reference and from the insistence on its process nature. This signifies a multiplicity of policies and services as a function of the processes of the production of homelessness: policies that 'stretch out' along the whole process of exclusion, from prevention to re-insertion. If it is true that prevention constitutes a decisive element at stake and that it is consistent with a correct interpretation of the processes that produce homelessness and provides an initial principle on which to articulate policies, then adequate attention must also be paid to the actually homeless in the direction of both reintegration policies and 'stabilisation' action. This also requires further and greater efforts with research.

If the accent is placed on housing exclusion, then a further (and partly different) set of policy problems opens up, which touches on the various points mentioned with regard to the 'housing thesis': the relationship between housing measures and social policies, the relationship between general housing policies and specific policies, etc.

The debate reported above leads us to question a common idea – often taken for granted by the homeless advocates – that good solutions to the problem homelessness must be essentially looked for in good housing policies, and that provision of cheap housing would be the main road to the solution.

The debate suggests instead a dual policy direction: for the homeless with no social integration problems, a specific affordability policy, aimed at providing very cheap accommodation; for the marginalised homeless, a provision of integrated packages in which accommodation is accompanied by other, social support services. This seems to prevent any simple identification of policies aimed at the homeless with (conventional) housing policies for low-income groups.

Of course this does not imply that a substantial supply of cheap housing is insignificant for the homeless – even for the extremely marginalised homeless. On one hand, the point raises the difficult question of the filtering mechanisms in housing markets, and on whether/how these mechanisms work for these segments of market. As has been said, the role of housing factors in the production of homelessness is an uncertain and still under-investigated research issue.

On the other hand, a distinction should be made between 'production' of homelessness and 'solutions'. In general no homology may be assumed between the (causal) chains and paths to homelessness on one side and the role assigned to housing in the solutions on the other. The importance that a home has in terms of solutions may be supported whatever interpretation is made of the factors. The availability of appropriate housing, for instance, is a requisite for 'integrated' actions aimed at social re-insertion of homeless persons.

The construction of the homeless is as important in 'making' the problem as are 'objective' factors such as labour market processes or family processes. The importance of the constructed character of the problem as a criterion for analysis and policy-oriented identification of it is a central theme of the debate.

The perception of homelessness as social construction has various consequences. First of all it has clear analytical implications. Attention to the constructed character involves a way of analysis: an analytical model based on 'interaction', not 'substantialist', but aimed at investigating the interactions that make the problem. There is the rejection of naturalistic viewpoints and attention – with regard to what 'makes' the problem of homelessness – to dimensions such as labelling processes, perceptions and self-perceptions, and policies as determinants of homelessness. The accent on the constructed nature of the problem also has direct consequences on how to imagine the policies and where to seek the most effective criteria for them.

Moreover, the accent on the constructed character of homelessness means that the various (opposing) points of view on the nature of homelessness and the processes that produce it must be discussed with reference to the function they perform in the game of construction and as the stakes in the conflict that develops with the construction. The great determinant is the conflict over the redefinition of social policies after the crisis of welfare systems, and the stake is what kind of 'reduction' to operate with respect to the universalistic forms of solidarity that have been typical of the Welfare State.

Some conflicting viewpoints in the construction of homelessness are structural and have accompanied the entire evolution of the debate. The main ones are that over social versus personal determinants, and that over the housing versus the 'social' definition of homelessness. The different points of view could even be incomprehensible if not set in the game of social/policy construction. Current simplifications could not be explained if they were not backed by the interrelationships between the representations proposed and the social construction of the problem, and appraised with reference to the political and public communication processes.

The category of homelessness itself may be seen as an element of this political game. The objections that have been aimed at the category of homelessness come from their policy implications. The criticisms are centred on two main arguments that proceed from the 'reifying' character of the category. On the one hand a strongly heterogeneous category is reduced to uniformity. Another aspect is that a reduction of the problem and of the policies would occur. Homeless would be 'cut off' with respect to other wider questions: poverty, the lack of affordable housing, etc. The identification between homeless and 'no abode' may accentuate this meaning.

As for the idea that homelessness is a housing or a right to housing problem, the difference between the opposing arguments centres essentially on the degree of inclusiveness it is wished to achieve and the relationships of continuity/discontinuity it is wished to claim with respect to the wider problems of poverty and housing poverty, and therefore on the meaning that should be given to targeted policies. The housing thesis has the merit of rejecting the 'emergency' approaches to homelessness, based on the split between normal and special housing that has been typical of the tradition of welfare housing policies. On the other side it risks not recognising the great innovation that is at the heart of the new trends in social housing policies: the attempt at 'taking responsibility in the housing field for the effects of the extension of the phenomena of poverty, precariousness and exclusion' (René Ballain) – a trend which also implies the integration of non-housing measures in housing policies.

Note

1   For references see the bibliography to chapter 4.

PART 2
THE RESEARCH OF HOMELESSNESS: DATA AND METHODOLOGY

6   Data Sources on Homelessness and Data Necessary for Needs-based Research

DRAGANA AVRAMOV

Introductory Considerations

Many social scientists take pride in the belief that their research is value-neutral. They fail to acknowledge that explicit and implicit aims of the research project influence the choice of the subject and the identification of research situations. Many will not venture into the value-loaded debate about policy implications of their findings. They will not monitor how research findings are used for policy purposes and how they are translated into measures and social practice.

While it may be argued that the interdependence between research, policies and practice may be less obvious and less consequential in some research domains, in the case of research of homelessness the acknowledgement of this link is essential. It is neither possible nor feasible to draw a line separating academic responsibility which researchers are prepared to accept in undertaking research from responsibility which they are willing to delegate to users of their work. Research, policies and social practice need to be considered as three pillars of informed social choices in tackling homelessness as a human condition and a social process.

Research of homelessness, like research about social exclusion in general, is inherently policy oriented. An academic interest in the subject is an indispensable component of research, but it is not a sufficient reason to address the issue. The ultimate justification of an academic input into research about homelessness lies in the social dimension of its aims. The mobilizing force is the aim to promote policies to prevent homelessness and to contribute to the development of effective instruments and measures to assist homeless people.

Thus, a synergy between researchers, policy makers and providers is a condition *sine qua non* of a successful enterprise. This '*synergysing*' builds upon a continuous flow of information between all the actors.

In order to establish a sound cooperation between researchers, policy makers and providers it is necessary to clarify what type of input can be expected from each partner. It is necessary to look at ways and means by which different contributors arrive at conclusions about what homelessness is and how to deal with it.

Research, policies and social practice are intrinsically interlinked. But in order to meet high standards of quality they each have to follow an approach-specific logic. How do we carry out research? How do we devise policies? How do we identify needs and provide services? A preliminary explanation is due by each party.

In this chapter I will focus on the research logic and discuss the research challenges and available empirical data from various sources which can be used for the analysis of homelessness. Taking stock of the current body of knowledge and identifying the weak and twilight zones is the starting point for developing policies and measures. It is also the starting point for setting the new research agenda.

Aims and Methodology of This Contribution

In this chapter I will give an overview of primary data on homelessness which, together with administrative and contextual data and secondary sources, constitute the material for the analysis of homelessness and housing deprivation. I will discuss how available data sources can be used for comparative studies of homelessness at the European level. In order to situate the debate about accuracy of available data within a comprehensive research framework I will operationalise the initial stages of a needs-based research project which are pertinent for data collection and analysis. Then I will formulate various research aims and match them against research subjects and research situations for which data are needed. I will discuss the available sources for research situations, which vary from literal homelessness to supported housing, and will identify aspects of the phenomena of housing deprivation which cannot be documented by available data and which require further research.

The general aim is to assess whether and how the empirical data on homelessness available in selected European countries (the 15 European Union members) can be used for comparative research. The specific aims are to take stock of available sources and to identify the under-researched areas.

The general aim is justified by a growing demand for comparative studies of causes, consequences and remedies to homelessness at the European level. There is ample evidence that the convergence criteria set and pursued in the economic sphere have multiple unintended, albeit not unexpected, repercussions in the social domain (Duffy, 1995; Avramov, 1995; European Commission, 1994; Council of Europe, 1993). Economic and political strategies do not only determine but also reflect how governments develop social inclusion policies and implement measures to tackle consequences of social exclusion. There is growing evidence that alongside with the privatisation of state functions in the housing domain an 'Europisation' of processess conducive to homelessness is occurring (Avramov, 1996).

In order to assess to what extent the available data sources on homelessness are comparable transnationally two main steps need to be taken. The first one is taking stock of data. The second is the assessment of the quality of the empirical basis and identification of under-researched areas.

I will focus on data for large aggregates (country, administrative region, capital city) which may be used to document the prevalence of homelessness and basic socio-demographic characteristics of homeless people. I will not attempt to take stock of small-scale surveys (e.g. those using 'capture-recapture' methods, counts of people sleeping rough on a particular night, turnover of homeless clients in services covering a municipality or sub-region, etc.). Only data currently available about the prevalence of homelessness and housing deprivation, personality characteristics and behavioural patterns conducive to homelessness will be identified. I will not discuss planned projects and diversified initiatives to gather new data in the forthcoming years.

In the first part I will identify main sources of primary, contextual data and secondary sources which can be used as background information to highlight the social context within which housing exclusion occurs. In the second part of the chapter I will identify and operationalise the research logic in terms of research aims, situation and data. Finally, I will indicate which research situations have not been adequately addressed and discuss future research needed in order to improve preventive and responsive policies to deal with homelessness.

Data Sources on Homelessness in the 15 European Union Countries

Targeted primary research of homelessness is rare at the national level and nonexistent at the European level. Surveys of the homeless population have typically focused on single problem areas, covered a small sample, were limited geographically to one locality and provided only patchwork data. Homelessness as a human condition and housing exclusion as a social process still remain under researched phenomena in the academic community. Due to lack of reliable empirical data the estimates of the prevalence of housing exclusion and identification of needs of the homeless population often have to be based on data gathered for the purpose of administration of services and for fund-raising. In the overwhelming majority of European countries researchers neither have the possibility to undertake primary research on a nationally representative sample nor do they have much choice in the selection of available data sources. Therefore, all attempts to compare data on homelessness in Europe must take into account the different nature of sources and acknowledge that data from research and non-research sources have a different degree of accuracy.

Empirical data which can be used as a starting point for the analysis of homelessness may be split into two main categories: data which directly address the condition of homelessness, and indirect sources. The first set includes research and non-research sources; the second, contextual data and secondary research.

Primary Sources

We can distinguish three main providers of data about the prevalence of homelessness and the socio-demographic profile of the homeless population: service providers, public administrations and researchers. Ideally, access to all three sources would give a complete picture of both manifest and hidden homelessness and of the extent to which a threat of homelessness did not materialize for groups at risk because effective protection is provided by the public services. A brief survey shows, however, that in the past very few countries have made a serious effort to gather information about the prevalence of homelessness from a variety of sources.

An overview of primary data sources in the Member States is given in Table 6.1. We can see that countries fall in five groups which range from no reliable primary sources to comprehensive national surveys on homelessness which pool information from multiple sources.

In Greece and Portugal there are no primary sources which are representative for the country as a whole or for administrative regions or large cities. Efforts by individual scholars (Sapounakis, 1995; Nascimento, 1993)

Table 6.1   Primary data sources on homelessness in the Member States

Country	Service providers (National data)	Source of data Public administration (National data) or the capital city)	Targeted surveys (Representative for the country
Austria	n.a.*	n.a.	Service users and people sleeping rough in Vienna surveyed in March 1993
Belgium	Turnover in night shelters over the course of one year and demographic characteristics of clients (annual statistics for the Flemish Community since 1988 and for the French Community since 1992)	n.a.	n.a.
Denmark	Number of 24 hour users of institutions for the homeless and socially excluded (annual statistics	n.a.	One day census of reception centres for homeless people and their clients (January 1992, published by Statistics Denmark) published by Statistics Denmark since 1977)
Germany	n.a.	n.a.	The registration system of the nongovernmental welfare organizations for the homeless (1990–1994). Empirical study conducted in 1992.
Spain	Turnover in night shelters between 1988 and 1990	n.a.	n.a.
Finland	Data on homeless persons living in institutions are included in	Central population register	Yearly survey of homelessness conducted by the Housing Fund of Finland (since 1986) the yearly survey on homelessness

Country	Source of data		
	Service providers (National data)	Public administration (National data) or the capital city)	Targeted surveys (Representative for the country
France	n.a.	n.a.	Survey of homeless people using night shelters, soup kitchens and those in temporary accommodation for homeless people in Paris (February–March 1995)
Greece	n.a.	n.a.	n.a.
Ireland	n.a.	Bi-annual assessment of homelessness conducted by the local authorities collated by the Department of Environment (since 1991)	n.a.
Italy	n.a.	n.a.	Survey on poverty and marginalization (1982; 1992)
Luxembourg	n.a.	n.a.	One day surveys among service providers about their clients (1994;1995)
Netherlands	Clients information system for caretaking (since 1994) flows and characteristics of service users over the course of one year	n.a.	Research project (1987–1989) and prognosis until the year 2000. Research project by local authorities (1989).
Portugal	n.a.	n.a.	n.a.
Sweden	Data from service providers are included in the national survey on homelessness	Local social authorities	National survey on homelessness by the National Board of Health and Welfare (1993)
UK	n.a.	Department of Environment annual statistics on households accepted by local authorities as homeless (since 1978).	Survey of people sleeping rough in central London (since 1991)

* n.a. = non available

to open the debate about the prevalence of homelessness on basis of personal experience and explorative work, have resulted in a series of tentative hypothesis which need to be tested in future field work. In Portugal, approximative estimates of the number of people sheltered in emergency accommodation are based on information from regional social security services and two main charities in Lisbon and Porto.

Shelters for homeless people are the only source of empirical information in Belgium and Spain. Although the source is the same, i.e. reports of activities by service providers, it must be stressed that the quality of information in these countries differs considerably. Data for Belgium cover the turnover of clients over a whole year in night shelters for homeless people. Data are gathered and published on annual basis by two associations which group all major service providers in the Dutch- and in the French-speaking communities of Belgium. They include detailed information about socio-demographic characteristics of service users. However, the turnover figures cannot be considered as counts of homeless people as they include multiple users. Data for Spain include an estimation of a turnover of clients over a three year period in night shelters in the late 1980s. Information provides elements for a preliminary typology of service users but not an analysis of socio-demographic characteristics of the sheltered population. In both countries it is service providers who gave information about their clients. Homeless people themselves were not directly interviewed.

In Ireland and in the United Kingdom only data from the public administration are available for the country as a whole. Figures for the UK do not include all the people who apply for assistance to the local authorities as homeless or threatened by homelessness, but only people who were accepted on the waiting lists for housing as priority groups. Data on the number of people officially recognized as homeless or potentially homeless under the Housing Act and guidelines for its implementation are published by the Department of Environment. A survey among people sleeping rough in central London is undertaken twice yearly since 1991. A nationally representative survey of mental health of the population as a whole enabled an identification of the subgroup of homeless people. The number of homeless people sheltered by private or voluntary organizations is not known.

In Ireland local authorities provide an assessments of the number of homeless people every two years. Not all homeless people are considered to be in need of permanent accommodation. Indeed, another survey is conducted to assess housing needs of the population. This assessment by local authorities is the basis for identifying homeless people who are considered to be in need of permanent accommodation.

In Austria, Germany, France, Italy and Luxembourg targeted surveys are the principal source of empirical data on homeless people. However, the theoretical framework, aims and methods used in these countries are radically different. The sample in Vienna was drawn from people using facilities for the homeless and those found in the train stations and selected subway stations. The sample in Paris included only people using emergency services for homeless people and long-stay shelters. Services encompassed night shelters and soup kitchens. The survey was implemented as a methodological study and not as a census. It did not have as its primary goal to estimate the extent of homelessness in Paris. Such an estimate, however, was possible and was made by Marpsat and Firdion (1996). In both Vienna and Paris homeless people were interviewed. In the case of Vienna an estimation of the total homeless population of the city was made on the basis of information gathered in interviews with people whose work is related to homelessness or brings them in contact with homeless people (see Kofler in this volume).

In Luxembourg a survey was undertaken among service providers who gave information about their clients. Data for Luxembourg were gathered in a one day survey undertaken by researchers in 1994 and 1995 (Wagner and Pels, 1995). On the basis of the report of activities of night shelters and other services for homeless people published by the Ministry of Housing and Ministry for Family, a complete list of services was compiled. Out of 28 consultation centres and shelters 22 in 1994 and 25 in 1995 provided information about the number and socio-demographic characteristics of their clients. The non-response by some service providers was not taken into account for the estimation of the total number of homeless people in Luxembourg. The survey does not enable an estimation of the total number of clients over a year nor does it take into account seasonal fluctuations. Persons sleeping rough, those threatened by eviction and people in severely substandard accommodation were not taken into account for the estimation of the homeless population.

The sub-sample which can be directly identified from an Italian survey on people living in extreme poverty includes only homeless people with no fixed abode. Tentative estimation of the number of people excluded from housing in Italy is made on the basis of information from the survey on poverty about people with no fixed abode, immigrants in marginal housing and travellers in extreme poverty. The survey in Germany includes an estimation of the population in housing need which is based on a variety of sources including data from local administrations. Empirical data of North Rhine-Westphalia for 1992 are used as a basis for the calculation of homeless people in West Germany (Busch-Geertsema and Ruhstrat, 1994).

It is only in Denmark, Finland, the Netherlands and Sweden that two or more representative sources can be used to estimate the prevalence of homelessness and to describe characteristics of homeless people. However, also in these countries the conceptual framework and the quality of data differ and are not strictly comparable between countries. The Danish data cover only service users in night shelters for the homeless. Data for Finland include both service users and other homeless people in housing need. Namely, persons living outdoors or in temporary shelters, persons living in night shelters or other shelters for the homeless, people living in institutions or institutional homes either temporarily or permanently due to lack of housing, prisoners soon to be released who have no housing, persons living temporarily with relatives and acquaintances due to lack of housing, families who have split up and are in temporary accommodation due to lack of housing (see Kärkkäinen in this volume). Similarly, in Sweden the population counted as homeless includes persons living in institutions and hostels who would have nowhere to live in the event of being discharged and persons living temporarily with friends or acquaintances. However, they do not include persons living temporarily with relatives (The National Board of Health and Welfare, 1995).

Before any comparison between countries can be made about the prevalence of homelessness and about characteristics and needs of homeless people, and before any extrapolation of data can be made from one source to the entire homeless population of a country, a number of theoretical and empirical hypothesis need to be developed and operationalised.

Furthermore, great caution is needed when using data from service providers. In the report for the European Observatory on Homelessness in 1992 the figure given as the number of homeless people in Germany is 1,030,000. This number is published in the second transnational report (FEANTSA, 1993). In the report for 1993 the figure is 850,000. No explanation was provided about this enormous difference in estimates in the national or the transnational reports (FEANTSA, 1994). Questions whether there was an substantial decline in homelessness, an error in counting and reporting or changes in the composition of the population considered to be homeless over a two-year period remained unanswered by the service providers.

Contextual Data and Secondary Sources

In addition to primary sources collected for the purpose of monitoring homelessness and services for homeless people, contextual data and secondary research sources constitute a valuable body of information which can be, and needs to be used by researchers. For countries with a weak institutional framework of assistance to homeless people and segmented research such as Greece and Portugal, but also Spain and Italy, contextual data and secondary sources provide most reliable indicators of the extent of housing deprivation.

Contextual data which document background structures and social processes which have an impact on homelessness are available from a variety of sources: population censuses, housing censuses, population registers, statistical yearbooks, housing and construction statistics, household surveys, statistics from the ministries of justice, of labour and of housing, economic and demographic yearbooks, statistics on social protection expenditures, welfare statistics. Most of these sources are collated by the intergovernmental agencies such as EUROSTAT, European Commission, Council of Europe and the specialised bodies of the United Nations. Although not always standardised, these sources generally meet minimum criteria of comparability.

Valuable secondary research sources are targeted research projects implemented in a variety of disciplines, from sociology, psychology, medicine, economy, demography, to urban planning. Although they may not be targeted explicitly at the homeless population research projects on poverty, social exclusion, health, living conditions, family and informal networks often include a housing component. Sometimes homeless people can be identified as a specific subgroup in the general sample. Such is the case, for example, in the Office of Population Censuses and Surveys on Psychiatric Morbidity in Great Britain.

The Research Logic

To what extent do those primary and secondary sources and contextual data contribute to the better understanding of the phenomenon of homelessness at the European level? Even a summary glance at a variety of sources makes us wonder whether data on homelessness are documenting the same phenomenon. Even when data originate from similar sources, be it statutory and voluntary services, public administration, or targeted research, they clearly have a different degree of accuracy. In order to use and compare the segmented sources we need to situate the available data in a research framework.

Research is a process and each stage builds upon the reliability of previous sequences. The key initial stage in social research is the identification of the problem to be addressed and clarification of its scientific and social importance.

In its preliminary stage the research process also includes the analysis of the literature, review of theories, formulation of the initial research hypothesis and definitions and gathering of data to substantiate or discard the hypothesis. The choice of methods and research techniques which will be developed and used to collect and analyse data will partially depend on the professional skills of researchers. But the quality of findings, their scientific relevance, their policy implications and practical consequences will not be determined by the technical precision at any single research stage. They will depend on the quality of the entire process.

The frustration of scholars sufficiently courageous to tackle homelessness as a research issue derives largely from the fact that they are seldom participants in the crucial initial stages vital for the reliability of research outputs. The political context characterised by the urgent need to know how to deal with homeless people coupled with a weak will to allocate resources for primary research implies that a researcher is only called to *make use of available data*. It is commonly believed that it suffices to apply a few techniques of frequency distribution and classification in order to describe the research subject, draw the conclusions and propose measures.

Under the EUROHOME project we did not have the financial resources needed to gather primary data. Since we could not collect pertinent data we set out to bring some clarity about research situations for which data are available and those for which we have no data whatsoever.

Operationalisation of the initial stages of research of homelessness includes a clear specification of research aims, identification of research subjects and nomenclature of research situations (Table 6.2) as the research framework within which available empirical data will be scrutinised. The development of the full research scheme with all its stages is out of the scope of this particular analysis and will not be further pursued than its initial stages.

A comprehensive research approach to homelessness as a condition and housing exclusion and inclusion as social processes would require information about all research situations. Ideally an interdisciplinary approach would involve several scientific disciplines and cover a variety of aspects of exclusion ranging from mental and physical health to family relations and social networks of the excluded, demography, economy and culture of the homeless, to the life-course analysis of exclusion processes. What we see in practice is that particular research situations are disproportionately represented while others remain under-researched.

Indeed, if we look at data available across Europe the situation is the following. Segmented research among homeless people sleeping rough and/

Table 6.2   Operationalisation of the initial stages of research about needs of homeless people and best practices

Research aim	Subject	Research situation
To asses the extent and type of needs of homeless people who remain outside the regular housing system and outside night shelters	Homeless people who rely on personal coping strategies	– sleeping rough – land squatting – squatting empty housing – illegal lettings – cheap furnished rooms – shared accommodation without contract
To assess the type of needs of homeless people who are currently receiving housing assistance	Homeless people who are using services for temporary accommodation	– night shelters – urgent and transitional accommodation (tents, containers, furnished rooms, boarding houses, temporary dwellings) provided and funded or co-funded by the services
To assess the housing needs of people in the sub-standard housing system and those who suffer severe economic hardship	Badly housed people and people who suffer severe housing stress due to high housing costs	– dwellings without basic sanitary amenities – poor quality buildings – overcrowded dwellings – households with rent arrears – households under eviction proceedings
To assess the extent and type of effective measures which are a buffer against homelessness	People in the regular housing system provided for groups at risk of deprivation and/or homelessness	– publicly funded or co-funded housing – publicly funded income transfers and housing benefits – supported housing

or using soup kitchens and night shelters has provided some basic data on the age and sex composition, and at best of the educational level, family of origin, marital status and health profile of clients of emergency services. These sources do not provide data about the prevalence of homelessness but can, in some cases, be used as basis for estimates. Data supplied by emergency service providers about the total number of clients over the course of a year include in their count of clients multiple users. They provide data on the turnover which can be used only as an indicator of how the existing capacities are used rather than as a measure of the extent of homelessness. One day censuses in emergency centres give a snapshot of a stock of clients on a given day. They do not provide information about the fluctuation of service users. They give reasonably accurate information about age, sex, educational level, marital status and health profile of those using emergency and transitional accommodation. But in general data provided by emergency services tell us about clients of particular providers rather than about the homeless population in a country.

Conclusions which may be drawn about characteristics, problems and needs of homeless people can be severely distorted when data gathered for a particular research situation are extrapolated to the entire homeless population. Typically, the prevalence of mental disorders measured among people sleeping rough is frequently extrapolated to the entire homeless population. Yet scientifically well founded research does throw a more nuance picture about the interrelationship between mental disorders and homelessness. Research results from a survey about the prevalence of psychiatric morbidity among homeless adults in the United Kingdom (Gill, Meltzer and Hinds, 1996) show to what extent the prevalence of neurotic and psychotic psychopathology varies according to the housing situation of homeless people, namely, residents of hostels, tenants of private sector leased accommodation, residents of night shelters and people sleeping rough, exhibit different psychiatric morbidity patterns.

If we match available data against research situations which need to be documented it is clear that a whole range of situations has not been adequately researched. Land squatting, squatting of empty housing, illegal lettings, cheap furnished rooms, shared accommodation without contract are conditions which we are not able to document. We can only hypothesise about the prevalence and the profile of people and can only make common sense conclusions about their needs.

It is clear that homeless people who remain outside the institutional framework of emergency services remain beyond statistics. This makes assessments of the level of unmet housing needs and needs for support and care weak unless complemented by other sources. The issue at stake is not only how to estimate potential clients or those *who would be* using services *if* services were there for them but also to understand what homeless people *need* by gaining insight into *how homeless people cope*. Knowledge about people who rely on their private coping strategies can contribute to a better understanding also about the role and functioning of family and informal networks of socially vulnerable people. If we knew more about the way people living under severely precarious housing conditions manage to cope we could do more to reinforce the existing informal networks, rather than just to continue channelling more and more resources and services to sheltering people once they fall through personal safety nets. In order to promote self help we need to learn more about borderline cases of housing exclusion and transitions in and out of homelessness.

Up to now, we could address the issue of hidden homelessness, or borderline cases of homelessness of people who have no access to adequate personal housing, only through secondary sources and contextual data. Population censuses and housing statistics provide some information about the number of people who are badly housed in terms of equipment, quality and size of dwellings. They provide data about the structure of the housing stock. Welfare statistics report on the number of beneficiaries of income transfers and housing benefits. Due to the impossibility of matching macro aggregate data against micro statistics it has never been possible to document the interaction between micro, meso and macro levels of causation. A population census or a housing survey provide information about the number of households living in overcrowded and severely substandard dwellings only targeted surveys could establish the link between housing deprivation and housing exclusion.

No European country has attempted to gather targeted information about the prevalence of homelessness by means of a general population and household census. Homeless people, of course, were included in the population census, to the extent to which they were not intentionally left out. People living in 'unconventional dwellings', those sleeping rough or in shelters for homeless people were counted, if found. But, no special efforts have been made to include all homeless people in the general population count. Furthermore, there are no official definition of homeless people for census purposes in any Member State. It is not possible to identify homeless people as a separate population subgroup purely on the basis of census data. The United States of America, which had put forward an explicit task of gathering data about homeless people in a general population census in 1990, did not achieve the best of results. Activities planned by the USA Census Bureau to count and describe homeless people in 2000 build around a specific methodology developed for a targeted survey among users of services for homeless people (Burt, 1995; National Law Center on Homelessness and Poverty, 1996).

In the European context targeted surveys among users of services for homeless people and samples drawn from social services in general and in particular among beneficiaries of minimum income and other welfare payments, guarantee a higher degree of probability of tracking down currently homeless people, those who may have experienced episodes of homelessness and those at risk of becoming homeless, than a general population census. Census as a massive and costly instrument can stratify collective households according to their function and can count users of night shelters on a reference day. But this can be achieved through targeted surveys in a less costly and more reliable way. Furthermore, only targeted surveys can trace those homeless people who are beyond population statistics. Only targeted surveys can provide information about fluctuation rates which are particularly high for the homeless population. Only targeted surveys can adequately deal with methodological and practical difficulties associated with finding and interviewing people who may have multiple problems and personality disorders. Only specially trained and motivated interviewers can approach the most handicapped part of the homeless population. Finally, population censuses are undertaken as a rule every 10 years and only in few countries at shorter intervals, usually only on a sample. The time span of 10 years is much too long for monitoring the phenomenon of homelessness which requires urgent social intervention on a continuous basis.

Prevalence of Homelessness: Why do we Need to Know?

The issue of numbers is one of most controversial aspects of the debate about homelessness and social exclusion in general. It raises perplexities about the 'game of numbers'. It is an issue on which ideologies clash between pressure groups who lobby by underestimating figures in order to minimise public responsibility and pressure groups who lobby to increase their political weight and resources by overestimating the number of their clients. A tiny body of reliable information is used to reinforce a multitude of conflicting opinions.

Do we really need to know the numbers? Why do we want to count people at all? Why do we want to count homeless people? In order to reach an agreement that it is unacceptable that people become homeless in the richest countries in the world we do not need to count the homeless. In order to reach an agreement that homeless people are not meritorious enough to share the wealth created by others we do not need to know their numbers. In both cases an ideological stand may suffice. Ideologies do not need figures; services do. We may not need figures to construct policies. We need figures to implement policies and monitor their efficacy.

The ultimate reason why authorities count the total population of a country (by means of a population and household census, population registers, vital statistics) is that figures are needed for the administration and planning of public services. When governments do not gather information about the homeless population in acute need of services it generally implies that there is a weak political commitment to planing services and to meeting housing needs of homeless people. It is, however, necessary to underline that what is needed is a sound basis for estimating the extent of the problem to be tackled and not a census of homeless people. Undertaking a census-type exercise in order to count homeless people is expensive, methodologically difficult to implement and inevitably superficial.

Counting homeless people is not necessary. But in order to assist homeless people we need to have an idea about the magnitude of the problem which we intend to tackle. In order to provide assistance to homeless people we need to identify problems associated with the condition and obstacles which homeless people encounter in accessing a home. In order to plan services we need to know both the number of current users and the number of people who are in need, those who would be using services if services were available.

Estimating the extent of homelessness may be redundant only in a minority of countries in which there is a strong commitment to housing as a public service: where publicly-funded housing is targeted at the entire population and where the supply of housing, supporting services and transfer payments matches the demand. Only in countries with a generous supply policy in which preferential access to housing by the homeless and people threatened by homelessness is preferential only in terms of the degree of urgency with which public authorities meet their housing needs may it be said that knowing numbers of people in great need is not important. Paradoxically, the few Member States which have traditionally had a strong housing component incorporated in their system of social protection also have best statistics about homelessness. One can go as far as to say that the level of knowledge about the prevalence of homelessness is a good indicator of the degree of commitment to eradicating homelessness.

Risks of Homelessness: Why do we Need to Know?

Knowing the number of people who are homeless at any given point in time may suffice to plan emergency night shelters, transitional accommodation and supported housing. It does not suffice to address the issue of prevention.

For that purpose we need information about risk factors which may precipitate homelessness.

Contextual data enable us to assess risk factors and to identify population subgroups at risk of housing exclusion. Typically, low income and lack of affordable housing are key background factors of housing exclusion. Levels of provision vary across Europe and economic, housing and welfare statistics enable us to illustrate the social context within which exclusion occurs and the impact of structural components of prevention of housing exclusion. Demographic parameters – namely decline in marriage rates, increase of divorce rates, increase in out-of-wedlock birth, changing leaving home patterns of young adults, increasing longevity – may contribute to our better understanding of mechanisms which may be eroding the caring capacity of the family. They do not enable us to explain why, within the subgroup of people with low education, low skills and low income, particular individuals become homeless. We do not know how the combination of background and personality characteristics lead to the erosion of family and social bonds and lead to a dead end condition of social detachment of homeless people. In order to understand ways in and out of homelessness we need to learn more about ways risks materialise.

In terms of individual characteristics which are conducive to homelessness, the current body of knowledge enables us to identify two main risk groups: risk-prone people and risk carriers. Typically, individuals with low educational achievement, low level of professional skills, who cannot access regular paid labour, who originate from a socially deprived family, who have experience family disruptions in childhood or adolescence, who have weak family and social networks are prone to the risk of homelessness. People who are drug addicts, alcoholics, or have clinical symptoms of mental disorders may be considered as risk carriers. What distinguishes these groups are not only paths into homelessness but also the ability to get out of the condition. The type and the duration of social support which may be needed will differ accordingly. Of course, all available data about characteristics of homeless people are cross-sectional. Therefore, the split between people who became homeless because they were risk-prone and those who became homeless because they were carriers of risks reflects the static nature of available empirical documentation. Only additional research which would be based on the life event analysis could document how risk-prone individuals may become risk carriers.

Clearly, in-depth studies and the use of advanced techniques of data collecting and analysis are needed to fill the missing links in the body of knowledge about homelessness. Such studies require long preparations, and are labour-intensive and costly. But investment of resources into research which would document how a sequence of events leading to social exclusion may result in lasting or even lifelong dependency on social support is more than justified by the enormous public cost of care and supported housing for people who have accumulate handicaps while being homeless. Indirect costs of containing crime and maintaining public spaces are rarely taken into account for the assessment of (financial) benefits of prevention.

Concluding Remarks

We have highlighted principal difficulties associated with the interpretation of available data on homelessness gathered for a variety of aims. One set of problems for data users derives from the fact that aims and methods used for targeted surveys and for administrative statistics do not follow the same logic. Data needed for scientific analysis and data needed for the administration of services do not require the same degree of precision in the choice of indicators and measurements. In order to describe in a quantitative way the composition of service users, a simple frequency distribution will be all that is needed. In order to gain insight into ways in and out of homelessness, complex life-event history analysis is needed.

In order to take a political stand, indicators of poverty, housing exclusion, social segregation, or simply the visible presence of homeless people in the streets of Europe's cities may be sufficient. In order to operationalise policies, and implement clusters of preventive and responsive measures reliable data and advance scientific techniques are needed. A high degree of scientific rigour is needed to identify targets, to develop the institutional set up, to devise means and allocate resources, to test methods and techniques and to monitor outcomes. In-depth studies are time and resource consuming.

This input may be difficult to justify from the point of view of short-term pragmatic responses to situations of great urgency, more particularly in view of current budgetary constraints in Europe. However, in a long-term perspective, prevention and early and adequate assistance is more effective and efficient. If we learn about processes which result in the social detachment of homeless people we might learn to control them. If we can control processes we might be able to prevent homelessness occurring on a large scale. We might be able to focus on meeting specific needs of people at risk of homelessness and truly assisting those who fall through all the existing private and public safety nets. Considerable public resources spent on running night shelters and keeping homeless people (temporarily) off the streets could be put to better use.

Bibliography

Avramov, D. (1995), *Homelessness in the European Union, Social and Legal Context of Housing Exclusion in the 1990s*, Brussels, FEANTSA.

Avramov, D. (1996), *The Invisible Hand of the Housing Market, A Study of Effects of Changes in the Housing Market on Homelessness in the European Union*, Brussels, FEANTSA.

Burt, M. (1995), 'Homeless survey and census methodology', paper presented at the *Meeting on Homeless Surveys*, 25 October, Institut National d'Etudes Démographiques (INED), Paris.

Busch-Geertsema, V. and Ruhstrat, E-U. (1994), *Wohnungsnotfälle. Sicherung der Wohnungsversorgung für wirtschaftlich oder sozial benachteiligte Haushalte*, ed. Bundesministerium für Raumordnung, Bauwesen und Städtebau and Bundesministerium für Familie und Senioren, Bonn.

Commission of the European Communities (1993), *Living in Europe, How we live in Europe and how we feel on the subject, A report on a survey of satisfaction with housing, housing costs and the areas in which people live*, Brussels, Directorate General V.

Council of Europe (1993), *Homelessness*, report prepared by the Study Group on Homelessness, 1991/1992 Co-ordinated Research Programme in the Social Field, Strasbourg, Council of Europe Press.

Duffy, K. (1995), *Human Dignity and Social Exclusion, Framework Document and Work Programme*, Strasbourg, Council of Europe.

European Commission (1993), *Statistics on Housing in the European Community*, Brussels, Directorate General V.

European Commission (1994), *Observatory on national policies to combat social exclusion, Third annual report*, Luxembourg, Office for Official Publications of the European Communities.

European Commission (1995), *Social Protection in Europe*, Brussels, Directorate-General Employment, Industrial Relations and Social Affairs.

FEANTSA (1993; 1994), Figures provided for the transnational reports drafted by Daly, M. Brussels.

Gill, B., Meltzer, H. and Hinds, K. (1996), 'The prevalence of psychiatric morbidity among homeless adults', *OPCS Surveys on Psychiatric Morbidity in Great Britain*, Bulletin No. 3, London, Office of Population Censuses and Surveys.

Gilli, A.G. (1972), *Come si fa ricerca*, Milano, Arnando Mondadori.

Marpsat, M. and Firdion, J-M. (1996), 'Devenir sans-domicile: ni fatalité, ni hasard', *Population & Sociétes*, May, no. 313

Nascimento, F. (1995), *Rapport national pour le Portugal, European Federation of National Organizations Working with the Homeless*, Brussels, FEANTSA.

National Law Center on Homeslessness and Poverty (1996), 'Homelessness in America', paper presented at the *International Forum on Homelessness*, 10 June, NGO Forum, Habitat II, Istanbul.

Sapounakis, A. (1995), *Annual Report on Homelessness in Greece, European Federation of National Organizations Working with the Homeless*, Brussels, FEANTSA.

The National Board of Health and Welfare – Socialstyrelsen (1995), *Homeless in Sweden*, Stockholm, Sweden, Socialstyrelsen.

Wagner, A. and Pels, M. (1995), *Enquete aupres des foyers d'accueil pour personnes sans abri*, Luxembourg, INSTEAD/CEPS.

7 Annual Survey on Homelessness in Finland: Definitions and Methodological Aspects

SIRKKA-LIISA KÄRKKÄINEN

Introduction[1]

Finland belongs to the Nordic group of countries which has adopted a distinct type of social policy sometimes called 'the Scandinavian model'. Typical of this model are the relatively strong redistribution of the income and universal social services and social benefits provided to individuals. The responsibility for social policy lies with society, the public sector and the municipalities. The success of social policy has, at least until recently, been evaluated by the degree and depth of social exclusion, by how well exclusion has been avoided in the society.

To carry out a universal social policy, much information on citizens' living conditions is needed. Part of the Nordic tradition is keeping population registers and gathering statistical information. This tradition was started by the church hundreds of years ago. Statistics have been gathered for the past 100 years, too.

The National Housing Board, the national authority responsible for the planning of housing policy measures and the authority granting loans for social housing and other subsidies for housing, has, since the beginning of the 1980s, conducted annual housing market surveys directed at local authorities. This work has been continued by the Housing Fund of Finland since 1994. The aim of these surveys has been to gather information about the housing conditions in municipalities and local areas in order to direct state funds to areas where there is a shortage of housing.

As part of the housing market survey a survey of homelessness and houselessness was started in 1986. This survey, which estimates the total extent of homelessness and houselessness, has been made yearly ever since.

This chapter describes the development of the concept, the definition of homelessness and houselessness in Finland and the methodology of the survey. The Finnish (and Scandinavian) administrative environment based on local authorities is described briefly in section 2. Section 3 contains a very short history of policy debate in Finland in the past few decades; during this debate the definition of homelessness and houselessness now used was developed. Section 4 the definition of homelessness or houselessness used in the survey.

After the description of the methodology of the survey (section 5), the definition and the results of the survey are evaluated against the theoretical debate on homelessness and against public debate and policy measures in Finland.

Social Welfare and Municipal Responsibility in Finland

The population of Finland is around five million. A good three-fifths of the population live in towns. The majority of the Finnish towns are, however, small, so that only one-third of Finns live in a town with more than 50,000 inhabitants. The greater Helsinki area has a population of just on 900,000, of which of half a million live in the City of Helsinki. Half the homeless and houseless are in Helsinki.

The municipalities have considerable autonomy and the right to levy taxes. The government passes the laws and appropriates funds to the local authorities for various purposes and the central administration has issued the instructions necessary to put the policy into practice; the number of instructions has been considerable reduced in recent years and the responsibility of the municipalities has grown.

Everyone is eligible for the basic social benefits and health services independent of his/her working career. Both the social security benefits and the services are mainly financed by taxes or other fees from employers or employees, collected by the state and the municipalities. The importance of private insurance is very modest in Finland. The role of non-governmental organisations (NGOs) as providers of social services in Finland is only a secondary one compared with that of the local authorities.

As a rule the municipalities have a good overall picture of the housing, welfare and health service needs of their inhabitants. To this end they use statistics and conduct investigations. The survey of homelessness and houselessness described in this article is one such annual survey used by a municipality as a means of planning. In particular the housing administration – the authority granting funds for social housing production – is in direct contact with the municipal administration; the information collected by the local authorities can thus easily be consolidated to form national statistics. In addition to the strong, uniform municipal administration, Finland's small size – only five million inhabitants – makes it possible to compile uniform data. The municipalities' capability for compiling and using statistics naturally varies according to their available human resources.

Background: The Development of the Definition of Homelessness as Part of Housing and Social Policy

Homelessness and houselessness was a large urban problem in the 1950s and 1960s. *Homelessness was, in the 1960s, regarded as a problem of alcoholism, unemployment and vagrancy.* A wide range of social care measures was duly devised with a view to solving these problems: homes for the care and treatment of alcoholics, emergency and halfway housing, and shelters. The local welfare authorities and the National Board of Social Welfare at central administration level began collecting precise statistics on the various groups of people living in institutions, homes for alcoholics, shelters and halfway homes (Puttonen, 1996, interview). There is no mention of the homeless or houseless or other special groups in housing policy documents. The official statistics revealed only the number of families living in cramped conditions.

The national housing programme in the middle of 1970s was the first document which stated that, '[a]ttention must be paid in developing the general housing policy system to the members of the population for which the government's housing measures are not sufficient for them to achieve a reasonable standard of housing' (Valtakunnallinen asunto-ohjelma, 1976). For the first time the housing policy report also dealt with persons living in shelters, but it did not yet speak of the homeless as a group. Housing and exclusion began to be connected in general discourse; the problem was *identified as lack of a home, and social care and control began to be abandoned as a sole solution.*

The local authorities were urged to draw up a housing programme for their areas and to take steps to improve the housing conditions of those in particularly poor conditions. According to the instructions to local authorities on drawing up a housing programme, *'[a] knowledge of the extent of problems is necessary in order to arrange housing'* (Kuntien asunto-ohjelmien laatimisohjeet, 1979 and 1984). In order to make it easier for the authorities to collect this information, a classification system was proposed for persons in substandard housing by the National Housing Board. The following groups were classified as homeless:

- persons living in institutions for lack of housing;
- families living apart for lack of housing;
- other homeless and houseless persons, i.e.
  - persons with no home at all (e.g. living outdoors)
  - persons in temporary shelters (caravans, etc.)
  - persons living in hostels, shelters, etc., for want of housing
  - subtenants
  - evicted persons
  - persons living in condemned buildings
  - persons released from institutions.

The housing, welfare and health authorities were urged to collaborate in collecting the statistics by, for example, keeping (confidential) registers. The instructions remained in force until the early 1990s, but many municipalities have continued to draw up their housing programmes according to the same principles.

In the 1970s the problems encountered by special groups and the homeless were, however, only just being recognised, and *not until the 1980s were any practical steps taken to eliminate homelessness and houselessness* (Saarenheimo and von Hertzen, 1996). *Nor was the time yet ripe for the systematic compiling of statistics on these issues.* Surveys of persons living in substandard and cramped conditions were made by the National Housing Board (Kosonen and Kärkkäinen, 1983; Harju, 1984), but not until the mid-1980s were more detailed statistics added to the official statistics compiled by Statistics Finland. The official, population register-based statistics were not, however, of much use in estimating the number of houseless people (any more than they are today; many houseless people are still registered under their former address and are not therefore classified as homeless and houseless).

In 1982 a doctoral dissertation in social medicine was published on homelessness and alcohol (Taipale 1982); this has been a significant source in Finnish debate on homelessness. This work also gave *a summary of the definitions of homelessness and houselessness used to date.* According to these, 'homeless and houseless' means persons who:

a) do not have a rented or owner-occupied home of their own and who

therefore have to live as subtenants;
b) are temporary lodgers, sharing their room with the host family;
c) are temporarily living with relatives or friends through lack of a home of their own;
d) are temporarily living in an institution and have no dwelling or home outside it;
e) are living in a building site hut or the equivalent (e.g. on board a ship) and have no dwelling or home outside it;
f) are living temporarily in an institutional home and have no dwelling or home outside it;
g) are living in a night shelter, hostel for the homeless or halfway home;
h) are living in some other type of temporary dwelling or shelter (e.g. a garden shed, sauna or outhouse);
i) are living outdoors.

Ilkka Taipale limited the word *koditon* (homeless) to mean

> a rootless person without a dwelling, a specific life circle or ties. Such persons, vagrants, are more often regarded as homeless than merely housingless. Houselessness can be avoided by producing and supplying housing. Reducing homelessness additionally calls for other support measures enhancing human relations and the environment. Housing is a vital prerequisite for the establishment of a home (Taipale, 1982).

The need of Finnish debate to try to break away from a definition founded on personal attributes was and still is evident. Finnish seldom uses the word *koditon* meaning homeless and has instead widely adopted the word *asunnoton* meaning houseless. The word *asunnoton* (houseless) has taken root in Finnish parlance.[2]

In 1983 a committee – the Homes for the Houseless Committee – was set up to debate the conditions of homeless and houseless people. The committee was anxious to define the concept of homelessness and houselessness as closely as possible so that the measures proposed in its report could be directed at those in the direst straits. It therefore defined as homeless (houseless)

> persons living outdoors, in shelters or other such temporary accommodation or who are, for want of housing, living in an institution (Asunnottomien asuntotoimikunta, 1984).

The committee nevertheless pointed out that the homeless should also be examined by population group, above all because different laws were applied to measures affecting different groups, and the organisation of measures calls for different means. These groups included:

- young people living in shelters or the like, or in youth homes under the Child Welfare Act;
- persons with substance abuse problems living outdoors, in temporary shelters, night shelters and various institutions for substance abusers;
- psychiatric patients living mainly in night shelters or in various kinds of institutions or hostels in accordance with the Mental Welfare Act;
- the mentally handicapped or severely disabled placed in institutions for want of housing;
- other persons who could be regarded as homeless or houseless according to the above definition.

The committee complained that the concept of homelessness or houseless had not yet been defined in unambiguous terms. In the absence of a precise definition, the number of homeless persons thus depended on the definition used. It was therefore proposed that the statistics on the homeless population should be improved throughout the country and in each municipality (Asunnottomien asuntotoimikunta, 1984).

The Homes for the Houseless Committee proposed a number of measures for eliminating homelessness and houselessness, the primary goal being to provide normal homes. Most of the committee's proposals were put into practice.

Stimulated by the International Year of shelter for Homeless people in 1987, *the government also announced its intention to eliminate homelessness and houselessness.* At that time there were, it was estimated, according to the survey described in the following, close on 20,000 houseless people (20,000 in 1986 and 18,000 in 1987).

The objectives were specified more closely in new planning instruments, in the programme for the development of housing conditions and in the national plan for the organisation of social welfare and health care services, both of which were approved by the government. According to the programme for the development of housing conditions, 18,000 homes (the number of homeless and houseless people was estimated to be 18,000 at the time of making the programme) were to be made available for the homeless and houseless over a period of five years. (Asunto-olojen kehittamisohjelmat, 1986, 1988). The local authorities had until the end of 1986 to investigate the number of persons living in institutions for want of housing, the homeless and persons living in extremely substandard homes, and to draw up a plan for providing them with a home (Asunto-olojen kehittomisohjelma, 1986).

As a result of these special measures, homelessness and houselessness was halved in 10 years, but the programmes aimed at eliminating homelessness and houselessness were, however, only partly successful. New homeless people have appeared as existing ones have been housed.

In both the development programme and the national plan the precise meaning of *homelessness and houselessness was defined for the first time.* This definition has since been used in Finland (see section 4). The Ministry of Social Affairs and Health further appointed a Houselessness Statistics Group to examine on the best way of establishing the number of homeless and houseless people (Asunnottomien tilastoryhmon muistio, 1986), although surveying of homelessness and houselessness had already been started.

The National Housing Board commissioned surveys of the housing market situation directed at the municipalities at the beginning of the 1980s. By the mid-1980s the survey had developed into a regular, and systematic way of collecting information about the housing markets. *In 1986 questions about the extent of homelessness and houselessness were added to the housing market survey.* The request expressed frequently in discussions for better, regular information about homelessness was thus answered this way.

Definition of Homelessness and Houselessness used in the Housing Market Survey

When the survey of homelessness and houselessness was started in 1986, there was no longer any difficulty in finding a definition after the long and lively debate. The national programmes approved by the government had defined the concept, too.

In the housing market survey, the homeless and houseless include the following categories:

- persons living outdoors or in temporary shelters;
- persons living in night shelters or other shelters for the homeless;
- persons living in institutions or institutional homes either temporarily or permanently due to lack of housing;
- prisoners soon to be released who have no housing;

- persons living temporarily with relatives and acquaintances due to lack of housing;
- families who have split up or are living in temporary housing due to lack of housing (Housing Market Surveys).

The more detailed instructions to the municipalities on how to fill in the survey form give the following guidelines:

- 'living outdoors or in temporary shelters' includes those living permanently outdoors and in various types of temporary shelter not intended as housing, such as garden sheds, sauna living rooms, huts, building site huts, caravans, etc.;
- 'living in night shelters etc.' includes those who, in addition to night shelters, live in hostels for the homeless;
- 'living in institutional homes due to lack of housing' includes those who live in various institutional homes which provide care (mostly institutional homes for alcoholics);
- 'living in an institution' includes those living in psychiatric hospitals, old people's homes, institutions for the mentally handicapped, etc. either temporarily or permanently due to lack of housing;
- 'prisoners soon to be released who have no housing' includes prisoners who have no housing and for whom no housing has been reserved by the Criminal Care Association or some other similar body;
- 'living temporarily with relatives or friends' includes persons who, according to the municipality's information or estimate, are living temporarily with relatives or friends due to lack of housing. This item does not include young people living in their childhood home;
- 'families who have split up or are living in temporary housing' includes families forced to live apart because of lack of housing, or in temporary accommodation, such as a boarding house, or temporarily with friends or relatives. Homeless families also include mothers in temporary mother-and-child homes without a home of their own and unmarried couples about to have a child but with no home of their own (Housing Market Survey, Housing Fund circular, 1995).

The instructions on how to define the various categories of homeless and houseless have not changed since 1986 (National Housing Board and Housing Fund circulars, 1986–95).

The number of homeless and houseless people was approximately 9,800 persons and 600 families and other households with more than one person at the end of the year 1997. A majority is single men (Tiitinen, 1996, 1997 and 1998). The trend since 1987 in the number of homeless and houseless people according to this definition can be seen in the article 'Housing Policy and Homelessness, Services in the Policy Context from the 1960s to the 1990s' later in this volume.

Methodology of the Survey

The Housing Market Survey

The form for surveying housing market is send to the municipal housing authorities by Housing Fund. The main items the municipalities are asked in the housing market survey were in 1995:

* the demand and supply of state-subsidised rental housing (social housing) during the course of a year and on a certain date;
* unoccupied state-subsidised rental housing;
* the housing situation of certain population groups;
  - young people
  - students
  - the elderly
  - refugees
  - the homeless and houseless;
* the demand for right-of-occupancy housing (a new tenure status);
* the demand and supply of state-subsidised owner-occupied housing;
* other information on the housing situation in the municipality.

All these are indicators of the housing market situation in the municipality. The questions (other than questions of the extent of homelessness) have changed more or less during 15 years: the items asked are meant to give information about the actual situation in the housing market; in the course of 15 years there have been fluctuations which have changed the situation sometimes even dramatically.

Local authorities send the completed forms to the Housing Fund, where they are read and checked. If the information given by municipality is supposed to be based on old information, or the changes are large compared with the information given by the municipality the previous year, the information is checked by discussions with the municipal authorities. The information on the housing market situation compiled over several years by the Housing Fund gives quite a reliable background for checking the information supplied by the municipality. In some cases the municipalities are asked to make a new survey.

The information yielded by the Housing Market Survey is then consolidated into a 'fact sheet' on the housing conditions in the municipality. The 'fact sheet' contains information from the official register-based statistics, too: the housing stock by tenure status, households living in overcrowded or insufficiently equipped dwellings in the municipality. All these are indicators of how things stand in relation to other areas. These data are used both in granting state subsidies for social housing production and as baseline data for the municipality's own planning. A large number of homeless and houseless people indicates that the housing situation is difficult in a municipality; the demand for rental housing exceeds the supply, often many times over.

The Total Homeless and Houseless Population on a Day Basis

The survey of homelessness and houselessness concerns the total homeless and houseless population in the municipality, not a sample. The aim of the survey is to get an overview of the extent of homelessness and houselessness in the municipality and in the country as a whole, not to collect detailed information on the personal characteristics of the homeless or on the reasons why the persons are homeless.

If an accurate figure for some groups of homeless or houseless is not available, the municipality is asked to give an estimate. The results of the survey cannot therefore be regarded as exact statistics or registration of homeless people. The decision to accept estimates if no accurate knowledge is available is an intentional one: if very accurate numbers were required, the task might be impossible and there would be a drop in the response.

The information is gathered on a day basis, and it tells the extent of homelessness and houselessness on a certain day. In 1995 the date was the 29 September. However, for many local authorities it is not possible to make a survey on that specific day; for this reason municipalities are instructed that 'information should be as up-to-date as possible (if, however, this is not the case, give the date to which it refers)' (Housing Market Survey, Housing Fund circular, 1995).

The decision to ask for the numbers on a certain day is based on a knowledge of the nature of homelessness. The homeless and houseless population does not remain the same over time, it is a stream of people. If persons in this stream are calculated on a yearly basis, the same persons may be counted several times and many people are no longer houseless when the calculation is made. This would not a good basis for planning measures. The survey has been made in spring or in autumn when the weather is cold in Finland; in summer the situation might be different.

In the instructions the local housing authorities are advised to gather the information together with other authorities, especially the social welfare authorities, who are responsible for providing services for homeless people.

The survey is directed at all municipalities, even through in most of municipalities there are no or few homeless people. Three-quarters of homeless and houseless people live in the 15 biggest cities and towns (Tiitinen, 1996). The information gathered by these municipalities is therefore crucial, but all the municipalities answered the survey, except a few small rural municipalities who sometimes drop out.

The Questions in the Survey

The municipal authorities are asked to give the number of single homeless persons on the date of the survey according to the categories included in the definition of the homeless:

- living outdoors or in temporary shelters;
- living in night shelters, etc.;
- living in institutional homes;
- living in various institutions;
- prisoners soon to be released who have no housing;
- living temporarily with relatives or acquaintances.

From these, the total number of single homeless persons can be counted.

The last group is families or other bigger households who have split up or are living in temporary housing due to lack of housing.

The municipal authorities are asked some further questions yearly concerning the policy to reduce homelessness: 'How has the municipality succeeded in providing housing for homeless and houseless people in 1994–1995 (= during the past year)? What are the main measures taken by the municipality? What are the main problems?' The answers are given in written form. They usually give much information about the municipal policy.

As the last question, the municipality is asked about the number of homeless and houseless people it has housed over a certain period (usually a year), single homeless and families separately. The total number of housed persons over a year in the country can be counted on the basis of the numbers given by the municipalities. Recently this number has been 3,000–4,000 persons, in the 1980s over 5,000 yearly.

In 1996 the numbers of homeless and houseless women and young people under the age of 25 years were asked in the survey. The extent of homeless and houseless women was 1,800 persons and that of young people 1,500 persons. The recent figures show a considerable increase in these figures (Tiitinen, 1998).

Surveying Homelessness and Houselessness at Local Level: Cooperation Between Different Actors

Gathering information at local level requires the cooperation of many actors from several authorities; the process of collecting may include many phases. The bigger the municipality is, the more partners there are. In small municipalities and even in minor towns the clients are known.

As I have said before, the instructions given to the municipalities about surveying and estimating the extent of homelessness are not very detailed, for several reasons:

- the municipalities have, depending on their size and on their administrative structures, different practices for administrating and handling matters concerning the homeless; services for homeless people can be provided by different service providers. Detailed guidelines are not possible;
- the municipalities use the information on homelessness and houselessness gathered by this survey in their own administrative planning. It would be contradictory to the idea of municipal autonomy to guide the surveying procedure too closely;
- the municipalities are not research institutes; the state authorities cannot expect the municipalities to have the resources to make surveys which require much research; some municipalities still make much larger surveys and finance research for their own purposes.

Authorities in five cities were interviewed for this article by an open interview scheme to check just how the numbers of homeless people in different groups are gathered. The following analyses the method of gathering information.[3]

The welfare authorities are usually familiar with those *living outdoors or in temporary shelters*. Helsinki keeps a register of persons living permanently outdoors and has a special social worker out in the field to keep abreast of the situation. The people living outdoors usually spend the night in shacks in the forest or on waste land, some of them in staircases and in rooms of the banking automatic teller machines. Many towns have had people living outdoors in winter, until recently. The welfare authorities forward their information to the housing authorities, which try to note the people living outdoors on the waiting list for council housing, too. The total number of homeless living outdoors or in temporary shelters is, according to the survey, close to 500 persons in 1995 (Tiitinen, 1996). In 1997 the figure was slightly more than 400 persons (Tiitinen, 1998).

Helsinki has a special welfare office responsible for the homeless. Each social worker is responsible for one *night shelter or hostel*; he/she pays the hostel on the city's behalf the daily charge for those not able to pay themselves (80–90 per cent). He/she is also responsible for granting social assistance, for welfare for substance abusers and other social work, and for housing the homeless. The social workers thus meet almost all the clients. From time to time they ask for a list of the paying inhabitants of the hostels.

Some towns have a register of those living in hostels and shelters; in others the information is collected with the help of the social workers. The housing authorities request information from the social welfare authorities on the collection date. Hostel residents are also taken from the waiting list for council housing (e.g. in 1995 in Helsinki approximately 500 hostel residents are waiting for council housing). Many middle-sized towns no longer have shelters; quite recently, however, the need to open the shelter again has become evident in some middle-sized towns, because several people have been found to be without any shelter.

All *the night shelter residents* are naturally counted as homeless. A night shelter is a temporary form of accommodation that must be vacated during the day, or at least the sleeping quarters must be vacated while cleaning is in progress. Hostel residents can spend all day in the hostel.

Of *the residents of the hostels*, almost all those in hostels charging a daily fee but not providing treatment are classified as homeless, even though these people may be more or less permanently resident there. In principle only those hostel residents who may be assumed as being capable of living independently but who are living in the hostel for want of housing should be classified as homeless or houseless. It is often difficult to draw the line, which is why the calculation practices differ from one town to another. Helsinki counts as homeless all persons living in the hostels and shelters for which the city's special welfare office acts as the central agent and in which a daily charge is made.

The total number of persons living in shelters and hostels was approximately 1,200 in autumn 1995 (Tiitinen, 1996); in 1997 the number was 1,300 persons (Tiitinen, 1998).

In contrast, the residents of hostels and institutional homes for psychiatric patients and the mentally handicapped, or of the halfway homes for persons with substance abuse problems, are not usually counted as homeless. They live in these homes either permanently or in order to get treatment.

The residents of the *rehabilitation homes for alcoholics* are there for treatment and are not counted as homeless for the duration of the treatment. The residents of *care homes for alcoholics* are long-term, and sometimes permanent ones. The majority of them do, however, tend to be counted as homeless or houseless in Helsinki. The residents of rehabilitation and care homes are not offered a home until the social workers consider they are capable of living independently. The practice is the same in the other towns.

It is not, therefore, altogether clear just how precisely the inhabitants of hostels, rehabilitation and care homes are differentiated for the purposes of the survey according to who could live elsewhere and who could not; the practice would appear to vary. The client's ability to live independently and his/her desire to leave the hostel community are not things that can be measured. There are probably some among those classified as homeless for whom a hostel or care home is a permanent, and possibly the most suitable, form of housing. The number of homeless persons living in rehabilitation and care homes alcoholics was counted to be close to 1,300 in 1995 and approximately 1,350 in 1997 (Tiitinen, 1996 and 1998).

Mental hospitals, institutions for the mentally handicapped and for substance abusers have some clients who may, through lack of housing, have had to spend longer in them than is strictly necessary for treatment. Some of the residents of old people's homes were at one time there because they had nowhere else to go; nowadays these people are provided with service housing.

Precise information on the number of persons living in institutions for want of housing is difficult to obtain. The staff of institutions or patients themselves apply for council housing, which means that these homeless people are on the housing waiting list. The municipalities also seek information from the hospital almoners. Some municipalities have held joint meetings for the authorities and hospitals looking into the housing situation of persons ready to be discharged and capable of living independently. Many patients cannot, however, be provided with housing, because the municipality does not have the resources to guarantee the client the daily assistance needed for him/her to cope in an ordinary apartment. The housing authorities thus try to avoid unnecessary evictions and other difficulties that have often arisen in such cases. Altogether 300 persons were estimated to be staying in institutions due lack of housing in 1995, while in 1997 the number had increased to 600 persons.

Helsinki has one social worker responsible for *prisoners about to be released*; he also knows of any such prisoners without a home to go to. The other towns, too, keep a register of or estimate the prisoners soon in need of housing. The prisoners themselves, the prisons and Criminal Care Association contact the housing authorities, which means that houseless prisoners are housing applicants. There were somewhat over 300 prisoners in the whole country in autumn 1995 who had no home to go to after being released. In 1997 the number had increased to 500.

The category of the homeless or houseless people most difficult to assess are *persons living temporarily with relatives or friends*. Some of them have applied for housing, some are clients of the special welfare office. The registers kept by the various authorities are not, however, compared in Helsinki. In Helsinki, the number is a pure estimate. What is more, a proportion of the persons living with relatives or friends do not apply for council housing because they do not believe they will get it, due to the difficult housing situation in Helsinki. Homelessness or houselessness of these persons can be of short duration, but it can be repeated. It is not possible to count this group in Helsinki.

In the smaller towns the number of homeless and houseless persons living with relatives or friends consists of persons on the housing waiting list, but it is to some extent based on estimate, too. Among them are a large number of housing applicants who have been evicted from council housing because of their disturbing behaviour or their failure to pay the rent and who will not be given a new apartment, for the time being. In the absence of any other accommodation, the members of this 'revolving door brigade' are camping with relatives or friends.

Homeless and houseless young people in particular seek accommodation with relatives or friends; they do not as a rule want to stay in a night shelter or hostel. This category of people is therefore becoming increasingly significant. In 1997 their estimated number was slightly more than 5,600 persons. (Tiitinen, 1998).

The houseless families have lost their homes for one reason or another (they have been given notice or evicted, they have lost their owner-occupied home through inability to pay off the mortgage, as a result of divorce, family violence, etc.). They are living with relatives or friends, the whole family together, or have been forced to split up, in mother-and-child homes, emergency apartments, temporary accommodation such as boarding houses, shared apartments, empty day nurseries. They are housing applicants and/or social welfare clients. Families with children, in particular, are without a home for a few weeks at most before being provided with ordinary housing or with supported housing in case of other problems, too.

Many towns and rural municipalities have no houseless families at all. The majority of the houseless families are in Helsinki, and at least half of them are Ingrian returnees or foreigners moving to Helsinki from other parts of Finland and on the waiting list for housing, staying in temporary accommodation. Quite recently the number of homeless families and other bigger households have increased, to 600 in 1997 (Tiitinen, 1998).

Evaluation

Data Analysis

As I have described above, the results of the survey are a combination of register data, exact statistics and estimates.

If the aim of the survey were to compile statistics on the homeless and houseless population, this survey would not meet the statistical requirements: the way the information is gathered varies from one municipality to another, and there are persons included as homeless whose homelessness or houselessness is a matter of definition. In this sense the definition is inadequate. It is uncertain, too, how well the registers of the social welfare authorities and the register of persons waiting for council housing are compared. There may be overlapping information, the same persons may have been counted twice. Finally, a part of the information is based on estimate.

The main aim of this survey is to get an overview of the situation, the extent of the problems which should be solved, the number of housing units or care units needed at local level and in the country as a whole. It is an example of a problem-solving approach in defining and surveying homelessness (Avramov, 1996). For this purpose the results of the survey have been sufficient in most of the municipalities; in the City of Helsinki, however, the methodology of the survey has proved to have relied perhaps too much on estimates in calculating the number of homeless and houseless people staying with relatives or friends.

The survey made on this basis does not give answers to following questions: how long the duration of homelessness or houselessness is, whether there are large fluctuations in the course of a year and what are the reasons a person is to be without a home. Some municipalities have studied and reported these issues for their own use, but the information has not been gathered on the level of the country.

The gender and the age of the homeless were not asked before the year 1996, even if many municipalities had that information. In 1996 the number of young homeless, too, was for the first time asked, especially for the purposes of the national report for European Observatory on Homelessness. The reason why the gender and the age of the homeless were not sought before was to avoid the survey to become too laborious for the municipalities. This could be seen to be a shortcoming, because the picture of homelessness has been changing.

The category 'families' has a partly misleading title; families with children are not homeless in Finland or they are houseless for a short time only. Most families who do not have a dwelling, i.e. a rental contract of their own, are housed in temporary dwellings and are thus not actually houseless. How many children homelessness affects in Finland yearly has not been estimated; the crucial issue in municipalities is to get a family with children housed as soon as possible. A considerable part of the homeless and houseless in the category 'houseless families' are couples without children. For this reason a better title might for this group might be 'multi-person households'.

One of the interviewed municipal authorities wished for the concepts to be defined more accurately in order to make it easier to collect information and not to leave the survey too open to various interpretations. This would make the comparisons between municipalities more reliable, too.

Definitional Aspects of Homelessness and Houselessness in the Research Literature

Homelessness and houselessness is defined in Nordic research from two opposing perspectives: 1) from the structural, social perspective; and 2) from the perspective of individual attributes, special group or asocial behaviour.

The structural explanations consider that the main cause of homelessness is marginalisation; the research is therefore concerned with the social structures and mechanisms as a result of which certain population groups find it difficult or impossible to earn a living and look after themselves. Among the most common factors are economic inequality, unemployment, and the shortcomings of the social welfare state. Homelessness and houselessness is thus analysed from the perspective of social exclusion, in which open homelessness is the culmination of a long process of social exclusion. In this respect research into homelessness ties in closely with research into poverty (e.g. Järvinen, 1992).

A sub-genre of the structural explanations are, in welfare society, the models focusing on the home or lack of it. Houselessness and evictions are partly due to the shortcomings of the housing markets and housing distribution mechanisms, and to the insufficient support for housing (Begreppet 'Hemlös', 1992; Juntto, 1990; Jokinen and Juhila, 1992; Sahlin, 1995). Research is also investigating where homeless and houseless people live and pass their days and nights. The research approach is no longer explicatory so much as descriptive.

The explanations based on individual attributes are older than the structural ones: the old concepts 'skid row' and 'vagrant' suggest a lifestyle, a subculture and asocial behaviour. These studies often analyse the culture of poverty, beginning with norms, identity and ideology (Järvinen, 1992). Many studies nevertheless combine structural models with explanations concerning subculture.

Structural models have dominated in the Nordic countries, especially Finland and Sweden, too. The choice of perspective is affected by the attitude to homelessness: the explanations focusing on structural processes of exclusion are based on the idea that economic inequality and poverty should be avoided, the housing markets and the distribution of housing should be restructured so that there would be no new homeless and houseless people and so that those who are already homeless could be helped. The research focusing on subculture and asocial behaviour describes the lives of the homeless just as they are. Viewed from this perspective, the homeless were previously regarded as objects of care, control, discipline and punishment.

Avramov's division of the European definition of homelessness comes close to the Nordic classification. Avramov (1996) proposes the following ways of defining homelessness:

1   ostensive definitions: the complex reality of homelessness and housing exclusion is reduced to its smallest, most visible dimension;

2   criminal justice definitions are based on juridical procedures and decision based on anti vagrancy laws;

3   administrative definition identifies those who should be helped. They are

usually based on legal terms which define who is entitled to assistance.

Also in the European discussion the definitions reveal the context within which a phenomenon is perceived. Some definitions are descriptive – used mostly by researchers. Many researchers nowadays use causal definitions which identify social processes focusing on mechanisms of exclusion. If we are able to identify causes of homelessness we may hope to become capable of controlling processes of exclusion. Finally, a definition can be persuasive; it aims at convincing people to a new use of a term. These kinds of definition are used in policy-oriented research (Avramov, 1996). Defining homelessness with a persuasive definition comes near to a problem-solving approach – the groups whose the problems should be solved are shown by the definition.

The Criteria for the Definition Used in Finland and its Criticism

The Finnish housing market survey is purely administrative and may be regarded as an example of the persuasive definition and problem-solving approach put forward by Avramov.

The survey concentrates in its definition on the housing question. Although it draws heavily on a structural explanation in the broader sense, it assumes that the best way to help someone who has been made homeless is to provide him with a home. For this reason the survey of homelessness and houselessness is a part of a housing market survey which gathers together several indicators of housing market about the demand and supply of housing. According to the Nordic welfare model, efforts should be made effectively to avoid homelessness and exclusion by providing various benefits and services; the structures, the mechanisms of exclusion, are thus the focus of attention.

The definition of homelessness and houselessness begins with the place where the homeless person is at a given moment and is in this sense descriptive. The emergence of this classification is largely due to the fact that it is thus easier to classify and find the homeless. The type or quality of the accommodation is not considered significant enough to describe in more detail; they are all substandard accommodations compared with the housing of normal standard and thus a problem which should be solved. The definition also seeks to limit the homeless and houseless to those who are already without a home: it does not include people under threat of eviction or people living in condemned buildings.

The definition has come in for a lot of criticism from those seeking to improve the housing conditions of young people because it does not class as houseless the young people forced to live with their parents for lack of a home of their own. Some of the definitions used in Sweden class these people as houseless, too. Defining these young people as homeless and houseless would have practical consequences: they would then be classed as housing applicants in urgent need of housing. Young people need housing and, because of family problems, some of them are also in urgent need of it; yet they are not houseless in the literal sense of the word.

The Finnish definition and the measures taken to eliminate homelessness and houselessness have deliberately tried to get away from the attitudes prevailing in the 1960s by which the homeless were classified according to their personal attributes (vagrant, workshy, alcoholic, etc.). These definitions branded people as being in need of care, control, isolation and discipline. This attitude was reflected in the measures taken: the homeless were provided with shelters, emergency housing, institutions for alcoholics, etc. Drunks found in the streets were taken to the police lockup (Savio, 1989).

To some extent this special-group attitude and special measures are still in evidence in the definition of homelessness and houselessness and action even today. The National Housing Board was widely criticised in the 1980s because it urged the local authorities to classify persons in substandard housing under various categories instead of urging them to find out how many low-income people they had living in substandard housing. The danger of branding is close at hand in such classifications. Classifications were, however, made to ease the work of those engaged in charting the situation.

The reasons why a person is homeless or houseless are not studied systematically either; it would be laborious. However, there is in the background the same fear as in analysing special groups; that of branding the people involved. In their verbal answers to the survey some municipalities describe the changes in the housing market and the ways some households lose their dwellings.

The local authorities are, however, in practice faced with the fact that people who are homeless for various reasons need different sorts of assistance and housing. Although this is not clearly stated in the definition used in the survey of homelessness, the idea is nevertheless present in the municipalities' own surveys and, particularly, the action taken: they cannot provide all the homeless with ordinary council housing and must instead find alternative solutions.

There have been one or two attempts to redefine homelessness and houselessness by reducing the definition to those in the most serious situation, i.e. to exclude from the definition and the survey people who are staying temporarily with relatives or friends. In this way the definition might become closer to the definitions which obviously are more general in Europe, referring to the personal attributes of the homeless people, to their inability to live 'normal' life. In Finland, however, it was thought that by redefining the concept and thus reducing the number of homeless and houseless people, from the point of view of the measures, the problem of homelessness would then have been easier to handle. No redefinitions have been made.

Social Policy and Housing Policy Implications of the Survey: Conclusions and Future Developments

Implications at the Local Level

The surveying of homelessness and houselessness in municipalities has become a routine. The answers to questions in the interview scheme directed at the city authorities concerning the importance and future of the survey revealed that they consider the survey important.

'Homelessness and houselessness has been defined unambiguously, this makes work at the local level easier.' All the interviewed local authorities found it necessary to make the survey yearly. The survey is important for the local authorities, because 'it makes it easier to get information about the needs and it is at the same time an instrument for following measures'. 'The survey produces results at the other end of the process, in measures.' 'Without the survey the measures would be too stereotyped.' 'It would be odd if the survey were not made', was one answer to the question on the future of the survey.

Too-detailed guidelines should be avoided; it is up to the municipality to plan and decide how to carry out the survey. This was one answer to the question of how to develop the survey while another wished more detailed definitions. No other desires to develop the survey were expressed. Instead the answers concentrated on how to develop the measures.

The number of homeless and houseless people has been written in municipal documents in most municipalities, especially housing programmes.

Quite another issue is nowadays that because of the cuts in municipal funds, resources for adequate measures may be more difficult to obtain. Due to economic difficulties and rent arrears in social housing, occupants for social housing are more easily chosen from applicants belonging more or less to the middle class or at least to that group of people who can pay their rents and assessment of the whether the applicant fits normal housing is made more carefully. The municipal authorities try to avoid a segregation of housing areas by choosing different kinds of occupants; this means in many cases that those in urgent need of housing must wait.

The numbers of homeless and houseless people have been used at counties, too. The duty of the county authorities has been to guide the local authorities in planning social policy and housing measures. Some county governments have done their own researches into homelessness and houselessness in their areas.

Implications on the Level of Society

The numbers of homeless and houseless people have been recorded in a large number of planning documents at governmental level during the past 10 years. They have been supplied with the basic information on the extent of the problem according to which the government has approved programmes aiming to eradicate homelessness.

The results of the housing market survey have been of crucial importance in directing funds for social housing have directed to the local level. In practice it has meant that a municipality with a considerable shortage of rental housing and extensive homelessness and houselessness has been granted funds to build one or two blocks of housing beyond the funds it would have been granted in a housing market situation with less of a housing shortage. This has applied especially in cases where the municipality has announced its plans to take special measures to house homeless and houseless people.

Even today the funds are still granted on the basis of housing market. The climate in housing policy debate has, however, changed lately. There are no national programmes for development of housing conditions and clearly announced intentions to eliminate homelessness. Fund for social housing were decreased in the 1990s, too.

The Finnish media are in the habit of telling the Finnish public the numbers of homeless and houseless people as new figures become available. They are especially interested in the trend in homelessness and houselessness. The articles dealing with homelessness always include background figures on the extent of the problem. There has even been a danger that the public will take the figures as too precise statistics.

The Future of the Survey and Developmental Needs

Homelessness is changing in all countries: far more young people are becoming homeless and more young homeless are women. The number of beds in mental institutions is being reduced, and there are more and more people with mental problems in danger of being excluded.

This 'new homelessness' is a phenomenon which should be studied in surveys of homelessness and houselessness. The survey in Finland does nowadays include some figures on the age and the gender of homeless and houseless people, but more information is needed. At local level, however, the municipal authorities are aware of the problem groups.

Young homeless people in Finland do not usually want to go to a shelter or hostel, so they do the rounds of their friends and relatives. The number of homeless people is becoming more and more difficult to count, especially in the big cities. Staying with friends often causes trouble not only for the homeless person but for the friends, too. The situation often results in eviction because of disturbances to the neighbours.

Developing the methodology to obtain more reliable knowledge of this homeless group is important now. However, due to the scarce personal resources in the municipalities the survey cannot be made too laborious.

The processes of becoming homeless may have changed in the 1990s, during the economic depression. Detailed studies of the processes cannot be included in the housing market survey, but it is important to obtain knowledge of the possible changes in the situation; more research work should be done.

Conclusion: Knowledge is a Prerequisite for Policy Changes

Social issues go through several stages in societal debate. The debate on homelessness and houselessness in Finland which I have described is an example of a case where a topic and a problem were originally considered solvable by segregating, neglecting and punishing. The problem has, stage by stage, through segregating care measures – to awareness of the societal disgrace that a problem like homelessness and especially houselessness can exist in a the welfare society – finally developed into a housing policy and social welfare problem. By developing housing policy measures it has been possible to resolve many controlling and segregating mechanisms in society. The measures taken by one authority provide opportunities for another to improve its operation.

Good knowledge is a prerequisite for taking adequate measures. It is a prerequisite for policy making to be able to move on from one stage to another. The methodology of surveying, the kind of knowledge gathered and the way it is collected are not therefore separate from other issues in society.

Notes

1   I have acquired the facts and views presented in this paper in the course of the many years I have worked with housing policy and homelessness. I was responsible for the housing survey conducted by the National Board of Housing at the time when the first surveys were being made of the number of the homeless people.

   Responsible for the housing market and homelessness survey at the moment is Virpi Tiitinen of the Housing Fund, with whom I have been in close cooperation, thereby greatly contributing to the writing of this paper. I also wish to thank Annikki Savio of STAKES for her very valuable comments.

   I wish to thank my discussant in the Vienna workshop, Volker Busch-Geertsema from Germany, for his very valuable comments and remarks on my preliminary paper. In the final version of the paper I have tried to take into considerations the issues he put forward.

2   In this text the both words 'homeless and houseless' is used here, because the word 'houseless' is not usual in the English language.

3   I wish to thank the housing authorities in Helsinki, Joensuu, Lahti, Mikkeli and Tampere and the special welfare office in Helsinki for their assistance. The following text contains some direct quotations from the replies given the city authorities. The names of the interviewees are given in the list of references.

Bibliography

Asunnottomien asuntotoimikunnan mietintö (1984), *Komiteanmietintö*, 18.

Asunnottomien tilastotyöryhmän muistio (1986), 'Sosiaali- ja terveysministeriö', *Työryhmämuistiö*, 37, Helsinki.

Asunto-olojen kehittämisohjelma vuosille 1987–91 (1986), *Ympäristöministeriö*, Helsinki.

Asunto-olojen kehittämisohjelma vuosille 1991–95 (1990), *Ympäristöministeriö*, Julkaisuja 1/1990, Helsinki.

Asuntopoliittisen toimikunnan mietintö (1965), *Komiteanmietintö*, A6.

Avramov, D. (1996), *The Invisible Hand of the Housing Market. A Study of Effects of Changes in the Housing Market on Homelessness in the European Union*, Brussels, FEANTSA.

Begreppet 'Hemlös' (1992), *En kritisk granskning av använda definitioner*, Karlskrona, Boverket.

Hallitusmuoto 1919/1995 (The Constitution).

Harju, H. (1984a), 'Epätyydyttävästi asuvat lääneittäin', *Asuntohallituksen tilastoselvityksiä*, 20.

Harju, H. (1984b), 'Epätyydyttävästi asuvat nuoret lapsiperheet', *Asuntohallituksen tilastoselvityksiä*, 10.

Harju, H. (1984c), 'Epätyydyttävästi asuvat vanhusasuntokunnat', *Asuntohallituksen tilastoselvityksiä*, 9.

Hemlöshet i Norden (1992), *NAD-publikationer*, no. 22, Helsingfors.

Irtolaislain kumoamisen vaikutuksia selvittävän toimikunnan mietintö (1986), Komiteanmietintö, 46, Helsinki.

Järvinen, M. (1992), 'Hemlöshetsforskning i Norden' in *Hemlöshet i Norden*, NAD-publikationer no. 22, Helsinki.

Jokinen, A. and Juhila, K. (1991), 'Pohjimmaiset asuntomarkkinat, Diskurssianalyysi kuntatason viranomaiskäytännöistä', *Sosiaaliturvan Keskusliitto ja asuntohallitus*, Helsinki.

Juntto, A. (1990), 'Asuntokysymys Suomessa Topeliuksesta tulopolitiikkaan', *Sosiaalipoliittisen yhdistyksen julkaisuja*, no. 50, Helsinki.

Kärkkäinen, S.-L. (ed.) (1996), *Homelessness in Finland*, Jyväskylä, STAKES, FEANTSA Group in Finland, Housing Fund of Finland, Y-Foundation.

Kärkkäinen, S.-L. and Vesanen, P. (1987), 'Asunnottomat vuonna 1986 ja toimenpiteet asunnottomuuden poistamiseksi vuosina 1987–1991', *Asuntohallituksen tilastoselvityksiä*, D1.

Kosonen, M. and Kärkkäinen, S.-L. (1983), 'Voestö – ja asuntolaskenta 1980: Asuntohallituksen erillisselvityksiä', *Asuntohallituksen tilastoselvityksiä*, 4.

Kunnan asunto-ohjelmien laatimisohjeet (1979), Asuntohallitus.

Kuntien asunto-ohjelmien laatimisohjeet (1984), Asuntohallituksen ohjekirja E1.1.

Näkökulmia huono-osaisuuteen (1990), *Sosiaalihallituksen julkaisuja* 16, Helsinki.

Saarenheimo, U. and von Hertzen, H. (1996), 'Asunnottomuus väheni Suomessa, *Määrätietoinen työ tuo tuloksia*, Suomen Ympäristö 49, Helsinki, Ympäristö ministeriö.

Sahlin, I. (1995), 'Excludering som strategi och definitionsprocess', en presentation på seminariet av det nordiska nätverket för forskning om bostadslöshet, Oslo, 16–17 November.

Savio, A. (1990), 'Purkamisen paineet ja potentiaalit, Laitoshuollon hajauttamisen edellytyksiä', *Sosiaalihallituksen julkaisuja* 13, Helsinki.

Summa, H. (1989), 'Hyvinvointipolitiikka ja suunnitteluretoriikka: tapaus asuntopolitiikka', *Yhdyskuntasuunnittelun täydennyskoulutuskeskus* A 17, Espoo.

Summa, H. (1990), 'Asunnoton hallinnon diskurssiobjektina' in *Näkäkulmia huono-osaisuuteen 1*, Sosiaalihallituksen julkaisuja 16, Helsinki.

Taipale, I. (1982), 'Asunnottomuus ja alkoholi, Sosiaalilääketieteellinen tutkimus vuosilta 1937–1977', *Alkoholitutkimussäätiön julkaisuja*, no. 32, Jyväskyl¨ä.

Tiitinen, V. (1996), 'Asuntokanta ja arava-asuntomarkkinat 1995', *Valtion asuntorahasto*, Selvityksiä 3.

Tiitinen, V. and Luukkainen, M.-L. (1990), 'Arava-asuntomarkkinat 1989', *Asuntohallituksen tilastoselityksiä*, D:2.

Tiitinen, V. and Hassi, L. (1993), 'Asunto-olot 1990-luvun alussa', *Asuntohallituksen tilastoselvityksiä*, D:4.

Tiitinen, V. and Seppelin, T. (1993), 'Arava-asuntomarkkinat 1991–1992', *Asuntohallituksen tilastoselvityksiä*, D:1.

Valtakunnallinen asunto-ohjelma vuosille 1976–85 (1976), *Komiteanmietintö*, 36.

Valtakunnalliset suunnitelmat sosiaalihuollon ja terveydenhuollon järjestämisestä vuosina 1987–91 (1986), Helsinki.

Vesanen, P. (1987), 'Asunnottomat vuosina 1986 ja 1987 ja toimenpiteet asunnottomuuden poistamiseksi vuosina 1987–1991', *Asuntohallituksen tilastoselvityksiä*, D:1.

Vesanen, P. (1989), 'Asunnottomat seko toimenpiteet asunnottomuuden poistamiseksi', *Asuntohallituksen tilastoselvityksiä*, D:1.

Other Material

Housing Market Surveys 1986–195, The National Housing Board and the Housing Fund of Finland.

8 Existing and Proposed Data Gathering Systems in the Netherlands Concerning the Homeless

HENK DE FEIJTER

Empirical research depends on data. In the field of homelessness, the availability and the quality of data are a problem. Every time national correspondents of FEANTSA meet, they complain about lack of data, lack of clear definitions of who is homeless, what are the characteristics and what might be the causes. At best, we have to rely on surveys on a limited scale. It is therefore important that in this research project explicit attention is paid to more systematic data-gathering systems and procedures, their advantages, problems and potentials.

This report could not have been written without the help of Josee Franken and Maria de Cock from the Federatie Opvang in Utrecht, who were very helpful to give me insight in the working of the KLIMOP data system. Andre Wierdsma from GGZ, Rotterdam was so kind as to inform me on his project on record linkage.

Introduction

The number of homeless in the Netherlands is, to a great extent, unknown: the Dutch Health Council, an advisory board to the Ministry of Health, issued a report last year in which it stated that the number might be between 20,000 and 30,000 (Health Council, 1995). More important than the remarks about numbers were the critical notes the Council made on the methodological flaws in various research projects. So, definitions on who to define as homeless are rarely comparable, most research projects are only directed to surveys at one point in time and most of those only refer to a limited local scale. Reliable national comparisons, general overviews of the whole population of homeless and roofless people are lacking.

The Dutch view on homelessness is dominated by the social-psychological approach. At the forefront appears a lack of social skills, which leads to an inability to develop and maintain contacts and (therefore) to inadequate social support. This approach can also be found in the set-up of the registration system described here. The institutions that register data on homelessness are welfare institutions, that have taken care of the traditional homeless for a long time. More structural causes of homelessness, such as came forward in the United States (poverty, lack of affordable housing, unemployment) have long been neglected in research.

The Health Council committee concluded that an integration between the social-psychological and structural approaches is required in order to provide better insights into the problems of the contemporary population of the 'roofless' and the 'homeless'. The Council takes the following definitions for the various groups: 'roofless' are those that are not guaranteed of shelter for the coming night; 'homeless' are those without a home, but with a shelter (mostly in an institution); and moreover, they define 'marginally accommodated people', living in unstable accommodation.

> In view of the fact that there is insufficient data available (other than information of a general nature) to enable a verdict to be reached on this population, the committee recommends that further studies be carried out. ... The committee feels that such studies must be longitudinal in design and epidemiological (data on characteristics, subpopulations, data like age, sex, marital status, health condition, addiction and the like) and ethnographical (life histories, attitudes, needs of the homeless themselves) methods should go hand in hand (Health Council, 1995, p. 22).

In this report, two projects that are meant to improve that situation are described. One is the Client Information System (KLIMOP) and the other is the proposed project for linking records of clients in the health care system of the municipality of Rotterdam (GTST).

Our aim here is not to go into the outcomes of the research, but to describe the system itself, its major advantages and shortcomings, its potentials for future improvements. We will also pay attention to the organisational and policy context in which these systems are set up and the prerequisites that should get attention when introducing such a data-gathering system.

The Klimop System

The Need for Information on Clients

Changes in society have engendered the development of new forms of care, especially between mental care and social care, with new groups of clients. Various developments in the welfare field, together with a growing attention for the position of women and of the homelessness, created the need for more information. The Ministry of Health, Welfare and Sport decided in 1993 to finance soft- and hardware for the development of a client registration system that could be applied in different fields of the welfare spectrum. Its main goal was the setting-up of a management information system: how many clients, how many refusals, how long did they stay in various institutions?

One of the major changes in the field of social care, which also had implications for the need for data, is that since 1994 the national government is no longer responsible for the realisation and financing of social care: instead this responsibility has been decentralised to local authorities.

The coordinator of the registration system is Federatie Opvang, a national cooperative body of some 120 institutions dealing with institutionalised social care. It coordinates contacts with the Department of Health, with the Association of Local Authorities, insurance companies and other care takers. Its office does not only implement the client registration system, but also handles the data, and promotes professionalisation, innovation and research projects in the field.

The project was called KLIMOP, which stands for Clients Information System in (Institutionalized) Social Care. Since 1 January 1994, various types of women's refuge centres, general crisis centres, evangelical crisis centres and shelters for the homeless have registered data on their clients in a uniform and automated way. Data on persons that apply for help, on persons admitted to the institution and on persons who have left the institution are registered.

For each of the various fields of care, separate modules have been developed, each with their own set of questions.

The primary aim of the system is to provide data on the number of clients who were treated in the institutions, and their characteristics.

The KLIMOP system was ready for use at the beginning of 1994. Institutions registered data of applicants and admissions to the institution with the help of the automated system. By the end of the calendar year these data (made anonymous) are sent in electronic form to the national office for further handling. In 1994 80 institutions sent in the information on disk, while some only registered during part of 1994. Some women's refuge centres did not register their clients individually but did so via a central reporting office.

Here, we only go into that part developed for shelters for the homeless, although in the other institutions also clients who could be defined as homeless may be accommodated, although in first instance their main problems are different. This could, for example, be the case in women's refuge centres.

Shelters for the homeless are aimed at giving shelter and taking care of homeless people. Those institutions are easy accessible (as a last resort), give practical help and do not have the intention to cure.

Most institutions are centred round their night shelters, in which accommodation, care and guidance is offered, sometimes 24 hours a day. Some also have programmes for daily activities, be it recreational or work. In some shelters nursing is available. Most institutions have also set up ambulant and day care for nonresidents in which all kinds of help are offered: meals, financial advice and medical care as well as forms of more independent living under guidance. Through KLIMOP data on residents in the shelters only are registered for the moment. From 1997 data on clients admitted in short stay facilities will also be registered (527 places)

Figures for 1994, the first year of operation, came from applications to 14 institutions with a total capacity of 1,073 beds. The response was 64 per cent (on a total number of beds of 1,659). The number of applications in 1994 was 3,500 clients. The shelters of the Salvation Army use their own registration system, but these data have been converted into the KLIMOP system and subsequently handled. Eight shelters did not send in their data. Extrapolation over all shelters the number of applicants for shelters for the homeless results in a number of 5,400.

Which Data are Gathered?

Three kinds of questionnaires are subsequently to be filled in when applying for help, on admission to and on departure from the institution. A number of data are only for administrative purposes, and are not nationally collected (names, addresses and numbers).

The questionnaires are highly pre-structured, giving a limited set of possible answer categories.

The questionnaire to be filled in when someone applies for help contains the following questions:

- registration number;

- personal code of the staff member who fills in the form;
- time and date of arrival;
- last residence: town/region/other regions/abroad/unknown;
- last address and postal code;
- client's name/surname;
- sex;
- reasons for not admitting the applicant:
  - lack of capacity;
  - no need for residence, ambulant help possible;
  - physical handicaps ;
  - possible serious psychic problems;
  - possible disturbing behaviour;
  - addiction;
  - legal status;
  - language problems;
  - needs secret address;
  - cannot take care of him/herself;
  - age of children;
  - number of children;
  - client did not show up;
  - client does not want help offered;
  - help offered not suitable;
  - client is too young/old;
  - only in need of residence;
  - circumvention of the law;
  - other reasons.

When an applicant is admitted, an admission form is completed, with questions regarding:

- last institution client was in during the last 12 months;
- if applicable, date of last departure;
- who sent client: list of services and institutions, including police, relatives, housing associations, etc.;
- main problems at time of arrival with a maximum of two:
  - sexual violence;
  - relational problems;
  - psychological problems;
  - material problems: debts, homeless (not having own accommodation),

no home (having no accommodation, no social network, no work, evicted from lodgings, house, other institution):
- addiction problems;
- pregnancy;
- psychiatric problems;
- cultural /integration problems;
- legal status problems;
- problems with justice;
- religious problems.

After having chosen the primary problem(s), a choice can be made of a maximum of three secondary problems, from the list cited above. The following information is also sought:

- source of income: no income, social benefits, wages, help form relatives/ parents/ student grants;
- gross income per month in three classes: under modal, modal, above modal;
- highest degree of education attained;
- client's native country, client's father's native country, client's mother's native;
- ethnic category.

When leaving the institution, another list is filled in, giving treatment, sometimes a more detailed description of the problems first stated at the time of admission, reasons for departure and next residence.

As stated, the KLIMOP system consists of two parts: one part is meant for national registration and does not contain personal information. Part two is meant for the institution itself and can be used in treating clients, setting the institution's own management goals, etc. Apart from the questionnaires mentioned above, the system allows the entry of specific data on clients, treatment schemes, medicine use and other particulars.

One weak spot is that, when people apply for help and there is no room available, the system expects forms to be filled in: of course, the willingness to go through the questionnaire is doubtful here. Moreover, clients continue to seek residence in alternative institutions when there is no room: double counts are hard to avoid, but the agreement is that the same person is only counted once if s/he applies for help with the same problem over a week.

GTST in Rotterdam

Linking Records of Homeless People from Different Sources

The project aims at listing the potentials for research based on data in already-existing registration systems. Its aim is not to develop a new kind of registration in which the administrations of institutions are combined, but a data set is developed based on data already there. The combination of data of different sources is essential so that individual patients can be traced on their way through the institutions and more accurate descriptions of problems can be found. From the existing registrations a data set can be built up over a number of years which then offers possibilities for longitudinal research and is at the same time a sampling frame for ethnographical research.

At first the project aims at homeless in the non-commercial shelters for the homeless. It means that roofless and homeless in commercial boarding houses are excluded. Of course people sleeping rough will also sometimes use shelters and then be part of the data set. It is not known how many of the roofless and otherwise sheltered will be found, though.

The research is limited to Greater Rotterdam and aims at answering the following questions:

- how many homeless have been treated by mental health care institutions or addiction care in 1994;
- what kind of help was last used by the homeless: intramural, extramural or semi-mural (psychiatric hospitals, addiction clinics, drug programmes, ambulant mental health care);
- how recent is their last contact;
- how was intense was the use of care over the last five years and are there patterns to be discerned;
- do heavy users have different characteristics from other homeless?

After the pilot project has succeeded, questions such as where the homeless came from, in what way they used care and where they went afterwards can be answered. Help-seeking behaviour and effectiveness of help for different categories will become clear. Through collecting data on all clients from the general social service, mental health care and care and treatment of addiction facilities, it can be seen which kind of clients become part of the homeless population so that risks of becoming homeless can be detected.

Existing Registration Systems

In the region of Rotterdam a number of registrations already exist which, when combined, can give a more complete view on the number of homeless and the 'careers' people make through different care institutions.

Short stay facilities and day care facilities: they register all clients that used these facilities. Other facilities might be included in the project later. Next to these administrations of institutions dealing with homeless are more general registration systems, such as:

- general social work;
- (psychiatric) crisis centres;
- drug care: data on all persons who applied for help in methadon programmes, alcohol and drugs care and clinics for addicts, regarding age, sex, marital status;
- medical data: health status, life-time prevalence of psychotic episodes, etc. and institutions that have referred to other institutions;
- mental health care: all municipal mental health care facilities register their clients: day care, ambulant care, mental hospitals, protected living arrangements: demographic characteristics, use of care, referrals from other institutions, legal status, diagnosis data of entering and leaving, etc.

Method Used: Record Linkage

Research among homeless mainly limits itself to surveys and non-structured interviews. Registered data are only rarely used. Combination of data of different registrations is possible without endangering the privacy of clients involved: through probabilistic linkage, on a limited number of personal identifying characteristics (first two characters of last name, date of birth, sex, etc.) records of clients in the homeless population can be matched with records of clients in other registrations. When applicable, the same number is applied to these records, which are considered, with a limited uncertainty, to be of the same person.

To protect privacy identifying data are only used during the linkage process. The procedure might be compared to what is usually done by mail surveys during which addresses are separated from survey data but used in order to be able to administer questionnaires sent back. After the linkage an anonymous new data set remains. Identification is still possible, but only in the institution from where the record originates. Thus, a sampling frame can be used.

Comments, Conclusions, Recommendations

Registering useful data on homelessness is a difficult matter. In this report we have described two examples of ways of getting data. Here we will comment on both.

KLIMOP

The institutions from which the data on homeless are collected are typical welfare institutions. Their autonomy is high and considered important, their work is to help clients and not to collect data. Moreover, registering data takes considerable time and money if it is to be done carefully. The need for data in this case originated in the subsidising bodies. Since decentralisation has meant that institutions' managements must present data on their performance to local authorities, the importance of a recognised registration system seems to be growing. Even so, the staff members who have to spend their time on filling in the forms have to be convinced that it is useful for them to register. The KLIMOP system allows itself to be extended for local use, where staff can benefit from data on treatment, extra characteristics they are interested in, etc. This possibility does not seem to be greatly used, which means that, as well as the KLIMOP system, institutions still operate their own systems.

The successful introduction of a central registration system takes a long time and should be done very carefully. Technical demands, but especially discussions on what items to enter in the questionnaire, which definitions to use, how to interpret different situations, etc., take considerable time. Moreover, since the field is continually changing, continuous updates are essential. A central help desk where institutions can get assistance in technical and interpretation matters is also essential.

Since the number of institutions that register data through KLIMOP will be extended, a more complete overview of the homeless population will be reached. Data that are registered up until now stress social-psychological factors, stemming from the traditional characteristics of the homeless and of the institutions themselves. This means that data from which more insight can be deduced in structural causes of homelessness are only marginally touched upon. Data on poverty over a longer period, for example, could be gathered. Another possible extension might be to gather more information on previous addresses and situations in order to build up a better view of the relationships between homelessness, rooflessness and being marginally accommodated. Also, more detailed information on the health situation might be helpful. Of course, this would involve considerable efforts, but might be worthwhile. Because the collected data on the national level are of great importance and the only data available, they should be accessible for researchers.

The Rotterdam Pilot Project

Since no new data are collected here, the problems of the introduction and careful use of the registration systems do not play a role. In effect, both systems are complementary. The Rotterdam approach allows researchers to go into considerable detail by carefully examining records of clients and if possible contacting homeless people individually, sampled from the sample population.

As with KLIMOP, in this project also no data will be available on the roofless and marginally housed people. However, as soon as these people contact a care institution they will be registered and then be part of the system. Only those who never contact these institutions will be excluded. Of course, the geographical scale is limited to the Rotterdam region.

The Rotterdam project promises a longitudinal approach; we must wait to see how accurate, complete and reliable data over a longer period will be.

Bibliography

Federatie Opvang (1995), *De maatschappelijke opvang in cijfers* [*(Institutionalized) Social care in figures: 1994*], Utrecht.

Health Council of The Netherlands: Committee on Roofless and Homeless (1995), *Roofless and Homeless*, The Hague: Health Council.

Wierdsma, A.I. and van Neijenhof, G.A.M. (1996), *Gemarginaliseerden, thuislozen in de stad Rotterdam, Aanzet voor een longitudinaal onderzoek naar thuisloosheid* [*Marginalised, homeless in the city of Rotterdam, proposal for a longitudinal research project into homelessness*], Rotterdam.

9   Living in the Streets of Vienna: The Methodology of the 1993 ICCR Study

ANGELIKA KOFLER

Introduction

Homelessness is a research topic not quite like any other. Empirical research about homelessness poses considerable methodological problems. Therefore, in many cases, homelessness researchers employ expert interviews with representatives of facilities for the homeless, secondary analyses of official statistics, or institutional studies that concern themselves with the theoretical effects of existing judicial and social regulations. Studies that orient themselves on the homeless population itself are the exception rather than the rule. If researchers do choose that approach, one finds typically two kinds of research designs, that is, either purely qualitative studies, mostly Masters theses or dissertations, or reports about the experiences of clients of specific facilities or investigations of certain policies. Naturally, all of these methods of compromise have inherent flaws and do not lead to more than the customary vague estimates about the extent of the homeless population and selective perspectives of their actual circumstances.

In the following, first, some of the idiosyncrasies of homelessness research as such will be pointed out. Second, the approach chosen by the 1993 study (Scharinger, 1993) of homelessness conducted by the Interdisciplinary Centre for Comparative Research in the Social Sciences – International (ICCR) that employed a combination of methods will be described[1] and commented upon in terms of the methodology that the researchers used. The case example is to illustrate how homelessness researchers have attempted to adapt standard methods to overcome some of the methodological difficulties in the exploration of the research populations' life situation and quality of life – or lack thereof.

The Idiosyncrasies of Homelessness Research

Theories

Just as empirical research of homelessness is the exception rather than the rule, theory development has a good way to go as well. So far, underlying assumptions that inform consequent definitions of terms can be roughly categorised into four theoretical models that researchers have been employing since the 1970s (Scharinger, 1993). Typically, the theories' starting points are either class, social ecology, the dysfunctional family, or the life situation.

The *Marxist model* presupposes material impoverishment within the capitalistic production system whose structure would be directly correlated with homelessness. Within this belief system, homelessness careers follow the temporary or permanent exclusion from the production process. Structural circumstances diminish the subjective capacity to act. Khella (1974) rejects the term 'marginalised group' and rather sees the homeless as members of a degraded proletariat. He holds societal and economic structures responsible for increasing poverty and consequent psychopathologies. This model assumes that all forms of physical and psychological deterioration of the homeless are directly caused by the production system. It also infers that all families or individuals would cope with structurally caused poverty in a uniform way. Moreover, the model assumes that the worker with access to housing and the homeless have identical interests and are bound by solidarity between them, thereby neglecting significant dimensions of social inequalities.

The *social ecology model* builds upon criticism of the class model. The social-ecological approach blames spatial segregation processes for homelessness thus assuming a correlation between spatial and social distance that insulates different population groups from each other. In cases of voluntary segregation, members of the same layers of society aggregate in certain neighbourhoods which creates distance to other groups. What can be held against this model is that forced segregation is a more complex phenomenon. Poverty and the resulting stigma can become even more problematic than the economic situation itself in that they increase the symbolic value of housing as indicator of social status even beyond its practical value.

The *dysfunction family model* focuses on consequences on the family system in the context of impoverishment and the resulting homelessness. Early predecessors of this model can already be found in nineteenth century literature where poor families were diagnosed with permanent dysfunction and consequently deprived of their potential entitlements. More recent advocates of this approach attempt to link the loss of a home with specific dysfunctional variables within the family. Weins (19983) sees death, illness, divorce or alcoholism as such indicators. It is indeed a reality that many of these factors are often part of the life histories of homeless individuals, yet direct causality cannot be assumed. Furthermore, the model implies that a particular family member is at fault and consequently structural changes in the social protection system would not be necessary. A distinction between 'innocent' and 'guilty', 'better' and 'worse' homeless people tends to reinforce simplistic perceptions of this population and makes for an ethically dangerous basis for social science research.

The *life situation concept* stresses three major factors that influence situational circumstances of the homeless: the structural environment, group values and family resources. The model uses the assumption of unequal distribution of resources as frame of reference for the analysis of societal structures, of predominant values in certain milieus and of individual coping strategies of the homeless. Several surveys of homeless families in asylums took that model as their starting point.

Independent from theoretical preferences, it can be safely assumed that the phenomenon of homelessness is a multifaceted one. Therefore, research as well as theoretical starting points have to take as many potential variables as possible into account when probing for the causes, the extent, and the circumstances of homelessness. A comprehensive contemporary theoretical model of homelessness, embedded in the context of social exclusion, in general, still needs to be developed. It should be based on empirical research and needs to do justice to the complexity of the phenomenon on the structural, the group, and the individual level.

Definitions

The pitfalls in carrying out homelessness research start already with defining the phenomenon. Definitions of 'homelessness' vary across the literature. One encounters a variety of attempts to operationalise the term that not only reflect particular attitudes and motivations but that also exemplify the difficulty of systematic research about homelessness itself. Concepts of 'home' or 'homelessness' are laden with implications and complications. Definitions, at times, surmise intent of the victim and distinguish between 'worthy' and 'not worthy' homeless persons – as happened to be the infamous practice during the Nazi regime. While this may be a drastic example of definitional consequences, the fact remains that to this day the way 'homelessness' is defined has consequences of an administrative as well as of a political nature.

Definitions currently in use may focus only on homeless people who use services to facilitate operationalisation; researchers may choose to consider someone as homeless only then when s/he has been without housing for a minimum period of time; it might be decided not to include individuals and families who live with relatives in the definition of homeless persons, even if their residential arrangements are not a matter of choice but the lack of their own housing; inadequate housing, in general, may or may not be considered homelessness; some researchers may define those in mental or drug treatment institutions as homeless, too; or wish to make a distinction between a family that has been evicted and someone that has been living in the streets for years. (For an overview of definitional approaches see Avramov, 1996, and also the conclusion to this section.)

Counting and Access

Estimates and access are further typical problems encountered. Due to the nature of the research population, estimates need to be approached with particular care. The methods that have been used for the purpose range from 'counting nights' in the 'darkest corners of the country' to mere expert interviews. In both cases, results are often disappointing and lead to the conclusion that this population simply cannot be counted, or if the attempt is made after all, double-counts or under-counts are a serious challenge to the researcher.

One of the central problems in empirical research about homelessness is to find a form of access to the population that can yield representative samples. What often follows is a research-pragmatic design. One possible consequence is that service providers become the spokespersons for the actual research population. Alternatively, researchers may refrain from empirical investigations altogether and rely on secondary sources.

Data

Empirical research about homelessness is in Austria as absent as in many other European countries. It is known to the housing authorities who and how many apply for public housing. Court records on eviction proceedings and consequent appeals, that can be filed based on the argument that the party is threatened by homelessness if evicted, are available. Service providers keep records that indicate basic data on their clients to varying degrees of reliability. Often these statistics are based on anonymised data, a practice which poses methodological problems – the likelihood of double-counts, for example – in itself. The authorities have data on recipients of Social Security and social welfare benefits.

In a non-systematic and hardly scientifically useful and accessible way, part of the homeless population in Austria can be traced, at least sporadically, for example, through records at either the facilities for the homeless or the social welfare authorities; but efforts to gather centralised and comparable data from service providers are only at their modest beginnings.

Coherent data on homelessness in Austria that could provide a sensible set of documentation sources that, moreover, would take regional differences into account, are yet missing. Furthermore, the availability of documentation depends often on the motivation and efforts of local actors. For scientific purposes none of these available records are meaningful for one or both of two reasons: either the data are not collected and analysed in a scientifically useful and reliable way as is often the case with records kept by service providers; or access restrictions apply as is the case with files on homeless individuals that are known to the social welfare authorities. Furthermore, these existing relevant records are neither linked in any systematic way, nor are they a source of information that can trace individual mobility or the development of the actual circumstances and histories of homelessness over time. None of the existing records allow conclusions about the number of homeless and their social circumstances without a legend of cautionary footnotes. In other words, in Austria, as in many other countries, usable data on homelessness is sparse and expressed in terms of practically nonexistent scientific criteria.

The Methodology of the Vienna Study

Objectives

The study was undertaken at a time when Austrian social scientists started to recognise homelessness as a research topic of importance and interest. Two studies from the 1980s made the feasibility and necessity of the enterprise particularly clear to the researchers: a controversial work of the Viennese sociologist Roland Girtler who portrayed the homeless as the creators of their own subculture who strive to bring about their own social network independent from society; and the 1987 empirical study of Wögerer et al., the only existing empirical investigation until then, that was limited to the perspective of service providers and above all suffered from methodological flaws that yielded contradictory data.

In order realistically to evaluate the social situation of the homeless, the researchers thought it crucial that, above all, the homeless themselves should be at the centre of attention and to keep in mind that homelessness is a multifarious phenomenon. This philosophy underlies the methodological approach that was developed. Furthermore, the study is understood as applied research; it was the objective that results should be applicable and a solid basis for social policy recommendations.

In order to achieve these goals, the researchers set out to compare the characteristics of the homeless population with the population as a whole; to verify or disprove the legitimacy of the perception of homeless people; to explore the connection between life histories and housing careers; to generate solid data that allows an estimate about the number of homeless people; to explore the connection between work histories and housing careers; and finally to identify risk factors to create a basis for policy-relevant recommendations. With these specific aims in mind, an innovative methodology customised to capture indigenous circumstances was developed.

Definitions

The definitions of homelessness that were chosen for this study follow Schuler and Sauter. These definitions had been already empirically tested and are based on situational facts rather than implied causes or personal characteristics and distinguish people who are actually homeless, threatened by homelessness, or potentially homeless.

Actual homelessness concerns individuals or families who lack a personal dwelling and live in the streets (in condemned buildings, railroad cars, public toilets, subway stations, under bridges, in open spaces) or in public emergency shelters, facilities for the homeless. The term also includes former inhabitants of such facilities whose permanent and sufficient accommodation is not yet ensured.

Threatened by homelessness are those who live under the immediate threat of losing their present residence, or live under unacceptable housing conditions because they are unable to access an adequate personal residence on their own, or live under circumstances of insecure tenure (no rent contract, staying with friends and family).

Potential homelessness concerns persons whose loss of their personal dwelling is not yet an immediate danger but for whom homelessness may still be a looming threat due to their insufficient income and the inadequacy of their present housing situation.

The study at hand has concerned itself almost exclusively with the social situation of the first category, that is, individuals who live under circumstances of *actual* homelessness.

Sample

The homeless The sample from the homeless population comprised individuals from heterogeneous backgrounds as far as age, sex, life experience, location or status of residence was concerned. During the first stage of data collection, in depth-interviews were conducted after which the standardised questionnaire, used for the sample of stage two, was developed.

In total, a sample of about 200 homeless people was envisioned, the actual stratified quota sample consisted of 235 homeless individuals. The homeless population targeted for the study, according to the working definition, included only men and women who were *actually* homeless, that is excluding those who may be potentially homeless or immediately threatened by homelessness but have not yet reached that stage. (For an overview of sample characteristics see Table 9.1.)

At the time of the interviews, 52 per cent of the respondents lived in hostels or other accommodation facilities for the homeless, 34 per cent lived in the streets, 11 per cent with friends or relatives, and three per cent in sub-let housing, communal residences or bed and breakfast places; 44 female (19 per cent) and 191 (81 per cent) male homeless persons were interviewed (N = 235). The apparent disproportionate number of men is not indicative of homelessness being a male problem, though. Instead it indicates differences along gender lines on a number of variables.

The majority of the homeless interview partners (85 per cent) were single at the time of the interviews. About half were never married, about 40 per cent divorced. More than a quarter of the subjects had children and custody for them. Twenty per cent of the females still lived with their children.

The respondents were between 18 and 80 years old, with the mode being 38 years. Ninety-two per cent were Austrian citizens, 48 per cent were born in Vienna. The majority of the non-Viennese originated from other federal states of Austria, in particular Upper and Lower Austria and Styria. Only 30 per cent of those not originally from Vienna came from rural areas, the majority migrated to Vienna from other Austrian cities.

It is of importance to note that the study dealt only in a limited way with

Table 9.1   Overview sample characteristics (N = 235)

Sex
Male	81 %
Female	19 %

Age
Range	62 years
Median	39.5 years
Mode	38 years

Marital status
Single	85 %
Living with partner	15 %

Geographical origin
Vienna	48 %
Austrian citizens	92 %
Other citizenship or no citizenship	8 %
Rural areas	30 %

Accommodation at time of interview
Hostels and other accommodation facilities for the homeless	52 %
Streets	34 %
Friends, relatives	11 %
Sub-leases, communal residence, bed & breakfast	3 %

Duration of homelessness
Range	40 years
Mean females	5 years
Mode males	6 years

the housing situation of individuals with non-Austrian citizenship. Only a relatively low percentage of non-Austrian citizens lives in a situation of actual homelessness. Reasons for this include specific forms of habitations, such as mass lodgings, short-term leases, situations of insecure tenure, extremely small apartments and family structures. However, the conclusion that non-Austrian citizens living in Vienna do not have to deal with the problem of homelessness cannot be drawn. Quite on the contrary: due to the described housing situations, foreigners form the majority of those who are threatened by homelessness according to the operational definition. At the time of the study, in 1993, about 58,000 non-Austrians and 14,000 Austrians lived in spaces with less than 10 square meters which for non-Austrian citizens means not only the potential loss of the dwelling but also the loss of their visa. These numbers alone exemplify very clearly the extent of those threatened by homelessness who, however, have not been the research population for this study.

Access to the sample of homeless subjects was gained through two kinds of locations: service facilities for the homeless and typical areas where homeless people can be found. That is, 21 facilities for the homeless, ranging from emergency shelters to transitory homes, three railway stations, and two busy subway stations. Based on a key, constructed in accordance with the number of clients in the facilities and expert estimates, the choice of locations and the corresponding number of interviews was selected.

The police and the experts A written request to comment on a number of key issues was sent to more than 100 police stations and followed by interviews at all 23 Viennese police precincts. Police were questioned about their perceptions of the homeless population. The data gained during this step contributed to the estimate of homeless persons and allowed important insights into the modes of communication between a marginalised group and the Viennese police.

In addition, experts whose work related to the homeless – social workers, civil servants of the housing authorities and social agencies as well as railroad officials – were approached. Starting points to access the sample of experts were thus sleeping places of homeless (interview partners ranged from railway stations officials to security personnel to shelter employees). Further types of experts were recruited from employment services for the homeless; from organisations providing legal advice (in terms of debt counselling, legal problems of psychiatric patients, eviction); from facilities for different target groups (ranging from homeless singles to homeless families, convicts, long-term unemployed, women, addicts, foreigners); and from specific services (such as day centres, street work, food supply schemes, and clothing distribution centres).

Instruments

The instruments used were developed in accordance with the objectives of the study as well as with the pragmatic considerations of the fieldwork in mind. The methodological approach comprised the use of the following methodological tools:

- guidelines for preliminary, structured qualitative in-depth interviews with homeless individuals;
- a standardised questionnaire for interviews with homeless individuals;
- guidelines for structured interviews with police; and

- guidelines for structured expert interviews with public and private service providers, housing agencies, and railroad officials.

Guidelines for structured in-depth interviews with the homeless These interviews were conducted to collect the qualitative, biographical data. The questions asked addressed three major thematic categories: social demographic status; experienced forms of housing; and work experiences. Special attention was paid to document paths of development and to probe for critical stages. Specifically, the questions addressed the following major themes: present housing problems; duration of present situation; worst housing situations; life story; major changes in housing career; types of households experienced; duration of housing problems and present situation; origin of present housing problems; desired housing form; relationship between housing and employment situation (and visa); health problems; the relationship between alcohol and homelessness; work experience and educational background; present occupation and circumstances; economic difficulties and context; legal problems and context; evaluation of the likelihood to find housing; desire for housing; social relationships; daily activities; and demographic features.

In addition, the interviewers were asked to evaluate the interview partners. They were asked to indicate their perception of the likelihood that the respondent will achieve desired outcomes (in terms of ability and of usage and knowledge of services); the fieldworkers also assessed the interview partners' level of marginalisation (temporary, permanent, institutionalised); the interview situation (chaotic, organised); and the respondents' ability for realistic judgments (self-image, motivation).

The questions were partly closed- and partly open-ended, thus allowing for in-depth narratives. This mixed format made for a maximum of qualitative data while at the same time keeping the wealth of data yielded manageable.

The standardised questionnaire Based on the results of these first in-depth interviews, the standardised instrument was developed. Some of the items of the questionnaire pertain specifically to the Austrian or Viennese situation for the homeless. That concerns, for example, specific forms of benefits from the social system, legal requirements for non-citizens, or questions regarding a very specific form of registration of residence, the so-called *Nichtmeldeschein*, an administrative device created particularly for the homeless to remove an obstacle homeless people have to overcome, namely the fact that registration of residence is the prerequisite for most dealings with the authorities.

The questionnaire covered basic demographic data (age, sex, educational background, work experience, marital status, children); for the cases of non-citizens their legal status; form of registration of residence; criminal record; reasons for moving to Vienna (where applicable); housing history; employment history; key problems leading to deterioration; daily activities; contacts with other homeless; typical and current sleeping places; satisfaction with 'housing' situation; evaluation of future housing situation; debts; forms and extent of income; health status (including addiction problems); desire to work; wishes for improvement; and also left room for other comments.

The standardised questionnaire, too, asked the interviewers to indicate their perceptions of the respondents and the interview situation. They were asked to comment upon the interview situation; the appearance of the respondents; the credibility and realism of the respondents' answers; the likelihood of the situation to be permanent or temporary, and perceived main problems.

Guidelines for structured interviews with police and experts The guidelines for the structured interviews with *police* probed for information covering the following points: locations of homeless people in the district; the number of homeless people observed there; the fluctuation of their numbers depending on the season and time of the day; information on specific categories (men/women, different age groups, drug addicts, singles and homeless families, foreigners); contacts with the homeless and consequent experiences and problems; reasons and initiating agent for contact, cooperation with other agencies; knowledge about the homeless individuals; perceived daily activities of homeless; changes in homeless environment and explanation; and knowledge about service providers for the homeless including experiences in these terms.

The guidelines for *expert interviews* at facilities for the homeless instructed the fieldworkers to gather information on the following: description of client population (demographic data, problem areas, previous accommodation, duration of care, housing desired); admission criteria; concept of institution; utilisation of facility in March 1993 and summer 1993; seasonal fluctuations; other fluctuation; description of institution (size, capacity, professional training of personnel, financing); wishes, recommendations, criticism of social policies (major problems).

For expert interviews with persons other than representatives of service providers, the questions were modified accordingly. Officials at the railway stations were thus asked in interview whether there are homeless people to be found at their station, if so, where (waiting rooms, railroad cars, condemned buildings); if they could estimate their number; seasonal fluctuation; they were asked to characterise the homeless (in terms of the male/female ratio, age, drugs, single, non-citizens, etc.); and also which problems does their administration would have with them, and if any major changes had been observed recently.

Procedure

Over a period of two months, August and September 1992, three certified social workers conducted exploratory interviews with 15 homeless men and women based on the guidelines described above and gained first insights about the life experiences and housing careers of their respondents. The interviewers had been instructed verbally and in written form about the specific procedure they had to follow. The interviews were recorded on audio tapes. The work during this phase contributed in a crucial way to the development of the standardised questionnaire that was used in the second stage.

The data gained by means of the standardised questionnaire was collected in the first week of March 1993 by students of the Social Academy. The students had also been instructed verbally and in written form about specific procedures and contextual background. Two hundred and seventeen such interviews with homeless individuals were conducted. An additional 18 had already been interviewed during the pretesting phase.

Expert interviews and interviews with police were conducted by members of the ICCR research staff themselves who also developed the design.

Data Analysis and Selected Results Relevant in Terms of Methodological Implications

The qualitative and quantitative data was coded and processed with standard statistical means via SPSS. No additional statistical techniques, such as applying weights, were deemed necessary. The researchers applied particular caution when they used the results of the study to estimate the number of homeless persons in Vienna. The estimate of the ICCR study is based on three independent sources which was also considered a means to safeguard as much as possible against double-counts and under-counts.

The following selected results will exemplify the kind of data that could be collected by means of the described methodology. As it is not the purpose of this article to present the complete set of results of this study but to discuss methodology, three areas have been selected that make a methodological point; first, the results gained from the variable 'registration of residence;' second, the numerical estimate; and third, gender differences between homeless men and women to exemplify methodological adaptation to indigenous characteristics.

Registration of residence

In Austria, everyone, citizens as well as non-citizens, has to register their place of residence with the police. This *Meldezettel* is the basis for most dealings with the authorities. For the homeless population it is particularly relevant in order to receive Social Welfare Assistance and other forms of public support. Thus, the City of Vienna created a so-called *Nichtmeldeschein* for the homeless that registers them despite the lack of housing and allows them to avoid obstacles in terms of administrative procedures.

The study showed that homeless individuals differ in their approach to registrations of residence. In the unique context of the Austrian system, form of accommodation and the form of registration of place are significantly linked. Different practices of the respondents led to conclusions about their individual characteristics: those not registered anywhere at all, neither *pro forma* at acquaintances' or relatives' places or at an institution, not even by means of this unique administrative device, tended to prefer withdrawal and being as little visible as possible; and importantly, this variable proved to be a valuable tool to estimate the number of homeless people.

Table 9.2   Form of registration of place (N = 235)

Form of registration	%
In facility for the homeless	54
Special registration for homeless people (*Nichtmeldeschein*)	20
Fake registration	7
No registration	19

What this variable exemplifies in terms of methodological implication is that unique local characteristics have to be taken into account in order to get a grasp on the research topic. Unique local features, such as a form documenting non-registration of residence may be a valuable data source. A different form of integrating indigenous features would be feasible if one were to study rural homelessness or any other area where local circumstances differ from other areas. In fact, one of the major points that this study makes is that innovative and creative concepts and combinations of standard methods are particularly appropriate and needed to overcome the difficulties in difficult research areas like homelessness.

The Numerical Estimate

The primary source for the numerical estimate was the questionnaires, particularly the responses to the items that asked for the number of other known homeless, their rate of fluctuation, and the form of registration of place. Based on the rate of registration of those living in facilities for the homeless, a first step towards a reasonable estimate could be achieved.

A second input source for the estimate was gained from the data collected from police. The comparison of these two data sources showed a surprisingly high correspondence. Where discrepancies were found, the third data source, that is, the interviews with railroad officials were used. In addition, for most railway stations, statistics were available that indicated the number of homeless that had been stopped by security personnel (*Wachdienst*).

Based on these three independent sources an estimate of about 1,500 to 1,700 actually homeless people living on the streets was made. This first procedure indicates mainly those homeless individuals who are most visible to police as well as other homeless people. As the research showed, however, some of those who live in the streets consciously avoid places where other homeless typically can be found and tend to withdraw from visibility as much as possible.

A more detailed analysis showed that the form of registration of residence and public visibility were clearly linked: individuals who were registered by means of the so-called *Nichtmeldeschein*, the unique form of registration of residence available to the homeless described above, and those who are fake-registered at a residence they do not actually live at, fall into the category of publicly visible homeless people. Those who are not registered in any way tend to live more withdrawn from the public eye. Estimates of these loners yielded a number of about 600–700 homeless individuals who are perceived only sporadically by others. Both groups together thus made for the number of 2,300–2,400 homeless persons living in the streets. In sum, the number of homeless in Vienna at the beginning of March 1993, was therefore estimated to amount to about 4,700–4,800 persons. This number, despite the inherent problems of counting the homeless, can be considered a solid guiding figure of actually homeless people.

Male and Female Homelessness

How crucial the development of innovative methodologies should be considered is also exemplified with another set of results: the study showed clear quantitative as well as qualitative differences between male and female homelessness. Differences emerged especially with regard to marital status, accommodation and form of registration of residence, education and work experience.

Especially the contextual biographical data showed causal factors as distinct between the sexes. While economic reasons are relevant for both, women, especially single mothers are at an increased risk. Moreover, homelessness of women has its origin mostly in personal conflicts which lead to severe financial problems caused by their economic dependence. Almost 40 per cent of women traced their homelessness back to relationship problems and personal crises. The majority lost their last secure housing situation through separation or divorce. For men, on the other hand, the loss of their job or stays in prison or an institution is more typically the immediate trigger of homelessness, apart from family and financial problems.

It appears that women not only fall into homelessness due to personal problems more often than men, they also are more likely to find personalised solutions such as looking for help from family and friends or trying to start over with another partner. One of the reasons for this gender difference in coping strategies might be the fact that about 40 per cent of the female respondents had custody of one or more children, and 20 per cent were still living with their children, whereas only one of the homeless men was still living with his child. If personal resources do not suffice, women are also more likely than men to look for shelter in facilities for the homeless. More than 80 per cent of the female respondents were registered at facilities for the homeless, compared to 45 per cent of the homeless men. Only 10 per cent of women lived in the streets, compared to 40 per cent of the males.

The clear gender differences that emerged do have methodological implications. The results indicate that female homelessness runs a different course, is less visible and therefore also more difficult to identify. That implies the necessity of gender-differentiated research methods. The methodological challenge of tracing hidden homelessness is thus particularly relevant for women. A similar method is needed to study those parts of the homeless population that have not been the focus of this study, namely those threatened by homelessness or those who may potentially become homeless.

Differences in accommodation strategies particularly point out the need

Table 9.3   Overview gender differences between homeless men and women (in %) (N = 235)

Variable	Homeless men	Homeless women
Age		
18–29 years	22.0	36.0
30–39	27.0	14.0
40–49	30.0	27.0
50–59	16.0	13.0
60–69	4.5	10.0
70–	0.5	–
Marital status		
Single	54.0	23.0
Married	8.0	27.0
Divorced	36.0	48.0
Widowed	2.0	2.0
Education		
Grade school	42.0	56.0
Vocational school	48.0	38.0
High school	4.0	2.0
College/university	2.0	2.0
No school finished	4.0	2.0
Job training		
None	30.0	56.0
Industry/business	55.0	16.0
Retail/transport	6.0	10.0
Service sector	4.0	10.0
Administration	2.0	5.0
Duration of homelessness		
6 months	10.0	16.0
6 months–1 year	10.0	14.0
1–3 year(s)	23.0	21.0
3–5 years	17.0	24.0
5–10 years	22.0	6.0
more than 10 years	18.0	19.0

to take gender as a variable into consideration when creating research designs (see Table 9.4).

Other Observations

The fact that several independent sources were used made this study highly

Table 9.4   Overview gender differences in accommodation (N = 235)

	Homeless men	Homeless women
Accommodation at time of interview		
Hostel, shelter	45	81
Street	39	11
Friends	11	8
Relatives	1	–
Sublease/communal residence/bed & breakfast	4	–
Main accommodation in winter		
Hostel, shelter	44	61
Street	37	16
Friends	10	9
Parents	1	4
With spouse	–	4
Sub-lease/communal residence/bed & breakfast	5	6
Prison	3	–
Main accommodation in summer		
Hostel/shelter	36	58
Street	40	16
Friends	7	17
Parents	–	–
With spouse	1	3
Sublease/communal residence/bed & breakfast	11	6
Prison	5	–
Experienced forms of housing		
Parents	109	132
Relatives	33	42
Friends	64	76
Children's home	40	60
Sub-let room	29	14
Own sub-let room	32	40
Own sub-let apartment	38	31
Apartment with spouse	45	53
Apartment provided by employer	19	21
Publicly funded apartment	22	31
Seasonal accommodation	15	5
Hostel/shelter	108	123
Bed & breakfast, hotel	14	12
Streets	120	67
Prison	84	12

	Homeless men	Homeless women
Last secure housing		
With spouse	20	23
Publicly funded apartment	17	15
Parents	17	15
Sub-lease	15	20
Own sub-lease	14	12
Apartment provided by employer	8	4
Relatives	3	5
Other (hostel, bed & breakfast, shelter)	6	6

representative. This is further evidenced by the rather high response rate that could be achieved. The reason for the high response rate might have been that the homeless in Vienna had not been subject to such inquiries before and therefore did not display the scepticism against researchers that might occur after repeated contacts with researchers without visible changes in their circumstances thereafter. During the first exploratory interviews with homeless men and women, the majority requested anonymity. However, after the interviews had been conducted, practically all interview partners requested to be quoted with their full names. Some indicated that the interviews had helped them to clarify their life situation and future plans. In most cases they explicitly stated the wish to continue the conversation. The willingness and – as it turned out in the course of the interview process – even eagerness of the homeless to cooperate with the researchers contributed to the fact that the achieved sample was actually larger than originally envisioned. Responsiveness of the experts and police had also been considerable. The police interviews could be conducted in all 23 Viennese districts, and the service facilities and railroad officials proved to be cooperative as well. The combination of these factors contributed significantly to facilitate the data analyses.

In terms of methodological implications for future research that is suggests great responsibility of researchers as well as of policy makers. When first approached, as has been the case with this study which was one of the first one's conducted in Austria, the respondents of the different populations are willing and even eager to cooperate. It can be assumed that this willingness is related to a certain confidence that research will also have an impact in terms of policy development. If it does not, however, attrition of potential respondents will most likely pose an additional problem to future researchers.

Conclusions

Despite the promising experiences and results of the study, a number of limitations are without doubt subject to discussion and warrant further research. Although it can be assumed that a large part of the Austrian homeless population can be found in the capital city, the fact that the presented study could cover only one city, albeit the largest, limits, of course, the possibility of drawing conclusions on homelessness in Austria as a whole. The numerical conclusions that can be drawn are limited to one Austrian city only. In addition, given that the practice of issuing a *Nichtmeldeschein* is not customary nationwide or in other countries, the method needs to be adjusted to the indigenous practices of other geographical locations were it to be applied elsewhere.

Another limitation is the fact that one of the important questions about homelessness that has implications for perceptions and policies could not be answered, namely how homelessness careers develop over time. To follow up this study and, even better, to develop an ongoing longitudinal project, could certainly contribute in a much more comprehensive way to the knowledge about the homeless and their social circumstances than a cross-sectional study can.

Of course, this desirable research design comes with its own methodological problems for which the present study has not provided answers either. How to follow the life histories of homeless individuals over time in order to assess to what extent homelessness is a temporary or permanent problem and how to make use of the insufficient official data and data from service providers are research questions in their own right that can only be addressed within the context of a long-term strategy. This is to say, links between data sources need to be established and existing forms of data collection need to be improved to provide a solid basis for a longitudinal project.

Another limitation of the described method is that it has been designed to research actual homelessness only. It does not and cannot trace hidden or invisible homelessness. The importance of researching not only actual homelessness but also risk populations can not be enough emphasised. Increasingly, risk groups, those segments of the population that is vulnerable to experience social deterioration, deserve attention. This, however, has not been the objective of this study. It follows that the methodology cannot be used for such purposes which is not to say that it should not be extended accordingly.

Its strength is certainly the combination of methods and sample populations that allow for a more comprehensive understanding of objective and subjective aspects of homelessness. The major methodological feature of this study is its use of more than one instrument and of several independent sources thus measuring the qualitative as well as the quantitative aspects of homelessness at a given point in time. The discourse on the topic at times questions the necessity of numerical estimates. Given how little empirical research on homelessness is available, one could argue that any data that helps to gain as comprehensive a picture as possible should be advocated – which by no means alleges that quantitative data is superior to qualitative data. It seems important to keep in mind as many factors as possible in order to do justice to the research objectives. Populations outside the system need to be seen from their own perspective as well as from the point of view of the integrated populations on whom they do depend to a greater or lesser degree. Furthermore, the structural environment has to provide the context to analyse data gained from either population. This study has attempted to take such a multifaceted approach.

Given the fact, that empirical and scientifically sound research about homelessness in Austria simply does not exist, the study, although it is by now several years old, did and does have impact on policies. The study, being the only one of its kind in Austria, is still used and quoted extensively by political actors, media representatives, and service providers lobbying for their special concerns. It shows that scientific research based on committed and imaginative scientists is needed and indispensable.

Note

1   This report is based on the work Interdisciplinary Centre for Comparative Research in the Social Sciences – International (ICCR) that carried out the research. Claudia Galehr supervised the fieldwork, Christian Scharinger wrote the research report. Ronald J. Pohoryles, the director of the institute, has been the initiator and catalyst that made the research possible.

Bibliography

Avramov, D. (1996), *The invisible hand of the housing market: A study of effects of changes in the housing market on homelessness in the European Union*, Brussels, FEANTSA.

Friedrich and Fränkel-Dahman (1979), *Soziale Deprivation und Familiendynamik: Studien zur psychosozialen Realität von unterprivilegierten Familien und ihrer Veränderung durch ausgewählte Formen sozialer Praxis*, Göttingen.

220   *Coping with Homelessness*

Girtler, R. (1980), *Vagabunden der Großstadt. Teilnehmende Beobachtung in der Lebenswelt der 'Sandler' Wiens*, Stuttgart.

Khella, (1974), *Theorie und Praxis der Sozialarbeit und Sozialpädagogik: Einführung*, Hamburg.

Scharinger, C. (1993), *Du wülst wissen, wo i schlof': Zur Situation von akut Obdachlosen in Wien*, Eine Studie des IFS-ICCR im Auftrag der MA12 der Stadt Wien.

Schuler and Sauter (1986), *Obdachlosigkeit und soziale Brennpunkte in Hessen: Umfang, Struktur und Entwicklung der Obdachlosigkeit*, Darmstadt, Institut Wohnen und Umwelt.

Weins (1983), *Problemfamilien im Gemeindekontext: Eine theoretische und empirische Analyse*, Stuttgart.

Wögerer, U., Spring, C., Florian, H. and Wögerer, H. (1987), *Obdachlosigkeit in Österreich: Ursachen, Folgen und Maßnahmen*, Österreichisches Komitee für Sozialarbeit im Auftrag des Bundesministeriums für Arbeit und Soziales.

10 The Homeless in Paris: A Representative Sample Survey of Users of Services for the Homeless

MARYSE MARPSAT AND JEAN-MARIE FIRDION[1]

Introduction and Survey Context

In what follows we present the details of the method used by the Institut National d'Etudes Démographiques (INED) to conduct its survey on a representative sample of homeless people using shelter and food services in Paris, in winter 1994–95. The INED survey adopted some elements of the sample design and survey methods from American work in this field (Urban Institute, Research Triangle Institute), and incorporated a number of lessons drawn from these surveys. The sampling method elaborated by INED was applied by another team in winter 1995–96, thereby demonstrating its suitability for generalisation.

Homelessness in France

France experienced a serious housing crisis in the 1950s, due notably to the slow pace of reconstruction and the *exode rural* or heavy rural out-migration after the second world war (Taffin, 1993; Paugam, 1995). The present housing crisis seems to be of a different nature. It occurs in a context of economic crisis and growing insecurity of employment, and at a time when social and family bonds are being seriously weakened: these conditions coincide with a gradual disappearance of the 'stock of de facto social housing', that is, the low quality but cheap housing, whose demolition or renovation is followed by its original inhabitants being replaced by the better-off.

A variety of observers are agreed that the number of homeless in France is on the increase, and that some of their characteristics are changing: they now include more women, young persons, and immigrants fleeing the political and economic situation in their own countries (particularly those of Eastern Europe in recent years). However, we remain poorly informed about this extremely heterogeneous population, due to the methodological difficulties of subjecting it to a statistical approach (CNIS, 1995). Indeed, while there is no shortage of 'unofficial' estimates of their number, a reliable estimate is to date lacking. Until now, there has been no genuinely representative statistical survey of this population.

For these reasons, a request was made in 1993 by representatives of voluntary organisations and trade unions present in the CNIS (Conseil National de l'Information Statistique — National Council for Statistical Information)[2] for a national survey of homelessness. Qualitative and quantitative information was to be sought with which to assess the scale of the phenomenon and to identify not only the people excluded from housing but those threatened with becoming homeless.

The Survey Aims

The survey of homeless service users conducted in Paris by INED is part of this larger project. A number of experimental surveys were conducted in France during winter 1994–95 and in limited geographical zones, with the aim of producing: 'an investigative schema to apprehend as scientifically as possible the situation of people excluded from housing, the processes responsible for this exclusion and the difficulties that they face when seeking housing' (CNIS, 1995):

- a survey of households threatened by eviction;
- surveys of the homeless *stricto sensu* (including that of INED);
- surveys on the housing conditions of very low-income households.

The INED experimentation adapts to France the methods in use in the United States for several years. The main aim of this first study was to explore the conditions in which this sort of survey could be conducted and their application on a larger scale, and to draw up proposals for improving coverage of the homeless in the general population census as well as in the surveys usually conducted only on households in 'normal' dwellings. It was also intended to provide a preliminary exploration of the processes that lead someone to a situation of homelessness.

The INED research was conducted under the auspices of the CNIS, and in partnership with voluntary organisations and other agencies working with the homeless. Financial support came from the Commission of the European Community, the French Ministry of the Environment, the Ministry of Health and Social and Urban Affairs, and the Abbé Pierre Foundation.

The Method

Earlier Studies in the United States and France

Studies in the United States Studies of the homeless in the United States have been carried out since the start of the 1980s (for a further discussion of the comparative advantages of each method, see Burt, 1992 and in this volume; Firdion and Marpsat, 1994). Among the methods devised to conduct surveys of persons who are homeless *at one point in time (point prevalence)*, several generations can be distinguished.

The first generation of studies was based on the opinions of experts: this was the case of the figures produced by the Community for Creative Non-Violence (CCNV) (Hombs and Snyder, 1983), which sparked off the national debate about the number of homeless people; and of the estimate by the HUD (US Department of Housing and Urban Development, 1984). The latter estimate, obtained using a more rigorous methodology though also based in part on consulting experts, was severely criticised by militants working with the homeless.

For the second generation of studies, the surveys were conducted on a given night, simultaneously in the street (and in other places not intended for habitation, such as gardens, car parks ...) and in the shelters, at a time when their doors have been closed, thereby minimising the risk of double counting.

Examples of this method are the studies by the Nashville Coalition for the Homeless (Wiegand, 1985) and those of Peter Rossi in Chicago (Rossi et al., 1986 and 1987). Although this method has more solid scientific bases, serious problems arise concerning the collection of data in the street. This was the method experimented with by the US Bureau of the Census in 1990 (Taeuber and Siegel, 1991).

In the third generation of studies, the surveys were conducted in the day and over a longer period, in the 'services' provided for people in difficulty. Works of this kind include those of Burnam and Koegel on the Los Angeles skid-row area, those of Martha Burt of the Urban Institute on a national sample of towns and cities, and those of Michael Dennis et al. of the Research Triangle

Institute, whose survey was in fact the 'homeless people' component of a survey on drug-taking among the whole population of the Washington, DC, metropolitan area (Burnam and Koegel, 1988; Burt and Cohen, 1989; Dennis and Iachan, 1993). In the Urban Institute study, for example, the survey was carried out among users of the services provided by the shelters and soup kitchens. The Urban Institute drew up a comprehensive list of these services and produced a sample of homeless persons, after stratification by size and the type of service (meal, shelter with meal, shelter without meal). Service users were then sampled in each shelter and soup kitchen.

The main difficulty with this type of survey is how to avoid double-counting and to calculate the weightings to produce a representative sample. Correction has to be made for the differences in individual probabilities of selection for the sample, due to varying levels of service use.

This method was employed by the Bureau of the Census for the national survey of homeless people in 1996. For the next United States Census, in the year 2000, it is also planned to rely on the networks of services and abandon the night-time surveys. The INED experimentation adapted this sampling method to the French case.

In addition, a number of other studies have been carried out about *people who have been homeless at least once in the course of a given period (period prevalence)*. These studies use administrative records containing retrospective data (Culhane et al., 1993, on Philadelphia and New York; this work is being extended to other cities, under the name of the ANCHOR project), panel study type surveys (Sosin, Piliavin and Westerfelt, 1990, for Minneapolis), or telephone surveys of households in which they are asked 'have you ever been homeless?' (for example, Link et al., 1994).

Some studies are based on methods such as capture-recapture modelling (Cowan, 1991), but several attempts to apply such methods in the United Kingdom seem to lead to the conclusion that the precision of their estimates is rather low.

Mention can also be made of works of an ethnographic type (for example, Kim Hopper, 1991b, or Snow and Anderson, 1993).

Studies in France Few statistical works producing reliable results have been carried out in France. The population census (particularly the last one, which took place in 1990) counted the homeless in the street on a given day, though they are not identified as such in the statistics. This enumeration presents many difficulties, which are responsible for both double-counting and underestimation. At present there is no official estimate of the number of homeless in France, despite the fact that the homeless are part of the census field (CNIS, 1995).

Sampling

The survey field The INED survey was aimed at adults who were homeless in the 'strict' or 'literal' sense, that is who slept in shelters (emergency or long-stay)[3] or in the 'street' (including car parks, stations and other places not intended for habitation). The survey has a representative coverage of the members of this population who use the shelter and food distribution (including soup and coffee, at night) services for homeless people. However, we also wanted to include in the survey the individuals met on the food distribution sites who were in similar or borderline situations: so people living in squats and those who were not regularly lodged answered the same questionnaire as people without housing; individuals who were regularly lodged or who had housing answered a very similar questionnaire but which describes their current housing conditions (in order to identify the situations of substandard housing, overcrowding, threat of eviction, and possible periods of homeless experienced in the past). Consequently the interview begins with a screening questionnaire which does not eliminate anyone from the survey but instead orientates respondents to the questionnaire relevant to their particular housing situation.

The survey does not, however, cover the situation of the people sleeping in the street, in squats, or staying with friends, who do not use the food distribution services. A test conducted on a single night during the survey and aimed at people sleeping in the street, indicated that the number of these who never used any of the food distribution services is low. This result is confirmed by a series of in-depth interviews with people sleeping in the street, carried out over a three-month period.[4] The other people are in principle covered, albeit imperfectly, by the standard surveys conducted on households. A better knowledge of these other badly-housed groups will be an aim of future INED research.

The survey was conducted on the users of service centres in Paris intra-muros, to which were added the Centre d'accueil et de soins hospitaliers at Nanterre and the Corentin Celton centre at Issy-les-Moulineaux, which is where people brought from Paris by bus are taken.

The sample design The INED survey takes place in the day, over the course of one month, on users of night shelters and food and meal distributions, including mobile or outreach services.

It is a two-stage sample-survey of service users in Paris intra-muros.[5] Because the list of each type of service had to be exhaustive, we restricted our attention to three types:

- free meal distributions and soup kitchens (whose service is a meal);
- emergency shelters (whose service is provision of a bed for the night);
- CHRS[6] and long-stay shelters (whose service is provision of a bed for the night).

The sampling method used was to draw a random sample of individual services from among the sites of the zone over a given period, and to interview the person who received them. When these services have been enumerated and sampled, the probability of being included for the individuals sampled is then calculated, allowing for the multiplicity of the sampling frame.

The primary sampling units are the 'site-days', that is, the total of services supplied by a given site on any particular a day of the survey.[7] Sampling is thus done by place and by day. Selection of the sites is proportional to the number of services they provide per week (to allow for closed days). For each of the four weeks of the survey, four of the five open days were selected at random and assigned to the sampled sites. Six sites were designated for each day of the survey, making 96 primary units (site-days) corresponding to 56 different sites.

To reduce the variance due to the heterogeneity of the service users, sampling without replacement was carried out after an implicit stratification, whereby for each of the two frames the night shelters were classified according to the category of population they served,[8] then in descending size order. The sites of food distribution were directly classified by size.

The sampling of the secondary units (the services) was carried out at random on the basis of six services per primary unit (site-day) in the survey. The relationship between service and service user is established by calculation of the weighting, which adjusts for the probability of the user being in the different sampling frames.

A total of 591 questionnaires (of 606 theoretically planned) were answered anonymously in three partially overlapping sampling frames:

- 219 questionnaires in emergency shelters;
- 137 questionnaires in CHRS or other long-stay shelters;
- 235 questionnaires in food distribution sites.

The weightings (see below) were adjusted so as to allow for, as far as was possible, errors over site capacities and the number of interviews completed each day, as well as for the degree of overlap between the sampling frames in the course of a day.

Questionnaire Design

The interviews began with a *'screening' questionnaire* (questionnaire 1) whose purpose was to identify the housing situation of the respondents. Depending on their answers to questionnaire 1, the service users then went on to answer either questionnaire 2, if they had housing, or questionnaire 3, if they did not.

Between 'having housing' and 'not having housing', there is in reality no clear-cut division but rather a continuum of situations. For example, while a person who spends one night in an emergency shelter can be classified as 'homeless' without difficulty, there are some who use the same shelter each night for years on end. Other hostels, such as the CHRS, are reserved for people undergoing social re-insertion and offer a more stable form of accommodation, where personal effects can be left. Some of the CHRS are intended for families and take the form of self-contained flats. Moreover, it is possible for a person to be lodged by a relative or friend on a stable and long-term basis. Clearly there cannot be a questionnaire for each housing situation, so they had to be put in one category or another. However, an effort was made to describe these situations as clearly as possible in the screening questionnaire and in questionnaires 2 and 3.

A large range of topics is treated in *questionnaires 2 and 3*. The interviewers were able to take their time and conditions of privacy were reasonably good. However, the problem of where to complete the questionnaire did arise when surveying the people using the mobile soup kitchens. These distributions of food take place outdoors (streets, squares, etc.) and it was often necessary to 'retreat' to a nearby cafe.

Approximately 30 minutes were required to complete questionnaire 1 plus questionnaire 2 or 3. The interviewers had instructions that those who wished to, be allowed to speak for as long as they liked, and to write this information on the back of the printed sheets or in the margin, where a space was provided for this purpose. The completion time of the questionnaires was thus often longer, with an average length of approximately 35 minutes.

Questionnaire 1 (screener) establishes the individual's housing situation, and questionnaires 2 and 3 differ only by their 'housing' section. They start with the demographic characteristics of the subject, followed by some questions about their use of the services in the course of the previous week – this part of the questionnaire allows the weightings to be established so as not to give too great an importance to individuals who make heavy use of the services. The questions on housing reconstitute the residential history, and describe the present housing of the people who are 'housed'. Subsequent questions explore the family history and the links with the family, then work, education and occupation. Finally, there are some questions on the origin (though not the amount) of their monetary resources.

The interviewers ask some subjects if they would agree to meet them again, for a more probing interview, in which case a time and date is arranged. The statistical questionnaire is then complemented by a semi-directive interview, the aim of which is to better understand the processes responsible for their situation and to check the retrospective information contained in the questionnaire.

The retrospective part of the questionnaire is all that is needed to compute the weightings. The topic considered can be modified according to the preoccupations of those conducting future surveys (as is shown by the example of the survey on health and access to health care, conducted using the same sampling method in winter 1995–96 by a medical research team).

The Data Collection

The interviewers The interviewers chosen were those considered to possess particular qualities for the task, though for different reasons: some were seasoned interviewers with experience of surveys in difficult conditions; others were chosen for their specialist knowledge of the milieu and their ease of contact with homeless people, due to their usual work (social workers, researchers in this field) or to their personal commitment (voluntary work). Indeed, the very diverse needs of those involved were a source of some problems in the training; for a larger-scale operation, a longer period of training would be desirable, with specific sections according to the background of the interviewers. The training for the INED survey comprised two half-day sessions, between which the interviewers had to get a questionnaire completed with a homeless person. The difficulties that arose in the completion of this questionnaire were examined in the second session. The end-of-survey meeting also occupied half a day.

For the survey of service users, 39 interviewers were recruited. Of these, 18 already belonged to a network of interviewers (INED, INSEE, Sofres, or other), 12 were social workers, three members of voluntary organisations, it being possible for an individual to be in more than one category. The remaining interviewers were students, usually in sociology or anthropology, and researchers from the same subjects. The team was occasionally completed by members of INED.

It is worth noting that no interviewer gave up in the course of the field work. Notwithstanding the difficulties stemming from the technical complexity of the random selection of interviewees and from the problematic survey conditions (thoroughfares, outdoors, cold, rain, violent incidents), and the behavioural problems of some interviewees (problems of memory, understanding, incoherence), all the interviewers continued to the end of their mission.

Listing services in Paris intra-muros The first stage in the survey was the drawing up of a comprehensive (as far as possible) list of the shelter and food distribution services in Paris intra-muros.

A list was first prepared from existing lists. Advice was also sought from the CETAF[9] which had already catalogued services for the homeless. This first list included all the forms of help available in Paris: shelter, food, clothing, hygiene, health, counselling, etc. Completion of the list involved much telephoning, consulting the Maison des Associations (which centralises information about voluntary organisations), seeking the opinion of people with field expertise we had come in contact with, and taking note of information published in the press, including in the so-called 'homeless' press.

A comparison of these different sources revealed a number of encouraging similarities but also visible divergences over the size and characteristics of the service provided and its exact location. These lists are prepared with aims that are not those of the statistician, which explains why, for example, the number and types of services provided are listed at the administrative headquarters, whereas we required the exact address of each site. In addition, the various guides had been prepared for specific purposes depending on their mission (insertion, emergency, etc.), which explains in part the differences of approach.

Several strategies were used to check the information: the telephone and Minitel (videotext terminals), a questionnaire sent to the sites via the representatives of the main voluntary organisations belonging to or associated with the Collectif Solidarité de Paris, whose help was considerable. Lastly, it often proved necessary to visit the actual sites, notably for the voluntary groups who were difficult to contact outside the times when services were being provided. Establishing contact is harder in the case of the numerous small associations who are not well known and who are less likely to be listed than the larger ones.

Some of the voluntary organisations were reluctant to supply the information requested, in the belief that they had already been asked for the same thing for the preparation of the lists mentioned above, and this at a time when they were extremely busy preparing for the winter. However, once our purpose had been explained to them, they were often extremely cooperative and supplied us with other addresses.

The drawing up of this list occupied two people working full time over three months, and the entire INED survey service was mobilised for the final checking. The sampling frame produced comprised 36 emergency shelters, 46 CHRS and long-stay shelters, and 58 food distribution sites. Experience was to show that some mistakes remained: a shelter for under-18 year olds only, a voluntary organisation that did not provide accommodation itself.

A number of problems arose from the use for statistical purposes of lists prepared for non-statistical purposes.

As regards the size of the sites: these are theoretical capacities, which may be either exceeded or not reached. In the case of accommodation for families, the figure given may be for the number of flats, that is, the number of families, or the number of adults, or the total number of individuals including under-18-year-olds.

Some of the centres registered as providing help for the destitute in fact take in very few homeless people and are more akin to student and young people's hostels.

The characteristic of a centre may change from one year to another (size, type of individual admitted).

Centres close down and others open, something that is especially true of the structures that provide specifically wintertime shelter.

As for the food distributions, they count the number of meals served and not the number of people who are present, figures which may diverge widely in the case of mobile or outreach distributions.

Another difficulty stems paradoxically from the improved response to the problems of the homeless. It is increasingly common for the centres that provide help to offer a total care for individuals (health, administrative documents, food, employment, clothing, etc.), so that it becomes hard to distinguish all the services available in a single site.

Manpower constraints meant that attention in the later stage of the project was limited to meals and shelter. However, pilot tests showed the interest of extending the survey to clothes distributions and free medical services, which are used by some people who are not encountered anywhere else (individuals housed by a relative, squatters).

Sampling the services The night shelters and hostels were stratified by type (emergency, CHRS and long-stay) and classified according to the category of population they served.[10] In this way it was possible to include in the sample a number of small centres which serve very specific populations (lone women, single-parent families). The distinction between emergency and long-stay is of course blurred. Some centres where individuals are allowed to stay for only 10–15 days were treated as emergency shelters.

The shelters were then selected in proportion to their theoretical capacity.

The midday and evening meals in a single place were counted as two different 'services' except when it was known that they were served to the same people. Meals provided in a shelter and to its users only were not included. It was decided not to survey at breakfast time. However, the distinction between breakfast and midday meal is also sometimes blurred. In some centres, for example, a sandwich can be eaten between nine and 11 in the morning. The distinction made between breakfast and midday meal is of course simply a statistical convenience, one which may be more or less removed from the reality of eating habits among the homeless.

The places where meals are distributed were then selected with a probability proportional to the average number of meals served per week, so that allowance could be made for the day (or days) in the week when they were closed.

In all, a total of 98 primary sampling units were used, equal to approximately six units per day over 16 days of the survey, corresponding to 60 sites.

Four open days per week were drawn at random for each of the four weeks of the survey, between 13 February and 10 March. Each shelter or place of food distribution was allocated to one or several days. It was decided not to conduct the survey at weekends, since practices were likely to be different then (staying with the family or with friends, for example).

A letter was sent initially to the places selected, but very few replies, even to refuse, were received. A posteriori, this is not really surprising in view of the heavy workload of the organisations in the middle of winter. Contact was then established by telephone with all the sites that had been selected. This procedure proved more time-consuming than planned, as it had been thought that the letter would enable some cases, at least of refusal, to be settled in advance. The small number of sites which refused to participate in the survey were replaced by a site of the same type and from the same strata. A few difficulties arose as a result of unexpected days of closure (during the school holidays, for example), and the days when the absence of the person in charge led to changing the date.

In all, there were only five definitive refusals. It is clear that such refusals can easily be explained by a laudable desire to protect the individuals one is helping, and also by a heavy workload at this time of the year (to which was no doubt added the task of allocating the requisitioned housing made available by the public authorities following the much-publicised rue du Dragon squat: the voluntary organisations sometimes had to mobilise at very short notice to decide who was to be offered this housing). The aims of the survey and our desire not to disrupt the centres or their users, had to be explained at several levels of responsibility in each of the 60 sites selected. In the field, when a site was operated by successive teams of voluntary workers, what had already been explained to the various levels of responsibility had to be explained to each new team. This desire to be informed is wholly legitimate, but seriously complicated our task. In addition, when the voluntary organisations have a more or less hierarchical structure, information does not always flow down between the levels.

It must be said that the contacts established with some agencies were particularly effective; those in charge passed on their orders and ensured continuity by supplying us with the names and addresses of the people running the sites.

Selection of the interviewees The INED team had to visit each site to elaborate a sampling plan that was adapted to the local context and as close as possible to the theoretical sample: on the sites for which no list existed, every third person in a queue was to be asked, and the first to accept was interviewed; for the sites with a list drawn up in advance, the sampling was the same systematic random sampling as that used by RTI (National Institute on Drug Abuse, 1993). In the mobile soup kitchens (distribution by lorries, outdoors, often at night), a difficulty arises from the fact that the users tend to arrive in compact groups and seldom stand in line.

The essential point for our purpose was to guarantee the random nature of the sample. Whenever possible, a member of the research team accompanied the interviewers on the day of the survey. Approximately six individuals had to be selected per site, and those selected were then invited to participate in the survey. The interviewer made clear that the survey was voluntary, totally anonymous and confidential.

For the CHRS, we initially tried to select the people in advance from a list and then sent them a letter (left in their pigeonhole) to arrange to meet them later. With a few exceptions this procedure proved ineffective: the individuals failed to turn up and did not inform the person in charge of the centre. Many of the people in these hostels have jobs and are not always back in time for a meeting usually fixed for 6.30–7.00 p.m. In response to these problems, we asked the supervisors to contact the people concerned after random sampling. The refusals were then far fewer, but this method went against our original intention (a desire for neutrality vis-à-vis those in charge of the facilities). Besides this difficulty, we sometimes had to face another problem: to limit the effects of refusals and to spare the interviewers unnecessary journeys, slightly more people were drawn than was actually necessary, with the result that the interview was sometimes accepted by too many people (and a solution had to be found so as not to disappoint those who had agreed to cooperate by answering the questionnaire). With more resources, a two-stage procedure could be envisaged: first, an informative meeting, then fixing a time for the survey itself. Here too, however, the number of people who could be reached by the informative meeting is not necessarily high (people absent, at work, unavailable, etc.).

The survey was not always welcomed by those in charge of the sites. We were particularly handicapped by the fact that a survey had been carried out shortly before by CSA for La Croix/La Rue/La FNARS, following which some supervisors wanted no more surveys in their centres. In some locations the INED survey was in 'competition' with the survey on the mental health of the homeless carried out for the Epidemiological Services of the Paris municipality, whose first tests took place on the same dates and in the same places as our survey. An agreement was reached with the organisers to reschedule the surveys, but it further complicated our task. It must be added that the services for the homeless are frequently visited by journalists, and some have even been victims of secret cameras. In these conditions it is not hard to understand the lack of enthusiasm of those in charge and their desire to protect the vulnerable individuals who turn to them for help.

The users contacted were sometimes hostile, though when the interview was accepted it was very successful. The interviewees were generally satisfied with the rapport established with the interviewer. Many of the interviews continued beyond the time needed for completion of the questionnaire. This was consistent with the instructions given to the interviewers but also reflected their personal investment in the survey. It is worth noting that the interviewers themselves were very pleased with their rapport with the survey subjects, and that despite the difficulties due to the originality of this type of survey and the fact that it was often necessary to improvise, none of the interviewers dropped out in the course of the survey.

The physical conditions in which the survey took place varied widely. In some sites it was hard to find somewhere a little out of the way where the questionnaire could be completed with an acceptable degree of privacy. By contrast, in others there was a room for each interviewer. In the street part of the survey (mobile soup kitchens), it was often necessary to go to a nearby cafe to get out of the cold and wet.

Particular importance was attached to recording the questionnaire *refusals* and the individuals who could not be interviewed (due to a language barrier, for example) on the special 'contact' form provided for this purpose. After the random selection of the person to be contacted, the interviewers were instructed to note as accurately as possible the outcome of this contact: questionnaire accepted; questionnaire refused, giving the reasons for this refusal; questionnaire postponed (the case, for example, of people who agreed to reply but only after their meal), giving the subsequent outcome (the questionnaire was completed, or the person did not return or could not be found, which in many cases was a disguised refusal); individuals who were 'incapable' (speaking a foreign language, ill, under the influence of drink, etc.) and giving the reasons for this incapacity. The interviewer also recorded the sex and the approximate age of the individual.

Quantitative aspects of the data collection When this survey was begun, we had no firm idea about the actual number of subjects. Unlike in the street survey experimented in the same winter, it did prove possible to obtain a large sample. The theoretical sample was composed of 606 questionnaires, 226 of which were in emergency shelters (37.3 per cent), 228 in food distribution sites (37.6 per cent) and 152 in CHRS and long-stay shelters (25.1 per cent).

A total of 591 completed questionnaires were obtained (plus 10 completed out-of-sample, see below), distributed as follows: 219 (37.1 per cent) in emergency shelters, 235 (39.8 per cent) in the food distribution sites, and 137 (23.2 per cent) in the CHRS and long-stay shelters.

What follows is based essentially on analysis of the contact forms.[11] As was seen above, the interviewers were instructed to note as accurately as possible the outcome of the initial contact with the person to be interviewed and if possible the reasons for this outcome. It may be noted that some of the reasons given for refusals also figured among the reasons for being judged 'incapable': for example, the fact of being foreign and not speaking French could be invoked either by an individual to justify a refusal to reply or by an interviewer who had been unable to make himself understood.

Two points can be made regarding the representativeness of the sample:

• from considerations of cost and operational complexity it was decided to conduct the interviews only in French. It is not practical to have interpreters on each site for all the different languages that may be met in Paris (Eastern European languages in particular), and unlike surveys on a housed population there is no guarantee that the foreign-language speakers will be found again to carry out the interview later with an interpreter. It follows that the sample cannot be completely representative. For a larger-scale survey this problem would have to be examined; it could perhaps be partly overcome by sending interpreters to those sites where it is known that many individuals of a particular nationality will be found. For the INED survey, it was decided simply to have a number of questionnaires completed out-of-sample in Russian by one of the interviewers, who was of east European origin and spoke fluent Russian. Half of those interviewed were Russian and half were from other East European countries. The aim here was not to construct a representative sample, but simply to explore certain itineraries associated with a particular situation.

• in sites where the users were constantly on the move or where the atmosphere was tense, the interviewers found it hard to apply the method of random selection that had been developed and to complete fully the contact sheet. As a result the number of contacts and refusals was underestimated, notably when refusal took the form of pretending not to hear the interviewer and moving quickly away.

Contacts and refusals A total of 997 contacts were recorded by the interviewers, distributed as follows: 833 (84 per cent) in Paris intra-muros and 164 (16 per cent) in the neighbouring Hauts-de-Seine department (at the Nanterre reception and medical care centre and the Salvation Army's Corentin Celton centre).

The contacts were established as follows: 407 (41 per cent) in an emergency shelter, 437 (44 per cent) in the food distribution services, and 153 (15 per cent) in an CHRS or long-stay shelter.

Among the recorded contacts, 406 persons (or 41 per cent) did not reply, either after a refusal, explicit or not, or through incapacity. This refusal rate is high: points to be remembered, however, are that the survey was not compulsory and was announced as such; that for both ethical reasons (see

Firdion, Marpsat and Bozon, 1995) (the person contacted would feel completely free to reply or not) and scientific reasons (the answer would not be influenced by information already supplied to the site supervisors), it was decided that contacts would be established not by those in charge of the sites but by the interviewers themselves. The refusals are in part linked to the proliferation of surveys and press stories during winter 1994–95: it is not unknown for some sites to have been surveyed every day of the week, by two or three different organisations. Since the homeless have seen no commensurate improvement in their condition, their interest in surveys has not surprisingly declined. This situation is doubtless typical of Paris.

In addition, so as not to influence the interviewees' freedom of choice, it was decided not to tell them until the end of the interview that they would receive a phonecard in return for their participation. According to our American colleagues, the fact of paying subjects ($10 for the Research Triangle Institute) contributed to their low refusal rates. The same might not necessarily be the case in France, where a large proportion of the refusals took the form of avoiding the contact (the interviewer was unable even to finish the sentence, let alone mention a possible payment). Moreover, a careful examination of the response rates in the RTI survey gives the following results, if a strictly equivalent calculation is made: the success rate in the street is 56 per cent; for the food distribution sites, the calculation cannot be made, since the RTI documents only give the rate of questionnaire completion once people have been declared eligible after the screener (approximately 85 per cent; for the INED survey the corresponding rate is 97.3 per cent, a rate due to the interruption of 16 questionnaires before the 'housing' section of questionnaires 2 or 3).

This refusal rate can be compared with that in other non-compulsory surveys in difficult conditions, or that in postal surveys. Mention can also be made of refusal rates in the different sites of the Poverty Survey by the CREDOC, which should be praised for its scientific integrity in not attempting to hide the difficulties met in some of its surveys:[12] 25 per cent in CHRS, 35 per cent in emergency shelters, 50 per cent in stations of the RER railway network. These figures are close to ours (see below). They are also estimates and are perhaps slightly underestimated, given that 'this estimate was made a posteriori, the interviewers having not made a precise record of the number of contacts established such as could have been compared with the number of questionnaires actually completed'.

The acceptance rate of the sites themselves was very good, since out of 56 sites contacted only five refused, one of which was very small and had agreed to participate in the pilot tests for the survey and whose users were the same as when the interviewers visited.

Of the 997 contacts recorded, 47 people asked to postpone the time of the interview; which is what actually happened in 16 cases.

A total of 22 individuals were judged incapable of replying, 12 of them on grounds of nationality. These individuals were only met in the emergency shelters and sites of food distribution.

We shall now examine the reasons given for refusal and some factors which appeared to have an influence on acceptance of the questionnaire.

Personal and collective factors in refusal Of the 353 people who refused the interview, 107 gave no reason for their refusal (in many cases they were people who had turned away from the interviewer or pretended not to hear), 58 said they were in a hurry, 32 were not French, 18 were tired or ill, and 18 claimed to have already replied. Various interpretations can be given for this last figure: the person could indeed have already been interviewed; it could be a polite way of refusing; the person may have been already asked to participate in one of the other surveys being conducted at this time (we had already obtained this reply on the very first day of the pilot test).

Women are less numerous (12 per cent) among the people contacted than among the completed questionnaires (20 per cent). Rather than a difference of behaviour due to sex, this doubtless reflects the better conditions for the survey in the shelters catering for women or couples, and which result in a higher acceptance rate.

For the sites as a whole, the success rate was 59 per cent. But it reached 90 per cent in the CHRS and long-stay shelters, as against 54 per cent in the emergency shelters and food distribution sites.

A number of reasons can be advanced to explain this difference. The actual conditions in which contact was established were much less propitious, for example, in the case of the mobile soup kitchens, at a cold and wet time of year (for completion of the questionnaire the interviewer was instructed to suggest going to the nearest cafe, whose agreement had been obtained), or in the case of certain emergency shelters where those present move through very quickly with little opportunity to stop. The differences in the composition of the 'clientele' of the various sites also appears to have had an impact. This can be linked to an observation by one of the interviewers to the effect that the 'ambiance' of a site, regardless of the physical conditions of comfort, has a strong influence on the acceptance rate (and the influence of these two factors appears to be confirmed by initial examination of the refusal rates across places of survey).

After completing the screening questionnaire, 44 people went on to complete a 'housed' questionnaire (four per cent of the contacts, seven per cent of the questionnaires) and 547 a 'not housed' questionnaire (55 per cent of contacts, 93 per cent of questionnaires). In fact, only 35 of those surveyed were really 'housed' (though in poor conditions), while the others resulted either from screening errors, or from the fact that it was decided to use the 'housed' questionnaire in some CHRS where residents were lodged in self-contained flats, since the form of the questionnaire was more suited to this situation (Gilles, 1995). Use of the screening questionnaire means that the survey can be conducted employing more or less strict definitions of the state of homelessness.

Lastly, the degree of overlap between different services shows the value of employing complex weightings so as to achieve a high degree of representativeness of the sample, while the proportion of soup kitchen and other food distribution users who do not also use the shelters shows the interest of also conducting the survey in these places, even though it sometimes presents greater technical difficulties.

Data collection difficulties and their statistical implications A number of difficulties met with in the course of the data collection distort the theoretical model:

- some sites that had been selected were subsequently found to be outside the survey field (for example, workers' hostels) or were closed at the time of the survey; they were replaced by the next site on the list used for sampling;
- five sites (three shelters, two soup kitchens) refused to participate and were replaced by the next on the list;
- some sites asked for the date of the survey to be postponed (for example, when the person in charge was to be absent on the selected day);
- a site which had been selected was found not to provide services for the category of population indicated by the criterion used to stratify the list of sites. In this case it was replaced by the next on the list;
- in some sites, the size (the average number of services provided per day, calculated from the number provided in a week) was inaccurate: theoretical size not corresponding to the size actually observed on the ground; size expressed in number of meals served in the mobile soup kitchens, whereas one person may be served more than once; size in number of beds but including the under-18 children of households;

- for organisational reasons, it was sometimes necessary to modify the number of questionnaires completed in a primary unit (though it remained around six);
- in the retrospective section on service use, some sites were not clearly identified, entries for some days were inadequately filled in, by either the interviewee or the interviewer;
- in some long-stay shelters, when the people selected at random from the list of rooms did not come forward (for example, because they were working at that particular time) they were replaced in a way that doubtless was not always random, with the help of the centre supervisor; the random character of the selection may also have been compromised in other sites.

These problems tend to introduce bias to the sample in two main ways:

- a selective effect on the interviewees produces a bias that cannot be measured and cannot be corrected for, though it is reasonable to think that it is negligible compared with the sampling error;
- variations in numbers (number of services, numbers of subjects) per primary unit distort the self-weighting character of the sample. A correction is straightforward to do at the level of the weighting of the service sampled, but not at the level of the weighting of the interviewee (see below).

Estimation and Weighting

An approach based on surveys of service users offers considerable advantages in terms of the cost of implementation. Methods which use the sites of service distribution to the homeless, such as food distribution and shelters, as sampling frames, provide an almost complete coverage of the homeless population and at much lower cost than those using street sites. One drawback with the service-based method is the risk of duplication of homeless persons counted on this occasion because they may be counted on more than one site. An aspect of the INED investigation is to test different means of eliminating, reducing or adjusting for such double-counting.

Duplication occurs when the same individual is counted in different places (sites of service distribution or shelters). In sample surveys, double-counting and unequal probabilities for individuals of inclusion in the sample arise when one secondary sampling unit is associated with more than one primary sampling unit. When the primary units are sites, differences in the probability of inclusion can arise because individuals move a) from one point of food distribution to another for different meals (in the same day or on different days), or b) between the points of food distribution and the shelters. These differences would still occur even if all the points of food distribution could be covered in the same day and all the shelters and hostels on the same night. When the survey period is longer, the two types of duplication increase in both quantity and complexity.

Two main approaches to this problem can be distinguished. The first involves the identification of the double-counts and their elimination from the result. Double-counting can be identified and eliminated by operations of manual or computerised sorting; it can also be identified by a direct question (for example, 'have you already been interviewed?'), or by combining the two approaches. We opted for the first solution.

The second approach involves an adjustment for the differential probabilities of inclusion in the sample, and requires gathering information about the use that the homeless persons interviewed make of the services. This information is also required for the approaches based on forms of the capture-recapture method, which have been proposed for surveys of homeless persons (Anderton, 1991; Laska and Meisner, 1993) for which a 'capture' stage only is needed. As will be seen below, the INED study, like the American studies whose methodology it adapts, uses weightings in which adjustment is made for these non-uniform probabilities (Marpsat et al., 1996). The method for calculating the weightings appears below.

The Probability of Selecting a Service and its Corrective Factors

Let $N_{th}(sj)$ and $M_{th}(sj)$ be the theoretical number of interviewed subjects and eligible subjects on day j in site s; $P_{th}(sj)$, the theoretical probability of selection at the first stage of site s on day j; $P_{th}(psj)$ the theoretical probability of selection at the first stage of the service p, on day j, in site s.[13]

Probability of selection and sampling rates The formula for calculating the theoretical probability of selection of a site service is: $P_{th}(psj)$ = *[probability of selection of the service in the site]* * *[probability of selection of the site]*.

Each primary unit selected corresponds to six completed questionnaires, that is N_{th} = 6 for all s, j; so the a priori probability of selection for a site of theoretical size $M_{th}(sj)$ on an average day, when $M_{th}(j) = SM_{th}(sj)$ is the sum of the theoretical sizes on an average day of the survey period (that is, 16 days) in the sites of the type being considered, and K is the number of primary units (each primary unit corresponds to six completed questionnaires) selected for this type of site:

$$P_{th} (psj) = K* [N_{th}/(M_{th} (sj) * 16)] * [(M_{th} (sj) * 16)/ (M_{th} (j) * 16)]$$

After cancellation this becomes:

$$P_{th} (psj) = K* N_{th}/(M_{th} (j) * 16) \text{ for any } s$$

that is, a uniform probability (self-weighting sample) whatever the site.

When sampling, it may be found that some sites refuse the survey, that others do not correspond to the expected average size, which results in a number of adjustments ($M_A (sj)$ being the adjusted number of eligible respondents in site s on day j, and $M_A (j)$ the sum of the adjusted numbers); which gives the adjusted probability of selection of the service in the sampling frame:

$$P_A (psj) = K* [N_{th}/(M_A (sj) * 16)] * [(M_A (sj) * 16)/ (M_A (j) * 16)]$$

which after cancellation gives the *adjusted* probability of selecting service p, of site s, on day j:

$$P_A (psj) = K* N_{th}/ (M_A (j) * 16)$$

Corrective factors A corrective factor must be used to adjust for the size of the sites observed on survey day j ($M_{ob} (sj)$ and $M_{ob} (j)$), which is known a posteriori. Taking the hypothesis of homogeneity (errors are assumed to occur at random and not to affect certain categories of site more than others) it is possible to say that there is no estimation bias even though there is a selection bias (errors of coverage). The latter are what we adjust for in the first correction coefficient. Allowing for the adjusted sizes, the probability was:

$$P_A (psj) = K* [N_{th}/(M_A (sj) * 16)] * [(M_A (sj) * 16)/ (M_A (j) * 16)]$$

To correct the sizes observed on survey days j (term: $1/M_{ob} (j)$), the observed number of completed questionnaires obtained on days j (N_{th}), and the average sizes over the period of the survey (term: $M_A (sj)/M_{ob} (j)$), the weighting of each observation will be expressed by:

$$Weight_{obs} = 1/[P_A (psj)* (correction\ coefficients)]$$

The first correction coefficient concerns only the sum of average sizes in the survey period (this is in some way a calibration against the data of the DDASS-Paris (Social Services) for each sampling frame):

$$Coeff\_1 = M_A\,(j)/M_{ob}\,(j)$$

The second correction coefficient adjusts for the difference between the expected number of questionnaires (N_{th}) and the number of questionnaires obtained $N_{ob}\,(sj)$, for site s on day j. For each site-day (that is the survey day j of site s), this is expressed:

$$Coeff\_2\,(s, j) = N_{ob}\,(sj)/\,N_{th}$$

The third correction coefficient adjusts for the observed size of site s on survey day j (known after or at the time of the survey):

$$Coeff\_3\,(s, j) = M_{ob}\,(sj)/M_A\,(sj)$$

For more details, see Marpsat and Firdion 1998.

From Weighting of Services to Weighting of Individuals

Here we deal with the weighting used for the estimation *for an average day of the survey period*. With the INED survey it is also possible (with some reservations) to calculate the weightings *for an average week*, though this point will not be examined here.

There is a difficulty to take into account when calculating these weightings: when subjects have been interviewed at lunchtime, nothing is known about where they will eat and sleep that evening (similarly, if they are interviewed at the evening meal, we do not know where they will sleep). This information has had to be completed by a process of imputation, established using the information on the past week.[14] Assume that these imputations have been performed. In the course of day j, the interviewee can have received between one and three services, involving (in principle) at most one of the two types of shelter plus two meals.

The probability of the interviewee being included in the sample on day j is thus:

$$P(E_j) = P(E_{jt}\ U\ E_{jt}{}'\ U\ E_{jt}{}'')$$

where E_{jt}, E_{jt}', E_{jt}'', are the samples on day j in the three types of services: midday meal, supper, bed for the night. The service for which the individual has been interviewed is denoted by t. Ignoring the corrective terms, we get:

$$P(E_j) = P(E_{jt}) + P(E_{jt}') + P(E_{jt}'')$$

The first term is known with the corrections from the collection which apply to this centre (see 2.6). For the two other services, the correction is only applicable in the case of primary units actually selected on day j.

All that remains is to sum the different daily samples. The estimations for an average day are obtained by taking an average of the 16 days of the survey.

Prospects for Reproducing the Survey

The INED survey appears to us to be the best solution currently available, and to be suitable for reproducing on a larger scale or in other countries.

To the question: have we done the 'thing right?' our reply is that the overall results are positive, and that the proposed methodological improvements, the details of which appear below, offer the possibility of improving the problems of data collection in particular. These improvements were incorporated by the team of medical researchers which carried out a survey using the INED sampling method in winter 1995–96.

To the question: was it the 'right thing' we would answer that the survey offers a good coverage of the homeless population at a particular point in time, and including some of the elements in its itinerary. By contrast, it does not supply information about how individuals may enter and depart from homelessness over a long period, such as a year. In particular, a person who has found housing will not appear in the sample. Such a study could no doubt be conducted using the site records (see the works of Dennis Culhane). But this requires a relatively complex organisation (all the sites must be computerised and use the same program), whereas the amount of information collected on each person is much smaller. Another limitation of the INED survey concerns the field and the fact that part of the target population is not observed (see below). Notwithstanding this, in the current state of knowledge this type of survey is the best available instrument.

A more detailed assessment follows.

Limitation of the Instrument

Field targeted, field covered

- *Field targeted*: all the adults who, over a period and in a zone, have slept in the night shelters or 'in the street', in an urban context. The limitation of our instrument stems from uncertainty over housing situations which theoretically are not in the field, because they concern persons who do have a roof over their heads, but which could be thought to have affinities with the two cases surveyed (night shelters and 'street'). These are: squats, people who are lodged by friends or relatives in overcrowded conditions, stays in institutions (hospital, for example). The persons in these situations have a minimum 'resource' which may mean that they do not have to use the services of help for the homeless such as shelter or meals. By contrast, those in the first two cases may make use of free medical services and distributions of clothes.
- *Field covered*: the persons who, in the period and zone considered, have slept in a night shelter, and, partially, those sleeping 'in the street', in squats, and, more generally, the people in situations of housing insecurity. The latter segments of population are only partially covered by this method since they are observed only if the people make use of the food distribution services. Also, no attempt was made to include underage persons in the survey, for whom special procedures would have to be developed. Lastly, foreigners who cannot or will not speak French are at present largely underestimated, since we have no means of recruiting interpreters or bilingual interviewers.

Data collection Four points must be made:

- rates of refusal and of inaptitude seem to be influenced much more by the type of place in which the survey is conducted than by the method and the interviewers;
- we experienced some difficulties in selecting people in the soup kitchens and social canteens. The large number of sites per day meant that members of the team were not always able to supervise (or help in) this form of selection;
- it was difficult to establish direct contact with the selected persons in the CHRS and social hostels. An improved collaboration with the site supervisors is indispensable for this aspect;

- our task was complicated by the recent or simultaneous presence at the same site of other surveys or of journalists, because of the fatigue this produces among site supervisors and the homeless themselves, who see a proliferation of surveys without any rapid change in their situation.

Reliability and accuracy of data

- The accuracy of the data is related to the quality of the sample design (stratification, complementary information) and of the sampling frame. Particular care must therefore be given to the list of services in the survey zone, which as far as possible should be based on checking and updating of existing computerised records.
- The reliability of the data depends on the quality of the information in the retrospective part (services used by the person in the previous seven days) of the questionnaire. The importance of this part of the questionnaire should be stressed during the training of interviewers, since it is from this that the weightings are calculated.

Review of the questionnaire design

- Some situations remain ill-defined in the section on work: undeclared work, odd jobs, payment in kind for casual work, etc. Despite many preliminary tests, it is hoped to improve this part of the questionnaire.
- The treatment of certain complex housing situations also needs to be improved.
- It is hoped to draw on the work of the CNIS group on nomenclature to improve the questions on this subject so as to get a better coverage of insecure housing and employment situations. A questionnaire on this topic has just been tested at INED, in collaboration with INSEE, the results of which are currently being analysed.
- The advice of linguists should be sought on how interviewers can reword the questions which are not understood, so that the same question could be put in several different ways.
- More work is needed on a number of topics that we had to omit from the questionnaire after failing to find a satisfactory formulation, for example, the sociability of the homeless, bonds of friendship, etc.

Recommendations

Repeating the survey? In what conditions? At what cost?

- It is suggested that the INED survey be conducted at the scale of an urban centre or group of towns of more than *n* inhabitants (more than 100,000 or 150,000 inhabitants, for example), including as a complement to a survey of the housed population (survey of employment, health). For this purpose it would be a good idea to prepare a list of the existing services that was suitable for statistical use, which would merely have to be updated by each survey organiser.
- By drawing on the local voluntary and institutional structures, the INSEE network in the case of France, and the university resources of each town and city.
- By scheduling the creation of the list of services, elaboration of the questionnaire, making contact with the services; the pilot tests could be carried out in the first year, while the sampling frame is being prepared, and the survey itself conducted in the second year.
- Repeat the survey at different times of the year using the same type of random sample.
- For the operation in Paris, the external cost was approximately 400,000FF (not counting the specific methodological operations which do not have to be repeated on a large scale) for 600 interviews (667FF per questionnaire).

Improvements

- We are not in favour of night-time street counts (costly and inefficient) even though a number of homeless persons who make no use of services can be reached using this method.
- As a substitute for a night-time operation we suggest completing the 'services' sample by a sample of daytime street survey sites that are known to be visited during the day by homeless persons. Qualitative studies currently being conducted, plus cooperation with voluntary bodies, may help us to identify these places. Thought should also be given to the possibility of using the information collected by the *Samu social* (mobile health care for homeless) in the urban centres where such a service exists.
- Repeating the survey in another country would require a preliminary investigation into the provision of services that existed there and into the additional information needed to complete the 'services' sample.

- The sample design must be strictly respected.
- The training of interviewers should be longer (notably to give the researchers time to read and check the first questionnaires completed by the interviewers during the training) so as to produce a more homogeneous data collection by interviewers from different backgrounds (professional interviewers and social workers, students, voluntary workers), while recognising that this diversity of recruitment is a source of numerous advantages in the field work.
- It is important that coverage of non-French speakers be improved.
- There is the problem of how to extend the field of services beyond shelter and food, to include free medical services and clothes distributions, for example, so as to increase the likelihood of observing the population that is less dependent on services of help to the homeless. Accommodation should be extended to the hotels used by voluntary organisations to lodge homeless persons. In this case, however, care must be taken not to introduce bias to the collection (these services cannot be precisely delimited) and to balance the cost of enlarging the sampling frame against the likely gains. Conducting the survey in urban centres other than Paris, however, where the development of services may have taken different forms, could lead to including day shelters, for example.
- The changes in modes of help for the homeless must be monitored, in collaboration with the relevant voluntary organisations and institutions, with whom a working group should be set up to produce as accurate a list as possible of services to be surveyed.
- As regards a broader spatial application of the survey, the work currently under way in the Ille-et-Vilaine department and the 1996 survey in the United States (countryside included) may supply answers to the question of the specificity of a rural context.
- For interviewing young people (whose presence at soup kitchens and stations is a disturbing phenomenon), specific procedures must be studied and developed. This was done by INED for its new survey on homeless youth, which will take place in Paris and its suburbs in February and march 1998.

Conclusion

The results of the INED survey are only just beginning to appear (Marpsat, Firdion, 1996 and 1998), so it is still too soon to know what impact it will have on social policy. These early results (Marpsat and Firdion, 1996) indicate that the processes which lead to homelessness may have very distant origins in the lives of those involved, and that policies to tackle the problem must take account not only of the difficulties of keeping people in housing and of providing access to housing, but also of the broader struggle against all aspects of poverty.

One of the positive things to emerge from this survey concerns its suitability for generalisation. This is among the recommendations of the CNIS report, and it is relevant to note that the sampling method developed by INED has already been applied in France by another team, working in Paris intra-muros, during winter 1995–96. The object here was to conduct a survey on the physical and mental health of homeless persons and their access to health care provision. This second survey, the first results of which can be found in Kovess and Mangin-Lazarus 1997, demonstrates that the INED survey method can be used in different circumstances and using different questionnaires. As said before, at the moment (February–March 1998), INED is conducting a survey in Paris and its suburbs, on the issue of homeless youth. This new survey adapts the method used for homeless adults to the specificities of young people (one of the differences is the inclusion of day centres in the field of services). And last (but not least), the French National Institute of Statistics (INSEE) is planning to conduct a *national survey on homelessness* around 2000, using the INED sampling method.

Notes

1   Maryse Marpsat and Jean-Marie Firdion belong to the Institut National d'Etudes Démographiques (INED, 133 Boulevard Davout, 75980, Paris Cedex 20, France). The theoretical weightings were calculated by Benoît Riandey (INED) and Olivier SAUTORY (INSEE). An article by Benoît RIANDEY detailing the methodology of the survey will appear in the volume of the *Travaux et Documents* series devoted to the INED research on the homeless.
2   The Conseil National d'Information Statistique (CNIS) is a forum for the producers and users of official statistics. It coordinates government statistical activities, and is responsible for drawing up a medium-term programme and an annual programme of compulsory surveys. The CNIS has an advisory role and its recommendations are made public. It brings together representatives of the trade unions, voluntary organisations, civil servants, academics, and specialists.
3   More than 15 days.
4   In collaboration with the Plan Urbain (Ministère de l'Equipement, des Transports, du Logement et de l'Urbanisme).

5   To which were added the two suburban shelters which receive people brought from Paris intra-muros by a special transport service.
6   CHRS-Centres d'hébergement et de réinsertion sociale (see glossary).
7   In this way no primary unit is sampled more than once, whereas certain sites are sampled on separate days, unlike in the RTI survey.
8   Shelters for men only; for men and women; for men and women and couples with children; for women with children; for women only.
9   Centre d'Etude, d'Animation, de Formation et de coordination en faveur du logement des populations en mutations économique et sociale.
10 See note 8.
11 These are provisional results.
12 These people were subsequently reclassified as 'not housed'
13 In the interest of clarity the French notation has been retained in the weighting calculations presented here. Hence j (jour) = day, s (service) = site, and p (prestation) = service [Tr.].
14 In a subsequent survey, subjects could be questioned about their plans.

Bibliography

Anderton, D.I. (1991), 'Using local longitudinal records to estimate transient and resident homeless populations', *Housing Policy Debate*, 2, pp. 833–900.

Bloor M., Shaw I, et al. (1994), *The Feasibility of Commissioning a Mark-Recapture Study of the Prevalence of Rooflessness in Scotland*, Cardiff, Social Research Unit, School of Social and Administrative Studies, University of Wales College.

Bramley, G., Doogan, K., Leather, P., Murie, A. and Watson, E. (1988), 'Homelessness and the London housing market', School for Advanced Urban Studies, University of Bristol, Occasional Paper no. 32.

Burnam, A., and Koegel, P. (1988), 'Methodology for Obtaining a Representative Sample of Homeless Persons: The Los Angeles Skid Row Study', *Evaluation review*, vol. 12, no. 2.

Burt, M.R. (1992), *Practical Methods for Counting Homeless People*, Washington, Interagency Council for the Homeless and Department of Housing and Urban Development.

Burt, M.R. (1996), 'Fifteen Years of U.S. Homeless Policy, Research, and Advocacy in Response to Growth and Change in the Homeless Population', *Sociétés Contemporaines*, (forthcoming).

Burt, M.R. and Cohen, B.E. (1989), *America's Homeless: Numbers, Characteristics, and Programs That Serve Them*, Washington, DC, The Urban Institute.

Conseil National de l'Information Statistique (1995), *Proposition pour un système statistique sur les sans abri et les personnes exclues du logement*, Interim Report, Paris, 12 April.

Conseil National de l'Information Statistique (1996), *Pour une meilleure connaissance statistique des sans-abri et de l'exclusion du logement*, Final Report, no. 29, Paris, March.

Cormack, R. (1989), 'Log-linear Models for Capture-recapture', *Biometrics*, no. 45, pp. 395–413.

Cowan, C.D. (1991), 'Estimating Census and Survey Undercounts Through Multiple Service Contacts', *Housing Policy Debate*, vol. 2, no. 3, papers presented at the Fannie Mae Annual Housing Conference, 'Counting the Homeless: The Methodologies, Policies, and Social Significance Behind the Numbers'.

Culhane, D.., Dejowski, E.F., Ibanez, J., Needham, E. and Macchia, I. (1993), *Public Shelter Admission Rates in Philadelphia and New-York City. The Implications of Turnover for Sheltered Population Counts*, Fannie Mae Working Paper, Office of Housing Research.

Dennis, M.L. and Iachan, R. (1993), 'A Multiple Frame Approach to Sampling the Homeless and Transient Population', *Journal of Official Statistics*, 9 (4).

Firdion, J.-M. and Marpsat, M. (1994), 'La statistique des sans domicile aux Etats-Unis', *Courrier des Statistiques*, nos 71–2, December.

Firdion, J.-M., Marpsat, M. and Bozon, M. (1995), 'Est-il légitime de mener des enquêtes statistiques auprès des sans-domicile? Une question éthique et scientifique', *Revue Française des Affaires Sociales*, no. 2–3, April–September.

Gilles, M.-O. (1995), 'Les spécificités des enquêtes quantitatives auprès de populations socialement marginales', CREDOC, *Cahier de Recherche*, 68, April.

HMSO (1993), *Social tTends*, 1993 edition, pp. 117–8.

Hombs, M.E. and Snyder, M. (1983), *Homelessness in America: A Forced March to Nowhere*, Washington, DC, Community for Creative Non-Violence.

Hopper, K. (1990), 'Public Shelter as "a Hybrid Institution": Homeless men in Historical Perspective', *Journal of Social Issues*, no. 46, pp. 13–9.

Hopper, K. (1991a), 'Homeless Old and New: the Matter of Definition', *Housing Policy Debate*, no. 2, pp. 757–814.

Hopper, K. (1991b), 'An ethnographic perspective on the S-night count', *Proceedings of the Annual Research Conference*, Washington, DC, Bureau of the Census.

Kovess, V. and Mangin-Lazarus C. (1997), 'La santé mentale des sans abri à Paris. Résultats d'une enquête épidémiologique', *Revue française de psychiatrie et de psychologie médicale*, no. 9, June.

Laska, E.M. and Meisner M. (1993), 'A Plant-Capture Method for Estimating the Size of a Population from a Single Sample', *Biometrics*, 49, pp. 209–20.

Link, B., Susser, E., Stueve, A., Phelan J., Moore R.and Struening, E. (1994), 'Lifetime and Five-year Prevalence of Homelessness in the United States', *American Journal of Public Health*, vol. 84, no. 12, pp. 1907–12.

Marpsat, M. and Firdion, J.-M. (1996), 'Becoming homeless: who is at risk ?', INED, *Population & Sociétés*, no. 313, May, English version of Marpsat, M. and Firdion, J.-M. (ibid.).

Marpsat, M. and Firdion, J.-M. (eds) (1998), *Sans domicile et mal-logés, Travaux et Documents*, INED, forthcoming.

Marpsat, M., Firdion, J.-M., Iachan, R. and Riandey, B. (1996), *Les sans-domicile à Washington et Paris deux études reposant sur les enquêtes auprès de la clientèle des services*, XXVIIIèmes journées de statistique de l'Association pour la Statistique et ses Utilisations, Québec, 27–30 May.

Murie, A. and Forrest, R. (1990), 'Les nouveaux sans domicile fixe (SDF) en Grande-Bretagne' in Ferrand-Bechmann, D. (ed.), *Pauvre et mal logé. Les enjeux sociaux de l'habitat*, Paris, L'Harmattan.

Murie, A. and Jeffers, S. (eds), (1987), 'Living in bed and breakfast: the experience of homelessness in London', School for Advanced Urban Studies, University of Bristol, working paper no. 71.

National Institute on Drug Abuse (NIDA) (1993), *Prevalence and Treatment of Drug Use and Correlated Problems in the Homeless and Transient Population: 1991*, Dennis, M.L., Iachan, R., Thornburry, J.P., Bray, R.M., Packer, L.E. and Bieler, G.S., final report under NIDA contract no. 271–89–8340, Washington, DC, Metropolitan Area Drug Study, Rockville, Md, NIDA.

Office for National Statistics (1996), 'Psychiatric morbidity among homeless people', *OPCS Surveys of psychiatric Morbidity in Great Britain*, Report 7.

OPCS (1991a), *1991 Census. Preliminary report for England and Wales. Supplementary monitor on people sleeping rough.*

OPCS (1991b), *1991 Census. Instructions for the enumeration of people sleeping rough.*

OPCS (1993), *Survey of psychiatric morbidity among homeless people: revised proposal.*

Paugam, S. (1995), 'Les sans-abri d'une crise à l'autre', *Fondations*, no. 1, special issue on the homeless, pp. 47–59.

Rossi, P.H., Fisher, G.A. and Willis, G., (1986), *The Conditions of the Homeless in Chicago*, Illinois, The University of Chicago Press.

Rossi, P.H., Wright, J.D., Fischer, G. A. and Willis, G. (1987), 'The Urban Homeless: Estimating Composition and Size', *Science*, 235, pp. 1336–41.

Santiago J.M., Bachrach, L.L., Berren, M.R. and Hannah, M.T. (1988), 'Defining the Homeless Mentally Ill: a Methodological note', *Hospital and Community Psychiatry*, no. 39, pp. 100–1.

Snow, D.A. and Anderson, L. (1993), *Down on Their Luck, A Study of Homeless Street People*, Berkeley, Ca., University of California Press.

Sosin, M., Piliavin, I. and Westerfelt, H. (1990), 'Toward a Longitudinal Analysis of Homelessness', *Journal of Social Issues*, 46 (4), pp. 157–74.

Taffin, C. (1993), 'Un siècle de politique du logement: l'Etat doit-il être acteur ou simple arbitre?', INSEE, *La Société Française, Données Sociales 1993*.

Taeuber, C.M. and Siegel, P.M. (1991), 'Counting the Nation's Homeless Population in the 1990 Census' in Taeuber, C. (ed.), *Conference Proceedings for Enumerating Homeless persons : Methods and Data Needs*, Washington, DC, Bureau of the Census.

US Department of Housing and Urban Development, Office of Policy Development and Research (1984), *A Report to the Secretary on the Homeless and Emergency Shelters*, Washington, DC, US Department of Housing and Urban Development, April, 18.

Wiegand, R.B. (1985), 'Counting the Homeless', *American Demographics*, 12.

Appendix

Glossary of terms and abbreviations

CREDOC: Centre de Recherche pour l'Etude et l'Observation des Conditions de Vie.

CHRS: Centres d'hébergement et de réinsertion sociale. These centres are run by public or private bodies (usually voluntary organisations), with the aim of making the people they serve independent and socially inserted. Their operating costs are paid by Aide Sociale (state) and they receive funds from the Directions départementales de l'action sanitaire et sociale (DDAS) (social services of each department). Persons are admitted for renewable periods of six months.

Emergency and long-stay shelters: the distinction we made between emergency and long-stay shelters is based not on their statute (CHRS, for example) which seemed very loosely related to the durability of the housing solution for the individual, but on the maximum length of stay allowed, the limit being fixed at 15 days.

FNARS: Fédération Nationale des Associations d'Accueil et de Réinsertion Sociale

INSEE: Institut National de la Statistique et des Etudes Economiques

'literally' homeless: people sleeping in a shelter or in a place not intended for habitation (street, car park, station, etc.).

11 Using 'Capture-Recapture' to Estimate the Size of the Homeless Population

MALCOLM WILLIAMS

Introduction

The purpose of this chapter is threefold. Firstly to discuss some key issues around the questions of definition and particularly, the measurement of urban homelessness. Secondly to show how these problems were tackled in a recent study in Plymouth. Thirdly to offer some observations on the usefulness of the approach used in Plymouth as a general method for the estimation of the size of homeless populations.

I will begin by briefly discussing the definitional problem of homelessness and how that impacts upon measurement. I will then describe some recent attempts at measuring the extent of homelessness in England and argue that the limited success of these studies in terms of numeric accuracy, results from both inadequate definition and the lack of reliable enumeration techniques. I will then go on to describe the approach to both enumeration and estimation used in Plymouth. Finally I will critically evaluate our experience in Plymouth with reference to the usefulness of the approach in studying homelessness in other locations.

The Problem of Definition

Definitional problems of homelessness can be described as resulting from local variations in what will count as homelessness.[1] In the UK, at least, more than one definition operates simultaneously. The first difficulty faced in attempts to enumerate a homeless population is which definition is to be used? The researcher is in fact on the horns of a dilemma. On one hand a narrow definition (such as that incorporated in the 1977 Housing (Homeless Persons)

Act in England and Wales) will not adequately describe the extent of severe housing need. On the other hand a much broader definition, perhaps one which adequately captures the subjective experience of homelessness (see for example Bramley, 1988), will be difficult to operationalise. Furthermore there is a moral burden upon the researcher insofar as what ends up being measured is what comes to count as homelessness in that location.

Whilst an understanding of the subjective experience of homelessness is crucial in its description in order to measure the extent of the phenomenon, it is unavoidable that objective quantifiable states must be determined. Having identified these states the question then arises about whether they will be visible in order to be measured. For example if it is decided that those in all forms of temporary accommodation will be considered as being homeless, is it the case that all of those in what is defined as temporary accommodation can be thus counted? Moreover the extent of visibility will vary from location to location, often crucially depending on the nature of official records kept. For example hostels operated by local authorities are likely to keep accurate client records, whereas there may be more variation amongst those in the private sector.

It is then a problem of operationalisation and can be summarised thus: whilst what is measured will depend on what is defined, what can be practically defined may well depend on what can be measured.

The Problem of Measurement

Whilst the problem of what can be defined may be one of visibility its solution will leave unresolved a further problem of accurately estimating the size of the homeless population p. We cannot easily know the extent of the p from the visibility of only some of its members. The homeless can be described as a 'rare and elusive' population. They are rare in that even in locations where homelessness is considered to be a major social problem, those who constitute p (however defined) will only ever comprise a small proportion of the general population P. Secondly they are elusive in that within P their numbers will vary and they will be geographically mobile. Indeed spatial mobility is usually regarded as an important characteristic of being homeless (Jenks, 1994, p.13). Specifically researchers are faced with three difficulties: *undercount* – however thorough an enumeration it is impossible to know whether all members of p are accounted for; *double counting* – conversely because members of p will be spatially mobile within the time span of the enumeration there are difficulties in knowing whether or not they have been previously counted; *process – p* may fluctuate in size. A single enumeration cannot tell us whether this is the case, or if it is the case the extent to which it is occurring. So even if, after one enumeration, we can generalise about the size of *p* in any given location are we entitled to generalise about its accuracy over time in that location?

The difficulties of measurement can be illustrated with three quite recent examples of attempts to enumerate and describe the homeless population in UK cities. In the first two examples it was intended to measure only the number of rough sleepers, although in the final example the definition of homelessness was broadened to include hostel dwellers.

In the 1991 Census of Population, in England and Wales, it was decided to attempt to count those sleeping rough. Though 1,312 sites were identified by voluntary organisations, churches and local authorities as places where people slept rough, the locational information was compiled one year prior to the census and only 453 of the sites were being used by census night. Moreover it was felt that inclement weather in many parts of the country on census night led to fewer persons being found than would be expected. In all 2,845 persons were enumerated (Dale and Marsh, 1994, pp. 24–5). Though the census does separately count those in institutions, specific identification of those in temporary hostels or night shelters is not possible. Had the rough sleeper count additionally identified this group then some imputation might have been made of the effect of weather conditions on the likelihood of sleeping rough. Given that this did not obtain and the local information was outdated then it is hard to see what was the value of the final enumerated figure.

Moore et al. (1991), in a survey commissioned by the Salvation Army, used 100 volunteers to 'comb the streets' of Central London for those sleeping rough. The figure from this count was combined with the numbers estimated to be in hotels, hostels or squats. In similar vein several organisations collaborated to count rough sleepers in Central London in May 1995 (Homeless Network, 1995). Pairs of 'outreach' workers collected anonymous details on a standard form and where people were sleeping rough a simple count and location were noted. Afterwards enumerators attempted to eliminate double counting in areas where counts were adjacent. In addition data on occupancy and number of applicants not accommodated was collected from Direct Access Hostels.

The third example concerns a UK Department of Environment-commissioned study (Anderson et al., 1993) aimed at collecting detailed data on the nature of single homelessness in England. Though it was never intended to produce a 'count' of homeless people (ibid., p. 3) there was an implicit imputation that the population had a certain size and characteristics and that moreover the findings were representative of the homeless population in general.

The sample in this case (described in Lynn 1992) was drawn from those using soup runs and day centres, for those sleeping rough, as well as those in hostels. Hostels, soup runs and day centres were selected on a probability basis whereby the resultant sample of users would reflect the overall number of clients, thus ensuring (as far as possible) an equal probability of selection (ibid., pp. 3–16). The size of the population was therefore known only within fairly wide parameters and may have fluctuated somewhat during the data collection period.

In the first two examples only 'rough sleepers' were to be counted, that is those who have no form of accommodation whatsoever and are sleeping in the open, or in makeshift shelters. Whilst it is laudable that attempts should be made to quantify this most severe manifestation of homelessness, 'rough sleepers' are a mobile and rapidly changing population. Whilst 32 per cent of those homeless in Plymouth had slept rough at sometime in the past 12 months, the periods in which most had slept rough were quite short.[2] Periods of sleeping rough are interspersed with other arrangements. Moreover those who are forced to sleep rough will often manage meagre resources in order to find alternatives in inclement weather. Finally, rough sleepers can be geographically mobile within relatively short periods and, because they often fear harassment and persecution, will be suspicious of known attempts at enumeration. The categorisation of any individual as a rough sleeper is likely to be very unstable. Even within the course of a single 'count' an individual may obtain temporary shelter. This unstable definition combined with the problem of spatial mobility over very short time periods renders counts (and especially single counts) of rough sleepers very unreliable.

Whilst these difficulties were recognised in the Anderson et al. study, the aim of which was description not enumeration, there must be some doubt as to the representative nature of descriptions based on a sample drawn from a population the total size of which (or key characteristics) is unknown. Whilst hostels and day centres were selected on a probability basis the locations of these sampling points were more subjectively decided. Indeed as Lynn notes (op cit., p. 3) it was important to 'select areas where there was a high incidence of homelessness in order to ensure the required number of interviews could be achieved.' In this particular research a non statutory definition of single homeless was used (ibid.) so it cannot be objectively known whether or not there was a 'high incidence' of homelessness (as defined) in particular areas.

The basis for the claim of high incidence is likely to rest upon agency records. However the existence of the agencies (and the records they keep) may simply render homelessness more visible in certain areas, or where services are offered, serve to increase the numbers homeless as they are attracted to those areas. The Anderson study, in effect, describes the characteristics not of a national single homeless population, but of the single homeless found in certain areas of the country.

4   Capture-Recapture

If for the above reasons it is the case that we cannot have confidence in attempts to produce a 100 per cent count of the homeless a reliable statistical method of estimation appears to offer the best hope for establishing the size of the population. Capture-recapture techniques (sometimes referred to as 'mark-recapture) utilise information from duplicate cases to allow the number of people otherwise unobserved to be calculated (Fisher et al., 1994, p. 27; Sudman et al., 1988; Bishop et al., 1975). For example in recent years Bloor et al. (1994) utilised this method to estimate the size of the injecting drug user population in Glasgow and Fisher et al. (1994) to estimate the number of homeless mentally ill people in northeast Westminster, London.

The technique rests on the principal of two or more independent observations of the same population. These observations can be simultaneously of two sources that represent approximately the same population, or they can be of the same source at two time points. In the latter case the observations should be at approximately the same time. In order to estimate the size of the population (N_t) the researcher needs to know the number of persons observed at the first count (N_1) the number of persons observed at the second (N_2) [or subsequent counts] and the number observed at both (M) [or each of subsequent] counts. Thus the estimate of the population (N_t) is:

$$N_t = (N_1 \times N_2)/M$$

The capture-recapture problem can be represented in a contingency table (Bishop et al., 1975, p. 231) where N is the total number of individuals in the population under consideration, N_1 the number of individuals in the first sample, N_2 the number in the second sample, and M the number in both the first and the second samples. The number of individuals observed in the second sample but not the first is $N_{21} = N_2 - M$, and the number observed in the first sample but not the second is $N_{1\,2} = N_1 - M$. Thus the contingency table is 2 X 2 with one missing cell.

Second Sample

First Sample	Present	Absent	
Present	M	$N_{1\,2}$	N_1
Absent	N_{21}	missing	
	N_2		

The model rests upon three key assumptions. Firstly each member of the population must have the same probability of capture in each sample though this does not have to be the same across all samples. Secondly dependency between samples should be avoided. An observation of an individual in one sample should not have any effect on the observation of that individual at subsequent counts. Finally the overall numbers in the population should not be different at the time of each sample.

The difficulty of fulfilling these requirements in the social world is discussed in a paper by Shaw et al. (1996). The problem of dependency (that is where there is a causal connection between presence in one sample and presence in subsequent samples) between samples is an especially difficult one mainly because we cannot know all of the ways in which presence in one sample may be related to presence in another. For example a client of a bed and breakfast 'hotel' (cheap hotels used by local authorities to house those who are statutorily homeless) will almost certainly be there as a result of referral from a local authority. Therefore if the two samples are taken at these locations those referred to bed and breakfast hotels will quite obviously have a greater probability of capture. Log linear modelling techniques have been used to model the degree of interdependence between samples, though this technique requires multiple samples. The aim being to construct the most parsimonious model judged acceptable from the chi-square statistic (Frischer et al., 1991). Whilst a number of types of dependency can be fitted to the model, and complex models could be constructed in which more and more dependencies are controlled for, this becomes little more than an exercise in statistical elegance when we simply can never know all of the ways our assumptions are undermined by the environmental characteristics of the research.

It has been noted above that a quintessential feature of homeless populations is their 'open' character. Again this is a problem that cannot be wholly overcome, however for this reason it is important that time series samples are approximate to each other. Secondly the model will rest on the assumption that the population will be relatively homogeneous and not subject to large fluctuation through large scale migration, births or deaths.

Finally and perhaps most crucially the validity and reliability of the samples will depend on how consistently and accurately the observations (the 'tagging') are made (Shaw et al., 1996, p. 78). The validity of the samples is directly related to the issue of definition. All observations must utilise the same definition of homelessness, which in itself must be a measurable characteristic. However even with valid definitions the reliability of the sample will be compromised by inaccurate recording of data, or mis-classification of observations. Clients presenting to agencies must be accurately 'screened' to check they fit the definition of homelessness adopted. Shaw et al. (ibid.) note that lack of validity and reliability will be manifested through the recording of 'false positives' and 'false negatives', whereby the former are those persons not homeless, but erroneously classed or recorded as such and in the second those people who are homeless, but are not so classed or recorded.

The Plymouth Research

Context

Before going on to describe how homelessness was defined and measured in Plymouth it may be useful to contextualise the project itself. Plymouth is a coastal city with a population of just over 250,000. In recent years a decline in traditional industries has given rise to very high structural unemployment (Payne, 1995). Despite this the city remains an economic focal point for a very large rural hinterland, some areas of which suffer even greater economic hardship (Payne, op cit.; Williams et al., 1995). It is then an important migratory destination. In recent years agencies in the city have reported increases in numbers in severe housing need. An incoming city administration shared the concern of these groups over an apparently growing problem and from this the research was born. Though some agencies in the city kept comprehensive client data, others did not and moreover the discontinuity of definition and recording mitigated against anything other than the most rudimentary estimate of numbers. Nevertheless some indication of the relative scale of the problem could be gleaned from a comparison of particular agency records over time. Plymouth offers a number of advantages for a project of this kind. Though, as I describe below, the sample comprised of data from a large number of agencies a very good and cooperative social network facilitated relatively unproblematic data collection. Just as importantly the city is geographical compact and is bounded by sea and river to the south and west and a very sparsely populated rural area to the north. This means that whilst there are significant migratory flows the isolation from large centres of population reduces short distance and short term movement into and out of the city.

Definition and Measurement

An earlier exploratory phase of the research in Plymouth (Williams and Cox, 1994) established that there were 47 agencies (or branches of agencies) who had some form of contact with homeless people. Agency, in this case, is defined as any organisation with which homeless people are likely to have contact. These may be voluntary, or statutory and in many case (for example the police, hospitals, etc.) do not specifically exist to assist the homeless. Not all kept records and there were many explicit and implicit definitions of homelessness operational in the agencies. Whilst nearly all agencies were happy to cooperate in data collection it was necessary to adopt a single definition of homelessness and to utilise the simplest possible screening form. Moreover because of the multiplicity of agencies, often dealing with quite different manifestations of homelessness, the decision was made to treat all as part of the same sample, but to sample at different time points.

The definition of homeless adopted required that a person be:

staying in a hostel;
staying in bed and breakfast; [3]
sleeping rough;[4]
staying in a squat;
staying temporarily with friends;
staying in no-residential institutions (such as hospitals) where no other accommodation was available;
staying in residential institutions catering for those excluded from, or unable to secure, other accommodation (e.g. homes for young offenders, women's refuges, etc.);

The research operated on the key assumption that most people so categorised would come into contact with one or more of the agencies collecting data. These agencies would not necessarily have a direct role in providing accommodation or housing advice, but might simply be places at which homeless people might receive benefits, or non housing advice and help. The agencies varied widely and included the City Housing Department, the Benefits Agency, the police, bed and breakfast hotels, advice agencies and hostels.

In order to 'tag' each observed person a unique identifier is required. In previous studies this has been name, date of birth and sex (see Fisher, et al., 1994) . Indeed in the Plymouth study this was the identifier used, except that respondents were asked for their initials in order to reassure them of anonymity. Additionally data on current 'accommodation' was gathered along with length of time in Plymouth. Cases were matched using the SORT procedure in SPSS/ Pc+ enabling them to be sorted in alphabetical order for non numeric values and in ascending order for numeric values.

Whilst more sophisticated models of capture-recapture are available (Sudman et al., 1988) it was decided that the simplest two-sample model would be adopted, but that the procedure would be repeated over time. Two samples were taken over a one week period at the end of February and beginning of March 1995. Further sets of two samples were taken at the end of April and the end of June. The additional enumeration periods provided data on the nature of change over time and in particular on numbers and characteristics of those moving into and out of the homeless population. Secondly though a mean of three enumerations would provide an estimate of numbers homeless across the study period, a comparison with the median figure would offer some measure of 'quality' control. The closeness of these two figures is not a guarantee of accuracy, however if they had been widely different the question of whether this was due to methodological inconsistency or environmental change would have to be answered.

Evaluation

The accuracy of the resulting estimations are of course critically linked to the quality of the data collection. In particular issues of validity and reliability resulted from the limited resources and time available to the study. Whilst most categories of homelessness were relatively straightforward and gave rise to few validity problems this was not the case for all. For example it was thought to be important that those living in squats be categorised as homeless, yet it is believed that a smaller proportion of this group may come into contact with agencies than others. Conversely, by definition, all hostel residents would be accounted for.

The concern over validity was somewhat less than that over reliability. Though the screening form (used to 'tag' those defined as homeless) was accompanied by guidelines on how the data should be collected, particularly how a homeless person should be so defined, briefing of agency staff was minimal. We simply cannot know the level of commitment to the accurate collection and recording of data. In cases where the study data could be taken directly from an agencies' own records quality could be verified to an extent. For most of the smaller voluntary sector agencies this was not possible. However more than 85 per cent of records were complete and in the case of incomplete records a relatively straightforward manual imputation procedure was successfully used. Nevertheless it seems fair to say that some recording of 'false negatives' and 'false positives' would have been inevitable even where records were complete and verifiable.

Dependency between samples is possibly the most intractable problem. Shaw et al. advocate the selection of agencies to participate in a 'capture-recapture' study rather than an attempt to enumerate at all agencies. A criterion for selection the agencies is absence of cross referral – a key factor in dependency between samples. If practicable the advantage of this would be obvious, yet in a city such as Plymouth if all cross referring agencies were deemed unsuitable then an enumeration would be impossible such is the extent of cross referral. Indeed a practical outcome of the study was a greater degree of coordination between agencies whereby referrals are more routinely made. In mitigation the method used in Plymouth allowed us to know the level and nature of cross referral. Indeed this information proved useful to agencies in so far as it indicated just how many agencies individuals approach, in a short space of time, to seek help.

The value of the approach used in Plymouth may possibly lie in the capture-recapture technique producing a more reliable population estimate than would have otherwise been produced, but additionally the repetition of the procedures over time allowed us to not only verify the accuracy of the capture- recapture estimates, but also to learn a great deal about the process of homelessness. Intra enumeration movement between agencies could be shown, as could disappearance and reappearance in the population. Indeed one of the more valuable findings of the research was that of the rate of turnover. Sixty per cent of cases recorded in the second and third enumerations were new cases. However only four per cent of total cases were recorded at the first and third enumerations. This figure was rather lower than had been anticipated given the hypothesis of fluidity in the homeless population. Our conclusion was that had the study period been longer – say one year, and not five months many more of those counted in the first enumeration period would have 'disappeared' only to 'reappear' at subsequent counts. This conjecture is based upon information subsequently gathered in the interview based stage of the research.

Conclusion

As Shaw et al. have noted difficulties of validity and reliability, specifically linked to 'tagging' and screening procedures are key determinants in whether the method will prove to be of value. Moreover the accuracy of estimation will rest on achieving non dependency between samples. Lastly, I would add, it is possible that other factors such as location and the ability to 'recruit' suitable agencies may be just as important in ensuring success. In Plymouth geographical advantages (described above) may have given a more 'closed' character to the population than would be the case in (say) a similar sized city surrounded, or abutted, by other large urban centres. The agency network is relatively well integrated and cooperative which meant no objections or difficulties were presented to the introduction of a standardised screening procedure. Whilst it is acknowledged that the Plymouth research was very much a first attempt and there is no claim that either the method was perfected or that the results are beyond technical reproach, it remains that the general approach outlined above might offer a best hope scenario. Homeless populations are quintessentially elusive and in principle it may be impossible to ever know with absolute certainty the size of such populations. That the need to know as accurately as possible the size of the homeless population in any given city or town is increasingly linked to funding to tackle the problem, may be the best reason for adopting such approaches, despite the identified deficiencies of the method. As Celsus remarked in AD54 'Diseases are cured by remedies not by rhetoric.'

Notes

1   In the UK the 1977 Housing (Homeless Persons Act), later consolidated into the Housing Act of 1985, defines homelessness as lacking secure accommodation free from violence,

or the threat of violence. The Act identified certain priority groups who can be termed as homeless and in application gave wide discretion to local authorities. Despite later legislation this remains substantially the position today with some local authorities accepting as homeless up to 80 per cent of applications and others as few as 20 per cent (CIPFA, 1994). With the exception of the sick, elderly, or disabled single people are mostly excluded as are those without connections to the locality, or those considered to have made themselves intentionally homeless.

Furthermore the definition of homelessness is interpreted in widely different ways by UK local authorities. Evans and Duncan (1988), in a Department of the Environment sponsored study of local authority responses to homelessness, found that four in 10 authorities surveyed reported difficulties in interpreting the legislation. The result was that the legislation was interpreted in widely different ways. For example all metropolitan authorities in the study reported that they would house childless battered women, compared 80 per cent of non-metropolitan authorities and 76 per cent of London authorities (1988, p. 17). Seven out of 10 authorities accepted applicants over retirement ages as priority needs cases and just under one-fifth would accept young single applicants. Finally there was huge variation in interpreting the concept of 'intentionally homeless', exemplified in the finding that half the authorities surveyed regarded a move to seek employment as becoming intentionally homeless.

2   A detailed face-to-face interview was conducted with a quota sample of those enumerated. This figure is taken from the survey data.

3   Where this is the only accommodation a person has and are in receipt of Housing Benefit.

4   It was anticipated that rough sleepers would at some time make contact with one or more agencies and indeed this proved to be the case. However a vigorous local debate about rough sleeping made a rough sleeper count 'politically' necessary. This was tackled in two ways.

- Firstly volunteers accompanied soup runs in the city during the enumeration periods. During these volunteers conducted a brief interview with the clients and obtained the same identifying information as that gathered in the monitoring.
- Secondly volunteers (including the research team) conducted a systematic rough sleeper count during each enumeration period. This had to be conducted between midnight and 6 a.m. so no identifier information was gathered. The results of these counts were compared with those of the main enumerations in order to obtain a measure of their accuracy.

Bibliography

Anderson, I. et al. (1993), *Single Homeless People*, London, Department of the Environment.

Bishop, Y. et al. (1975), *Discrete Multivariate Analysis,* Cambridge, Mass., MIT Press.

Bloor, M et al. (1994), 'Tideline and Turn: Possible reasons for the continuing low HIV prevalence among Glasgow's injecting drug users', *Sociological Review*, pp. 738–55.

Bramley, G (1988), 'The Definition and Measurement of Homelessness' in Bramley, G. (ed.) *Homelessness and the London Housing Market*, Bristol, SAUS.

CIPFA (1994), *Homeless Statistics 1992–3*, London, The Chartered Institute of Public Finance and Accountancy.

Dale, A. and Marsh, C. (1993), *The 1991 Census User's Guide*, London, HMSO.

Evans, A. and Duncan, S. (1988), *Responding to Homelessness: local authority policy and practice,* London, HMSO.

Fisher, N. et al. (1994), 'Estimating numbers of homeless and homeless mentally ill people in north east Westminster by using capture-recapture analysis', *British Medical Journal*, 308.

Frischer, M. et al. (1991), 'A New Method of Estimating Prevalence of Injecting Drug Use in an Urban Population: Results from a Scottish City', *International Journal of Epidemiology*, vol. 20, 4, pp. 997–1000.

Jencks, C. (1994), *The Homeless*, Cambridge Mass., Harvard University Press.

Lynn, P. (1992), *Survey of Single Homeless People*, London, Social and Community Planning Research.

Moore, J. et al. (1991), *Faces of Homelessness*, Guildford, University of Surrey, Psychology Department, The Housing Research Unit.

Payne, J. (1995), *Interpreting the Index of Local Conditions in Devon and Cornwall*, Plymouth, Plymouth Business School.

Shaw, I. et al. (1996), 'Estimating the Prevalence of Hard-to-Reach Populations: The Illustration of Mark-Recapture Methods in the Study of Homelessness', *Social Policy and Administration*, vol. 30, 1, pp. 69–85.

Sudman, S. et al. (1988), 'Sampling Rare and Elusive Populations', *Science*, 240, pp. 991–6.

Watson, S. (1984) 'Definitions of homelessness: a feminist perspective', *Critical Social Policy*, 11, p. 60–73.

Watson, S. (1988), 'Vulnerable groups and homelessness' in Bramley, G. et al. (eds), *Homelessness and the London Housing Market*, Occasional Paper 32, School for Advanced Urban Studies. Bristol, University of Bristol.

Williams, M. et al. (1995), *Movers and Stayers: Population and Social Change in Cornwall 1971–91*, Plymouth, University of Plymouth, Department of Sociology.

Williams, M. et al. (1995) *Homelessness in Plymouth: Report of research – Stage Two*, Plymouth, University of Plymouth.

Williams, M. and Cox, S. (1994), *Homelessness in Plymouth: Report of research – Stage One*, Plymouth, University of Plymouth, Department of Applied Social Science.

12 US Homeless Research During the 1980s and Early 1990s: Approaches, Lessons Learned, and Methodological Options

MARTHA R. BURT

In this chapter on research on homelessness in the United States since the early 1980s, I will try to describe the different types of studies that have been conducted, who they reach, advances in methodology, and the latest thinking and practice in collecting data to affect policy related to the homeless.

Early Research Efforts – 1983–86

The first simple attempts to count and describe homeless populations occurred during the early and mid-1980s. These studies were usually simple counts, organised to be done on a single night and to count the people in shelters and people on the streets. Pittsburgh, Phoenix, Washington, DC, and other cities conducted such counts (see General Accounting Office, 1988). Boston and Nashville began what became a series of annual (Boston) and twice-yearly (Nashville) counts using the a consistent methodology (see Lee, 1989 for a summary of the Nashville studies). These counts were funded by local governments, foundations, and/or advocacy organisations, and relied heavily on volunteers for data collection.

During the mid-1980s the federal government also started to fund research on homeless populations and homelessness, thus stimulating more sophisticated methodologies and studies describing the homeless. One group of these studies that described homeless people but did not try to estimate the size of the population was supported by the National Institute of Mental Health.

266

These studies, conducted in Los Angeles, St Louis, Detroit, Boston, and the state of Ohio, produced the first important information about the prevalence and problems of homeless people who had a serious mental illness (summarised in Tessler and Dennis, 1989).

Another study, conducted in 1984 by the federal Department of Housing and Urban Development (HUD), did try to estimate the total number of homeless people, and also the number of shelter beds available in the country (Department of Housing and Urban Development, 1984). This was the first effort to make a national estimate, and it ran into a great deal of controversy. The estimate of the number of shelter beds, 110,000, was not in dispute. But HUD tried four different methods for developing an estimate of all homeless people in the United States. These included several ways to extrapolate from shelter bed counts, plus one approach that relied on the opinions of local homeless experts. HUD came up with a range of 192,000 to 586,000 and what it called a 'most reasonable range' of 250,000 to 350,000 based on all four of the methods used. This 'reasonable range' figure, and indeed all of the figures, were considered much too low by homeless advocacy groups, some of whom had been saying that there were almost 10 times that number – 2–3 million (others used more reasonable numbers derived from more adequate methodologies). The advocacy groups sued HUD, Congressional hearings were held, there were many arguments about the methodologies HUD used, and the whole mess meant that HUD never again tried to develop an estimate of population size, despite repeating the shelter survey in 1988 and developing a second estimate of the number of shelter beds (Department of Housing and Urban Development, 1989).

For all that, subsequent research has suggested that the 1984 HUD estimate was probably not too far wrong, as a one-night count. But the advocacy strategy at the time seemed to assume that no one would make serious efforts to solve the problem unless the numbers were very high. So high numbers were needed, they thought, to increase the probability that the problem would be taken seriously enough for the federal government to act. Low numbers, in advocacy eyes, appeared to be an effort to make the problem appear trivial. Some people, even at this time, argued that very high numbers made the problem seem unsolvable, and that lower numbers were more likely to inspire government action because they appeared more manageable. But these arguments did not carry the day in the advocacy community. And, in reality, we do not know in what ways policy has been affected by estimates of population size.

Adding to the numbers controversy were the results of a very important study conducted in Chicago and directed by Peter Rossi (1989). Rossi developed the first sophisticated methodology for estimating the number of homeless people found in outdoor and other non-shelter locations. His method relied on assigning every block in the city of Chicago a probability (low, medium, high, certainty) of finding homeless people on it during a night-time search. Researchers then selected a stratified probability sample of blocks, and went out to count homeless people. Any homeless person found on a block could be assigned a weight, based on the probability of the block being selected and the number of blocks in its stratum. Using this method, which for the first time established a way to generalise to a population estimate from a sample of homeless persons found on the streets, Rossi conducted two surveys in Chicago, one in the autumn of 1985 and another in the winter of 1986.

The estimates of the numbers of homeless on Chicago's streets that Rossi produced using his new method were much lower than expected; they were only one-half to one-third of the figures generally given by advocates in Chicago. The Rossi results were quickly written off by the policy community, but his method was replicated (with some modifications), in two other landmark US studies, the RAND Corporation's surveys in three California counties in 1988 (Vernez et al., 1988), and the Washington, DC Metropolitan Area Drug Study in 1991 (Bray, Dennis and Lambert ,1993). In varying degrees, these studies also produced estimates that were lower than advocacy claims for the same geographical areas, as have most other studies that try to make a count. The difference between expectations and research findings arise in part from the difficulties involved in making an accurate count of the homeless population. However, other factors that are no easier to resolve also play a part, including what definition one is using to identify someone as homeless (discussed in more detail below), whether it is more important to be able to estimate service need (which may include one person using more than one service) the total number of separate individuals, and the period of time for which the count is to be made (one day, one week, one month, etc.).

Developing More Sophisticated Methods to Count and Describe the Homeless – 1987–92

Major research efforts were completed during this period that offered reliable new data on homeless population size and characteristics. These research projects were federally funded; federal agency motivations for supporting them included a desire to have sophisticated and reliable data on which to base federal policy. More than most research, the results of these studies have actually influenced policy and have the potential to continue to do so.

The Urban Institute Study

In 1987, the Food and Nutrition Service of the US Department of Agriculture contracted with the Urban Institute to conduct a study of homeless users of shelters and soup kitchens in cities with 100,000 or more population (Burt and Cohen, 1989, 1988). This survey was the first in the United States to use a probability-based sampling methodology and to collect identical data using identical procedures from homeless people in many cities across the country. Thus the study provides the only *national* picture of the homeless, albeit this picture is restricted to the urban homeless who use services. The study was able to identify the proportion male and female, the proportion from different racial/ethnic groups, the proportion with children (i.e., families), and various other important population characteristics.

The study's funder was an agency whose mission is to improve food access and nutrition for poor people. Thus the study focused on the food needs of the homeless, with the consequence that the design included soup kitchens as well as shelters in its sampling frame. The serendipitous result of including soup kitchens was that the study achieved a reasonably high degree of coverage of that part of the homeless population that did not use shelters, without having to conduct searches of street locations at odd hours of the night. This methodological innovation has proved to be a very important element of other research designs.

Because the Urban Institute study used a probability sampling approach, it could also produce an estimate of the size of the entire urban service-using homeless population, and could use this estimate to extrapolate to a figure for the entire country. This national figure, of 500,000–600,000 homeless persons on any average day, became the figure accepted by government agencies for policy and planning purposes.

The DC Metropolitan Area Drug Study (DC*MADS)

The DC*MADS study (Bray, Dennis and Lambert 1993), funded by the National Institute on Drug Abuse and conducted by the Research Triangle Institute, combined two innovative research methodologies to perform the ultimate investigation of homelessness in an entire metropolitan area (the city of Washington, DC and 16 surrounding counties). For its search of outdoor (non-shelter) locations, the study used the block probability method developed by Rossi for his Chicago studies. It also used a shelter sampling frame, and augmented this with a soup kitchen sampling frame following the Urban Institute methodology. The DC*MADS study thus contained three distinct sampling frames, and could calculate the coverage of the entire homeless population one would achieve using one, two, or all three of the frames. For the service-rich metropolitan area of Washington, DC and its environs, the DC*MADS study found that a study which went only to shelters would capture only 56 per cent of the homeless, but that going to both shelters and soup kitchens would provide better than 90 per cent coverage of the literally homeless. Street searches using the block probability method, which took about two-thirds of the study budget, contributed only about seven per cent of the final count who would not also have been counted at either soup kitchens or shelters. For urban areas similar to Washington, DC that have many services for the homeless, the results of this study strongly suggest that research money would be best spent on covering shelters and soup kitchens, rather than attempting street searches.

The DC*MADS study also was able to help reconcile the ubiquitous discrepancies between formal counts and provider/advocate estimates of the homeless population. The DC*MADS study found that on a given day homeless people made about 15,000 *service contacts* at either shelters or soup kitchens. This figure corresponds quite well with advocate estimates of the size of the homeless population in the Washington DC metropolitan area. However, when the DC*MADS researchers took into account the fact that many homeless people use more than one service on a given day, they arrived at an estimate of 10,000 homeless *people* who had made the 15,000 service contacts. The study concluded that both figures are important. The 15,000 figure indicates the level of service need in the community on a given day, while the 10,000 figure indicates the number of homeless people who would have to be helped if we wanted to eliminate all homelessness (on that day).

1993 to the Present

Evidence for Widespread Homelessness

Two new types of data became available during the mid-1990s – data from shelter tracking databases, and data from telephone surveys. These data provided startling new evidence that the number of people affected by homelessness in a year's time could be as much as six times higher than the number homeless at any given time (Burt, 1994; Culhane et al., 1994), and that the proportion of the population experiencing homelessness within the past five years could be as high as three per cent (7–8 million people – Link et al., 1995, 1994).

Culhane and his colleagues used computerised administrative shelter records from New York City and Philadelphia. These data can be unduplicated, so that each person is counted only once regardless of how many times he or she used the shelter system in either New York or Philadelphia. Using three years of data in Philadelphia, Culhane and colleagues documented that almost three per cent (2.8 per cent) of the city's population had been in a shelter in the years 1990 through 1992. In New York City, more than three per cent (3.3 per cent) of the city's population had been in shelters at least once over the five year period covered by the database. These figures for the proportion of the city population who experienced homelessness are accurate, and are not inflated by counting people in shelter more than once.

Culhane and colleagues found that the average number of days that a person stayed in the shelter system during a year was 120 in New York and 60 in Philadelphia. Since the level of shelter use remained fairly constant throughout the year in both cities, these figures implied that in New York, three times as many people used the shelters in a year's time as were present at any given time; in Philadelphia the corresponding figure was six times as many people. Burt (1994) assembled and summarised similar or more startling figures for both annual levels of homelessness and shelter turnover rates in smaller jurisdictions, indicating that this level of homelessness was not confined only to the nation's largest cities. New data systems are being developed that will supply information on service use and client characteristics from this type of shelter tracking database for more US cities.

The New York and Philadelphia figures, hovering around three per cent of the population, were corroborated from a completely different source – household telephone surveys conducted by Link and his colleagues (1995, 1994). They asked a random sample of adults, reached through a random digit dialling techniques, whether they had ever experienced a period of homelessness in their lives, and whether they had experienced such a period within the past five years. Respondents were also asked to describe their homeless episode(s), so the researchers could classify episodes by whether they did or did not meet definitions of literal homelessness. Their data reveal that 6.5 per cent of American adults had a lifetime experience of literal homelessness, with about three per cent experiencing literal homelessness within the past five years.

Obviously, most of these homeless experiences did not last a very long time, or the one-day homeless population would be considerably higher than the 500,000–600,000 commonly thought to be a reasonable estimate for a 24-hour period. The new data has caused both researchers and policy makers to rethink programmes for the homeless and to consider what services might be relevant for someone who just needs a little help to leave homelessness, as well as for someone who needs a lot of help.

Antecedents and Patterns of Homelessness

Longitudinal studies of homeless cohorts became available in the 1990s for the first time. Several research projects (in Minneapolis, Minnesota and Los Angeles and Oakland, California) undertook to *follow* a sample of homeless people over extended periods of time. These efforts (see, for example, Koegel and Burnam, 1991; Koegel, Burnam and Morton, 1996; Piliavin, Sosin and Westerfelt, 1993; Robertson, Zlotnick and Westerfelt, 1997) revealed in great detail the complexity of homeless careers. While some people may have only one homeless episode, during which they are 'on the streets' for the entire time, many people who are homeless at the time a sample is taken have been found to move in and out of housing quite frequently, depending on how much money they have, how long it lasts, and what other supports they can muster from family, friends, and neighbours. The results of longitudinal research studies help us understand how difficult it is for many homeless people to leave homelessness, and what it will take to truly *end* this type of homeless career.

Longitudinal studies have documented some of the near-term causes of homeless episodes, and shown just how fragile is the hold some people have on stable housing. Both longitudinal and other studies have also highlighted strong associations of negative childhood experiences with homelessness (Bassuk et al., 1997; Caton et al., 1994; Herman et al., 1997; Koegel, Melamid and Burnam, 1995; Mangine, Royse and Wiehe, 1990; Susser, Struening and Conover, 1987; Susser et al., 1991; Weitzman, Knickman and Shinn, 1992; Wood et al., 1990). In particular, histories of foster care and other out-of-home placement, physical and sexual abuse (which often precede out-of-home placement), parental substance abuse, and residential instability and homelessness with one's family as a child are much more common among people who have experienced adult homelessness than among people who have not.

Another important new type of research documents the contribution of certain environments to homelessness, even after one considers the individual characteristics and histories of those who become homeless while living in these environments. Culhane, Lee and Wachter (1996) analyse the addresses of families applying for emergency shelter in New York City and Philadelphia, and find them much more concentrated geographically than poverty in general. Neighbourhoods producing high levels of family homelessness have high concentrations of poor African-American and Hispanic female-headed households that include children under six years of age. The housing is the poorest in the city, and despite the fact that rents are the lowest available, residents still cannot afford them, with the consequence that housing is overcrowded and many families double up, even though apartment vacancy rates are high. The limited amount of research available on service outcomes for homeless families (Rog and Gutman, 1997; Wong, Culhane and Kuhn, 1997) indicates the efficacy of providing housing subsidies as a means of stabilising residential patterns among homeless families and suggests that without such subsidies, these families' personal resources, skills and human capital are not adequate to maintain themselves in housing and otherwise take care of family responsibilities. These are also the families likely to be the least capable of finding employment at the level of self-sufficiency, and therefore to be the hardest hit by welfare reform provisions limiting the time of welfare receipt. Loss of welfare income may precipitate episodes of homelessness.

State Surveys

In recent years, the Department of Housing and Urban Development (HUD) has required systematic data on homeless populations as a condition of receiving federal homeless funds. To help state and local governments meet this obligation, HUD sponsored the development of a manual (Burt, 1992) detailing a variety of methodologies for counting and describing the homeless, including names and phone numbers of people at the state and local level who had used the methods and could be called upon for assistance. The data requirement has for the first time led some states to conduct statewide surveys that went beyond counting people in shelters. New Jersey conducted a statewide survey that went to both shelters and soup kitchens (places that serve prepared meals) (New Jersey Department of Human Services, 1994). Utah surveyed people in shelters, but also included some households staying in motels (State of Utah, 1994). These were people (often families with children) with no other place to stay, usually in communities without a homeless shelter, who did not have enough money to afford the rent on an apartment or house. They stayed in motels for two or three weeks out of every month, or as long as their money lasted, and in their cars for the rest of the time. The Utah agency doing the survey could identify many of these motels and therefore could include them in their count of the homeless.

Some state surveys broke new methodological ground. Two surveys in predominantly rural states, Kentucky and North Dakota, were among them. Their surveys were done over a period of time (two months for Kentucky, two weeks for North Dakota), and reached homeless people through a wide variety of agencies (for example, welfare offices, community action agencies, mental health agencies, police departments, libraries, food pantries and soup kitchens, other food distribution programmes and churches, as well as formal shelters where these existed). They used a screener to determine who was homeless, asking everyone who came to each agency where they were living and whether their living arrangements were stable. If the answer was no, the person was asked to complete the rest of the questionnaire, which took only about two minutes. The questionnaire asked about issues or problems related to the person's homelessness, what services the person needed, and also collected identifying information so that any potential duplications arising from use of more than one agency, or one agency more than one time, could be eliminated. The survey obtained counts and descriptive information for a single day (the first day of the survey) and for the entire period of time covered by the survey. In Kentucky, they also used homeless people to help the researchers find others who were homeless and staying in remote outdoor locations (Kentucky Housing Corporation, 1993).

The results of these expanded state data collection efforts included far more detailed information about local homeless populations than had previously been available to policy makers. Also, in the case of Kentucky where the researchers were particularly thorough, the survey documented a level of need (a level of homelessness) that had not previously been acknowledged as existing in rural areas. This information will influence the distribution of resources in the State of Kentucky, and hopefully also at the national level.

Services Research

Federal government agencies with responsibilities for services to persons with certain disabilities (notably, mental illness, drug abuse, and alcoholism) sponsored demonstration research projects to identify models of care and supported housing that could be successful in bringing some of the most difficult-to-help long-term homeless into stable housing situations. This research has documented quite clearly that we *can* create housing environments with appropriate supportive services that will be attractive to the long-term homeless, will serve their needs, and will succeed in keeping them off the streets (much of this research with respect to the severely mentally ill is summarised by the National Resource Center on Homelessness and Mental Illness, 1992). Now that we know what *will* work, we come directly to the issue of whether the political will exists to create the types of housing and services that are known to help people.

The 1996 National Survey of Homeless Assistance Providers and Clients (NSHAPC)

The lack of national data on the homeless since 1987 has been remedied by a new national survey of the homeless. Funding was a joint effort of twelve federal agencies with responsibilities for homeless programmes; the Census Bureau collected the data. Provider data was assembled between October 1995 and October 1996, and data from service users was collected from mid-October through mid-November 1996.

The design for this survey benefited from all of the methodological breakthroughs during the past decade. The design was based on the 1987 Urban Institute survey, but expanded it in several important ways. First, the new survey used 76 primary sampling units (PSUs) that in combination cover smaller urban, suburban and rural areas, as well as large cities. Most PSUs were metropolitan statistical areas (MSAs). The 28 largest MSAs were selected with certainty; 24 other MSAs were selected using a sampling strategy based on stratification by geographical region and size of MSA. The remaining 24 PSUs were rural areas selected at random from among the catchment areas of a type of social service agency (Community Action Agencies) that covers virtually all rural areas in the United States. This greater geographical representation permits comparison of the situation of homelessness in dense urban areas, in more suburban areas, and in rural areas.

Second, the survey had two parts, a provider component and a client component. The provider component gathered information to describe the entire homeless service network of agencies in each of the 76 PSUs, covering 15 specific types of homeless service plus an 'other' category. The client component drew samples of service users from 10 of the 15 service types (emergency and transitional shelters, permanent housing programmes for formerly homeless people, programmes distributing vouchers for temporary hotel/motel accommodations, soup kitchens, mobile food programmes, outreach programmes, drop-in centres, migrant housing used for homeless people in the off-season, and food pantries in rural areas only).

Third, coverage for service users was improved in two respects: the issues covered, and the range of people included in the interviews. The questions asked of service users were much more extensive in many important areas of policy, including homeless children, the housing and homelessness histories of respondents, medical needs, and conditions of mental illness and substance abuse (both alcohol and drugs). The addition of outreach programmes and food pantries to the traditional soup kitchens and shelters, as sites through which the survey reached homeless people, improved coverage of the homeless population.

Fourth, the survey took place over a one-month period, and went back to particular service providers several times to interview their homeless clients. Therefore, the questionnaire instrument included questions to elicit data for making more accurate projections of service use during the one-month period of data collection (to be able to unduplicate across and within frames). The instrument also asked quite sophisticated questions about period of time homeless and experiences since last leaving a stable living environment; these questions will allow a better assessment of population turnover, exit, and re-entry.

With all of these changes, the coverage of the 1996 survey was considerably greater than was true for the 1987 survey, and provides important new information to feed the policy decisions of the participating federal agencies. Data on service systems should be available publicly in late spring 1998, with client data following in late fall 1998.

Structural Analyses

Several attempts have been made in the United States to understand what factors affect differing rates of homelessness among US cities. Three different databases have been used as the source of the dependent variable – homeless rates per 10,000 population: 1) HUD's 1984 estimates of the numbers of homeless in 60 urban areas (Elliott and Krivo, 1990; Quigley, 1990); 2) number of shelter beds per 10,000 population available in all 178 US cities over 100,000 in population in 1986 (Burt, 1992); and 3) the 1990 decennial census count of sheltered and street homeless on the night and early morning of 20–21 March 1990 (Benjamin, 1995). These analyses can only be as good as their databases allow, and each database has received considerable criticism. Nevertheless, these are the only multi-city databases available, so people have used them to conduct structural analyses, which they accompany with caveats about the appropriateness of the data used for the dependent variable.

Predictive factors examined have all been characteristics of the geographic areas studied. Some have reflected the characteristics of the people who become homeless, such as the poverty rate for the geographic area, its proportion of female-headed households, the rate of publicly subsidised housing units in the area, and other factors associated with the very poor. Other factors were chosen to reflect the pressure on the housing supply from people who were *not* poor, such as the proportion of dwelling units occupied by single middle class people, the amount of convention and tourist business and hotel accommodations, middle class population growth, growth in good-paying jobs, and so on. The most interesting findings from these analyses are that the traditional 'poverty' measures do very little to predict intercity differences in homeless rates, whereas the measures of housing pressure produce much more satisfactory levels of statistical explanation. These findings suggest that the structural factors stimulating increased homelessness may have little to do with the characteristics of the people who actually fall off the bottom of the housing ladder. The most vulnerable fall off, even if they are not a very large part of the local population.

Issues of Survey Design and Population Coverage

The remainder of this paper concentrates on definitions of homelessness, how these definitions affect which people one should target for one's homeless research, and the implications of decisions about definitions for a survey design that tries to reach particular parts of the homeless population. It looks first at definitions, then at potential sampling frames, and finally at potential combination designs. It ends with a discussion of the possible relevance of the US experience for European researchers.

Who Are the Homeless? – Defining the Population of Interest

Any survey involving in-person interviews with homeless people must have a highly-specified mechanism for determining who should and who should not be interviewed – that is, who is and who is not homeless. However, developing such a mechanism is anything but a straightforward task, since a great deal of controversy surrounds definitions of homelessness. There is substantial agreement about the literally homeless – those sleeping on the streets or in shelters. The controversy becomes most heated when considering how to treat people who sleep in conventional dwellings. This segment of the population is known by many terms, including 'the doubled-up', 'the precariously housed', and those 'at imminent risk' of becoming literally homeless. Each term has slightly different implications for who would be included as 'homeless' or 'near-homeless'. The following are definitions of the literally homeless population and of segments of the population sleeping in conventional dwellings who might be considered homeless or at imminent risk of homelessness (i.e., at imminent risk of residing on the streets or in shelters). These definitions will be used as the basis of the present discussion.

Adults, children and youth sleeping in places not meant for human habitation: 'places not meant for human habitation' include streets, parks, alleys, parking ramps, parts of the highway system, transportation depots and other parts of transportation systems (e.g., subway tunnels, railroad cars), abandoned buildings, squatter situations, building roofs or stairwells, chicken coops and other farm outbuildings, caves, camp grounds (with no other usual residence), vehicles, all-night commercial establishments (e.g., cinemas, restaurants, launderettes), and other similar places.

Adults, children and youth in shelters: 'shelters' include all emergency shelters and transitional shelters for homeless persons, all domestic violence shelters, all shelters and residential centres or programmes for runaway and homeless youth, and any hotel/motel/apartment voucher arrangement paid because the person or family is homeless.

Adults, children and youth at imminent risk of residing on the streets or in shelters:

- *children in institutions* – children or youths who, because of their own or a parent's homelessness or abandonment, reside temporarily, and for a short anticipated duration, in hospitals, residential treatment facilities, emergency foster care, detention facilities and the like, and whose legal care has not (yet) been assumed by a foster care agency;
- *adults in institutions* – adults currently residing in mental health facilities, chemical dependency facilities, or short-term criminal justice holding facilities, who at the time of their entry into the facility had no home of their own, no known address, or whose address was a shelter for the homeless, or another facility such as a soup kitchen serving the homeless;

- *adults, children and youth living 'doubled-up' in conventional dwellings –* the categories described below are subsets of the larger category commonly referred to as 'the doubled-up.' If being doubled-up means that a dwelling unit is occupied by two or more sub-households, then the very large majority of doubled-up households are voluntary arrangements and do not imply homelessness or an imminent risk of homelessness – e.g., a teen mother and her child living with her mother, an elderly couple residing in the home of their adult child, or roommate and college student group house arrangements. The definition given here of people at imminent risk is designed to identify the people in doubled-up situations who might be considered most likely to find themselves literally homeless – that is, residing on the streets or in shelters.

1 One category is the 'precariously housed'. For people sleeping in conventional dwelling units to be considered 'precariously housed', their housing situation must:

   a have arisen from an inability to pay for one's own housing due to an emergency; and
   b be of short anticipated duration (less than 60 days).[1]

2 The most severe risk category is a precariously housed child, youth, adult, or family who has:

   a no plans or prospects for stable housing; and
   b no financial resources to obtain housing.

Pragmatically, a set of screening questions would be used to determine the degree of imminent risk among the doubled-up, such as:

   a left last stable housing situation due to financial emergency;
   b anticipated length of stay (less than 60 days);
   c not contributing to rent;
   d no safe place to go if told to leave;
   e income of sub-household at or below poverty level.

Where Are the Homeless? – Selecting Appropriate Sampling Frames

Conducting a survey of homeless people requires first locating them. While this statement would be trivial if applied to people residing in conventional dwelling units, it presents the second set of issues with respect to the homeless – where to find them, and how hard to search.

The definitions of the homeless presented above provide some sense of the different locations where homeless people may be found – in shelters, in 'places not meant for human habitation', and in conventional dwellings. But there is no simple one-to-one association between these locations and preferred methods or sampling strategies. Nor will any single approach capture a very high proportion of the population of interest.

In deciding which sampling frames to include, it is helpful to divide the population of potential interest into the literally homeless (those in the first two definitional categories), and those at imminent risk of residing on the streets or in shelters (the remaining definitional categories). There can be little question that any study of the homeless must attempt to locate and interview a representative sample of the literally homeless. There is more room for debate as to the extent of coverage necessary or desirable for those at imminent risk of literal homelessness, and the methods required to reach this second subgroup are quite different from those that will reach the literally homeless.

Each of these two broad categories is further subdivided into service users and non-users – a distinction that is helpful in selecting strategies for finding homeless people. Most studies of the homeless go to shelters to find homeless people. Thus a primary research strategy in the homeless area relies on a type of service agency, namely shelters, as a sampling frame.

A number of studies have used soup kitchens, a second type of service agency, as an additional sampling frame. In the Urban Institute's 1987 national study, 29 per cent of the final sample were found to have used soup kitchens but not shelters within the week prior to the interview. Further, among homeless people interviewed on the streets, 68 per cent had used either a soup kitchen or a shelter within the previous seven days, giving some sense of the coverage obtainable when both shelters and soup kitchens are included in the design. This coverage increases to approximately 85 per cent of the literally homeless when the time period is extended to the previous 30 days (see Bray, Dennis and Lambert, 1993 for the Washington, DC metropolitan area; Farr, Koegel and Burnam, 1986 for downtown Los Angeles).

The strategy of locating homeless people through the services they use has thus proved to be efficient and reasonably thorough in urban areas, where studies have concentrated on homeless-specific services. An informal survey (conducted by the author for the Census Bureau) of key informants in several non-MSA areas selected from different geographical regions indicates that an approach using service networks will also be able to reach most of the homeless in these areas, especially in the winter months. In these rural areas, the service networks included homeless-specific services where those existed, and many other types of agency. Key informant estimates of 'most' ranged from about 60 per cent to 90 per cent, in 10 of 11 areas examined. In only one area, New Mexico, was the informant sceptical of reaching even half of the non-MSA homeless through service networks. The experience of the Kentucky Housing Corporation study (1993) confirms this impression that many of the homeless can be reached even in rural areas through their contacts with a wide range of homeless and non-homeless services (examples of the latter include mental health services, libraries, and jails).

Figure 12.1 displays the four subgroups of potential interest – service users and non-users among the literally homeless and those at imminent risk – and examines the ability of various research strategies to locate and interview people belonging to each subgroup. In addition to the strategies that locate shelter and soup kitchen users, Figure 12.1 also looks at strategies that might result in including literally homeless users of other services and non-service users, and strategies to locate and interview people at imminent risk of literal homelessness. The following discussion pertains to conditions in the United States.

Shelters and Soup Kitchens

The first two rows of Figure 12.1 give the probable coverage resulting from designs that use shelters or soup kitchens as locations for contacting homeless people. A design combining these two frames was used in the Urban Institute's 1987 national study, and is illustrated on the second page of Figure 12.1 as the first row under 'Combination Options – Urban'.

The shelter frame covers homeless people who use shelters, which may be 35–40 per cent of the homeless on any given night, and about 50 per cent over the course of a week.[2] If performed on a one-night basis, the shelter sampling frame taken by itself will miss many homeless who use shelters infrequently, homeless service users who do not use shelters but do use soup kitchens and other services, and homeless people who do not use any services. If data collection involves repeated samples from the same shelters over the

Sampling frame for survey	Literally homeless		At imminent risk		Comments – these reflect US situation, and may differ in other countries
	Non-service users*	Service users*	Non-service users*	Service users*	
a Shelters	No	Some[1]	No	No	Easiest
b Soup kitchens	No	Some[2]	No	Some[3]	Easiest
c Outreach programmes	Yes	Some	No	No	Good way to reach street 'encampments' if they exist; also populations such as youth and the mentally ill homeless who are often difficult to find
d Other service sites for homeless (e.g., health, drop-in)	No	Some[4]	No	No	Not often included for client surveys, heavy overlap with a & b, low apparent payoff
e Street – block/area probability approach	Some[4]	Some[4]	No	No	Little increased coverage for much more effort
f Institutions	Some	Some	No	No	Little increased coverage for much more effort
g Generic service sites (welfare, service and charity agencies)	No	Few	No	More than b	Only worth effort if want 'imminent risk' and cannot do h, or if have few or no homeless-specific services (a, b, c or d)
h Survey of conventional dwelling units	No	No	Yes	Yes	Add-on to existing survey, or special survey. Only way to get statistically representative reading on 'imminent risk' population

Figure 12.1   Research strategies to locate literally homeless service users and non-users and those at imminent risk

Sampling frame for survey	Literally homeless		At imminent risk		Comments – these reflect US situation, and may differ in other countries
	Non-service users*	Service users*	Non-service users*	Service users*	
Combination Options – Urban					
a & b	No	Most	No	Some	Probably gets 70–80% of literally homeless[5]
a, b & c	Yes-many	Most	No	Some	Probably gets 85-90% of literally homeless[5]
a, b, d & f	No	Most	No	Some	Not much more than a & b; probably less than a, b & c
a, b, c, d, & g	**Yes – many**	**Most**	**Some**	**Some**	**Worth doing if the programmes in c & d are screened to include only those without much overlap in clients with a & b**
a, b, c & h	Yes – many	Most	Most	Most	Very comprehensive, but much expense devoted to covering at-risk population
all (a through h)	Yes – many	Most	Most	Most	Most comprehensive, but expensive for the additional coverage
Combination Options – Rural[6]					
a, b & c	Yes – many	Most	No	Some	Adequate for covering literally homeless
a, b, c & g	Some	Most	No	Some	**Including g may identify some of the doubled up**
a, b, c, d, g, & h	Some	Most	Most	Most	H is probably needed if one wants a reliable reading of those at imminent risk

* A 'service user' is anyone who uses shelters *or* soup kitchens *or* other services for the homeless *or* generic services. A 'non-service user' is anyone who does not use any of these services. Data in footnotes 1, 2, and 3 are from the 1987 Urban Institute study; see Burt and Cohen, 1989.

1 In urban areas, about 55 per cent also use soup kitchens.

2 In urban areas, about 57 per cent are homeless; of these 57% also use shelters.

3 In urban areas, about 43 per cent of soup kitchen users reside in conventional dwellings; we do not know, however, what proportion this represents of domiciled households at imminent risk of literal homelessness.

4 Heavy overlap with a and b.

5 Assumes the jurisdiction(s) to be covered have a reasonable number of these services; assumes a 30-day interviewing schedule, with repeat visits to sites. Even this may not be adequate to cover rural areas with few services.

6 For rural options, 'b' (soup kitchens) includes food pantries and similar food distribution mechanisms.

course of a week or a month, a considerably higher proportion of the homeless (perhaps as high as 70 per cent) is likely to be captured through a methodology based on shelters.

The soup kitchen sampling frame, taken by itself over the course of a week, will probably pick up about 45 per cent of the total homeless population, and an unknown proportion of very poor people residing in conventional dwellings who may turn out to be at imminent risk of homelessness.[3] It will miss about half of the shelter-using homeless, and all of the non-service using homeless and at-risk populations. Taken together and performed over the course of a week, the shelter and soup kitchen frames will probably cover about 70 per cent of the literally homeless and a small but unknown proportion of the service-using at-risk population. If data collection is stretched to a month, the coverage will be even greater – perhaps as high as 85–90 per cent of the literally homeless.

Outreach Programmes

In many cities, the array of services for the homeless include one or more outreach programmes. These programmes may be operated by a shelter, a soup kitchen, a drop-in centre, a health care centre, neighbourhood centre, or other service facility. Their target population is homeless people who do not routinely use shelters or soup kitchens. The outreach programmes typically distribute food, and sometimes blankets or warm clothing. Specialised outreach teams may also do psychiatric diagnoses, assist people to apply for public benefits, or help them get in touch with needed services. Outreach teams typically follow a route that covers the known locations frequented by homeless street people, or at which homeless street people assemble at the time they know the 'food wagon' will come by. Including outreach programmes in a design as a sampling frame allows one to maintain the control and efficiency associated with sampling service programmes and their users, while still reaching the 'reachable' portion of the street homeless population.

The outreach services that distribute food could be included in the sampling frame for soup kitchens, even if the overall category of outreach programmes were not made a sampling frame of its own. But the specialised outreach efforts focused on homeless youth, or on the chronically mentally ill, often do not distribute food – they merely keep in touch with their target populations and offer assistance as needed. Since these specialised populations are among the hardest to reach and the least likely to use 'stationary' services, creating an explicit sampling frame to include them has distinct advantages in enhancing study coverage for far less additional cost than would be required by an area probability approach based on streets or blocks.

Other Homeless Service Sites

Some studies of the homeless have augmented the shelter/soup kitchen sampling frames by including other homeless service sites such as drop-in centres and health care programmes. If a drop-in centre serves one or more meals, it should be classified as a soup kitchen and included in that sampling frame. Health care for the homeless service delivery sites tend to be located in soup kitchens or shelters, since to increase access they often set up service in places where homeless people congregate. Given the actual patterns of service use among the homeless, the inclusion of these additional service sites would probably not provide access to many more homeless people than would be covered by going only to shelters and soup kitchens, and would do nothing to increase coverage of the at-risk population (unless there is reason to suspect that many users of health care for the homeless services are not literally homeless).

Street-Block/Area Probability Frame

Many homeless people (probably 70–85 per cent) who appear on the streets during the daytime actually use services, and can be counted and interviewed through a design based on service sites. However, because a certain proportion of the homeless population do not use any services, no research design based exclusively on access through the usual service sites of shelters and soup kitchens will include them. The issues with respect to these non-service users are what proportion they comprise of the whole homeless population, and how important it is, in relation to cost and effort, to represent their numbers accurately in any particular study.

Methods have been developed for urban areas to conduct statistically generalisable street surveys, but these tend to be very expensive in relation to the number of homeless people they actually add to the count. In general, the findings of several studies using these methods (Bray, Dennis and Lambert, 1993; Rossi, Fisher and Willis, 1986; Vernez et al., 1988) are that *very* few homeless people are identified in the sweeps of most blocks. The exceptions are those few blocks/areas which Rossi called 'super blocks' and Michael Dennis has begun to call 'encampments.' These are locations identified by the virtual certainty of finding homeless people sleeping there on any given night. These encampments are relatively easy to identify; most cities do not have an overwhelming number of them (Dennis found 17 in the whole Washington metropolitan area), the homeless people found in them comprise a high proportion of the total street count for the homeless, and a relatively high proportion (15–20 per cent, according to Dennis) do not use either shelters or conventional soup kitchens. A design which augmented a basic shelter/soup kitchen strategy by including street encampments would probably succeed in covering close to 90 per cent of the literally homeless.

The most efficient way to include the encampments in a national survey is to rely on outreach programmes (see above). If one were doing a street probability survey, outreach teams would be the researcher's best source of up-to-date information on the location of encampments and the probability of finding homeless people in particular settings. It is far more efficient, and easier to handle statistically when weighting the results, to reach the street population directly through the outreach programmes, thus maintaining all sampling frames as 'service' frames. Including the outreach programmes, and thereby the encampments, would provide the ability to describe most non-users of standard services at relatively little additional cost. To do other than this in an effort to improve coverage would add significantly to the cost of a study without much payoff.

Institutions

Some people who currently reside in institutions such as general hospitals, mental hospitals, chemical dependency treatment programmes, jails, detention centres, and the like either were literally homeless when they entered the institution, or will be literally homeless when they leave (or both). Yet while they are institutionalised, they are not literally homeless. Furthermore, the anticipated length of stay for people in some institutions such as prisons may be so long that trying to guess their condition upon release, or asking them whether they would be homeless if they had to leave today, are purely hypothetical exercises. Still, some studies have tried to identify those people currently in institutions who were or will be literally homeless, and to include them in a count and description of the homeless population. Thus whether or not to do so in a national study is a decision that must be made.

The big questions with respect to this segment of the homeless population are, how big is it (and therefore how important is its inclusion), and can we get the same people without actually going to the institutions. In all probability, homeless people in institutions are a very small proportion of the total homeless population at any given time. Further, average length of stay in most of the institutions in question is quite short – short enough so that if data collection for a design that included shelters, soup kitchens, and outreach programmes were scheduled over a month's time, most of them would be counted either before they entered institutions or after they were released.

Including institutions in the study design would require adding an entirely new second stage sampling frame and involve considerably more work, for very limited payoff given the alternative ways to count the same people. In a report recently sent to Congress from the Department of Education which presented designs for counting homeless children and youth, even the representatives of advocacy organisations on the advisory group agreed that the numbers in institutions were insignificant in relation to the effort required to learn about them, and that study designs should therefore exclude institutions (Burt, 1991).

Generic Service Sites

In general, studies show that currently literally homeless people are not heavy users of generic services. The only exceptions are homeless households that include children, which in the US often receive AFDC or General Assistance, and homeless people in rural areas where there are no homeless-specific services. In urban areas, these households of interest also are virtually all in shelters or vouchered hotel/motel arrangements (often paid for by AFDC-Emergency Assistance, at least through 1997), so they would be captured through shelter surveys. Most other literally homeless urban users of generic services such as General Assistance will also be found at service sites, which often help them apply for these benefits. However, in rural areas it may be necessary or advisable to include generic service sites in a study design, since these types of programmes may be all there is.

Other than in rural areas, the primary reason to include generic service sites in the study design is to capture a larger proportion than would otherwise be possible of the population residing in conventional dwellings but at imminent risk of becoming literally homeless. It may be assumed (but has not been demonstrated) that many of those at imminent risk will be found among people poor enough to be receiving a variety of benefits through generic government programmes; therefore these sites should be included if reaching the at-risk population is a high priority and if it is impossible to include a survey of conventional dwelling units in the design.

In rural areas, the few studies that exist have tended to include in their counts of the homeless people whom we defined above as part of the 'imminent risk' group – that is, people in doubled-up situations whose circumstances arose from a crisis or emergency, and who were not able to stay in their current living arrangement for more than 45 days (Toomey's operational definition in Ohio; 43 per cent of homeless people counted fell into this category – however, most of these people had experienced an episode of literal homelessness during the six months that the study went on). There may be some reasonableness in counting such people as homeless in rural areas, as they would probably be in shelters if there were any shelters to be in. Such results from rural areas tend to be interpreted as 'rural homelessness is different than urban homelessness,' but in fact the same design has never been used in urban areas. If it had been, undoubtedly large numbers of urban households in conventional dwellings would also show up as homeless (meaning there are a lot of desperate people everywhere).

Anyone, regardless of country, who is designing a national study and wants to go to both rural and urban areas *and use the same design in both* should take seriously the possible need to include generic service sites as one second-stage sampling frame that would make it possible to tap the at-risk population. In the US, the NSHAPC abandoned the criterion of using the same design in both, and included food pantries (a type of generic agency) in rural areas only. A better solution, of course, but a significantly more expensive one, would be a survey of conventional dwelling units themselves, as described below. Another alternative for tapping this population is to add several questions to an already existing national household survey.

Conventional Dwelling Units

A survey of conventional dwelling units, through which one asks about people within each unit who meet the criteria for being at imminent risk, is the only way to get a complete and reliable view of this component of the homeless population. The priority given to including this approach in an overall study of the homeless will depend on how politically or scientifically necessary it is judged to be to cover the at-risk population.

There appear to be two routes to consider if one wants to include conventional dwelling units in the overall design. The first is to add questions onto an already existing national survey. The second is to conduct a special survey of dwelling units in the same PSUs selected for the surveys of shelters, soup kitchens, and encampments.

The second page of Figure 12.1 shows my expectation of the coverage of each population segment obtainable using different combinations of methods. The options in bold are the recommended study designs for urban and rural areas. As noted earlier in this article, the NSHAPC used these two options as the sampling frames for its client component (food pantries were the only generic agency included in rural areas). However, in the provider component of the NSHAPC, every variety of homeless-specific agency was surveyed, and its services documented.

Relevance of the American Experience to European Studies of the Homeless

Conditions of service systems, homeless populations, and survey resources are very different in each European country and in the United States. Countries without well-developed service systems for the homeless might be more like rural areas in the United States in their inability to reach the homeless through homeless-specific services because few such services exist. On the other hand, most European countries have much better developed systems of 'safety net' services, and these might be expected to *prevent* homelessness among a great number of households and individuals who might be at risk of homelessness in the United States. Europeans might therefore be much more interested in learning about the part of the population who are at risk of homelessness, so they could be helped through the generic service systems. The remaining population who become literally homeless may be quite different in Europe and the United States, with the European homeless more closely resembling those in the United States who avoid homeless-specific services and basically forage on their own. This would certainly affect the research strategies one would choose to reach them.

The best way for European researchers to benefit from the US experience of conducting homeless research for the past 15 years is to think very carefully about the known characteristics of your homeless populations and of your service systems, and also about which parts of the homeless and near-homeless population it is important for you to reach. With this information in hand, you will be better able to focus on the methodological developments in the United States that have the most relevance to your situation. Since we have certainly made every mistake there is to make in doing this research, and have capitalised on what we have learned from making them to improve our methodological approaches, we are happy to have others benefit from our years in the trenches.

Notes

1   If the person in question is a youth (unaccompanied minor), who would not normally be expected to pay for his/her own housing, the emergency might include being a runaway, pushout, or throwaway.

2   From the Urban Institute study results, we can posit that service users comprise at least 70 per cent, and non-service users no more than 30 per cent, of the homeless. Of service users, 53 per cent (37 per cent of total population) had spent the previous night in a shelter, and 71 per cent (49 per cent of total population) had spent at least one night in a shelter during the previous week.

3   According to the Urban Institute study, 43 per cent of soup kitchen users are not literally homeless. Both the DC*MADS study (Bray, Dennis and Lambert ,1993) and Sosin's research in Chicago (Sosin, Colson and Grossman, 1986) indicate that about one half of currently domiciled soup kitchen users have been homeless at least once in the past, suggesting the general risk level of soup kitchen users, even if currently living in conventional housing.

Bibliography

Bassuk, E.L., Buckner, J.C., Weinreb, L.F., Browne, A., Bassuk, S.S., Dawson, R. and Perloff, J.N. (1997), 'Homelessness in female-headed families: Childhood and adult risk and protective factors', *American Journal of Public Health*, 87 (2), pp. 241–8.

Benjamin, R. (1995), 'Inter-city homeless rates and housing and social indicators', Washington, DC, Department of Housing and Urban Development, unpublished document.

Bray, R.M., Dennis, M.L. and Lambert, E.Y. (1993), *Prevalence of Drug Use in the Washington, DC Metropolitan Area Homeless and Transient Population: 1991*, Rockville, Md, National Institute on Drug Abuse, Division of Epidemiology and Prevention Research.

Burt, M.R. (1991), *Alternative Methods for Counting Homeless Children and Youth*, prepared for the Department of Education, Report to Congress, 26 July.

Burt, M.R. (1992), *Over the Edge: The Growth of Homelessness in the 1980s*, New York and Washington, DC, Russell Sage Foundation and the Urban Institute.

Burt, M.R. (1992), *Practical Methods for Counting Homeless People: A Manual for State and Local Governments*, Washington, DC, Interagency Council on the Homeless and Department of Housing and Urban Development.

Burt, M.R. (1994), comment on Dennis P. Culhane, Edmund F. Dejowski, Julie Ibañez, Elizabeth Needham and Irene Macchia's 'Public shelter admission rates in Philadelphia and New York City: The implications of turnover for sheltered population counts', *Housing Policy Debate*, 5 (2), pp. 141–52.

Burt, M.R. and Cohen, B.E. (1989), *America's Homeless: Numbers, Characteristics, and the Programs that Serve Them*, Washington, DC, Urban Institute Press.

Burt, M.R. and Cohen, B.E. (1998), *Feeding the Homeless: Does the Prepared Meals Provision Help?*, Washington, DC, The Urban Institute.

Caton, C.L.M., Shrout, P.E., Eagle, P.F., Opler, L.A., Felix, A. and Dominguez, B. (1994), 'Risk factors for homelessness among schizophrenic men: A case-control study', *American Journal of Public Health*, 84, pp. 265–70.

Culhane, D., Dejowski, E., Ibañez, J., Needham, E. and Macchia, I. (1994), 'Public shelter admission rates in Philadelphia and New York City: Implications for sheltered population counts', *Housing Policy Debate*, 5 (2), pp. 107–40.

Culhane, D.P., Lee, C.M. and Wachter, S.M. (1996), 'Where the homeless come from: A study of the prior address distribution of families admitted to public shelters in New York city and Philadelphia', *Housing Policy Debate*, 7 (2), pp. 327–66.

Department of Housing and Urban Development (1984), *A Report to the Secretary on the Homeless and Emergency Shelters*, Washington, DC, Department of Housing and Urban Development, Office of Policy Development and Research.

Department of Housing and Urban Development (1989), *A Report on the 1988 National Survey of Shelters for the Homeless*, Washington, DC, Department of Housing and Urban Development, Office of Policy Development and Research.

Elliott, M. and Krivo, L. (1991), 'Structural determinants of homelessness in the United States', *Social Problems*, 38 (1), pp. 113–31.

Farr, R., Koegel, P. and Burnam, M.A. (1986), *A Study of Homelessness and Mental Illness in the Skid Row Area of Los Angeles*, Los Angeles, Los Angeles County Department of Mental Health.

General Accounting Office (1988), *The Homeless Mentally Ill: Problems and Options in Estimating Numbers and Trends*, Washington, DC, USGPO, GAO/RCED-88-63.

Herman, D.B., Susser, E.S., Struening, E.L. and Link, B.L (1997), 'Adverse childhood experiences: Are they risk factors for adult homelessness?', *American Journal of Public Health*, 87 (2), pp. 249–55.

Kentucky Housing Corporation (1993), *Kentucky Homeless Survey Preliminary Findings*, Lexington, KY, Kentucky Housing Corporation.

Koegel, P. and Burnam, M.A. (1991), 'The Course of Homelessness Study: Aims and Designs', paper presented at the 119th Annual Meeting of the American Public Health Association, November 1, Atlanta, Ga., Santa Monica, Ca., RAND Corporation.

Koegel, P., Burnam, M.A. and Morton, S.C. (1996), 'Enumerating homeless people: alternative strategies and their consequences', *Evaluation Review*, 20, pp. 378–403.

Koegel, P., Melamid, E. and Burnam, M.A. (1995), 'Childhood risk factors for homelessness among homeless adults', *American Journal of Public Health*, 85 (12), pp. 1642–9.

Lee, B. (1989), 'Stability and change in an urban homeless population', *Demography*, 26 (2), pp. 323–34.

Link, B. Phelan, J., Bresnahan, M., Stueve, A., Moore, R. and Susser, E. (1995), 'Lifetime and five-year prevalence of homelessness in the United States: New evidence on an old debate', *American Journal of Orthopsychiatry*, 65 (3), pp. 347–54.

Link, B., Susser, E., Stueve, A., Phelan, J., Moore, R. and Struening, E. (1994), 'Lifetime and five-year prevalence of homelessness in the United States' *American Journal of Public Health*, 84, pp. 1907–12.

Mangine, S.J., Royse, D. and Wiehe, V.R. (1990), 'Homelessness among adults raised as foster children: a survey of drop-in center users' *Psychological Reports*, 67, pp. 739–45.

National Resource Center on Homelessness and Mental Illness (1992), *Annotated Bibliography: Developing Housing for Homeless Persons with Severe Mental Illnesses*, Delmar, NY, Policy Research Associates, Inc., March and September.

New Jersey Department of Human Services (1994), *A Demographic Profile of New Jersey's Homeless Population*, Trenton, NJ, New Jersey Department of Human Services.

Piliavin, I., Sosin, M. and Westerfelt, A.H. (1993), 'The duration of homeless careers: An exploratory study', *Social Service Review*, 67, pp. 576–98.

Quigley, J.M. (1990), 'Does rent control cause homelessness?: Taking the claim seriously', *Journal of Policy Analysis and Management*, 9, pp. 88–93.

Robertson, M.J., Zlotnick, C. and Westerfelt, A. (1997), 'Drug use disorders and treatment contact among homeless adults in Alameda County, California', *American Journal of Public Health*, 87 (2), pp. 217–20.

Rog, D.J. and Gutman, M. (1997), 'The Homeless Families Program: A summary of key findings' in Isaacs, S. and Knickman, J.R. (eds), *To Improve Health and Health Care, 199: The Robert Wood Johnson Anthology*, San Francisco, Jossey-Bass.

Rossi, P. (1989), *Down and Out in America: The Origins of Homelessness*, Chicago, Il., The University of Chicago Press.

Rossi, P.H., Fisher, G.A. and Willis, G. (1986), *The Condition of the Homeless in Chicago*, Amherst, Ma. and Chicago, Social and Demographic Research Institute and the National Opinion Research Center.

Sosin, M.R., Colson, P. and Grossman, S. (1988), *Homelessness in Chicago: Poverty and Pathology, Social Institutions and Social Change*, Chicago, Chicago Community Trust.

State of Utah (1994), *Utah 1993 Homeless Count*, Salt Lake City, UT, Community Development Division, Department of Community and Economic Development.

Susser, E.S., Struening, E.L. and Conover, S.A. (1987), 'Childhood experiences of homeless men', *American Journal of Psychiatry*, 144, pp. 1599–601.

Susser, E.S., Lin, S.P., Conover, S.A. and Struening, E.L. (1991), 'Childhood antecedents of homelessness in psychiatric patients', *American Journal of Psychiatry*, 148, pp. 1026–30.

Tessler, R.C. and Dennis, D.L. (1989), *A Synthesis of NIMH-funded Research Concerning Persons Who Are Homeless and Mentally Ill*, Rockville, Md, National Institute of Mental Health, Division of Education and Service Systems Liaison, Program for the Homeless Mentally Ill.

Vernez, G., Burnam, M.A., McGlynn, E.A., Trude, S. and Mittman, B. (1988), *Review of California's Program for the Homeless Mentally Disabled*, Santa Monica, Ca., The RAND Corporation.

Weitzman, B.C., Knickman, J.R. and Shinn, M. (1992), 'Predictors of shelter use among low-income families: psychiatric history, substance abuse, and victimization', *American Journal of Public Health*, 82, pp. 1547–50.

Wong, I., Culhane, D.P. and Kuhn, R. (1997), 'Predictors of shelter exit and return among homeless families in New York City', *Social Service Review*, 71 (3), pp. 441–62.

Wood, D., Valdez, R.B., Hayashi, T. and Shen, A. (1990), 'Homeless and housed families in Los Angeles: A study comparing demographic, economic, and family function characteristics', *American Journal of Public Health*, 80, pp. 1049–52.

13 Conclusions and Policy Implications

ANGELIKA KOFLER

Introduction

Homelessness research faces unique challenges and thus the question of appropriate methods is crucial in order to obtain data at the national as well as at the European level that can be used as a solid foundation for policy development. The following summarises the idiosyncrasies of this field of research, the status quo of currently available data in Europe, provides subsequent conclusions, and points out major policy implications.

Challenges and Methodologies

Unique Challenges in Homelessness Research

Typical challenges in homelessness research are related to the nature of the research population and are an ongoing subject of refinement and improvement in order to generate comparable data across countries. Even before defining the homeless as a sub-population, the conceptual question arises of whether homelessness needs to be seen as a phenomenon in itself or as a symptom of a larger phenomenon in the context of housing exclusion, social exclusion and poverty.

More than is the case with other topics, research about homelessness is prone to the influence of ideological underpinnings. Whether homelessness is seen as a phenomenon caused by individual characteristics or whether it is seen as the result of structural deterioration impacts on the nature of research and ensuing policy recommendations. The focus on the individual can provide insights into individual coping behaviour and the way service providers can assist in this process. The structural focus at the macro level stresses deteriorating or improving circumstances. Either focus can provide information, yet care has to be taken under what assumptions it is collected and used. Furthermore, quantitative data, in particular numerical estimates of homeless people, have to be examined within the country-specific context, related to policies and likely outcomes, particularly when comparisons among countries are made.

These considerations, naturally, inform the various definitions of homelessness that are used in research. It appears that in some European countries such as Germany, Finland or the UK a trend towards changing paradigms away from investigations of individual traits of the homeless towards contextual studies that take structural factors such as poverty, unemployment and housing shortages into account can already be observed. The need to integrate homelessness research into the body of knowledge on related issues still needs to be emphasised.

In sum, definitions of homelessness on which consequent research is based are closely related to ideological preconceptions on the cause of homelessness as well as to pragmatic methodological decisions. It is clear that homelessness is a multifarious problem, and, especially if the emphasis of research designs is on housing, care needs to be taken not to neglect the wider social context. It is crucial to pay attention to how the phenomenon is studied. Ideally, homelessness research will be defined as investigations of the *processes* that lead to homelessness, investigations of *actual homelessness* as well as investigations of homelessness careers *over time* (which may well include periods of time were individuals are not homeless).

Concepts and definitions The different aims as well as the resources available lead to a variety of operationalisations of homelessness. Currently, as can also be seen in the chapters of this book, research definitions on different levels of accuracy are in use and include distinctions such as the following:

- *service-users* and *non-users*;
- *long-term* homeless and *temporarily* homeless people (with parameters of x days defined);
- *actually homeless*, individuals *threatened by homelessness*; *potential homelessness* individuals presently *having housing* and individuals *not having housing* according to that definition;
- staying in a *hostel, bed and breakfast*, staying in a *squat*, temporarily with *friends, nonresidential institutions, residential institutions, sleeping rough;*
- living *outdoors or in temporary* shelters, in *night shelters or other shelters* for the homeless, in *institutions, prisoners* soon to be released who have

no housing, persons living temporarily *with relatives and acquaintances*, families who have *split up or are living in temporary* housing;
* *homeless, roofless, marginally housed.*

Regardless of the definition chosen, categories are not mutually exclusive. Moreover, one definition will probably not suffice for all purposes. Rather, careful consideration of research objectives needs to inform the choice of any given research design, paying particular attention to the questions that unclear situations can raise.

It has to be decided if the defined homeless population will, for example, include those in mental or drug treatment institutions or correction facilities or people staying with families or friends for lack of income to afford independent housing. Another consideration regards potential qualitative distinctions in housing situations between, for example, those who are staying with friends temporarily and young people who cannot leave the parental home for lack of resources to afford own housing; people resigned to their fate in overcrowded or otherwise inadequate lodgings as compared to those registered on application lists for social housing; or someone evicted and temporarily homeless versus someone living in the streets for years.

Particular attention in the definition of research populations needs to be paid to vulnerable groups who are potentially at risk to fall into homelessness in order to understand the processes leading to homelessness and to enable the formulation of preventive measures. For risk groups, too, definitions are required. Dragana Avramov distinguishes risk-prone people and risk carriers while at the same time, however, conceding that the only available data about the homeless is cross-sectional. Therefore this distinction escapes empirical documentation. In other words, definitions of risk groups will depend not only on the requirements of research designs but also on the accumulation of knowledge about causal factors leading to homelessness which may or may not be included in research designs.

To decide if someone with unstable housing scenarios is homeless, whose standards apply, especially across countries, or how often an individual has to sleep in shelters or in makeshift accommodation and for how long in order to be considered a member of the homeless population are crucial in the conceptualisation of the research design and also relate to the problem of relative or absolute standards of accommodation as well as of poverty.

In sum, conceptual questions relate mostly to the following domains: the period of time without housing or without adequate housing that defines homelessness; the point of view that defines homelessness; and the definition of adequate housing or housing norms which may go beyond physical housing norms and include (or exclude) notions of autonomy. The chosen concept and consequent data that studies provide are closely related to the translation of such data into policy measures targeted at the homeless population and its subgroups or related populations such as those that are not actually homeless but can be considered at risk of homelessness.

Ethics and numbers Homelessness research is as much an issue of ethics as it is one of methodology. Ethical questions are involved at different levels: the purpose of the research effort, the research design, the research procedure itself, and finally the usage of the data that research yields. To deal with these issues, the following questions need to be addressed: Who is benefiting from the research efforts? Which issues does the research address and whose problems is it trying to solve? What happens with the data and research results, particularly with numerical estimates, after they are published?

Numerical estimates of homeless populations which are such attractive elements of research for policy makers and the public alike are typically faced with distinct problems: under-counts, double counts, and the problem of covering mobility. A population subgroup for which the problem of under-counting is particularly relevant might be illegal aliens. However, estimates of numbers are possible with surveys whose point is the understanding of processes such as in the surveys done in Paris, Vienna and in some of the US studies. Still, counting is a double-edged sword. It is sometimes in the interest of service providers to indicate higher numbers to receive funding. It is sometimes in the interest of governments to indicate lower numbers to reduce public responsibility, and it has been argued that counting should not be the focus of research. Researchers may prefer to emphasise the need to discuss homelessness within the wider context of social exclusion and stress the importance of linking research (and communication) strategies to the social construction of homelessness and of policies against homelessness rather than the accumulation of statistics.

Realistically, both, numbers and deeper analytic insights which come from case studies on coping strategies or housing stress or income deficiency, are necessary. Trends in the extent of homelessness constitute early warning systems based on leading indicators, and numbers are relevant for policy formulation and evaluations.

Homelessness research is de facto action research. Regardless of one's position on the necessity of numbers or the emphasis on them, pragmatic considerations will call for some quantitative data. The way policy processes most likely unfold, concrete numbers are a required tool. In order to create efficient instruments to combat homelessness, numbers are needed to at least gauge the balance between supply and demand in services. At the same time keeping underlying processes in mind is certainly crucial.

To these and other specific research considerations, different data and different methods offer answers to different but equally significant questions.

Data on Homelessness in Europe

As Avramov observes in her article, data on homelessness is typically derived from two types of sources. *Primary* sources are those *specifically concerned with homelessness*. *Secondary* sources provide contextual information and secondary analyses of sources that are *indirectly related to homelessness*. All in all, European data on homelessness can be described as patchwork at best. Existing research in the Member States varies greatly with regard to its extent, the methodologies used and, consequently, also the reliability of the data. How to coordinate the different sources to make for a coherent data set remains without doubt a challenging task.

Studies

Since the early 1980s when the first systematic investigations of homelessness were attempted, methodologies have become more sophisticated. Marpsat and Firdion observe *three generations of homelessness research*: the first relied mostly on expert opinions; the second conducted night surveys in the streets and shelters; and the third began to cover longer periods of time, during daytime, as well as such approaches as the use of administrative records, panel studies, capture-recapture, ethnographic studies or telephone surveys of households to probe for homelessness in the past.

Recent European studies employed various methods: The 1993–94 *Paris* two-stage sample survey targeted the adult homeless population that uses services. (The project was part of a larger one.) It provides qualitative and quantitative data, including a numerical estimate of the population as defined. Basically any item can be included in a questionnaire of this kind and could be used in wider areas. The study gives point prevalence only.

The 1993 ICCR survey in *Vienna* focused on actually homeless people using the available accommodation facilities as well as those living in the streets and included the perspectives of the homeless themselves, that of service providers as well as the perspective of the authorities. The study yielded qualitative and quantitative data, including an estimate, gained from different populations and their respective points of view which were considered as increasing data reliability. The study covers point as well as period prevalence through inquiries about seasonal changes, albeit based on self-report.

In the *Netherlands*, administrative local and national data gathering systems are emerging that cover the nation's shelters and institutions. On a regional/municipal level, methods are being developed to integrate more detailed information from files on clients from different sources in order to get an integral view on causes and consequences of homelessness. Numerical estimates are not included in either data set.

In *Finland*, an annual housing market survey that is administered locally and collected into a national survey by the Housing Fund of Finland integrates data collection about the homeless population. The survey is conceptualised as an instrument for quantitative data collection and provides point prevalence. Individual municipalities may supplement the data with own surveys providing more detailed information.

Other European research activities include an ongoing *Spanish* project that currently concentrates on three lines of research that developed out of an earlier project on mental illness among homeless people: the focus is on the cross-cultural dimension, life histories, and estimates of the Madrid homeless population. The project is designed longitudinally over a three-year period and is implemented by means of structured interviews. It is planned to maintain contact with the selected sample through monthly contacts to minimise missing data. One of the objectives is to achieve what has been identified as a crucial flaw in the European data: comparability with other European cities. The *Plymouth* survey exemplifies the potential and limitations of the capture-recapture method which is based on more than one observation of the same population and provides numerical estimates.

Databases

In addition to national data, European databases, potentially, can provide some additional information. EUROSTAT has not been a major source for data on European homelessness so far. As the reasoning goes, EUROSTAT is embedded in, and constrained by, an institutional environment and consequently generally reactive rather than pro-active; it has to carry national statistical offices with it and be responsive to the administrators in Brussels. Thus, the priority EUROSTAT gives to statistics on the homeless will largely reflect the importance attached to this subject by its partners. In addition to this point of view, in the spirit of subsidiarity and its mechanisms, another factor is most likely also the methodological difficulty to integrate different national data sets – if they are available at all – into a European information source. The *Taskforce on Homelessness,* another potential instrument at the European level, is currently dormant.

Databases with marginal relevance to homelessness studies include the family budget surveys, used to derive poverty indicators; the harmonised labour force survey, which sheds light on labour market exclusion, one of the precursors to homelessness; the population census, which, unlike the household surveys, cover the institutional populations and is a potentially more useful source of data.

Potentially the most useful source may be the EC household panel. It shares the limitation of other household surveys in that it excludes non-private households without a fixed abode. However, homelessness is not just a stock concept but a process encompassing many social and economic deprivation antecedents, such as labour market exclusion, income insufficiency, housing stress, disintegration of social networks, indebtedness, family breakdown and so on. All these events are covered in the ECHP. Moreover, the ECHP is longitudinal, which would allow for the possibility to trace mobility into and out of homelessness, and it was designed to generate comparable data, thereby permitting some research on 'best practices'.

However, as the panel excludes non-private households and households without a fixed abode, the ECHP needs to be extended to cover target groups, to truly use its potential. The question of panel attrition regarding the sub-population of interest is subject to regional differences, however, also an additional argument for extension to target groups.

In sum, databases available at the European level, so far, are a negligible source for data on homelessness. While surveys that target the labour market, family budgets or households can provide some contextual information, they do not include specific items on homelessness. Theoretically, questions on homelessness could be added to the population census. However, this is not the case at the present time.

Research Gaps and Their Reasons

As Avramov observes, at the national level, targeted primary research of homelessness is rare. It is nonexistent at the European level. Household surveys are typically limited to either single problem areas, cover small samples, are restricted geographically and yield fragmented data. Estimates therefore are often based on data gathered for other purposes such as administration of services or fund raisers. Also, longitudinal research is not the norm, which limits the conclusions that can be drawn from snapshots of homelessness at a certain point in time, which do not allow insights into the processes involved.

Often the quality and in all cases the comparability of these data leave much to be desired. *It is clear then that without primary research on the European level no profound assessment of homelessness in Europe is possible.* Without that, a unified battle against homelessness whereby resources can be allocated in a sensible way is *undeniably obstructed.*

Furthermore, given the fact that certain research situations are *disproportionately represented* while others remain *under-researched*, the danger of severely distorted conclusions about characteristics and needs of homeless populations cannot be avoided. Typically, research does not cover topics which are crucial to understanding border situations and risks of homelessness. These topics include land squatting, squatting of empty housing, illegal lettings, cheap furnished rooms, shared accommodation without contract, vulnerable groups, housing (homeless) careers over time, coping modes over time.

As Tosi and others have pointed out, it is not customary, although it is necessary, to link the number of homeless people and other information that surveys may yield to the processes that lead to homelessness. We know very little about the direct causal relationships between certain factors such as poverty and homelessness and what combination of factors pushes which segment of risk populations over the edge into homelessness. It is for this reason that homelessness research needs to be linked to risk factors such as unemployment, access barriers to housing or family distress. Research needs to be integrated in research about social exclusion.

The active commitment and contribution of key actors is needed in order to do the necessary policy-relevant research. While EUROSTAT has taken some initiatives, it has not been able to provide data on the homeless population, which tends to be outside the technical scope of conventional household surveys. Neither has FEANTSA been in a position to compile cross-nationally comparable data. While consensus seems to be established about the necessity and feasibility of research about homelessness, concerted efforts to stimulate according activities are yet amiss.

In general, the available information on homelessness is simply not sufficient. Two steps are necessary to deal with that situation. Research designs must provide the opportunity to collect and analyse cross-nationally comparable data, and funding bodies must be approached and motivated to attach the appropriate importance to social exclusion, in general, and the phenomenon of homelessness in particular.

Homelessness goes beyond the mere fact of homelessness. It is part of the wider issue of social exclusion and social protection. Homelessness is but a symptom of weakening social solidarity and a breach of the social contract. Profound data on homelessness in Europe that is the basis for adequate policies and measures is amiss despite ongoing more or less sporadic efforts in the Member States.

Research is needed. The commitment of key actors at the national and the European level is indispensable to achieve the ultimate goal, i.e. successfully to combat social exclusion in spirit already expressed in the Medium-term Social Action Programme 1995–1997: *'The Commission will continue to promote cooperation on housing issues, social developments in urban areas, and homelessness ...'* (European Commission, DGV (1995), *Medium-term Social Action Programme 1995–1997*).

Summary Conclusions and Policy Recommendations

General

- Innovative and appropriate methodologies and data are a crucial prerequisite for scientifically sound research about homelessness and an indispensable input into policy development and implementation
- Available data on homelessness in Europe are embarrassingly sparse and non-comparable. National data differ in quality and quantity. Comparable data across Europe do not exist.
- As has been documented, the most costly form of fighting homelessness is crisis intervention after the fact. Prevention is not only more desirable from a humanistic point of view, but also cheaper for the public. Sound research needs to provide the basis for prevention.
- Proven, potentially feasible methodologies are available. The main obstacles are not the lack of policy-relevant research expertise but rather weak underlying data, insufficient inter-institutional linkages and imperfect mechanisms to harness that expertise.
- Cooperation between all key actors needs to be particularly emphasised: researchers, service providers, official national statistical offices, policy

makers as well as funding bodies have to join forces. This issue concerns particularly the European level, where research about homelessness is almost nonexistent yet much needed if the objective of a social Europe for all is to be attained.

- It is necessary to persevere with empirical research about homelessness at the European level that yields, and is based on, qualitative and quantitative data that is reliable and comparable as a first, basic step towards the development of policy designed to combat social exclusion, in general, and, within it, homelessness in particular.

Methodological Recommendations

- No single method of data collection will provide comprehensive knowledge about homelessness. An effort to combine all existing resources and forces, with the institutions concerned forging the necessary collaboration, is needed, i.e. studies of methods for dovetailing data derived from different sources, in particular from administrative and survey sources. An assessment of the different data integration approaches should be closely linked to the specific research objectives concerned.

- Empirical research is necessary because without concrete knowledge of the problem, its extent, its reasons and its long-term outcomes, the solutions are but guesswork at best. Primary research is clearly superior to the use of secondary sources, however necessary and useful the latter are to providing contextual information.

- To gain data about homelessness in Europe, studies using comparable premises must be carried out in the Member States.

- Research efforts need to take into consideration the precursors of homelessness. Little is known so far about the causal factors of homelessness that can be generalised to the heterogeneous homeless population. Vulnerable groups that are at risk of becoming homeless have to be part of the research efforts.

- Theoretical underpinnings of research need to be developed and structural factors analysed in relation to the research population concerned, and research designed accordingly.

- Decisions regarding research objectives need to distinguish between description and enumeration. In descriptive studies there may be more room to elaborate on a comprehensive definition of homelessness. Studies that aim at enumerating or counting are typically based on definitions that encompass only a particular subgroup of the population. In the interest of comparability, the problem of definition in a standardised form is even more complex.

- For applied research, it needs to be clarified beforehand whether the research attempts to provide the basis for preventive approaches (such as planning of housing or prevention of evictions) or for crisis intervention (such as planning for service measures). In the first case, the inclusion of the risk population or vulnerable groups, in addition to those defined as actually homeless is inevitable. In the latter case, reliance on service providers would be necessary. These policy choices have also financial implications. From a long-term perspective, it is documented that prevention is more cost-efficient.
- Another crucial element is time, i.e. the distinction between cross-sectional or longitudinal data, as they play different roles. Cross-sectional data can be gathered more easily and are necessary for policy reasons such as to provide estimates of current service needs. Longitudinal data collection provides beyond that a better insight in causes and consequences and requires more time and funding resources. There is no doubt that research results and their usefulness will differ considerably between these two sources. Longitudinal data should be collected wherever possible.
- The importance of constructing reliable sampling frames that take account of the heterogeneity and mobility of the research population needs to be stressed. Common causal factors may lead to homelessness but different sub-populations may still require different solutions.
- In sum, research objectives and designs have to be decided upon around the following considerations: definition of target population, enumeration or description, pragmatic and practical questions of sampling frame (cost-benefit of certain potential steps, enumeration purpose).

Specific Methodological Requirements

Ideally research about homelessness would:

- develop sampling frames and sample designs to reach the greatest possible coverage of the homeless population without duplication (i.e. users of shelters, soup kitchens, outreach programmes);
- consider more than one client group to allow for more than one perspective (homeless, service providers, authorities);
- consider risk populations as part of homelessness research in order to learn more about processes and dynamics and hence inform preventive measures;

- collect longitudinal data in order to know about homelessness as a process and also to yield more meaningful estimates of the target population as a whole;
- apply methods in research designs that would counteract technical difficulties in research about homelessness (i.e. double-counting, under-counting, access, communication barriers);
- include rural homelessness as a potentially qualitatively different yet certainly under-researched topic;
- devise designs covering particularly unclear and thus under-researched situations (i.e. squats, forced cohabitation and other forms of makeshift albeit on the surface more or less conventional housing);
- develop research frameworks that reflect the policy interconnections (social protection, housing) within which measures to fight homelessness are, or should be, tackled;
- given that no one data source can be sufficient to capture the full range of information required on homelessness, develop methodologies for integrating data;
- data improvements on homelessness should be undertaken in close collaboration with, or as an integral part of, the activities on national statistical offices that should be involved to the extent national policies provide them with the potential to do so.

Necessary Steps and Accompanying Measures

In order to carry out research along these lines it is necessary:

- for key actors to collaborate across agencies and across countries and to raise the funds necessary to do so.

This includes the following accompanying measures:

- the presently dormant *Taskforce On Homelessness*, set up by EUROSTAT, has been a step in the right direction. It needs to be reactivated and receive the necessary support in order to be effective;
- furthermore, working groups concerned with related issues – housing, social protection, poverty, social exclusion in general – should cooperate closely and on a regular basis with researchers on homelessness. Homelessness is but one of the manifestations of failing social protection systems and, in order for homelessness to be fought effectively, research needs to be

included into frameworks that are concerned with the maintenance and development of social protection measures;

- these considerations have an important bearing on costs, which are often quoted as the reason for limited public action to alleviate homelessness. The workshop participants agreed that more research in more countries should be carried out to estimate the cost of preventive measures compared with the actual cost (for example, the health bill) of addressing the problem after it has arisen;
- the recognition of homelessness as a social problem, regardless of the number of homeless people in Europe, is needed. If there were only one homeless person, it would already be one too many;
- input from agencies such as EUROSTAT is much welcome and needed. EUROSTAT can provide support in several ways: encourage national statistical offices to include questions relating to homelessness in their next population census; stimulate, encourage and monitor improvements in existing national data; provide input in the development of sample frames and designs that make for comparable and reliable European data; analyse data from the European Community Household Panel on risks to homelessness and – last, but not least – encourage national statistical offices and research institutes to set up a comparative European Community Panel Study focused on households suffering severe economic and housing stress;
- policy makers and research funding bodies are key actors in the fight against European homelessness. Collaboration is called for on two levels: to systematise and organise existing data and to stimulate and make possible the collection of missing data, nationally and comparably across Member States;
- sophisticated and continuously developing methodologies are available; competent research capacities are available; data are not, neither is funding. The reasons for this may be manifold. They need to be addressed urgently.

PART 3
VALUES AND POLICIES IN RELATION TO HOMELESSNESS

14 Regimes of Social Policy in Europe and the Patterning of Homelessness

MARY DALY

It is by now a truism to say that homelessness is a social phenomenon which reaches far broader than housing and housing policy. But the significance and meaning of this is not always appreciated. In this chapter I want to explore some dimensions of the societal meaning of homelessness by researching the relationship between nations' configuration of social policies and their approach to homelessness. In taking a much broader canvass than housing policy, I am essentially making a claim that it is not only the narrow policy domain which counts but in addition the overall set of ideologies and social provision which prevails in a nation. With a European Union-wide scope, I seek to identify if a systematic relationship exists between different models of social policy and the prevalence of and approach to homelessness. In its more descriptive vein, the chapter examines whether and how variations in homelessness are related to variations in social policy. The 15 members of the European Union provide an ideal setting within which to seek answers to these questions for they embody a number of distinct approaches to social policy and to homelessness. The chapter comprises three parts. The first describes and classifies the social policy approaches of the different Member States. The second part focuses first on the background to homelessness. Since homelessness is best conceived of as located upon a continuum of precariousness, poverty and long-term unemployment will be considered in this part as well. These are high risk factors for homelessness. Further parts of this section of the chapter go on to consider the prevalence of homelessness, to the extent that it is known, and the policy context in terms of key aspects of housing policy. In its third concluding part, the chapter analyses the relationship and patterning which exists between homelessness and different approaches to social policy within the European Union.

Social Policy Regimes in Europe: Making Sense of Diversity

Within the social sciences there exists a large body of work on social policy and the welfare state. Two main approaches are distinguishable within this literature. The first branch of study – the *social policy approach* – focuses upon the substance of social policies, seeking to understand how particular policies have developed and operate in fields like social security, housing, health and education. The British social administration school (see Titmus, 1974; Lee and Raban, 1988; Glennerster, 1989) is the most well-known body of work within this approach. It holds the view that social policies are as interesting for how they represent particular responses to need or social problems as for their outcomes or effects. Most of the work which has been done on homelessness could be said to fall within this general approach for it tends to treat policies on housing and homelessness in isolation from social policy models in general. But this social policy approach is generally less popular today, especially among scholars in continental Europe and the United States where the *political economy approach* dominates. This second way of looking at welfare states interests itself most in how welfare policies alter the distribution of power, income and life chances. In other words, welfare-related policies and institutions are situated within their broader social and economic context. This body of work places great emphasis on politics – both formal and informal – as explaining the form and content of the welfare state within and across national settings. While each has its strong points, the political economy approach is more suitable to the present endeavour for a number of reasons. The first is because it views social policies in a broad sense, not just in terms of a composite of a number of types of measures (cash transfers, taxation and social services) but also taking account of the significance of policy outcomes for social structures themselves. A second characteristic of the political economy approach which makes it attractive for the present purpose is that it has almost always been strongly comparative – to identify and explain cross-national variations in welfare state policies has been for long a key objective. This has yielded rich fruit in the large body of work which has been accumulated on how welfare state programmes across national frontiers can be compared and the degree to which they resemble each other.

In fact, attempts at typologising have become increasingly common in recent years. The underlying assumption is that there exists a number of basic approaches to social security or social welfare and that the systems which are in existence in the European nations all draw their origins from one of a number of basic models. According to Sainsbury (1991), two particular approaches have figured prominently in discussions on types of welfare state or variations in social policy. The first is deductive in nature, constructing analytical models based on contrasting ideal types (Titmuss, 1974; Wilensky, 1975; Korpi, 1980; Jones 1985). Titmuss (1974), for example, sketched three models on the basis of the tasks or functions attributed to social policy: the *residual* model, *the industrial performance achievement* model and the *institutional redistributive* model. Although underdeveloped by Titmuss, the models themselves, and the analytical task of modelling welfare state variations, were to prove influential. Korpi (1980), for example, usefully distinguished between *marginal* and *institutional* welfare states, each an ideal type epitomising extremes in possible welfare state forms. The marginal represents a minimal welfare commitment, whereas the institutional state undertakes a wider range of welfare responsibilities. The distinction rests upon a number of criteria among which are: the proportion of the national income spent on welfare programmes; the proportion of the population receiving some welfare state benefits; the universality or selectivity of welfare policies; the progressivity of the taxation system; and the importance of full employment. In another variant of this approach, Jones (1985) used the concept of welfare capitalism to classify states, obtaining a continuum from *welfare* capitalist states to those which are welfare *capitalist*.[1] In the former, social policy is focused on the welfare of individuals or families whereas welfare *capitalist* social policies are intended to support and reinforce a capitalist system. Jones derived her continuum on the basis of three criteria: the funding of social policies and in particular the degree of reliance on revenues from income tax and social security contributions; the types of social provision that exist; the effects of such provisions on social inequalities and life opportunities.

A second approach to typology building has been more inductive in nature, starting with a particular country or set of countries and seeking to pinpoint the distinctive features of the welfare state(s) in question. Furniss and Tilton (1977) decipher three models on the basis of linkages between the extent, form, aims and beneficiaries of state intervention. They distinguish between the *positive state*, the *social security state* and the *social welfare state*. This approach to model building has some shortcomings, however. In the case of Furniss and Tilton, Sainsbury points out that the dimensions of variation underlying the three models remain implicit and that the approach's emphasis on the most salient features in each case can easily obscure the fact that the same features characterise the other state types, although they are less prominent (1991, p. 5). Also, given that the models are derived from three specific countries, the US, Britain and Sweden respectively, their broader application to other systems remains in some doubt.

The interest in typologising has grown apace and the most interesting aspects of welfare states are now seen to reside in how they resemble or differ from each other. The work of Esping-Andersen (1990) was undoubtedly the precipitator of the recent interest in typologising, not least because it overcame some of the shortcomings of earlier attempts to model welfare states. His work was more systematic and broader in scope, developing and applying a relatively innovative set of indicators to 18 welfare states. His focus embraces qualitative and quantitative variations across states, not just in terms of the organisational features of welfare programmes but also welfare programmes' relations with surrounding institutions (such as the market and family for example). Esping-Andersen's work has made it commonplace to speak in terms of 'social policy regimes' – a concept generally taken to refer to nations' configurations of institutional arrangements around work and welfare (Esping-Andersen, 1987, p. 6) and understood as 'structures which carry common logics of mediation, alleviation and regulation' (Shaver, 1990, p. 2).

For Esping-Andersen contemporary welfare states are best differentiated from each other on the basis of three criteria: their logic of organisation (especially their capacity to de-commodify individuals by loosening dependence on the market); their social stratification effects; and their configuration of state-market-family relations. Esping-Andersen operationalised these three criteria in a manner which captured, among other things, the relative generosity of benefits, the inequality in the average benefits received by people, some of the primary conditions of benefit receipt, the power relations which typically underpin different kinds of welfare state, the groups most and least privileged and so on. The following are the specific indicators which he used.

Evaluated on these characteristics, 18 advanced capitalist welfare states (including all of the 15 Member States of the European Union, apart from Greece, Luxembourg, Portugal and Spain) are judged by Esping-Andersen to derive from three base types of social policy regime: liberal, conservative and social democratic. First there is the world of the selectivist *liberal welfare state* where means-tested benefits and a liberal stratification system prevail. This type of state pays modest if not mean benefits directed mainly to low income groups, subsidises private welfare and limits social reform by a strong work ethic. The United States, Canada, New Zealand, Australia, and, less comfortably so, Britain and Ireland are countries with, according to Esping-Andersen, liberal welfare state regimes. The second world, labelled *'conservative'*, embraces Germany, Austria, France and Italy, among others.

Conceptual Focus	Empirical indicators
Degree of de-commodification	wage replacement rates; length of contribution periods; method of financing of transfers; degree of equality in the value of transfers;
Principles of stratification	degree of corporatism; degree of etatism; significance of means-tested poor relief; significance of private pensions; significance of private health spending; average universalism; average benefit equality; range of entitlements;
State/market relations	state/market mix in pension provision; conditions under which individuals exit from and enter the labour market.

Figure 14.1 Criteria used by Esping-Andersen to typologize welfare states

Here rights are linked to work performance, being founded on the earnings-related principle. Given its status maintenance character, the stratification system is typically conservative and corporatist. Finally, there is the *social democratic* world of welfare capitalism in which citizenship rights are well-established, the welfare system resting on universal benefits and displaying a high level of benefit equality. In these societies, mainly the Scandinavian states, the stratification principle is depicted as socialist.

Esping-Andersen's work was greeted with acclaim in most quarters but strident critique in some. Two themes have formed the heart of the critique: that his work neglects crucial aspects of the welfare state; that it misclassifies or has no place for particular national welfare systems.

With regard to the first, it is important to note that Esping-Andersen's classification is not based on all welfare state programmes but only on old-age pensions, sickness insurance and unemployment insurance. Among the notable exclusions are the safety-net social assistance programmes, all family-related and women's programmes as well as state-provided or -funded services. The first and the last are very important from the point of view of homelessness. Other aspects of Esping-Andersen's method of classifying welfare states have also provoked criticism. Feminists have been especially vocal in drawing attention to how they perceive that his work ignored welfare states' treatment of women, gender relations and the family. They have pointed out that welfare states can play an important role in commodifying people, women especially. For example, the degree of provision of public caring-related services can directly and indirectly enable women to participate in the labour market. Also absent from what Esping-Andersen considers as the actors shaping the welfare state are non-worker groups and non-state actors. Pressure groups other than those which are embedded in a worker/employer/political party nexus have no role in Esping-Andersen's explanation of how welfare states came about and operate. In addition, his work takes no account of the particular character of the welfare mix wherein a host of other providers – voluntary groups, community groups, religious groups – usually exist side by side with the statutory authorities.

The second set of criticisms that met Esping-Andersen's work converged upon his regime types themselves and whether particular countries were appropriately classified. Judging from the spate of objections which emerged from scholars in different countries, it is only a slight exaggeration to say that Sweden and the United States are the only countries which are uncontroversially placed in his classification. However, not all of the country-specific objections to the regime clusters rest upon sound argumentation. Some of them certainly have been of the 'oh no – what has he done to my welfare state' calibre, a response which may owe more to the pique aroused by a sense of lost national uniqueness than to inaccuracies in Esping-Andersen's interpretation. There are in my view two points in this whole debate worth retaining. First, some country cases are definitely problematic for the purposes of regime clustering à la Esping-Andersen. Failing to emerge clearly from his empirical work, they have had to be dragged kicking and screaming by Esping-Andersen and others into particular clusters. The Netherlands and Italy are especially notable as outliers. The United Kingdom and Ireland are also problematic if one includes them in a cluster with the United States, Canada, Australia and New Zealand. Secondly, there is a valid critique to be made about the completeness of Esping-Andersen's clusters. Castles and Mitchell (1990), for example, suggest that greater attention to how welfare states vary in (the extent and means of) redistribution reveals a further regime type – the 'radical' – with Australia, Canada and the United Kingdom as the constituent countries. And then, there is the question of where the southern European countries fit in, for they are, apart from Italy, excluded from Esping-Andersen's analysis.

While the designation of both nations and types continues to be controversial, most analysts would agree that the differences and similarities among European welfare states are such that one can speak of four approaches to welfare within the European Union. These are: a *Nordic model*, a *continental European model*, and two other less easily definable models which include a *liberal model* along the lines of the United Kingdom and Ireland and what we might call a *Mediterranean model* which encapsulates arrangements in Greece, Italy, Portugal and Spain.[2] Figure 14.2 overleaf classifies the Member States accordingly. The criteria which I use here are broader than those of Esping-Andersen. All income support policies, both in terms of their general principles and also their potential to lead to divisions, have been included. In addition, the volume and nature of social service provision, so important for homelessness, is also taken account of.[3] However, the classification is very broad and is in some ways less systematic than Esping-Andersen's. It is intended as a heuristic device, to provide an overview of European social policy models, and so should be treated with care.

To a large extent, the four models of European social policy are differentiated from each other by the degree of state intervention, and, in turn, the effects and effectiveness of public policies. In the Nordic countries the welfare state tends to reach very wide, intervening not just in the labour market but also in the community and family. The continental type of welfare state, found in Germany, Austria and some neighbouring countries, tends to play a strong role in relation to supporting the economy but intervenes in the family and civil society only reluctantly, more or less when it cannot be avoided. The liberal welfare state model is less interventionist again as compared with the conservative. The provision of a minimum social safety net and the alleviation of poverty are the dominant goals of welfare in this model. However, there is an exception, in Britain anyway, with regard to social service provision in that the state undertakes a wide range of service responsibilities. In the Mediterranean countries, where welfare state institutions are still in the process of being developed, social service provision is especially rudimentary and the coverage and generosity of cash transfers tends to be more fragmented and dualistic than elsewhere in the Union.

We can greater appreciate the similarities and differences by taking provision in one country as exemplary of the overall approach. In the Nordic model, with Sweden to the fore, social insurance is the main type of benefit but the high potential for inequality inherent in this model is offset by a number of factors. First, the idea of a basic benefit is well-established so that only part of the payment is usually earnings-related. Secondly, with the meaning of full

Type	Countries	Main Features
Nordic	Sweden Denmark Finland	the benefit system is a mixture of flat-rate payments plus a wage-related second tier; citizenship or residence is a common basis of entitlement, family status is infrequently used; public services are widespread;
Continental European	Germany Austria Belgium France Luxembourg Netherlands	social insurance benefits dominate the cash transfer system; employment contributions are the main basis of entitlement to benefits; the value of benefits is tied closely to the recipient's former wages; services are available on a low to medium basis;
Liberal	United Kingdom Ireland	the benefit system is a more or less equal mix of social insurance and means-tested payments; employment contributions and need are twin pillars of entitlement; benefits are flat-rate and low level; public services have a medium (but decreasing) availability;
Mediterranean	Italy Greece Portugal Spain	social insurance is the main plank of the benefit system; a social safety net, means-tested or otherwise, is practically nonexistent; employment contribution is the most common basis of entitlement; public services are poorly developed.

Figure 14.2 A typology of European welfare states

employment interpreted broadly, most people are likely to be in the labour market. This acts to temper the unequalising potential of social insurance. This kind of model places a high emphasis not just on service provision but on public service provision. Thirdly, citizenship (more recently residence) is a very important basis of entitlement in Sweden. So benefits and services which in other countries are limited to the securely employed are available in the Swedish model on a wider basis. The continental European model, such as that which exists in Germany for example, strikes a stark contrast. Here, male employment is strongly privileged by public policy. The cash transfers tend to be generous but only when earned through a lifetime's employment. This leads to big differences in the value of benefits, and also among benefit recipients especially those who rely on insurance and social assistance. Those who prove themselves a success in the labour market are the real winners in this model. State-provided services are rare for the subsidiarity principle ordains that the state should keep a distance and encourage community and other forms of initiative. Voluntary and community service providers take the place of the 'strong state' in the Nordic model. In the third model, represented by liberal Britain, labour market participation for all is encouraged and indeed rendered necessary by low social payments (and low wages). The benefit system is a more or less equal mix of social insurance and means-tested benefits. This is a differentiation which has few stratification consequences for in Britain all benefits are low-level. There are no winners among benefit recipients in this welfare state model – the real winners are those who can avoid having to depend on benefits by providing for themselves in the labour market and through private insurance. A relatively wide network of state-provided social services was for long an integral element of the British approach to the welfare state, but this has been undermined by Conservative governments during the last decade and a half. In general, this model does not so much promote dependence on the state as personal independence for everybody. Among the Mediterranean countries, there is quite a lot of variation, not least because social policies are still developing. These countries' cash transfer systems tend in general to rely on a social insurance model but the risks covered tend to be delimited. Furthermore, there is typically no general social safety net provision. In relation to Italy, which has the most highly developed social security system amongst the southern countries, Trifiletti speaks of coverage of a small number of 'first order' social risks, in other words risks which the family cannot sufficiently protect itself against (1995, p. 2). Such risks tend to be well-protected while other social risks are assumed to be taken care of, and left to, the family. Because coverage is far from universal and has many gaps, private systems of support (especially the nuclear and extended family) are of high importance. The network of social services is only thinly developed in these welfare states.

What is clear is that the continental European model, embracing Austria, Germany, Belgium, Luxembourg, France and partly the Netherlands, is the most widespread type of social security arrangement within the European Union. Thus, while there are important variations within and across these national contexts, a social insurance model which ties benefits to past employment and wage rates is the primary means of organising income support in the Union today. This is also the welfare state model which leads to the greatest income inequalities between insiders (those receiving insurance benefits) and outsiders (those with no personal claim to a benefit and so must depend on means-tested benefits or on private means of support). The Mediterranean model, which is similar in its reliance on social insurance but dissimilar in the relatively low degree of coverage and high diversity among its schemes and the extent to which there is a safety-net provision, is the next most widespread type of welfare state model. The liberal type of welfare arrangement, to be found in the United Kingdom and partly Ireland, and the Nordic model which characterises Denmark, Finland and Sweden, are the least widespread.

Composed in such a manner, the policy configuration of welfare state models have different types of outcomes or consequences. The next section concentrates on homelessness, seeking to identify how it is distributed and its characteristics within the members states of the European Union. The risk factors associated with homelessness are also considered.

Homelessness: Risk Factors, Patterns and Policies

It is notoriously difficult to define homelessness, not to mind measure it in a satisfactory manner. The problems of definition hinge especially on how inclusive the definition should be. Should one include only those who are on the street or availing of designated public services? Or should one go broader and include people who have a roof over their heads but one which is neither theirs nor secure? In general, organisations and individuals involved in the study of homelessness have tended to opt for the broader definition. For example, the EUROHOME project, the progenitor of this monograph, defines homelessness as 'the lack of access to adequate personal accommodation'. Homeless persons are, accordingly, defined as 'those who are unable to access and maintain an adequate dwelling from their own resources, and people unable to maintain personal accommodation unless secured community care'. However, almost regardless of how one defines it, the measurement of homelessness is beset by data problems. As Avramov (1996b) points out, the main sources of information not only vary widely from country to country but information gathered by official sources is the exception within the Union. Most often, we are dependent on information collected by the service providers since targeted surveys are also very rare. Hence great care must be exercised in interpreting the information which is available for particular countries as well as in making cross-national comparisons.

In order to get a first idea of how the phenomenon of homelessness is constituted in different countries and how it is related to different approaches to social policy, I will look at factors which are background, perhaps formative, characteristics of homelessness and social exclusion. In a very real sense, homelessness is one stage, albeit a relatively advanced one, in the process of social exclusion overall. This renders conditions like unemployment, low income and poverty crucial in shaping the transition to homelessness for individuals and formative for the extent and characteristics of homelessness at a national level. On the other hand, issues pertaining to the supply and distribution of housing are also key. Relevant factors here include the supply and state of housing in general, and of social housing in particular. Each of these will be considered in turn, with a special eye to whether there is a patterning along social policy regime lines. The general policy approach to homelessness will also be considered in a later part of this section.

Risk Factors Associated with Homelessness

Homelessness is not an isolated phenomenon but is part of a process of a broader phenomenon of social exclusion. It exists therefore within a context of factors which either precipitate or prevent housing exclusion. The evidence is at this stage quite persuasive about the relationship between homelessness and other factors which are either an indicator of social exclusion or associated with high social risk. Two such factors are poverty and long-term unemployment. Table 14.1 shows how the then 12 Member States of the Union compare on these two social phenomena in the early 1990s.

The degree of variation which exists within the Union is very striking, in regard to both poverty and long-term unemployment (measured on the basis of the proportion of the unemployed who are out of work for one year or longer). Poverty rates vary from six per cent to 26 per cent and long-term unemployment from 32 per cent to 62 per cent. There is a cross-national patterning to be seen though, some of which conforms to the social policy models set out earlier. Denmark, the sole representative of the Nordic approach to welfare in these statistics, is the EU member state with the lowest poverty rate (six per cent). The continental European countries, Belgium, Germany, France, Luxembourg and the Netherlands, are close to each other and occupy a 'middle' position with regard to poverty. Those countries which have the highest poverty rates belong to either the 'liberal' or 'Mediterranean' models

Table 14.1   The extent of poverty and long-term unemployment

	Individuals living in poor households in 1993 (%)*	% of the unemployed out of work for 1 year or more, 1994
Belgium	13	58
Germany	11	44
Denmark	6	32
Spain	20	54
France	14	38
Greece	22	52
Ireland	21	59
Italy	20	62
Luxembourg	15	33
Netherlands	13	50
Portugal	26	43
United Kingdom	22	45
EU 12	17	48

*   a person is defined as poor if s/he lives in a household which has a net income below 50% of the average net income in her/his country.

Source: Poverty: EAPN Newsletter June/July 1997; Unemployment: European Commission, 1995, Table 33.

of welfare. The cross-national patterning of long-term unemployment is less clear and concise. Denmark is once again the country with the least long-term unemployment whereas Belgium, Greece, Ireland and Italy cluster at the other pole of high long-term unemployment.

There is also some covariation between poverty and long-term unemployment. The Mediterranean countries tend to have a rather high prevalence of both and Ireland also tends to be a poverty and long-term unemployment black-spot. Denmark is, on the other hand, the country from among these 12 with the lowest prevalence of both poverty and long-term unemployment. Most of the other countries are characterised by moderate poverty and long-term unemployment levels. There are two exceptions though, countries where the rates of unemployment and poverty are not very closely related. Britain is one such country: it has high poverty levels but its rate of long-term unemployment is below the European average. Belgium is the second exception with a patterning that is the reverse of that found in Britain. Overall, though, these data do indicate some patterning along policy regime lines. In particular, there is evidence of a closeness among the Mediterranean countries and, with the exception of Belgium, the continental European nations also experience similar, middle-range, levels of poverty and long-term unemployment. Britain and Ireland are also close in terms of their (relatively high) poverty rates but Ireland has a considerably more severe long-term unemployment problem.

The Extent of Homelessness

What is the relationship between these risk factors and homelessness? This is a question that cannot be answered with a high degree of precision because of the aforementioned definition, measurement and data problems in regard to homelessness. The closest that we have been able to come to a measure of those who are homeless are the calculations made available by FEANTSA and the European Observatory on Homelessness estimating the numbers of people who have been dependent upon public and voluntary services for homeless people during a particular period of time. The following is how the fifteen Member States compared on the basis of the absolute number of users of such services over the course of one year in the early 1990s and the proportion these form of the population as a whole.

The degree of variation is striking here so much so that there is no immediate cross-national patterning. At most, one can espy some tendency for the larger countries to manifest the greatest prevalence of homelessness (with Italy and Spain as the exceptions to this pattern). Thus, Germany is the European leader with slightly over one per cent of the population availing of services for the homeless over the course of a year. It is followed by Britain and France. There is a very big gap between these three and all the other nations in the European Union where recourse to services for the homeless is much rarer. Sweden followed by Italy, Finland and Ireland has the next highest prevalence of use of services for the homeless whereas the nations which evince the least use are Luxembourg, Spain, Portugal and Greece. If one relates these patterns to those on the social policy models outlined in Figure 14.2 above, one can say that the Mediterranean followed by the Scandinavian welfare models have the lowest prevalence of the use of services for the homeless. It is not easy to reach conclusions for the other models though. The continental European type of welfare regime, incorporating countries such as Germany, France, Luxembourg, Belgium and the Netherlands, clearly displays a very mixed record on the use of services for the homeless, containing the country with the highest prevalence (Germany) and that with the lowest

Table 14.2   Estimate average annual number of people who may have been dependent on public and voluntary services for homeless persons in the early 1990s

	Number of users over the course of a year	As a proportion of the national population
Austria	8,400	.10%
Belgium	5,500	.06%
Germany	876,450	1.10%
Denmark	4,000	.08%
Spain	11,000	.03%
Finland	5,500	.11%
France	346,000	.61%
Greece	7.700	.08%
Ireland	3,700	.11%
Italy	78,000	.14%
Luxembourg	200	.05%
Netherlands	12,000	.08%
Portugal	4,000	.04%
Sweden	14,000	.16%
United Kingdom	460,000	.80%

Source: Avramov, 1996a, Table 5.

(Luxembourg). The liberal welfare state model, comprising the United Kingdom and Ireland, tends to be characterised by relatively high levels of recorded homelessness, although this cluster of countries is not internally all that consistent (since Ireland has a much smaller incidence than the United Kingdom).

Lest we over- or misinterpret this information, it is important to draw attention to its limits and sources of bias. In fact, the reported prevalence of the use of services for the homeless cannot be taken as a reliable indicator of the prevalence of homelessness given that it is itself a function of service provision. That is, since most of this information comes from service providers, the statistics are dependent in the first instance on the existence of services and in the second on the quality of reporting from the relevant services. Given that the latter depends especially upon resources, it may be that the reported prevalence of homelessness is highest in those countries which have the best-resourced services. Hence it is not impossible that the reported prevalence of homelessness in a country is a reflection of the resources made available to deal with the phenomenon in that country. And this may well be the reason why the largest countries tend to manifest the highest use of service provision for the homeless. Available information suggests that Germany, France and Britain, the three countries with the highest prevalence of use of services for the homeless, have a level of service provision which exceeds that of the other countries (Daly, 1992). While there are some exceptions and the relationship is far from perfect, this does tend to confirm that statistics which derive from service providers are unreliable as estimates of the extent of homelessness. Another reason why these data are unreliable as estimations of homelessness is that they exclude the hidden homeless as well as people who are potentially homeless. For these reasons, the information above should be treated with caution.

Policies on Homelessness

If homelessness is an essentially social phenomenon, then it follows that it is shaped and affected by a broad set of policy areas. The broad contours of policies of Member States were set out in the first part of this chapter. Here we examine those domains of policy which are closest to homelessness. Accommodation and financial and social support are the main needs of the individual homeless person to which public policy must respond. This makes housing policy and income assistance with housing costs the two most relevant domains of policy for the present purpose. In regard to the first, the supply of social housing and the nature of state policies governing access to it are crucial. With regard to the second, the most important issues are whether and how states subsidise and assist people with the costs of their housing. To identify the broader context, I also consider a third issue: whether a particular or specific policy exists with regard to homelessness and whether homeless people have a right to housing. Since these are each very complex areas in their own right, my intention here is to offer an overview of the main patterning which exists among Member States of the European Union in regard to relevant policies.

In terms of the first issue, housing stock and housing supply, what is of great significance from the point of view of homelessness is the availability of affordable housing. This is by no means an easy matter to establish: one would need to undertake a detailed study of the quality and distribution of available accommodation. Not only is such information lacking on a European-wide basis but there is no perfect indicator of the availability of affordable housing either. As a rough proxy, I take the availability of social housing for rent. Social housing as used here refers to housing which is intended to ensure, by means of specific or general providers, the provision of a particular quantity of housing services, in addition to those available on the open market, at a particular cost for which part of the price is paid by the state (Ghékière, 1997, p. 42). The following is how Member States compare on this dimension of policy.

Table 14.3   Proportion of social housing for rent in the total housing stock of Member States in the 1990s

0–10%	11–20%	20–30%	30–40%
Greece (0%)	Ireland (11%)	Sweden (22%)	Netherlands (36%)
Spain (2%)	Finland (14%)	Austria (23%)	
Luxembourg (2%)	France (17%)	United Kingdom (24%)	
Portugal (4%)	Denmark (18%)		
Italy (6%)			
Belgium (7%)			
Germany (8%)			

Source: Ghékière, 1997, p. 44.

Clearly, there is considerable variation in the availability of social housing for rent within the European Union. The Netherlands is the member state with the highest proportion (36 per cent) of its housing stock in this form. It is followed by Sweden, Austria and the United Kingdom which have between a quarter and a fifth of their housing stock in this sector. Next come Ireland, Finland, France and Denmark with between a tenth and a fifth. Most of these countries operate to an ideology of public housing as a public or universal good. They tend, therefore, not to impose income ceilings as a condition of entitlement although most do use priority criteria (Ghékière, 1997, p. 46). This is a policy which tends to draw its roots from anti-segregation and the avoidance of discrimination. The Mediterranean countries, together with Belgium and Germany, are those with the lowest proportion of social housing among their stock of housing. Taking this information as a whole, two points are striking. First the degree of variation is high. Secondly, the clustering among countries in regard to their social housing is quite different to that found for the general approach to social policy.

A key element of a nation's housing policy, along with the proportion of social housing, is how it grants access to that housing. In this regard Avramov (1995) provides a useful classification of European countries. She differentiates national approaches in this regard in terms of three classifications: statutory access to social housing, preferential access to low cost housing and low-priority access for homeless people to subsidised housing. In the first type of approach, which characterises the United Kingdom and France, homeless and potentially homeless people are eligible for social housing and legal instruments have been introduced to give effect to that entitlement. In the second approach, local authorities are not obliged to house the homeless but criteria defining preferential access to social housing are set out either in legislation or in custom and practice. The countries which fall into this group are Belgium, Denmark, Germany, Ireland Luxembourg and the Netherlands. The last group comprises the four Mediterranean countries in which there is limited direct public investment in funding for social housing and homeless or potentially homeless people have no enforceable right to housing.

We now turn to the second domain of policy – whether and how states assist people with the costs involved in housing. Most Member States have either a particular scheme to assist with the cost of housing or they have a provision within their means-tested social assistance programme for this purpose (Eardley et al., 1996, pp. 67–71). However, Italy and Spain are unique within the Union in having no national scheme to assist with the costs of housing (it should also be remembered that neither of these countries has a general safety net income scheme). Five countries have a particular scheme though which it is possible for people with a low income to receive assistance with their housing costs: Denmark, France, Germany, Sweden and the United Kingdom. In general these countries also tend to offer the highest level of assistance: once they prove their need people can usually receive assistance with the full costs of their accommodation and also for as long as their situation of need lasts. However, it should be noted that the United Kingdom is exceptional among this group of countries by virtue of the fact that its social security benefits tend to be much lower in absolute and relative terms. In addition to these countries, Portugal also has a general scheme to assist with housing costs but the receipt of assistance is time-limited. Finland and Greece have more limited schemes for certain categories of people. A second policy option is where the general safety net scheme also includes the possibility of additional assistance with housing costs. This is the case in Austria, Ireland and Luxembourg. Finally, there are two countries – Belgium and the Netherlands – where the payment of social assistance is assumed to (and presumably calculated on the basis that it does) cover the costs associated with recipients' housing. When it is insufficient, people in the Netherlands can make recourse to a regulated benefit but no option exists in Belgium in this scenario other than purely discretionary local payments. Apart from these general tendencies, there are quite considerable variations in the details of support with housing costs between countries. Countries vary for example in the extent to which they offer support to owner occupiers as well as renters. In general though, Member States tend to offer financial assistance to house buyers and tenants alike (ibid., p. 71).

The third aspect of the policy architecture which is relevant is whether or not countries have a national policy on homelessness and what kind of housing rights they confer on those who are in need of housing. While the European policy landscape could be characterised as one of inadequate services and supports, there is really no European policy norm in regard to the treatment of homelessness. But some common patterns are identifiable. At one extreme are countries like Greece, Luxembourg, Italy, Portugal and Spain which have little or no coordinated national policy on homelessness (Daly, 1992; Avramov, 1995). The absence of a nationally coordinated response to homelessness makes for fragmentation in services, variation from place to place and generally inadequate provision. It may in general be taken as evidence of a lack of official priority attributed to homelessness. Four countries could be said to comprise the other extreme in that they have adopted national laws so as to transform the right to housing into concrete regulations which address the condition of homelessness (Avramov, 1995, 26). These are Belgium, France, Ireland and the United Kingdom. The French law, elaborated within a broad approach towards combating poverty and marginalisation, is perhaps the most explicit and far-reaching, asserting clearly and in a detailed manner the right to housing for all citizens. To realise this right, a programme of measures has been put in place which on the one hand seeks to improve the supply and availability of a diversified stock of accommodation and on the other strives to (re-)integrate the homeless person through the provision of psychological and other forms of support and counselling. None of the other countries goes this far although the legislation introduced in Belgium in 1993 addressed some of the needs of homeless people especially by granting them access to social assistance. In the United Kingdom a legally enforceable claim to housing exists for certain subgroups of the population and this is realised by legal obligations on the local housing authorities. No legally enforceable right or claim to housing exists in Ireland but the local authorities do have designated responsibilities towards homeless people. These do not include a responsibility to house homeless people but to establish priorities for accommodation and to assign a proportion of available dwellings to low-income persons. The remaining countries for which information is available – Germany and

Denmark – form a middle group between these two extremes. These are countries which recognise some obligations towards the homeless and which have instituted some policies so as to make that recognition a reality. While there are considerable variations between them, they could be said to be policy regimes which have made homelessness a focus of policy, albeit that the resultant policies are piecemeal and fragmented.

Overview: the Links between Social Policy, Housing-related Policy and Homelessness

Europe has not by any means a singular experience of homelessness nor indeed a single approach to social policy. There is a good deal of variation to be seen but then there is also considerable patterning. Although the particular placement of countries may be at times controversial, it seems fairly clear that the general social policy approaches of the Member States divide into four main types. The Scandinavian countries resemble each other in having instituted welfare states which provide a comprehensive range of services and a set of income supports which are made available on the basis of citizenship or residence. The countries in the European heartland – Austria, Belgium, France, Germany and Luxembourg – also resemble each other in their approach to welfare tending to place a strong emphasis on a social insurance, and hence labour market participation, model of social security. Then there are two other approaches: that exemplified by the United Kingdom and Ireland and that to be found in the Mediterranean countries. In the former, an anti-poverty approach dominates which means that benefits are quite low in value and distributed on the basis of tests of need. In the Mediterranean countries, income support and social services tend to be underdeveloped but the main model of income support where it exists is social insurance.

Provision and policy for homelessness does not follow in any simplistic way from social policies writ large. There are, however, some clearly observable tendencies. The two poles of Europe, North and South, are not only geographically distant from each other but represent two extremes within the available European approaches to and experiences of homelessness. In the Nordic countries, the relatively widespread availability of and access to social supports of all kinds is in effect, if not always in intent, a policy of prevention. Although these countries do have homelessness, in comparative terms it is low. The prevalence of measured homelessness is also low in the Mediterranean countries. This is not, though, due to the same factors as in

Scandinavia. First, these societies are amongst the most 'traditional' in Europe. In the context of homelessness this means that family, neighbourhood and other informal ties are more likely to act as mechanisms of prevention than say social services. In addition, the availability of social services for homeless people is very inadequate in these countries and, given that the only figures which we have available on the prevalence of homelessness are based on counts of users of services, it may also be that the statistics are artificially suppressed by the low level of service provision. The remaining two sets of countries – the continental European nations and the United Kingdom and Ireland – fall somewhere in the middle between these two extremes. They are nations with middle to high levels of homelessness and a rather mixed set of policies. The variations within and across these two sets of countries suggest that the relationship between homelessness and social policy is not by any means a simple one. In terms of the prevalence of homelessness, the big countries – Britain, France and Germany – have the most severe homelessness problem. This is despite the fact that they have adopted quite different approaches to homelessness and that their general social policy models are also different. There is no perfect fit and no easy predictions can be made about homelessness from the type of social policy model which is in place in a country overall. The very northern and southern parts of Europe are easiest to classify but overall one should resist the temptation of very general classifications and comparisons. This is a very complex field.

On a policy level, homelessness is not addressed by any simple approach. However, it must be said that the Nordic countries are exceptional in policy terms in that their generally generous model of provision has a preventive effect when it comes to homelessness (and other social problems). Three features distinguish the Nordic approach to social policy: generous cash benefits; a widespread network of social services; citizenship or residence as a fairly widespread criterion governing access to services and cash benefits. Further to the south things get more complicated. The continental European countries more or less share a common approach to social policy: generous benefits but only when earned through labour market participation, and a network of social services which is primarily voluntary in character. But these countries vary considerably in their experience of and approach to homelessness. Germany and France for example have each a high incidence of homelessness but have very different policy approaches to homelessness. Of the two, France has by far the most extensive and coordinated set of policies in this regard. On the basis of this comparison and the experience of other countries, one must conclude that the factors which generate homelessness can only be understood and combated beyond a narrow policy landscape.

On an academic level, bringing homelessness in to social policy typologies in general poses a real challenge to conventional approaches. It is not just a matter of including service provision – itself a real advantage given that most of the social policy typologies to date have been based only on income transfers. Rather bringing in homelessness means treating housing as a constituent domain of social policy and homelessness as an outcome of particular approaches to social policy. The latter inclusion of homelessness as an outcome of policies is very important. Almost all existing typologies of welfare states rest upon an analysis of inputs to policy, such as the structure or provision, the architecture of entitlement and so forth. Bringing homelessness in presents, therefore, a powerful challenge to conventional ways of understanding the welfare state.

Notes

1 This framework has been subsequently developed and extended by Leibfried (1990).
2 For further detail, see Castles and Mitchell (1990), Esping-Andersen (1990), Leibfried (1990) and Daly (1996).
3 But see Anttonen and Sipilä (1995) for a classification of welfare states which rests specifically upon service provision for social care.

Bibliography

Anttonen, A. and Sipilä, J. (1995), 'Five regimes of social care services', paper presented to the Eighth Nordic Social Policy Research Seminar, Stockholm, 9–11 February.
Avramov, D. (1995), *Homelessness in the European Union Social and Legal Context of housing exclusion in the 1990s*, Brussels, FEANTSA.
Avramov, D. (1996a), *The Invisible Hand of the Housing Market*, Brussels, FEANTSA.
Avramov, D. (1998) (see chapter 6 in this book)..
Castles, F.G. and Mitchell, D. (1990), *Three Worlds of Welfare Capitalism or Four?*, Australia, Australian National University Public Policy Programme Discussion Paper no 21.
Daly, M. (1992), *European Homelessness – The rising tide*, Brussels, FEANTSA.
Daly, M. (1996), *Social Security, Gender and Equality in the European Union*, Brussels, Commission of the European Communities.
EAPN Newsletter June/July 1997, Brussels, European Anti Poverty Network.
Eardley, T. et al. (1996), *Social Assistance in OECD Countries*, London, HMSO, Department of Social Security Report no 46, Volume 1.
Esping-Andersen, G. (1990), *The Three Worlds of Welfare Capitalism*, Cambridge, Polity Press.
European Commission (1995), *Social Protection in Europe*, Brussels/Luxembourg.

Furniss, N. and Tilton, T. (1977), *The Case for the Welfare State: From social security to social equality*, Bloomington, Ind., Indiana University Press.

Ghékière, L. (1997), 'Allocation of social housing in Europe' in Parmentier, C. (ed.), *Where to sleep tonight? Where to sleep tomorrow? Orientations for Future Action*, Brussels, FEANTSA.

Glennerster, H. (1989), 'Swimming against the tide: the prospects for social policy' in Bulmer, M., Lewis, J. and Piachaud ,D. (eds). *The Goals of Social Policy*, London, Unwin Hyman.

Jones, C. (1985), 'Types of welfare capitalism', *Government and Opposition*, vol. 20, no. 3, pp. 328–42

Korpi, W. (1980), 'Social policy and distributional conflict in the capitalist democracies. A preliminary comparative framework', *West European Politics*, vol. 3, no. 3, pp. 296–316.

Kvist, J. and Torfin,g J. (1996), *Changing Welfare State Models*, Copenhagen, Centre for Welfare State Research, CWR Working Paper 5.

Lee, P. and Raban, C. (1988), *Welfare Theory and Social Policy*, London, Sage.

Leibfried, S. (1990), 'Income transfers and poverty in EC perspective. On Europe's slipping into Anglo-American welfare models', paper presented at EC seminar *Poverty, Marginalisation and Social Exclusion in the Europe of the '90s*, Alghero, Italy, 23–25 April.

Sainsbury, D. (1991), 'Analysing welfare state variations: The merits and limitations of models based on the residual-institutional distinction', *Scandinavian Political Studies*, vol. 14, no. 1, pp. 1–30

Shaver, S. (1990), *Gender, Social Policy Regimes and the Welfare State*, Australia, Social Policy Research Centre, The University of New South Wales, Discussion Paper no. 26.

Titmuss, R.M. (1974), *Social Policy An Introduction*, London, Unwin Hyman.

Trifiletti, R. (1995), 'The gendered "rationalization" of Italian social policies in the nineties', paper presented at the Second European Sociological Association Conference 'European Societies: Fusion or Fission', Budapest, Hungary, 30 August–2 September.

Wilensky, H. (1975), *The Welfare State and Equality: Structural and ideological roots of public expenditure*, Berkeley, Ca., University of California Press.

15 Different Policy Approaches to Homelessness

JAN VRANKEN

The key idea of this chapter is that social problems and related policies are socially constructed and that in this process of social construction different views on person and society play an eminent role. This argument is developed as follows. First, I try to identify the specificity of the phenomenon of homelessness, which generates questions such as: does the change in concepts that are being used indicate a change in perspective? If this is the case, does this reflect developments in the socioeconomic and demographic composition of the homeless population or in the nature of homelessness itself? Or does it just reflect a development in the way we perceive homelessness? Secondly, the 'social (re)construction' of homelessness is analysed by using the social problem context. Because of their importance in the definition of a social problem, specific attention is paid to of standards ('perspectives' or 'models'). Next, the relation between the social problem perspective on homelessness and policy approaches is discussed. In the end, four models of homelessness policies are developed and some of their implication are discussed.

Models are difficult to construct and at the same time a most important element of scientific activity (Vranken, 1997). They are most difficult, because the construction of models presupposes at least one well-developed theory, the identification of relevant variables and their specification into indicators. They are the most important part for roughly the same reasons: only scientific endeavours that arrive at constructing a model are really successful. Models contribute to a better understanding how (a given part of) reality works. Models also can be targeted to policy making variables. Even if this is not the case, policies always is one of the main variables.

Researchers' and policy makers' interests do meet here, because – as Comte already wrote – 'savoir pour prévoir, prévoir pour pouvoir'; reality can only be controlled and changed if one can foresee its developments and in order to do so one needs to know reality. This does not mean that their interests always coincide, because the theoretical context and related indicators can be selected either with a focus on better understanding society, or rather at changing society. In the former case, the model will include rather structural – and therefore less manageable – dimensions of society, whereas in the latter case more attention will be paid to policy relevant dimensions, which can be managed and even manipulated by policy makers.

It should be clear that this contribution is but an attempt to link policy models of homelessness to some elements from the sociology of social problems and policy making. It is meant to form the starting point for the development of a framework for empirical research.

Factors and Developments, Concepts and Models

The Social Construction of Homelessness

There seems to be an inverse relation between the visibility of certain socially excluded groups, such as the homeless, and our knowledge of them. Their visibility undoubtedly has increased; extreme forms of homelessness in particular are getting through to the front pages of newspapers and are receiving ample attention on TV. Beggars have become part of the picture in chic shopping streets, stations and other public places are populated by 'rough sleepers'. At present, the 'fourth world' has an easier access to royal palaces or government offices than the average citizen.

In spite of their visibility, we know very little about the homeless. This is not unique; it goes for the poor in general. The main reason is that the dominant form of social research contributes very little to our knowledge of excluded population groups. This is so because social research focuses on dimensions such as income and work, which are not very discriminating when it comes to identifying extreme forms of social exclusion. Moreover, in its large scale surveys extremely marginalised groups such as illegals, (inter)generational poor or the homeless are heavily under-represented and often close to absent.

Even then, information about the number of excluded persons and the 'incidence of exclusion' is less scarce than knowledge about the structures and processes of social exclusion. We are referring both to processes and structures at the macro and meso level and to 'the structures of daily life' of socially excluded groups and persons. However, this is the kind of information we need most to develop a coherent set of policy measures to efficiently combat social exclusion in general and in its specific forms.

This discrepancy between lack of knowledge and high visibility results from factual developments but it also is the result of changing perceptions and thus of the way(s) in which 'homelessness is being constructed'. That homelessness is presently being recognised as a 'social problem' and is not being reduced to an 'individual problem' is a most important shift; it is the condition for homelessness to become the subject of social policy. Since social policy is developed in response to the problematisation of societal conditions, it is necessary to discuss both elements of a social problem somewhat more in detail.

The Making of a Social Problem

A social problem is a discrepancy between a given reality and a set of standards, a discrepancy that is judged dysfunctional by relevant groups and that is the subject of reduction through collective action. In such an approach several elements are crucial.

The first one is the discrepancy between reality and standards. Standards refer to values, norms, goals or expectations that are implicitly or explicitly present in a society; their most explicit formulation being the 'social rights' component of certain constitutions or the establishment of these rights in (national) positive law (see Avramov, 1995, pp. 20–30). At least as important is, however, the prevalence of well-housed people in contemporary societies, which makes 'manifest forms of poverty, homelessness and bad housing ... unacceptable today' (ibid., 141). The living conditions of the majority of the population thus become the standard and since the living conditions of a significant minority are deviating from this standard, they are subject to being problematised. It is the latter 'reality' that is being referred to in the second component of a social problem. This 'reality' can apply to a group's living conditions in general or to a specific element such as service provision; that is, to the difficult access or the lack of access to services of these groups, what is sometimes referred to as the 'Matthew-effect' (Deleeck, 1983).

A second element is the social actors involved in the definition of the social problem. Most marginalised population groups play but a minor role in the 'social discovery' of their plight. It is different with the homeless, for two main reasons. Firstly, because of their visibility, the homeless tend to be perceived by the general public (and by politicians) as a kind of 'dangerous class' (*classe dangereuse*). It often has led public authorities to order their eviction from public places, a substantial but often neglected component of homelessness policies. Secondly, their position in this process of problematisation has been stronger than is the case with other socially excluded groups in most countries. Indeed, well-organised associations were taking care of the interests of the homeless long before the recent rise in public and political attention.

Thirdly, the means needed to remedy the social problem must be present and one of these means is collective action. It is, of course, not enough that the homeless themselves are aware that something has to be done or even that they present solutions to their problems. The identified social problem has to pass through a number of stages, the most important one being that public authorities accept their responsibilities in combating the social problem. This acceptance is most clearly expressed in the development of a policy plan and in steps being taken for its implementation.[1]

What, then, are the consequences of such a social problem approach for conceptual and policy frameworks? In the course of a social problem formulation, practical concerns of policy makers, social administrators and social workers 'to do something about the situation' become more prominent than the objective of social scientists to better understand the situation and its relation to larger social processes and structures. The difference is, in the end, a very profound one. From the social problem approach – and thus from the policy makers' point of view – homelessness is something quite irrational, particularly if the social resources are available for improving living conditions or for promoting social integration.

This is not, however, the case from the research problem point of view. For the social scientist, homelessness, as social exclusion and poverty, is a perfectly rational phenomenon; it can and should be explained by the organisation and functioning of society and its institutions. Questions to be asked, then, are: could a society function without forms of social exclusion such as homelessness? Does not any society need some form of exclusion in order to obtain the minimum level of coherence required by any system? Does it produce the degrees of liberty needed for inducing internal mobility and change? Will homelessness be differently organised in different societies, according to their demographical, cultural, political, social and economic structures or are identical processes working in most or even all societies? These reflections lead to the important conclusion that a better knowledge and understanding of homelessness come through comparing its forms and processes of production in different types of society. This comparative perspective can be historical, but should at least be cultural. Theory development and model building, the latter also for policy purposes, are the results of this process.

An approach in terms of rationality, however, does not imply that all social scientists agree on the causes of homelessness; their selection of causes will be guided by their different societal perspectives. Before embarking on this issue, I shall discuss both dimensions of the 'social problem' of homelessness. First, I shall discuss its specificity and secondly I shall develop a typology of policy approaches to homelessness, aware of the fact that other typologies are possible and relevant.

The Specificity of Homelessness

That the homeless constitute a very heterogeneous category of persons is well-known. Durlacher's characterisation of the poor certainly applies to them: they are 'a heterogeneous population with a common fate' (Durlacher, 1973, p. 49). The heterogeneity is well illustrated by Koch Nielsen (1998): apart from the traditional homeless she includes bag-ladies, drug abusers, mental patients and street children in her typology. Regardless of how 'typical' these types are, a typology based on individual characteristics adds but very little to our understanding of the phenomenon. What we need is a typology that is based on situational characteristics: a typology of homeless*ness*.

According to Daly (1994, p. 2), homelessness has to be located on a continuum, which implies that the relation between the different stages is gradual. The sequence I have in mind, however, contains discontinuities and could best be pictured as a cascade. Our 'homelessness sequence' runs from inferior or substandard housing on the one end to complicated rooflessness (as illustrated by tramps, sleeping rough, street youth) on the other; the situations in-between being – from 'bad' to 'worse' – insecure accommodation ('furnished rooms'), houselessness (or 'simple' rooflessness), homelessness. Moreover, this sequence is not exclusively composed of housing factors, although these do form its hard core. Other factors are relevant in two ways. The first and rather evident role of factors such as (un)employment or (lack of) income or (low) education is that they interact directly with housing deprivation in the production of homelessness. The other is that persons who at one or another point of this 'homelessness sequence' have not necessarily entered it at the starting point but could have done so at any point, coming from other sequences ('streams') that are running parallel to the 'homelessness sequence', such as an 'employment sequence', an 'educational sequence' or an 'income (debts) sequence'.

Indeed, the factors leading to homelessness are manifold. Their more general context is formed by demographic, economic, social, cultural and political developments that have direct and specific consequences for definite population groups. Labour market restructuring is resulting in long-term unemployment for many unskilled workers; exclusion from the labour market is very significant in societies where income, status, social relations and power primarily depend upon ability to work. This growing exclusion from the labour market has been accompanied by changes in family and community relations, which together aggravate both scale and depth of social exclusion. Indeed, changing demographic patterns are leading to changes in family patterns: declining family size, increasing marital breakdown and more one-parent families.

Protection provided by welfare state arrangements such as social housing and income maintenance programmes is weakening and the introduction of 'activating' approaches in these programmes is speeding up this process. In most European societies social protection is losing its integrating philosophy of benefit protection through insurance contribution, because of the growing number of persons who are unable to contribute and who therefore are obliged into dependency upon means-tested social assistance benefits. Alcock (1996) attributes a central role to this phenomenon in his analysis of growing social division and social exclusion. Indeed, whilst social insurance operates on an inclusive model of protection, social assistance is based upon a separation between those who contribute (taxpayers) and those who receive (unemployed and non-employed claimants).

In his most recent book, Jordan (1997) discusses the social exclusion (and integration) which results from non-membership (or membership) of community groups and social organisations. He specifically draws attention to the fact that membership of, participation in and contribution to social groups are essential dimensions of citizenship in all societies. More in general, community structures and networks have been changing and shifting. Associational life is being replaced by social networks that provide less social help and protection, particularly for those who do not have the human capital to develop networks and maintain by themselves.

It should by now be quite clear that these developments and particularly their effects are not isolated, but operate in a combined fashion. A most relevant illustration of how larger developments are affecting the situation of households and individuals, is provided by the concept of 'stressed families' (Ecoter, 1987, p. 29 as mentioned in Tosi, 1997, p. 19). It refers to the coexistence of two opposed and even contradictory developments: the family becomes more important as a protecting agency and at the same time, its capacity to protect is reduced (Tosi, 1997, p. 5). Both factors, however, result from the same 'crisis of the welfare state': the welfare state shifts part of its burden to other social institutions, mainly at the intermediate or meso level, withdrawing or reducing at the same time the means necessary for taking up these new responsibilities. Because of the increasing risk of youth unemployment, the young are obliged to live with their parents for a much longer period than before, thus increasing the financial, social and relational requirements to be met by the family; at the same time, unemployment benefits are reduced and entitlement conditions become stricter, so that the family is not compensated for this increased burden.

So, homelessness is not just 'housing deprivation' but is closely related to other disadvantages and discriminations that are resulting from social divisions in society. Therefore, is not that easy to be precise about the specificity of homelessness. It is quite clear that it refers to some kind of housing deprivation. 'Housing, after all is much more than shelter: it provides social status, access to jobs, education and other services, a framework for the conduct of household work, and a way of structuring economic, social and political relations' (Achterberg and Marcuse, 1983, pp. 474–83). As poverty, homelessness is a complex phenomenon in which a large number of deprivations are closely connected. We could even see it as a specific type of poverty, as an accumulated result of deprivation on housing and social networks (Stevens and Vranken, 1983).

Different Perspectives on Homelessness, as a Form of Social Exclusion

The search for causes of homelessness is a very central one in the literature on homelessness. According to Deben and Greshof (1995, pp. 258–9, 267) 'for no other social problem the question is asked so persistently about what is cause and what consequence, what is choice and what not'. They distinguish between three traditions in defining homelessness. The first one is based upon the material and physical living conditions of the 'literally homeless' (Rossi, 1989). A second approach focuses on social integration and relational networks; it thus links personal situation and social fragility and puts them into a larger social context. A third perspective starts from social conditions, such as a deficient housing and labour market and insufficient social services and analyses their effect upon persons and groups with fewer resources.

It thus is clear that homelessness is being defined and analysed from specific perspectives, as is the case with other forms of social exclusion. These perspectives can be classified according to whether they look for causes at the individual level or the level of society and to whether these causes are seen as inherent or accidental. The resulting perspectives are – explicitly or implicitly – structuring theoretical debates, empirical research, policy making, welfare and public opinion and they relate these different types of social action to one another.

Causes	Status	
Level	*Inherent (intrinsic)*	*Accidental (extrinsic)*
Individual	Deficiency model	Accident model
Societal	Structural model	Cyclical model

Figure 15.1 Different perspectives on forms of social exclusion (poverty, homelessness)

Undoubtedly, the individual models are still prevailing: in social sciences and in public perception. Micro-models based upon individual behaviour are most developed by economists and psychologists. Economists tend to see people's behaviour as the result of an optimisation of their welfare or utility. If one introduces uncertainty and erroneous perceptions about the constraints subject to which utility is maximised, as well as uncertainty about the consequences of one's decisions, then it is possible to explain, at least partly, social exclusion as an unfortunate result of an unsuccessful attempt to maximise welfare. They are still dominating in public and political perception, whether they explain homelessness in terms of personal deficiency, deviant behaviour or social accident. The 'personal deficiency model' in particular leads to the promotion of a 'therapeutical' approach. Lately, this personal deficiency model has regained importance in the Anglo-Saxon world not least because of its usefulness for the dominant political discourse. Its spokesman is Charles Murray, who already in 1984 had argued that welfare payments targeted on the poor promote a dependency culture, in which state support replaces paid work as the lifelong income generating source (Murray, 1984). In 1994 he even associated the 'deepening crisis in the social order' with the undesirable lifestyles of the members of the underclass, especially with that of young single mothers (ibid.). It clearly is a case of 'blaming the victim': the poor and the socially excluded are not only the authors of their own misfortune but even of that of the other social classes.

On the other side, the cyclical approach refers to phenomenons such as economic crises or rapid social change. The structural approach tries to identify the production processes of homelessness and thus looks for its explanation in the way(s) society is organised. This approach goes further than an institutional approach. Indeed, a structural model implies that homelessness is not something that 'happens' to society, but is produced by the way society is organised and by the processes that are generated by this organisation. From this perspective, society's organisation is the problem, not homelessness.

In the meantime, it should have become clear that this model inspires our argument. I developed such a structural model for the analysis of poverty; its main conceptual elements remain relevant for a better understanding of the production of homelessness (Vranken, 1972, 1977, 1997)

The first idea is that society has a number of *dominant* features (or *centres*). In spite of all changes that Western society has undergone, societal fields still are organised as functions of the economic process of production. Social actors (individuals or social groups) occupy positions in regard to these centres, which highly determine their chance of being marginalised; see also social, economic and cultural capital (Bourdieu, 1989). Processes through which individuals or groups are reduced to a low degree of participation are subsumed under the heading of 'marginalisation'.

The distance between these positions and the centres is expressed in terms of *differential participation*. Participation is not always continuous; it often is interrupted by *discontinuities* (or societal *'fault lines'*) that can take different forms. The most radical is the one between 'participation' and 'non-participation'. However, even equal (quantitative) degrees of reduction in participation do not always have the same (qualitative) effects on the distance to the centre. We also must reckon with the phenomenon of 'negative participation', which refers to participation at negatively evaluated processes or institutions, such as criminality.

Some authors maintain that groups living in society's margins have a culture of their own, often called a *'culture of poverty'*, which enables them to survive in poverty but at the same time prevents them from using the resources if and when they become available. Others stick to the hypothesis that the poor just adapt their behaviour to changing circumstances, without values and norms being involved. The most plausible hypothesis probably is that of a dynamic relation between on the one hand values and norms and on the other hand living conditions (or available resources); the positions that the poor occupy then serve as the relating factor between both. This approach is called the 'adaptational' one.

This last approach, however, still does not refer explicitly to the organisation of society. This dimension can be analysed with the help of 'social networks'. The final question then is, whether these networks take the form of social groups and which is the status of these excluded groups in the class structure. This is a most important political question, because the socially excluded will only be able to improve their position or condition when they develop a collective identity. If this is not the case, they will remain dependent upon the willingness of other social actors to support their demands.

A structural approach means that both concepts of 'homelessness' and 'the homeless' are to be clearly distinguished. Homelessness refers to a network of positions characterised by a low degree of access to the dominant economic, social, political and cultural resources of society. They lead to an accumulation of individual and collective deprivations which separate the homeless to such a degree from the rest of society that they are unable to bridge this gap on their own.

The homeless are persons or groups who are living in homelessness. In our societies, individuals or groups are given a position because of their 'score' on characteristics that matter for the functioning and maintenance (survival) of this specific type of social organisation. A positive score on these relevant characteristics brings them closer to the centre(s) of social organisation, a negative feature keeps them away from these centre(s) and eventually pushes them into society's periphery. What is valid for individual members applies to social groups (families, ethnic communities, social classes) because, in the end, they are based on one or more of these social features.

There are, of course, internal and external limits to a structural approach. The main external one is that our model starts includes a number of presuppositions, the basic one being the central role of the economic production process. The internal limit is that we will have to complete the structural framework with non-structural elements.

Policy Making and Policy Models

Policy and Policy Making

The word 'policy' sometimes refers to a goal, sometimes to a course of action and sometimes to a set of procedures or rules. Policy clearly implies a process, that of 'policy making', of which policy formulation, policy planning, policy implementation and policy evaluation are important dimensions.

I shall not discuss these different stages of policy making, but focus on the standards (defined in terms of 'models' or 'perspectives') which cut through these different stages. Indeed, policy making not only is a conscious attempt to solve problems and control the course of future events by foresight, systematic thinking, investigation but also 'the exercise of value preferences in choosing among alternative lines of actions' (Gilbert and Specht, 1977, p.1). The rational model of policy making states that, faced with a given problem, policy makers first clarify their goals, organise (eventually rank) them, list all possible policies for achieving the goals, investigate all the important consequences from each of these policies, compare these consequences with the goals and finally select the policy alternative that most closely matches the goals. In practice, many factors interfere with this rational model of policy making. First, different levels (policy, programme and service) are being mixed up. The service can be seen as part of a programme and the programme as part of a policy. Particularly concerning homelessness, it often is to a collection of services that one is referring when using the word 'homeless(ness) policy'. Secondly, all levels are inspired by values and other standards. This especially is so with policy implementation, since it involves the matching of policy goals and (political) values. Although considerations of political, economic and technical feasibility are part of this matching, its context is made up of the degree of conflict and consensus, of coordination and cooperation, the time frame of reference (short, medium, long) and the spatial frame of reference (a community, a local area, a region, a nation-state or the European Union).

Policy evaluation often is ignored or at least played down by policy makers, although it is poor policy to plan programmes and to take actions without providing for their evaluation. Difficulties thus lie not only in the methodological and technical issues that hamper the development of evaluation techniques, but also in the area of political manipulation, both of the policy programmes and the evaluation studies. It therefore is important to outline some of the main decisions that are always taken, implicitly or explicitly, when developing a policy. I shall, of course, focus on social policies concerning social exclusion.

Elements of Policies to Combat Social Exclusion (and Homelessness)

I shall present these elements as sets of alternatives. It will be clear, or become so in the course of our presentation, that in our opinion one element of each pair of concepts is to be preferred over the other. This choice will be further discussed in the last paragraph. It should also be clear that in practice, there will always be a mixture of both alternatives.

Multifaceted or mono-faceted According to whether 'homelessness' is defined in terms of 'housing deprivation' alone or as a set of related deprivations in which the housing component dominates, different homelessness policies will be the result. In the former case, it is expected that the dominant feature, if tackled, will 'automatically' influence the whole of the living conditions. It implies a strong interaction between the different domains.

Integrated or segmented Even a multifaceted policy is not necessarily an integrated policy. It will remain segmented if multiple objectives are targeted separately. Integration goes one step further. It supposes a coherent political plan that clearly defines its goals, the interactions between the different fields of political action, different methods for realising the goals and different partners (public authorities and private associations) at different levels (from the local to the European level). One step further would be the development of an 'inclusive' policy: a homelessness policy that would be included into 'normal' policies, without losing its specificity.

Long- or short-term A homelessness policy can focus on the immediate needs of homeless people, such as is most clearly the case with emergency programmes. A long-term perspective, on the other hand, accepts that the problems of the homeless and the condition of homelessness are generated by the persistence of processes and situations of social exclusion. If the medium- and long-term perspective are focused upon, the structural and preventive dimensions will become prominent.

Preventive or curative A preventive approach means that interventions should first prevent the creation of situations favouring the development of homelessness in particular and poverty or social exclusion in general. This does not imply that the curative dimension should be left out from policy programmes, but they are rather seen as necessary corrections resulting from the unforeseen effects of social dynamics. It is, indeed, impossible to know, to understand and to control at every moment and at every level the totality of societal developments and mechanisms that lead to homelessness and other forms of social exclusion and which one must know to combat homelessness effectively. A curative approach implies that it is irrelevant and even impossible to intervene in societal production processes and that policies just should control and/or alleviate the consequences of these processes.

Structural versus individual Schematically, this opposition can be presented as follows: one can set up a policy for the homeless or a homelessness policy. The first focuses on the victims, the second on the societal processes and structures that generate homeless people. An 'individual' policy intends to assist socially excluded persons, in this case the homeless, to improve their living conditions and to stimulate escape out of that situation (individual mobility). A structural policy focuses on elements such as mechanisms of distribution and redistribution of social goods and opportunities (income, power status). Both types of politics, however, are not necessarily antagonistic, particularly if one takes a closer look at the word 'structural'. It does not only refer to large societal units, such as social classes or the labour market but also to 'structures of daily life'. Indeed, social life imposes symbolic, social and material structures on our way of life; even within the four walls of our dwelling.

With participation of the homeless or imposed by public authorities Policies concerning matters of social exclusion face a problem that is less present in other social policy fields: that the world of the poor or the homeless is characterised by destructuration and powerlessness. That they are being excluded from society (*Gesellschaft*) does not imply that they are living in a community (*Gemeinschaft*), characterised by face-to-face relations and informal help. On the contrary, homeless persons are isolated individuals, who are not very well informed and who, anyhow, have very little or no control over the powers that organise their lives. We could characterise them as 'nomads who are monads'. Because of this situation, the socially excluded in general and the homeless in particular have but very few opportunities to organise and even less so to start social movements. In this respect, their situation is not comparable with that of the (unskilled and poor) workers of the nineteenth century. Until recently, only the non-homeless have succeeded in bringing the problems of the homeless into the public and political spotlights. It is true that at present the situation is changing and that associations working with socially excluded people are being accepted as spokespersons by public authorities.

Informed (research-based) or intuitive policies What kind of knowledge should inform policy making? Is the intuition of the policy maker or of the field worker sufficient or do we also need research? Several factors are implying the need for research. Firstly, in our society processes and situations of social exclusion are manifold, complex and often hidden. Moreover, persons and groups that are well informed about the target groups often are too deeply engaged in militant work and identify too much with their problems and interests; they lack the intellectual distance to situate specific problems into a larger context, which is needed for effective policies. This research can be quantitative (populations counts, profiles) or qualitative; the latter pays attention to the structures of the daily life of the homeless.

A Typology of Homelessness Policies

Our typology is based on two sets of variables that have been discussed above:

a) whether the focus is on *standards*, as expressed in values and norms, rights and entitlements, or on *situations*. This dimension relates to the two main components of a social problem which are the main targets for any policy;

b) whether the homelessness policy is *specific* or *integrated*. This is a proxy variable for an number of characteristics: 'curative versus preventive', 'short term versus long term', 'personal versus structural'.

Using these criteria, we are able to construct four policy models.

	Focus on standards	Focus on situations
Specific policies	*'Social right' model*	*'Housing (policy)' model*
Integrated policies	*'Solidarity' model*	*'Poverty (policy)' model*

Figure 15.2 Models of homelessness policies: a typology

In using these models, we obtain clearer answers to the question of how the social problem gap between standards and reality being is being bridged. The most current view is: by improving the social position and the living conditions of homeless persons, so that they are brought closer to the 'general accepted standards of society'. Is this the way the gap is being closed at present? Or is it the other way round, adapting values and norms related to homelessness in such a way that the homeless person's position and living conditions are no longer perceived as problematic by the population, because it is seen as their 'natural' condition, or as the result of personal deficiencies. This 'stigmatising the homeless' perspective clearly does not fit into this scheme, although it still is helpful in explaining the attitude of numbers of policy makers. However, it is not a policy model as such, but only a collection of stereotypes. In a certain sense, this perspective can be seen as the negation of any policy model.

In the next pages, I shall briefly discuss these four models. I shall describe some of their characteristics and assess some of their implications. However, I shall not systematically analyse actual 'homelessness policies' in the different countries; the scope of this contribution is rather too modest for that.

The 'Social Right' Model

The origin of the 'social right' model is to be found in T.H. Marshall (1963). He proposes to divide citizenship (in a welfare state context) into three elements: a civil, a political and a social element. By the social element, he means the whole range 'from the right to a modicum of economic welfare and security to the right to share to the full in the social heritage and to live the life of a civilised being according to the standards prevailing in the society' (Marshall and Bottomore, 1992, p. 8). Social rights are important because they provide the inspiration for laws and 'laws are important instruments of standard-setting. ... They are, ultimately, the explicit statement of society's values, concerns and the level and nature of its sentiments of social solidarity' (Avramov, 1995, p. 160).

Two important questions should be asked regarding this model. Firstly, do social rights provide us with just a general inspirational context or are they implemented through laws? Secondly, even an elaborated legal framework does not guarantee that means are provided for the realisation of social rights.

Let us take up under this point the relation between constitutional social rights and laws and leave the second question for the next one. Since the specific '(social) right to housing' is very well analysed by Avramov (ibid., 153), I shall turn to her 'Homelessness in the European Union' for a brief discussion of this model.

The advantages of legal codification are evident: they guarantees more permanency because it is more difficult to revoke than social policy measures; Avramov calls it an 'insurance policy for the future' (ibid., p. 159). Legal codification may seem superfluous in culturally homogeneous societies or in times when there is a consensus about homelessness as an important social problem. In more fragmented societies or when there is not such a high degree of consensus between the main political actors about homelessness, legal codification may be the best way to guarantee the acquired provisions. However, even in countries where the 'right to housing' is included in the constitution (Belgium, the Netherlands, Portugal and Spain), individual legal claims cannot be made exclusively upon this constitutional 'statement of intent'. It requires the operationalisation of this fundamental right through legal provisions. A chain of obstacles can hamper this establishment of the right to housing as an individual entitlement.

In addition to the lack of a clear and explicit recognition of the right to housing as an individual entitlement, the lack of enforceability of the existing legislation, the lack of clear identification of responsibilities and duties of governments and administrations, the lack of comprehensive identification of target groups, the inconsistent monitoring of implementation, the uncritical evaluation of the efficacy of used legal instruments and policy measures, and the insufficient allocation of resources (ibid., p. 158).

The sole existence of specific legislation, on the other hand, also does not suffice. In countries that have passed laws which specifically address the condition of the homeless, they do not necessarily imply a general right to housing. Even worse, housing legislation may include a statutory priority for homeless people in accessing public (or social) housing, 'it may even exclude them from access to publicly funded or state-subsidised housing' (ibid., p. 156). It is, indeed, important to realise that measures not promoting the access of deprived population groups to provisions are as intrinsically a part of policies as are the more positive ones. 'The result is that homeless people have low-priority access to subsidised housing and may be weak competitors under the prevailing distribution system' (ibid., p. 158).

The right to adequate housing should then be defined as an individual entitlement that can be claimed; only so can it be fully and legally established and adequately implemented. This implies at the same time that the target groups, the terms of preferential treatment and the public authorities responsible for policy measures are clearly identified.

It requires a firm policy commitment of governments to enhance the right to housing, it implies the establishment of the right in national legislation, the provision of means to enable equitable access to the right, the monitoring of the implementation of juridical and social policy dispositions, and may need the continuous affirmation and reaffirmation of principles by the social partners and citizens in order to promote and to maintain the acquired rights (ibid., p. 154).

That the effect of laws and regulations is not always and everywhere as big as could be expected thus could be due to an insufficient or ineffective implementation or application. However, even a legal framework that possesses all the required characteristics will not always and necessarily result in the removal of structural obstacles to access the markets of adequate housing. What is needed is a set of policy initiatives aiming at the provision of (financial means for the production of) sufficient dwelling places. This facet is prominent in a second model, the 'housing policy model'.

The 'Housing Policy' Model

The core idea in this model is not 'rights' but 'provision of means', in particular the provision of affordable dwelling places for low-income groups. Means can be directed to several specific housing purposes: to rent subsidies, to (hard or soft) renovation of the existing housing stock, to the setting up of 'social rent offices', to improve deprived neighbourhoods. It is, however, the production of social rented housing that is most frequently understood under this heading. Indeed, this type of policy

> is intended to ensure the production, by means of specific providers or general providers, of a quantity of housing services in addition to those available on the open market, in which a part of the price is paid by the State in order to put pressure on the overall equilibrium of the rented market and enable groups in need of housing to acquire a home (Ghékière, 1997, p. 42).

Several questions arise and nearly all are related to allocation. First, how is the target group defined? Secondly, what kind of resources are made available? Thirdly, by which methods is the allocation of these resources to the target groups guaranteed? To ask the question, seems to answer them; at least in this context.

Target groups can be defined according to a number of criteria: income ceilings, need, location or population group. Need is the most differentiated criterion since it can apply to all kinds of housing condition, such as overcrowding or lack of minimal sanitary provisions. Resources may be more or less appropriate to the situation of the homeless and more or less targeted at their needs. With 'appropriateness' of these resources, I am referring to whether only financial means are being provided or a larger array of resources is made available, directly or indirectly.

Regarding the allocation of the resources, we have to take account of all policies that affect homelessness. It is quite clear that relations of all kinds exist between these policies, the most harmful of which are called 'perverse policy effects'. A useful pair of concepts to analyse them is that of 'direct' and 'indirect' policies. Policies are direct insofar as they are targeted at a definite situation (education, poverty or homelessness) or population group (migrants, the elderly, the homeless). With respect to a given domain, policies are indirect insofar as their are targeted to another domain but have significant effects on, in our case, housing or homelessness policies. This means that most policies can be either direct or indirect, depending upon the perspective taken.

Concerning the provision of resources for homelessness policies, three levels are important. The first one is that of general (social) policies such as labour market and employment policies, general housing policies or social security. At the intermediate level we find policies such as the ones focusing on 'poverty and social exclusion'. Programmes to combat homelessness and actions to assist the homeless constitute the most specific level. A given set of policies can be 'indirect' or 'direct' according to our focus. Social housing or subsistence income programmes are 'direct policies' when we are targeting poverty or social exclusion in general; they will, however, become 'indirect' when we take homelessness as our focus and measures to increase the number of shelters or to improve the homeless' entitlement to guaranteed subsistence income programmes (cf. 'le minimex de rue'/'minimex dans la rue'; Deschamps, 1996) will then become 'direct policies' for the homeless (or for combating homelessness).

At first sight, in societies that have developed a good set of social policy measures at all levels, no additional benefits seem to result from the codification of the right to housing as an individual entitlement that is discussed in the first model. However, both entitlements and provision should be integrated into policy making and the difference between policy models then becomes rather one of degree, depending upon smaller shifts in the balance between 'rights' and 'means' (or 'entitlements' and 'provision').

There remains, however, another dimension of policy models to be discussed. Is the policy approach rather specific or rather integrated? Both former models were rather focused on one specific dimension, housing; both next models, the 'solidarity model' and the 'poverty model' are examples of integrated policy approaches. The distinction between 'direct' and 'indirect' policies already referred to this debate; far from covering it, however.

The 'Solidarity' Model

This model focuses on systems through which the mutual interdependence of members of a society is institutionalised. Therefore, solidarity should be primarily defined in terms of 'structural solidarity' or 'institutional solidarity' and attention should go to mechanisms through which the complementary interests and needs of individuals and population groups are being linked. This definition of solidarity refers to a wide range of institutions, from the division of labour to systems of social security; in short to the 'welfare state'. The policy making model discussed here consequently covers the same wide array of policies, stretching from labour market reorganisation to social security (re-)arrangements.

Our focus on mechanisms of structural solidarity does not, however, mean that the 'value of solidarity', as it is expressed in forms of 'spontaneous' solidarity, can be put aside. The problems our institutionalised forms of solidarity meet with today, are caused by the weakening and even disappearance of this 'value of solidarity', which is important in reinforcing social cohesion. Especially at the level of society, 'the common good' (or 'the common interest') is less tangible than at the smaller and more homogeneous group level, where it is easier to calculate personal benefits.

Institutional forms of solidarity such as social security and social services, imply the transfer of resources and services between individuals, generations and groups. Their core idea is that these institutions should be accessible to all members of society who are able to enter in social exchange relations. That is why systems of guaranteed subsistence income are not part of social security systems. In a certain sense, this is the model that has dominated Western European social policy during the first 30 postwar years; 'les trente glorieuses', as Fourastié has named them.

The most prominent expression of this model are social security systems and particularly their so-called 'continental' (or Bismarckian) variety. They are promoting intergenerational and 'intersituational' solidarity and include intended 'horizontal' transfers from the healthy to the sick, the employed to the unemployed, from the young to the old, from childless families to families with children and intended 'vertical' transfers from the richer to the poorer. Unintended 'vertical' transfers, however, are not absent from this 'solidarity' model and they can be subsumed under the already mentioned 'Matthew-effect', which implies vertical transfers from poorer to richer individuals and households.

No explicit attention is paid to persons, households or groups which either are not sufficiently covered by these programmes or are not taking up the benefits or provisions to which they are entitled. It is presumed that the general systems of social protection are functioning in such a way that extreme forms of social exclusion are excluded. However, since the early 1970s it has become clear that people who are outside the labour market, and who constituted a rapidly increasing group, had either to rely on entitlements derived from family members or where excluded from these institutional forms of social solidarity. These developments have led to the questioning of the welfare state type of solidarity and to an increasing attention paid to systems of guaranteed subsistence income and to other, non-income dimensions of the living conditions of excluded groups and persons. Homeless people not only answer the labour market criterion, but others as well. The result is that the 'solidarity model', at least in its traditional form, does not take enough account of the specificity of homelessness and is not very appropriate for the analysis and developing of related policies.

The 'Poverty' Model

'Poverty' cannot be reduced to a question of income, an idea which is most clearly expressed by Townsend in his classic work *Poverty in the UK* (1979, pp. 54–9). Indeed, the term 'poverty' has for quite a long time been used to refer to a wide range of specific manifestations, without this resulting in these manifestations losing their singularity. The use of that one term 'poverty' quite rightly calls attention to the comparable social construction of the underlying reality, which essentially may be reduced to forms of exclusion from the dominant integration-generating institution: the labour market (Vranken, 1972, 1977).

Recently, attention has been focused on social exclusion. Social exclusion refers to, among other things, situations and processes such as polarisation, discrimination, poverty and inaccessibility. In recent years, much has been published in the way of theoretical perspectives on the phenomenon of social exclusion (see Rodgers et al., 1995; Room, 1995; Paugam, 1996; Jordan, 1996). According to Paugam (1996: 7); exclusion is now the outstanding paradigm from which society reflects upon itself and its dysfunctions, and sometimes also tries to find solutions.

Social exclusion arises when there is not merely a hierarchical relationship between the units observed (individuals, positions or groups), but when they are also separated by a clearly discernible fault line – which may manifest itself as a gap, a wall, or a barrier – that leads to a division between 'in' and 'out'. Some fault lines are generated through collective intervention (e.g. subsistence income or institutional isolation), while others arise without any explicit and deliberate intervention on the part of the social actors.

I distinguish between three types: relational, spatial and societal fault lines. *Relational* fault lines have to do with the kind of networks to which the poor belong. These are networks that provide no or very limited access to important social commodities (or to economic, social and cultural capital). The central question in case of *societal* fault lines is whether society as a whole or important areas of it are developing into sub-societies. This hypothesis is illustrated by developments concerning income generation (living on 'earned' income versus a lifelong dependence on 'unearned' income), the labour market (dual labour market) or the housing market (primary versus secondary housing market).

Spatial fault lines are a consequence of social polarisation in (urban) environments due to increasing dislocation and a modifying class structure. This classification might be further refined, but the three types of fault line mentioned above suffice for the purpose of gaining insight into the phenomenon of social exclusion and its specific forms.

First and foremost, we must however try and answer what is probably the most crucial question with regard to social exclusion, namely exclusion from what? (see among others Silver, 1995, p. 60). Depending on whether it concerns a culturally homogenous or heterogeneous society, social exclusion has fundamentally different implications. In heterogeneous societies, exclusion from one sub-society still leaves open the possibility of inclusion in another; in a homogenous society this is, by definition, impossible. The latter type of society usually is structured according to a centre/periphery relationship, while society's social goods (or its economic, social and cultural capital) is unequally distributed and only partly within reach of less powerful groups.

What, then, is poverty? 'Poverty is a network of forms of social exclusion that stretches across several areas of individual and collective existence. It separates the poor from society's generally accepted patterns of life. They are unable to bridge this gap on their own' (Vranken et al., 1997). How exactly do poverty and social exclusion relate? Poverty has all the characteristics of social exclusion: limited means (inequality), fault lines (social exclusion); they connect poverty with the broader context of society. Poverty, too, is characterised by the unbridgeable gap that is so typical of social exclusion. So are the two concepts identical after all? What, conceptually speaking, sets poverty apart from social exclusion? And, last but not least, how can poverty be distinguished from other types of social exclusion such as homelessness?

What makes poverty special is that it concerns a *'network of exclusions'*; it is, in other words, a multifaceted phenomenon. Poverty has to do with the more limited participation in various societal commodities such as income, labour, education, housing, health, administration of justice, collective provisions and culture. These areas are interrelated. I have argued that poverty can also occur as a result of an accumulation of situations of near-exclusion in these areas (Vranken, 1997, pp. 23–32): multifarious quantitative peripheral situations can accumulate to a degree that together they make a qualitative difference (exclusion).

In other words, poverty is a special case of social exclusion, it is an aggregate of interrelated instances of exclusion. These instances of exclusion concern various areas of social and individual life, and they can manifest themselves in specific ways in each of these areas. This is the essence of poverty. The fact that poverty must by its very nature concern a network of exclusion distinguishes it from other instances of social exclusion, such as homelessness, discrimination, inaccessibility, institutional confinement. Of course, these other, specific manifestations of exclusion *may* be characterised by exclusion in various areas, but this need not necessarily be the case: homelessness is a form of exclusion even when it merely concerns the housing situation (and is called rooflessness). Also, these various forms of exclusion are interrelated, which finds expression in, among other things, the floating character of the boundaries between illiteracy, homelessness, and poverty. It is also evident from the fact that an instance of exclusion may constitute a phase in a process.

Conclusion

Years of economic growth and a fall in the number of the unemployed clearly did not contribute to a significant reduction of problems of homelessness; the long-term social effects of the economic crisis are still alive and kicking and determine the political debate: drastic reorganisation – read reduction – of social security, impoverishment of inner city neighbourhoods, increased tension between ethnic communities, increasing success of extreme right-wing parties.

It is in this context that the debate on models of homelessness policies should take place. Partly because it is a new policy domain, it has been characterised by experiments and innovation. The multi-faceted nature of phenomena such as poverty and homelessness, however, already contains the risk of a fragmented approach. The scattering of political responsibilities over different levels of decision-making and over several departments only contributes to this fragmentation. That this increases the risk of parallel initiatives, perverse effects and uncovered situations, does not need further explanation. Countering these shortcomings requires more than good will, of which the policy makers and administration are undoubtedly not short. Our attempt to introduce more coherence in homelessness policies proves this point.

We need an overall concept in which general policies, poverty policies (social exclusion included) and specific homelessness policies are integrated. General policies must provide the general context, poverty policies can reduce risks directly leading to homelessness and homelessness policies are rather apt at combating the specific problems related with it and which are not taken into account by general and poverty policies.

What are the characteristics of such a model? It is important to clearly distinguish between projects, programmes and a policy. A collection of projects is not a programme and certainly not a policy, just as a collection of programmes is not a policy. Moreover, a structural approach seems to be more productive in reducing homelessness, without leading to the perverse effect of combating the homeless. If we define 'homelessness' as a specific form of social exclusion, then it remains possible to advocate one of the specific models of homelessness policy ('social right' or 'social housing'). If, however, we rather see homelessness as a type of poverty, one in which the 'housing' component dominates, then we must accept the multi-faceted character of homelessness and take this characteristic into account when defining a homelessness policy. Clearly, a policy that only focuses on one, although dominant, facet never will generate the expected results. It has, at least, to take into account what happens on other policy domains, because most of them interact directly or indirectly. Every specific measure will reinforce the positive or negative effect of the others. It is, of course, preferable to take into consideration from the start the multi-faceted characteristic of homelessness in the definition of a homelessness policy.

However, even a multi-faceted policy is not necessarily an integrated policy. It will remain segmented if multiple objectives are targeted separately. Integration supposes a coherent policy that clearly defines its goals, the interactions between the different fields of political action, different methods for realising the goals and different partners (public authorities and private associations) at different levels (from the local to the European level). One step further would be the development of an 'inclusive' policy.

This idea of an 'inclusive' policy implies that improving the quality of policy making at the local level is perhaps one of the highest priorities in the actual context. That the idea of partnerships between public authorities and the large variety of private initiatives is well received in many places offers an inviting context for developing an 'inclusive homelessness policy'. 'Inclusive' means that a homelessness policy should not be isolated from other policy fields. All departments should be (made) aware of the problem and should try to prevent this form of social exclusion. Combating homelessness has to be 'included' in the so-called 'hard' sectors: employment, housing and education. It offers an intellectual context for the promotion of coherent and effective homelessness policies.

A homelessness policy should, evidently, also take care of the immediate needs of homeless people. Because of their powerlessness, the homeless have but very few opportunities to organise and even less so to create a social movement of their own. Until recently, only the non-homeless have succeeded in bringing the problems of the homeless into the public and political spotlights. It is true that at present the situation is changing and that associations working with all groups of socially excluded persons are being accepted as spokespersons by public authorities.

Note

1   In this sense, every social problem has its own 'history'. The classical definition of this 'history of a social problem', that is of its development from a 'social situation' into a 'social policy', remains Blumer's five stages model (Blumer, 1997). We must, however, refrain from applying this model because of the amount of empirical research that it required.

Bibliography

Achterberg, E.P. and Marcuse, P. (1986), *Toward the decommodification of housing* in Bratt, R.G., Hartmann, C. and Meyerson, A. (eds), *Critical perspectives on housing*, Philadelphia, Temple University Press.
Alcock, P. (1993), *Understanding Poverty*, Houndmills, Macmillan.
Alcock, P. (1996), 'The Advantages and Disadvantages of the Contribution Base in Targeting Benefits: A Social Analysis of the Insurance Scheme in the United Kingdom', *International Social Security Review*, 49, 1, pp. 31–51.
Avramov, D. (1995), *Homelessness in the European Union. Social and Legal Context of Housing Exclusion in the 1990s*, Brussels, FEANTSA.
Avramov, D. (1996a), *Exclusion from housing: causes and processes*, Brussels, FEANTSA.
Avramov, D. (1996b), *The Invisible Hand of the Housing Market*, Brussels, FEANTSA.
Blumer, H. (1979), 'Social problems as collective behaviour', *Social Problems*, 18 (3), pp. 298–306.
Bourdieu, P. (1989), *Opstellen over smaak, habitus en en het veldbegrip (gekozen door Dirk Pels)*, Amsterdam, Van Gennep.
Daly, M. (1993), *European homelessness – the rising tide. The first report of the European Observatory on Homelessness, 1992*, Berchem.
Daly, M. (1994), *Abandoned: Profile of Europe's homeless people. The second report of the European Observatory on Homelessness, 1993*, Brussels, FEANTSA.
Daly, M. (1995), *The right to a home, the right to a future. Third report of the European Observatory on Homelessness, 1994*, Brussels, FEANTSA.
Deben, L. and Greshof, D. (1995), *Thuisloosheid: Sociale feiten en perspectieven* in Nuij, M. and van de Lisdonk, E. (eds), *Medicus en Maatschappij*, Utrecht, SWP.
Dechamps, I. (1966), 'A propos du "minimex de rue"', *Bruxelles Informations Sociales*, 136, pp. 26–7.
Deleeck, H. et al. (1983), *Het Mattheüseffect. De ongelijke verdeling van de sociale overheidsuitgaven in België*, Antwerpen, Kluwer.

Durlacher, G. (1973), 'Armoede: een poging tot analyse',*Mens en Onderneming*, 27, 1, pp. 45–65.

ECOTER (1987), *Urban environment, accommodation, social cohesion: the implications for young people. Italy*, Dublin, European Foundation for the Improvement of Living and Working Conditions.

Ghékière, L. (1997), *Allocation and social housing in Europe* in Parmentier, C. (ed.), *Where to sleep tonight? Where to live tomorrow? Orientation for future action* (Third International Feantsa Congress), Brussels, FEANTSA.

Gilbert, N. and Specht, H. (eds) (1977), *Planning for Social Welfare*, Englewood Cliffs, NJ, Prentice Hall.

Jordan, B. (1996), *A Theory of Poverty and Social Exclusion*, Cambridge, Polity Press.

Koch-Neilsen, I. and Børner Stax, T. (1998) (see chapter 20 in this book).

Marshall, T.H. (1963), *Sociology at the crossroads and other essays*, London.

Marshall, T.H. and Bottomore, T. (1992), *Citizenship and Social Class*, London, Pluto Press.

Murray, C. (1984), *Losing ground: American social policy, 1950–1980*, New York, Basic Books.

Murray, C. (1994), *Underclass: The Crisis Deepens*, Institute for Economic Affairs, London.

Paugam, S. (ed.) (1996), *L'exclusion: l'état des savoirs*, Paris, La Découverte.

Rodgers et al. (eds) (1995), *Social Exclusion: rhetoric, reality, responses*, Geneva, International Labour Office.

Room, G. (ed.) (1995), *Beyond the Threshold. The Measurement and Analysis of Social Exclusion*, Bristol, The Policy Press.

Rossi, P. (1989), *Down and out in America: The origins of homelessness*, Chicago, The University of Chicago Press.

Silver, H. (1995), *Reconceptualising social disadvantage: Three paradigms of social exclusion* in Rodgers, G. et al. (eds) (1995) *Social Exclusion: rhetoric, reality, responses*, Geneva, International Labour Office.

Stevens, A. and Vranken, J. (1983), *Armoede: een kwalitatieve benadering*, Brussels, Koning Boudewijnstichting.

Tosi, A. (1997), *Marginalisation processes and youth homelessness in Italy*, report for FEANTSA, Brussels, FEANTSA.

Townsend, P. (1979), *Poverty in the United Kingdom. A Survey of Household Resources and Standards of Living*, Harmondsworth, Penguin Books.

Vranken, J. (1977), *Armoede in de welvaartsstaat. Een poging tot historische en structurele plaatsing*, Antwerpen, UIA.

Vranken, J. (1997), 'Modelling in social sciences and models on social exclusion and social integration' in European Commission, Science Research Development, *Social Indicators: problematic issues* (TSER, Targeted Socio-Economic Research Programme), European Commission, D.G. XII, Brussels.

Vranken, J. and Geldof, D. (1992), *Armoede en sociale uitsluiting, Jaarboek 1991*, Leuven/ Amersfoort, Acco.

Vranken, J. et al. (1972), *Armoede in België*, Antwerpen/Utrecht, De Nederlandsche Boekhandel.

Vranken, J. et al. (1997), *Armoede en Sociale Uitsluiting. Jaarboek 1997*, Leuven/Amersfoort, Acco.

16 Housing Policy and Homelessness: The Danish Case

HANS KRISTENSEN

Introduction

Since the second world war the Danish housing policy has been able to ensure a sufficient supply of housing to cover housing need in Denmark. As such there are no 'normal' Danes who do not have a dwelling – at any rate not for long. The relatively few without a dwelling are to a large degree maladjusted persons who are in need of a special type of dwelling. So when talking about homelessness one can say that the Danish housing policy has been a success. Homelessness is practically nonexistent in Denmark!

The homelessness in Denmark which resembles the one we know from the international debate mainly comprises persons with problems related to alcohol, drugs and psychical disorders, who, for a shorter or longer period, do not have a dwelling. Most of them live in different forms of institutions. This group may also include persons who may have a dwelling, but do not consider their dwelling a home and are unable to use their dwelling as such. The majority of this group, however, cannot be helped through housing policy measures but should rather be helped through more social-policy efforts – or through non-traditional measures taken in grassroot-like housing areas.

The Danish conception of a homeless person in everyday language means a person who has nowhere to live, i.e. it is synonymous with a person without a dwelling. In order to define the conception of homeless I will be discuss it in the first part. I shall try to illustrate the extent of the problem.

Next, the main elements of the postwar Danish housing policy will be described, stressing how the social considerations of the housing policy have been observed. This review will be concluded by a look at the main elements our housing policy today.

In the final part of the chapter I shall discuss which social housing problems

– including homelessness – need special attention and which measures have been taken already. This discussion will concern both housing and social policy.

Who Is and How Many Are Homeless?

A report from the Danish National Institut of Social Research (SFI, 1995) about homelessness has the paradoxical title *Homeless With or Without a Dwelling* (Jensen, 1995). At first sight this title is incomprehensible in the Danish daily language universe. If you have a dwelling you are by definition not homeless. Not having a dwelling you are, by definition, homeless. But in the report it is argued that a broader definition of the concept should be used, stressing that the possession of a dwelling is only a necessary prerequisite for having a home. The transformation of a dwelling into a home presupposes that the occupant has established a mental and social feeling of belonging to the dwelling, which makes it a place where you can at minimum endure living.

This makes it a very difficult task to evaluate the number of homeless persons. It is no longer sufficient to ascertain whether a person has a leasing contract or owns a dwelling, one has to go a step further to be able to decide whether the person considers his dwelling a safe and nice place to stay. This kind of information is not included in the Danish statistics.

In another SFI report, attempts have been made to evaluate how many persons can be categorised as homeless. In this report the evaluation has been based on how many persons on a given day in January – which is the coldest month of the year and when very few people can sleep outdoors – spend the night in institutions for the homeless. In the report the figure of 2,218 'homeless' is reached (Børner, 1997, p. 8). It is, however, pointed out in the report that the figure depends on how you define homelessness.

If young people who want to leave home and persons who stay temporarily with family or friends while looking for a dwelling of their own are included there is no doubt that the figure will be considerably higher. How high depends on the individual's urge to move without being able to.

Finally there is a group of persons who live in 'nonexistent' dwellings, e.g. in self-made, illegal houses at Christiania,[1] in summer allotment houses, in summerhouses and other forms of interim dwellings. This category of 'homeless' has a home ... but not a dwelling. Although they actually have no dwelling they are not relevant as part of the description of the problem, but the type of dwelling might be relevant as a part-solution to some of the more psychosocial problems concerning homelessness; problems which cannot be solved by the allocation of a standard dwelling in for instance a non-profit housing corporation.

All in all, the problem of homelessness in Denmark is limited, perhaps 2,000–3,000 persons by a narrow definition and up to 6,000–7,000 by a more broad definition out of a population of 5.2 million, and 2.2 million dwellings.

The Most Important Elements of the Housing Policy

The immediate reaction to the above-mentioned figures may be that housing policy has succeeded in creating a sufficiently extensive and sufficiently varied supply of dwellings in Denmark. People who for a long time have not had or have been unable to obtain a dwelling are normally not victims of a housing policy 'error', but in general victims of a social policy inadequacy. In general it is a question of people who have problems with alcohol or drugs or people with psychic problems so serious that they are unable to live with other people in an ordinary dwelling or, conversely, other people cannot live with them. That means that homelessness in Denmark in general is a social policy problem.

The housing policy measures which have led to this 'happy' condition have, during the entire postwar period in Denmark, mainly consisted of a tax-financed subsidy of house building and housing consumption, a control of the housing market, in particular rental housing, and in the creation of a large non-profit housing sector. In the following will be described some of the most important housing policy elements which have been applied after the second world war. The description is based on various reports on the development of the housing policy and on my own views (Ministry of Housing and Building, 1997; Danish National Report to Habitat II, 1996; Ministry of Housing and Building, 1995; Andersen et al., 1993).

During the second world war the production of dwellings almost ground to a halt due to lack of materials. Simultaneously a brake on rents in rental housing was introduced, with the effect that most people experienced a decrease in their relative housing expenditure. As the population increased owing to the birth rate during the war, dwellings became very much in demand and towards the end of the war in 1945 the country was experiencing a 'housing shortage'.

In 1946 a Housing Subsidy Act was passed with the aim of increasing the production of dwellings. The instrument to reach this goal was low interest long-term government loans. The government loans were granted both to rental housing and owner-occupied houses. This started a gradual increase of housing production as the shortage of materials in the late 1940s and early 1950s diminished. Up until the end of the 1950s, at which time government loans were abolished, 240,000 dwellings were built, out of which 90 per cent received government loans.

The general economic situation had, however, improved to the extent that the rules were modified in 1958, whereafter the right to deduct interest from the owners' taxable income became the more 'hidden' subsidy of this type of dwelling. Throughout the 1960s owner-occupied dwelling, especially the detached single-family house, became extremely popular, helped along by a growing inflation, which meant that during this period owner-occupied dwellings became available to almost everybody with a stable, not necessarily high, income. The tenancy area, in the form of non-profit housing corporations, was, during the same period, subsidized by government guarantees for the loans and by rent subsidies. A considerable production of subsidised non-profit dwellings took place during the entire period, while private rental housing production nearly stopped. The size and quality of subsidised non-profit dwellings developed in step with those of owner-occupied houses. In the late 1960s it was not uncommon that non-profit dwellings measured 120-130 square metres and contained 4–5 rooms and two toilets and bathrooms. In the early 1970s many skilled workers, salaried employees, and young highly-skilled university graduates chose non-profit dwellings as their first family dwelling, although the single-family house was a tempting alternative. The somewhat higher economic threshold and the initial, expensive years in an owner-occupied house prevented some families from choosing this type of dwelling.

During the period 1958–74 approximately 700,000 dwellings were built, topping in 1973, when 56,000 dwellings were completed. The oil crisis in 1973/74, combined with rising building expenditures and the introduction of VAT on building, caused a decline in building during the following years. Although a great deal of urban renewal took place during this period, when old and obsolete buildings were torn down, an explosive growth in the housing mass took place. In 1945 there were 1,180,000 dwellings for a population of four million. In 1975 there were 1,942,000 dwellings for a population numbering five million. Calculated as dwellings per 100 inhabitants, the figure was 29 in 1945 and 38 in 1975.

Already in 1966 a housing agreement had been made with the aim of normalising the housing market, i.e. removing subsidies as well as rent control. The agreement did not, however, have the desired effect. In 1976, 10 years later, it was illustrated how homeowners and tenants were subsidised. It appeared that considerable subsidies were still in force and that the distribution was uneven. On an average owners received three times as much as tenants (Andersen et al., 1980). After another decade a serious cut in the subsidies for owner-occupied houses was made, while in 1987 a gradual reduction of the rent deduction right was introduced. This made it more expensive to live in an owner-occupied house.

On several occasions there have been attempts to remove part of the subsidies of the public housing, including rent subsidies. On the whole, however, the construction was subsidised through favourable loans as well as housing consumption being subsidised through rent subsidies related to income. Today all types of housing consumption are still subsidised, but contra the situation 20 years ago, the subsidies per dwelling is larger in the non-profit sector than in the owner-occupied sector.

The low economic activity with rising unemployment from the late 1970s until the early 1990s resulted in a division of the population: the majority with a job, and an unemployed or totally rejected minority. The unemployed and the rejected today make up approximately one-quarter of the adult (non-retired) population. This has made its impact on the housing pattern of the population. The owner-occupied houses are now, as previously, occupied by the middle and upper class but a large percentage of the workers also live in owner-occupied houses. The non-profit housing sector especially has experienced a dramatic change, from mainly being dwellings for workers and salaried employees with moderate or medium incomes, to containing today a large part of unemployed and socially rejected persons on different forms of welfare. Also, more and more housing estates contain a growing number of immigrants and refugees. All in all, the housing market has been more segregated during the last 15–20 years.

The political discussion during the last 10 years has been characterised by large oscillations. During the period up to the early 1980s there was, in reality, a rather high degree of political agreement on the level of subsidies to non-profit housing and owner-occupied housing. But in the mid-1980s Denmark had a conservative government, which meant that non-profit housing as a social democratic 'project' came under fire. A government committee was set up, headed by a conservative mayor, who scrutinized the role of non-profit housing on the housing market

The conclusion of the committee's work came in 1987 (Ministry of Housing and Building, 1987) and was to a large degree favourably inclined towards the public non-profit sector. The conclusion of the committee was that this sector was solving its social-housing task well and ensured good dwellings for the weakest groups of our society. In the report it was also stressed, however, that the composition of tenants due to the great attraction of the owner-occupied houses for many of the original 'regular tenants' – the skilled, married worker with two children – had weakened both economically and socially. The many unemployed and rejected had replaced these people and that had become a problem to the subsidised areas.

Before the publication of the report, a government shuffle took place and the Ministry of Housing and Building got an ultra-liberal minister. His attitude to the role of the subsidized sector on the housing market was far more negative than the report warranted. Therefore he set up a new committee headed by a well-known liberal Professor of Economics with the task of examining the function and problems of the entire housing market. During the period 1988–93 this committee published three discussion papers which strongly recommended the liberalisation and application of the free market mechanisms to the housing market and a reduction of subsidies (Ministry of Housing and Building, 1988, 1990, 1993). In the argumentation for this policy, demographically-based models were introduced which showed that a saturation of the housing market was near. Consequently there was no need for subsidising new building.

When a social-democratic government took over in 1993 the committee was thanked for its work and dismissed. Since then the demand for housing has been on the increase, owing to the favourable economic development in Denmark since the beginning of the 1990s, but also due to an increasing demographically-based demand due to immigration (and in the long run the higher fertility of the immigrants). These changed political and 'objective' conditions have had the effect that today's discussion is about where, what and how much should be built, parallel to an already increased building activity. Prior to this new development the annual number of dwellings built had reached an historic low, with only 13,100 new dwellings in 1995. At the same time the total amount of dwellings was 2,437,000 and the population numbered 5,251,000, or 46 dwellings per 100 inhabitants. So, although the building of houses over the years has decreased the total housing supply has continued to rise.

During the entire postwar period, publicly financed urban renewal efforts have been going on where obsolete buildings have either been removed – that was the dominating procedure until the late 1970s – or renovated. Together with extensive privately-financed improvements of owner-occupied buildings over the years, urban renewal has improved the average standard of the dwellings. This has also resulted in rent increases but, owing to rent regulation and especially owing to the very favourable subsidy rules connected with urban renewal, it has to a large degree been possible for the previous tenants to return to their renovated flats. The rent increase will not be felt until after 5–10 years. So in the short run, urban renewal has not created more homelessness – but in the long run the average higher rent level may work in that direction. However, a lot depends on the municipal obligations towards people looking for a dwelling.

At the moment the important question of the Danish housing policy is: Can government subsidy of the housing consumption and control of the rental housing market be removed? Experience from the latest large intervention in connection with the interest deduction tax entitlement – where the value of the deduction over several years was reduced – resulted in price fluctuations for owner-occupied houses, thus creating great problems for many people who had bought a house trusting in stable or rising prices. As regards rent control, a Rent Act Commission was set up to discuss rent control, including the transition to a totally free market. In spite of the intensive work of the committee, no agreement was reached. In other words, it has proved very difficult to change the economic rules and the finely balanced situation in the distribution of subsidies surrounding dwellings.

The second important question of housing policy concerns the social situation regarding the dwelling in a series of problem-ridden housing estates and urban areas. In 1993 a ministerial committee was set up with the task of identifying (new) social problems and solutions concerning dwellings. Due to a heated newspaper debate, immigrant problems were in focus during the first round on the housing estates and urban areas where the proportion of immigrants is high. The efforts range from club activities and teaching of Danish, to employment and education projects. Several types of projects have been started focusing more on 'Danish' problems in the same areas and housing estates: unemployment, rootlessness, alcoholism, violence and vandalism. These efforts consist of various forms of activities, clubs, social support, cultural arrangements and education. These broad efforts are of a sociopolitical nature. Very large funds are spent, however, on the physical improvement of the sad impression of wear and tear of the areas. Further development of these efforts is now called 'a lift to urban areas'. The six projects, which have been agreed upon between the state and the municipalities in question, have elements in them of urban planning and renewal, improvement of dwellings, social, educational and employment efforts and ecological projects.

The third theme of the housing policy is the renewal of towns and dwellings. In the latest legislation – from the spring of 1997 – public financing of urban renewal continues on practically the same level as previously, but there are possibilities of renewal where public and private funds to a large degree are combined in preventive efforts in areas which are not yet totally run down.

Finally, housing policy has lately given high priority to special groups; housing for the elderly especially has undergone several changes, from focusing on nursing homes and old people's homes to increased efforts to keep the elderly in their own home as long as possible and later on to develop dwellings with good access and often some form of light surveillance/help in their daily life. The field of disabled persons has been characterised by attempts to find and develop types of dwellings which put the disabled in a position to help themselves

Finally several dwellings have been built for the young people who are leaving home and entering the ordinary housing market.

Homelessness and Housing Policy – a Discussion

Danish housing policy has thus ensured a constant growth of housing mass which has been considerably higher than population growth; from an average of 29 dwellings per 100 inhabitants in 1945 to 46 dwellings per 100 inhabitants in 1995. At the same time, the average size and standard of equipment of the dwellings have increased considerably. It is hard to say whether there are enough dwellings. But a pressing demand does not exist today. And so the *first* condition of avoiding homelessness has been fulfilled.

The *second* condition is that the dwellings should be within reach economically. In this area, also, housing policy (together with tax policies) through regulation of the rental market, ensures that even people with low incomes – or totally without incomes – can settle down in a modern, fairly large flat. The rent level is controlled and the municipalities are in a position to grant people a favourable loan to pay for possible deposits, and under certain circumstances even pay the rent. This, however, is not common procedure. But almost half of all tenants receive a rent subsidy, enabling them to live in fairly large modern flats without economic deprivation.

The *third* condition is that no mechanisms of exclusion should exist preventing certain categories of people from getting a flat. In order to avoid such hindrances, the municipalities have a right to dispose of one-quarter of all vacant, subsidised flats – a right only used by half of Danish municipalities. The municipality takes on an economic responsibility when it utilises this right, as it guarantees the building association payment of the rent as well as of possible repair costs in connection with moving.

Finally, the *fourth* condition is a municipal obligation according to a national law to ensure the families of the municipality a decent dwelling. This obligation does not include single persons, but many municipalities do help them also to find a dwelling. When it is not possible to integrate a person into an ordinary dwelling it is the responsibility of the municipality, together with the regional authorities, to find a suitable institution for that person.

These four elements have, on the whole, made homelessness practically nonexistent in Denmark.

There are people, however, who live in institutions and who therefore are included in the category of homeless, who might be able to live in a sort of dwelling somewhere between their own home and an institution, if a social function of support was offered to support them. During the last decade Denmark has been subjected to a de-institutionalisation which in particular has included the closing down of some psychiatric institutions. The consequences of this policy have been that a number of subsidised housing estates – on the recommendation of the municipalities – have been forced to make dwellings available to people who would have previously been living in an institution. Parallel with this, a district psychiatric service was established which was supposed to help these people in their own new dwelling. From a series of investigations of housing estates where these maladjusted people have settled, the messages have been the same: a housing estate can handle a few, but not too many and too maladjusted persons and that the supervision and assistance to these people have been inadequate. Often one gets the impression that the responsible authorities had hoped that neighbours and the social network could help these maladjusted people to lead a fairly normal life. But experience shows that this task is too overwhelming for ordinary people. This has let to a series of unhappy situations where the maladjusted have lived in misery in their dwelling and where the neighbours have suffered from noise, threats, and indescribable filthiness, etc. In short, many of this type of potentially homeless people cannot be integrated in an ordinary dwelling.

An alternative to an ordinary dwelling has been the establishment of different forms of 'social settlement forms', i.e. different forms of dwellings combined with a more intensive local support function. These new forms were established during the same period – but in step with the de-institutionalisation. In a recently published report from the Danish Building Research Institute and the Danish National Institute of Social Research a series of the 'social living quarters' have been evaluated (Jensen et al., 1997). The social living quarters in this evaluation comprise the following dwelling types:

- support in your own ordinary flat;
- alternative shelters;
- staircase communities with common premises;
- digs, hostels, boarding houses;
- social housing communities;
- temporary support dwellings.

The physical design and social support vary a lot. For instance, an alternative shelter was established in railway coaches on an old shunting yard in Copenhagen. More conventional joint living quarters were also established in villas, which were converted into a kind of housing communities.

It was not possible to reach a simple conclusion as to which type of dwelling (a combination of physical design and social support) was the most suitable for certain kinds of homeless or potentially homeless, maladjusted characters. So the recommendation to the municipalities – from the evaluation – is to build up a variety of offers of social living quarters both with a view to the physical design and the social support.

While the above-mentioned forms of social living quarters are an initiative from the municipality and as such subject to a series of formal rules and regulations, a number of 'unusual housing areas' have emerged, especially in Copenhagen, but probably also in some of the large provincial towns. One example is garden allotment areas, where the houses gradually – and illegally – have turned into all-year habitations. Shanty towns of temporary character have become permanent but quite illegal homes built by people themselves on the outskirts of refuse dumps, along the outfall of main sewers etc. and Klondike-like, unregulated shacks/dwellings have emerged. In a report (Sørensen, 993) some of these dwelling areas were investigated to find out *how* they have emerged, *who* live there and *how* the areas function socially. The report points out that these areas, as a rule, have a strong social network which are in a position to support even very malfunctioning individuals and make them function without the support from the public authorities (apart from a sort of pension or other form of transfer income when – typically – there is no salary). Of course there are limits to what an informal, voluntary community can handle – but the limits are higher than in an ordinary housing estate. The main point of the report is that although these housing areas violate rules of the building regulations and the planning laws, they have emerged and will continue to do so because they contain a type of dwelling suitable for certain people who otherwise would have been homeless or unfit for more conventional dwellings. Therefore the report concludes by suggesting – as a paradox – a more planned and targeted effort from the municipalities, for instance that the municipality make exemptions to existing rules (or turn a blind eye) when such housing areas gradually emerge, if they are not a nuisance to other people. And that municipalities perhaps even point out areas where new Klondike-buildings are allowed to spread. One single municipality (Århus) has, since the publication of the report, taken up the idea and is about to find a suitable area as well as interested builders.

The final conclusion is that in Denmark homelessness is very limited and that it can hardly be solved through housing policy measures. Most of the homeless today are so maladjusted that they are unable to live under normal circumstances in a subsidised rental dwelling. To procure a home for them a strategy is necessary where the municipal offers of different forms of social support combined with the dwelling are given with the greatest possible variety and furthermore, there is probably a need for ensuring more possibilities of establishing 'free dwelling forms' through exemptions to existing rules in 'unusual housing areas' in a number of different places in the country.

Notes

1   A community of nearly 1,000 persons living in a former army-barracks in Copenhagen occupied by hippies and other groups since the early 1970s.

Bibliography

Andersen, H.S. and Bonke, J. (1980), *Boligsektorens fordelingsmæssige virkninger*, København, SBI og Lavindkomstkommissionens sekretariat.
Boliger og byggeri (1995), København, Boligministeriet.
Boligmarkedet og boligpolitikken – et debatoplæg (1988), København, Boligministeriet.
Boligmarkedet og boligpolitikken – et debatoplæg (1990), København, Boligministeriet.
Boligmarkedet og huslejespænd – et debatoplæg (1993), København, Boligministeriet.
Børner, T. (1997), *Youth Homelessness in Denmark*, Copenhagen, SFI.
Danish National Report to Habitat II (1996), Ministry of Foreign Affairs, Housing, Environment and Energy.
Den almennyttige boligsektors rolle på boligmarkedet (1987), København, Boligministeriet.
Hansen, K.E. and Andersen, H.S. (1993), *Strategier for regulering af bolig- og byfornyelsen i Norden*, Hørsholm, SBI.

Kjær Jensen, M. (1995), *Hjemløse med og uden egen bolig*, København, Boligministeriet.
Kjær Jensen, M. (1997), 'Ole Kirkegaard og Michael Varming', *Sociale boformer*, København, Boligministeriet.
Koch-Nielsen, I. and Kristensen, H. (1977), 'Preventive and responsive policies' in *Where to sleep tonight?*, report from Third International FEANTSA Congress.
Legelovskommissionen (1997), *Bilag til betænkningen*, København.
Legerforhold-bilag (1997), *Legelovskommissionens betænkning*, Boligministeriet.
Lorang Sørensen, P. (1997), *Drømmenes port*, København, SUS.

17 Housing Policy and Homelessness in Finland

SIRKKA-LIISA KÄRKKÄINEN

Prologue

While I was writing this chapter at home, there was a ring at my door. A Gallup interviewer, an elderly man, asked for an interview. I told him that I was busy writing an article, and that I could give a short interview only. After the interview he was curious to know the subject of my chapter. 'Does that issue interest anyone any more?' he asked, after hearing that I was writing about homelessness.

Introduction

The history of service provision in Finland cannot be analysed without describing the trends in housing policy and in welfare policy. The social and policy context of the development of services for homeless people has undergone some major changes since the 1960s. The services considered most useful for the majority of homeless people in the late 1960s and well into the 1970s are nowadays considered necessary only for a small minority of homeless people. While in the 1960s and 1970s the service provision made a vast shift from night shelters to care and treatment measures, an even greater shift has taken place since then, to the dominance of housing policy measures combined with other social welfare measures. Can we now expect yet another shift towards more support-orientated service provision, or will the welfare resources be cut even more, resulting in a shift back to the shelters? The following pages will give an overview of these trends, the shifts from the 1960s until the present day.

The following chapter begins with a conceptual discussion of homelessness. This is an issue which at first glance does not seem to belong in a report the aim of which is to give the facts about service provision. However, the concepts and the shift in concepts have in the Finnish context had a great influence on 'the debate on homelessness and on the policy formulations, too.

The services and the work of individual service providers will not be described in detail in this chapter, for two reasons. First, the social and policy context of service provision is a big enough subject for a whole chapter. Second, service provision has not been evaluated and described systematically.

The Concepts 'Homeless' and 'Houseless' in Policy Making and Research

Homelessness is a phenomenon which is understood differently in different countries, depending on the circumstances in the particular country and on the tradition how the problem has been perceived. Due to this fact, within the European Federation of National Organizations Working With the Homeless (FEANTSA) homelessness has not been defined unambiguously. With the aim of including both housing exclusion and other dimensions of exclusion as well as broad range of living conditions which can be perceived as homelessness, Avramov (1996) proposes the following definition for homelessness:

> Homelessness is the absence of a personal, adequate dwelling. Homeless people are those who are unable to access a personal, permanent, adequate dwelling or maintain such a dwelling due to financial constraints or other social barriers, and those people who are unable to access and maintain such a dwelling because they are unable to lead a fully independent life and need care support but not institutionalisation.

This definition includes the diverse dimensions of the phenomena: housing deprivation, poverty or insufficient economic resources of a homeless person and personal incapabilities of a homeless person. An adequate definition could be further developed on this basis. This proposition has, however, not yet been discussed within FEANTSA. While there is no consensus on the concept of homelessness at the European level, researchers and policy makers in every country use their own definitions, each different.

Homelessness vs. Houselessness in the Finnish Debate

In Finland we do not speak about homeless people. After the war, until the 1960s, the concept was used much more. The names of the NGOs founded in the 1950s – 'Support for the Homeless' and 'Friends of the Sorely Tried' – reflect the vocabulary used at that time. These associations are still active, but otherwise the concept 'homeless' (in Finnish *koditon*) is very seldom used.

Instead we speak about houseless people (in Finnish *asunnoton*; a literal translation would be 'dwellingless'). This concept has been fully rooted in the Finnish everyday and official vocabulary since the 1970s.

The concept 'homeless' (*koditon*) is, perhaps, associated in everyday Finnish speech with the idea that nobody is interested in the particular person, nobody takes care of him. To my ears the concept refers to the feelings of the speaker towards a homeless person, but at the same time it refers to the feelings of the homeless person himself. That person is more or less a vagrant. The concept 'houseless' (*asunnoton*) is more rational: the particular person does not have a place of his own to live in, a dwelling at his disposal. Indirectly, society may be able to do something about the feelings and the misery of the homeless person. However, the concept 'houseless' implies that a person could be helped directly, by providing him with housing, social benefits and other help. Welfare society is interested in him. In this way the concept has a normative connotation.

In his doctoral dissertation of 1982 Ilkka Taipale limited the word *koditon* (homeless) to meaning

> a rootless person without a dwelling, a specific life circle or ties. Such persons, vagrants, are more often regarded as homeless than merely houseless. Houselessness can be avoided by producing and supplying housing. Reducing homelessness additionally calls for other support measures enhancing human relations and the environment. Housing is a vital prerequisite for the establishment of a home.

The debate stimulated by Taipale has become firmly entrenched in Finnish thinking. The administrative use of the word is at least here to stay. There has been a clear need in the Finnish debate about homelessness or houselessness to try to break away from a definition founded on personal attributes. Sweden has also been debating the difference in meaning between the words *hemlös* (homeless) and *bostadlös* (housingless) (Begreppet 'Hemlös', 1992; Järvinen, 1992).

Homelessness and Houselessness – Some Dimensions of the Problem

Tosi (1997) has discussed the conceptual uncertainties and ambiguities that characterise the debate on homelessness. According to him, there is a polarisation around two meanings: on the one hand the lack of an 'own space' and on the other, the absence of social relations or ties, which in turn reveal situations of social exclusion or marginalisation. The most commonly accepted meaning of the term 'homeless' refers to a situation of extreme poverty and marginalisation (Tosi, see ch. 4; de Feijter and Blok, 1997), to persons who lack a home (where the term 'home' is referring to more than the actual walls, roof, etc., to the social activities taking place inside the structure) and who lack the capability to use social institutions (considered part of a 'normal life') or personal relations (Børner, 1997).

Tosi argues that we lose the multidimensionality of the problem by concentrating on one parameter – the lack of housing. This is certainly apparent. The issue of multidimensionality can, however, be seen in a different light, depending on the framework in which we look at the problem:

1 as *a pure research problem* the multidimensionality of the problem 'homelessness' is more or less, or should be taken into account, the interests of the researcher usually being far-reaching, simultaneously including various dimensions of the problem. Even here, however, there are two main approaches, the socio-psychological one and the structural one, which are interested in different sides of the multidimensional problem 'homelessness';

2 another starting point to the question of 'homelessness' is that of *policy making and measures.* A policy making process usually starts with a specific problem and has or should have clear goals. For effective intervention, in order to make the problem and the policy goals operational – practical enough to be implemented – some aspects (such as the need for care and treatment or the lack of housing) are studied more precisely than others. Considering that, if all the multidimensional, often conflicting, aspects of the phenomenon were taken into consideration simultaneously in making a plan for a policy, one may ask whether the policy plan will ever be made. It is only possible to say in retrospect whether the problems and goals were the right ones and the key problems of the problem area.

The eradication or reduction of homelessness and houselessness is an example of a goal which can be striven for; later on, during the implementation of the policy process, other aspects of the multidimensional problem are more or less taken into account, in practice usually with the help of social workers and, if possible, within the four walls of a dwelling. These walls are supposed to give the particular homeless person a chance to try to find solutions to his other problems himself. This introduction briefly describes the policy orientation towards homeless and houseless people in Finland; and the prevailing orientation has had its effect on the terminology.[1]

Examples of Some Research Approaches in Finland

Finnish researchers have studied the psychosocial backgrounds of homeless people by interviewing them in order to understand the personal reasons for their becoming homeless. However, the policy issues aiming at reducing homelessness and houselessness have been so dominant in Finnish debate that even the research community has concentrated greatly on studying, critically, the approaches of policy making and policy implementation on the different levels of administration. Their research orientation is thus societal, structural. The personal processes of a homeless person as such have not interested the researchers within this orientation.

Jokinen and Juhila have in their discourse-analysis research studied the process of assessing the ability of homeless and houseless people to live in normal housing; according to them through their assessments and actions the local authorities maintain a circle of poor-standard housing. Some of the homeless housing applicants are stated in the administrative evaluations as being 'not fit for housing', meaning incapable of living in ordinary rental housing because of some personal attribute (inadequate, irresponsible, weak-willed), and they are sent on a round of the night shelters, hostels, poor-standard housing and rehabilitation institutions. Using this analysis as a basis, Jokinen and Juhila have developed a concept, 'the bottom-end housing market', for use in Finnish debate on homelessness and houselessness (Jokinen and Juhila, 1991).

The presence of special-group thinking in classifying homeless persons and others in substandard housing has, according to Jokinen and Juhila, even meant that the criteria have overshadowed the common denominator shared by all people living in substandard housing, and that is a poor economic situation (ibid.).

Summa, in her research into the rhetoric of housing policy, has stated that the reports of the homelessness surveys (Kärkkäinen and Vesanen, 1987; Vesanen, 1989) clearly try to separate the concept of homelessness and houselessness from the individual attributes of persons without a home by classifying them according to the conditions in which they live. Yet, she says, there prevails an ambivalence between the official debate and the actual situation of homeless and houseless people: on the one hand the official is eager to hold on to 'normality' and to avoid branding, while on the other, he considers it essential to define and analyse the state of these people and the nature of their personal problems as closely as possible in order that measures may be directed in a way that 'allows for individual needs' (Summa, 1990.) One may ask whether multidimensionality has gained too much emphasis, according to this statement.

However, the whole policy process from governmental policy statements right down to local housing schemes and other service provision has not been studied by any researcher. Nor has any sizeable comparative study evaluating the effect of the measures taken been made.

All researchers, regardless of their research approach, use the concept *asunnoton*, houseless and not *koditon*, homeless. If they want to describe the persons they are studying further, they have used descriptive concepts like 'an alcoholic'.

Who are Defined as Houseless in Finland?

As I have stated above, the concept 'houseless' is the one generally used in Finland. It was deliberately introduced in administration and policy in the 1970s. In the 1960s the homeless were labelled according to their personal attributes (vagrant, workshy, alcoholic, etc.). Even the concept 'homeless' was not used as much. These definitions branded people, as policy objects, as being in need of care, control, isolation and discipline.

The Finnish definition of 'houseless' people used since the mid-1980s begins with the physical place where a homeless person is at a given moment. The emergence of this classification is largely due to the fact that it is thus easier to classify and discover where homeless people actually live. The reasons why a person is homeless or houseless – his personal relations, activities or personal capacities – are, or at least should be taken into consideration by the local social workers and housing authorities; they are not used as criteria for classification.

People are defined as 'houseless' if they:

- live outdoors or in a temporary shelter not intended as housing, such as a garden shed, sauna cottage, hut, building site hut, caravan, etc.;
- live in a night shelter or a hostel for the homeless;
- live in an institutional home providing care due to lack of housing (mostly institutional homes for alcoholics);

- live in an institution such as a psychiatric hospital, old people's home, institution for the mentally handicapped, etc., either temporarily or permanently, due to lack of housing;
- are prisoners soon to be released who have no housing and for whom no housing has been reserved by the Criminal Care Association or some similar body;
- live temporarily with relatives or friends: includes persons who, according to the municipality's information or estimate, are living temporarily with relatives or friends due to lack of housing. This item does not include young people living in their childhood home;
- are families and other households with more than one person who are forced to live apart because of lack of housing, or in temporary accommodation, such as a boarding house, or temporarily with friends or relatives. Homeless families also include mothers in temporary mother-and-child homes without a home of their own and unmarried couples about to have a child but with no home of their own (Housing Market Survey, Housing Fund circular, 1995).

The number of houseless people has been counted (and partly estimated) annually (since 1986) by the municipal housing and social authorities. The data are collected by the Housing Fund of Finland. The definition used and the instructions on how to define the various categories of homeless or houseless people have not changed since 1986 (National Housing Board and Housing Fund circulars, 1986–95). (The survey is described more fully in Kärkkäinen, 1996.)

Are These People Homeless, Too?

The majority of persons belonging to the first five categories could be called homeless, too, if by the term 'homeless' we are referring to social relations and activities and to inability to use the normal social institutions. Some persons and households belonging to the last two categories share these definitions, too, but not all. Many or most of the persons and households belonging to the two last categories need housing only, and not much other support. There are, however, no precise data on the proportion of homeless or houseless persons who could and who actually do manage without any other significant support measures after getting a dwelling.

The number of homeless (houseless) people was estimated at approximately 9,600 single persons and 360 larger households in autumn 1996.

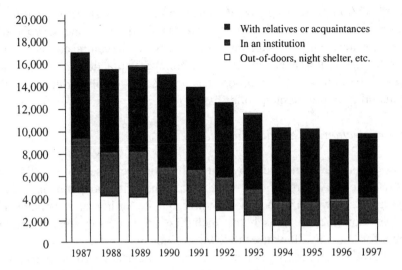

Figure 17.1 Single homeless people 1987–97 in Finland

Source: *Housing Market Surveys*, Housing Fund of Finland.

The majority are single men. Approximately 60 per cent of the single houseless belong to the category living temporarily with relatives and friends (Tiitinen, 1997). The number of houseless people has decreased from 18,000 since 1987, particularly in those categories in which most people need other support and welfare measures and who thus can be called homeless in international terms, in groups of persons who sleep rough, live in shelters or hostels or in an institution due to lack of housing. The numbers of such homeless persons has more than halved since 1987. Quite recent number for the year 1997 show a slight increase in the extend of homelessness and houselessness; 9800 single houseless persons and 600 larger households (Housing Market Surveys, 1998).

Some Brief Facts about Finnish Society as Background Information

The Municipalities Have Great Authority

The fact that Finland has a small population of only about five million makes policy formulation and administration much easier than in a big country. The basic administrative units, the 455 municipalities, have considerable autonomy and the right to levy taxes. The basic responsibility for the planning and implementation of housing, social welfare policy and service provision lies with the local authorities. The government passes the laws and appropriates funds to the local authorities for various purposes and the central administration issues the instructions necessary to put the policy into practice. In recent years, however, the number of instructions has been considerably reduced and the responsibility of the municipalities has grown.

Social Protection and Service Provision

All residents of Finland are provided with basic social security, social and health services. All are eligible for the basic benefits independent of their working career, which is an important prerequisite for homeless persons, for example. Low-income households, including single person households, are eligible for housing allowances to lower the housing costs.

Both the social security benefits and the services are mainly financed by taxes or other contributions from employers or employees collected by the state and the municipalities. The importance of private insurance is very modest in Finland. The role of non-governmental organisations (NGOs) as providers of social services is only a secondary and complementary one compared with that of the local authorities. The voluntary organisations usually receive their funds from the local or government authorities or from the Finnish Slot Machine Association subject to government control.[2] Usually the services provided by NGOs are purchased by the municipality, which means that the municipality has a coordinating role over the work of the NGOs. The role of the NGOs has recently become more important in service provision; they provide innovative services. However, at the same time the City of Helsinki has taken over more and more of the service provision for homeless people from the voluntary service providers in order to guarantee better quality. Some services provided by the private sector have been of poor quality.

The system of general social protection has been effective in preventing extreme marginalisation in Finland; recently, however, the level of benefits has been lowered, especially the benefits meant for minimum subsistence. The unemployment rate has been very high; although the economy has now recovered from the recession, the unemployment rate is still 13 per cent (young people 20 per cent). These issues are being widely debated in Finland today.

Housing

Finland has 2.2 million households, 66 per cent of which consist of only one or two persons. In cities the percentage is higher than on average and growing. The average size of a household is 2.3 persons (Buildings, dwelling and housing conditions, 1995, 1997). The demand is thus increasingly for small and medium-sized apartments rather than for family homes.

Finnish housing policy has relied on owner-occupancy of dwellings. Slightly more than 60 per cent of households live in owner-occupied dwellings, some 30 per cent of rental dwellings. Thus the proportion of rental housing stock is small in Finland compared with many other EU member states. The percentage of owner-occupied dwellings has, however, decreased in 10 years from 68 per cent to 62 per cent. Due to the economic difficulties, fewer households can buy an owner-occupied dwelling.

Half the rental housing stock is state-subsidised social housing and consequently regulated. More than half of these dwellings are council apartments. The state imposes certain price and quality criteria on the housing it subsidises. This has resulted in practical dwellings of a good basic amenity level. The applicants for social housing dwellings must be low- or mid-dle-income households. Priority is given to applicants who are in urgent need of housing. These guidelines are given by the government.

Several thousand homeless and houseless people have been allocated a dwelling from the social housing stock every year. Special housing, housing built for special groups (service housing for elderly or disabled people, group homes for demented elderly people or mentally retarded people, dwellings for homeless people) are included in the social housing stock as well and are subsidised by the state in the same way as other social housing.

There is very little cheap rental housing with a low amenity level in Finland, especially in the cities and towns; the idea of housing poor people in low quality housing has not been popular.

Housing Policy – a Hotly-debated Topic in Finland

The social housing stock in Finland is, however, far too small to satisfy the need and the demand. The number of applicants for social housing has increased recently. There were 2.7 applicant households on average for every vacant dwelling, and in 1996 only slightly more than one third could get a dwelling. In Helsinki the number of applicants per dwelling was much higher (Tiitinen, 1997). In 1997 the number of applicants has increased further, there were 2.8 applicant household per dwelling (Lehdistötiedote 10.2.1998, Housing Fund of Finland).

Housing policy is a highly debated and criticised issue in Finland and it has been considered one of the weakest links in the welfare policies. The large proportion of owner-occupied housing stock and the financial support granted for owner occupancy has been criticised for decades. At the same time, the shortage of rental dwellings has been a common problem for most young people. Now that rent control for non-state subsidised dwellings has been abolished, there are more rental flats available, but the rents are high for low-income people.

Housing policy measures have similar basic structures in all the Scandinavian countries, relying on state loans and rent subsidies for housing production and renovation and housing allowances for low-income households. The resources available for housing have, however, been and still are considerably higher in, say, Denmark, than in Finland, and consequently Denmark has a higher proportion of social housing, too. The average housing area per inhabitant is over 50 square metres in Denmark, as against 33 square metres (in 1995) in Finland. Homelessness emerges in a different light in these two Nordic countries: in Denmark it is no longer a housing problem; dwellings are available for those homeless people who are assessed to be capable of living in normal housing (Kristensen, 1997). This is not the case in Finland, one of the significant reasons for homelessness being the shortage of affordable rental housing.

Since the second world war, two opposing visions of housing policy – visions of how the housing market should function – have been competing in Finland: according to the first one, housing policy should rely much more than at present on the free housing market. In the early 1990s this vision gained dominance in policy making and today, too, these views have a strong position. Some say that all should pay their own housing costs. Some have likewise questioned whether housing policy should even be part of social welfare policy.

According to the other vision, which is based on the ideas of solidarity, all citizens who cannot afford or maintain a dwelling on the free market should be provided with housing on the social housing estates. This was the dominant ideology from the 1970s to the end of the 1980s. The campaign against homelessness and houselessness was part of this period and ideology; this policy will be scrutinised more closely in the following text.

According to the second vision, housing policy includes not only the usual means of regulating the supply and demand of dwellings by, for example, financial measures and by state interventions in the form of state loans, subsidies, town planning, building regulations and rent control, but also the measures which guarantee housing for the least privileged, providing the kind of special, supported housing the particular group and individual needs.

Homeless and Houseless People Gradually Emerge in Policy Formulations

While Finnish housing policy has been criticised for being inefficient, it has, together with social welfare policy, been effective in reducing homelessness and houselessness. Why? In what follows, this question will be studied by describing the development of housing policy and social welfare measures aimed at eliminating homelessness. The discussion will be based on Jan Vranken's theoretical analysis in ch. 15, which analyses the framework of the policy, in this case the policy to reduce homelessness. He also makes a typology of policies adopted. The Finnish policy will be monitored within this in the concluding part.

The following discussion describes the past, the historical developments, the shifts in the paradigm in the discourse about homeless people and other groups living in precarious housing conditions. Since then societies, the world economy and the climate of opinion, maybe even the values, have undergone considerable changes in Europe and in Finland. This paper will not and cannot answer the important questions: what kind of policy is possible now and in the future, and if the policy of the past is no longer possible, what are the basic reasons why it will not be possible? The situation today will, however, also be described.

The 1950s and 1960s, the Period of Barracks and Shelters

How was the phenomenon 'homelessness', 'houselessness' *discovered* as a social problem in Finland?

Urban homelessness was a major problem in Finland after the second world war. It was aggravated by the large number of workers moving into the towns in search of a job. They stayed in barracks maintained by religious and other voluntary organizations and for the workers on the construction sites by the employers. In the 1950s the number of these people rose to 100,000 (Juntto, 1990; Taipale, 1982). Some of these workers stayed in night shelters for a long time. In the 1960s, the inhabitants of the night shelters and streets were for the most part excluded persons, and most of them had drinking problems. Homelessness was very visible, and elderly homeless persons with severe drinking problems (known as *puliukko*, or lushes in Finnish) were very often seen in the streets. Homeless people were *visible* but at the same time *overshadowed* as objects for any kind of policy, except for shelters provided by voluntary organisations.

The plight and problems of the homeless were taken up by a civil movement called *Marraskuun liike* (The November Movement). The severe winter of 1967, when many homeless people were found dead in the snow, helped the public and the media to discover the problem. This aroused a moral reaction. *Collective action* was needed before the problem was really officially *discovered*. Soon the problem was accepted as one requiring special social policy measures, since the *emergency measures were not considered to be sufficient*. It became a concern of the *social administrators and social workers*, who insisted that something must be done. Their *concern was practical*.

Homelessness was in the 1960s regarded as a problem of alcoholism, unemployment and vagrancy. A wide range of *special social care measures* was duly devised with a view to solving these problems: homes for the care and treatment of alcoholics, emergency and halfway housing, and shelters. Besides providing care and treatment, the aim of these measures was to guarantee a stable society (Savio, 1989).

The Housing Shortage – a Big Social Problem

When *social housing production* was first introduced in Finland after the second world war, the aim was to alleviate the housing shortage in the towns by producing new homes. The housing shortage was enormous after the war and affected all kinds of households. It was the job of housing policy *to provide homes for families with children*. At the beginning, however, the state- loaned new dwellings, mostly owner-occupied, were allocated to rather well-to-do families, but soon it was pointed out that the homes financed by government loans should be given to low-income families, in other words, to prevent the housing exclusion of these groups. A report issued by the Housing Policy Committee in 1965 states that 'it is essential, in order to achieve the social housing goals, for families with children to be able to acquire a sufficiently sized home for themselves'. 'The building of homes should be directed more than at present towards production of family homes (at least three rooms and a kitchen)' (Asuntopoliittisen toimikunnan ..., 1965). There is no mention of the homeless or other special groups. The homelessness or houselessness of single persons did not concern policy makers in this field at all.

Special Groups Gradually Enter the Debate

The national housing programme in the mid-1970s was the first to state that:

> Attention must be paid in developing the general housing policy system to the members of the population for which the government's housing measures are not sufficient for them to achieve a reasonable standard of housing. These special housing-policy groups either have exceptional difficulty in obtaining or financing a home, or they need exceptional structural facilities or amenities in their homes, or their housing is closely tied in with the other social services targeted at the group in question (Valtakunnallinen asunto-ohjelma, 1976).

Special groups, and groups in need of special support in finding a home, had made their appearance in housing policy. For the first time the housing policy report also dealt with persons living in shelters, but it did not yet speak of the homeless as a group. This was the first – not a step, because nothing was done – but the first *recognition of the necessity of direct special housing policy measures* in order to provide housing for special groups; the *indirect measures*, of which the production of social housing is one of the most important, were not enough.

First Contacts on a Multi-professional Basis

The phenomenon of 'homelessness' was (and is to some extent even today) like many other social problems a totally *irrational* one for the traditional policy maker or administrator working *within housing policy.* The policy maker within housing policy follows the logic of the supply and demand of housing, combined with subsidies to cover housing costs. *Multi-professional cooperation was needed.* Authorities at this time became aware of this necessity.

The first *links between the housing authorities and the social welfare and health authorities* were built in the 1970s. Until then, neither had been able to envisage the needs of the other, the professional languages differed, officials in different sectors had difficulty understanding each other. The perspective was narrow on both sides, and this had an impact on the measures taken. (Saarenheimo and von Hertzen, 1996). A joint working group with representatives from both sectors clearly stated towards the end of the decade that 'the primary aim should be to provide homes for special groups within the confines of the general housing policy'. This happened in 1979. (Puutteellisesti asuvien ...,1979). *Housing and exclusion began to be connected in general discourse*; homelessness was identified as lack of a home, too, and social care and control began to be abandoned as a sole solution. In the language of today, people asked whether services for homeless and houseless people could be provided as part of the *ordinary services* in the municipality.

More Knowledge Required

The importance of *adequate knowledge* began to be emphasised. The housing, welfare and health authorities were urged to collaborate in collecting statistics by, for example, keeping (confidential) registers. The aim was *to make the problem visible for the policy makers*, both at local level and at the governmental level.

The local authorities were urged to draw up *a housing programme* for the municipality and to take steps to improve the housing conditions of those in particularly poor conditions. *Instructions* on this and on how to collect information were given by the National Housing Board, which was the governmental body responsible for housing matters.

Thus we can say that in the 1970s the problems encountered by special groups and the homeless were only just being recognised, and not until the 1980s were any practical steps taken to eliminate homelessness (Saarenheimo and von Hertzen, 1996). Sets of *rules and procedures* were thus developed, but there still were *no clear political goals* given by the policy makers. The measures were only administrative ones.

The Period of Policy Measures

A Committee is Set Up

The new government taking office in 1983 was the first to state the elimination of homelessness as one of its *goals*. But *still no policy formulation* was given by the government. In that same year a committee – the Homes for the Houseless Committee – was set up to debate the conditions of the homeless and to make suggestions for policy formulation. Because *policy planning needs systematic thinking* and investigation, the committee was anxious *to define the concept of homelessness* as closely as possible so that the measures proposed in its report could be directed at those in the direst straits.

The Homes for the Houseless Committee proposed a number of *measures* for eliminating homelessness and houselessness, *the primary goal being to provide normal homes*. Most of the committee's proposals were put into practice, and *implemented* within the policy process which had already been planned earlier (Asunnottomien asuntotoimikunta, 1984).

Homelessness and houselessness had thus been highlighted as *a separate problem* in housing policy debate, and as a problem *requiring specific measures*. In other words *direct measures* were taken to reduce homelessness, not only aimed at producing social housing or measures against poverty, which both *indirectly* help homeless people, too. Networking of public bodies working in various sectors and levels of the administration, together with NGOs, was initiated at that time. It has made the coordination of services considerably easier.

The International Year of Shelter for Homeless People

In the background was the resolution passed by the UN General Assembly in 1981 to name 1987 the Year of Shelter for Homeless People. This created, or strengthened a new *climate of opinion*: the resolution was taken seriously and in an atmosphere where homelessness was considered to be *a disgrace* in a welfare state. All the political parties agreed with this.

The UN resolution actually made it easier for the civil servants planning measures to justify their action (Saarenheimo and von Hertzen, 1996). The *administrative dimension* was very strong in this policy making all the time. At that time the municipalities, even though they had always had great authority, were guided considerably by the central authorities, in these issues by the National Housing Board and the National Board of Welfare. These bodies granted money to the municipalities for different purposes. This meant that *cooperation between different levels of the administration* was rather easy to arrange. The *practical policy implementation and the practical constraints* of policy making were left to the local level. Most municipalities succeeded very well in their service provision, but some did not. They were nevertheless *encouraged by the resources* from the government in implementing their plans.

New Legislation is Needed

The fact that homeless people (and other special groups) had been acknowledged as groups requiring special measures had its effect on the *legislation*, too.

The Act on the Development of Housing Conditions of 1986 states that the *municipal authorities must create the general prerequisites for the development of housing conditions in their area*. To this end they must ensure that such measures are directed especially at improving the conditions of the homeless and those living in substandard housing (Act on the Development of Housing Conditions, 1985.)

A couple of years earlier, in 1984, the Social Welfare Act covering the provision of social and health services as well as last resort income maintenance in the municipality had already stated that housing services must be provided to persons who for some special reason require help or support in the arrangement of housing or a dwelling. The Act also goes on to say that the municipality must establish, supply or otherwise reserve service housing and support dwellings as well as institutional care facilities according to the local need (Social Welfare Act, 1982, revised 1984.)

Although these laws were only *skeleton laws, and not binding*, they did (and still do) have a *guiding function*.

Furthermore, the Vagrancy Act, according to which living as a vagrant had been punishable, was abolished 1987, resulting in more homeless applicants for council housing (Irtolaislain …, 1986).

The right to housing, as one of the basic rights of a citizen, had been discussed for a long time and there was quite large opinion in favour of it. One of the arguments against the legislation, which would have guaranteed the individual's right to housing, was: how does *a law, a goal* help if the municipality does not have the *resources* to provide enough housing for its people? The paragraph stating the right to housing was added to the Constitution as late as 1995; it, too, states the public authorities' obligation to arrange housing, not the individual's right to demand it. The paragraph has not yet had any juridical consequences (Constitution, 1919/1995).

A Governmental Goal and a Formulated Policy

Finally, stimulated by the International Year of Shelter for Homeless People in 1987, *the government also announced its intention to eliminate homelessness* by 1991. At that time there were, it was estimated, close on 20,000 homeless people. Now, finally, there was *both a clear goal and a policy formulation* (described in the following). *The policy procedure* had already been established.

The objectives were specified more closely in *new planning instruments*, in the programme for the development of housing conditions and in the national plan for the organisation of social welfare and health care services, both of which were *approved by the government*. According to the programme for the development of housing conditions, 18,000 homes were to be made available for the homeless over a period of five years (Asunto-olojen kehittämisohjelmat, 1986, 1988).

The national plan for social and health care services placed the local authorities under obligation to provide a home of a minimum standard for every homeless person in need of housing services (Valtakunnallinen suunnitelma ..., 1986). The local authorities had until the end of 1986 to investigate the number of persons living in institutions for want of housing, the homeless and persons living in extremely substandard homes, and to draw up a plan for providing them with a home (Asunto-olojen kehittämisohjelma, 1986).

The Measures and Services Grow

The *measures became more concrete*. As the 1987 Year of Shelter for Homeless People approached, *special funds* were set aside in the national budget to permit the local authorities and certain organisations to purchase housing for the homeless and houseless. State loans for rental housing production were, furthermore, to be directed especially at municipalities with a large homeless and houseless population. Attempts were made to make the *goals and resources complementary*, but in this respect the policy did not quite succeed.

In addition to the guidelines and financial support to encourage the municipalities to match the policy goals, *a nationwide organisation*, the Y-Foundation, was set up in 1985 to provide housing for the homeless and houseless and refugees. This was founded by the Association of Finnish Local Authorities, five of the biggest Finnish cities, the Finnish Red Cross, the Finnish Association for Mental Health, the state alcohol monopoly ALKO, and the central construction employers and workers unions. This Foundation chiefly purchases individual apartments in normal housing companies in an attempt to avoid the formation of areas and blocks of houses with a social bias. The Foundation works in close operation with the municipalities.

All the measures announced on the national level aimed at providing as many homeless and houseless people as possible with normal housing. Other services, support and social work necessary to help homeless people were entrusted to local welfare authorities and voluntary organisations working with the municipal authorities. As was stated earlier in this article, the researchers criticised the authorities more for not being willing to assess a person as capable of living in normal housing than for not providing adequate other services for homeless people. The belief in every person's ability to guide his or her life in a more normal direction was and still is great in Finland's homelessness policy.

Effects of the Policy

As a result of these special measures, homelessness was halved in 10 years, but the special programmes aimed at eliminating homelessness were only partly successful. Instead of 18,000 apartments built with special financing, only 13,000 were provided in five years. At the same time, however, the municipalities allocated 5,000–6,000 apartments a year to homeless people. But new homeless people have appeared as existing ones have been housed.

The housing market situation in the municipalities has been surveyed annually since the beginning of the 1980s as directed by the National Housing Board. In 1986 questions about the extent of homelessness were added to the housing market survey. The results of the annual housing market survey were and still are the *basic information* in allocating *resources*, state loans and allowances for social housing to municipalities.

The survey has had an evaluative function in the Finnish debate. The figures raised the public awareness in the mid-1980s. Judging from the figures, the policy is considered to have been successful even though the persons using these figures are warned about their weaknesses. On the local level the figures are more reliable and used in more detail for planning local policy measures.

No real evaluation of these policy measures and the effect of the services has, however, yet *been made.* This has been left to the local authorities, which have not made any special evaluation studies either; the success at local level is evaluated in practical work, examining whether the client's problems continue, whether he or she needs further support or not. The criteria for integration have not, however, been developed as a research problem, and the evaluation of the criteria has mostly been left to the field, the housing authorities and social workers.

The 1990s, a Decade of Major Changes

Economic Aspects Dominate

The 1980s was a decade of economic growth. Growing material welfare made it possible to allocate resources to various purposes, including social ones. The increase in funds made it possible for society and the policy makers 'to be social', to take solidarity issues more seriously into consideration than in times of economic recession. The economic recession in Finland began in the early 1990s. The economy has now recovered, but the resources available for social purposes do not seem not have increased.

We are now experiencing a period of social policy rethinking in Europe and in Finland. Social issues are more or less being set aside in the policy orientation. The language of politics has changed, the 'common story' of growing welfare is breaking down, the only language which really sounds common is money (Hänninen, 1997). The prevailing paradigm is one of emergency instead of one of progress. Something ought to be done immediately, but nobody knows what (Soulet ,1997).

Instead of the rationally devised political objectives in social policy, many fragmentary policy issues have come to prevail; the role of local communities is increasing, local activities, and the self-governance and activation of marginalised people are topical issues. Long-term programmes and action have given way to immediate action.

Since the beginning of the 1990s there has in Finland been waning interest at government level in problems such as homelessness and houselessness. Housing policy has been overshadowed by economic policy; this applies especially to social housing policy. At the same time social benefits have been cut considerably, which has made it more difficult for low-income people to obtain and to maintain affordable housing. Since the present government was appointed, attitudes and values have changed a little, back to the earlier ones, but still the economic, often rather short-term economic aspects dominate.

The number of persons on the waiting lists for social housing has increased. As in the 1960s, many people are moving away from the rural regions into the towns and cities, especially to the capital. Finland is once again experiencing a migration. In the 1960s and especially the early 1970s the migration was quite soon met by social housing production; no such reaction can be witnessed now. On the contrary, the level of social housing production has at least until recently been kept low in order to prevent an economic boom in the construction sector.

Although the survey figures do not show a considerable increase in homelessness and houselessness, quite recently, however, homelessness (not just houselessness) seems to have increased in the Helsinki region and in some major towns (Tiitinen, 1998). New emergency measures are needed, the Helsinki shelters were full in the autumn and more beds had to be found.

Homelessness Has not Been a Topical Issue Lately

Going back to the policy analysis, it is not yet possible to evaluate the actual situation with the same concepts as in the past. Some of the issues can, however, be described and some questions can be asked.

Although the problems of marginalisation and the risks of homelessness have been increasing for some years now, homelessness *has not been recognised* in official policy making as a separate problem, neither as a problem requiring preventive measure nor the one requiring repairing measures. Only the State Auditor has reminded the authorities of the necessity of evaluating the homelessness policies. Quite recently, however, the Minister of Social Affairs and Health, who is also the Minister of Housing, expressed her concern about the situation. This statement was connected with the collective action on Homelessness Day during which the media discussed the topic, too. The problem is, perhaps, being *rediscovered*.

Indirect housing measures, the production of housing and the allocation of social housing units *does not meet the demand*, especially in the cities and towns, the population of which is growing. The allocation at local level of governmental resources for the production and renovation of housing does still allow for the local housing demand in general and the demand for special housing, but the problems of special groups, particularly of homeless and houseless people, do not have the same significance as earlier. The Housing Fund continues collecting annual data on the housing market situation in municipalities, one item being *data on homelessness and houselessness*. *Special funds* for housing homeless and houseless people have continued to be set aside in the budget, but the sums have been *small*. Whether or not more resources are needed for this purpose is a topic which has recently entered the debate.

The Policy Orientation Today

There is *no clear policy goal* for eliminating or reducing homelessness and none is foreseeable. *The legislation* stating the municipalities' responsibility to develop the housing conditions and to provide housing for persons who for some reason require help or support in the arrangement of housing has *not changed*.

The *government planning instruments*, however, have *lost much of their guiding influence*. No national programmes for the development of housing conditions are being drawn up. Instead the Ministry of the Environment regularly presents parliament with an action plan for housing policy. This programme is not a planning instrument of the government. The introductory chapter to the latest programme refers to the Constitution, which states that the public authorities are obliged to promote the right to housing of every citizen and to decrease the inequality in housing conditions between different population groups. Bad housing conditions can lead to other social problems, the programme says. However, the programme states that the citizen himself is responsible for arranging his housing. The duty of society is to provide the potential for people to manage by themselves. It is crucial to promote competition on the housing market in order to make the housing market efficient (Asuntopolitiikan tavoitteet ...,1996).

The programme emphasises the role of the municipalities in the development of housing conditions. The municipality should direct its measures at the promotion of the housing conditions of homeless people and the people living in cramped housing and housing with low amenity level. The programme does not, contrary to the programmes of 1980s, suggest any detailed ways of implementing these goals or say with what resources.

The national plan for social welfare and health care still approved by the government has changed its title to 'The Goals of Municipal Social Welfare and Health Care'. It emphasises the preventive measures in social welfare and health care and states that homelessness has not been eliminated despite the measures taken for this purpose. The programme stresses that it is important to develop measures to prevent marginalisation. The social welfare and health authorities must actively cooperate with the housing authorities. Detailed plans for the implementation of these goals are not included in the programme (Kunnallisen sosiaali- ja terveydenhuollon tavoitteet, 1997).

The National Housing Board and the National Board of Welfare, *the administrative bodies* which had a firm guiding function at government level in the 1980s, have both *been abolished*. The guiding role of the central authorities is no longer considered to be necessary, and the emphasis has shifted from norms to *guiding by information*. The role of the government authorities has thus changed. A new ambivalence prevails as to the role of the civil servants; according to Hänninen, there is nowadays a 'freely floating body of civil servants': the ideal way of working is networking, and policy orientation may even be disturbing (Hänninen, 1997).

The Responsibility for and Measures to Reduce Homelessness at Municipal Level

At local level, the municipalities are responsible for taking measures to reduce homelessness and houselessness. Earlier, in the 1980s, the measures taken more or less implemented the goals put forward by the government. In the 1990s *the responsibility of the municipalities has increased* as the government level has receded. Allocations in the national budget are still the main *resources* for implementing social welfare and housing policy but the local authorities have been given greater authority to allocate these resources as they see fit.

The resources from the national budget have, *however, been cut* considerably. The unemployment rate, which has been high for several years, has reduced the municipalities' revenue on their own taxes. The demand for benefits has grown. These are some of the reasons why many municipalities are in great economic difficulty. This fact diminishes their ability to plan and implement measures to promote various social goals.

The administrative procedures developed in the 1980s for providing housing and services for homeless people are *still the same* and are well rooted in the everyday routines of the municipalities. The multi-professional cooperation learnt at that time functions well in most of the municipalities, but there is also considerable variation. In 1997 the municipalities housed 3,800 homeless and houseless people (Tiitinen, 1998). This is a little more than half the average figure for the 1980s.

The social housing estates, functioning on the basis of self- financing (the management and capital costs must be covered by own income, by rents) are, however, in great difficulty because of the tenants' weakened financial ability to pay their rents. This situation can and has in practice led to harder values in allocating dwellings: there is a temptation to give first priority to applicants who can pay their rents themselves.

There are other reasons, too, why homeless people are confronted with difficulties when applying for dwellings, the biggest being the shortage of small dwellings. Since the demand for social housing greatly exceeds the supply, choosing only persons and households with severe problems may result in a tense atmosphere in some blocks of flats and some quarters. In order to avoid this kind of segregation, 'ordinary' tenants must be chosen, too.

Policy procedures and services established in the 1980s have been continued and developed

The Y-Foundation, set up 10 years ago to provide housing for homeless and houseless people, has continued its activities, on average purchasing 200–

400 dwellings a year for homeless people and refugees in several cities and towns, Helsinki included.

Many middle-sized towns have closed their emergency shelters and concentrated on other measures, on ordinary or supported housing for homeless people. It remains to be seen whether new emergency measures will be needed in the towns and cities, whether homelessness will increase if other options are not available.

Helsinki, where half the homeless or houseless population of nearly 5,000 lives (the total population of Helsinki is half a million), has more than halved the number of beds in shelters and hostels since 1985 (from 2,000 to 900). According to the Helsinki welfare authorities, unsuitable hostel accommodation should be minimised by providing the homeless with a dwelling in the normal housing stock. To this end, the special social services office runs a housing service system consisting of 600 beds in support homes or housing and 1,400 independent apartments. Just recently the City of Helsinki purchased three hostels from private service providers; the quality of these hostels was poor. Two of them have already been closed and instead the City has established a hostel with 74 single rooms in a block previously used as a nursing home for elderly people (Leijo, 1998; Suuri muutto …,1997).

The City of Helsinki has a special social services office which is responsible for the provision of housing services for single homeless adults in Helsinki. In most other municipalities services for homeless and houseless people are provided as a part of the ordinary service provision. The aim of the Helsinki special social services office is to offer the homeless in Helsinki housing to suit their individual ability and their need for rehabilitation. The special social service office provides both emergency services, support homes for people in capable of living independently (temporarily or permanently) and housing services in normal housing for the homeless. (For more details see Kärkkäinen, 1995.)

The City of Helsinki has a goal to purchase, in cooperation with the Y-Foundation, approximately 300 dwellings a year on the private market for homeless people and for other persons in need of support. This activity is, according to the City housing programme, to continue on the same scale in 1998–2002. (Helsingin asunto-ohjelma, 1998–2002). The housing prices have, however, risen during the past two years and this has become an obstacle for the City, which is trying to buy dwellings at reasonable prices; the City was not able to reach its target in 1997. Some members of the City Council have issued a written enquiry to the City Board about this, referring to the increasing numbers of homeless people and fearing that new emergency shelter places will be needed. The members of the Council stress that immediate measures must be taken to ease the situation.

In addition to dwellings purchased specially for homeless and houseless people, the City allocates dwellings from the council housing stock for homeless and houseless people. However, while the number of applicants for social housing has increased, the shortage of small dwellings has become more serious; in 1996 only 15 per cent of all the applicants for a City dwelling with one room and a kitchen or kitchenette could be given one.

Support for Previously Homeless People now Living in Ordinary Housing

The fact is that some homeless people cannot or are not even willing to live in normal housing. For many of them, this kind of housing does not succeed without special help; living in normal housing often results in eviction.

Some municipal service providers, the Y-Foundation and other organisations, are developing methods by which the previously homeless people, alcoholics or people with mental problems can be supported in normal housing. The public authorities, private organisations and voluntary persons should form a network to help these people in their everyday lives. This field of service provision is a developing one.

Concluding Remarks

In chapter 15 of this book Jan Vranken divides homelessness policies into four types:

- the right to (adequate) housing model;
- the public housing model;
- the solidarity model;
- the social exclusion model.

The *'right to housing'* ideas are founded on the discrepancy between the prevailing standards of housing and the living conditions of homeless people. These egalitarian ideas were a clear starting point for the policy formulations and for the official policy goals in Finland in the 1980s. Although the constitutional right to housing was discussed, the issue was not pressing enough in the 1980s. Other measures were considered to be more effective. In 1995 a paragraph stating the municipal obligation was added to the Constitution;

however, the issue has not been discussed much lately.

Solidarity is part of the Nordic way of thinking, related to the right to housing. Solidarity is an issue the significance of which now seems to be changing. We are experiencing a period of social policy rethinking; it is still difficult to say how much this change in values will influence homelessness policies and especially local measures to combat homelessness and houselessness in Finland. In recent years, as the number of homeless and houseless people has steadily decreased, it has been easier to forget homelessness in public debate. If homelessness and houselessness goes on increasing, the solidarity will be tested.

Finland has relied on *the public housing policy* to reduce its homelessness and houselessness. Special, direct housing measures were found to be necessary only because the general public housing policy did not alone succeed in providing housing for the houseless people. Other measures, indirect and direct welfare measures have been of crucial importance; without social protection and social benefits, housing policy cannot help deprived people. The personal problems of homeless people were not of any great significance in the policy debates in the 1980s. Only a minority of homeless people was considered to be in need of care and treatment primarily. These aspects were left to the local level, to the social workers. However, the support measures needed by many previously homeless people have so far been insufficient. There are people who really are unfit to live in normal housing, but some could manage in normal housing with qualified support.

Although the Finnish measures to combat homelessness and houselessness have concentrated on housing issues, *the prevention of social exclusion* has been the aim, even though the concept was not used much at the time the policy was formulated. *Long- or at least medium-term* programmes were found to be necessary and, furthermore, the administrative procedures were designed to last. Today, the shortage of available resources and the changes in the social paradigm have deleted long-term thinking from the topical agenda. The administrative way of working at local level still continues, providing as many homeless and houseless people as possible with housing.

Although the main aim of the homelessness policy has been to provide normal housing for homeless people, the policy was formulated as a *multi-professional* venture at all levels of the administration. The practical success of policy implementation depends on how well the cooperation is arranged at local level.

Homelessness and houselessness was a special policy issue in the 1980s. But it was *integrated* with normal housing and with the social welfare policy.

Most of the services for the homeless are provided as part of *the ordinary service structure*, the responsibility lying with the municipality. The City of Helsinki is the only authority with a special municipal office providing services for homeless people – not only emergency services and hostels, but also housing in collaboration with the City housing authorities. Several NGOs provide services, too, in Helsinki and other towns, but *the municipalities have a coordinative role*. The NGOs get most of their finances from the public sector.

Social protection and housing policy are the basic *preventive* measures by which marginalisation can be avoided. Special housing and special care measures for homeless and houseless people aim at preventing further marginalisation. If homelessness is seen to have been generated mostly by societal structures, as has been seen in the Finnish debate, the policy should aim at changing the structures or at least protecting low-income people from becoming homeless. Curative, individual measures are necessary for some people, too. The significance of preventive measures has become visible as the risks of marginalisation increase.

The homelessness and houselessness policies have been *formulated by public authorities* at all levels of the administration. There are some good examples of active participation by homeless people and their organisations, but the decisions are mostly made by the authorities. A comprehensive policy has its advantages, yet it may well be asked whether the decisions have too often been based on what the authorities think is best for the homeless.

The policy formulations have *not been based on research recommendations*. However, *information* on the extent of the problem has been *gathered systematically* for 10 years; this has been extremely important for policy making. But no evaluation has been made of how a particular measure or service has actually helped the person to break away from the vicious circle, of how it has helped the person to integrate with society. Such an evaluation is vital for future policy formulations to be made, especially now that the risks of becoming homeless are increasing and the homeless and houseless population is changing, since new, more severe problems are becoming common.

To conclude: we are experiencing a change of paradigm. The long-term programme has given way to short-term projects. Projects are necessary in order to obtain deeper knowledge of particular problems, but can social exclusion be prevented solely by projects?

Notes

1 The concept 'homeless', meaning both homeless and houseless, will be used in this English text although the direct Finnish translation is not used in Finnish. The word 'houseless' is not common in English.

2 Finland's Slot Machine Association RAY has a legal monopoly on slot machine and casino game operation in Finland. Income from this is distributed to voluntary organisations.

Bibliography

Asunnottomien asuntotoimikunnan mietintö (1984), *Komiteanmietintö 1984*, 18, Helsinki.

Asunto-olojen kehittämisohjelma vuosille 1987–1991 (1986), Ministry of Environment, Helsinki.

Asuntopoliittisen toimikunnan mietintö (1965), *Komiteanmietintö 1965*, A6, Helsinki.

Avramov, D. (1996), *The Invisible Hand of the Housing Market. A Study of the Effects of Changes in the Housing Market on Homelessness in the European Union*, Brussels, FEANTSA.

Begreppet 'Hemlös' (1992), *En kritisk granskning av använda definitioner*, Karlskrona, Boverket.

Børner, T. (1997), *Youth Homelessness in Denmark, National Report for FEANTSA 1996*, Copenhagen, The Danish Institute of Social Research.

de Feijter, H. and Blok, H. (1997), *Youth Homelessness in the Netherlands, Nature, Policy and Practices*, National Report for FEANTSA, Amsterdam, AME/University of Amsterdam.

Hallitusmuoto 1919/1995 (The Constitution).

Hänninen, S. (1997), 'Sosiaalipolitiikan syrjäytymisestä' in Simonen, L.,Elovainio, M. and Valtonen, H. (eds), *Sosiaalitutkimuksen valossa*, Jyväskylä, STAKES.

Helsingin asunto-ohjelma 1998–2002, City of Helsinki, kaupunginvaltuusto.

Hemlöshet i Norden (1992), *NAD-publikationer*, no. 22, Helsingfors.

Järvinen, M. (1992), 'Hemlöshetsforskning i Norden', *Hemlöshet i Norden*, NAD-publikationer no. 22, Helsingfors.

Jokinen, A. and Juhila, K. (1991), 'Pohjimmaiset asuntomarkkinat, Diskurssianalyysi kuntatason viranomaiskäytännöistä', *Sosiaaliturvan Keskusliitto ja asuntohallitus*, Helsinki.

Juntto, A. (1990), 'Asuntokysymys Suomessa Topeliuksesta tulopolitiikkaan', *Sosiaalipoliittisen yhdistyksen julkaisuja*, no. 50, Helsinki.

Kärkkäinen, S.-L. (ed.) (1996), *Homelessness in Finland*, Jyväskylä, STAKES, Feantsa Group in Finland, Housing Fund of Finland, Y-Foundation.

Kärkkäinen, S.-L. and Vesanen, P. (1987), 'Asunnottomat vuonna 1986 ja toimenpiteet asunnottomuuden poistamiseksi vuosina 1987–1991', *Asuntohallituksen tilastoselvityksiä* D1.

Kristensen, H. (see chapter 16 in this book).

Kunnallisen sosiaali- ja terveydenhuollon tavoitteet (1997), *Valtakunnallinen suunnitelma sosiaali- ja terveydenhuollon järjestämisestä vuosina 1998–2001*, Helsinki.

Laki asunto-olojen kehittämisestä 919/85 (1985), Helsinki.

Puutteellisesti asuvien vähävaraisten väestöryhmien asunto-olojen parantamista selvittävän työryhmän mietintö (1979), Sisäasianministeriö, Helsinki.

Rakentaminen ja asuminen, Vuosikirja 1996 (Construction and Housing Yearbook 1996) (1996), *Statistics Finland, Housing Construction 1996*, 2, Helsinki.

Saarenheimo, U. and von Hertzen, H. (1996), *Asunnottomuus väheni Suomessa, Määrätietoinen työ tuo tuloksia, Suomen Ympäristö 49/1996*, Helsinki, Ministry of Environment.

Savio, A. (1990), 'Purkamisen paineet ja potentiaalit, Laitoshuollon hajauttamisen edellytyksiä', *Sosiaalihallituksen julkaisuja* 13/1989, Helsinki.

Sosiaalihuoltolaki 710/1982 (The Social Welfare Act) (1984), Helsinki.

Soulet, M.-H. (1997), *How Homelessness is so Real?*, Copenhagen, EUROHOME Workshop on Models and Best Practice.

Summa, H. (1989), 'Hyvinvointipolitiikka ja suunnitteluretoriikka: tapaus asuntopolitiikka', *Yhdyskuntasuunnittelun täydennyskoulutuskeskus*, A 17, Espoo.

Suuri muutto, yömajasta yksiöön, Sosiaalikehitys Oy 7/1997.

Taipale, I. (1982), 'Asunnottomuus ja alkoholi, Sosiaalilääketieteellinen tutkimus vuosilta 1937– 1977', *Alkoholitutkimussäätiön julkaisuja*, no. 32, Jyväskylä .

Tiitinen, V. (1997), 'Arava-asuntomarkkinat', *Valtion asuntorahasto*, Selvityksiä 5/97.

Tosi, A. (1997) (see chapter 4 in this book).

Valtakunnallinen asunto-ohjelma vuosille 1976–85 (1976), *Komiteanmietintö*, 36.

Valtakunnalliset suunnitelmat sosiaalihuollon ja terveydenhuollon järjestämisestä vuosina 1987– 1991 (1986), Helsinki.

Vesanen, P. (1989), 'Asunnottomat sekä toimenpiteet asunnottomuuden poistamiseksi', *Asuntohallituksen tilastoselvityksiä* D1.

Vranken, J. (1997) (see chapter 15 in this book).

Other Material

Housing Market Surveys 1986–95, The National Housing Board and the Housing Fund of Finland.

Housing Market Surveys 1997, Housing Fund of Finland.

18 Conclusions and Policy Implications

INGER KOCH-NIELSEN

Introduction

The four chapters in this section have all somehow tried to answer the question: What is the connection between welfare policies and homelessness? The aim of dealing with this question is, of course, not only to develop a new theoretical understanding of homelessness, but in the end to influence policies and to provide measures to prevent or combat homelessness.

In the first part of this chapter I will emphasise the arguments and conclusions of policy relevance in the four chapters. In the second part I will present the policy recommendations that have emerged to me through the work with the EUROHOME network. They should be considered as my – I hope sound – conclusions.

Welfare Regimes and Social Policy Models

Mary Daly introduces us to the (different) theories of comparative welfare studies trying to apply those systematic approaches to the issue of homelessness. As has been the case all way through the work of EUROHOME she also encounters the difficulties in measuring the prevalence of homelessness. Accordingly she cautions the conclusions to be drawn from the statistics, because probably they mainly reflect the scope of national service provision and the ability of the service providers to measure and report to the system: 'Hence it is not impossible that the reported prevalence of homelessness in a country is a reflection of the resources made available to deal with the phenomenon in that country.'

Instead she tries to scrutinise the policies supposed to be linked to homelessness: the proportion of social housing and the access to such housing, state payment towards towards costs involved in housing, and whether the state has a national policy on homelessness either expressed in legislation or through some forms of obligations for the authorities to provide housing or to care for the homeless. Again it seems as if there are no easy predictions about homelessness to be made from the nature of the social policy approach in a country. On the other hand, she ventures to conclude that the Nordic approach to social policy has three distinct features that seem to have had a preventive effect when it comes to homelessness: a system of generous cash benefits; a widespread network of social services; and citizenship or residence (and not the position in the labourmarket) as the criterion governing access to services and cash benefits.

> On the basis of this comparison and the experience of other countries, one must conclude that the factors which generate homelessness can only be understood and combated beyond a narrow policy landscape.

Jan Vranken discusses the prerequisites and forms of a functional policy on homelessness. Before we have a policy on a social phenomenon this phenomenon must be recognised as 'a social problem'. A social problem is defined as 'a discrepancy between a given reality and a set of standards, a discrepancy that is judged dysfunctional by relevant groups and that is subject of reduction through collective action'. And homelessness has definitely for some time been considered a social problem in Europe. According to Vranken the efforts to solve the problem can be categorised into four policy models – different from those that Daly used for her analysis:

- a right to housing model;
- the public housing policy model;
- the solidarity model;
- the social exclusion model.

In societies that have developed a good set of policy measures it can be discussed whether the codification of *the right to housing* as an individual entitlement provides any additional benefits. Nevertheless, it is argued that laws are important instruments of standard setting and might turn out as useful instruments in times of change or if homelessness is disappearing from the political agenda.

The *public housing policy model* focuses on the provisions of means to ensure the availability of adequate housing.

The *solidarity model* focuses on the defining of basic social rights and on the distribution of goods. This model is reflected in the social security systems. In this system, however, no special attention is paid to groups not covered by the programmes or the non-taking-up of rights.

In the *social exclusion model* homelessness is explained by societal processes, and as Vranken considers this to be the ideal model for as well explaining as combating homelessness, he sets up six requirements for effective policies to combat homelessness *as a form of social exclusion.* The policies should be: 1) multifaceted, not only focusing on one albeit dominant factor as housing, but on other domains of policy as well; 2) integrated, meaning that policy towards homelessness must be part of the general policy, but still maintaining its originality; 3) long-term, not only taking care of the immediate needs of homeless people, but also of the problems generated by homelessness in society; 4) preventive; 5) structural vs. individual, meaning a policy towards homelessness – not for the homeless; 6) with participation of the homeless (not only the NGO's representing them); and 7) informed and research-based.

The four above mentioned models do not seem to convene very much with the welfare regimes or social policy regimes used by Daly. It might be claimed, though, that the conservative, continental model comes close to the solidarity model and that the social democratic, Nordic model might be subsumed under the social exclusion model – at least intentionally (as far as 1–5 are concerned).

The Nordic Model

The two chapters by Hans Kristensen (Denmark) and Sirkka-Liisa Kärkkäinen (Finland) are so to speak 'case-studies' of the Nordic model. Here the intention has been to take a closer look at the regimes considered to be preventive, integrated, generous, with an extensive network of social services, etc. What kind of homelessness – if any – do we encounter in these countries. Have the general policies succeeded? Generally speaking: yes – but ...!

There is a remarkable difference between the two countries: in Finland there has been a lack of housing while in Denmark there is a sufficient stock of housing in general and of social housing in particular.

Thus in Finland homelessness has been considered and treated as – in the first place – a housing problem (which is also reflected in the language: the Finnish word for homeless is dwellingless), while in Denmark, due to the housing policy, homelessness is considered a social problem.

Apart from this difference both countries have, up to now, avoided serious marginalisation problems due to the relatively generous social benefits. Secondly, there has been state support for the construction and consumption of housing, enabling low-income families to live in dwellings of a good amenity level. Finally, the local authorities have had an general obligation to provide housing and a specific obligation to provide shelter.

Kärkkäinen attaches importance to the fact that the Finnish policy on the one hand did not consider emergency measures to be sufficient, while, on the other, it recognised that general housing measures were not enough. Special measures had to be taken to assure housing for the vulnerable groups. The primary aim was to provide housing for the special groups but within the confines of general housing policies. But she also stresses the dilemma: trying not to brand the homeless while at the same time looking for targeted measures that require an individual approach to the homeless.

The picture of a homeless person in Denmark is that of a single man, but it can also be a woman with many other problems than the lack of a dwelling. Not infrequently they might even have a residence that they do not want to make use of or rather are not able to make use of because of mental and social insufficiencies.

So in countries where basic social problems and housing problems have been solved due to the general welfare policies, homelessness still exists, but in another shape: those who are considered homeless have for several years been characterised as persons with mental problems and alcohol or drug abuse. So homelessness in Denmark tends to be explained by individual factors and the policy measures to be individual and targeted.

Kristensen presents us with a provocative suggestion: provided that we are not facing a housing problem, but rather facing people with a preference for another way of living – originating from a wish not to be fenced in, in a flat situated in a big housing area away from the preferred environment like the central city or the waterfront, etc. – should we not allow for an alternative way of living, below the technical standards that we otherwise demand? He stresses that this way of living should not be considered as part of the problem – but as a solution. In another section of this volume, another Danish contributor, Preben Brandt, ventures the idea of introducing new asylums, or 'villages for unusual people' allowing them to live a segregated and different life. The groups in focus of Kristensen and Brandt are indeed different. But behind both suggestions is the idea that we should accept the different, the deviant and not try to 'integrate' every person into mainstream society.

It must be stressed, in order to avoid misinterpretations, that these suggestions are put forward on the background of the encompassing and general welfare system, where the overall responsibility for homelessness (still) lies with the state.

Reflections and Dilemmas

So where does this take us? Are there applicable lessons for policy makers to be learned from this? No – and yes.

First a caution: the European countries represent different welfare regimes and as we have seen within each regime there exist great differences. Their national welfare systems are rooted in history and ideologies, so systems cannot just be transferred from one country to another – and if they were, we would not be sure of the outcomes. It is probably more useful and relevant to transfer experiences about specific measures for specific groups (see section 4).

1   Nevertheless there is enough evidence to conclude, that the first sine qua non prerequisite for the prevention of homelessness is the *availability of sufficient (affordable) housing*. But this is not enough – the authorities must also have an obligation to provide housing and a right to access special groups into housing. This might on the one hand be characterised as a too commonplace consideration – but on the other hand it is a consideration which there is a tendency to 'forget' in a period where there seems to be a political preference for targeted measures more than for general measures. So whether or not a clear path can be found from the welfare regimes to the prevalence of homelessness it is important to insist on this.

2   The other general prerequisite is the existence of a policy against social exclusion and serious marginalisation, a policy including *cash benefits and housing support of a sufficient size*, allowing for a decent life not only a life out of poverty. In the Nordic model those general measures were, of course, not introduced or sustained just with the aim of preventing *homelessness* nor just to prevent poverty. In the Nordic model it is a question of *distribution of goods and of equality in life*. Equality has of course not been obtained, but studies of the effect of the distributional policies through taxation and income-transfers in Denmark give a very clear picture of how 'poverty' or low-income is reduced due to this policy.

3   A third general factor of importance that has not till now been touched upon in this section is sudden or encompassing changes in the structure,

accessibility or practice of services/institutions (e.g. hospitals, prisons). The same might be the case with changes in the (pre)-pension system or in the conditions for obtaining other benefits. Often the consequences of those changes are not taken into account until the result shows in the scope or composition of homelessness. What I claim here is not that this will always be the case – but that it might be worth while considering the effect on exactly homelessness when introducing such changes. Again this could probably not be done at an European level – but a general knowledge of effects of different kinds could be expected to exist. And often the service providers might have a rather good idea about what the effects of proposed changes might be.

4   Even in countries where the general prerequisites mentioned above have been fulfilled (more or less) a phenomenon called homelessness still exists. We can only grasp this contradiction if homelessness is understood as a category that different categories of people can float in to. In this perspective homelessness is best defined by the concept of *emergency*, as argued by Soulet in section 1. And in different countries and in different periods of history this urgent need for help is present in new groups.

What are the policy implications of this? Not that the general measures mentioned above are of less importance, but that there will (always) be a need for institutions fit to meet urgent, but probably *quickly changing* needs. But we cannot leave it there. Meeting the urgent need for food and shelter cannot be considered sufficient in a welfare state. There must also be a system, with an obligation to assist those people in getting out of their emergency situation. This demand immediately raises two important questions not to be answered that easily:

1   should the necessary assistance be provided by the institutions for the homeless or rather by the ordinary social welfare services – local or regional? The ordinary services are not probably really able to cope with those problems – if they were the urgent need should, theoretically, not have been there. This might be for many reasons, but the lack of experience and relevant education of the social workers of the ordinary services might be one important answer. On the other hand the wish to avoid branding of the persons might count in favour of leaving the job of integration with the general services. We are here again facing the dilemma of whether targeted measures – though more fit to meet the needs – have at the same time the

effects of further stigmatisation and exclusion?

2   must the way out of the emergency necessarily be a way into mainstream society? Here we have sufficient experience to give the answer: no it is not necessary – not even fruitful. As can be seen in section 4 on service provisions there is a need for a broad range of 'halfway housing' or 'supported housing'.

Finally we might raise the question of the importance of self-organisation and self-representation of the homeless. History tells us that important improvement in the living situation of a group will not occur, until the group can stand up and speak for itself. Or is this just another way of suppressing the powerless – asking them to fend for themselves? From a theoretical point of view supporting self-organisation – even at a very low scale – might be recommended. For some groups it is of course not feasible, but that should not prevent the experiment for others. The next question is who should be the promoter of such an organisation? Can we expect the organisations *for* the homeless to do this, or should we rather ask the state to support such steps?

A more general observation that might also be of policy relevance is that homelessness can be considered a *thermometer* indicating that something has gone wrong, that somewhere in the system there is a 'disease'. This means that monitoring and studying homelessness will supply us with indicators of dysfunctions and even of where they originate. But the indicators might, as mentioned above, change very quickly – from one year to another. Therefore monitoring of homelessness is most useful if it is done regularly and gives rise to the question: What does this reveal about ongoing changes in society as a whole?

PART 4
SERVICES FOR HOMELESS PEOPLE – NEEDS AND PROVISIONS

19 Social Emergency: Between Myth and Reality

MARC-HENRY SOULET

> Emergency is a method but not a finality ... What will get this policy in the end is wanting to treat all forms of exclusion with the methods of emergency. For everyone can see emergency, and that is what affords it media attention, but the damage of exclusion cannot be repaired by emergency. The social worker who worked in emergency would discredit the professional action which makes prevention and the long-term necessary ... A different process, different personnel (Xavier Emmanuelli, founder of the SAMU Social, Paris).[1]

For quite some time, social emergency has been in the limelight of the media and, as winter approaches, it occupies the forefront of our minds, the cold serving as a reminder of the misery of fellow citizens, of the distress of those who are in need of food and lodgings. In a more general way, beyond the loud demonstrations, emergency has quietly taken root in the social landscape and has progressively acquired credentials by becoming one of the components, among other older ones, of social intervention, so much so that one is justified in asking if one is not partaking of a new understanding of social problems, at least of the most critical ones, which calls for new practices capable of providing a better response to social needs.

Yet, paradoxically, so omnipresent is the reference to emergency in the representations and daily actions that it remains a theoretical unthinkability. Not only does it constitute an umbrella term whose polysemy explains recourse to it and its efficacy, but, above all, its use and mobilisation are auto-sufficient. Moreover, the semantic field of social emergency is marked by a metonymic reasoning with catastrophe and death. Thus, social emergency is qualified by the evidence of a relation to limited time, with reference to medical emergency. By an analogical shift, the medical is superimposed on the social, inspiring it with the ways of administering extreme situations and marking its field and means of action around prescribed responses, effective because they are quick. The mutilated body of the injured person informs as it were the intervention on a suffering person's behalf who, in turn, represents the homeless figure, the archetypal figure of disconnection.

But this evidence merits interrogation in so far as, on reflection, it appears problematic. This article wishes to participate in this sense in the clarification of the concept of social emergency by putting it to the test, i.e. firstly, to confront it with its universe of reference, especially those of death, of time and of the action beforehand, and secondly, to examine what it covers *in fine* and how it participates in the recomposition of social action and, more specifically, how it imprints the social representation of homelessness.

The Referentials of Social Emergency

Social urgency is part of a universal referential which confers meaning and legitimacy, making it thus undisputed and evident in its essence and exempting it from specifying what emergency consists of, that which gives it its very name and identifies it. And no doubt that which specifies better the latter is the ancient rule of classical drama, that of tragedy: unity of time, unity of place and unity of action (Guihard, 1987, p. 112).

Emergency: A Philosophy of Action

'To respond to an emergency situation, is not in its origin, a professional or scientific act, it is an ethical act' (Ginisty, 1987, p. 14). To put forward that moral competency is at the heart of the action in an emergency situation amounts, as it were, to engraving in golden letters on the baptismal font of emergency that it is incontestable, that it would not be subject to criticism, unless criticism in this respect exposed it to the purpose of non receiving, because it must be in reference to the supreme good which it means to preserve, i.e. the integrity of the human being. By calling on a feat of conscience in view of the intolerable, it constrains one to act without any bargaining; it does not admit of any circumvention by analysis, classing and dissecting before acting. 'Is emergency not a political trick which, by resorting to it, sees its enterprises as evident and irreducible? Does it not involve an invulnerable procedure of legitimisation always ready in case of trouble to serve authority proving by decree the pertinence of action?' (Beauchard, 1986, p. 6).

This priority of action seems to be at the opposite pole of any possibility of its being technologised, since it puts the personal implication in the forefront, which is at the same time a definer and a component of the reality of emergency. This philosophy of emergency action seems in fact to be situated in radical opposition to what one is accustomed to calling emergency jobs, medical emergency and catastrophes, firemen, sea or mountains rescuers, etc.; those who rely on highly skilful professional competencies and know-how as well as on sophisticated technologies, as we shall see further on. But at the same time, they feed on the same ground since they base all their efficacy on a very high-powered prior analytical breakdown so that while the act in an emergency situation is being carried out, it is not subject to any decisional interference; this is to ensure that the completion of the ethical exigency to preserve human integrity will be effective as quickly as possible. That which is imposed by emergency is not so much in this sense a denial of all means or of professional instruments but the obligation to 'act without thinking' (Stiegler, 1987, p. 21).

Emergency: The Conjuration of the Threat

To act in an emergency situation is to act without delay, but to act because there is still some time left, no matter how little, otherwise the emergency situation gains the upper hand, as doctors relate of those for whom there is no need to act because nothing can be done, because the outcome is certain, no matter how upsetting it may be. If, therefore, emergency does not include impossible action, it is because it implies the idea of its being manageable: the situation is controllable, the problem reducible and the catastrophe avoidable. But this in a very short space of time, because the menacing catastrophe reigns. If emergency works with duration, or, one should say it makes duration work, it is because it tries to conjure threat, or, at least to make sure that the threat is not realised. By doing so, because it places the threat at the heart of its obligation to act, more than the effects of this by the way, emergency is based on relativity. It is above all an appreciation of the threat, an assessment of its potential to produce what it predicts. Before becoming urgent, a situation is threatening, at least it must be judged as such.

Emergency

> is a challenge to the threat: whoever says emergency, is uttering a project of immediate struggle against the intolerable, fatality, all kinds of distress which experienced by anticipation, call for preventative action and for the constraint of an obligation of a result and at the least the prevention of a catastrophic course of events (Beauchard, 1986, p. 5).

Urgency occurs with reference to the objective of the contention of the situation and to the preservation of the existing one, even if to do so, exceptional means have to be mobilised.

In a certain way, emergency is a socially salvatory utopia, and this in a double sense: on the one hand, it is a vehicle of the belief in the possibility of conjuring the threat by a rhetoric of salvation as much as by the mobilisation of a particular technology; on the other hand, it justifies the collective and social prevention as it constrains the social body to accept, for itself and for a part of its members, to work on its environment and to work on oneself by anticipation to conjure the threat which precisely emergency should be used to fight.[2] But at the same time, emergency is an exceptional situation, a state of urgency, if one likes, which, by imposing itself as necessary and inevitable, imposes in a similar way the possible transgression of a situation of rights, the likelihood of the public sphere treading on the private or intimate one, the probable superimposition of heteronomy on autonomy, in the name of the superior interest which has founded its existence. These risks are, of course, obvious in natural catastrophes, collective accidents or attacks in public places, but they are all also present in the voluntary rehousing of the homeless. The situation, which has to be controlled to conjure the threat, is in fact tempting, not to say logical, and to do so at all cost, beyond the free will of the persons concerned, or to perpetuate the mechanism, that by its nature was intended to be transitory, against which it is meant to fight.

Thus one understands better why and how, year in, year out, as soon as winter sets in, emergency measures for the homeless appear: the threat of the liquefaction of the social body in face of the sight of the intolerable which it could have produced is always present. Thus, only the doubling of means, only the reorganisational reinforcement of the structure, only the professionalisation of the action could act as a damn, ignoring the fact, however, that the conjuration of the threat only makes sense if by the consubstantial development of an etiological action on what makes it possible. Just as catastrophe can enhance the salvation aspects by the élan of solidarity, which it evokes to ease the effects, the action in reference to social emergency participates in a 'ritual of social restoration' (Beauchard, 1986, p. 7) by reminding one of the fragility of the social bond and the necessary work of constant mobilisation to perpetuate it (Gilbert, 1992, p. 102). And in this context, the call on individual and collective energies to struggle against this figure of the unthinkable which constitutes, for contemporary societies, the homeless, because at once an ethical exigency and a feat of citizenship, it constitutes one of the mainsprings of these restructurisation/revitalisation of the social bond.

Emergency: Working Against Time

> With regard to these categories of activity, characterised by instability, the right *per se* is incontestably more dependable than emergency. It interacts on general conditions, not only on particular situations; paradoxically, it endeavours to be woven into a stable definition, but that only comes with time. It aims to create, in the same way a de-dramatisation, since it enables an identification of the issues involved and tries to situate it beyond particularities (Guihard, 1997, p. 115).

Emergency is at odds with such a logic because it is directly involved in the event and because it is constrained to produce a result. At the opposite poles of the regulations which lay down the directives and determine the normal state of action, i.e. which produce as it were routine by formulating the norm, emergency refers exclusively to the exception. Because the modes of institutionalised or vernacular regulation have become irrelevant as they are judged inefficient for conjuring the threat, because the course of events has been ruptured faced with an accident, emergency, in so much as it is a referential as being, at the same time, a way of action, can only inscribe itself in a short time span, as its essence is drawn from the reign of necessity. Because it is a reflexive activity made mute by the exigency of saving, it privileges the present and cannot allow itself the luxury of being viewed from a distance. The aim, to restore the normal state of affairs in face of a peril judged to be extreme, justifies the imperative of immediate results and imposes 'the direct feasibility of the produced effort' (Bindé, 1997, p. 22).

But paradoxically, emergency, when it imposes itself as a paradigmatic figure of social-political action (as is the case for humanity of the interior for the homeless), because it is condemned to managing the events, is constrained by these and limits considerably its margin of manoeuvre and, more seriously, the efficacy of its own action. Or, if one wishes, its demand for immediate return and tangible results in the short term constructs the conditions of its weak efficacy on the middle- and long-term basis. Moreover, one must consider it as an antinomy since it is a form of devaluing the future (Laïdi, 1998, p. 135). By overloading the present, the short-term, aiming at a definite economic response, it breaks from a perspective of the project, which it in turn deliberately conceives of as a durable response, even if hypothetical.

In this sense, emergency brings about a process of auto-care of the immediate while conserving the situation in its state without allowing oneself the luxury of the bypass of a political project which would loosen the stranglehold of the constraint in order to act structurally.[3] Then can emergency action be considered as a policy if it does not afford us a grasp of the ensemble of the society in which it is deployed? That is to say, if it in no way regulates the status of individuals in a given society. Can it pursue its ultimate objective of the preservation of human integrity without the parallel upholding or developing the political capacity to act socially, without the possibility, in other words, for all the members of any given society, to gain access to a social citizenship? To base the intervention on a topic of emergency refers in this sense to the status of an object of the above mentioned social attention. Should not one fear the development of a process of uncivilisation, in the etymological sense of the term civil, even of a decitizenship, referring to the debate on the citizenship of the homeless.[4]

Medical Emergency: The Symbolic and Organisational Matrix

> The emergency worker is led to consider the organism as an object denuded of any significant dimension in order to be able to restore, after the rescue manoeuvres, the whole dimension of the subject ... But often this dimension disappears on behalf of purely technical actions which consider rescue work and immediate repair as the ultimate goal of the intervention (Emmanuelli and Emmanuelli, 1996, p. 62).

Medical emergency serves as a usual consensus-based reference to social emergency, for legitimised to a large extent as much by its ends as by its proven efficacy, even if it does not raise any questions itself. The sharing of the same philosophy by two universes is translated into names (in France the same term *SAMU social* refers to so much since the abbreviation SAMU means *Service d'Aide Médicale d'Urgence*, Service of Medical Emergency Aid, the strong medical inspiration in the symbolisation of the intervention of social emergency) but also and above all in the processing methods of the emergency call. It is a matter of reacting immediately on the basis of an idea according to which no human being should succumb or be derobed of his human condition on the grounds of negligence or the selfishness of others and /or of the social body. Of course, large differences remain beyond the will to act without a deadline, especially: 1) the fact that social emergency originates, mostly, in a predicament which is characterised by duration and whose emergency character results from a phenomenon of 'simple' degradation or amplification, whereas medical emergency is set off by an accident or a catastrophe; 2) the fact that medical emergency aims at getting sophisticated means to the place of the catastrophe, whereas social emergency aims at supplementing the ordinary existing services in the name of their inefficiency or their weak performance (Sassier, 1997, p. 185);[5] 3) the fact that, in a general way, action in the context of emergency necessarily implies a continuity and, above all, a prolongation, as much as emergency surgery, as uncomfortable as were the conditions of carrying it out, cannot but continue 'naturally' in the post-operatory phase in the ordinary context of hospital, (i.e. medicine which only served emergency would be as inefficient as meaningless), as much as the logic of a continuum of intervention within the framework of social emergency is more than problematic, at least in its practical modalities for the passage from asociability to assistance then to autonomy (Bergier, 1996), if there is a strong incantatory value in the justification of social emergency still remains quite unrealistic.[6]

But, fundamentally, the matrix universe is identical; thus a strong similarity is observable between the mechanisms of medical and social emergency: 1) in setting up a prescribed system which can manage emergency situations; 2) in the systematic establishment of a diagnosis *ante* action based on the breaking down of the situation into an many points which can possibly be acted on; 3) in the clear-cut hierarchisation of the different modalities of action inherent at the different levels of the intervention in order to achieve the goal, by harmonious adjustment.

The rationalisation of the means in view of maximising the intervention *in situ* underlies any organisation of emergency mechanisms. It only makes sense in reference to a strategic approach which privileges analytical reasoning, i.e. the decontextualisation of the patient by cutting him off from his history, his environment, his belongings in order to privilege the biological dimension of survival. This extreme functionality leads thus to consider that 'emergency medicine marks a rupture with the humanist tradition and leans on a very mechanical concept of the body' (Emmanuelli and Emmanuelli, 1996, p. 57), as everything to be seen in the rise of power of the reference to emergency in the field of social intervention which leads to a process of technocratisation of this to the detriment of its clinical dimension, the latter aims not to perceive the Other suffering as an object but to apprehend him as a subject (Renaud, 1997).

Besides, emergency intervention and action which is out of the ordinary are alike in that they confer on the interventionist, medical or social, an unquestionable legitimacy and extreme power. It is this which makes possible and even logical – in the name of efficacy in view of achieving the ultimate goal shared by each one – the transgression of the basic principles on which ordinary social action is based (the professional secret and the intimate conviction of the social worker or the doctor as the foundation of his action).

Emergency: A Model of Professionalism

'Risk management supposes prevision work, planning which is at first sight the very opposite of emergency, the latter being by definition unpredictable and non-planned' (Bouillier and Chevrier, 1995, p. 9). Emergency jobs produce theoreticians and technicians of risk. It is a matter of transmuting the event experienced or the catastrophe into the consequence of a risk which one has already, by anticipation, dealt or simulated. The professional expertise of emergency, for the fireman, for the rescuer at sea or for the doctor sent to catastrophes, lies in an anticipated accumulation of experiences, by enacting a disaster before its very existence so as to be able to deal with it in a routine way when it occurs. It amounts to foreseeing the unpredictable in order – at the moment of the intervention in a context of extreme urgency – to play a laid out game, a simple set of coordinated standardised actions so as not to let oneself be carried away by the disorganising force of hazard, so as not to be reduced to asking oneself what in the emergency is really an emergency, when everything is an emergency. This is explained by the fact that any intervention of the emergency jobs is based on a logic of an instrumental strategy which decomposes the problem, breaks down the acts, codifies the rules and rationalises the articulations between the different phases of action.

But to provide an answer, immediate, guaranteed and adapted, the emergency must first be a reliable and precise diagnosis. Hence the capital importance of the centres of treatment of alert and of remote controlled diagnostic orientation, sorting the calls, regulating the panic and dispatching the most suitable information to the typical actor to reduce at the most the emergency to a normal situation. This phase is essential. It enables, for example, in hospital emergency units the sorting out of the 'real' emergencies, those of a lethal nature, from the 'felt' emergencies which depend at least as much on the objective state of the suffering as the perception of the danger by the suffering person himself or by his environment.

The professionalism of these emergency jobs is thus based on a triptype: time, decision, automated treatment. It is the function of these three variables and can be resumed as $U = f (T, D, Ta)$ (Mouton, 1986, p. 26).

1   Time is crucial for, faced with a catastrophe catalogued as irreversible, i.e. it is impossible to avoid or to make do with ordinary measures, one must gather speed to cancel or to reduce the harmful effects as much as possible. The reference to time is in this sense twofold: it is a matter, on the one hand, of the time it takes to act as much as possible in a short time, that is

in real time, on the other hand, to anticipate in order to foresee as much the outcome of the catastrophes forecasted as well as to preconstruct responses to them.

2   Emergency imposes a state of affairs and annuls even the idea of a decider. The situation itself dictates the line of behaviour. 'Emergency imposes the constraint that there is no time possible for reflection and for the constitution of a decider' (Mouton, 1986, p. 27). This configuration is stamped by the tactic which compels field action, without reflecting as it were, in order to get out of the situation as well as possible in virtue of the ultimate objective of the preservation of the integrity of the human being (or human beings) at peril in the situation. It can only be counteracted by the reinscription of this 'crisis without enemy' (Gilbert, 1992, p. 167) in the strategic logic isolating one Other subject from wanting or being able to against whom it is possible to act.[7] The heart of professionalism of emergency lies in this transmutation which, by integrating the innateness of the catastrophe and thus the fact that its existence should be defined by the situation, can reinscribe the management of this crisis in the normal order of things, i.e. in the chain of technical coordinated and finalised acts, thanks to the predictability and to the anticipation which have allowed the application of an instrumental rationality. Otherwise, if faced with this threatening and catastrophic situation, there has not been this preceding work which leads to accomplishing technical acts in a reflexive way, meaningful and finalised at a preceding point of time, there is only room for good will, that is, only the closest person can act and who will do it with all his heart and all his energy but as an amateur.

3   But to combine speed of action and efficacy of means in order to reach optimal results, emergency imposes a reflexive action but conceived and experimented a priori. The pre-organisation is essential for the automatic handling of a catastrophic situation which calls for emergency intervention. The automation of carrying it out reflects the necessary struggle against all improvisation. If every act has not been thought right through, nor wanted, when it comes to an emergency intervention, it is indeed because well before the appearance of risk, it occurred before and has been adjusted to others in an operational mechanism (a fortiori in the case of an intervention supposing an action of several differentiated actors: police, fire brigade, doctors ...).

Such a model of professionalism raises the question of social emergency. The latter refers to this both to establish his competence to act in substitution of the ordinary organisms and services and not to be put off, particularly because of its strong benevolent component to work for amateurs justified simply by the presence, by the capacity to be there when faced with a menacing situation. However, at the same time, it cannot but distance itself, for this model of military-scientific-technocratic as the emotions, which form the humanitarian substratum of social emergency, are poles apart from the logical resources and practices of which is disposes to establish its action.

The Issues at Stake in Social Emergency

Taking first and foremost into consideration the suffering experienced by the human being, i.e. privileging his biological animal dimension over the political animal subject to rights and duties, emergency constrains action with reference to watching the unbearable and to bearing the intolerable. Everyone can act, but at the same time this action is reserved for those who possess the essential virtue which is 'the intelligence of the poor' (Faure, 1991) which, by intropathy, enables one to enter the point of view of the poor and to share their suffering. For it is this empathetic proximity to the suffering being, this extreme attention, which founds the irrepressible need to act and which also legitimises the competency to do so.[8] Thus are situated the direct and indirect issues of the professionalism of social emergency, beyond which the forms of voluntary action constitute the architecture, and of the legitimacy of this type of intervention in relation to other modes of professional social action. It is in this sense that social emergency, not only modifies the context in which it is born, but besides imposes a profound mutation of the meaning accorded to social intervention by devising new instruments and modes of action.

The Relativity of Social Emergency

> It appears clear that it is the notion of danger which is going to determine on the one hand the action directed at the family and on the other hand the emergency to protect the child: it is thus necessary for the professional to evaluate the danger and this can only be done in a minimum of time (Gabel, 1997, p. 53).

Contrary to civil or medical emergency, social emergency appears as a confused notion especially in relation to the very idea of threat or at least to evidence thereof. While emergency, in a general way, as shown above, supposes a rapid interpretation of undeniable risks, the appreciation of the threat is uncertain in the case of social emergency. Nevertheless, it is subject to variation according to the values, the commitment, the proximity and the sensitivity of the individuals faced with the event. In other words, 'Going upstream, the interpretation of the danger is complex' (Beauchard, 1990, p. 64), it is even itself a social issue of definition. While the paradigm of emergency is based on a simplified reality, so simplified that the situation imposes itself as catastrophic and bears irreversible consequences if nothing is undertaken, the social emergency is, in its basis, to be treated with caution, i.e. the very nature of the emergency, by reason of the complexity which has to be made statutory. In fact, the unacceptable character of social emergency is above all a question of perception: it is at least just as relative to the situation which the victim is familiar with as the emotion felt by the witness. The tolerance threshold of third party persons (professionals, politicians, media, public opinion ...) is a key element of the appreciation of the gravity of the situation. Emergency is thus to a certain extent imagined, for want of being imaginary, for it is a matter of ideology or of sensibility.

> The evident reality of emergency does not concern only the bodies. There is no social emergency: at the most an emergency 'resembling that of a social one' which is concentrated in the scandalous risks of murder, of fire, of suicide, of famine (Mouton, 1986, p. 29).

Thus, that which seemed evident, that which followed naturally, i.e. the necessity to act immediately, disintegrates: and within that which founds the necessity to act and within that which justifies the immediacy of action, immediacy meant at one and the same time the absence of a deadline and the absence of mediation. The technical decision of how to act best in the face of emergency in general, is now substituted first and foremost by social emergency by the political decision of why to act. The decision is an issue, a collective issue, the object of opposition and of conflict about values and norms of action as particular or collective interests.

> If urgency aggregates a consensus as soon as the physical integrity or the life of a person is endangered, the evaluation and the management of social emergency imply taking the parameters into account which are infinitely more complex (Bouquet, 1987, p. 77).

And paradoxically, in order to avoid acting on sentiment, a documented evaluation is very often necessary despite the apparent critical nature of the situation; sometimes it is necessary 'to take time for emergency' (Gabel, 1997, 59).

For how is one to recognise the urgent demand of the 'real emergency'? Does it require, in response to a given situation, a rapid intervention or an emergency intervention? This is not playing with words. Wherein lies the essential character of real danger which justifies the second? After all, faced with a situation which has lasted for a long time, even too long, a rapid response, one which simply speeds up the administrative action, is perhaps all that is necessary. And, if this is so, the register of emergencies is but one symbolic arm used in the rhetoric of the interventionist to get a case settled, to get the beginning of the treatment under way or even to allow an out of the ordinary case i.e. one beyond the framework of the regulations for taking charge, to be taken into consideration. The social categorical imperative which represents emergency is stamped as it were when this is qualified as social in order to leave room for an army of experts that decide on the nature of the emergency at the risk of non-action (the time to assemble the preceding documentation into a consensus file takes the place of the immediacy of the response to the threat), or the normative imposition as a result of approval: an actor occupies from then on a hegemonic position, quite often that of the 'intelligence of the poor' in defining the socially and ethically alarming character of the situation as irremediable, and thus it is qualified as an emergency.

Social Emergency and Recomposition of Social Action

The emergency of a situation leads to the process of the depoliticisation of the social on several levels: recomposition of the norms of intervention, imprisonment in the inevitable response to emergency, revaluation of what is 'concrete' instead of a social policy (Cochart, 1986, p. 13).

The recurring referent to emergency actually informs profoundly contemporary social action. Thus the issues of professionalism pitting social workers against benevolent, 'old' and 'new' professionals in the social sphere, social policy and humanitarian action, social emergency has undeniably been drawing up new forms of action. The first among these is characterised by a strong inclination to individualising poverty and to depoliticising action. Individualisation because poverty is incarnated in the suffering bodies; it becomes visible through the extreme demonstrations of social deterioration. To fight against it is to somewhat relieve the ordeal, put an end to this individual expression of what is unacceptable in the social sphere. 'The emergency services manage what is unbearable to see, get rid of the idea that our society can kill instead of embarking on the wish to repair' (Sassier, 1997, p. 190). Depoliticisation because the exposition of individual cases contributes to covering up the social reality of poverty by decontextualising it, by reducing it to the immediate apprehension of the spectator who cannot but react while, at the same time, calling the public powers, that are supposed to be there precisely to avoid this, to account for themselves, and so the failings of the social protection system are shown up. In this sense this depoliticisation is only a facade for it contributes considerably to accelerating the process of questioning the welfare state by calling on exceptional means, those claimed in the name of emergency, in so far as the ordinary modalitites seem inefficient to contain the wave of exclusion threatening the social body. Moreover, this depoliticisation/repoliticisation is also a form of deproblematisation, in spite of the complexity of the definition of the character of emergency, the tendency is strong to reify what is visible and to fossilise the circumstances in their catastrophic aspect in order to impose the necessity to act. In doing so, by precipitating 'the moment of qualification' of the emergency, a precocious model is induced and above all not discussed of the situation and of the means to set in motion to reabsorb it. 'In other words, the more the emergency is dealt with in the immediacy of the factual situation, the greater the risk of becoming a kind of management 'in real time'. By dismissing the likelihood of a response in a differentiated time frame which would allow the conciliation of 'reception without conditions' with an 'intersubjective analysis of the situation, social emergency remains in the order of the accidental and of threat' (Jeudy, 1986, p. 109).

The second norm of intervention which contributes to the imposition of social emergency is without a doubt 'reception conditions', the unconditional right to assistance. But this itself entraps the beneficiary in the need, in the setting up and the ritualisation of a real need, to be able to be the receiver of social emergency help. For the only vector which guarantees this unconditional right is the receptiveness and the sensitivity of the social body. What is essentially extraordinary becomes, as it were, a commonplace in order to uphold the perpetuation of aid. The granting of emergency aid merely by an effect of symbolic reversal – that is to say, to persons who outwardly look the part – thus becomes one of the conditions of this 'reception without conditions', as not only do the subjectivity and ambiguity of the determination of needs play a role, but also the scarcity of resources means that these are concentrated on manifest expressions of the most immediate and the most extreme of these needs. *In fine*, interrogated are the very foundations of social policies which postulate the necessary equity in the dealing with people faced with a problem if the mechanisms of the auto-declaration of need, the dramatisation of the situation and the unequal implantation of emergency social services in the territory come to be a principle of the distribution or not of those services (Lipsky and Smith, 1989).

Social Emergency and Homelessness

Firstly, one is tempted to consider that the strong reality of homelessness gives strength to social emergency, it founds it on emotion for want of a rational basis. Thus, it seems appropriate to interrogate this evidence and to put it the other way around by asking in what way emergency, as a new referential value, contributes to making homelessness real.

Such a question does not refer to the factors that create homelessness (the case in point is representations not causes). The question could be reformulated like this: Which values have made homelessness so present and so important in the current social debate? Which basic values have appeared and have produced this unbearable situation which makes us fight against homelessness or, more precisely, which makes us speak about it and try to do something?

As Merton (Merton and Nisbet, 1976) said about social problems, the central interrogation is the gap between what ought to be and what actually is, this moral gap, which represents an evident social reality, namely, that of homelessness. From this point of view, the problem is not to establish that so many people are in a homeless situation but to understand why homelessness is now so real in our minds and in our priorities.

What makes homelessness possible is not the result of a change of a central value (the decrease of solidarity or the emergence of an amoral and individualistic society), rather it results from a conjunction of changing norms, that is, of a network of new basic values. The most important trends that make homelessness so intolerable and so real can be characterised by two points.

Firstly, the paradigm of emergency has taken the place of the paradigm of progress. Emergency nowadays takes up more and more place in our basic values and also in the basic principles of our policies. It is not only a category of action (something must be done; it is impossible not to intervene) but it is mainly a category of representation of our societies, of their problems, of their future, or, more precisely, of their absence of future. But if there is no future, everything is at stake here and now, *hic et nunc*. It is not only the tyranny of constraint, but rather too great an emphasis on the present. This is the reason why, for example, giving shelter to a homeless person one night, and not another night, is absolutely necessary and even a good thing, but almost enough. To choose the present, in that sense, is to act against the future.

The increase of emergency also means that ordinary processes and ordinary policies are insufficient and no longer credible because they are based on long-term action. Something must be done right away; but then the immediate action often becomes *instead of* the long-term action. It must be admitted that the most important capacity of emergency is to wipe out all representation of time, except that of the very moment, that is, the here and now. And, if one used to say that progress has no end in itself, the same can be said of emergency. Emergency provokes emergency again and again, just as progress provokes progress again and again. Maybe the difference is that progress was the son of the Enlightenment and emergency is the daughter of emotion.

Secondly, the paradigm of lay compassion and civil *agape* (originally a kind of Christian love for everybody because everybody is a human being) instead of the paradigm of public solidarity. We can, in fact, see a new wave of basic values meaning the end of entire welfare. As Polanyi (1983) said about the liberalism that failed in the nineteenth century, to live alone, to live only on one's own principles, and brought about the need to introduce social principles that progressively led to the welfare state. At present two trends must be admitted:

1 a clear-cut and all-embracing welfare state seems impossible; besides, few would really want that. So what is being witnessed is more and more the development of a part of social action, and also of social policy, based on voluntary action and personal commitment to a sense of civic duty. The warmth of compassion complements the chilliness of public solidarity;

2 just as pure liberalism failed during the nineteenth century to live on itself, i.e. to live solely on the basis of its own principles, and had to resort to the progressive introduction of social principles which led to the welfare state (Polanyi, 1983), there appears at present a syncretic overlapping of different registers of action of men in society. The third industrial revolution, an apparent success of the liberal spirit that symbolises deregulation of the global economy consecrating again the failure of liberalism to lean on its own principles finds it necessary to promote/support some new values to counterbalance the social effect of the globalisation of the economy. And so one can observe the necessary humanisation of the new global order to

make it more tolerable and to enable it to last, but this time on a dimension no longer mainly on the basis of social principles like social solidarity, assurance reciprocity and redistribution which make up the social debt, but rather on compassion and pity. Not in a new kind of 'peace and love' but more in sort of 'profit and *agape*'. In this respect, Princess Diana was *post mortem* a figure of this kind of humanitarian love, although her action represented the lowest degree of social action.

In fact, this is not a good example because this kind of humanitarian love must be considered as a civic love. Pity felt for some people, e.g. homeless people, because they are considered to be like everyone else, but, of course, one realises at the same time that they have not had the opportunity to be really like the rest – never or perhaps for a long time. They belong to the human condition but they cannot exercise this human citizenship. This is the reason why one feels the urge to help them. It is not an individual responsibility, rather it is a collective duty. And homeless people symbolise at best this incapacity to be citizens, as they might otherwise be, and at the same time the necessity to act in order to restore this basic human right.

Active involvement in voluntary organisations comes about not only because public action and welfare policies have failed, but also because the general representation of suffering has also changed. Now society seems divided into two camps, the winners and the losers, or more precisely, those who are lucky and those who are unlucky. And who in our society suffers more than homeless people? Who is unluckier ? Who is so close to the rest of society and yet so far removed? The best neighbour for *agape* that we can find. So real and so little danger for the social order.

Unfortunate people are subjects who suffer but also subjects who can, and who sometimes want to act. This is the reason why misfortune (being unlucky in this sense) is so unbearable and why there is commitment to voluntary actions by personal exposition, by a gift of oneself.

> The will to act quickly also finds strength in the choice of committing oneself to fight the misery commensurate with one's means and capacities, for what is unbearable for the other becomes unbearable for oneself (Sassier, 1997, p. 183).[9]

It is not a question of wanting to re-educate or to normalise marginal people by assistance and educational programmes as formerly; rather a matter of making such unfortunate people responsible for themselves and helping them to find once again their place in society, to become again a citizen and a member of the human condition. And one wants to do this by an act of *agape*, by personal exposition, and by doing so, to show them that they can do the same: be the actor of their life.[10]

In fact, the underlying model of integration is not assimilation, the incorporation of external values, but access to the collectivity by being in control of one's life. Being a citizen is, after all, in that sense, a matter of working out and on one's personal identity. And as everybody knows, identity is frail. This is the reason why one wants to help people to rebuild their broken identity and retrieve their human condition. And by doing so, one reassures oneself of one's own identity and reinforces one's own human condition. Nothing is free of charge. Remember Diana: to fight against bulimia, anorexia, devalued self-identity, marital troubles, nothing was better than to kiss a poor young African refugee or shake hand with a person suffering of AIDS.

That paradigm leads to the emergence of a strange kind of policy, a mix based on a gap between, on the one hand, a biological animal in need of humanitarian and voluntary action, and, on the other hand, a political animal in need of social policies and public solidarity (though with a little help from oneself). In other words, one saves them and helps them to survive thus giving them the opportunity to be citizens through their own use of citizenship.

The emergence of exclusion has modified the general representation of poverty. Previously, poverty was seen as an accumulation of disadvantages, a social relation which rendered a category of people unable to obtain certain goods because, by definition, profit demands domination and exploitation. Now exclusion is an accumulation of lacks, it is the fruit of misfortune that makes some people fall down the social ladder to the point of exclusion because they are not useful in terms of profit and are, therefore, not useful for anything. Exclusion is a way of explaining and reformulating the survival of poverty in developed societies that have created welfare. But how is it possible to maintain a symbolic difference between the poor and the poorest if too many people are out of the game, but in the game, or, if one wishes, are out of the economic game even if they are still, that is a basic principle of the social order, members of the collectivity? In other words, what is on the verge of exclusion but different from exclusion? Homelessness. Homeless people are out of the economic and social game but also out of the civil game. That is their problem and our problem. But by being so, they represent the ideal *pharmakos*, the perfect scapegoat: they can show that excluded people are in fact members of ordinary society even if they are not true members. The poorest of the poor, homeless people show through their very existence to excluded people that exclusion is a different but a quite normal way of being a member of society.

When a person has no job but a flat, when one has no money, only social benefits but a family, when one cannot afford holidays but has friends and neighbours, when one watches homeless people sleeping rough in the street, one thanks God or Fortune, as one likes; one can also thank the existence of homeless people for revealing conditions worse than one's own. In short, they have the effect of making one's own situation more acceptable and perhaps more comfortable.

In fact, there is a common phenomenon underlying these two changes in basic values. This is the naturalisation of social problems. As has been pointed out, a rising value is the description of social oppositions in terms of unhappiness and happiness and the explanation of them in terms of unfortunate people and fortunate people. There are a lot of victims but no guilty party. Those victims are, of course, created by certain economic, political and social factors, but concretely, they exist by chance. They are unemployed, excluded, homeless by chance, because they were at a particular place at a particular time – in the wrong place at the wrong time – in short, because they were unlucky. Take, for example, the recent debate about the Renault enterprise. The decision to close a factory in Belgium was a financial and economic strategy to maximise the strength of this enterprise on the car sales market. But concretely for the workers, if they work in Vilvorde factory, it means bad luck for them, they will lose their job and maybe more; if they work in Flins, for example, another Renault factory in France, they have some hope of maintaining their working activity and their place in society for the next few years. Why? It is the same job, they have the same qualifications, the same way of life. Even though the difference and the inequality are produced by an industrial strategy, these factors seem to be only the fruit of fate for most people.

Perhaps this is the most important change in the representation of social order: social differences and social inequalities are considered more and more as the result of misfortune. If one is still in a modern society explained without the help of God, if one continues to maintain that men and women always draw and produce society, it must be admitted that fate has made a comeback. A growing number of social factors are nowadays explained, in the scientific community also, by, for example, the notion of events 'crashing' at a certain point or by one key moment, by chance or misfortune.[11] But what can one do against the strength of fate? Nothing, except do the maximum oneself to give no chance to fate and help those who have been struck by bad luck. And the unluckiest are the homeless. In fact, homelessness is possible and so present in people's minds and preoccupations because it symbolises the potent weight of fate. And at the moment this weight of fate seems the only explanation, or the more admissible socially, for the gap between what ought to be and what actually is.

To conclude, we must admit that our initial question – what does the notion of social emergency really mean? – is still present. Is social emergency a theoretically grounded principle? As has been pointed out, it is not even a descriptive category, but simply a category for action. The problem is that it is also a category for representing situations. Therefore, if emergency is not a given fact but a social construction, how is a situation to be defined as an emergency and why is there emergency? It is easy to understand why there is emergency in certain situations: fire, sea rescue operations, natural disasters, attacks etc. Thus it is clear what professional action must entail (firemen, sea-rescuers, emergency medical services ...) and why it must be professional. Emergency is understood because it is recognisable: strictly speaking, it involves saving life. This is an absolute emergency while social emergency is relative. Where precisely is emergency in what is called social emergency? Although it remains difficult to pinpoint, emergency is considered to exist for normative reasons, in so far as the expression commonly used 'that is intolerable, unacceptable' or the like. This assumption informs our action and has several consequences

First consequence: emergency is an unthinkable element that obstructs thinking otherwise about the situation. Immediate action come first. Emergency action is an imperative, it is a necessity in itself. This is precisely why a critique of emergency is so difficult. Emergency invites action without imposing any conditions, thus skipping the stage of analysis. Emergency action is thus revealed as management in real time of the situation and refuses to put off a solution to a later moment.

Second consequence: what is emergency action? Is it an action against the clock, as rescuers who must gain whatever time they can by rationalising their activity in an endeavour to save life? For example, how does it solve the mediation between rescue and solidarity?

Third consequence: emergency is a non-political way of perceiving a situation, not in terms of political issues. The more response there is to social emergency, the less chance there is of changing the situation. This is why emergency breeds emergency. In this sense, emergency action is the very opposite of the idea of social change because immediate action leaves no room for the mediation of a project.

Therefore, from the theoretical point of view, emergency must be considered as an epistemological obstacle because one cannot but perceive and admit the extreme dimensions of the given situations. Thus faced with social emergency, perhaps the following position should be adopted: resist emergency by never considering emergency in terms of emergency. Or, to be more provocative: beware of emergency, do nothing because, as Talleyrand said, 'When it is urgent, it is already too late'.

That is so in theory. Alas, practically and ethically it is impossible to follow such a maxim. And that is the crux of the problem.

Notes

1   Emmanuelli Xavier (1998), 52nd congress of the National Association of Social Service.
2   Emergency is in this sense close to precariousness which very strongly symbolised the image of the new poverty. 'If there is a resurgence of the debate, an amplification of the issues at stake and a change of the connotations concerning the "new poverty", it is probably especially because nowadays the middle classes feel the threat (and it suffices to be perceived as such). The anticipation, the fear of an economic setback of an uncontrollable nature in a precarious situation justify foresight and saving just as much as a certain form of solidarity on a daily basis' (Martin and Soulet, 1983, p. 93).
3   Wherever, in the name of a logic of compassion and emergency, one uses a reasoning based on moral or social evidence in humanitarian interference, is a differentiated understanding of the basic problems not be feared? This is what Zaki Laïdi stresses when he calls for an intellectual feat to 'fight emergency not so much as a category of action, but as a central category in the representation of our societies, of their problems and their future' (Laïdi, 1995).
4   'Torn from himself, the humanitarian "game" is, by the way, more often shown as lying, lifeless, submissive. There is neither language nor face. He is a mere pretext for affliction, distress, pitiable and even infra-human. He is the object of pity and not the subject of rights' (Guillebaud, 1994, p. 84) Cf. likewise Robert Redeker's humanitarian critique of the interior. 'Humanitarian aid has nothing to do with ethics: it sees man as a biological animal whose existence one must preserve; the humanitarian duties have nothing to do with ethical duties: it is simply a matter of duties faced with man as a living being; in fact humanitarian aid is profoundly nihilistic in so far as it entails the negation of man as anything else but a mortal animal' (Redeker, 1994, p. 34).
5   Zaki Laïdi develops an analogical idea when he remarks that, in a general way, emergency occurs when other modalities of action are no longer or not to be envisaged. It does not ask if one cannot 'see in the rise of the power of emergency an expression of the will to have recourse to exceptional mechanisms of action in face of the deadlock of the ordinary procedures and institutions. Therefore, the generalisation of the logic of emergency would reveal the inadequacy of the structures and of the institutions in relation to the social expectations and demands' (Laïdi, 1998, p. 41).
6   The ways of social re-insertion remain in this sense more mysterious than those of curing, at least in that the element of uncertainty is more pronounced.
7   To take up the famous distinction between tactic and strategy made by Michel de Certeau (de Certeau and Giard, 1980)

8 'Everything seems to work as if those who have approached misery or suffering could become retainers, even owners of a particular form of knowledge that is difficult to share, which would confer on them a secret power when it comes to "what must be done in a particular case", a right of ownership, or, at least, a right of recognition' (Sassier, 1997, p. 183).

9 One must consider the all-importance of the effect of public commitment for the personal and social identity of those who undertake it. Commitment is simultaneously work on oneself and a test of one's affiliation.

10 A new analytical couple thus appears substituting that of individual/society, henceforth classical even obsolete, that of 'personalisation/publicisation' (Ion and Peroni, 1997, p. 9).

11 Pierre Bourdieu (1991, p. 9) in his survey on social misery attributed this idea of *fatum* as one of the current interpretations of social situations. ' I received every word, every sentence, and above all the tone of the voice, the facial expressions or body language, as evidence of this sort of collective bad luck which strikes, like fatality, all who are gathered in places of *social relegation,* where the miseries of each are doubled by all the miseries that are born of the coexistence and of the cohabitation of all who are miserable.'

Bibliography

Beauchard, J. (1986), 'L'urgence et l'insupportable', *Actions et Recherches Sociales*, 'L'urgence sociale', 3.

Beauchard, J. (1990), 'L'urgence sociale', *Etudes psychothérapiques*, 'Urgence', 2.

Belorgey, J.-M. (1987), 'Urgence sociale ?', *Actions et Recherches Sociales*, 'L'urgence', 2.

Bergier, B. (1996), *Les Affranchis. Parcours de réinsertion*, Paris, Desclée de Brouwer.

Bindé, J. (1997), 'L'éthique du futur. Pourquoi faut-il retrouver le temps perdu', *Futuribles*, 226.

Boullier, D. and Chevrier, S. (1995), 'Grammaire de l'urgence: les sapeurs pompiers, experts du risque', *Les Cahiers de la Sécurité Intérieure*, 'Les métiers de l'urgence', 22.

Bouquet, B. (1987), 'L'urgence incontournable', *Actions et Recherches Sociales*, 'L'urgence', 2.

Bourdieu, P. (1991), 'L'ordre des choses', *Actes de la recherche en sciences sociales*, 90.

Cochart, D. (1986), 'Fin d'une politique sociale? Individualisation de la pauvreté', *Actions et Recherches Sociales*, 'L'urgence sociale', 3.

de Certeau, M. and Giard, L. (1980), *L'invention du quotidien*, Paris, UGE.

Emmanuelli, X. and Emanuelli, J. (1996), *Au secours la vie, la médecine d'urgence*, Paris, Gallimard.

Faure, A.(1991), 'L'intelligence des pauvres' in Collectif, *Démocratie et pauvreté*, Paris, Albin Michel.

Gabel, M. (1997), 'Maltraitance : vraie ou fausse urgence', *Le groupe familial*, 'Quelle urgence pour l'urgence', 154.

Gilbert, C. (992), *Le Pouvoir en situation extrême. Catastrophes et politique*, Paris, L'Harmattan.

Ginisty, B. (1987), 'Face à l'urgence, une philosophie de l'action, *Actions et Recherches Sociales*, 'L'urgence', 2.

Guihard, J.-L. (1987), 'Urgence, droit et politique', *Actions et Recherches Sociales*, 'L'urgence', 2.

Guillebaud, J.-C. (1994), *La Trahison des Lumières*, Paris, Le Seuil.

Ion, J. and Peroni, M. (eds) (1997), *Engagement public et exposition de la personne*, La Tour d'Aigues, éditions de l'Aube.

Jeudy, H.-P. (1986), 'L'état d'alerte et le silence des mots', *Actions et Recherches Sociales*, 'L'urgence sociale', 3.

Laïdi, Z. (1995), 'Les problèmes de fond s'enlisent dans l'urgence', *Libération*, March.

Laïdi, Z. (1998), 'L'urgence ou la dévalorisation culturelle de l'avenir' in Soulet, M.-H. (ed.), *Urgence, souffrance, misère: lutte humanitaire ou politique sociale*, Fribourg, Editions Universitaires.

Lipsky, M. and Smith, S.R. (1989), 'When Social Problems Are Treated as Emergencies', *Social Service Review*, 63, 1.

Martin, C. and Soulet, M.-H. (1983), 'Quelle nouvelle pauvreté?', *Actions et Recherches Sociales*, 'auvreté et action sociale', 4.

Merton, R. and Nisbet, R. (eds) (1976), *Contemporary Social Problems*, New York, Harcourt Brace Jovanovich.

Mouton, R. (1986), 'Urgences: conflictualité interorganisationnelle et paradoxes de la prévention spécialisée', *Actions et Recherches Sociales*, 'L'urgence sociale', 3.

Mouton, R. (1987), 'Sur l'urgence dépassée', *Actions et Recherches Sociales*, 'L'urgence', 2.

Polanyi, K. (1983), *La Grande transformation. Aux origines politiques et économiques de notre temps*, Paris, Gallimard.

Redeker, R. (1994), 'Qu'est-ce que l'humanitaire de l'intérieur?', *Les Temps modernes*, 579.

Renaud, G. (1997), 'L'intervention: de la technique à la clinique ou de l'objet au sujet' in Nélisse, C. and Zuniga, R. (eds), *L'intervention: les savoirs en action*, Sherbrooke, GGC Editions.

Sassier, M. (1997), 'Action sociale et action humanitaire: les avatars d'une liaison dangereuse' in de Ridder, G. (ed.), *Les nouvelles frontières de l'intervention sociale*, Paris, L'Harmattan.

Stiegler, B. (1987), 'Urgence technologique, technologique du temps', *Actions et Recherches Sociales*, 'L'urgence', 2.

20 The Heterogeneity of Homelessness and the Consequences for Service Provision

INGER KOCH-NIELSEN AND TOBIAS BØRNER STAX

Introduction

The general aim of this chapter is to describe the need for urgent accommodations for the homeless. But, in order to do so it is necessary, first, to deal with the heterogeneity of homelessness and the related concept of social exclusion; it is necessary briefly to discuss and clarify the concepts and to dwell shortly on the question of accommodation. In a Danish context the question of accommodation is closely linked to preventive and reintegrative measures. In this chapter some examples of recent measures – general as well as more targeted – will be given. We will present some difficulties connected with evaluating the outcome of measures and experiments in this field, especially at a European level. The chapter is first and foremost based on ongoing evaluations of accommodation, and on reports of a qualitative kind about different types of the homeless population.

The Heterogeneity – and Stability – of Homelessness

Though it is not the actual aim of this chapter to discuss the concept of homelessness and social exclusion it seems impossible to avoid the subject, as the differentiated need for service provisions is a consequence of the composition of the homeless population.

Somehow homelessness is a sub-category of social exclusion, though the definitions are not very clear. In a Danish context the socially excluded are very broadly defined as persons who are not able to support themselves or to care for themselves (or their families) in a manner acceptable to society or acceptable to the person her/himself. Implicit in the term exclusion is also an unmet need for integration (Fridberg, 1992).

A broader description – but aiming at the same group – is given by Brandt, who takes a historical and critical view on the excluded population and the response hereto by society.

> At least through the last 400 years we have been discussing and reflecting over the socially excluded, launching measures with the aim of getting rid of exclusion. The measures have consisted in upbringing, vocational training, in punishment or placement and isolation in institutions. Basically the methods have been the same apart from the tendency of each period in history to give priority to one of the 4–5 methods mentioned. Somehow it seems as if there has been a constant kind of fight going on between the excluded and the represent-atives of society – a fight (so it seems) about who is best at cheating the other. At the same time it has been the general belief that the constantly improving welfare policy would prevent the upcoming of new generations of excluded.
>
> So – in spite of changes in the economy, in the social legislation, in the dominant attitudes and ideas – we have had and still have human beings on the margins of society – either human beings who – according to our own temperament and to the distance we have to those people – are considered to live an unattractive life, a hard life, or to be a physical threat to us or our private property. They have been considered as frightening and threatening, they are different in their relations to rules and regulations. And they are not humble in so far as they try to live a quiet, industrious, working and targeted life … The excluded today are people not socialised to solve the tasks in society in the usual way. They are not a random sample of the Danish population, but persons who have not in their early years been taught the difficult art of socialisation (Brandt, 1995, our translation).

We take this statement as a starting point for our chapter, as it reflects that most homeless are not homeless only because of the Danish housing situation. The statement does not imply that poverty, homelessness and social exclusion as such are caused by personal factors. The statement does indicate, however, that there will always be a group of homeless, though their background and composition may well change, and that this change ought to be reflected in the provisions for the different groups. If one agrees with Brandt – as we do – an analysis of the homeless along the lines of a typology similar to the one presented below is needed. But first we need a brief clarification of who we are talking about. Again, we can return to Brandt. He has proposed this definition of a homeless person:

a person is homeless if she/he does not have a home that can be regarded as stable or permanent and meets one's demands to a reasonable standard of a dwelling. He/she is furthermore incapable of using the different relations and institutions offered by society – e.g. family, network, and private and public institutions of every kind.[1] The reason for this can be some open or hidden conditions inherent in the person her/himself or in the societal organisation (Brandt, 1992, our translation).

We have now outlined two central concepts for an understanding and evaluation of homelessness in the Danish society: the concept of homelessness itself and the concept of social exclusion. But how can we relate these two concepts to each other? Is homelessness a sub-category of social exclusion, or are the two concepts to be separated if our understanding is to enable a more efficient policy formulation?

Homelessness in Numbers

A little numerical information might enlighten us in this regard - as well as contextualise the rest of this paper.

Lets first look briefly at a one-day census among users of different kinds of help-programmes in Copenhagen, including the 105-institutions, drop-ins and other public and private programmes.[2] The study attempts, for one thing, to establish whether or not there is a degree of correlation between the socially excluded and the homeless. Through questionnaires answered by the staff at 143 programmes and the 4,341 users these programmes could include[3] the study analyses to what degree homelessness, dwellinglessness, mental illness, drug abuse, etc. are reasons for using institutions provided for socially excluded (Eskelinen et.al., 1994). The result of the study is reproduced in Table 20.1.

Of special interest to this chapter is that 22 per cent of the users included in the survey stated that homelessness was one of the two major reasons for their current situation. Nine per cent felt that dwellinglessness was one of these two most important reasons. One sees in the table that there is a myriad of reasons for the current situation. This indicates that an important aspect in an evaluation of which services appeal to and are of use for which groups is to be aware of the differences within the group using institutions and services for homeless, and then try to connect the different measures with these types of homeless. That is the topic of sections 3 and 4 of this chapter.

A second study which can provide a briefing on the quantity of the different types of homeless and other socially excluded is a recent paper which outlines

Table 20.1   Indicated causes and main cause for the use of institution or help programme for socially excluded or threatened in Copenhagen metropolitan area

Problems	Causes (n=2,592)*		Main Cause (n=1,749)**	
	No.	%	No.	%
Homelessness	576	22	73	8
Dwellinglessness	224	9	21	2
Need of assistance	55	2	37	4
Domestic problems	199	8	32	3
Substance abuse	896	35	251	27
Physical health problems	105	4	24	3
Mental problems	502	19	297	32
Need of psychological/ social support	1,055	41	72	8
Loneliness	307	12	118	13
Other	608	23	–	–
In total	–	–	**925**	**100**

*   Two causes could be given.
**   Only one cause could be given.

Source: Eskelinen et al., 1994, pp. 49 and 51.

potentially fruitful studies for furthering the understanding of homelessness (Børner, 1996). The paper includes an overview of the different estimates which exist today in regard to homelessness. In Table A in the Appendix we have provided a translation of this overview

What is not shown in that table – or elsewhere for that matter – is dynamics within or between the different groups of homeless. To obtain a dynamic picture is pretty difficult in Denmark. We do not possess any information which can serve for that purpose in regard to homelessness – yet – but it is part of a research project which we are currently trying set up.

The composition of homelessness is most frequently – for practical reasons – described on the basis of the users of the 105-institutions.[4] In recent years the following changes have been reported – some of which might well reflect changes also in administrative definitions as well as changes in the actual composition of the homeless population. The reported changes should be read carefully – they are tentative not yet verified findings which we in the future will attempt to evaluate. However, what is often presented as the current development is:

- a decreasing average age;
- an increasing ratio of women;
- an increase in the ratio of drug abusers;
- an increasing ratio of psychiatric patients;
- an increase in heavy multi-problem clients.

The latest reports from Copenhagen – still at an impressionistic level – tell about an overall *de*crease in users of 105-institutions, a *de*crease in the psychiatric clients, but an *in*crease in heavy drug abusers, and in immigrants and refugees. We still need to have this confirmed at a more general level. From the provincial towns, on the other hand, we receive reports of an *in*crease in those who need a cheap abode – indicating an increase in what we might call dwellingless – and indicating the possibility of a new important tendency in Denmark. The changes may however be due to changes in praxis of registration and counting as well as changes in legislation just as well as they might reflect changes and tendencies among the composition of the homeless.

Different Types of Homeless

Speaking of homelessness one is often prone to focus on the lack of an *abode*. As we shall show later, the problem is more frequently that of a lack of a *home* as a base for establishing a social network.

In order to get closer to the very differentiated needs for services for this (those) group(s) that might be called homeless or socially excluded/exposed we shall try to set up a typology. This typology is constructed along the dimension of *relational ties* and *micro breakups* (Guidicini et al., 1996): from a point where only a few relational ties have been broken and to the extreme end where no ties at all exist. The relational ties taken into consideration are those of family and network, of the labour market, of the social services especially those directed towards the homeless and of the ties to society as such. The dimension is not envisaged as a line where a person starts his career towards homelessness at the one end ending as extreme excluded at the other. The entrance into the dimension can take place everywhere along the line. The examples of the typologies come from recent studies and surveys. The idea has not been to provide quantitative information on the different types, but to outline some characteristics which the different types might carry, and the hope is that a typology will enable us better to grasp the many faces of homelessness, thereby enable a more efficient policy formulation.[5]

The street children Street children are first and foremost characterised by the lack of family ties, but also by broken relations to institutions such as schools and the social welfare system. They might be defined as

> children and young persons under 18 years of age who for shorter or longer periods of time spend their lives in special street environments, around the Central station, in buildings occupied by squatters, in shopping malls, and in other more temporary places in the city. They include young people who are uprooted and whose primary attachment is to groups in the street environment. Formally they may have an address with their parents or at an institution, but the crucial difference is that they actually spend little time there *and that there are no adults – represented by parents, schools, institutions and social welfare authorities – with whom they have a binding relationship* (Juul, 1991, our translation).

A street child does have some kind of a network of peers around him/her. There is no question of a real friendship, nor of a subculture, if by subculture we mean a group reflecting a collective ideology. The children are living on the edge between what the researchers envisage as a culture of survival and a sheer deviant culture: the group is on the one hand the condition for personal survival but, on the other hand, group life often centres on pot and other substances. Consequently, the young person most certainly will have broken the law, and be at serious risk of falling into addiction and crime, the latter caused by, for example, debt to some loan shark.

The child will be well acquainted with the social service departments but feels that he or she has been turned down so many times that it is of no use applying there for help – except for receiving a survival assistance – as it has been their experience that the system gives priority to the problems of the parents, not of the child.

For some, the life as a street child will be a transitional phase. For those where this is not the case they will turn into young homeless, without any social network – no family ties and almost no relation to the labour market.

The traditional homeless This group will also have broken family relations behind them, as well as broken relations to the labour market with which they might once have had a more or less stable relationship. Their relations to the institutions of society as a whole are not broken but problematic, and they are not considered as dangerous.

They are the relatively well functioning middle-aged men staying at reception centres for several years, but who could or might be moving out either to a private flat or probably to a sheltered flat connected to the centre. Those users are *well-acquainted with reception centres*. Their actual reason for staying at the centre might be a split up of a partnership, perhaps caused by violent behaviour, alcohol abuse, or a mixture thereof. Because of indebtedness (due to arrears of tax, child maintenance benefit or rent) and a consequent inability to borrow money for a requested down-payment, some have no possibility of finding another flat. At times the heavy alcohol abuse may come under control, and for some a capacity to perform daily and regular activities might be restored during the stay at the institution.

They have often had a connection to the labour market for many years, but the connection might have been characterised by a high degree of mobility in the young and job-active years: e.g. as a sailor, a trucker, or even as an artist in a circus – jobs that do not demand much formal education but demand vitality and strength, and perhaps jobs that promote the habit of drinking. Their derailment might have been caused by sickness or a traffic or work accident, accompanied by unemployment or perhaps a divorce.

The mental patients Here we find persons who might never have had any stable relational ties at all. They are characterised by a chronic psychosis and have repeatedly been discharged from a psychiatric institution to either their parents' or their own flat. So the very fragile relational ties that they might have had (to an institution) have been broken – not by them, but by society due to the idea of de-institutionalisation. Either because of conflicts with parents, or the housing association, or because they do not dare to live alone, they will leave the residence and turn to a reception centre – perhaps after living for a period on the street. Others dare not go out and will stay isolated for a long time in solitude in a flat until either neighbours or social workers manage to get them out. Many of these 'revolving door' patients will know the institutions for homeless rather well as they have been there a couple of times before. Much time will be spent in shelters and drop-ins, some of which are public and other private.

They have had almost no relationship to the labour market and they have often been granted an invalidity pension several years ago. They will appear confused, and at times also frightening and incomprehensible to others (non-professionals). Furthermore, a personal contact might be impossible to establish because of a mixed substance abuse.

The most conspicuous group among the mental patients are those known as bag-ladies/men. They are persons with considerable mental problems who are almost impossible to contact. They take daily shelter in the same public place, so they are well known to the public. The shelter can be the Central station, a certain square, etc. They are very lonely people – not necessarily without a dwelling somewhere, but, definitely incapable of using it. They attract much attention, but cause no fear – and they are very few.

The drug addicts The most marginalised group – and the group most difficult to reach from the welfare system – are the drug addicts.

We find men as well as women mainly in the age-group of 16–40 years. They might have a child with one of their often-changing partners. The child will now and then be placed away from the mother and at intervals come back to her when there is the slightest prospect of improvement. *No ties exist to a family of origin*, as they have been broken many years ago; accordingly the social network consists of other abusers. They will almost certainly *never have been in touch with the labour market*, having lived on social assistance since they left school. They are probably now in a state where they are applying for – or have been granted – a social pension. Because of substance abuse they are regularly involved in *criminal activities and/or prostitution*. They might also suffer from a borderline psychosis or just from a neurosis, perhaps caused by the abuse. They live on the streets, with acquaintances, or sometimes in the reception centres, where they are now and then ejected because of their frightening and distasteful behaviour.

They live at the borderline of society.

***

What we have tried to illustrate with a presentation of these four types – all being part of the larger group of homeless – is that we are talking about a variety of people who are having various problems, each – at least partially – with their own solution. By approaching the research and the policy formation on homelessness through a focus on plurality rather than as a uni-dimensional problem, we direct the evaluative aspect of the rest of this chapter – which presents measures directed towards homelessness – to the width of the measures, rather than attempting to establish parameters for comparing the different measures with each other.

General Policy Measures – Integration and Normalisation

Basically all Danish social services – and cash benefits as well – are provided by the municipality (though the central government will cover half of the expenses for the cash benefits). The idea behind this is that a citizen in need of help or assistance should only have to apply at one location – the municipal social office – and here receive all the professional and financial assistance deemed necessary. It is also the responsibility of the municipality to provide sufficient housing in general and to provide the individual with a proper place to live. *And this obligation is, of course, the most important general measure in preventing homelessness as a more widespread phenomenon.* Recently this obligation has been expanded from families to encompassing also single persons.

During the summer of 1996 the Ministry of Social affairs conducted a survey among 30 of the larger municipalities in Denmark. They tried to obtain information on how often the municipalities had assigned dwellings to single persons over the course of one year and two month. In the 30 municipalities, 2,800 persons had been assigned to a dwelling. Of these, 1,600 had obtained a permanent dwelling and 1,200 had been enrolled into temporary accommodation. In regard to the latter, the municipalities were currently working on providing permanent dwellings to a little over half of the 1,200 persons.

The estimate for the country as a whole by the Ministry of Social Affairs was that 7,000 (1.3 per thousand inhabitants) had been assigned to a dwelling from 1 April 1995– 31 May 1996 (Ministry of Social Affairs, 1996).

But one should be careful with interpretation and analysis based on these figures. Let us briefly attempt a critical reading of the national estimate: 1.3 per thousand. 1.3 is the figure one gets by dividing the figure on assigned persons by the Danish population as a whole. If one excludes the population under the ages of 18 the rate raises to 1.7. Furthermore the figure does not include the number of families assigned to a dwelling, and therefore cannot be regarded as an estimate of the yearly pressure on the municipalities for the assignment of dwellings. Finally, there is a critical point to be made about who we are obtaining information on. We are not talking about persons without a dwelling – the persons in the survey have been provided with accommodation. From the survey we do not obtain information on how many people which are presently without a roof. Only under the assumption that the municipalities fulfil there legal obligations in regard to § 31 in the Social Assistance Act[6] can the estimate on 7,000 people be taken as an illustration of the number of people which are dwellingless during a year. Whether or not this assumption is correct we do not know.

But despite the intentions in the Social Assistance Act institutions for the homeless do exist (see below). They are administered at the regional level by the counties, as are institutions for handicapped, mentally ill, and drug abusers. On the general level the important aspect to notice is the ideology of *de-institutionalisation and community care*. This ideology has influenced the composition of and provisions for the homeless in ways to be only briefly recalled here: the closing down of the big psychiatric institutions and the reduction in the capacity in the hospital sector have in Denmark as in other countries – for a period at least – had an impact on the composition of homelessness, with a heavy increase in the mentally ill among the users as its result. For some people the erosion of institutional room – even though they might be discursively incorrect institutions – is an erosion of a home or of a place to be. The closing down of large institutions does leave some people on the streets, even if an equal amount of alternative, smaller, and local possibilities for temporary stays are provided. The smaller, local, and less-institutionalised is not what everyone seem to fit into. Formulated more formally: it demands a feeling of belonging to a locality to benefit from the de-institutionalisation

But it is not just the psychiatric sector that is being de-institutionalised; this is also the case in regard to homelessness itself – an effort which is connected to the ideology of *integration or normalisation*.

Recently this trend of decentralisation, normalisation and integration into local communities has been questioned for a number of reasons: first, it seems as if the municipalities (especially the small ones) do not give priority to those groups and that they do not possess the experience and knowledge necessary to tackle those problems. Also, it seems as if the so-called local community is not very eager to receive these people. Finally reintegration into the overall society is does not just happen. It demands different kinds of professional assistance as we shall return to later on.

Targeted Measures

We will first introduce a couple of measures which are directed towards the homeless as one group and thereafter direct our attention towards a couple of measures targeted on the different types presented in the typology above.

Targeting the Homeless

If we briefly look at the legal security provided for homeless, the important bill is the Social Assistance Act. This legislation states which kind of persons the shelters, reception centres, etc. (so called Section 105-institutions, are obliged to receive. The 105-institutions are the most fundamental measure directed towards homeless. The latest amendment (from January 1995) reflects that there has been a broadening in the target group for the 105-institutions. This paragraph now explicitly mentions persons *with* an abode as well as persons without:

> **§ 105** ... *Persons who are without a dwelling or who are unable to stay in it and because of special social need require special accommodations or activating support and care, not provided according to the otherwise existing regulations in the social or any other legislation.*

Through the change of paragraph 105 in 1995 the concept of homelessness disappeared from the legislation. The indicator for help is now formulated as 'special social need'. Nevertheless the concept is widely used in the public debate and the institutions and living arrangements mentioned here are considered as services to the homeless. We will also continue to use the term in this chapter.

There are other measures included in the Social Assistance Act which are directed towards homelessness. One – also a consequence of the amendment in January 1995 – is the possibilities for *communal living* which can now be provided by the municipality:

> **§ 68b** *To persons with special social difficulties the municipality can offer a stay in communal living or in other living arrangements and can provide the assistance (staff) needed.*

Below there is a presentation of some of the preliminary findings in regard to the use of communal living.[7]

The last measure which we will present prior to the outline of various instruments directed towards the different types of homeless is the *personal action plans*. Recently the municipalities and the reception centres have become obliged to set up such action plans for the users of the centres within three months (from the admittance into the centre). The aim is to force the relevant institutions to evaluate how to get the actual person back into society. We do not yet know how this measure will work – but it is an interesting aspect in future research on homelessness.

Targeting the Different Types of Homeless

Trying to use the typologies constructed above, we will now focus on different measures targeted on those types. Reflecting our current state of knowledge and the direction of the resources used on homelessness we shall not deal with either the bag-ladies or the street children in of this chapter.[8]

The traditional homeless This group consists mostly of single 35–55 years old men *with a previous attachment to the labour market*. The findings are primarily based on a report by Jensen (1995) and one by Rostgaard and Koch-Nielsen (1994). Regarding the living arrangements described below, the primary source is a forthcoming report by the Danish Building Research Institute and the Danish National Institute of Social Research (SBI and SFI, 1996).

The importance of – and current possibilities for – work Some of the measures and results reported focuses on different means of integration established through the labour market or other occupational activities, which is considered to be the vital link for this group of homeless.

The first possibility is a *return to the labour market*. To reintegrate the homeless into the labour market is a difficult option. But for a few of the interviewed persons in Jensen (1995) it has been done. A couple of generalities might be drawn from his study. First – and not surprisingly – it is often more of an option if the person is young; the older they are the more difficult it is. Second, it is probably important that the institution at which the homeless is staying is active and supporting in regard to obtaining a job. Third, the attitude of the place of work seems of importance. There might be a need for the workplace to accept that the homeless is having other problems than a 'normal' worker, e.g. alcohol abuse. It is important that the workplace becomes an active part in solving these problems.

Overall the conclusion might be that a workplace provides the homeless with the feeling of being members of society, and that inclusion in the labour market can initiate a process through which the individual becomes capable of reintegration in other aspects, although it often demands special caring and attention if an integration is to be successful.

The second possibility is connected to *education/rehabilitation programmes*. The homeless have, as any other Danish citizen, the right to join an education/rehabilitation programme. In Jensen's report there are two examples of such. In both instances the programmes have been working –

and the persons interviewed have been reintegrated into the labour market. But there is a second finding outlining a problematic: the welfare system sometimes has to be under pressure before the homeless are included in the programmes. And here the 105-institutions play an important role. They are often those who are capable of applying the pressure on the welfare office's decision.

The third possibility consists in *alternative ways of working*.

> Not everyone has the possibility of being reintegrated at the labour market but other ways exist. The majority of the larger institutions for homeless are able to offer different kinds of employment[, also] for those who have moved out. Only a smaller share of the former homeless make use of this offer but for those who do it represents a vital part of their life. They maintain the contact to the staff who can then help them in difficult times and prevent that they loose the grip of their dwelling
>
> Being involved in a production and the subsequent self-respect is the most important factor of having a job. The work place might as well be situated outside the institution but some of the interviewed emphasise the importance of being able to get help from the staff whom they know very well by now and being able to use the other facilities available at the institutions (Rostgaard and Koch-Nielsen, 1994, pp. 49–51).

Living arrangements: to create a home As part of the comprehensive attempt at integration and the combating of social exclusion in the bigger cities, several experiments have been set up under the so-called 50 Million Pool Scheme. Some of the experiments are aimed at this best-functioning group among the users of the institutions for homeless. The 50 Million Pool Scheme was established by parliament in 1992. It was decided to direct 50 million DKK towards experimental housing, drop-ins, and contact persons[9] for homeless and socially excluded in 1993. In subsequent years between 70–80 million DKK per year has been directed into the pool scheme.

The living arrangements launched under the programme can be grouped into:[10]

1   *support in own apartment*: the individuals live in their own apartments and receive support there. The support can come from the reception centre or from a municipal centre, and can be of different kind. It can range from practical help with the cleaning on a weekly visit, to daily visiting and helping;

2   *staircase communities*: the individuals also live in their own apartments, but the apartments are located in the same staircase (or in blocks near each other). One apartment in the staircase (or in a nearby block) functions as a common area for the inhabitants. This apartment often includes facilities for collective activities (e.g. dining together or hobby-minded work) and often has an office which is staffed during the daytime;

3   *shared dwellings*: these are collective dwellings located in a flat or house. Each inhabitant has their own room and then shares the other facilities such as kitchen, bathroom, living room, etc. There can be staff connected to the shared dwelling, who might either have an office in the dwelling – often the case – or come around once in while;

4   *dormitories*: the dormitories are in-between shared dwelling and one's own flat. They are like the dormitories often provided for students. Each tenant has their own bath, but they share a common kitchen. There is also staff connected who drop by once in a while;

5   *other alternative housing arrangements*: this group includes different projects. As an illustrative example we have taken a project located in three outdated train wagons. Two of these have been transformed into dwellings, with two compartments constituting one housing unit. Furthermore, the wagons have had bathrooms installed. The third wagon functions as common area with kitchen, living room, etc. Besides the fact that the inhabitants live in a train, the project functions basically as a shared dwelling.

We have selected an example to illustrate how some of these different measures works for the group of traditional homeless.

Example 1: Shared accommodation for inhabitants at a shelter in Copenhagen

One of the experiments under the 50 Million Pool Scheme has been established in connection with a shelter in inner Copenhagen and consists of three shared dwelling arrangements: one shared dwelling in a small apartment with room for two, another in a shared flat with three inhabitants, and the third in a large house with four people. There is a paid staff consisting of two persons connected to the project. Their job is to look for social activities useful for the inhabitants and to be the link to the social authorities and to the shelter from which the inhabitants are recruited. The group of homeless targeted for this project includes those who have been in the § 105 system for a while, and who – according to one employed in the project – would tend to keep hanging on there if they were not helped. The project is not for those who at present have any serious drug abuse problem. According to one working in the project, it would demand a larger amount of resources should they deal with drug abusers. But a couple of the tenants do have minor alcohol problems.

The intention with the shared dwelling is to slowly make the tenants 'normally' functioning citizens. The project has a time limit of one year on how long the tenants can stay. It should, however, be noted that it is possible to obtain a dispensation from the limitation if it is judged as positive for the tenant by the staff. But the intention of the plan is that after a year the tenants will be able to move into their own dwelling with support from either the employed in the shared dwelling or from those working at the shelter.

The inhabitants – who have no serious problems, e.g. of a mental character or in regard to drugs – neverthelesshave problems with finding a suitable dwelling, according to themselves because of indebtedness and according to the staff because of indebtedness combined with an inability to manage their own financial affairs. They are also characterised by rootlessness and a high degree of mobility. Still, the inhabitants can be classified as traditional homeless.

Some conclusions can be drawn – but only with caution, as we are talking of a project aimed at 10 persons which is no more than two years old.

A prerequisite to making such shared living arrangements a success is the way the inhabitants are accessed to the project. The basic rule of thumb is, that if the inhabitants do not get on together, they will quite simply move out (which often means back to the shelter). That provides us with the most important preliminary finding in regard to the establishing of shared dwellings: there needs to exist a prior knowledge of the potential tenants. A second finding is that the inhabitants appreciate that they have privacy and yet are not alone, but it is important for the different projects to be aware of this distinction, and to be willing to move any existing boarder between the private and the common sphere if needed. (Interviews for the report are published in SBI and SFI, 1996.) What is interesting in this project is that it includes three types of living arrangements – and that they are using all three in the process of reintegrating their users. There is the house which has a connected office for the staff and four inhabitants. Here there is room for people who need close contact to somebody who can be supportive. Secondly, there is the shared dwelling with three inhabitants. Here the staff drops by a couple of times a week – and the tenants thus have to be more self-reliant. Finally, there is the small apartment with room for two. Here those who are thinking about moving out of the project can move in for a shorter period, to work out if establishing their own home is the right thing to do. There are no arranged visits to such an apartment, but the inhabitants can, of course, call the staff if needed. It is still too early for conclusions on the degree of success, but so far it seems that the possibility of internal mobility is having positive consequences for some of the tenants.

The drug addicts and the mentally ill The measures that we shall report on in this section can be considered as provisions for homeless as well as provisions for the mentally ill in order to prevent them from either homelessness or from having to go back into a hospital. Some of the presented measures might not even attempt to reintegrate but 'just' try to provide a better quality in life for (former) patients or drug abusers.

It should be added that the mentally ill currently receive the greatest political attention and that the pressure on the authorities to solve the problem for the mentally ill is great. The rise in pressure might be explained by a recent increase in media attention on the mental state of criminals, and especially explained with reference to a couple of concrete instances where the police had to resort to shooting to protect others or themselves.

The following is also based on results from the above-mentioned evaluation by SBI and SFI(Jensen et al., 1997). We will give some examples of the different kinds of provisions set up under the 50 Million Pool Scheme.

Example 2: Living arrangements by the Municipality of Copenhagen for mentally ill

Four different arrangements have been set up by the Municipality of Copenhagen:

1 *single apartments in a 'staircase community'*: up to now, we are talking about 16 flats where each inhabitant has their own apartment located near a common flat placed in a nearby block. This means that tenants have to leave their own apartments and buildings in order to meet the others. The flats are meant to be permanent flats for those mentally ill who do not want too close a contact with the other inhabitants or the staff; on the other hand they do not want to be or cannot handle being totally on their own.

The access to these flats is either through personal request or through different kinds of psychiatric services. Drug abusers are not accepted, but alcoholics are if they do not cause problems for the other inhabitants. The inhabitants have so far been mostly men living on social pensions. Some of them are undergoing psychiatric treatment. Their educational and family background is not that bad. They have been very stable inhabitants and seem to be very satisfied with the arrangement. The staff connected to the project are members of a team, and one of the team will be present in the common flat during the afternoon and part of the evening. The local community, e.g. neighbours, have not been told about the project, and up to now there have been no problems;

2   different kinds of *shared dwellings* where the inhabitants have only one room to themselves and then share the rest of the flat, e.g. kitchen, bath and living room.

  The target group for these shared dwellings set up by the Municipality of Copenhagen is schizophrenics with a low intelligence who do, furthermore, have a mixed abuse. For this group, the alternative would be an institution – not necessarily an institution for the homeless but one for the mentally ill – e.g. a nursing home. The staff from the municipal home-help centre carries out all the practical work (cooking, cleaning, shopping) and is present all day, but not during night. The users keep the room if they go to hospital for shorter stays (Børner and Koch-Nielsen, 1996);

3   intermediate arrangements meant for inhabitants who have treated their flat in such a way that they cannot themselves live in it, or meant for patients on their way out of hospital until another arrangement has been found;

4   30 private apartments with support from five home assistants as a supplement to a home-nurse and home-help programme;

Example 3: Living arrangements for mentally ill and substance abusers from Sundholm[11]

While it might be debated whether the first-mentioned project is directly related to homelessness, this one certainly is, as it concerns the inhabitants of the reception centre Sundholm in Copenhagen. The team set up for this project consists of two staff members (a social worker and the head of one of

Sundholm's sections) with the task of finding suitable dwellings. The main idea is that providing these inhabitants with a dwelling is not sufficient to keep them out of homelessness. It is necessary to keep up the contact and the cooperation between staff and former users, because they are not able to manage on their own – the target group being the mentally ill with a substance abuse, alcoholics and HIV-positive abusers. From the very beginning of the project it has not been an easy task. Often it is difficult to find a place where they are not viewed as intruders and are thus unwanted by the neighbours. Presently there are four people living in the project, which is supposed to include eight. Due to personal as well as practical and juridical problems there has been some substitution among one-half of those enrolled in the project. But again it is difficult to come up with general statements – for some within this group it does work: this is the case, for example, for three middle-aged men, who for the last three years, have been living in a well-functioning shared dwelling.

Example 4: Shared dwellings for former alcoholics

This arrangement encompasses 10 small apartments for eight users and two volunteers – the use of volunteers being a very unusual phenomenon in this field and country. The volunteers are recruited from the national organisation for alcohol treatment 'The Chain'. The volunteers will, among other things, be present in the project during evenings and nights. The paid staff consists of the manager of the project and a psychiatrist who is present a few hours every week.

The eight inhabitants are alcohol abusers, most of them homeless – often because they have been kicked out by their partners. They are accessed through the nearby hospitals. Being in treatment is a condition for being accessed to this project. The keywords for the 'treatment' are rehabilitation, care, and service. The intention is to give some positive experiences to the inhabitants. Service will include assistance with transportation, addressing public authorities, helping to move out (back), and contact afterwards if it is wanted.

During the stay users participate in running the project. They are involved in cleaning, in gardening, and take part in the cooking. Furthermore there is the possibility of working in a small workshop. Alcohol is not allowed. Because of the location of the project there have been no problems with the local community.

The researchers consider this to be something quite new and different: the close connection between the living arrangements, medical treatment and the patient's organisation working with volunteers has not been seen before in Denmark.

But such project is not for everybody, but for those who want to make a serious effort to get rid of their abuse. The alternative for several of the inhabitants would be a 105-institution.

Some of the success is attributed to the manager who, apart from being educated in social work, is also a strong personality.

Example 5: Drop-ins of different kinds

Drop-ins are seen as a special service for excluded and exposed persons in general. They are set up all over the country – most of them by private non-profit organisations and a few by the municipalities. They are day centres aiming to provide a place for contact and activities for the homeless and socially excluded. As a measure towards homelessness, the drop-ins were included in the 50 Million Pool Scheme. They cover a variety of target groups and activities. Some are cafes partially staffed by the homeless themselves – thereby providing a few job opportunities. Others are activity centres where one can do hobby-minded work. The different types of drop-ins demand different resources. Some (especially those with a target group of the mentally ill) need a professional and well-educated staff, while others rely more on voluntary engagement.

The variety indicates what is supposedly the intention in the experiment with drop-ins: to provide an alternative to the more formalised public system. In the drop-ins it is preferably the users who decide on the activities, and engage in the practical work (Seemann, 1996).

For the group of traditional homeless mentioned above this does not seem to be the right service, as they consider them to be targeted towards drug abusers and the really excluded (thus indicating a hierarchy in exclusion). But other groups seem to benefit from these projects. There are in Copenhagen two projects directed towards youngsters, and here the preliminary indications are somewhat positive.

Presently we have descriptions of those drop-ins – but actual evaluations are hard to get. An interesting and specific thing about the drop-ins is that they employ volunteers – often the former 'guests' or users who, through this activity, are said to become more resourceful and integrated.

We have now presented different measures directed towards homelessness, both some measures of a general character in that they are directed towards all people considered to be part of the socially excluded, but also more specific measures. In particular the housing arrangements which we have been presenting have been outlined in connection with a type of homelessness. Our point in connecting the different types of homeless with different kinds of accommodation has been, first, to show how it turned out in Denmark when different groups established measures under the 50 Million Pool Scheme – how did the organisations actually implement the funding. Second, we think that it is necessary to avoid grouping all the homeless together into one bunch. They are different people with different problems. Some of these problems might be solved through the establishment of different housing arrangements. Especially in the case of the traditional homeless, the least mentally ill, or people with a minor substance abuse, this seems to be a good solution. But for some this might not be the required solution. For some many other measures need to be provided. For a third group, a helping hand in acquiring their own apartment might be enough. Yet there is no information which would enable an in-depth clarification of the connections between the types of homeless and the size and shape of the helping hand needed despite its being an area which needs a lot of future attention.

Summing up the preliminary Danish experience with housing arrangements especially, the researchers behind the report evaluating the 50 Million Pool Scheme state that:

> The social aspect of the human dwelling is for most people present without further reflection. The dwelling is thus the physical frame for the social life with families, friends, colleagues, and others who constitute the social network.
>
> For people at the margins of society it is the other way round. For them the apartment can turn into a place of isolation where they every day encounter the lack of purpose with getting up in the morning to the daily life, not to mention a perspective on life as such. The social aspects of the housing arrangements aims at filling out the empty space left by the lack of family, friends, etc. Furthermore, the housing arrangement can be followed up by different forms of support systems necessary because of special circumstances by the inhabitants ... Thus, the task (in the experiments) has been to create living arrangements where the basic physical frame can meet the need of the inhabitants while at the same time optimize the conditions for the re-establishing of a social life assisted by a necessary support system. Considering the differentiation in the group of inhabitants and the difficulties in re-establishing a social life, this is a very difficult and complex task (SBI and SFI, 1996a).

Discussion: Where Can We Go From Here?

Very briefly at the end of this chapter we would like to raise some questions on the possibility of not just descrbing but also evaluating different measures of provisions for homeless – (how) can this be accomplished? And at a European level?

Some questions and terms need to be discussed and clarified in depth prior to engaging in such project. Here are just a few:

1 the terms 'accommodation' and 'provision' are not very precise and encompass such different measures as housing, the whole social welfare system, the provision of shelters and centres, the services they render apart from just a bed and a shelter (rehabilitation, methadone, social activities, etc.) and connected reintegration projects as here described;

2 evaluations are always difficult but it seems as if we are here facing more problems than usual: the groups are small, no control groups exist (can they?), and success seems to depend very much on the right mix of the individual with the provision. So even though the categories set up in the introduction are not necessary not useful, they are certainly too broad and imprecise when it comes to establishing possibilities for cross-national evaluation and the comparison of measures;

3 moreover evaluation takes time and requires good records. If not we are left with the expressed satisfaction of the users and the staff. Perhaps we cannot get any further but can we come up with methods (standards) which will enable a closer/better comparison of the different nationally created evaluations?

The overall question that draws our attention is of course: which kinds of policies seems to affect homelessness?

a) At the *individual level* one answer to the question might be found in this chapter: results based upon more or less impressionistic cases – studies from the countries can be compared qualitatively and perhaps certain general patterns might appear.

Another possibility would be to follow selected groups who have been exposed to the same kind of reintegrational measures. For such project we need groups of a certain size, registers, uniform descriptions of the 'measures' and common success criteria.

A third possibility for answering the question is to return to the idea of typology. Is it possible to present some archetypes of homeless with a precise description of their characteristics? Is it then possible that each country could find one (or maybe more) person matching these outlined characteristics, and then follow that person's career – encounters with the public system, encounters with private help organisations, with shelters, with different types of accommodation, etc. through a certain time period, or until the person becomes reintegrated (or is given up)? This could perhaps be combined with a theoretical construction of the person's expected route – or a description of how it should have been had each and every rule been followed.

b) At the *societal level* the effect of the different policies should show up in the size and perhaps more the composition of homelessness (see also section 3). In order to give such a description we should have as a base a European survey among service providers combined with a census among the users. One problem here is in the selection of the service providers – and in ensuring that programmes such as those mentioned above are included in the same way in each national survey.

Notes

1   A short modification of Brandt's definition is needed. A person will be homeless if she/he is capable of using only the institutions provided by society *for* homeless, e.g. the below described 105-institutions. The institutions referred to by Brandt must be taken as institutions considered as part of a 'normalised' life, not institutions which are established with the excluded as their target group.

2   Sections 3 and 4 of this chapter will present some of these programmes in more depth.

3   The questionnaire was originally send to 173 programmes allowing room for about 5,640 users. Thirty institutions did not participate for various reasons, leaving the number of users at 4,341.

4   The institutions are presented in section 4 below as institutions targeting the homeless.

5   A typology has previously been presented in *National Report 1994* (Rostgaard and Koch-Nielsen).

6   § 31 of the Social Assistance Act is the paragraph that states that everybody has the right to a dwelling. But, as it is also stated, this right can – if nothing else is available – be fulfilled temporarily through visitation to a § 105-institution (see below).

7   In the *National Report 1995* (Børner and Koch-Nielsen) there is a presentation of two such projects.

8   Street-children are a central part in the forthcoming *National Report 1996* to FEANTSA.

9   We will leave the contact persons out of this paper since at present we are aware of very little evaluation of this measure.
10 The different types of living arrangements presented here are not solely directed towards traditional homeless – as will become clear below. We have chosen first to present all the different types together hoping thereby to provide an illustration of the variety in the arrangements. During the rest of section 4 some of the arrangements will then be knitted together with the different types of homelessness, and thereby be presented in more depth.
11 Sundholm is the biggest Danish reception centre and is located in Copenhagen.

Bibliography

Børner, T. (1996), *Hjemløshed: begreber, tal og metoder*, Copenhagen, The Danish National Institute of Social Research.

Børner, T. and Koch-Nielsen, I. (1996), *National Report 1995 Denmark*, Brussels, FEANTSA.

Brandt, P. (1992), *Unge Hjemløse i København,* Copenhagen, DK:FADL' Forlag.

Brandt, P. (1994), personal correspondence.

Brandt, P. (1995), *Nogle skal ydmyges*, Copenhagen, Ministry of Social Affairs.

CASA and SUS (1996), *Væresteder – et sted at være*, 2, delrapport, Copenhagen, CASA.

Danmarks Statistik (1996), 'Den sociale ressourceopgørelse 18. januar 1995' in *Socialstatistik 1996*, 9, Copenhagen, Danmarks Statistik.

Eskelinen, L. et al. (1994), *Socialt Udstødte i Københavns Kommune*, Copenhagen, Institute of Local Government Studies, Denmark.

Fridberg, T. (1992), *De socialt udstødte*, Copenhagen, The Danish National Institute of Social Research.

Guidicini, P., Pieretti, G. and Bergamaschi, M. (1996), *Extreme Urban Poverties en Europe*, Franco Angeli, Milano.

Jensen, M.K. (1993), *De Udstødte*, Copenhagen, The Danish National Institute of Social Research, pjece 38.

Jensen, M.K. (1995), *Hjemløse med og uden egen bolig*, Copenhagen, The Danish National Institute of Social Research.

Jensen, M.K. (1997), *Sociale Boformer*, The Danish National Building Research Institute and the Danish National Research Institute.

Juul, S. (1991), *Gadebørn i Storkøbenhavn*, Copenhagen, The Danish National Institute of Social Research.

Ministry of Social Affairs (1994), *Den sociale indsats for sindslidende og socialt udstødte.* Copenhagen, Ministry of Social Affairs.

Ministry of Social Affairs (1995), *Social Assistance Act, the,* legislation #333 of 1974 with changes, Copenhagen, Ministry of Social Affairs.

Ministry of Social Affairs (1996), *Undersøgelse af indsatsen for hjemløse m.fl.*, Notat from Analysekontoret. J.no. 7225–4, 17 September.

Rostgaard, T. and Koch-Nielsen, I. (1994), *Homelessness in Denmark: FEANTSA national report*, Copenhagen, The Danish National Institute of Social Research.

Seemann, J. (1996), *Storbypuljen – nogle organisatoriske overvejelser,* paper, Aalborg, Aalborg University.

Wendt, P. (1991), *Byggeri og boligforhold*, Copenhagen, Handelshøjskolens Forlag.

Appendix

Table A   An overview of concepts, definitions and figures in Danish research on homelessness

Concept	Definition	Source	Number/year
Categories of homeless			
Working homeless	Those who do not have their own dwelling, or who are not capable of using such and who have a connection to the labour market.	Fridberg, 1992	Less than 23% of 105-users
Addressless	Those registered by the Danish authority as not having their own address, where this cannot be explained as a consequence of their job.		n.a.
Assigned	Those who have been assigned to a dwelling by the public.	Min. of Soc. Aff. 1996	7,000 singles during a year/1995–96
Dwellingless	Those who do not possess their own dwelling despite a explicated wish thereof.	Eskelinen, 1994	2% or 9% of those enrolled in a 105-institution.
Street children	Those below the age of 18 who do not live with their parents, a guardian, or in their own dwelling.		n.a.
Homeless without their own dwelling	Those who do not possess their own dwelling.	Jensen, 1993 and Fridberg, 1992	A little more than 50% of the 105-users
Homeless with their own dwelling	Those who officially are in possession of their own dwelling but who in reality are not capable of using it and therefore are staying somewhere else.	Jensen, 1993 and Fridberg, 1992	A little less than 50% of the 105-users
Homeless with an abuse problem	Those who do not have their own dwelling, or who are not capable of using such and have an abuse problem of some kind.		n.a.
Publicly-sanctioned homeless	Those who by the authority have been forced to leave their dwelling and thus are presently without their own abode.		n.a.
Bag-ladies	Those (both male and female) who sleep rough in places not meant for sleeping.	Brandt, 1994	900/1991
Mentally ill homeless	Those who do not have their own dwelling, or who are not capable of using such and have a mental diagnosis.	Jensen, 1993	400–600 are among the most excluded
Erratic dwellers	Those who for a while are sleeping over in friends' or family's dwellings.	Brandt, 1994	2,000 each day in Copenhagen

Concept	Definition	Source	Number/year
Categories of homeless			
Traditional homeless	Those who have previously been connected to the labour market and who do not have their own dwelling, or who are not capable of using such.		n.a.
Unacceptable dwellings	Households lacking at least one of the following installations: kitchen, bath, toilet, hot water or central heating.	ECHP, 1995	14% of all households/ 1995
Unacceptable dwellers	Those living in dwellings of an unacceptable standard	Levevilkår, 1986	7% of population 1986
Users of 24H-institutions			
§ 105 users (both day and 24H users)	Those who during a week are enrolled at an institution established under § 105 in the Social Assistance Act.	Danmarks Statistik, 1996	2,770/1995
§ 105 users (24H)	Those who sleep in an institution established under § 105 in the Social Assistance Act estimated over a year.	Fridberg, 1992	12,000–13,000/1992
Homeless users of institutions not established for homeless	Those who stay temporarily in an institution established with a different purpose than the 105-institutions where the person in case falls under the category for whom the institution is established but where the person does not posses their own dwelling.	Brandt, 1994	300
Homeless 'institution abusers'	Those who stay temporarily in an institution established with a different purpose than the 105-institutions where the person in case does not fall under the category for whom the institution is established and where the person does not posses an own dwelling.		n.a.
Socially Excluded			
Socially excluded	Those who without help are incapable of providing for or taking care of themselves in a manner acceptable to the society or the individual.	Min. of Soc. Aff., 1994	27,500–31,500/1994
Socially excluded	Those who without help are incapable of providing for or taking care of themselves in a manner acceptable to the society or the individual.	CASA, 1996:5	40,000–50,000
The unhelpable	Those who are seen as unfit for any of the measures provided by the authority today.	Min. of Soc. Aff., 1994	8,000–10,000

Source: Børner, 1996.

21 Temporary Accommodation for Homeless People in Germany with Special Focus on the Provision for Immigrants and Asylum Seekers

VOLKER BUSCH-GEERTSEMA

Preface

When I was asked to prepare a chapter on temporary accommodation with special focus on the German experience in assisting immigrants and asylum seekers, I had some reservations whether it would be possible to make statements valid for the whole territory of Germany, as it concerns a sector which is mainly in the responsibility of municipalities with different legal regulations in each *Bundesland* and different local conditions in each municipality. Still worse, there are hardly any empirical studies on the practice of temporary accommodation of homeless people which could claim nationwide representativeness, and even less primary research is done on the temporary accommodation of immigrants than on the temporary accommodation of 'native' homeless people.

As the available means do not allow primary research, the following chapter can only compile a patchwork of the most different detail studies on certain regions of Germany. Referring to my knowledge, which results from my own research work on social marginalisation and problems of homelessness, I will combine the results of these studies and try to give a comprehensive survey on the topic. It will soon become evident both that the 'special focus' on temporary accommodation of immigrants is only partly possible because there is not sufficient information about it and that the situation of an essential part of Germany – the East German *Bundesländer* in the territory of the former GDR – has to remain in the dark because, up to now, there is hardly any empirical material on the topic of temporary accommodation from this region. That means that most of the following observations refer to the situation in West Germany. Only sometimes is it possible to deal especially with the conditions in East Germany.

In the following, first of all the main groups of persons in need of temporary accommodation will be distinguished and trends in the need for temporary accommodation in the last 10 years will be analysed, as well as a prognosis given which reaches into the next millennium. The main focus is on the incongruity between demand and supply of normal permanent housing, on migration and on the relationship between housing wealth and housing distress.

The second part of the chapter will describe the supply of temporary accommodation and the practice of municipalities in lodging homeless people, distinguishing between immigrants and the non-immigrant homeless. It also describes the legal framework and responsibilities, as well as the provision of assistance for people in temporary accommodation. Among many negative examples some positive approaches to a solution of the problem are to be presented. The third part considers the costs of temporary accommodation and compares provisions of different quality concerning their economical aspect. Finally the fourth part deals with the question 'How temporary is temporary accommodation?' and therefore with the duration of stay in temporary shelters, with social effects of temporary accommodation and with the chances of homeless households being reintegrated into normal permanent housing. The results of this analysis will be summarised and assessed in a short résumé.

Who Needs Temporary Accommodation?

Three Main Groups in Need of Temporary Accommodation

To describe temporary accommodation of homeless persons in Germany we have to distinguish between three main subgroups: firstly there are German homeless people who had to leave their dwellings due to actions for eviction or other reasons or who were dismissed from institutions like prisons, hospitals, therapeutic institutions, homes for young people etc. into homelessness (at this point further specification is necessary and is to be given later). Secondly there are immigrants with German origin (*Aussiedler*) who had lived in Eastern

Europe after the second world war and who have moved to Germany in recent years. Concerning essential legal rights as well as the provision with normal housing, they basically possess the same status as other Germans, but they are usually accommodated in temporary accommodation separate from the provisions for the first-mentioned group. And finally there is the group of asylum seekers and other refugees. Most of them stay in Germany only for a limited time and have no legal claim to be provided with permanent housing. Only a relatively small proportion of asylum seekers is legally approved as entitled to asylum. In recent years the rates of legal approval were between 3.2 –7.3 per cent (Fleischer and Sommer, 1995). After being approved as entitled to asylum, their legal status concerning temporary or permanent provision with housing is similar or equal to the status of the first-mentioned group. However, as long as their applications for asylum are being dealt with, asylum seekers are excluded from provision with normal housing and are mostly accommodated in shelters. In addition there are several special groups among refugees who enjoy a right to stay – in most cases for a fixed time – due to special regulations and who are sometimes provided with normal permanent housing but sometimes only with temporary housing.

Trends in the Demand for Housing in Germany Between 1985–95 and Forecasts for the Future

Demographic trends and the development of households: an increasing demand for housing Although there has been a clear increase in the construction of new housing since the beginning of the 1990s and although it is said that the housing market has relaxed since the end of 1993, there is still a definite mismatch between housing demand and housing supply. The sector of cheap housing is particularly affected by this incongruity.

In 1985 the number of inhabitants of West Germany had reached an absolute minimum of just over 61 million. Since then it has risen by more than five million inhabitants, mainly as a consequence of migration. At the beginning of 1995 it amounted to 66 million inhabitants in West Germany. Even considering the whole territory of Germany, there was a clear increase between 1985–95, although the population figure in East Germany has dropped since German unification in 1990. At the beginning of 1995 the population figure for Germany was at 81.5 million altogether.

Latest forecasts about future population trends assume a further increase of the population of Germany. Until the year 2010 a further increase of more than four million inhabitants is expected, so that the total population figure

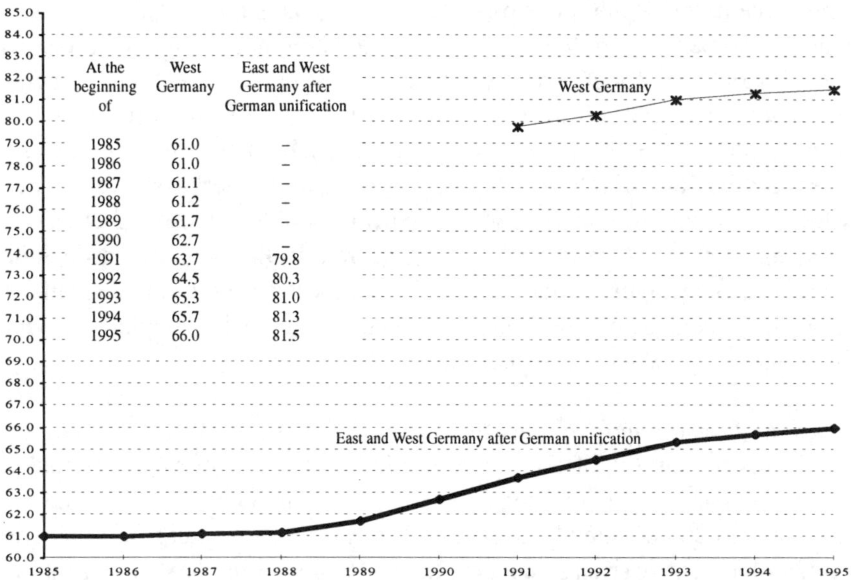

At the beginning of	West Germany	East and West Germany after German unification
1985	61.0	–
1986	61.0	–
1987	61.1	–
1988	61.2	–
1989	61.7	–
1990	62.7	–
1991	63.7	79.8
1992	64.5	80.3
1993	65.3	81.0
1994	65.7	81.3
1995	66.0	81.5

Figure 21.1 Population of Germany (in millions of inhabitants)

will be 85.7 million persons. The natural population change would cause a decline, but this trend will be reversed by external migration. As in previous years the population increase will affect mainly West Germany, whereas for East Germany further decreases in population are prognosticated (Bucher, Kocks and Siedhoff, 1994).

Even more important than the increase in population which is mainly caused by migration is the development of private households. After all, it is the development of households with which the supply of housing has to keep pace. One can assume that even without gains by external migration the number of private households would definitely have increased in previous years and is further going to increase. The number of households has risen more strongly than the population figure (increase in population figure in West Germany between 1985–94: 8.5 per cent; increase in households: 13.4 per cent). This trend is going to continue: until the year 2010 a clear increase in the number of households in East and West Germany is prognosticated. By then an increase of altogether about two million households (from 36.7 million households in 1994 to 38.7 million households in 2010) is expected. The main reason for this trend is the reduction of household sizes. While the average household size in 1985 was at 2.31 person per household in West Germany, it was only at 2.21 in 1994 and will be at 2.17 in the year 2010, according to latest forecasts.

The percentage of one- or two-person households is on a steady increase. It was at 63.4 per cent in West Germany in 1985, but had risen to 67.3 per cent by 1994. For the year 2010 a percentage of 69.3 per cent one- and two-person households is expected (all figures mentioned above from Voit, 1996). The number of single households is increased by the ongoing trend of individualisation, which mainly affects young and elderly persons. Factors which contribute to the trend of smaller households are, among others, the growing number of childless adults, a decline in the birthrate, a declining number of marriages, an increase in the number of divorces and finally the growing percentage of elderly couples living together without children, which is caused by growing life expectancy.

Does the housing market meet the demand of housing? In the beginning of the 1990s a shortage of about two million housing units was assumed for West Germany. After the construction of new housing had dropped to a minimum of 209,000 newly-constructed housing units in 1988, the completion number has clearly risen since then. In 1994 again more than half a million of housing units were newly erected, and in 1995 the construction boom reached a peak, with about 550,000 flats (Guttmann, 1995; BMBAU, 1996, p. 15). For the future, a declining trend in housing construction is expected again.

In 1996 there were clear indications of a slump in the construction business and of marketing difficulties, especially for expensive new flats. Nevertheless, existing prognoses predict a need for about 470,000 newly-constructed flats per annum by the year 2000 to provide a growing number of households and to cover the increased demand of housing space.

Anyhow, analyses of the shortage of housing mainly refer to the ratio of supply to solvent demand. The needs of persons who are not able to articulate their demand as a solvent demand for housing (e.g. the residents of institutions) are often ignored. On the other hand, solvent demand and the development of incomes are important factors for the consumption of housing space and therefore for the question whether the existing housing supply is sufficient for the housing provision of the total population. In a pointed way one could say that in the postwar years in West Germany, housing need and an increasing demand for temporary accommodation always went along with a greater demand for housing (or housing space) increased by an economic boom, whereas a relaxed situation of the housing market or even housing vacancies were apparent when economic crises led to a decline in housing demand (Ulbrich, 1991). So there is a direct link between housing need and housing wealth in Germany.

In any case, in dealing with the issue of temporary accommodation we are mainly interested in that sector of housing which is suitable for persons who come from institutions of temporary accommodation. These households need reasonably cheap dwellings and dwellings on which the state has some influence concerning their allocation. A considerable part of German *Aussiedler* households which immigrated to Germany in recent years are for example supposed to have been integrated into permanent housing because they were given priority in the allocation of social housing. But as social obligations for housing originally built as social housing are limited to a certain time and as the greatest part of social housing was constructed in the 1950s and 1960s, these social obligations have been expiring for some time. The supply of social housing has been shrinking for years: by the year 2000 more than one third of those 2.7 million social flats in West Germany which in 1993 had a limited rent and were reserved for households with low incomes will have lost their social obligations according to the federal government (BMBAU, 1996, p. 23). So municipalities lose their influence on the allocation of these dwellings. The influence of municipalities, however, is an important precondition for the integration of persons in temporary accommodation into normal housing.

The development of external migration Immigration to Germany is of double importance to the need of temporary accommodation. Firstly it is an important cause of the incongruity between housing supply and housing demand. Housing allocated to immigrated German *Aussiedler* is no longer available for other households with low incomes and in need of support in the provision with housing. Secondly the immigrated groups themselves constitute a great part of those persons in temporary accommodation in Germany.

German Aussiedler German *Aussiedler* are persons of German origin who had lived in different Eastern European countries after the second world war and who moved to Germany in recent years. *Aussiedler* have a legal claim on German citizenship. Their immigration to Germany was politically welcomed and supported and promoted by numerous financial state aids. Meanwhile their immigration is only tolerated and limited in numbers. Immigration of *Aussiedler* to Germany increased strongly after the political changes in Poland and in the former Soviet Union at the end of the 1980s. In 1990 the number of immigration cases of *Aussiedler* reached its peak at almost 400,000. Afterwards the legal admission procedures were changed: since July 1990 *Aussiedler* have to make an application for the acknowledgement of their affiliation to the German population group and for the entry to Germany in their East

European residences. Only when their application has been approved are they permitted to settle permanently in Germany. Through this new procedure the annual number of immigration cases has been halved again. Since 1992 it has been limited to 220,000–225,000 *Aussiedler* as an annual admission rate (Heeler et al., 1993, p. 17). Between 1985 and 1995 about 2.25 million *Aussiedler* moved to Germany.

Since 1992 the distribution of *Aussiedler* to the different *Bundesländer* (federal states) has also been fixed to rates. In the *Bundesländer Aussiedler* are first registered in central reception agencies and, if necessary, accommodated for a short time. Afterwards municipalities are responsible for their accommodation in transitional hostels or other forms of temporary accommodation for which these municipalities receive some financial aid from the *Bundesländer*. There are only few available data on quantity, quality and duration of accommodation of *Aussiedler* by municipalities, which only provide a very incomplete picture on a national scale. There will be more about this later, but it is to be mentioned here that, considering the total number of immigrating *Aussiedler*, up to now they have been integrated rather successfully into normal housing. According to an estimation based on inquiries of municipalities in North Rhine-Westphalia and Schleswig-Holstein on one fixed day in the middle of the year 1992 (30 June 1992) about 260,000–320,000 *Aussiedler* were accommodated temporarily in shelters in West Germany (Busch-Geertsema and Ruhstrat, 1994, p. 60). As about 20 per cent of newly-arriving *Aussiedler* are assigned to East German *Bundesländer*, the number of *Aussiedler* in temporary accommodation there may be estimated – without any empirical evidence and with reservation – at about 52,000–64,000 persons on the same fixed day. So the total number for Germany of *Aussiedler* in temporary shelters on this day in 1992 may be estimated at about 312,000–384,000. This number is clearly higher than the number of *Aussiedler* arriving in Germany every year, and the number of homeless *Aussiedler* is therefore about the same or even higher than the number of non-immigrant homeless people in Germany at the same time (cf. the confirming results of an inquiry in Hesse, in IWU, 1994). But a comparison with the total number of *Aussiedler* having immigrated within the last 10 years shows that many hundreds of thousands could either provide themselves with normal housing or were provided for by the state.

The average household size of *Aussiedler* is higher than that of the rest of the German population. A representative inquiry of *Aussiedler* in temporary accommodation in 1992 showed an average household size of 3.5 persons (for the rest of the German population it is at 2.24). Only 7.7 per cent of all

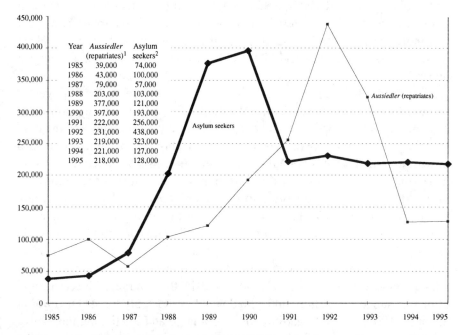

Year	Aussiedler (repatriates)[1]	Asylum seekers[2]
1985	39,000	74,000
1986	43,000	100,000
1987	79,000	57,000
1988	203,000	103,000
1989	377,000	121,000
1990	397,000	193,000
1991	222,000	256,000
1992	231,000	438,000
1993	219,000	323,000
1994	221,000	127,000
1995	218,000	128,000

1   Source: *Statistisches Jahrbuch*; numbers for 1995 from Bundesverwaltungsamt, Köln.
2   Source: *Statistisches Bundesamt*, 1995, p. 88; numbers for 1995 from Bundesamt für die Anerkennung ausländischer Flüchtlinge, Nürnberg.

Figure 21.2 Migration to Germany*

*   Until 1990 only for West Germany.

Aussiedler live in single households (Heller et al 1993, p. 47).

Asylum seekers and other refugees The immigration of asylum seekers to Germany also increased strongly at the end of the 1980s. In 1992 it reached a peak at 438,000. In the middle of 1993 the German Basic Constitutional Law, and as a consequence the legal provisions for asylum procedures, were changed in order to limit immigration and to accelerate the deportation of asylum seekers. One essential innovation is the rule that nobody may be granted asylum in Germany who has travelled to Germany from 'safe countries of origin' or via 'safe third countries'. At the same time the provisions for state support for asylum seekers were removed from the Federal Welfare Act and were ruled by a special act (*Asylbewerberleistungsgesetz*). Claims on material support have been lowered, payments in kind and vouchers are preferred to direct financial support, and asylum seekers are explicitly excluded from a number of other benefits. The new legal provisions had effects even in the same year and more clearly in following years, as the immigration of asylum seekers declined strongly. In 1994 and 1995 the annual immigration figures were just under 130,000.

Between 1985 and 1995 about 1.92 million asylum seekers altogether came to Germany. However, unlike the *Aussiedler* only a small proportion of asylum seekers is supposed to have managed to stay in Germany and many of them left the country again when their application for asylum was turned down. Nevertheless, it is not only asylum seekers entitled to asylum who stay in Germany. A proportion of those asylum seekers whose application was turned down cannot be deported to their home countries for humanitarian, political or legal reasons. The number of these de facto refugees, which includes refugees who have not applied for asylum at all, amounted to 550,000 at the end of 1995, which is nearly double the number of *people entitled to asylum* who live in Germany (about 258,600 at the end of 1995). The number of so-called quota refugees (who are admitted in the course of international humanitarian rescue actions and who do not have to apply for asylum) was at about 91,100 in 1995. In addition there is a large and fluctuating number of war refugees in Germany who were admitted, for example, because of the war in former Yugoslavia (at the end of 1995: 320,000 persons) (all figures from BMI, 1996).

Asylum seekers are only allowed to stay in Germany to prosecute their asylum procedures. They are distributed to the different *Bundesländer* by quotas as well. For the first three months of their residence in Germany they are usually obliged to stay in central mass shelters of the *Bundesländer*. Within this time applications for asylum which are considered as 'obviously unfounded' are to be decided. Those asylum seekers whose procedures for approval have not been settled during this time usually have to go on living in shelters after having been assigned to municipalities which are responsible for their further accommodation after three months. The freedom to move of those asylum seekers is severely restricted and there are several restrictions which exclude asylum seekers from important social basic benefits (e.g. concerning health care, family support or social benefit).

When an asylum seeker is granted asylum, he receives an unlimited residence permit and is no longer obliged to stay in shelters. He may look for a dwelling of his own. His legal status is similar to that of a non-immigrant German homeless. When an asylum seekers is not granted asylum – as happens much more often – he receives an order for departure or he is immediately deported unless he is entitled to a limited residence permit as a *de facto refugee*.

There are no official statistics about the household structure of asylum seekers. It may be assumed that a great part of them are single persons. However, there are important differences depending on the countries of origin of asylum seekers. An estimation for 1990 assumes an average household size of 1.6 persons (Weeber und Partner, 1991, p. 43).

Databases and available information on the accommodation of asylum seekers are much more fragmentary and are even less suitable for providing a general view than the information concerning the accommodation of *Aussiedler*. So in the following we are only able to consider single examples.

The development of homeless figures in the sector of municipal provision of temporary accommodation for non-immigrant Germans In Germany there are no permanent and nationwide statistics on homelessness. So the question about the development of the number of homeless people in temporary accommodation who are not immigrants (*Aussiedler* and refugees) is difficult to answer.

However, there are clear indications that the number of non-immigrant German homeless persons in temporary accommodation increased in the late 1980s until the mid-1990s. Only in 1995 were there first signs of a decline of the number of cases of temporary accommodation. One of the few *Bundesländer* with annual statistics for a fixed day on those homeless people who are provided with temporary accommodation by measures of the police law is North-Rhine Westphalia, which is also the *Bundesland* with the highest population figure. Although these statistics contain only a part of the homeless in temporary accommodation (because, for example, homeless persons in particular social institutions or in hotels, pensions etc. are not accommodated under the police law but by provisions of the Social Welfare Act), it gives some clues for assessing the development over the years. It is clear that the number of homeless persons registered on the fixed date of the 30 June of each year increased from its historical minimum in 1988 by more than 62 per cent by the year 1994. Between 1994–95 there was a first decline by 7.4 per cent.

The number of homeless persons in temporary accommodation (except *Aussiedler* and refugees) in West Germany was estimated at just under 260,000 on the 30 June 1992 (Busch-Geertsema and Ruhstrat, 1994a, p. 73). Later data are not available. Up to now there are no comparable estimations for East Germany. However, data from some towns in East Germany indicate that the number of homeless people in temporary accommodation there is (up

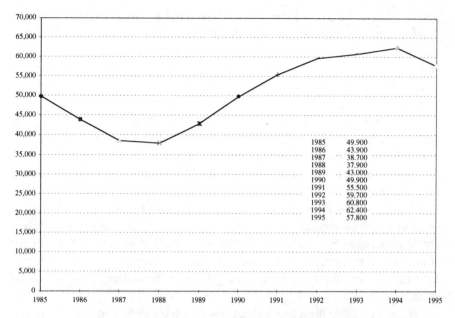

Figure 21.3 Homeless persons who are temporarily accommodated under the police law (Ornungsbehördengesetz) in North Rhine-Westphalia (30 June each year)

to now) smaller than in West Germany, but that, in contrast to West Germany, it is strongly on the increase.

The average household size of the non-immigrant homeless in the sector of accommodation under the police law (Ordnungsbehördengesetz) is 2.7 persons (Busch-Geertsema and Ruhstrat, 1994a, p. 79); for the total number of homeless households in temporary accommodation it is probably far below this value. (According to a survey about the *Bundesland* Hesse from 1994 the average household size there was just 1.9; cf. IWU, 1994, p. 60.) There are many reasons to believe that more than half of the homeless in temporary accommodation are one-person households.

As by definition this group of homeless in temporary accommodation is not affected by immigration, flight or expulsion, some of the reasons or occasions for homelessness are to be mentioned. One can assume that the greatest part of non-immigrant homeless households have lost their dwellings due to notice to quit because of rent arrears and that therefore they had to be provided with temporary accommodation. Surveys about single homeless clients of service-providers in the voluntary sector, however, have revealed as well that a considerable part of these homeless did not become homeless as a result of notice to quit, but (in order of frequency) as a consequence of separation from partners, of leaving parents' homes, of being released from institutions like prisons, hospitals etc. and by the loss of tied accommodation (for further detail see Busch-Geertsema, 1995, p. 25–27 and Evers and Ruhstrat, 1994, p. 223–8).

The Sector of Temporary Accommodation in Germany

Responsibilities and Legal Backgrounds

In Germany the responsibility for the accommodation of the homeless lies mainly with municipalities. For the first months after the arrival of asylum seekers and *Aussiedler* only, the *Bundesländer* provide for their accommodation in central institutions for a limited time until the immigrants are assigned to municipalities. The *Bundesländer* are also partly involved in the costs of temporary accommodation of immigrants by municipalities. Finally there are special institutions for homeless people who are categorised as so-called persons with an unsettled way of living and for people released from prison, which are financed by administrations of the *Bundesländer*. But apart from these exceptions, the general responsibility for the provision and financing of temporary accommodation lies with municipalities. They also have to bear all the costs of temporary accommodation for the non-immigrant homeless. When commercial enterprises or organisations of the non-profit sector offer accommodation, they usually act on behalf of municipalities and are paid by them.

In most municipalities the responsibilities for different groups of homeless are assigned to different offices and administrative departments. Immigrants are usually accommodated by special departments of social welfare offices, and as a rule – though not always – *Aussiedler* and refugees are separately accommodated. In many municipalities departments for public order and security are responsible for non-immigrant homeless persons, whose temporary accommodation is usually separate from the accommodation of immigrants. This is a result of the definition of homelessness as a danger to public safety and order by the law in force, which obliges municipalities to accommodate homeless persons according to police laws. However, most bigger cities have started to entrust the accommodation of non-immigrant homeless people to social welfare offices. Social welfare offices are anyhow obliged to grant support to persons 'without sufficient accommodation' according to the Federal Welfare Act (para. 72) and to bear the costs of accommodation (according to para. 11), if the homeless cannot afford them. But within social welfare offices there is usually a separation of responsibilities for the accommodation of immigrants and other homeless persons as well.

The distribution of responsibilities correspondent to different target groups is the cause of the fact that homeless persons are often accommodated by sectors which are not mainly responsible for the accommodation of the homeless. For example many persons released from prison are temporarily accommodated by voluntary organisations for offenders; some towns have made extensive accommodation arrangements exclusively for homeless drug addicts; and there is temporary accommodation provided by youth welfare services. Women who have become victims of domestic violence and who cannot or do not want to live in their former dwellings find temporary accommodation in homes for battered women. Homes for mothers with children also accommodate persons who would otherwise be homeless, etc. Voluntary organisations which offer accommodation mainly exist within the sectors just mentioned and in the sector of institutions for so-called persons with an unsettled way of living. The diversity of responsibilities, of different target groups and specific offers of temporary accommodation as well as distinctive differences in the organisation of housing provision by different municipalities complicate a general survey on quantity and types of temporary accommodation of homeless people.

Types of Accommodation

The accommodation of non-immigrant homeless people Starting with a description of temporary accommodation of the non-immigrant homeless we get the following picture.

Various surveys about West Germany point out that a majority of homeless people is accommodated temporarily by measures of police laws.

The police laws of the *Bundesländer* make it possible to assign homeless persons to accommodation provided by local authorities for temporary accommodation, which either belongs to the municipalities or is rented by them. This accommodation may consist of whole housing estates erected for the temporary accommodation of the homeless – mostly at very unattractive and isolated locations (near railroad tracks, in industrial areas, in the outskirts of a city, etc.) and with deliberately low housing standards (no current hot water, heating by stove, bad insulation, etc.). However, estates of this kind were pulled down, modernised and redeveloped into normal housing in many towns – though not in all, by far – during the last 20 years. The housing standards of estates for the homeless have been partly improved. Sometimes single houses are used for the accommodation of homeless people, either with individual dwellings for the homeless or with shared dwellings containing several rooms, which are usually occupied by more than one person, communal bathrooms and sometimes self-catering facilities. Another type of temporary accommodation is shelters for so-called 'passers-by' (*Durchwanderer*) in which the stay is limited to a few nights, though single homeless persons who insist on staying at a certain place by law have to be accommodated there for a longer time until they can be provided with normal housing.

At the end of the 1980s the number of homeless persons in need of temporary accommodation increased considerably; this had not been expected by local authorities. As a consequence many new types of provisional accommodation were used, for example shacks and containers, air-raid shelters and shelters with emergency beds which were only opened during the winter months.

German jurisdiction prescribes only rather low minimum standards concerning municipal accommodation (cf. von Aken and Derleder, 1994). Temporary accommodation provided by municipalities explicitly does not have to comply with German tenancy law. It should be 'fit for human beings', but a heatable room which protects against the weather is sufficient. Certain basic demands concerning hygiene have to be fulfilled, there have to be enough sanitary facilities (bathrooms and toilets) and a plain furnishing with beds and wardrobes as well as electrical lighting. A person in need of temporary accommodation has no right to a room of his or her own. In particular single homeless persons have to tolerate shared bedrooms and sometimes also a separation of bedrooms for the night and rooms where they can stay during the day. 'Living space' of five square metres per person is considered as appropriate. Homeless persons in temporary accommodation can be displaced to another place of temporary accommodation at any time, and they have no claim on a specific accommodation.

A part of the houses, flats and shelters used for temporary accommodation is in possession of municipalities. Except for government flats, caretaker flats etc., temporary housing for the homeless is often the only housing owned directly by municipalities. Rented housing for permanent housing provision is owned by independent companies or organisations and private landlords, even in the sector of social housing, though sometimes municipalities are associates or even owners of such housing organisations. Sometimes they have also transferred the administration of municipal temporary accommodation to these housing associations. This has happened more often in recent years, as has the practice that municipalities rent dwellings from housing organisations to use them for the temporary accommodation of homeless persons.

On the other hand police laws allow the confiscation of dwellings belonging to third persons to accommodate homeless persons. This occurs rather often in big cities in particular and especially affects social housing organisations. Usually households threatened by eviction are then reassigned to their own dwellings to prevent homelessness. In confiscating the dwelling the responsible local administration guarantees the owner rent payment as well as compensation for all costs caused by the use of the dwelling. The household reassigned to the flat is no longer considered as a tenant, its legal rights are severely restricted and it can be displaced at any time to another accommodation by administrative action. Usually a reassignment is limited to a fixed time, and after half a year at the latest the household has to leave the dwelling finally. But in some towns reassignment is possible for a longer time and is carried out in agreement with the housing organisation. The economic risk for housing organisations is reduced to almost nil as administrations guarantee the compensation for all costs.

Compared with other alternatives, reassignment to their own dwellings is often a good form of temporary accommodation for households threatened by eviction. It gives them time to look for alternative permanent housing without having to move to temporary housing first, they do not have to present a stigmatised address when looking for a new dwelling etc. However, reassignments mainly take place in big cities and rather seldom in smaller towns, though some cities do not apply them at all. Very often reassignments are only carried out in cases of families threatened by homelessness, whereas single persons are referred to existing forms of temporary accommodation. Finally, reassignment is considered by jurisdiction as *ultima ratio*, because a tenant is more or less forced on a landlord against his will. If a landlord refuses to accept this measure, it can only be kept up as far as the municipality proves definitely that no other form of temporary accommodation is available at the time. In cases like this local authorities have to provide other forms of temporary accommodation as soon as possible – even if this means putting up containers or making arrangements for a denser use of existing shelters.

Apart from measures of temporary accommodation under the police law there are other forms of temporary accommodation for which social administrations have come to an agreement with private providers or non-profit institutions in the voluntary sector and for which they assume the costs. These forms of accommodation are, firstly, mainly beds in hotels or pensions and, secondly, hostels for single homeless persons in the voluntary sector.

In particular in big cities hotel accommodation is important for the provision of homeless persons with temporary accommodation. In Berlin about 4,100 homeless households (predominantly single homeless persons) were accommodated in hotels or with other commercial landlords at the end of the second quarter of 1995 (Senatsverwaltung für Soziales Berlin, 1995). In Munich about 900 German households with more than 1,100 persons were accommodated in hotels in November 1994 (almost 90 per cent of them were one-person households, cf. Romaus, 1996, p. 5). In Hamburg there were still more than 2,000 homeless persons in hotels in March 1995: an effort of the municipality to reduce this expensive form of temporary accommodation brought the figure down to just under 1,400 persons in January 1996 (Hamburg, 1996, p. 8).

In hotels single bedsteads are often rented according to requirements and paid for by the number of night's lodgings. But there are also hotels which offer their whole capacity to municipalities for the accommodation of homeless people for which they receive a fixed monthly amount. In most cases the homeless are accommodated in rooms with more than one bed, but sometimes single bedrooms are used for temporary accommodation as well. The number of beds in rooms with more than one bed usually varies between two and six beds per hotel room. The standards of the hotel rooms vary considerably. There are common tourist hotels in which only single rooms are used for the accommodation of homeless persons, but more often hotels for the temporary accommodation of the homeless have very low standards. A survey on hotel accommodation of single homeless persons in Hamburg complains that facilities and hygienic conditions of the majority of rooms are disastrous. It reports damp walls, rotten and damaged windows, worn-out and soiled furniture and further about the dissemination of vermin (Mehnert, 1990, p. 63). In Berlin a popular expression for these hotels is 'louse pensions'. The length of stay in these pensions may be very long. In Munich the average length of stay of German homeless persons accommodated in pensions was found out to be two years and 11 months. Just under 45 per cent had stayed longer than two years in pensions (Romaus, 1996, p. 24, 25).

Hostels for single homeless persons in the voluntary sector are predominantly institutions which also offer support by social workers and which were mainly directed to so-called persons with an unsettled way of living in the past. As the strict distinction between single homeless persons who have become homeless at the place of relief and homeless persons who have changed places after their home loss has been increasingly questioned (like the definition of the term 'persons with an unsettled way of living') a growing number of institutions in the voluntary sector is open for all single homeless persons. Because of different responsibilities concerning the assumption of costs (administrations of the *Bundesländer* instead of municipal administrations are responsible for 'persons with an unsettled way of living') these distinctions are still necessary. The service providers for the homeless in the voluntary sector are in the vast majority members of the big welfare agencies of the Protestant and the Catholic church. Except for a minimal part which these providers have to bear, all costs for accommodation and assistance of the homeless in this sector are taken over by social administrations of municipalities or *Bundesländer*.

Hostels of voluntary providers can have fewer than 10 up to more than 200 beds. The number of beds per room varies enormously. In institutions with an approach of rehabilitation one- or two-bed rooms are more common, while dormitories with four or more beds prevail in hostels mainly for overnight and temporary stays (as a survey on the accommodation of single homeless persons in the *Bundesland* Baden-Württemberg shows, Käpple et al., 1993, pp. 109–44). Usually showers and toilets have to be shared. Often all meals are provided, but sometimes self-catering is possible.

There is no general survey on the local distribution and standards of the types of accommodation mentioned above. But it is possible to derive some indicators from several regional studies. They show that accommodation in dwellings with low standards under the police law prevails in smaller towns, whereas this form of accommodation is of minor importance in big cities. Accommodation in hostels and hotels is predominant there. In towns with more than 300,000 inhabitants in North Rhine-Westphalia, 56.6 per cent of all beds used for temporary accommodation belonged to these types of accommodation (Busch-Geertsema and Ruhstrat 1994a, p. 138), and in towns with more than 100,000 inhabitants in Hesse, 48 per cent of all beds for temporary accommodation (IWU, 1994, p. 45). At the same time it is obvious that the proportion of single homeless persons among the homeless in temporary accommodation is much greater in big cities than in smaller municipalities. It has already been pointed out that reassignment of households which are officially homeless into their own dwellings under police law is mainly practised in big cities: in towns in Hesse with more than 100,000 inhabitants no less than 17 per cent of all persons in temporary accommodation had been reassigned to their former dwellings (ibid.).

Considering the total capacities of accommodation used for the accommodation of non-immigrant homeless persons, we get the following picture about the density of accommodation: 43 per cent of all homeless persons are accommodated in rooms with three or more persons, every fifth household has to share a room with another household (Busch-Geertsema and Ruhstrat 1994a, p. 140).

The highest average standard of temporary accommodation of homeless people is usually to be found where normal housing is formally converted into temporary accommodation by reassignment. The lowest standard is found in short stay night shelters and in 'winter emergency projects' of big cities. For example the city of Hamburg provided 100 emergency beds in public shelters in the winter of 1995/1996 (50 of them were emergency beds on a ship) and 100 beds in containers erected on church property (Hamburg, 1996, p. 8).

The temporary accommodation of immigrants Temporary accommodation of immigrant refugees and *Aussiedler* is not principally different from temporary accommodation of non-immigrant homeless people, though in most cases these groups are accommodated separately. However, in general it is to be assumed that accommodation in shelters for immigrants is even more crowded, that makeshift shelters erected in times of especially high immigration figures are more common and that accommodation standards – in particular for immigrated refugees – are lower than for non-immigrant homeless (for example more beds per room, more people have to share kitchens and sanitary facilities, etc.). Reassignments are by definition ruled out and usually there are no hostels with more intensive care by social workers or pedagogues. But refugees are also accommodated in hotels. For example, 53.9 per cent of altogether about 2,500 persons in hotels in Munich were foreigners. Most of them were refugees with a – perhaps limited – right to stay. During their asylum procedures asylum seekers are usually accommodated temporarily in shelters.

Altogether 30 transitional hostels for foreign refugees in 10 towns were visited for a study in North Rhine-Westphalia (MAGS, 1994). The summarising report states:

> In providing accommodation and support of foreign refugees the different towns and municipalities are faced with great problems (lack of buildings, property, high organisational demands etc.). The ways in which municipalities deal with these problems vary. Refugees are accommodated in reconstructed old buildings

(former factories, office buildings, hotels, restaurants, schools, departmental stores, military barracks, shelters for the homeless, railway stations etc.), in houses built like containers, in railway wagons, sometimes also in new buildings. There is a wide range of standards of transitional hostels: from rotten, old, draughty and little suitable to live in to solid, acceptable and fit for human beings. The location of the transitional hostels that were visited is very different, but in most cases rather bad (in industrial areas, near railroad tracks, by big roads, motorways or in socially marginalised quarters of the town). Dependent on size and quality of the grounds they either look like ghettos or housing estates. The condition of the grounds is very different: it ranges from dull and neglected to clean, green, with playgrounds (MAGS, 1994, pp. 62–3).

In the following it is pointed out that in most cases there are no communal rooms and that the estates often have a repellent effect on the refugees themselves as well as on the people who look after them and on neighbours. Many transitional hostels are crowded (with 100–200 persons) and in a bad condition. Although it is often tried not to lodge more than four single persons in one room, there were transitional hostels in which 10 persons share one room under extremely crowded conditions. Families often share a room.

Other research reports are also critical that the building quality of rooms used for the temporary accommodation of asylum seekers and *Aussiedler* is often not adequate to climatic conditions and the number of people living in the rooms. This results in dampness, mouldiness and excessive wear. Often many rooms (in particular toilets, showers and kitchens) have to be shared by many households. These shelters were often clearly separated from other housing estates and difficult to reach. This enforced discriminations and stigmatisations which anyhow afflicted immigrant homeless people because of their social situation. 'Particular aggravations result from the lack of most essentials of what is considered as "having a home" in our society. A close individual or familiar sphere in which everything is possible which belongs to housekeeping' (Weeber and Partner, 1991, p. 272).

In most shelters where asylum seekers are accommodated after their allocation to municipalities, the immigrants receive communal feeding or food vouchers and only little pocket money. These shelters are often provided by municipalities, or municipalities order (municipal) housing organisations to provide shelters. If there is any assistance for the people in the shelters at all, in most cases voluntary organisations look after the shelters and provide the meals. But there are also initiatives by commercial service providers who offer, for example, a combination of accommodation, meals and assistance. The city of Bremen, for example, has rented a ship for five years to accommodate 400 asylum seekers, who are lodged in two-bed cabins. The commercial provider receives a monthly lump sum as a rent which is independent from the actual number of asylum seekers lodged on the ship. Many other cities, like for example Hamburg and Köln, also use ships to accommodate asylum seekers. Especially repellent and inhumane provisional shelters were used in the past for the temporary accommodation of asylum seekers. In Bremen, for example, refugees were accommodated in air-raid shelters without windows for some time, and in Hanover more than 1,700 refugees were accommodated in tents in July 1992 (cf. Heller et al., 1993, p. 153).

There are similarities between the temporary accommodation of *Aussiedler* and the temporary accommodation of refugees. But we must keep in mind that in Germany *Aussiedler* have a completely different status from foreign immigrants. The immigration of *Aussiedler* is politically accepted, though limited in quantity. A more positive attitude of politics and administration towards this group of immigrants often becomes obvious in better standards of the buildings used for temporary accommodation. *Aussiedler* are German citizens and have the chance to provide themselves with permanent housing from the first day of their stay in Germany. They are entitled to social housing and as a special target group they even enjoy priority in the allocation of social housing. Though in the course of a more restrictive immigration policy some benefits of the past have been abolished for *Aussiedler* as well (integrative measures like languages courses, cheap state loans for furnishing and several special social benefits for *Aussiedler*), they have not been excluded from regular benefits of the German social system – in contrast with asylum seekers. But for *Aussiedler* it is also difficult to find permanent normal housing after their arrival in Germany. Usually their incomes are low, after their arrival they have problems with the German language and they are affected by the scarce supply of social housing. An inquiry among *Aussiedler* in 1992 revealed that only 10.6 per cent were able to move into permanent housing without having to use some form of provisional accommodation first. Most of them (44.5 per cent) were accommodated in hostels first, others (in order of frequency) in hotels, in flats rented for temporary accommodation, in gymnasiums, containers, camps, youth hostels and schools. Just 0.9 per cent were accommodated by relatives immediately after their arrival. More than half of all *Aussiedler* had to change temporary accommodation at least twice before they were able to rent a dwelling. More than one third of the *Aussiedler* households questioned in transitional hostels and other forms of emergency accommodation had lived there longer than two years at the time of the inquiry in 1992. On the other hand, about half of those who were able to provide themselves with permanent housing managed to find a dwelling within six months after they had started to look for a flat (Heller et al., 1993, pp. 56–8).

Positive examples of temporary accommodation of Aussiedler: how an integration of homeless persons is possible The immigration of *Aussiedler* provides some interesting positive examples of temporary accommodation and of an active policy of the integration of households in temporary accommodation into the permanent housing provision.

In several *Bundesländer* there were model projects in which *Aussiedler* were accommodated temporarily in flats which were built quickly and at low prices according to the standards of social housing. It was realised that provisional buildings – like, for example, container estates or wooden shacks – are of short durability and are on the whole expensive because of high operating costs and high wear. In addition, their isolated location, their outer appearance as special institutions like camps and the crowded, enforced communal form of accommodation often infringe upon human dignity. So some *Bundesländer* and municipalities supported the construction of normal houses with long-term usability instead of provisional buildings for temporary accommodation. In these normal houses, however, more people than usual were accommodated for some time. There is a long list of positive examples (cf. Weeber and Partner, 1991, pp. 129 ff.; Großhans, 1996). They range from the construction of prefabricated houses with the purpose of temporary accommodation of *Aussiedler* (cf. Ruhstrat, 1989) over housing construction schemes with extra quotas for *Aussiedler* to so-called two-stage models, in which houses are firstly built as *Aussiedler* hostels for a limited time, but are to be developed into social housing in a second construction stage, as was already intended in the original planning. There are important advantages in the temporary use of new buildings of social housing for the provisional accommodation of *Aussiedler*. On the one hand an acute need for temporary accommodation may be satisfied, and on the other, the provision of permanent housing for the population can be improved by building normal houses which are needed in the long term. When the acute pressure of accommodating homeless persons on a temporary basis eases off, the houses may be used for the provision of permanent housing. Ideally, some of the *Aussiedler* who have been accommodated temporarily in houses like this may even go on living there permanently. New buildings of this sort are also much easier to integrate into residential areas with a good infrastructure than, for example, estates of shacks or containers, and therefore enhance their residents' chances of social integration. The construction of these houses, which are used for the temporary accommodation of immigrants for a limited time, takes a little longer than the erection of container camps or shacks, though the preparations for the construction of such provisional low-standard shelters may also take a long time due to necessary authorising procedures and poor acceptance of camps like these by the local population – at least in Germany.

However, normal houses can be used for a much longer time, their practical value is much higher, and on a long-term basis, they are considerably cheaper.

Until 1990 measures like these could be financed by a special loan scheme of the federal government, if they served the temporary accommodation of *Aussiedler* (or of households from the former GDR which had moved to West Germany).

Another point in this context is construction schemes aiming at the permanent provision of normal housing for *Aussiedler*. At the end of the 1980s a scheme like this was launched by the federal government (Eekhoff and Hamm, 1989), but it was given up later in the course of efforts at public consolidation.

Assistance

As to the assistance of homeless persons in temporary accommodation, only few general statements are possible. Institutions of voluntary organisations directed to certain target groups of the homeless (like 'persons with an unsettled way of living', ex-offenders or battered women) have relatively high ratios of social workers. Overnight shelters with rooms with more than one bed need more personnel – though not necessarily social workers – to guarantee 24-hour management and because conflicts between clients are much more common than in individual forms of temporary accommodation. Homeless persons who are accommodated in hotels are often expected to call on advice centres of municipalities or voluntary providers if they need support. In municipal estates for the homeless, assistance is provided partly by general municipal social services, but there are municipalities which finance the assistance of homeless households offered by social workers from voluntary organisations. Often there are special measures to support children and young people from homeless families (day homes for school children, remedial classes, etc.).

In the sector of temporary accommodation for asylum seekers the provision of assistance is often much restricted. But there are great local differences. While for example the city of Bremen has a ratio of 2.5 caring personnel to

100 refugees in temporary accommodation (Heintze and Plücker, 1995, p. 14), there are ratios ranging from one per 60 to one per 500 refugees in North Rhine-Westphalia (MAGS, 1994, p. 86). The caring personnel are often almost fully occupied with administrative work, sometimes also with caretaker chores, so there is only very little time left for talking to clients and offering useful assistance.

Costs of Temporary Accommodation

It is almost commonplace to point out that prevention of homelessness is cheaper than the provision of homeless households with temporary accommodation and the staff necessary to run such accommodation. There are different examples of calculations: for example, the city of Cologne compared the costs between measures for the prevention of home losses and measures of temporary accommodation for the homeless in 1986 and recognised that temporary accommodation costs about seven times as much as the necessary means for securing dwellings (especially for assumption of rent arrears) (DST, 1987, appendix 1). A similar calculation for the town Leipzig led to the result of a ratio of 1:4. The difference is also dependent on the forms of temporary accommodation and on the duration of stay of the homeless in them. If a household has to be accommodated temporarily in a hotel because it was evicted from its dwelling due to rent arrears, and if it stays there for one year because it cannot find a new permanent dwelling as a consequence of its existing rent arrears, the costs of temporary accommodation may amount to 20 or 30 times as much as an assumption of rent arrears would have cost. In cases of temporary accommodation of homeless persons in hostels of voluntary organisations where social assistance is provided the results are similar (cf. Busch-Geertsema and Ruhstrat ,1994b, pp. 39–51).

However, it is not always possible to avoid homelessness by maintaining prior homes. In particular in the case of immigrants this is impossible. But costs for temporary accommodation may also be very different.

A study on 'Provisional and graduated solutions' concerning the temporary accommodation of homeless persons (Weeber and Partner, 1991) has proved that apparently 'cheap' provisional solutions like shacks or containers erected by many municipalities for the temporary accommodation of refugees often, under an extreme time pressure, turn out to be very expensive when balanced economically. These provisional buildings were often erected on public premises which were to be used otherwise in the near future (for example for the construction of a street or for the development of industrial areas). The difficult problem of finding premises is solved this way, but in many cases the development of the property creates high costs, because it was not meant to be used for housing. Usually the service life of shacks and containers is very short, so their depreciation creates high annual costs. One examination discovered, for example, that containers used for the temporary accommodation of asylum seekers showed considerable wear after just four years (rust, seeping-in of rainwater etc.). Often provisional solutions like these are offered by commercial providers to municipalities, and the rent for them already contains the costs of depreciation (and because of the great demand by municipalities and the dominant position of single providers on the market a high profit rate). One example of a calculation from 1990 showed a monthly cost-induced rent (containing rent and municipal costs for the development) of 16.40 ECU per square metre for a two-storey container camp with 48 beds. As the insulation of shacks and containers is very bad, costs for heating in particular are extremely high. Compared with normal housing used for the temporary accommodation of immigrants, the costs for heating and hot water in containers and shacks amounted to five to nine times as much (Weeber and Partner, 1991, p. 108). Other provisional solutions often cause unexpectedly high costs as well because the buildings are not designed for housing. In Münster, for example, the costs for providing temporary accommodation in caravans came to more than 1,000 DM (about 530 ECU) per bed and month in 1993, because expensive sanitary containers had to be erected. The costs for landing places of ships used for temporary accommodation often amount to several hundred thousands ECU (Busch-Geertsema and Ruhstrat, 1994b, p. 34).

The efforts of municipalities to save costs when erecting shelters for immigrants by choosing cheap constructions and low standards have often turned out to be contra-productive when durability and maintenance costs have been taken into account. The option to provide only few sanitary and cooking facilities for many rooms is very problematic for the inhabitants. Under certain circumstances it seems to be justifiable to save costs by reducing the living space per person (compared with the living space in normal housing) and by using newly-constructed houses as an interim measure. The use of existing and vacant buildings as hostels for the homeless for a limited time is sometimes also justifiable (Weeber and Partner, 1991, pp. 275–7). So a higher degree of 'normality' in temporary accommodation for the homeless may actually be cheaper. This is also true for the temporary accommodation of non-immigrant homeless people. The reassignment of an evicted household into its prior dwelling creates just a fraction of the costs incurred by its temporary accommodation in an estate for the homeless. Provision and maintenance of concentrated temporary accommodation in estates for the homeless is often more expensive than decentralised accommodation in flats rented for temporary accommodation. The indispensable 24-hour management of temporary accommodation in rooms with a greater number of beds (which is necessary if only to settle conflicts that inevitably arise) swallows up more money than can be saved by dispensing with more individual forms of accommodation (cf. Busch-Geertsema and Ruhstrat, 1994b).

Because of their high personnel costs, voluntary organisations' hostels which offer assistance by social workers are often extremely expensive. The costs per day and person are between 40–70 ECU (that is about 1,220–2,130 ECU a month for one bed). Temporary accommodation in hotel rooms also costs a lot of money. The city of Hamburg alone still spent more than 8.5 million ECU for the temporary accommodation of homeless persons in hotels in 1995 (Hamburg, 1996, p. 8; author's calculations). Even for so-called cheap hotels, prices of between 16–30 ECU (and often more) per night and bed (without the costs of assistance) are common in many bigger towns (so a bed in a hotel room with more than one bed may easily amount to more than 910 ECU a month). In contrast to that, in the sector of normal housing in big cities departments of social services accept a monthly rent up to the maximum limit of about 265–320 ECU for a one-person flat.

The city of Cologne has made a survey of all of its forms of temporary accommodation and has come to the conclusion that accommodation in hotels and the erection of containers is much more expensive for the city than providing social housing for the same target group through municipal subsidies. Even a so-called rent model, which means that the city encourages private investors to build rented housing by renting it for a lump sum for the temporary accommodation of homeless persons and guaranteeing a relatively high rent for 10 years, is cheaper than some of the frequently used measures of temporary accommodation of the homeless (cf. Schleicher, 1996).

It is not possible to assess the costs and subsequent costs caused by the effects of living in low-standard shelters, of segregation and social marginalisation on homeless households, which reduce their chances of a normal life. But certainly indispensable measures caused by low-standard accommodation (ranging from the expensive redevelopment of shelters to special measures for children and young people in temporary accommodation and therapeutic and police intervention) add up to the direct costs of temporary accommodation.

(1 DM = 0.53 ECU)

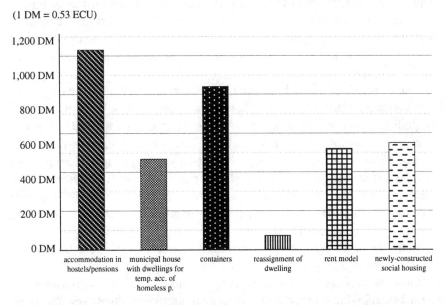

Figure 21.4 Costs of accommodation: comparison of costs between emergency accommodation schemes and schemes for the construction of new housing in the City of Cologne (monthly costs of accommodation per person)

How Temporary is Temporary Accommodation?

The Longevity of Provisional Solutions

Unfortunately many measures planned as temporary accommodation for homeless persons up to the time of their reintegration into normal permanent housing turn out to be long-term forms of accommodation which do not facilitate integration into normal housing, but, rather, hamper it severely. The consequence is a long-term exclusion of homeless people from the housing market. In many estates for the homeless the frequency of removals is lower than the average frequency of removals within normal housing. In other sectors of temporary accommodation there is a high fluctuation, but it is at least partly caused by frequent changes, especially of single homeless people, between different types of temporary accommodation which do not lead to their provision with permanent housing. Administrative measures also enforce a mobility of households in temporary accommodation within the system of temporary accommodation. One example is night shelters for so-called passers-by (with a limit on stay). But in the sector of temporary accommodation for *Aussiedler* there are also complaints about frequent changes enforced by administrations.

The example of Munich, which has been mentioned above, has shown a high average duration of stay of homeless people in hotels. In Schleswig-Holstein the average duration of stay was ascertained for 5,000 places of temporary accommodation. For more than 60 per cent of these places the average duration of stay was longer than two years. Though a longitudinal study as a basis for a methodically better research on 'the dynamics' of temporary accommodation does not exist, there are clear signs of a high percentage of long-term homeless persons who are not able to leave the system of temporary accommodation.

In the sector of temporary accommodation of *Aussiedler*, the duration of stay is often very long as well, at least for a proportion of them. While one section of the *Aussiedler* is successful in providing themselves with permanent accommodation fairly quickly, the average duration of stay of *Aussiedler* living in transitory hostels in 1992 who were questioned was about 15 months. About 60 per cent of these had been there for less than one year, but more than 30 per cent had been there for one to three years, and almost 10 per cent for longer than three years (Heller et al., 1993, p. 80).

As was to be expected, the duration of stay in temporary accommodation also depends on housing market supply. At the beginning of the 1990s *Aussiedler* had more problems in finding permanent housing than before, because certain special support schemes for this group had been abolished and because the mismatch between demand and supply of social housing was especially obvious. Since the middle of 1990s it has been reported from some German cities that the housing provision for *Aussiedler* has clearly increased again.

Asylum seekers are often at a disadvantage compared with *Aussiedler*. While *Aussiedler* are able to promote their integration from the first day of their stay, asylum seekers – if they may stay at all – depend on temporary accommodation in shelters for a very long time, if only because of the long duration of their asylum procedures. Only when these procedures have been brought to a successful close or when the asylum seekers have received a long-term residence permit (*Duldung*) are they allowed to look for permanent housing, and even then they belong to the group of homeless people which is most severely discriminated against.

Social Effects of Enforced Communal Accommodation

To sum up, it can be said that temporary accommodation of homeless persons has several negative sides compared with normal housing provision. It is temporary by definition, though this does not mean that it cannot last for years. In any case, homeless persons in temporary accommodation have no right to stay permanently in their current dwelling or shelter. Their private sphere is much restricted. Small households in particular, but many family households in temporary accommodation as well, mostly have no possibility of independent housekeeping. They have to form enforced communities with other people they have not chosen, and it is obvious that conflicts must arise from this situation (see also Specht, 1994, 1992).

In shelters for asylum seekers conditions are especially extreme. Asylum seekers are often allocated to these lodgings without any consideration of their countries of origin, their ethnic backgrounds and the size of their households. So, very often people of the most different cultural conditioning and in completely different personal and familial situations have to share cramped quarters: people from Europe, Asia, Africa, America, women as well as men, from newborn babies to old people, singles, couples and families. They speak different languages, belong to different religions and have different political views. Their level of education may range from illiteracy to academic grades. Living together is often difficult and charged with conflicts, all the more as most refugees have to struggle with special strains caused by the reasons for their flight, the loss of their homes and the insecurity of their future lives. Children and young people in the shelters grow up under difficult conditions. Within the families difficult conflicts may occur as well. This extreme situation, and the often bad physical and psychic state of health of refugees, hampers initiative and self-organisation necessary for the management of present problems.

But enforced communal accommodation is a great problem for non-immigrant homeless people as well. A considerable part of those single homeless people who live in the streets and refuse the offers of temporary accommodation by municipalities and voluntary organisations act like this, because for them the conflicts in night shelters, frequent thefts, unrest and the total lack of privacy are just unbearable.

Reintegration of Homeless People into Normal Housing

There are various problems for homeless people in temporary accommodation to find normal permanent housing. Finding a dwelling with private landlords often fails because of the high amount of rents which are demanded. The barriers in the housing market, however, are not only of an economic nature, but are often socially founded: the criteria of a landlord choosing a tenant are determined by his interest in long-term tenancies, in regular and punctual rent payments, in a careful use of the flat and in avoiding conflicts among his tenants or within the neighbourhood. If it is doubtful whether an applicant for a dwelling matches these criteria, his chances of success are low as against other competitors. Basically, the same is the case with providers of social housing. Surveys show that, for example, foreigners meet with great reservations (Osenberg, 1991). This is also true for homeless people, especially when they have been affected by action for eviction before, when they have debts or when they are identifiable as homeless by their addresses. Homeless persons are often generalised as having problems and lacking social adaptability.

Therefore these groups are dependent on further state support in the provision of housing, which goes beyond influencing rent prices. The right of municipalities to make suggestions for the allocation of dwellings is especially important in this context. A right to make suggestions concerning the allocation has existed mainly in the sector of social housing. As social obligations – including this right – have considerably expired, the municipal influence in allocating housing is on the decrease. Additionally, municipal housing departments often refuse to accept consistent preferential treatment of homeless people, because they fear a spatial concentration of 'problematic cases' in the remaining supply of social housing. Finally, a proportion of the homeless is labelled as 'not capable to cope in normal housing' and in this way excluded from the provision with normal housing. Another aspect is the fact that a considerable part of homeless people are single, while social housing used to be directed to families. So providing single homeless people with permanent housing is particularly difficult.

The chances of homeless people being provided with normal housing might be improved by gaining concessions to allocate tenants as well as by contractual agreements with landlords (for example with the aim of allocating a certain rate of dwellings to homeless people in temporary accommodation). Finally, municipalities can remove risks which landlords might fear by giving guarantees, e. g. for rent payments, but, if necessary, through ensuring social assistance for tenants by social workers as well. In general sufficient advantage is not taken of these possible measures in Germany.

There has been a series of schemes for *Aussiedler* in the sector of normal permanent housing (some of them have been mentioned above) which show that the integration of a very high number of immigrants from temporary accommodation into normal housing is possible if it is politically willed. The concession of legal priority in the provision of social housing for *Aussiedler* belongs to them (for a long time the introduction of a corresponding priority for all homeless people into the German Housing Construction Law has been demanded) as well as housing construction schemes directed to *Aussiedler* and the promotion of the acquisition of housing property by *Aussiedler* households. Measures aiming at the provision of permanent housing for other homeless households have only been discussed seriously in recent years (at the moment the federal government supports a model scheme with seven model projects for permanent housing provision for homeless people; a research programme to analyse cooperation agreements between municipalities, voluntary organisations and housing business for a better housing provision of emergency cases has just been resumed). In this context it has become clear that new forms of assistance and support by social work are necessary to include homeless people with social problems into a permanent provision with normal housing.

Concluding Remarks

Temporary accommodation is often expensive, leads to a long-term exclusion of homeless people from provision with normal permanent housing and has negative effects on the social situation of the homeless people.

It is therefore important to strive for a maximal provision of homeless people with normal permanent housing (whether they have become homeless at the place of relief or not). At least in Germany it is not an extension of provisional shelters which is needed. Instead, the sector of temporary accommodation should be reduced and expensive institutions of temporary accommodation should gradually be removed. What is needed is more normal permanent housing which is affordable and available for persons living in temporary accommodation. For this purpose, municipalities must have more influence on the allocation of flats (concerning the existing supply of housing as well as the subsidy of construction of new housing). The provision of assistance by social workers should be clearly extended for (formerly homeless) people in permanent housing, if they need it.

However, provisions for the temporary accommodation of homeless people will never be completely dispensable. As long as temporary accommodation is necessary, every effort should be made to keep it temporary; that means permanent housing should be provided as soon as possible. Certain minimal standards for temporary accommodation must be observed: the shelters should enable a minimum of privacy, an enforced communal use of rooms (bedrooms, sanitary and kitchen facilities) by persons who are neither relatives nor friends should be avoided. Institutions for the temporary accommodation of homeless people should be integrated into normal residential areas and should be within easy reach if possible. Most suitable are decentralised forms of temporary accommodation like rented flats of normal housing. Construction schemes providing housing with normal standards which is used as an interim measure for temporary accommodation are the most reasonable solution and, on a long-term basis, cheaper than apparently fast and cheap provisions with high subsequent costs. Positive examples for this have been mentioned. Nevertheless, whenever it is possible, impending homelessness should be avoided by taking preventive measures, and an appropriate housing construction planning and subsidy should ensure a sufficient provision or normal housing for the population (including the expected number of immigrants).

Bibliography

Bartholmai, B. (1994), 'Bevölkerungsentwicklung und Einkommensverteilung – Auswirkungen auf den Wohnungsbau', *Wohnungswirtschaft und Mietrecht*, 11.
BMBAU, Bundesminsisterium für Raumordnung, Bauwesen und Staedtebau (1996), *Wohngeld und Mietenbericht 1995*, Bonn.
BMI, Bundesminnisterium des Innern (1996), 'Auslaendische Flüchtlinge in der Bundesrepublik Deutschland,' unpublished paper, Bonn
Bucher, H., Kocks, M. and Siedhoff, M. (1994), 'Die künftige Bevölkerungsentwicklung in den Regionen Deutschlands bis 2010', Annahmen und Ergebnisse einer BfLR-Bevölkerungsprognose in Bundesforschungsanstalt für Landeskunde und Raumordnung (ed.), *Informationen zur Raumentwicklung*, 12, pp. 815–52.
Busch-Geertsema, V. (1995), *Insecurity of Tenure and Prevention of Homelessness in Germany*, National Report 1995 for the European Observatory on Homelessness, Brussels, FEANTSA.
Busch-Geertsema, V. and Ruhstrat, E.-U. (1994a) (eds), *Wohnungsnotfaelle. Sicherung der Wohnungsversorgung für wirtschaftlich oder sozial benachteiligte Haushalte*, Bonn, Bundesministerium für Raumordnung, Bauwesen und Staedtebau and Bundesministerium für Familie und Senioren.
Busch-Geertsema, V. and Ruhstrat, E.-U. (1994b) (eds), *Wirkungsanalyse wohnungs- und sozialpolitischer Maßnahmen zur Sicherung der Wohnungsversorgungsozial und*

wirtschaftlich benachteiligter Haushalte, Bremen and Bonn, Bundesministerium für Raumordnung, Bauwesen und Staedtebau for the Commission of Experts on Housing Policy.

DST, Deutscher Staedtetag (1987), *Sicherung der Wohnungsversorgung in Wohnungsnotfaellen und Verbesserung der Lebensbedingungen in sozialen Brennpunkten*, Düsseldorf.

Eekhoff, J. and Hamm, H.(1989), 'Das Aussiedlerwohnungsprogramm 1989', *Der langfristige Kresit*, 40. no. 1.

Evers, J. and Ruhstrat, E.-U. (1994), *Wohnungsnotfaelle in Schleswig-Holstein. Im Spannungsfeld zwischen Sozial-, Ordnungs- und Wohnungspolitik*, Ministerium für Arbeit, Soziales, Jugend und Gersundheit des Landes Schleswig-Holstein und Diakonisches Werk Schleswig-Holstein (ed.) Kiel,

Fleischer, H. and Sommer, B. (1995), 'Bevölkerungsentwicklung 1994', *Wirtschaft und Statistik*, 12.

Goeddecke-Stellmann, J. (1994), 'Raeumliche Implikationen der Zuwanderung von Aussiedlern und Auslaendern', *Informationen zur Raumentwicklung*, Heft 5/6.

Großhans, H. (1996), 'Wohnungsunternehmen und ihre Rolle bei der Wohnungsversorgung Benachteiligter' in Specht-Kittler, T. (ed.), *Wohnungswirtschaft und Wohlfahrtspflege* (Materialien zur Wohnungslosenhilfe, 29), Bielefeld.

Guttmann, E. (1995), 'Zur Entwicklung des Wohnungsbaus in Deutschland in der ersten Haelfte der neunziger Jahre', *Wirtschaft und Statistik*, 5.

Hamburg, F., Hamburg, H. and Arbeitsgemeinschaft der Freien Wohlfahrtspflege Hamburg e.V.(eds) (1996), *Obdachlose, 'auf der Straße' lebende Menschen in Hamburg*, Hamburg.

Heller, W., Felgentreff, C., Kramp,E., Rolirad, T. and Seitz, C. (1993), *Integration von Aussiedlern und anderen Zuwanderen in den deutschen Wohnungsmarkt*, Bundesministerium für Raumordnung (ed.), Bonn, Bauwesen und Staedtebau.

IWU, Institut fuer Wohnen und Umwelt (ed.) (1994), *Wohnungsnotfaelle in Hessen. Problembeschreibung und Erfahrungen mit Konzepten zur dauerhaften Wohnungsversorgung* (Dilcher, R., Schaefer, H., Schuler-Wallner, G. and Ulbrich, R.), Darmstadt.

Knäpple, A., Rümmele, A., Goll, E. and Nette-Hauber, G. (1993), *Fortschreibung der Kommunalen Konzeption zur Hilfe für alleinstehende Wohnungslose (Nichtseßhafte) in Baden-Württemberg*, on behalf of Landeswohlfahrtsverbaende Baden und Württemberg Hohenzollern, Stuttgart.

Koch, F., Hard, G. and Tristram, P. (1993), *Landessozialbericht, Band 2: Wohnungsnot und Obdachlosigkeit, Soziale Folgeprobleme und Entwicklungstendenzen*, Ministerium für Arbeit (ed.), Gesundheit und Soziales des Landes Nordrhein-Westfalen.

Landesamt für Datenverarbeitung und Statistik Nordrhein-Westfalen (different years) *Statistische Berichte. Die Obdachlosigkeit in Nordrhein-Westfalen*, Düsseldorf.

MAGS, Ministerium für Arbeit, Gesundheit und Soziales des Landes Nordrhein-Westfalen (ed.) (1994), *Unterbringung von Flüchtlingen in Nachbarschaft zu Einheimischen*, Düsseldorf, Forschungsgruppe Kommunikation und Sozialanalysen GmbH.

Mehnert, J. (1990), *Hotel- und Pensionsunterbringungen von alleinlebenden Wohnungslosen in Hamburg - Umfang, Lebensbedingungen*, Handlungsansaetze, Hamburg.

Osenberg, H. (1991), *Auf Sozialwohnungen angewiesen. Die Bedeutung der Vermittlung von Sozialmietwohnungen durch das Wohnungsamt für Bevölkerungsgruppen mit besonderen Problemen am Wohnungsmarkt*, Bundesministerium für Raumordnung (ed.), Bauwesen und Staedtebau, Bonn.

Romaus, R. (1996), *Obdachlose in Münchner Pensionen*, Landeshauptstadt München, Sozialreferat (ed.) München.

Ruhstrat, E.-U. (1989), 'Warum billig, wenn es auch teuer geht?' in *Gefaehrdetenhilfe*, 1.

Schleicher, M. (1996), 'Kommunen als Akteure am Wohnungsmarkt zwischen freier Wohl-fahrtspflege und Wohnungsunternehmen' in Specht-Kittler, T. (ed.), *Wohnungswirtschaft und Wohlfahrtspflege* (Materialien zur Wohnungslosenhilfe, 29), Bielefeld.

Senatsverwaltung für Soziales Berlin (1995), 'Wohnungslose Haushaltstypen nach Haushalts-typen und Ort der Unterbringung am Ende des 2. Quartals 1995', unpublished, Berlin.

Specht-Kittler, T. (1992), 'Obdachlosigkeit in der Bundesrepublik Deutschland', *Aus Politik und Zeitgeschichte. Beilage zur Wochenzeitung Das Parlament*, 27 November.

Specht-Kittler, T. (1994), *Housing poverty in a rich Society: Houselessness and unacceptable housing conditions in Germany*, National Report for the European Observatory on Homeless-ness 1994, Brussels, FEANTSA.

Specht-Kittler, T. (ed.) (1996), *Wohnungswirtschaft und Wohlfahrtspflege* (Materialien zur Woh-nungslosenhilfe, 29), Bielefeld.

Statistisches Bundesamt (1995), *Fachserie 1, Bevölkerung und Erwerbstaetigkeit, Reihe 2, Auslaender 1994*, Wiesbaden.

Ulbrich, R. (1991), 'Wohnungsmarktsituationin den westlichen Bundeslaendern', *Wohnungswirtschaft und Mietrecht*, 5.

von Aken, J.C. and Derleder, P. (1998), 'Rechtliche Aspekte und Rahmenbedingungen im Zusammenhang mit der Wohnungsnotfallproblematik' in Busch-Geertsema, V. and Ruhstrat (eds), E.-U., *Wohnungsnotfaelle. Sicherung der Wohnungsversorgung für wirtschaftlich oder sozial benachteiligte Haushalte*, Bonn, Bundesministerium für Raumordnung, Bauwesen und Staedtebau and Bundesministerium für Familie und Senioren.

Veith, K. (1994), 'Überlegungen zur Zuwanderung am Beispiel Aussiedler', *Informationen zur Raumentwicklung*, Heft 5/6.

Voit, H. (1996), 'Entwicklung der Privathaushalte bis 2015', *Wirtschaft und Statistik*, 2.

Weeber, H., Weeber, R., Hasemaier, M. and Ruoff H. (1991), *Wohnungsengpässe: Provisorien und Stufenlösungen*, Stuttgart.

22 Urgent Accommodation Shelters for Homeless People in Greece: Who Provides Services and Who Uses Them?

ARISTIDES SAPOUNAKIS

Introduction

Homelessness and Greek Society

In Greece, as indeed in other Mediterranean countries, homelessness as a social problem has become apparent quite recently. The phenomenon of homeless people wandering around or sleeping in the streets in big cities is fairly new. The general public is not familiar with it and tends to believe that homelessness does not exist in Greece or at least that it is not a social problem with significant dimensions that is worth taking seriously. In fact, up until recently, such attitudes were expressed even by government officials responsible for social welfare. It is only in the last few years that homelessness has escalated, due, to a great extent, to the influx of large numbers of immigrants mainly from Albania, the countries of southeastern Europe and the Middle East. The issue has, therefore, only recently been acknowledged and attracted attention and publicity, while any attempts to address its present form and extent through service provision, remain as yet, insufficient and fragmentary.

Despite the recent sensitisation of state officials and public opinion, no institute, NGO or even public authority in Greece, deals with homeless people as a special group. Although the Greek Constitution states that the provision of accommodation to people who are homeless or housed in unsuitable conditions constitutes a special task for the state and a legal framework for the provision of social housing to people of low income does exist, there is no statutory obligation of local authorities or central government to provide accommodation and support to any individuals or social groups defined as 'vulnerable'.

Greece has generally followed the pattern of other southern European countries in that social welfare – housing being an important aspect of it – has tended to be primarily a responsibility of the family rather than the state. In other words, family solidarity has been filling the gaps left by insufficient welfare provision. It is therefore a widespread and acceptable feature of the Greek society that accommodation problems are dealt with within families and reliance on services is usually a last resort for those who lack family support.

This picture, however, has somewhat changed in recent years. The massive rise in immigration has had a strong impact on Greek society and especially on the labour and the housing market. The number of Greek-origin people that repatriated following the collapse of the socialist regime in the ex-USSR has escalated to over 60,000, which generated the necessity for special measures and programmes to be introduced to address their immediate housing and other needs. At the same time, there has been a huge increase in the inflow of – mainly illegal – labour force from countries of southeastern Europe and the Middle East. The majority of these economic refugees come from neighbouring Albania. Their exact number is difficult to specify the records of the Ministry of Public Order – according to which nearly 220,000 Albanians were deported to Albania in 1993, while in 1994 the number reached 250,000 – give some indication of the extent of the problem. The Greek government distinguishes between illegal Albanian immigrants and Greek repatriates from Northern Epirus (i.e. Southern Albania), who are of Greek origin, orthodox and speak Greek, towards whom they are more sympathetic. The Ministry of Foreign Affairs reports that, in total, there are 500,000–600,000 illegal labour immigrants in Greece today. The presence of these social groups – primarily individuals without family support or whole families in great financial and housing need – has reshaped radically the employment scene in Greece. At the same time, it has exerted a great amount of additional pressure on the already fragile market of cheap housing.

As poverty and unemployment figures have become more gruesome, the housing conditions of sizeable portions of the population have been deteriorating. As far as rented accommodation is concerned, the rise in unemployment and rent prices makes it increasingly difficult for many tenants to keep their homes or even find suitable, cheaper accommodation. The threat – or reality – of homelessness and substandard housing is becoming increasingly pressing. As a result, the need for effective services to address the needs of homeless people, is becoming more and more evident.

State intervention into housing in Greece has always remained too modest to cope effectively with the level of need. Housing loans on favourable terms as well as a number of benefits are available only to social groups that meet specific criteria relating to status and employment record, and who are not necessarily the most needy. As housing integration is an important component, if not a prerequisite, for wider social integration, a growing portion of the population tends to become socially excluded. In most cases homelessness is paired with inability to work either due to individual circumstances or as a result of high unemployment affecting particularly certain groups – e.g. young ex-offenders or care-leavers, people aged 55–65, those suffering from chronic diseases etc., people who have just come out of an institution whether prison, reform school or mental hospital, etc. Such vulnerable social groups find it particularly difficult to cross the bridge towards integration and are forced into poverty and social exclusion as a result.

There is some vagueness surrounding the very definition of 'homelessness', partly due to the fact that the Greek word for 'homeless' means literally 'roofless' (*astegos* as opposed to *aspitos*, which is not a term generally used). The term seems to refer to the group of people we would normally call 'street homeless'. It reflects a narrow definition and understanding of homelessness – endorsed by many – which overshadows the fact that large numbers of people have no access to secure accommodation that is appropriate to their needs, despite the fact that they do not actually sleep on the streets. For the purposes of this chapter we shall define the homeless population as 'people who are excluded from decent, appropriate housing either of their own or in the form of a tenancy'.

From the point of view of services for homeless people, Albanian and other economic refugees and nomads, cannot be regarded as homeless, insofar as they have 'put themselves into this situation', either by leaving their homes in order to seek better economic gains elsewhere, or by choosing a particular lifestyle. Moreover, foreign labour is not always economically excluded from the housing and rental market, but rather they themselves are often reluctant to spend the money they earn on rent so that at the end of the day they can save and export it to their homeland. Nevertheless, their case needs to be mentioned as, in recent years, they have had a strong impact on the housing market, especially insofar as low-cost rented accommodation is concerned, as well as because they share the housing problems of the rest of the homeless population in Greece.

Social Housing Provision in Greece

Provision of housing for the poor in Greece, has been minimal. The Workers' Housing Association (OEK) has a construction programme of ready-made dwellings that are distributed to its beneficiaries via a lottery system. OEK beneficiaries may enjoy the privilege either of acquiring a house through this system or of being offered a subsidised housing loan in order to buy, refurbish or construct the house they wish, provided they are first-time buyers. A rent subsidy scheme has recently been introduced and constitutes an important measure against insecurity of tenure for nearly a tenth of OEK beneficiaries (20,000 out of 200,000) who are eligible for it. Despite its limitations, OEK offers an important service to its beneficiaries, who are normally low-income employees with a more or less consistent working record. It is not, however, in any way connected to services for homeless people and is not, in effect, concerned with the poorest section of the population. It is important to note that there is no rental sector of public housing in Greece.

The Welfare Section of the Department of Health, Welfare and Social Security which, in the past, has had a sizeable output of social housing activity – such as provision of ready-made dwellings and favourable loans for construction of houses – has, in recent years, limited its activity to providing assistance to the disaster-stricken and welfare benefits to those in need. It is interesting to note that there has been a revival in construction activity put in effect last year through a number of housing projects, which aim to address the housing needs of a diversified range of beneficiaries throughout the country. The outcome, however, has been too modest to cover these needs.

A relatively extensive system of housing loans, also aims at promoting access to housing for the poor. These loans are directly or indirectly linked to social housing policies, in so far as they aim to address the housing needs of primarily working people with low income. The housing loan market, however, cannot address the needs of people who do not have a regular job and income, and are not, therefore, capable of repaying a loan.

On the whole, it has to be noted that social housing provision in Greece, although important for many people in need, is not in any way linked to emergency or transitory housing services for homeless people. It is directed towards specific groups – mainly people of low income with a more or less consistent working record – and excludes large groups of people who may be in desperate need, but do not meet the criteria for becoming beneficiaries of welfare organisations.

The Role of the Family

The role of the Greek family in filling the gap left by the absence of a well-developed welfare state is crucial. With regard to housing a stable system of family solidarity has developed over time, which aims at helping family members in need. The recipients of such help – that is often available to the extended as well as the immediate family – are, naturally, the ones in greatest need, i.e. newly-married couples, elderly, lonely or disabled relatives, etc. The most common form of housing provision is the 'dowry', that is, the allowance granted to nearly every married couple by the bride's family, often in the form of a house or flat. Even though the institution of the dowry has been abolished in the legal sense, it remains a strong element in the Greek tradition, as most Greek families would provide a house or flat for a newly-married couple, whenever financially possible.

Cohabitation of parents and adult children, as well as amongst other family members, is also very common in Greek families. It is partly directed by financial necessity as few young people are able to afford independent housing. To some extent, however, it is also due to the fact that the extended, as opposed to the nuclear family is still the most dominant form of family organisation in Greek society. In most Greek families adult children would not be expected to leave the family home before marriage and elderly relatives would normally come to live with the younger generation, especially after the death of one spouse.

The close family bonds are also manifest in the support available to family members facing insecurity of tenure. It has the form of help with paying the rent, offered to young couples seeking housing – usually by the bride's family in cases when provision of a flat or house is not possible – or even to other members of the extended family. As houses become smaller in size and family bonds are gradually slackening, in recent years cohabitation is often being replaced by financial assistance to those in need. Social changes and the gradual loosening of family bonds suggest that family solidarity, although still quite strong, may not have quite such a central role in Greek society in the future as it has had traditionally up to now.

Overview of Services for Homeless People in Greece

There are a number of different services offering emergency as well as longer-term accommodation and support to homeless people. Their governing bodies, their goals as well as their target groups vary widely. Some services target social groups with specific types of other problems distinct from but usually related to their state of homelessness. We shall present an outline of the range of services available for homeless people – along with a profile of their users – in five main groups, although in some cases there is a partial overlap. It must be noted, however, that the overview of services presented is mainly based on first-hand data collected for the European Observatory, as there is no official body in the country surveying this field. In view of this fact, it is expected that allowances should be made for any gaps.

Statutory Hostels for Homeless People

There are three statutory hostels providing emergency accommodation in Athens, with a total capacity of 155 beds. The first one is situated in Omonia, an inner city area notorious for high levels of homelessness, and the other two in the Greater Athens areas of Careas and Bouliagmeni. Their target group is single homeless people from the streets, as well as people facing a range of personal and social problems that result in temporary or long-term homelessness – e.g. young people (over 18) leaving care institutions, ex-prisoners, people who became homeless through a family crisis or break-up, elderly people with no family support who need a place to stay until they can make a longer term arrangement, etc. A number of beds are occupied on a fairly regular basis by people from all over the country visiting Athens for various reasons – often to receive outpatient medical treatment or to accompany a relative receiving treatment in hospital – who cannot afford to pay for proper accommodation, but who, obviously, cannot be termed 'homeless'. Two of the three shelters only accept single people or couples without children while the one in Bouliagmeni can also accommodate families as well as single women with children.

Referrals to the shelters are made by various welfare institutions, the church, children's homes, community organisations, hospitals, etc. They also accept self-referrals by homeless people themselves. With regard to the criteria for admission, prospective residents have to be Greek nationals – with the exception of some Greek-origin people from southern Albania and Greek repatriates from Pontos – and must not suffer from any infectious disease, or have any psychiatric problems or problems related to alcoholism or drug addiction. Proof of identity and proof of low income as well as medical certificates are required for admission and the admission procedure may take some time, which seems to make access to the shelters problematic for people in crisis or people sleeping in the streets who would need direct access or would find it quite difficult to produce the documents required.

The shelters have links with health, employment and other welfare services and the residents receive social work support in their effort to make longer-term arrangements. Meals are provided either on the premises or in the form of meal-vouchers. However, the length of stay is officially limited to 3–4 months and can only be extended in exceptional cases, at the discretion of the social workers. Residents are responsible for making further accommodation arrangements for after they leave. Often, in theory, this amounts to the prospect of getting a job so as to be able to afford private rented accommodation. The shelters purport to offer the space and time people need to be able to do that, however unrealistic this may be for many of their residents. The shelters themselves have no link to permanent housing and can take no responsibility for the resettlement of their residents.

Although the brief stay at the shelters can offer important help to people whose state of homelessness is the result of a particular life-crisis, to a few people who can be referred to some other supportive environment (e.g. to old people's homes) or to poor people visiting Athens for a limited period, it offers no real solution to chaotic, long-term unemployed and homeless people. These people's level of functioning would not normally allow them to get work and find rented accommodation within the few months of their stay, and the shelters cannot offer any more help towards that direction. As a result, the very people who are most vulnerable and in need of support often have to return to the streets.

The three shelters differ slightly in some of their rules and regulations and in the way they are managed. They operate independently of one another despite the view expressed by staff that there should be more contact and cooperation amongst them so as to ensure that residents are placed to the one that is more suitable to their individual needs (e.g. in terms of location and access to particular facilities) or that the situation does not arise where there are vacancies in one shelter while there may be a waiting list in another one. There also seem to be cases where people attempt to move into one hostel after leaving another one and it is felt that they should be prevented from doing so in cases when they have not been able or prepared to use constructively their stay in a shelter in the first place.

However, cooperation seems to be obstructed by communication problems and different degrees of involvement by senior management, as well as by differences in some of the regulations and style of operation. In particular, it appears that in the shelter located in Bouliagmeni, there is less day-to-day involvement from senior management and more is left to the individual social worker's judgment and discretion. As a result, in this shelter there seems to be a lot more flexibility than in the other two, in terms of internal regulations, decisions about a prospective resident's suitability, admission procedure and length of stay. A person, for instance, self-referring and in urgent need could be admitted immediately, even if unable to produce at the time of admission the documents normally required. Similarly, a person genuinely in need and unable to get work so as to pay for accommodation or someone whose move on plans depend on factors beyond their control would not be put under pressure to leave by a certain date.

All shelters, like most welfare services in Greece, face chronic financial and staffing problems. In the Careas shelter, in particular, less than half of the 50 beds available for homeless people are currently occupied, while there is a need for a further reduction of the number of residents to a maximum of 12, due to cuts in funding, despite a higher demand for beds. The day-to-day operation of the services is often obstructed by bureaucratic delays, ineffective procedures, and problems on senior management level. Nevertheless, it must be noted that the service provided is of good standard and staff seem to be dedicated to providing a good quality service within the limits of what these shelters are able to offer.

Services Run by Local Authorities

In Greece, local authorities were never empowered to take on an active role in relation to issues arising in their territory, let alone to launch programmes aiming to combat specific social problems. This is largely due to the fact that funding and decision making processes have traditionally been centralised and local authorities have lacked the money and authority to take the initiative in setting up services.

Nevertheless, a number of services have been set up on the initiative of various local authorities. In particular, there are 'public poorhouses' in various parts of Greece, offering accommodation to elderly people lacking an income and family support. There is also meals provided for the poor in several municipalities.

In recent years, the Athens City Council set up a women's refuge. The refuge provides emergency accommodation, practical assistance and psychological support to women who are victims of domestic violence, and their children.

An important new service for homeless people, set up by Athens City

Council is about to start its operation. It is a day centre, offering meals, washing and laundry facilities and primary health care to homeless street people. An emergency night shelter is scheduled to operate in the next few months in parallel to the day centre. A description of this service, which constitutes a novelty for Greece as it is the first of its kind in the country, is the subject of a separate presentation.

Hostels and Guest Houses of the Voluntary Sector

There are several types of hostels and guest houses all over Greece which offer emergency as well as long-term accommodation to people in need. There are estimated to be approximately 2,500 people living in such hostels. These hostels are neither statutory nor connected to any health services and they vary according to governing and sponsoring body, length of stay granted, target-groups, etc. Their common ground is that the majority of their residents are homeless and are not requested to pay for their stay.

Most of these services are charities, run by the church or various NGOs. Some of them are funded by the Department of Health and Social Welfare or directly by the church itself; others rely on charitable donations, or a combination of external funding and donations, or even contributions of the residents according to their means. The majority of these hostels are homes for the elderly. In this chapter we distinguish them from the numerous private homes for the elderly across the country that operate on a profit-making basis and whose residents are not considered as homeless. They offer accommodation to elderly people with low incomes who have no other home, and residents can stay there for the rest of their lives. The main factor resulting in these people's state of homelessness is lack of family support, which is cited as the main criterion for admission to most of these homes.

There is a variety of other hostels in this category, some of them targeting specific social groups: a YWCA hostel, for instance, offers accommodation for up to 2–3 years to up to 111 homeless young women studying or working in Athens, as well as to refugees.

The Guest House of Mother Theresa also provides accommodation and support to women refugees and their children. The House of Christian Love, is a hostel divided in two wings, one of them providing long-stay accommodation, meals, health care, etc., to homeless elderly women, the other one accommodating girls (from five years old upwards) and young women, who are either orphaned or became homeless through family breakdown or because of an unsuitable family environment; it has up to 60 residents and there is no limit in the length of stay allowed; the young women normally stay till they complete their education and are able to get a job so as to afford rented accommodation. The Centre for Infants 'Mitera' is the best known organisation in Athens that deals primarily with the care and protection of children under five and arranges for fostering and adoption placements. It also offers accommodation and support to homeless pregnant women and unmarried mothers and their children.

Onissimos is an organisation that provides accommodation and social support to ex-offenders. It runs hostels for adults as well as one that is specifically for women ex-offenders and their children. Arsis is a voluntary organisation that operates a drop-in centre, vocational training schemes and a small guesthouse providing emergency accommodation to homeless young people (aged 15–22). Arsis aims to provide training and social support to vulnerable young people, many of whom are ex-offenders, with a view to promoting their longer-term social reintegration.

Finally, an important specialised service is a guesthouse for people with HIV and AIDS, which is an annex of the Centre for the Control of Infectious Diseases (part of the Department of Health). It offers accommodation, medical care and support to up to 16 people with HIV and AIDS, many of whom became homeless for reasons related to their medical condition. Although the official length of stay is for a maximum of six months, residents are allowed to stay indefinitely in cases when they have nowhere else to go or need medical care. In recent years, there has been a growing emphasis on the medical care provided at the hostel, as there is a growing number of long-stay residents in advanced stages of the disease.

Not all hostels and guesthouses in the country falling into this category have been recorded; in the context of the present study, we aimed to give an overview of the main services found in the Greater Athens area. The above list illustrates the range of services available that offer accommodation and support to particular categories of homeless people, many of whom face serious social problems in addition, but usually closely related, to their state of homelessness.

Housing Provision for Refugees and Repatriates

Refugees There are 8,000 officially recognised refugees in Greece today, most of them originating from Turkey, Iran, Iraq, Syria, Somalia, Sudan and Sri Lanka, as well as the former Yugoslavia. The influx of people seeking asylum in Greece is constant, and, has in fact increased in recent years. The UN High

Commissioner for Refugees supports three non-governmental organisations, the Foundation of Social Service, the Greek Council for Refugees and the International Social Service, which provide legal and practical assistance as well as social support to asylum-seekers and refugees. The Greek government provides accommodation to up to 350 refugees in the Lavrion Refugee Camp, as well as education and health care in all public services in the country.

These people stay at the refugee camp until their status is officially clarified as well as while waiting to be moved elsewhere. The length of their stay may vary, depending on whether or not permission to emigrate to another country is granted and on how long this procedure may take. It is estimated that approximately 75 per cent of these refugees stay in Greece after leaving the camp. They are normally expected to get a job and move into rented accommodation, as there is no longer-term housing provision for them after leaving the camp. It must be noted, however, that the standards of hygiene in the camp are low and the general living conditions quite poor, which results in many people being discouraged from using the service.

Greek repatriates from Pontos (the northern and eastern Black Sea coasts)
According to the records of the Ministry of Foreign Affairs, the figure of 20,598 people from Pontos who repatriated to Greece between 1966 and 1988 has escalated to over 60,000 in the last 6–7 years, following the collapse of the socialist regime in the ex-USSR. The majority of repatriates from Pontos (84 per cent) have headed for the two biggest urban centres, while 61 per cent have chosen to settle in Athens and its suburbs. Although the vast majority of the families repatriated between 1966–89 did not get any support from the state, the Greek government started the implementation of an accommodation scheme for repatriates from Pontos even prior to the emergence of political changes in the ex-USSR. The Department of Health, Welfare and Social Security, in cooperation with the Department of the Environment and Public Works and the Agricultural Bank, set up a scheme for the distribution of 324 dwellings from the newly-constructed projects of EKTENEPOL (a quasi-public construction company) in Xanthi and Komotini to expatriate households from Pontos in the late 1980s. These dwellings were handed out via interest-free loans subsidised by the Greek government by 35 per cent.

In 1990, a special body called EIYAAPOE was set up by the Home Office. It aims to assist Greek repatriates to become integrated into the Greek society through a four phase programme, which includes provision of transitory accommodation as well as of other forms of support (practical assistance, psychological support, training, etc.). As part of this programme, EIYAAPOE has set up a number of guesthouses and organised admission camps offering temporary accommodation to repatriates, in a process of gradual integration into permanent housing.

According to EIYAAPOE records, 64,000 repatriates have arrived in Greece since 1990. Fifteen thousand of them have approached the organisation for assistance and have been participating in its various housing programmes: 600 are accommodated in the guesthouses at any time, and 3,000 are temporarily housed in the special 'admission camps', which is the second stage of the housing programme, prior to the final move to permanent housing. Nine thousand five hundred people have so far moved into permanent rented accommodation (2,600 dwellings), while another 2,000 people have moved into 448 dwellings allocated to families by EIYAAPOE through an interest-free loan system. Fifty households have settled in existing apartments provided by EKTENEPOL in northern Greece. In the same area, a new programme is currently being planned aiming at the construction of 2000 dwellings in a 55 ha. plot provided by the National Mortgage Bank of Greece.

In addition to the above, a number of benefits have been introduced by various government departments, aiming to contribute to the urgent financial needs of the repatriate population. Apart from the various economic benefits, repatriates are granted other privileges, such as special licences to maintain flea-market stalls.

The EIYAPOE programmes, although quite ambitious, have only been able to cover the housing needs of about a quarter of the repatriate population. The majority of the remainder are forced either to seek assistance from friends and relatives or to cope on their own. Thus, apart from the 15,000 people participating in the housing programme, as many as 20,000 Greek repatriates live with friends and relatives in areas like Kallithea and Liosia in Athens, about 10,000 live in caravans in Menidi and other deprived areas in the periphery of Athens and, finally, another 20,000–30,000 are scattered all over the country, some of them having managed to find proper accommodation in Thrace, others living in substandard conditions in areas like Aspropyrgos.

De-institutionalisation Programmes that Include Accommodation Facilities

Hospital patients and people in prisons, asylums or other institutions are not regarded as homeless. However, those accommodated in hospitals' special annexes or in various rehabilitation centres, with no other home to return to, do fall into this category.

Since the mid-1980s, in line with the EEC Regulation 815/84, which funded psychiatric reform in Greece, a number of rehabilitation and community mental health services have been set up. Since 1985, a number of rehabilitation programmes have been launched in all nine public psychiatric hospitals in the country. The implementation of the individual programmes has been undertaken either by the hospitals themselves or by non-governmental mental health organisations. A presentation of the de-institutionalisation programmes in each hospital, in conjunction with the community services involved would amount to a presentation of the whole network of mental health services set up in Greece in recent years and falls outside the scope of this chapter. The programmes generally combine housing rehabilitation with some form of vocational training. The housing provided is either in short-stay guesthouses or in long-stay residential care hostels, with a longer-term view of moving patients on to private-rented supported flats. At the same time there are special schemes offering vocational training, according to people's capacities, leading on to work placements, either arranged specially with employers in the private sector, or in special projects that are part of the rehabilitation programme. Long-term housing resettlement, at least in theory, amounts to the former patient being able to live – either alone or with others – in private-rented accommodation, the rent of which is covered either by a disability pension or by the earnings or other income of the patient, with the supervision and support of community mental health services, unless he/she can be rehabilitated within their family environment.

In the case of best known example in the field, the psychiatric asylum of Leros, the Department of Health funded the creation of 11 medium- to long-stay residential care hostels in seven Greek cities, with a total capacity to accommodate 110 patients (Madianos, 1994). The main criterion for placement in a particular hostel has been patients' place of origin prior to their hospitalisation. At the same time it has to be noted that significant steps were taken in order to upgrade the patients' living conditions in the hospital itself, to rearrange and improve the physical environment at the hospital, to attract qualified staff, to introduce various therapeutic activities, etc. In 1990, an agricultural co-op was established on the island, employing 20 members/patients while, in 1992, 12 patients were moved to two supported flats and another 17 to two guesthouses operating on the island. There were plans for setting up a third guesthouse to accommodate 12 patients and another one based within the hospital premises for another 10 patients attending a pre-vocational training programme. In 1993, there were a total of 29 patients living outside the hospital premises in Leros, although they officially maintain the status of hospital patient.

However hopeful and pioneering these changes in an asylum that for decades resembled a dumping ground, they have merely been the government's response to a much wider proposal put forward by a special Committee of the Greek Psychiatric Society set up to assess the situation in Leros. According to this committee, about 1,100 patients had to be placed in 44 supportive hostels in 12 cities over a five-year period so that the asylum gradually closes down. This highlights the fact that only a fraction of the problem has been addressed in Leros. The same holds for the other public psychiatric hospitals where similar rehabilitation programmes have been launched.

Madianos (1994, p. 169) points out that 768 new beds in supportive community housing projects are required to cover the real needs of psychiatric patients countrywide. This figure results from an estimate of the number of chronic hospital patients in immediate need of rehabilitation. In other words, although these people are 'hospital patients' and therefore not regarded as homeless, it is in actual fact the absence of appropriate supportive housing, as well as other mental health services, that forces them to remain in hospital. It is important to note also that the existing projects are currently at risk and their future highly uncertain as the EU funding runs out in 1999 and there is no official commitment by the Department of Health concerning their future. In view of this, ex-patients may face the possibility of being forced to return to an asylum.

De-institutionalisation difficulties are also faced by young people leaving care homes, ex-offenders coming out of prison or people in drug rehabilitation centres. Evidence shows that a notable proportion of such people face homelessness, often an unsurpassable obstacle towards social integration. Many of them lack family support and have particular difficulties in getting work that would allow them to pay for rented accommodation. Some people in the above categories may find temporary accommodation in the shelters and hostels mentioned above, yet there exists very little provision of long-term housing. The only service providers currently addressing this target group, and especially young ex-offenders, are Arsis and, to an extent, Onissimos. Lack of funding, however, an issue pertinent to NGO's of the voluntary sector, has kept the output of these bodies minimal despite the rising needs.

People completing residential drug rehabilitation programmes face similar difficulties as those leaving other institutions as regards housing and wider social integration. Although all therapeutic programmes include a strong emphasis on future reintegration, getting a job and being able to afford to pay rent is often very difficult, the danger for relapse remaining eminent. OKANA, a body set up by the Department of Health for matters relating to drug-services, is currently contemplating the introduction of rent subsidy for a period of one year after people complete a residential drug-rehabilitation programme.

Evaluation

The evaluation of service provision for the homeless in Greece, should develop along two directions: a) the appraisal of existing services as such; and b) an overview of social groups that are not using the services or whose needs are not addressed by these services. The evaluation should take place with reference to a set of criteria applied to various services which take into account the standards of service provision, the accessibility by the various target groups, the prospects of reintegration into proper and permanent housing and the overall management of the service. In the context of the present study however, the reader must be reminded of the limitations of the data available concerning individual service providers.

Evaluation of Existing Services

The opening of statutory hostels for the homeless in the mid-1980s marks an official acknowledgement of the problem of homelessness and the need for specialised services in the field. As shown above, the shelters can offer important help to people in crisis, poor people from around the country coming to Athens for a particular purpose or people needing space and time as well as psychological and social support in order to work out solutions for themselves.

They offer a reasonably good standard of accommodation in terms of hygiene, facilities, provision of meals and access to basic health care. In terms of the operation of these services, it appears that it is often obstructed by problems on senior management level (i.e. Department of Health), bureaucratic procedures and inconsistencies in funding. As a result, the shelters remain understaffed and under-occupied, despite a high demand for beds. Failure to achieve full occupancy is also due to admission procedures, which are often lengthy, as people have to produce medical certificates and other documents, which makes access to the shelters difficult for people who are chaotic and have problems in their social functioning. Furthermore, many vulnerable groups of people such as those with psychiatric problems or problems related to alcohol or drug dependency are excluded and often have to remain in the streets in the absence of adequate specialised services that could provide the level of support they need.

The most important limitation, however, in the function and scope of the urgent accommodation hostels, is that they have no transition facilities and no link to permanent housing provision. They are not connected to agencies responsible for social housing and do not undertake any responsibility for the resettlement of their residents. Although hostels aim at helping their guests to address their problems during their stay the search for employment and housing is seldom realistic. In their present function, therefore, these shelters seem to offer a kind of respite to their client group, a form of breathing space for the better-functioning homeless people. Thus statutory hostels are incapable of providing real solutions to the most vulnerable, the more chaotic people they accommodate.

The same holds for non-governmental hostels and guesthouses, although some of them offer long-term accommodation and support and in the cases of certain groups, as for example elderly people, resettlement does not arise as an issue. Standards of service provision vary widely, as there is a comparatively great number of different services falling into this category (see Table A3, Appendix). Many of these hostels are run by the church or by non-governmental organisations and are characterised by a high degree of commitment and care, aiming to offer a supportive, homelike environment for their clients. Their self-governing character however, suggests that in many cases there may be a lack adequate procedures for quality control as well as more room for arbitrary action on the part of staff or management, which may leave residents in a very powerless position in case a problem or disagreement arises.

A number of services in this category are able to become more flexible than the statutory shelters with regard to the length of stay and support they offer to their users, thus allowing them to work out solutions for proper resettlement. Ultimately, however, the only option open to users of such services with regard to social integration is getting a job and moving into private-rented accommodation, which, especially given present-day salaries and rents, is extremely difficult for most people who have found themselves in this situation in the first place.

The EIYAAPOE housing programme for Greek repatriates from Pontos is amongst the most ambitious and in some respects well thought-out housing schemes in operation in Greece. The first two stages of the programme, during which accommodation is provided in guesthouses and organised camps, constitute a rare example of transitory housing proper, in the sense that they are part of a scheme facilitating the residents' transition to permanent quality housing. In some respects, the EIYAAPOE programme resembles the rehabilitation programme set up during the 1920s in Greece, which housed more than a million refugees of Greek origin from Asia Minor. Nowadays, however, EIYAAPOE covers the needs of merely a quarter of the repatriate population, the majority of whom live in conditions of extreme poverty and face severe difficulties in the process of their integration into the Greek society. It must further be noted that living standards in the camps are not what they should be, while people often have to wait for years before they are forwarded to the next phase. On the whole, however, the rehabilitation programme is thought of as being good in principle yet too modest in its application.

The EU-funded de-institutionalisation programmes for people with psychiatric problems can boast some pioneer and efficient work in terms of the creation of supportive community housing projects and rehabilitation programmes for former asylum patients. As pointed out in the section on these services, however, we still have to bear in mind that the absence of adequate and appropriate accommodation facilities in the community results in many people continuing to live in asylums, while it is not required by their illness as such that this should be so. In connection to that we also have noted the impending crisis of already-existing projects by the time the EU funding commitment expires in 1999 as there is no commitment by the Department of Health as yet that funding will be provided after that date, as was originally planned. As a result, a number of people who have been through a process of rehabilitation over the last few years face the prospect of actually having to return to hospitals.

With regard to issues of equal opportunities, it has to be noted that several services target specific minority groups and therefore cater for their particular needs. There is, for example, a home for the elderly directed specifically towards people of Russian origin, one for Armenians, a hostel for people suffering from HIV/AIDS who face prejudice and discrimination, special services for refugees, etc. However, the notion of an official equal opportunities policy and of special provisions for specific minority groups is not generally known in most services in Greece. The statutory hostels, under their official regulations, only accept Greek nationals and exceptions to this rule may only take place unofficially, resting on the discretion of individual social workers. It obviously follows from this, that any question of provisions for non-Greek speakers or people from a different cultural background does not even arise. Although no extensive research on the matter has taken place in Greece as yet, it seems reasonable to assume that people from minority groups may not find the general services as accessible or as appropriate to their needs as the rest of the public, and therefore, they may be reluctant to approach them.

Categories of Homeless People who do not Benefit from Existing Services

The long-term homeless population According to social workers working with the homeless, people sleeping in the streets are estimated to be about 350. About 150 of them live in Athens and its periphery, 120 in Piraeus and Salonica, while the rest in other urban areas. To this figure one should add about 50 people staying in emergency hostels as well as a percentage of those squatting or staying in boarding houses. By and large, one may refer to as many as 1,000 people being practically roofless in Greece, many of whom may be regarded as long-term homeless. Naturally, the figure is approximate while there has been no systematic attempt to collect data or even to count the specific target group. Evidence suggests that the majority of the long-term homeless population in Greece are older people who are unable to work and to cope with reality.

The street homeless are the main target group of the statutory emergency hostels in Athens. However, many of them fail to meet the requirements of the admission procedures of these services, and even when admitted to a shelter for a short period of time, they are unable to get work and achieve integration into permanent housing. The limited period of stay granted, along with the absence of mechanisms able to ensure resettlement, forces people to return to the streets. Thus, the long-term homeless sleep on park benches and railroad stations in-between periods of stay in accommodation centres, hospitals, etc. Although the extent of the problem is not as great in Athens as in other European cities, the street homeless are increasing in number and they constitute a special and very vulnerable group who are not, in effect, recipients of any services.

People with psychiatric problems or drug dependency Despite the de-institutionalisation and reintegration programmes in mental hospitals or drug rehabilitation centres, many people with mental health problems or former drug users face insurmountable problems in getting a job and achieving access to proper housing. The reason for this failure is that there are no shelters or other services to provide housing to people with mental health or drug- and alcohol-related problems who do not participate in organised rehabilitation programmes. Their position is made worse by the refusal of admission they face when they apply for urgent accommodation in the statutory hostels. Although there has been little research on the issue, social workers believe that the a large part of the long-term homeless population frequenting the streets of Athens belong to this category.

In this context we must also note the absence of emergency shelters that allow for direct access to everybody, for short periods of time. The existence of such shelters could provide to people with psychiatric problems or drug dependency some 'breathing space' as well as facilitate access to other services.

Young institution leavers and one parent families The existing system of services is not particularly thoughtful of young institution-leavers or one parent families. Two out of the three statutory emergency hostels do not accept people who are younger than 18 even when accompanied by a parent. Thus pregnant women or women with children under five years old must seek accommodation in the 'Mitera' Centre, while there are very few hostels that accept young people under 18.

Illegal immigrants As noted earlier, illegal immigrants may not be termed 'homeless' even though they follow similar patterns of behaviour. In many cases the reason for this rests with their limited motivation to become integrated, which urges them to travel to and from their native country, while in most cases they prefer to economise rather than spend money on accommodation. Yet it must be noted that very few emergency shelters accept foreigners, who are often compelled to find refuge in small deserted barns or huts in the outskirts of big cities or in the fields, depending on the kind of jobs they expect to find. From estimates of the Department of Public Order as well as our own experience it appears reasonable to assume that nearly a third of the Albanian immigrants in Greece fall into this category. In Calamata, for instance, 200 of the small prefab dwellings once used by victims of the 1985 earthquake are known to have been taken over by Albanians.

Gypsies and other population groups living in marginal accommodation Another category of homeless people who do not benefit from existing services are those living in tents, caravans, containers, etc. There are as many as 60,000 people living in accommodation of this kind, including about 45,000 gypsies. The gypsy population, however, are not officially regarded as homeless, as their type of accommodation is regarded as the result of choice related to their tradition rather than the outcome of real life necessity. Their living conditions, however, are often appalling, posing threats to the hygiene of the settlements and it is now becoming apparent that treating the whole situation simply as a cultural choice overshadows the absence of any effective state intervention to improve these conditions. Very recently, gypsies requested the provision of a set of services that will improve living standards of gypsy settlements and contribute to their already expressed need to become socially integrated. We must note the initial sympathetic reaction of both central government as well as a number of local authorities to these demands.

Conclusion

Summary of Findings

There is roughly an estimated 15,000 homeless people in Greece. This figure does not include people with ownership problems as regards their dwelling, those staying with another person or family while being capable of having a home of their own, gypsies living in tents or people in substandard housing conditions. The above figure also ignores the approximately 100,000 homeless economic refugees who are not officially considered as homeless. The number of these people fluctuates and is very difficult to specify.

Social housing provision, although quite important for many people of low income, is not linked to emergency or transitory housing services for the homeless; in fact, it does not even address several categories of homeless people. It is restricted to certain social groups, mainly workers and low income employees or other groups meeting specific criteria. People who are in the greatest need for social housing or rent subsidy would not be eligible for them as they do not meet the criteria for becoming beneficiaries of welfare organisations. Entitlement criteria, therefore, do not seem to take adequately into account present-day needs and more recent features of inner city homelessness, such as the link between homelessness and unemployment. It appears evident that existing services only address a fraction of the problem.

At the same time, family solidarity which has always been important in the Greek society, remains the main source of support for most people in housing need. Statistics reveal that the degree of family intervention in the provision of housing surpasses by far any action by the state. Similarly, the stronger the family bonds the more likely that people will be aided at times of need.

People who rely on services for the homeless are, therefore, primarily those who are for various reasons excluded from the labour market and lack family support. By definition, these population groups are the most vulnerable within the Greek society and find it increasingly difficult to cope. As housing integration is an important component if not a prerequisite for wider social integration, a growing number of people tend to become socially excluded on a long-term basis.

Provisions seem to be inadequate for certain social groups particularly vulnerable to social exclusion – young people, older people, immigrants, one-parent families, people with specific needs, ex-offenders and institution-leavers, etc.

The growing awareness of the issue of homelessness on the part of the government as well as the public in general has provided the ground for the development of the means to combat the problem. In recent years, a number of services for homeless people have been set up, which despite a number of difficulties they face, offer a fairly good standard of service and address the immediate and urgent needs of at least part of the homeless population. The main problem and limitation in the function of these services is that they are not in a position to offer resettlement into what we may term 'proper' housing as such. They therefore need to be further developed so as to tackle the problem of homelessness on a more permanent basis.

Recommendations

As has already been pointed out, a most significant issue in relation to social housing policy is the absence of any link between services for homeless people and provision of permanent housing. It seems important that the Welfare Section of the Department of Health, Welfare and Social Security, following the revival of its housing support schemes through the production of new housing estates, should consider implementing support schemes for those below the poverty line. It also seems important that housing programmes are introduced aiming at the reintegration into proper housing of people who do not have a consistent work record and, may be facing the spectre of long-term social exclusion. One way of tackling this issue could be the introduction of flexible low cost processes for housing people who would otherwise stay either in shelters or in the street. Buildings which have been vacated for long periods of time and may not easily yield profit to the owner (i.e. the state) may be utilised for this purpose.

The inadequacy of service provision for certain population groups that face a higher risk of long-term social exclusion, and the lack of special provisions for minority groups, highlight the need for more services that target specific vulnerable groups as well as the need that equal opportunities for all societal groups be integrated into planning policies and structures. The incorporation of an effective residents' complaints procedure within the services' internal rules and regulations could also be an important step towards empowering the users of these services and promoting democratisation in their operation.

As regards information and access to services, many homeless people have little or no information about their rights and about provisions that could be available to them. This problem could be tackled with the compilation in a practical guide of information on homeless people's rights and privileges as well as on the services and facilities they may use. Such a move would also make existing services more accessible and effective. In relation to this issue, there also seems to be a need for direct-access street services, providing assessment, information and practical assistance to the more chaotic long-term homeless people, thus facilitating their access to residential services.

Finally, the need for a national scale body dealing with homelessness as such has to be noted. As mentioned above, there is neither a statutory nor a non-governmental organisation or body of this sort at present. Its absence is evident both in as much as survey and analysis of the problem as well as action and policy making are concerned. Such a body could also relate to the provision of information to homeless people about services available and vacancies in shelters and hostels on a day-to-day basis. Homelessness in Greece has matured enough to convince central and local government officials of the need for more positive action to address it. The establishment of an organisation which may not necessarily belong to the public sector but at least have the state's backing and support appears to be essential towards this end.

Bibliography

Department of Housing and Public Works (1996), *National Report for Greece*, document prepared for the Habitat II Conference in Istabul, June.

EOP (1992), unpublished extracts of the survey on social and economic parameters conducted in 1991 in Greece by the National Technical University of Athens (EMP) for the National Organisation of Welfare (EOP), Athens.

ESYE (National Statistical Agency) unpublished results of the 1991 General Population and Housing Survey, Athens.

Madianos M.(1994), *Psycho-social Rehabilitation – from the asylum to the community*, Athens, Greek Letters Pub.

Sapounakis, A. (1993), 'Housing conditions of new settlers; the case of the Gypsy settlement of Aliveri, Volos, Greece', paper presented at the conference organised by the Poverty 3 Programme in Perama, Athens (to be published in Greece).

Sapounakis, A. (1994), *Annual Report on Homelessness in Greece – 1994*, European Observatory on Homelessness.

Sapounakis, A. (1995), *Annual Report on Homelessness in Greece – 1995*, European Observatory on Homelessness.

Vrychea A. et al. (1996), *Housing of Underprivileged Social Groups in Greece Today*, study prepared for the Greek Chamber of Engineers.

23 Reflections on Homelessness as Seen from an Institution for the Homeless in Copenhagen

PREBEN BRANDT

Homelessness is just as well-known a phenomenon in welfare Denmark as in other Western countries. Apparently, fewer people in Denmark live openly on the streets, but that may be because we have no tradition for wishing to see them. The number in relative terms is actually essentially the same as for other comparable countries. Denmark has, however, a strong century-old tradition for institutionalising homelessness. Throughout the last several hundred years, with periodic variations, there have been 2,000–4,000 beds available in institutions for homeless. Today, institutions can shelter 2,000 persons out of a population of over five million; or four out of every 10,000 persons can find shelter in an institution for homeless each night. In addition, at least an equal number of homeless can stay overnight in jails, hospitals and other institutions, and just as many again on the streets or with friends or acquaintances. In other words, a considerable number of persons, presumably at least two out of every 1,000 of the whole population, are to some degree homeless, also in a welfare society like Denmark (Amtsrådsforeningen i Danmark, 1990; Koch-Nielsen and Rostgaard, 1993; Brandt and Munk-Jørgensen, 1996).

Here, I have assumed that it is possible to estimate homelessness, that the number of homeless is measurable. This demands an operational definition of homelessness in which the decisive factor is whether a person has housing or not. In reality, I find that such a definition is insufficient, at least if one wishes to understand the essence of homelessness. For homelessness is something other than the lack of housing.

In 1855, a Jewish-Danish author, Meïr Goldschmidt, published a novel entitled *Homeless*, published several years later in English. It is far from a

510

social-realistic novel about at person who lives on the street as homeless, but rather a novel about a man's development. The main character obtains an education and later a job; and throughout his life he has his own place to live, even though he moves often. But he never adjusts, never feels accepted and never acts according to accepted standards of behaviour. He does not belong.

That is homelessness. That is how the homeless are. They are people who are 'wrong' in relation to what we others consider to be 'right'; they behave differently. They do not live in a way that we find right, and cannot utilise society's institutions, in the term's broadest sense. From the point of view of ordinary citizens, the homeless are different in a negative sense, and we exclude them from our ordinary social life. We do not like them.

It is practical to maintain the assumption that homelessness is also a social condition characterised by lack of housing, but above all homelessness must be understood as an existential-dialectical condition – a keeping oneself outside and a being kept outside. On the basis of the following text, I will conclude by proposing a definition of homelessness that includes these qualitative considerations.

Even though we have always been able to meet the beggar on the street, and even though deviant personalities living as homeless have always existed, a special focus on the homeless has developed during the last couple of decades and in the whole of the Western world. Much has been written about the homeless and homelessness, and many studies have been initiated that try to account for the number of homeless and reveal the conditions of their existence (Brandt and Munk-Jørgensen, 1996; Rossi et al., 1987; Salicath, 1992). In Denmark during the last 20 years, the situation has changed similarly. Earlier, it took special occasions to arouse an interest in the conditions of the homeless; today, there is almost constant focus on homeless institutions and the people who live on the street. There is also great interest in homeless who are mentally ill, the so-called bag-people, and initiatives are taken to care for those who are often called double outcasts, those homeless who are mentally ill and have problems of abuse. At the same time, a similarly great interest can be observed in the homeless in other welfare societies with a strong sense of public obligation, such as Sweden and Norway, as well as Southern European countries and countries with much larger and distinctly urban societies, such as the USA.

The homeless are on the agenda. Hopefully for their own benefit, so that they achieve better living conditions and receive respect for their individual possibilities and resources.

Danish Society's Institutions for the Homeless

From the Middle Ages' houses for lepers and victims of the plague to industrialisation's work houses and poor farms and to the large mental hospitals and shelters for homeless, society has housed those among the homeless and the outcasts who could be forced into institutions or who for one reason or another have themselves sought them out.

This has been done out of charity, in order to resocialise and in order to control. Correspondingly, the homeless have been considered to be poor wretched creatures, incorrigible loafers, and dangerous deviants.

In the following, I will describe the considerations that form the basis of my understanding of the essence of homelessness and attempt to analyse the motives for and the quality of the initiatives being taken. My examination of the Danish situation takes as its point of departure the large social care institution in Copenhagen, Sundholm, which, with its 208 beds, is Denmark's largest institution for the homeless and also has deep historical roots. Sundholm's present buildings for the homeless were first used in 1908. There was room for approximately 1,000 persons in this closed institution with gates, fences and a moat, which, it should be noted in all fairness, also and perhaps primarily had a draining function.

The institution was situated then at the edge of the city, a couple of kilometres from the centre. The moat existed until the beginning of the 1960s and the fences and control at the gates until toward the end of the 1980s.

Sundholm is still a large institution with many buildings. Many people are to be found of course on the grounds between buildings and many activities are carried out indoors, both organised and spontaneous and both acceptable and unacceptable. There are workshops, various kinds of recreational activities and living rooms. There is a reception and an administration department with offices for registration and economy. Here also is the archive, where the institution's history is collected, old posters with rules and regulations, weekly menus, old registration books, etc.

Not only Sundholm in Copenhagen can be thus described; there are 30–40 similar but smaller institutions in Copenhagen and elsewhere in the country.

Some years ago, I visited Centro de Acogida san Isidro, situated outside central Madrid and like, Sundholm, a large old public, city-owned and city-run institution for homeless. To my surprise, not only did the inhabitants resemble those I knew from Sundholm in Copenhagen, but so did everything else. Even the old posters. Both places had proclaimed that it was forbidden to spit on the floor, and both places had earlier demanded that those who lived there had to be diligent and hard-working; at both places the focus is now on social counselling and retraining of everyday skills in order that those living there can take care of themselves in their own or in communal housing. And both places have found that those coming to their institutions are increasingly suffering from mental illness and drug and alcohol abuse. Also in Madrid, the new homeless are requiring new considerations about new special initiatives.

Introducing the Homeless at Sundholm

Every year, Sundholm with its 208 beds is used by a total of about 1,200 different persons as a place to find shelter for the day/night. By far the majority of these know about the institution and come on their own initiative. There is a significant percentage that come more than once, at least when viewed over a period of time. No statistics exist showing how long a period individuals use the institution, but my experience tells me that most users return again and again over a period of several years, three to four years for most, but of course there are variations, from a single short visit to very long stays or repeated visits over several decades.

Only 15–20 years ago, the majority of Sundholm's residents were older alcoholic men who came here at the end of a social decline. They were often people who had some difficulties early in life, for example, problems adjusting or behaving normally, but without growing up with very serious problems from childhood.

At that time, most lived in the institution for many years, often instead of an actual old people's home, and their only contacts were with other residents and the personnel. Contact with their families had usually been broken off far earlier.

It was obvious that the conditions offered the elder residents at Sundholm, in relation to those available to other old people in Denmark at that time, were poor, humble and also often unworthy, both in regard to the physical facilities and to the respect shown to the individual.

In the mid-1980s, political and administrative decisions were made to change these conditions. The desired change was to offer an apartment and the necessary support to the elder alcoholic or as an alternative admit him to a nursing home. It was hoped that this change would lead to a reduction in the need for shelters for the homeless, and perhaps there would no longer be any need for these large institutions.

Of course, it did not work out that way.

Changes Within the Group of Homeless

It had been experienced earlier in the history of the Danish homeless that the group of homeless had changed. The most marked example (Brandt, 1992) comes from the end of the 1800s, when the number of homeless women dropped sharply from 80 per cent of the users of homeless institutions to 40 per cent, and just after 1891 to 10 per cent. The explanation is found in the changed attitude in the population toward the concept of 'worthy needy'. Most homeless women were elderly widows without any means of earning a living, but who had otherwise lived exemplary lives. During this period, the will to support these elderly worthy needy grew, and the great social reform in 1891 initiated general old-age pensions for this group. The fact that at the same time the number of homeless men increased, so that the total number of homeless did not fall significantly, was due to other social changes which will not be analysed here.

As mentioned above, in the 1980s a planned effort was initiated to move the older homeless from a situation where their only residence was on the street or in an institution for homeless to a situation where they, just as other citizens, had access to housing that was stable with the possibility of obtaining a lease and with a standard that was average for society as a whole.

The results of the change described here in the homeless population of Sundholm in Copenhagen are the same as for earlier changes. A particular dominant group of homeless has been 'moved' from the position of homeless outcast to that of participants in what one could call ordinary social life. There was no significant change in the total number of residents at Sundholm during the period 1980–90 (Brandt, 1987), so the old people were immediately replaced by a new group that took over the arena and became the next dominant problem group of homeless and outcasts.

The term problem group is consciously chosen. I do not mean that I understand the homeless to be one or two groups with identical histories. It is clear that we are dealing with different persons, each with their own story and their own fate. However, it is obvious that there are some common characteristics shared by most homeless, and some particularly characteristic conditions which are especially relevant during certain periods.

The change that is described above did not only happen in one institution in Copenhagen. It is a change that affected institutions for the homeless throughout Denmark; elsewhere in the world similar changes have also been described. Focus has been especially directed toward the increase in more serious psychiatric problems among the homeless (Jones, 1986; Isaac and

Armat, 1990; Munk-Jørgensen et al., 1992).

Sundholm thus had, since the beginning of the 1990s, a group of homeless that was younger than experienced earlier and had new serious problems, primarily drug abuse and serious mental health problems.

Danish laws in this area expect the institutions that receive homeless not only to provide shelter, but also to work toward resocialisation. One might indeed ask whether the possibilities available to the homeless in Denmark in the form of shelters can live up to these expectations, especially in light of the sudden appearance of the group of younger homeless that, at least at that time, we were only superficially acquainted with.

Sundholm, an Institution for Homeless and for People who are Different

As already described, Sundholm is an old institution that can shelter 208 persons overnight. Sundholm has four sections, each with 20–80 residents, which function for the most part independently. Each section has its own target group. The hostel functions also as the receiving section; here, there are mostly double rooms, the rest being single rooms. It was originally intended that this section should house short-term residents, but there are many who stay for longer periods. Only a few years ago, one could have a bed for the night but had to spend the day outside the institution as best one could. Today, people are admitted and have a bed at their disposition around the clock. They pay a fixed daily price for the bed equal to about one-sixtieth of the normal welfare payment or about half of the welfare amount received monthly.

Two other sections have somewhat the same functions and cost the same, but they have only single rooms and are used for residence over longer periods. One of these sections requires the residents to have full board and to pay for it separately.

The fourth section can best be compared to a small hospital ward. There are 22 beds and the personnel group is the same as in a Danish psychiatric hospital ward. The residents here have more or less serious physical or mental health problems; they cannot manage to live either on the street or in ordinary institutions for homeless, and they are not ill enough to be admitted to an ordinary hospital. Or else they are ill enough but are so deviant or difficult that an ordinary hospital does not wish to admit them.

In addition, Sundholm offers various workshops and other work opportunities, and there is a residents' council. A house organ is published for both the personnel and the residents, and part of the editorial staff of the Danish homeless-magazine *Hus Forbi* published by and for homeless resident at Sundholm.

Over the past few years, some new members have been added to the staff, professionals who go outside the institution to seek out and support earlier residents after they have moved into ordinary apartments, and an external service has been established at Copenhagen's railway stations to support homeless there.

To this picture of a large institution that receives people with the great social problem of not having anywhere to live, as well as people with significant psychosocial and health problems, belongs also a description of the personnel who have contact with and responsibility for helping the homeless. Some of the personnel have an education that answers to the functions they perform, but about half have no formal relevant educational background.

When the fences around the institution were torn down, more was accomplished than giving easier entrance; the institution in fact opened itself to the surrounding society. It is no longer the police who deliver the destitute to the institution against their will, but people who come on their own and ask for shelter. And after their stay, some ask to continue to come and, for example, work in the workshops, take their meals or just have a place where they can come and talk to others.

One can choose to only give weight to the positive qualities to be found in an institution offering shelter to the homeless of a high quality and equipped to meet many different needs.

But one can and ought to question an institution like Sundholm, due to its double and not always clearly defined functions. Sundholm provides necessary shelter as an alternative to life outdoors in the streets, but also insists on providing services that have resocialisation as their goal. The user usually comes to find shelter, perhaps also to find acute social help, and in some cases, to find help for health problems. But the boundary between the importance given by the homeless to these different functions and the personnel's judgment about the needs of the homeless can be and often is unclear. Thereby, the motives for doing these things are often unclear as well. The means used are also just as imprecise and it is difficult to know whether the functions performed also express what the homeless themselves judge their needs to be or a paternalistic personnel's projected ideas about homeless people's possibilities and wishes.

Do we know the Homeless Well Enough?

I consider it to involve a significant risk in relationship to initiatives for the homeless if the questions I have just raised are not included in the continuing debate among those who work with homelessness and the homeless. Do we really understand living conditions for homeless and their background for living under these conditions, when we concern ourselves with homeless who do not only have a housing problem? In order to try to understand how well we understand their lives and their individual backgrounds, I will return to the new group of homeless who in the 1980s appeared at Sundholm and in homeless institutions throughout Denmark. This group of course represents only itself and thus only a part of homelessness, but that does not prevent us, through gaining better insight into this group's situation, from learning something that could have significance for understanding both the essence of homelessness and our tendency to create myths and to disregard essential problems for a particular, and especially a particularly vulnerable, group of citizens – perhaps because their problems seem too hard to bear.

During the course of 12 months in 1988/89, I registered all those aged 18–35 that used homeless institutions in Copenhagen (Brandt, 1992). These totalled 960 different individuals of whom 171 (18 per cent) were women. The 960 persons used a total of 105,644 bed-days out of the 269,771 available or over one-third.

Of the 960 persons, two-thirds were only admitted once; however, 10 per cent lived at the institutions all year without interruption.

About 20 per cent received an early pension as compared with 0.9 per cent in the same age group in the population as a whole. Less than 10 per cent earned any income or were being educated as compared to 85 per cent in the same age group as a whole.

The only remarkable thing about these figures is that a group of young people – for men it is one per cent of all men in Copenhagen in the same age group and for women 0.3 per cent – in the course of a chance year each used the city's institutions for homeless as an overnight shelter an average of 110 days. One could conclude that as long as homelessness is seen as a social phenomenon that only relates to a shortage of housing, there is nothing disturbing in these figures.

One could however also choose to focus on the fact that this small amount of quantitative data presents a picture of a group of citizens who are perhaps seriously marginalised. They are probably young people who are excluded from the labour market. But how bad is their situation otherwise? When did this process of marginalisation start? Was it the economic situation, unemployment and bad times that sent them onto the streets? Or one might also like to know: where were these young people as children?

Of the registered 960 younger homeless, I interviewed a representative sample of 129 persons. The interview treated their actual situation and their background. Young people from all social classes were represented, but otherwise they had little in common with other young people living in Copenhagen.

Half of all those interviewed said that one or both of their parents used drugs. Most common was severe alcohol or medicinal drug abuse.

Most (about 80 per cent) described growing up under insecure conditions combined with a severe lack of emotional support and a tyrannical or rigid upbringing.

About half of those interviewed told of a childhood home characterised by economic need, where they often experienced a lack of food, and normally were not able to buy new clothes or other necessities.

In addition, about half claim to have suffered various forms of psychological symptoms during childhood.

It is therefore not surprising that 60 per cent of those interviewed said that their drug or alcohol abuse started before the age of 18, and half of these experienced themselves as abusers before they were 16.

This group of younger homeless has thus been exposed to many severely damaging conditions while growing up. From their descriptions of these conditions, it becomes evident again and again that it is the women that have been hardest hit by destructive conditions early in life.

Only five persons out of the 129 interviewed, or about 30–40 of the group of 960 younger homeless, can say they had a completely normal and respectable childhood with stable parents who had no problems of abuse, that conditions at home were secure, not violent, and without severe economic problems, and that they themselves had no severe work, behaviour or abuse problems and were therefore physically and mentally healthy.

Is it possible to avoid supposing that these young people who end up in a situation of homelessness do so, at least in part, because of the conditions that have so heavily contributed to pervade the way in which each of them has come to exist?

These conditions, which can be understood as the psychosocial situation for the adult younger homeless, are also characterised by the fact that as they describe it, their network is very weak and often in fact nonexistent, in any case in relation to ordinary established society.

Criminality and other forms of deviant behaviour for the purpose of supplementing official income are very common in the group investigated. Such behaviour is not only an economic necessity, but also part of the special behaviour pattern of the subculture.

Members of the group also describe great mobility. They move around a great deal and find random and temporary places to stay, among them 'the street'.

It is hard to avoid trying to place these younger homeless in diagnostic categories. In a mixed psychosocial context, they can be categorised as suffering from schizophrenia, borderline psychosis, severe brain damage and personality disorders. Some are drug addicts, some are alcoholics.

The descriptions those interviewed presented of their living conditions while growing up indicate very clearly that there is a connection between early emotional failure and risk of becoming a social outcast and homeless. It does not relate so much to which social class an individual comes from, but much more to the care – or lack of it – he or she receives. Perhaps most interesting is the fact that the investigation shows that the authorities have often been in contact with the family earlier, without it having been possible to change the course of development. Already at an early age, the later homeless had been stigmatised as an outcast.

Considerations about Resocialising Homeless

As stated earlier, it is of course not possible to generalise about the homeless' background and earlier living conditions, the conditions for their upbringing and eventual lacking socialisation or their exclusion as a result of their deviant behaviour, on the basis of a study of a little group of younger homeless in Copenhagen. I will, however, put forth the hypothesis that what we see in the younger homeless is a common element of the essence of homelessness. And from there I will try to consider alternatives to the ways in which we respond to the homeless – alternatives especially to the air of superiority and the urge to re-educate and control that are in themselves attitudes that contribute to feelings of exclusion. I fear that these are very common attitudes, and as I pointed out in my description of Sundholm, they seem to be the rule when attempting to do something for the homeless. As a consequence, this way of responding is part of the dialectical conflict between the honest attempt to improve conditions for the homeless and the desire to normalise those who live and behave otherwise.

Due primarily to my 20 years of working with homeless people, I dare to put forth a series of generalised considerations on the basis of what is actually documented for some special few. From my experience, I have the feeling that the mechanisms that develop homelessness often resemble those described in relation to the younger homeless, but that reality is hidden behind a romanticised or respectable facade. I also find support for my idea about the generality of these considerations in the descriptions that can be found primarily in much earlier and contemporary literature about the lives and fates of outcasts and homeless.

The child psychiatrist, Alice Miller, writes ironically about our usual way of reacting to the deviant behaviour of children who have been forsaken:

> Most people do not show the least interest in the question of why a child has become so or so. When one draws attention to the causes, the father's brutality, the mother's self-absorption, they say: 'That is no excuse for stealing. Everyone has been through hardships during their childhood without becoming criminals.' That the cause of this difference in development lies in the degree of the attention the individual has received does not interest them.

And further:

> ... Everyone will exert themselves to discipline these people, to bring them something positive, but no one wishes to know about the tragedy of their existence (Miller, 1988).

For several hundred years, it has been good practice to try to discipline the homeless. The obvious motives have been compassion, a demand for self-sufficiency on conditions dictated by society, or the wish to control those who are different. Attempts to discipline have seldom succeeded. The fact that we continue anyway must either be due to an aversion to or anxiety about those who are different, or perhaps an unformulated wish to protect ourselves from the homeless by institutionalising them while also 'maintaining them'. In this way, we ordinary citizens have the opportunity to see our own dark side, in the distance and without gettin in touch with it.

It is thus questionable whether there is any social interest whatsoever in contributing anything at all to the homeless, other than what is completely traditional and absolutely basic. It is in fact surprising to see that numerous attempts have been made to extend help toward a better existence to many people who function very badly, as, for example, the younger homeless, by completely traditional means and with no or only temporary results or – one could fear – with the opposite of the desired results.

In addition, it would seem that the already-existing institutions have a tendency to exclude those who function worst, because it is not possible to achieve anything with them and to show any results. This practice creates a group that has such heavy and complex psychiatric and abuse problems that they 'are too badly off' to be able to receive treatment or other forms of help from either psychiatric hospitals or narcotics or alcohol treatment centres, and they are not especially welcome in the homeless institutions either.

All this makes one wonder whether we are doing anything right.

The law says that measures shall be taken to bring the homeless back into ordinary life in society, and this principle is the usual basis for most of the social and also medical work being carried out. The goal is the best possible resocialisation.

But when this is not possible – and we often see this first after several attempts at resocialisation – the homeless are categorised as impossible, all treatment, both purely social and sociomedical, is withdrawn, and they are left to shift for themselves.

Maybe we are making a mistake.

Maybe we should consider, when planning initiatives to be taken regarding both treatment, resocialisation and other kinds of social help, whether we should change some of our traditional ideas about the kinds of measures that should be taken, their content and goals. We could also ask ourselves whether the usual separation between social and medical initiatives is valid, based as it is on the idea that a person has a distinct set of social problems and a distinct set of health problems.

To follow other roads than that of resocialisation could be part of a course of action that could provide much more quality and dignity, especially for those who, for one reason or another, cannot meet the ordinary demands of society. This process could also be one of a set of social and social-medical tools, so that 'non-resocialisation' would not just be an undesirable side effect of a complicated social system or an expression of the dissolution of social relationships that indicates that things are going badly.

'Non-resocialisation' could then be part of a process that eventually creates the possibility to conduct another kind of socialisation or to find a lasting living standard, even though this standard might not seem acceptable to an outside observer. An example can perhaps describe what I am thinking of here.

A 52-year-old man lived at a homeless institution from the age of 29– 34 without interruption. He received welfare and drank excessively. He had lost contact with his family. Except for three periods of one to three months, he had never had a job. He named himself 'Jens Drunk'. Besides a character defect, he did not suffer from any serious psychopathology.

He first rejected the suggestion that he apply for an early pension, but several conversations revealed that he considered himself to be far too low on the social scale to be able to imagine that he could be considered for 'something so high and unattainable as an early pension'. This early pension, which he was then awarded and which would normally be an indication that everyone had given up on him, meant for him that he had changed his identity. He was now 'Pensioner Jens'. Contact with his family could be renewed, he moved into an apartment, bought furniture and other necessities and has since then had intermittent work in protected workshops. He still drinks, but much less.

Receiving an early pension was here a decisive factor in a long process of improvement of this man's living conditions.

It must be possible to find a level in the work of helping homeless who are abusers and mentally ill by developing an attitude that can best be described by the expression 'optimistic nihilism'.

We must learn to combine an intense sense of duty with honest realism.

It is completely unrealistic to work with a group of people who are for the most part so severely wounded and vulnerable without facing the fact that their problems are chronic and that visible growth and change in the traditional sense will probably be impossible.

On the other hand, this must not lead to just letting problems continue as they are and labelling these people's condition as hopeless and impossible to treat. Change is possible, although slow and perhaps limited, and possibly in a completely different direction than the one traditionally attempted – a good life is not the same as an ordinary life within the confines of established society.

It is necessary to develop a special will to understand the person as he or she is, combined with an ability to see the limits of the possible. It is necessary to see, to understand, to avoid rejection, and dare to be able to maintain a long-lasting treatment in spite of interruptions, resistance and negative responses. Maybe we could do a bit better if our treatment and social work were not so goal-oriented. If only we could stop evaluating the means we use on the basis of the value of the goal – that is, by holding tight to a kind of 'the end justifies the means' attitude.

I believe that the means, the social work, if it is 'good' in itself, is of value even if no goal is reached.

What Could be Good Practice?

My experience tells me that no people exist who reject attempts at help and contact, if only the help and contact offered have the right character. Nevertheless, we continue to talk about meeting lack of motivation and lack of the will and desire to change on the part of people who are living a marginalised existence. First reactions toward us, the ones with all the correct ideas and initiatives, must of course be ones of rejection.

My proposal is that we try to create as good living conditions as possible for those who live differently, without at the same time maintaining that we know best what *the good life* is.

That we also ensure room and resources for those who are different and that we dare to live with them in society.

That we give the excluded homeless the possibility to come to the systems designed to help them in order to have their needs met, without immediately 'getting their ears caught in the machine'.

That we reconsider who is threatening and who is threatened.

That we understand that integration does not necessarily demand normalisation.

Just to name some obvious examples, there must be room:

to treat a sore on the shin, for example, without regard for whether the person continues to drink or cannot keep appointments;
to ensure housing, in shelters, collectives or some other form, for the deviant and excluded mentally ill who will not conform;
to also consider uncommon occupations as work;
to accept those who are different as they are. Not in blind indifference. Not as an expression of just letting things continue as they are, but rather as a generous acceptance of the fact that we are all different, that the world is a world in chaos, that it can be difficult to determine what is right and what is wrong, and what is better and what is worse.

I could wish that the word 'treatment' were not only applied to efforts leading to better health, but that it also had the connotation: TO TREAT EACH OTHER – WELL OR BADLY, and that care was not seen as something secondary or less respectable, and that we were not afraid of everything different.

To admonish, demand, exert pressure in order that others should change is seldom anything more than moralism. And moralism can only please dilettantes and those who think they know best.

I do not mean that we should not offer treatment and resocialisation; of course, we should. But it should not stand alone. Treatment must be available and measures that can lead to resocialisation must be offered also to the socially weakest. But these should not be either the primary or most important measures; they must, however, be of the best quality – committed, visionary and based on respect.

Could we wish, for example, for modern asylums? And would socially weak and excluded persons wish to live in modern asylums?

Integration can be costly for a person who is lonely and lacks the room to satisfy special needs and interests. Segregation does not only need to be a negative concept. The Norwegian criminologist, Nils Christie has described villages for unusual people (Christie, 1989). In connection with considerations about also allowing people to live a 'non-socialised' existence, this idea could inspire us to imagine new types of asylums – places that would provide a framework for building living conditions and cultures that give those who wish it a fair chance to live decent lives. Such asylums could be part of existing institutions or be placed outside them as independent organisations. They should be places that could room the desires of those who were to live there, both in regard to living arrangements, activities, working arrangements and cultural life. They should be built up around residents' own wishes, needs and possibilities, and planned in a cooperation between these residents and people who are visionary enough to have ideas and also democratic enough to allow everyone to contribute to how things should be. That is to say, asylums that provide living space for those who are different, but not places for treatment or re-education.

In Copenhagen, there have been established one or two such small asylums where mentally ill homeless with severe abuse problems, also of illegal drugs, could live permanently with a contractual right to stay at the asylum, which thus became their home. Here, they were not met with demands to be drug-free or absolutely and without discussion to submit to psychopharmacological treatment. Nor were there demands to submit to other forms of treatment or activities that the personnel considered meaningful.

Demands were made, however. To the personnel, that they should give care and support according to the needs of those living there.

This attitude should also be the basis of the necessary work being done at the street level. Homeless people will always be found living on the street, and the efforts to help them must be sufficient, in both form and content.

To Understand What Homelessness Is

On the basis of the considerations I have tried to formulate here, it should be possible to propose a qualitative definition of homelessness.

Even though homelessness is primarily considered to be a social housing problem, and being 'homeless' understood as synonymous with being 'housingless', a definition that only includes the housing aspect will be too narrow and meaningless, except perhaps in relation to a purely demographic discussion.

> A person is homeless when he or she does not have a place to live that can be considered to be stable, permanent and of a reasonable housing standard. At the same time, this person is not able to make use of society's relations and institutions (understood in the broadest sense, such as family networks and private and public institutions of all kinds) due to either apparent or hidden causes relating to the individual or to the way in which society functions (Brandt, 1987).

This definition, in any case, covers the problems presented by the group of younger homeless that I have studied, and I believe that it most probably also applies to other groups of homeless: those living on the street, other age groups of homeless and also the large group that can be considered relatively homeless – those who live under unstable conditions with acquaintances and family.

That there exists a basic rule of society that there is a need for people who can serve as scapegoats must here remain a postulate, but when one can read that exclusion and homelessness have existed in different cultures and at different times, largely unchanged in spite of apparently superficial changes, and when one combines this with the often uninspired efforts that basically build on the same few principles, also in different cultures and times, it is easy to support this postulate. As a consequence, I could understand homelessness in a completely different way: homelessness is symptomatic of a society that does not satisfy the basic needs of certain of its citizens.

Bibliography

Amtsrådsforeningen i Danmark (The Association of County Councils in Denmark) (1990), *Amterne og videreudviklingen af § 105-institutionerne (The counties and the development of the § 105-institutions)*.

Brandt, P. (1987), 'Hjemløshed og psykisk lidelse' ('Homelessness and mental illness'), *Nord Psykiatr Tidskr*, 41, pp. 295–301.

Brandt, P. (1992), 'Yngre hjemløse i København', disputats, ('Young homeless in Copenhagen', thesis), Fadl's forlag, København..

Brandt, P. and Munk-Jørgensen, P. (1996), 'Homelessness in Denmark' in Bhugra, D. (ed.), *Homelessness and Mental Health*, Cambridge, Cambridge University Press.

Christie, N. (1989), *Om landsbyer for udsedvanlige mennesker* (*About villages for unusual people*), Oslo, Univeritetsforlaget.Koch-Nielsen, I. and Rostgaard, T. (1993), *Homelessness in Denmark*, National Report for FEANTSA, Copenhagen, The Danish National Institute of Social Research.

Isaac, R.J. and Armat, V.C. (1990), *Madness in the Streets*, New York, The Free Press.

Jones, B.E. (ed.), *Treating the Homeless: Urban Psychiatry's Challenge*, Washington, DC, American Psychiatric Press.

Miller, A. (1988), *Das verbannte Wissen*, Frankfurt (tr. from the Danish).

Munk-Jørgensen, P., Flensted-Nielsen, J., Brandt, P., Krusell, J.B., Borg, L., Hansen, S.S. and Petersen, B (1992), 'Hjemløse psykisk syge, en registerundersøgelse af klienter på herberg og forsorgshjem' ('Psychiatric patients with no fixed abode. Registration of clients in hostels and care homes'), *Ugeskr Læger*, 154, pp. 1271–5.

Rossi, P.H., Wright, J.D., Fisher, G.A. and Willis, G. (1987), 'The Urban Homeless: Estimating Composition and Size', *Science*, 235, pp. 1336–41.

Salicath, N. (ed.), *Homelessness in Industrialised Countries*, Netherlands, International Federation for Housing and Planning.

24 Conclusions and Policy Implications

SIRKKA-LIISA KÄRKKÄINEN

The chapters presented in this section show how difficult it is to analyse the services provided for homeless people, since they are not regarded as part of the ordinary service provision for the nation at large. The planning of services for the homeless is nevertheless part of social policy, of the way society is prepared to assume responsibility for those in need. Each of the European countries seems to have adopted a path of its own founded on its own social institutions in its attitude to homelessness. As a result, the criteria on which services for the homeless are based differ from country to country. Seldom have countries looked abroad to see how others have addressed the problem. The active authorities and NGOs have greatly affected the nature of the policy adopted and the types of services provided for homeless people. Some EU Member States have in fact only recently become aware of homelessness as a problem in society; all in all the problems associated with poverty are so vast that homelessness used not to be recognised as a problem in its own right. There is also one major factor that cannot be predicted, and that is immigration; the social upheavals and unrest in neighbouring territories have presented many countries with large numbers of immigrants, all of whom need housing.

Perceptions of Homelessness and Conceptualisation of Services

Authors of the chapters have stressed that homeless people are *poor* people of *no fixed abode*, and that many of them are *deviant in their behaviour and incapable of using the institutions in society*. Some of them are, furthermore, aliens, i.e. immigrants.

These descriptions of homeless people and their way of life have been accompanied by debate on the reasons for homelessness. These are felt to be either socio-psychological or structural, or both. The definition proposed by Brandt (see above) with its stress on deviation, looks in both directions for

527

the reasons: 'A homeless person is not able to make use of society's relations and institutions (understood in the broadest sense, such as family networks and private and public institutions of all kinds) due to either apparent or hidden causes relating to the individual or to the way society functions'. The reason for homelessness may, according to this definition, thus lie in either the individual or society.

Brandt's definition just goes to show how widely opinions of homelessness may differ (see also Børner Stak and Koch-Nielsen). The reason for homelessness, however it is viewed, seems to have a considerable impact on the types of services provided for homeless people. Even if these people are characterised by all the attributes mentioned – poverty, lack of a home and deviant behaviour – the nature of the services provided for them appears to differ according to which of the characteristics carries most weight.

In examining the services provided for homeless people, we have given some thought to what we regard as the objective. Some of the homeless people may perhaps not be capable of handling their affairs as normal tenants, of bearing the responsibility required by a rental agreement. In most cases they nevertheless need decent housing, either for themselves alone or shared with others, which they can hopefully look upon as a home. The service provider may see to the paying of the rent and many other practical matters. In this case quality is the primary objective for the apartment, since these people are not fully independent.

This issue has also been examined to some extent via the concepts of housing and home (and houseless and homeless). Housing is a space within four walls, a space that can be made into a home, a place for social relations. The matter becomes a problem when the occupant is unable to make the space into a home and to look upon it as his/her home. He/she is not 'houseless', because he/she has housing, but is nevertheless (according to several authors) 'homeless'. Should we nevertheless aim to provide such a person with housing, a space which can be in principle convert into a home, and help him/her to stay in it? If this potential has never even existed, the person will be eternally homeless. There are major differences of opinion over this distinction in the European countries, and they greatly affect the types of services provided for homeless people.

What do the services thus primarily seek to eliminate: houselessness or homelessness? The provision of care and treatment for the homeless person aims to induce a change so that he/she becomes capable of establishing social relations. If, after this care and treatment, that person is no longer mentally 'homeless' but does not have housing (is housingless), has the service provision chain truly fulfilled its purpose?

In the same way we may ask whether the service provision has been successful if a homeless person is given housing but cannot use it or cannot look upon it as his/her home. If that person is incapable of changing, would it be better after all to provide a roof over his/her head in a way that is worthy of human dignity, in special housing?

Deviation as the Basis for Service Provision

Deviation, a person's inability to make use of society's institutions (regardless of whether the reason is felt to lie in the individual, the prevailing conditions or society), creates a need to provide emergency services, to care for and rehabilitate him, to change and normalise him. This need to change, to lead a different sort of life, often springs from the homeless person himself, but by no means always.

Attempts have been made to cure people of deviant behaviour, regardless of whether or not it is regarded as a disease, by means of a broad network of institutions and care homes that vary enormously in their nature and care practices from one society to another. Even if the treatment fails, at least an attempt has been made to isolate these people from others in various kinds of institutions, or else they once again become homeless.

A homeless person must, according to this concept first change before being given a normal home. But when, and on what conditions, is a person regarded as being sufficiently normal to live in a normal home? Countries differ considerably on their views on this, and the issue will always be a problem for any country.

* Unless policy makers pay sufficient attention to the problems of deviant homeless people and unless resources for services are allocated to improve the living conditions of these people, who themselves have very little or no resources to improve their situation themselves, homeless people will be doomed to become the (often permanent) occupants of housing designed only as a temporary measure, or they return to being homeless. This situation is the most urgent one to be prevented.

* Treating deviation to help homeless people, to normalise the clients and integrate them with society, often in a stepwise process, is a necessary effort, especially if based on the wishes of the client, too. But a person

should not be required to change, to become normalised before providing him/her with decent human living conditions. Using the requirement of normalisation as a prerequisite for the provision of good quality services usually dooms a person to a vicious circle; while living under inhuman living conditions the effort to change one's life and the way of living may be impossible.

* Caution is needed in identifying what integration really means, over the community or human environment with which the client is expected to integrate and which environments are accepted as the ones the person should integrate with. Who in fact prescribes the objectives of this integration and how much say does the homeless person himself have in the matter? These issues should be researched and the concept of integration clarified.

Poverty as the Basis for Housing Provision

Homeless people are poor, often desperately so. Being poor, they do not have access to or cannot afford a normal home. This may be the result of many factors: unemployment, sickness, deviant behaviour, exclusion, being a refugee, etc. Those who are unable to make use of society's institutions are particularly threatened by poverty. Whatever the reason for their poverty, the society in which they live either does not wish to or cannot afford to provide sufficient financial resources to ensure them even a minimum standard of living. The social security systems vary and are not fully adequate. Homeless people may not necessarily be entitled to benefits, especially if they are immigrants. Not all countries are currently able to lower their housing costs by means of housing benefits or some other such system, and unemployment causes problems in all countries.

In most countries of the European Union the average level of income and welfare is already high enough to able to guarantee the basic resources for living. Sufficient minimum financial resources, in the form of benefits and allowances, should be provided to all people in order to prevent them from becoming homeless solely due to poverty. Sufficient welfare benefit should be targeted also to all citizens independently of their working career.

Housing Exclusion and Substandard Housing as the Basis for Housing Provision to Socially Vulnerable

Some countries have solved the housing problem of their low-income population by preserving cheap, substandard housing, in the old inner cities, for example. Demolishing these houses would reduce the supply of cheap housing and raise the risk of homelessness.

By contrast, other countries regard the housing of poor people in substandard stock as running contrary to the ideals of equality and solidarity; the provision of sufficient social housing and the criteria for its allocation are regarded as social issues. Once again the question presents itself of what makes a person so deviant that he cannot be given a home in social housing, and above all, how the sick and deviant can be helped to keep their homes and helped with their everyday problems so that they are not evicted.

Most countries cannot provide enough alternative housing for persons who cannot or do not wish to live according to the norms of the majority. The alternative housing is often in substandard communal housing or old stock, or in housing built by members of the community themselves (such as Christiana in Copenhagen). These communes tend to be illegal and hence temporary.

* Examining homelessness primarily as a housing exclusion problem guaranteeing a sufficient stock of housing, and above all social housing, is of major importance. The criteria for allocating housing should be such that homeless people and other socially voluntary groups also have a chance of being granted a home.

* The support helping the occupant to live in this housing once it has been granted is a field of social welfare which should urgently be developed in order to help vulnerable groups to maintain the housing and to prevent evictions. Eviction may spark off deviant behaviour and other problems, marking the start of a downward spiral for substance abusers and the like. And vice versa, being provided with housing may be an opportunity to begin a new life and to become integrated with society or the community.

* Alternative housing for people who are not capable or willing to live in normal housing, even with support measures, should be developed. The alternative housing does not, however, need to be of a low standard. There are examples in a number of countries of high-standard alternative housing for homeless people and other vulnerable groups either separate from or

within the social housing stock. The housing, the apartments are good standard apartments, only way in which it differs is that it is subject to special regulations and support.

* If homelessness is examined purely as a shortage of housing, and providing normal housing is the only way of solving the problem, there is a danger that the homeless people who also have other problems will be excluded and end up in night shelters and hostels. Alternative housing is called for, along with care and treatment.

Emergency Services – the First Step on a Continuum?

Emergency is an unexpected event which creates an urgent, pressing need. Usually it refers to very specific situations, the clearest example being the need to survive, i.e. the case in which someone's life is threatened. The emergency measures are an immediate response to the situation of a person in urgent need of help.

The chapters in this section show that emergency services are mostly provided by several voluntary organisations. Each service provider focuses on its emergency tasks; coordination between service providers is not very common. There is not necessarily anywhere to send a homeless person who is no longer in need of this particular kind of service. So he stays in the shelter or other temporary accommodation. The situation is that of long-prevailing precariousness, and no longer of emergency.

The question of the continuum of services, the coordination of services, is also addressed. Some of unanswered questions may be summarised as: Which authority should be responsible for this coordination? Voluntary organisations are often funded by public authorities. Funds from the government or other public authorities are granted separately for each organisation. Whether or not the funding body requires coordination amongst the different services funded is often unclear and depends on the administrative system of the particular country.

* The chapters confirm that there are advantages if the service provision of different service providers are coordinated to each forming a chain along which a client can proceed. Therefore coordination should be developed. How this will be done depends on the overall system of service provision in the particular country.

* In some countries the services provided by the voluntary sector are comp-lementary to municipal services and at least partly financed by the local authorities. Municipalities have the ultimate responsibility for providing services for homeless people; this makes the coordination much easier to arrange, but how well the coordination is arranged depends on the initiatives and resources of the local authorities. Govermental authorities could in some case urge the municipalities to take measures.

* In some other countries the service provision is based on services provided by the voluntary sector. In most cases, however, the providers get their finances from the public sector. The financing organisation should set requirement on coordination of services before granting resources.

* The provision of emergency social services should ultimately aim at minimising the demand. However, because there is little or no possibility of the service providers being able to direct clients elsewhere, there is a steady demand for new emergency services. Those who apply for help are in permanent need of help. When there is a distinct lack of overall coordination, the notion of the continuity of services fails to have any meaning. This is a situation which should be urgently tackled with in all Member States.

Separate Services or Services as Part of the Ordinary Provision?

Services for homeless people are usually provided separately from other, ordinary services. Is this necessary, and does it guarantee better quality? Ordinary welfare and health services are provided for every citizen or for those eligible, depending on the welfare system of the country. There are notable differences in the way services are managed and financed in the various countries. In some, however, the most excluded part of the population is denied access to services as they fail to meet specific eligibility criteria.

In other countries all citizens are eligible for the same services, homeless and other vulnerable groups as well. Special services are provided only if the ordinary service provision is not capable of providing proper services for these people. Services are often ordered in such a way that their coordination and continuity make it possible to guide the excluded person on to the other services he needs. Voluntary service providers, which often show initiative in their service provision, may play a considerable role in the change of services, thus being able to provide services for the very people who derive most benefit from them.

* Although the social housing services differ to a greater or lesser degree from the social welfare, the cooperation and the coordination of measures between these sector is absolutely necessary. Inasmuch as services for homeless people and those at risk of becoming homeless are concerned, it appears that both sectors must be well coordinated in order to maintain the required continuity of service provision, including special housing provision.

Temporary Accommodation – Often a Permanent Low-quality Solution

Emergency action usually results in the provision of temporary accommodation; but how do we define 'temporary'? Shelters and hostels clearly aim to provide accommodation for a short period of time. Many clients (such as elderly homeless people) do, however, spend years in shelters. Emergency can thus often lead to 'long-term temporary' solutions. Thus a number of homeless people who have stayed in hostels for years do not even wish to move to an apartment of their own any more. They have social contacts in the hostel, and they are perhaps not even capable of living in normal housing.

Must temporary and emergency accommodation facilities necessarily be substandard, as is often the case? Are there any reasons why temporary accommodation should be inferior even if the client will only be staying there for a few days?

* One must question the role and, hence, the use of temporary accommodation. Surely temporary accommodation should be provided only in situations where the client is expected to move on to some other form of accommodation or housing in the very near future.

* The standard of temporary accommodations should be evaluated. The reasons why the standard is kept low should be asked. There are several examples of good practice in the various countries by which good quality housing is available on a temporary basis. In some countries there are special 'crisis dwellings', e.g. for victims of domestic violence and other families with children which need accommodation in an emergency; the

aim is to prevent mothers with children from becoming homeless and to guarantee proper accommodation even during the first emergency period.

The Step Model – How Far is it Needed?

In many temporary accommodation projects providing socio-psychological support the clients have to go through a number of stages in a programme of social reintegration before they are considered capable of living on their own.

A number of such projects have succeeded in reintegrating a significant percentage of homeless people. However, clients often have to go through long temporary periods living in socio-therapeutic communities.

* Research is needed to determine to what extent the stepwise measures are really necessary. Although the aim of this process is to socialise the client to the normal society, does it really do so? Does the long temporary stay alienate him from normal life rather than integrating him in normal society? The alternative would be to allocate an apartment in an ordinary housing environment and to provide support in order to help him deal with everyday life.

Special Housing Provision

It is evident that there are people who are not capable of living independently, even with support measures, in ordinary housing. Ordinary housing provision and the housing management staff are not capable of dealing with people with specific problems. Although many such people may need socio-psychological support, they do not necessarily require institutional care.

Why must housing for these people be arranged on a temporary basis? Their problems often demand a permanent housing solution which also incorporates the provision of the socio-psychological help they require.

* Special housing with daily support and help is needed for these people. Special housing is a term not very common in all European countries. It in some cases refers to low standard housing; however, special housing need not be of lower physical standard than other housing. It should refer to good standard housing with which some kind of other service provision is connected.

* There are specific population groups whose needs demand specific facilities and services, e.g. elderly people, disabled people, mentally retarded people. In most welfare states the quality of the special housing (service housing, care homes, etc.) provided for these people is high or at least good. In the case of excluded population groups like former psychiatric patients, homeless people and immigrants the categorisation often results in lower quality housing, thus treating these groups as second class citizens.

    These citizens should not be treated as the ones not deserving decent housing. This division should be prevented.

Housing and Home

Researchers have stressed that it is not always entirely clear what is meant by normal housing and normal mainstream housing. The definition of housing can be founded in the architecture of the dwelling: does it satisfy the requirements of a building intended for human habitation, are the rooms a sufficient size, does the dwelling have washing and cooking facilities? If the answer is 'no', then the building is a hostel or some kind of shelter.

* Except for the architectural plan it is characteristic for normal housing that people in normal housing sign a rental agreement or own the apartment, in which case the ability to live independently and to sign a rental agreement is a prerequisite for the definition of normal housing. However, in the case of vulnerable persons and households, this prerequisite need not be valid; the apartment can be a normal one, but the rent payment is and should be guaranteed by the service provider, which also can provide other support services.

Preventive and Responsive Services

A distinction is drawn in discussions between the measures aiming to prevent homelessness and the services provided for those who are already homeless. Being excluded from housing, eviction, is naturally a major dividing line.

* The services targeted at people who are already homeless should also be regarded as preventive measures since they prevent the homeless person from sliding down the spiral to rooflessness. Some of these measures may

be the same as those designed to help the rest of the population, such as unemployment benefits, social security and above all housing provision, while others are special services targeted specifically at homeless people. The broader the social security is, and the sooner a person is provided with services on becoming homeless, the more the downward spiral can be prevented.

Uniform Recommendations Hindered by Differences Between Countries

It is impossible to make a direct comparison of the services for the homeless and their standard from one country to another. The major social differences between countries make such a comparison either difficult or downright impossible. The differences are greatest between southern and northern Europe, the Nordic countries and northern Central Europe. The climate alone gives homelessness a different dimension: unlike in the warm south, it is vital to have somewhere warm to go to for the night in the cold northern winter.

There are also major differences between European countries in the income level of their populations and the level and structure of their social security systems. In some countries the basic social security system is the family, while in others social security is targeted mainly at the individual. A person's working history also carries different importance in the granting of benefits designed to ensure a basic subsistence. In particular the right of single people to basic social security differs from country to country, and this affects a single person's ability to obtain and maintain a home. In certain countries some of the homeless people are families or mothers with children, while in others these groups take priority in the granting of social protection and the allocation of housing and are not therefore homeless inhabitants of hostels and night shelters.

A country's housing policy, the groups at which housing policy measures are targeted, the size of the social housing stock and the criteria for allocating housing likewise all affect the structure of homelessness for both single people and families. The proportion of rental housing in the total housing stock also varies greatly from one country to another. Many countries try to reduce the housing costs by means of a housing allowance or benefit, but not all. There are also differences in the use of cheaper, often substandard housing.

The most significant factor of all is, however, probably the extent of the homelessness problem. In countries with few homeless people it is easier to seek solutions and to provide services according to the need. The number of immigrants is of decisive significance: countries that have over the past decade been the receivers of hundreds of thousands and even millions of refugees or other immigrants, either legal or illegal, face a completely different situation from countries where the problem is confined more or less to the native population.

The number and proportion of the most difficult homeless cases, especially of drug addicts, drug-medicine abusers and people with serious mental health problems likewise varies from one country to another. The traditional alcoholic, the most common type of homeless person in the Nordic countries in particular, is less of a problem. The number of homeless people with more serious problems such as drug addiction and HIV, especially young homeless people, seems to be growing in all European countries. These problems are already very considerable in a number of cities. There seem to be few ways of helping these homeless people.

* However, in spite of these national differences, some general principals and goal should be outlined for the service provision for homeless people in the Europe.

Reflections and Dilemmas

Homeless people, like all other human beings, need basic security:

- economic resources, money to live our everyday lives;
- a permanent place where to live, an apartment;
- social contacts or/and social support;
- something meaningful to do.

A street homeless, a person sleeping rough, cannot meet many of the basic needs in his everyday life. Often, he/she is so deprived that they do not even expect to meet these needs. Services for homeless people aim at making the living conditions of a homeless person better. Which needs on the list above are the ones which have had a priority in developing the services and which of them are taken into consideration? Or expressed the other way round; should all these be taken into consideration in the service provision in order be able to help a homeless person properly? The answer is probably yes; the possibilities, the chances for a person to become integrated after a period of homeless are better, the more multidimensional service provision is, the more the services allow opportunities for a homeless person to use his own abilities and initiatives, too.

One can ask, however, which goal has the priority in the service provision, to help a homeless person to gain human conditions for his living or to treat, to cure and to normalise him? Even if these goals are not, primarily, contrary to each others, there seems often to be a need to make the requirement of a personal change as a condition for providing other services of better quality. Would it be possible for us, so-called ordinary people, to advance in a process of profound personal change while living in very precarious living conditions? And if the person is incapable of changing, must he be doomed to precarious living conditions for the rest of his life?

Emergency services are the services which are available for these people in most European cities. Accommodation is provided on temporary basis. While there are often few possibilities for a homeless person to go further, to services which would satisfy better his diversified needs, he stays: temporary accommodation becomes a long-term temporary solution for him. To prevent this situation, coordination between different service providers and different kinds of services should urgently be developed in the European cities, a coordination which embraces the whole chain of services from emergency shelters up to mainstream housing provision and even, if possible, to opportunities to integrate into the labour market. Especially during times of unemployment, the opportunities for homeless people to get work are not good; for this reason other activities, from supported working opportunities to self-managed cooperation are important, to satisfy the need to have something meaningful to do. This issue has not been much dealt with yet in the discussion of homelessness.

The decision-makers are often reluctant to invest societal economic resources on nonproductive people, especially on homeless people or immigrants. However, some studies have indicated that it is often much more expensive for a society to arrange the living conditions of these people on temporary basis, by building and providing temporary accommodations. The cost can be several times higher than the cost of providing these people with normal housing, although the rent must be paid by the society. In case of street homeless people, a high cost will be paid by the society if a homeless person must often be taken into custody, and furthermore even higher if he is taken to hospital care because of serious health problems caused by homelessness and severe abuse problems connected to it. Further research is needed to address the cost-benefit aspect of service provision.

The most serious problems connected to homelessness seem to be increasing; numbers of substance abusers using drugs, medicines or several intoxicants simultaneously are increasing. These problems are often connected to serious mental problems, too. Measures to treat these persons and to provide services for them are certainly the problems which should be tackled more concretely while studying homelessness and services for homeless people.

We are experiencing a period of social policy rethinking in Europe. The prevailing paradigm, the prevailing discourse is emergency, instead of one of progress which during the previous decade was expressed by govermental programmes, especially social programmes. In the present day it is essential that something is done immediately. In this light we may ask if we can look forward to the announcement of any goal-orientated measures by governments that would aim at reducing homelessness by planned and coordinated provision of services?

PART 5
THE RESEARCH AGENDA

25 Reflections on Needs for Future Research

What Have We Learned From the EUROHOME Project?

The main conclusions may be summarised as follows.

1   Innovative and appropriate methodologies and data are a crucial prerequisite for scientifically sound research about homelessness and an indispensable input into policy development and implementation.

2   While acknowledging that progress has been made in recent years in research, serious gaps which impair the development of informed policies have been identified (see Kofler in this volume).

3   Available data on homelessness in Europe is sparse and non-comparable. At the national level targeted primary research of homelessness is rare. It is nonexistent at the European level.

4   The expert group has developed methodological recommendations, identified methodological requirements and proposed the necessary steps and accompanying measures in order to carry out pertinent policy oriented research about homelessness (see Kofler in this volume).

5   The risk concept is important for understanding homelessness. Risk situations are affecting more people due to the employment crisis and new policy trends and vulnerability factors are multiplying due to the growing exposure to risks of deprivation and loosening of social bonds. The area of vulnerability is potentially more of a problem than the entity of current exclusion would suggest (see Tosi in this volume).

6   The whole range of policies for fighting poverty and ensuring social

protection are important but that they are not sufficient, as is shown by the actual existence of homelessness even in systems with widespread general protection.

7   The policies for fighting homelessness which are identified as feasible are: multifaceted (as opposed to monofaceted), integrated (versus segmented), long-term (versus short-term), preventive (versus curative) structural (versus individual), with participation of the homeless (versus imposed by public authorities) (see Vranken in this volume).

8   It is noted that there are two trends in service provision. The first one is a kind of 'supermarket approach' as is focused on provision of services without examining whether these are actually determined by client needs. The second one is based on a more thoroughgoing assessment of problems to be tackled (see Kärkkäinen in this volume).

9   Better understanding of the identity crises of homeless people and their self-perception could be of great policy value and be employed in the evaluation of services.

10 It is necessary to learn more about the role and functioning of family and informal networks of socially vulnerable people so that targeted measures could be developed and benefits transferred to reinforce the existing networks, rather than just to continue channelling more and more resources and services to sheltering and assisting people once they fall through the personal safety nets.

11 Integrated policy models developed in Denmark and Finland are identified and described as models of best policy and practice in preventing homelessness and assisting homeless people. It is acknowledged, however, that even in these countries people with multiple problems fall out of the system of standard social and welfare protection. Complementary services for crisis intervention are needed and exist even in countries with a strong integrated policy approach. Services for the homeless who have multiple, albeit, fast-changing problems prove to be efficient instruments of reintegration providing that there is a continuation between general social and welfare protection and crisis intervention (see Koch-Nielsen in this volume).

12 In addressing the issue of models of good practice we could not go beyond the descriptive level as no resources were available for field research. Only contextual conclusions could be drawn about the impact of policies to combat housing exclusion. The future research agenda is determined by the need to implement policy impact studies using modern methodologies.

13 In the current stocktaking of practice in the domain of service provision models of good practice are generally identified on the basis of what service providers intend to achieve and on self-evaluation. Criteria for the measurement of success are usually set by service providers and outputs and outcomes remain beyond the critical analysis of performance from the point of view of other institutions and clients.

What More Can Researchers Say About Homelessness?

14 Researchers can further contribute to the development of the conceptual and methodological aspects of homelessness as a specific condition and as part of broader phenomena of social integration and exclusion in advanced welfare states.

15 Researchers can improve data and make extensive use of modern method for data analysis in order to end the 'game of numbers' about homelessness and housing aspects of deprivation. Researchers have the know-how to gather credible information to shape effective policies and efficient services.

16 The composition of the homeless population varies between countries and over time. Researchers can monitor which social processes are contributing to *'fragilisation'* of particular risk groups and which risks are conducive to homelessness.

17 Researchers can contribute to the better understanding of exclusion processes and can identify requirements for an effective social inclusion by further analysing coping strategies of people living under severe housing stress in dilapidated housing estates, crime-ridden neighbourhoods, conflict-burdened households, overcrowded apartments, overburdened by housing costs or living in transitional emergency accommodation or supported housing.

18 Researchers can study changes in patterns of homelessness between countries and over time in order to distinguish temporary maladjustment which can be addressed through palliative measures from structurally-induced housing deprivation which may be of more lasting nature and which may require fundamental changes in mainstream housing, social and welfare policies.

19 Researchers can contribute to the assessment of the monetary and nonmonetary costs of social and housing integration and monetary and nonmonetary benefits for the public and individuals and families affected by deprivation.

20 The domain of service provision is a policy twilight zone.

21 Researchers can break the dead lock of the mainstream debate about services and new partnerships which is more based on ideologies than on sound knowledge. The debate about *innovative-models-which-are-(presumably)-transferable-although-we-do-not-know-whether-they-actually-work -and- how-much-they-actually-cost* has not contributed much to tackling homelessness or social exclusion for that matter. Researchers can analyse effectiveness and efficacy of crisis intervention.

22 We know that services are mushrooming and there are suspicions that they may be operating as revolving doors for the homeless, that they may be providing more care that the client need and/or wish to receive. Researchers can analyse effectiveness and efficacy of crisis intervention.

23 We know that there is fragmentation of services, competition between service providers, lack of cooperation between specialised services. Researchers can analyse effectiveness and efficacy of crisis intervention and supported housing.

24 We know that services for homeless people are highly costly, are not sufficiently needs-based and their success rate in terms of outputs and outcomes is generally unknown.

What Can Researchers Further Say About Policies and Services?

25 Researchers have recognised that there is an urgent cognitive and policy

need to undertake methodologically sound evaluations of policies and services by means of:

- policy impact studies;
- performance measurements of services from the point of view of providers, other institutions and clients.

26 Researchers can develop a methodology for housing and welfare policy impact studies.

27 Researchers can develop service performance measurement methodology.

28 Researchers can develop standards of service delivery in the field of supported accommodation assistance which take into account the needs and the points of view of users.

As researchers we learned to think long and work fast. We have already translated most pertinent components from the above list of 'could be done' into project proposals and have submitted them to funding agencies. We have proposed the concrete outputs and are now waiting for concrete outcomes.

Contributors

Dr Dragana Avramov is a former director of the Demographic Research Centre, Institute of Social Sciences, University of Belgrade, Yugoslavia, and is currently director of the Population and Social Policy Consultants, Brussels, Belgium. She is senior scientific fellow, has lectured at several European universities, has served as a consultant for the United Nations and Council of Europe and was Council Member of the International Union for the Scientific Study of Population (IUSSP). Dr Avramov has received her PhD in sociology, MSc in sociology of culture and cultural policy and BA in sociology. She has published seven books and over 70 scientific articles in several languages in the domain of family and population sociology, social policy and social protection and housing exclusion in Europe. Her publication include the monographs *Individual, Family and Population in Mismatch* (1992), *Demographic Problems and Population Policy in Kosovo* (1992), *Homelessness in the European Union* (1995), *The Invisible Hand of the Housing Market* (1996) and *Youth Homelessness in the European Union* (1998).

Address: Population and Social Policy Consultants, Maria Louizasquare
            33:B1, 1000 Brussel, Belgium
Phone: + 32 2 230 02 24
Fax: + 32 2 230 91 92
E-mail: psp@innet.be

Tobias Børner Stax is an associated researcher at the Danish National Institute of Social Research where he is doing research on social exclusion and homelessness. He also teaches sociology at Copenhagen University. He graduated with an MA in political science from Copenhagen University in 1996 with a thesis on ethics and science in a postmodernist perspective and graduated with an MA – also in political science – from Washington State University in 1994 with a thesis on structuration theory in international politics. He has conducted research on the connection between homelessness and the housing market, on youth homelessness and on homelessness in a longitudinal perspective with focus on the mortality rate, the institutional history and the current living conditions of previously homeless people. Among his publications are the annual reports on 'Homelessness in Denmark' for the European Observatory on Homelessness (FEANTSA) (1995, 1996 and 1997), Om hjemløshed: begreber, typer, tal og metoder' (About Homelessness: Concepts, Types, Numbers and Methods) (1997), Youth Homelessness in Denmark (1997) and Homelessness in Denmark (1998).

Address: SFI, Herluf Trollesgade 11, 1052 Copenhagen, Denmark
Phone: + 45 33 48 08 00
Fax: + 45 33 48 08 33
E-mail: tob@smsfi.dk

Preben Brandt was employed from 1972–81 in various larger psychiatric hospitals. From 1981–97 he has been the leading psychiatrist at Sundholm, the largest institution for homeless people in Copenhagen. In conjunction to this, since 1990 he has done voluntary work with homeless people on the streets. He completed his doctoral thesis in 1991 ('Yngre hjemløse i København' ('Younger homeless people in Copenhagen')). Since then he has published *Socialpsykiatri – en humanistisk psykiatri* (*Social-psychiatry – a humanistic psychiatry*) and various scientific articles and discussion papers on social exclusion, drug abuse and social psychiatry in Danish and international publications. Since 1993 he has been involved in the work of Mental Health – Social Exclusion, a transEuropean committee concerned with mentally ill homeless people, under the auspices of the European Regional Council of World Federation of Mental Health. Since 1995 he has been Chair of the Danish National Narcotics Council. In 1997, Preben Brandt was the initiator and founder of Projekt UDENFOR (Project Outside), a non-profit private foundation involved in practical street level work with homeless people as well as research on social exclusion and social psychiatry, both in a social as well as health perspective, of which he is now the director.

Address: Projekt UDENFOR, Frederiksborggade 42, 1.tv 1360 Copenhagen, Denmark
Phone: + 45 33 17 66 77
Fax: + 45 32 54 71 67

Dr Martha R. Burt is the Director of the Social Services Research Program at the Urban Institute in Washington, DC. She received her PhD in sociology in 1972 from the University of Wisconsin-Madison. Her work on homelessness began in 1983, and in 1987 she directed the first US national survey of homeless individuals. That study focused on soup kitchen and shelter users in cities over 100,000 population and is reported in *Americans Homeless: Numbers, Characteristics, and the Programs that Serve Them* (1989). In 1992 she published *Over the Edge: The Growth of Homelessness in the 1980s*, which analyses why homelessness became a major social problem in that decade. Also in 1992 she compiled *Practical Methods for Counting Homeless People: A Manual for State and Local Jurisdictions*, which has been widely disseminated and used. She continues to conduct research and policy analysis on homelessness and residential instability, analysing results from the 1996 National Survey of Homeless Assistance Providers and Clients supported by the Interagency Council on the Homeless and data on residential instability from the National Survey of American Families (which is part of the Urban Institute's Assessing the New Federalism project examining the impacts of welfare reform).

Address: The Urban Institute, 2100 M Street NW, Washington DC, USA
Phone: + 1 202 857 8551
Fax: + 1 202 463 8522
E-mail: mburt@ui.urban.org

Volker Busch-Geertsema is a sociologist and works as a senior research fellow of the Association for Social Planning and Social Research (Gesellschaft für Innovative Sozialforschung und Sozialplanung – GISS) in Bremen, Germany. Since 1995 he has been national correspondent for Germany at the European Observatory on Homelessness and has produced three national reports on different aspects of homelessness. In Germany he has published a book about poverty and three books (and a number of articles) focusing on different regional and thematic aspects of homelessness together with his colleague Ekke-Ulf Ruhstrat (the latest publication was a study on homelessness in East Germany, Wohnungslosigkeit in Sachsen Anhalt, Bielefeld, 1997). He has prepared several expert reports for national and federal ministries in Germany.

Address: GISS, Hemmstrasse 163, 28215 Bremen, Germany
Phone: + 49 421 339 88 33
Fax: + 49 421 339 88 35

Mary Daly is Professor of Sociology at Queen's University, Belfast. A native of Ireland, she has published widely on the subject of European welfare states from a comparative perspective. Her work on homelessness in the European context is well known.

Address: Department of Sociology, Queen's University, Belfast, BT7 1LN, Northern Ireland
Phone: + 44 1232 335985
Fax: + 44 1232 320668
E-mail: m.daly@qub.ac.uk

Katherine Duffy trained as an economist and her research interests are in social policy and urban regeneration. For many years she was active in social initiatives in her local community and this is the foundation of her continuing commitment to combating poverty and social exclusion. She is currently a member of the England Committee of the UK Anti-Poverty Network. Katherine was UK programme manager for the Poverty 3 programme (1989–94), an initiative of D-G V of the European Commission. She has recently worked as consultant for both D-G V and D-G XII, on the Commission's contribution to combating social exclusion, and on evaluation of the targeted socioeconomic research programme. She is currently Director of Research for the Council of Europe initiative on Human Dignity and Social Exclusion (1996–98). The research will result in a major report and a new plan of action for the Council of Europe.

Address: Leicester Business School, de Montfort University, Leicester LE19 9BH, UK
Phone: + 44 116 257 7227
Fax: + 44 116 251 7548

Dr Henk de Feijter is demographic and urban planner at the Amsterdam Study Centre for the Metropolitan Environment of the University of Amsterdam and has worked with FEANTSA since 1994.

Address: Universiteit van Amsterdam, Nieuwe Prinsengracht 130, 1018 VZ Amsterdam, The Netherlands
Phone: + 31 20 525 40 40
Fax: + 31 20 525 40 41
E-mail: feyter@ivip.frw.uva.nl

Jean-Marie Firdion is Surveys Service Manager at the French Institute of Demographic Studies (INED) and a member of the International Association of Survey Statisticians (IASS). He worked with the ACSF team (Analysis of Sexual Behaviour in France) on methodological issues about data collection, sensitive questions and the accuracy of survey results. As one of the rapporteurs of the CNIS (National Council for Statistical Information) Working Group on Homelessness and Exclusion from Housing, he contributed to methodological studies and reports. Thus he conducted, under the leadership of Maryse Marpsat, the first French statistical survey on a representative sample of homeless people (March 1995). This survey (with a services-based methodology) was conducted in the inner city area of Paris. He has just finished, with Maryse Marpsat, a new survey on homeless youths (16–24 years old) in Paris and the suburbs (February–March 1998), with an improved methodology. His publications include articles in journals and edited volumes, many in conjunction with Maryse Marpsat (q.v.)

Address: INED, 33 Boulevard Davoult, 75980 Paris cedex 20, France
Phone: + 33 1 56 06 20 00
Fax: + 33 1 40 25 12 32
E-mail: firdion@ined.fr

Sirkka-Liisa Kärkkäinen works as researcher in the National Research and Development Centre for Welfare and Health, STAKES. Her areas of expertise are housing conditions and housing policy, social housing and the housing market. She has particularly studied the housing of elderly people and that of people who need special services both in housing provision and in support in their everyday life. She has participated in several development projects which have studied social requirements in the renewal of housing and living environment, looking especially from the point of view of the people who need help and special arrangements in order to be able to live in an ordinary environment. She has also studied tenants' democracy and participation in the management of social housing. Homelessness has been one of her areas of expertise since the 1980s, when she worked in the National Housing Board in Finland and participated in the development of homelessness policies and services for homeless people in Finland. She has been the national correspondent for FEANTSA since 1995 and has written research reports and articles in the research network. She has published numerous articles and contributed to several publications on all her research issues.

Address: STAKES, Box 220, SF-00531 Helsinki, Finland
Phone: + 358 939 67 20 68
Fax: + 358 939 67 20 54
E-mail: sirkkali@stakes.fi

Inger Koch-Nielsen was awarded the degree of Master of Law from the University of Copenhagen in 1965. Since 1982 she has been Head of the Research Unit of the Danish National Institute of Social Research. From 1982–87 she was responsible for the research unit engaged in equality research and health and working conditions. Since 1987 she has been responsible for the research unit engaged in social policy research on immigrants and refugees, the elderly, the disabled and the socially excluded. Her present fields of research are those of homelessness, the voluntary sector and social services. Prior to that she was engaged in divorce research. She has been a member of the advisory research group for the Poverty 3 research programme, the National Research Unit of the ECHP pilot study, the working group for the preparation of a European time budget survey (EUR-OSTAT), the Danish Social Science Research Council, the Governmental Committee on Volunteering in Social Work. Presently she is a member of the organisational committee for the Nordic policy research seminars, the Observatory on Homelessness (FEANTSA) and the Board of the Danish National Volunteer Centre.

Address: SFI, Herluf Trollesgade 11, 1052 Copenhagen, Denmark
Phone: + 45 33 480800
Fax: + 45 33 480833
E-mail: ikn@sfi.dk

Angelika Kofler is a research fellow at the Interdisciplinary Centre for Comparative Research in Social Sciences – International (ICCR) in Vienna. Her responsibilities at the ICCR include research in the areas of social as well as science and technology policy. She is also active as research coordinator and editor of *Innovation – The European Journal of Social Sciences*. Her research activities and publications include work in the subject areas of homelessness, gender and ethnic identity, multiculturalism, emotions, the information society and East-West cooperation in research and technological development. Before her scientific career, she held positions as news anchor and writer for the Austrian radio and television network ORF and as a print journalist in the US, where she was also active in a PR agency. Her educational background includes degrees in sociology and social psychology as well as in

English and comparative literature.

Address: ICCR, Hamburger Strasse 14–20, 1050 Vienna, Austria
Phone: + 43 1587 39 73 15
Fax: + 43 1587 39 73 10
E-mail: kofler@iccr.co.at

Hans Kristensen is deputy director of the Danish Building Research Institute, where he is also head of the research division on Housing and Urban Research. He was awarded an MA in sociology from the University of Copenhagen in 1982. Since then he has worked primarily with regional, urban and housing research, and also with development research in Kenya as well as with low-income problems as head of the scientific secretariat to the Danish Low Income Commission. He has been a member of the Danish Social Science Research Council for seven years, and is now adviser to the Norwegian Research Council. Most of his publications are reports for Danish ministries, written in Danish.

Address: SBI, Postbox 119, 2970 Horsholm, Denmark
Phone: + 45 45 86 55 33
Fax: + 45 45 86 75 35
E-mail: hk@sbi.dk

Maryse Marpsat is a member of the French National Institute of Statistics and Economic Studies (INSEE). She is now working as a researcher at INED, where she is in charge of the research programme on the issue of homelessness. This programme includes two representative statistical surveys (one about the living conditions and biographies of homeless people aged 18 and over, the other on homeless youth aged 16–24) and in-depth interviews. She participated in the writing of the National Statistical Council (CNIS) report on homelessness in 1995, 'Pour une meilleure connaissance des sans-abri et de l'exclusion du logement'. She is also working on spatial segregation and neighbourhood effects. Other publications include 'La statistique des sans domicile aux Etats-Unis', *Courrier des Statistiques* (1994) and 'Devenie sans-domicile: ni fatalité, ni hasard' ('Becoming Homeless: Who is at Risk?'), *Population et Sociétés* (1996) both with Jean-Marie Firdion. She has also edited a special issue of *Sociétiés Contemporaines* on homelessness in France and the USA (1998), and was co-author of 'Est-il légitime de mener des enquêtes statistiques auprès des sans-domicile? Une question éthique et scientifique' *Revue Française des Affaires Sociales* (1995).

Address: INED, 33 Boulevard Davoult, 75980 Paris cedex 20, France
Phone: + 33 1 56 06 20 00
Fax: + 33 1 40 25 12 32
E-mail: marpsat@ined.fr

Serge Paugam is a sociologist at the CNRS. He works in the Observatoire Sociologique du Changement (FNSP/CNRS) and at the Laboratoire de Sociologie Quantitative (CREST/INSEE). He teaches at l'Ecole des Hautes Etudes en Sciences Sociales and at the Institut d'Etudes Politiques de Paris. His main publications include 'La disqualification sociale, essai sur la nouvelle pauvreté' (PUF), 'La societé française et ses pauvres, l'experience du revenu minimum d'insertion' (PUF) and edited 'L'exclusion, l'etat des savoirs' (La Decouverte). Currently he is coordinating a European research project on the themes of 'Employment Precocity, Unemployment and Social Exclusion', with Duncan Gallie of Nuffield College, Oxford.

Address: CREST, Batiment Malakoff 2, Bd Gabriel Péri, 92245 Malakoff, France
Phone: + 33 1 41 17 77 21
Fax: + 33 1 41 17 57 55

Dr Aristides Sapounakis is a self-employed architect and planner. He also lectures at the School of Regional Planning and Peripheral Development at the University of Thessaly in Volos, Greece, and is also cooperating with the Research Institute 'Kivotos', being mainly responsible for research and policy planning on the issue of homelessness in Greece. As a planning expert he has been involved in studies on urban and regional development and the protection of the environment. The research topics in which he is concerned also include social exclusion and housing policy, access to housing for the least privileged social groups, improvement of the conditions in modern cities through the amelioration of the image of the urban environment and the expansion of pedestrian space.

Address: KIVOTOS, Ag. Pyrri 9, 11527 Athens, Greece
Phone: + 30 1 771 33 57
Fax: + 30 1 771 08 16
E-mail: arsapki@athena.compulint.gr

Marc-Henry Soulet is Professor of Sociology and Titular Chair of Social Work at the University of Fribourg in Switzerland. He held an academic position at the University of Caen and has been Fellow at the University of Montreal. His research activities are in the field of social policy, social problems and the sociology of social work. His publications include *Le systéme de la recherche sociale* (1987), *La recherche sociale en miettes* (1988), *De la non-intégration* (1994), *Crise et recomposition des solidarités* (1996), *Petite grammaire indigène du travail social* (1997), *Les transformation des métiers du social* (1998) and numerous articles and contributions in edited volumes.

Address: Chair, Francophone de Travail Social, Université de Fribourg, Rte
             des Bonnefontaines 11, 1700 Fribourg, Switzerland
Phone: + 41 2 63 00 77 80
Fax: + 41 2 63 00 97 15
E-mail: marc-henry.soulet@unifr.ch

Antonio Tosi is Professor of Urban Sociology at the Polytechnic of Milan and member of the Scientific Steering Group of the European Observatory on Homelessness (FEANTSA). He held academic positions at the Catholic University of Milan, the University of Camerino and the University of Genoa. He is currently working on urban poverty and the relationships between poverty and housing exclusion, homelessness, housing for immigrants and community participation in distressed urban areas. He is the author of *Ideologie della casa* (1978), *Immigrati e senza casa* (1993), *La casa: il rischio e l'exclusione* (1994) and *Abitanti. Le nuove strategie dell'azione abitativa* (1994).

Address: DST, Politecnico di Milano, Via Bonardi 3, 20133 Milan, Italy
Phone: + 39 2 23 99 54 17
Fax: + 39 2 23 99 54 35

Jan Vranken is Professor of Sociology and Social Policy at the University of Antwerpen (Ufsia), where he is in charge of the Research Unit on Poverty, Social Exclusion and Minorities (CASUM). His research activities have resulted in many books and reports on these matters. Since 1991 he has been the editor of the *Yearbook on Poverty and Social Exclusion* (in Dutch). Recent publications include a handbook on sociology (*Het Speelveld en de Spelregels*, 1996), *Naar het Middelpunt der Armoede?* (*To the Centre of Poverty?*) and *20 Ans CPAS. Vers une actualisation du projet de société* (1998). He is a member of the Scientific Committee of FEANTSA.

Address: UFSIA University of Antwerpen, Priensstraat 13, 2000 Antwerpen, Belgium
Phone: + 32 3 220 43 20
Fax: + 32 3 220 44 20
E-mail: jan.vranken@ufsia.ac.be

Malcolm Williams is Senior Lecturer in Sociology at the University of Plymouth and Visiting Research Fellow at City University, London. His research interests combine methodological questions and empirical research. Empirical work has been in the area of housing need, housing deprivation and urban-rural migration. Methodological work has included papers on probability, measurement and operationalisation. Recent monographs include *Housing Deprivation and Social Change* (1996) with Angela Dale and Brian Dodgeon (HMSO), *Philosophy of Social Research* (1996), with Tim May (UCL Press), *Knowing the Social World* (1998) edited with Tim May (Open University Press). Current work includes a measurement of youth homelessness in Torbay, England and a book on science and social science.

Address: University of Plymouth, Plymouth PL1 8AA, Devon, UK
Phone: + 44 1752 233217
Fax: + 44 1752 233201
E-mail: mwilliams@plymouth.ac.uk

Contributing Organisations

FEANTSA

FEANTSA – the European Federation of National Organisations Working with the Homeless was founded in 1989. At present, FEANTSA brings together more than 50 members in the countries of the European Union and other European Countries. FEANTSA is funded by the European Commission. It is supported by the European Parliament, and has consultative status at the Council of Europe.

One of FEANTSA's principal objectives is to engage in dialogue with the European institutions and with national governments in order to promote the development and implementation of effective measures to tackle the causes of homelessness and to facilitate access to decent and affordable housing.

FEANTSA is in charge of a research structure, the European Observatory on Homelessness, which is composed of a network of national correspondents who collect information concerning homelessness and relevant policy measures in the EU Member States. Each year, the Observatory produces a series of national reports on a specific research theme, and these findings are published in a European report which also presents an analysis of transnational trends. Since 1991, the European Observatory on Homelessness has completed research on the following themes and issues:

- existing sources of information and statistics on homelessness;
- the causes of homelessness and the most vulnerable groups;
- the recognition and implementation of the right to housing;
- the possibilities for low income groups to access decent housing;
- homelessness among young people;
- the emergence of new schemes of services for homelessness people.

Address: FEANTSA 1, rue Defacqz B. 1000 Brussel
Phone: + 32 2 538 66 69
Fax: + 32 2 539 41 74
E-mail: feantsa@compuserve.com

The Interdisciplinary Centre for Comparative Research in the Social Sciences (ICCR)

The Interdisciplinary Centre for Comparative Research in the Social Sciences – International (ICCR) was founded in 1986 with the aim of designing and promoting interdisciplinary and transnational research. The mission and research programme of the ICCR is inspired by Austria's unique geographical position in Central Europe at the crossroads of East and West. Thus, the ICCR is involved in many research projects dealing with East-West relations and the integration processes which are under way in the European Union to meet the challenges of European sociopolitical changes.

In learning from the experiences and mistakes of other international organizations, the ICCR has aimed to establish an international research institute with a concise research programme that relies on a clear comparative methodology, an interdisciplinary academic network and a flexible, albeit disciplined, organizational structure. ICCR research is guided by the conviction that the current societal issues can only be analyzed in a meaningful way in cooperation with other scientific disciplines. Thus, ICCR built an interdisciplinary, academic network. (ICCR is, for example, a founding member of the research network RESER which is located in Milan.)

The ICCR is an independent international non-profit institution which is largely financed by research contracts from various Austrian ministries, governmental bodies, international organizations and other research funds. An international board that meets twice a year decided upon and supervises the interdisciplinary and transnational research programme.

Address: ICCR Hamburgerstraße 14–20, A. 1050 Vienna, Austria.
Phone: +43 1 587 39 73 15
Fax: +44 1 587 39 73 10

Danish National Institute of Social Research (SFI)

The Danish National Institute of Social Research is an independent institution under the Ministry of Social Affairs.

The institute was established in order to conduct and disseminate research on social policy, working life, the social aspects of housing and health conditions and also living conditions amongst the population in general and the family in particular.

The Institute is especially involved in applied research connected with political and administrative decision-making. According to the provisions of the law the Institute may:

- conduct its own research work and undertake research assignments at the request of public authorities and private organisations;
- assist in research projects conducted outside the Institute;
- give advice to public authorities in connection with the preparation and implementation of legislation and in connection with planning.

The Danish National Institute of Social Research was set up by law in 1958 and during the subsequent years independent and impartial applied research has been published based on the Institute's research result.

Address: Danish National Institute of Social Research, Herluf Trollesgade 11, DK – 1050 Copenhagen K
Phone: + 45 33 48 08 00
Fax: + 45 33 48 08 33
E-mail: ikn@sfi.dk

Dipartimento di Scienze del Territorio (DST)

The Dipartimento di Scienze del Territorio (DST), established in 1981 as a department of the Polytechnic of Milan, has worked extensively on the various aspects of urban studies. A focus on the policy and planning relevance of research has been a characterising trait of this work. Members of the DST have carried out research in the field of social welfare and housing policies, with a strong interest in comparative studies. Main focal points of study include urban poverty and housing exclusion, homelessness, housing for immigrants, neighbourhood in crisis. On these subjects the DST cooperates with various local and national government agencies, and is involved in various transnational projects. Since 1992 the DST has published a quarterly journal, *Territorio*.

Address: DST, via Bonardi 3, 20133 Milano, Italy
Phone: + 39 2 23 99 54 17
Fax: + 39 2 23 99 54 35

STAKES

The National Research and Development Centre for Welfare and Health (STAKES) is a unit subordinate to the Ministry of Social Affairs and Health.

Mission: STAKES is committed to safeguarding the future of social welfare and health, to enhancing the health and social well-being of the nation and to promoting social welfare and health services that are of a high quality and cost-effective, for all citizens alike.

Objectives: STAKES aims to be:

- a nationally significant and internationally recognised research establishment engaging in applied research into services in the field of social welfare and health;
- the main centre of innovative development in its field, seeking new modes of operation and helping to construct cooperation networks; and
- a statistical and register authority on social welfare and health providing good, efficient service and developing its knowledge resources together with its clients.

Address: STAKES, Siltqsqarenkatu 18, PO Box 220, 00531 Helsinki, Finland
Phone: + 358 9 396 71
Fax: + 358 9 761 307
E-mail: viestint@stakes.fi

KIVOTOS

Kivotos is a newly-founded (1992), non-profit organisation based in Athens, Greece, which aims at the promotion of scientific thinking and research in key sectors related to the development of contemporary societies. Its objective is achieved through: a) scientific research in key sectors; b) dissemination of ideas and proposals through publications; and c) organisation of relevant actions and policies.

Based on the above, KIVOTOS is chiefly interested in promoting scientific thinking in the following issues:

- urban and regional planning, especially as regards the alleviation of urban poverty and the protection of environment;
- institutional strengthening and institutional efficiency in key sectors of

education, health and family planning;
- social aspects of housing (such as the definition of affordable housing);
- social integration of excluded population groups;
- the characteristics of poverty in the developed and developing countries;
- transformations in the production process and the labour market with specific reference to issues such as industrial relations and the repercussions of affordable modern technologies.

Address: KIVOTOS, Scientific research Institute Ag. Pyrri 9, Athens 11527, Greece
Phone: + 30 17 70 33 57
Fax: + 30 17 71 08 16
E-mail: arsapki@athena.compulint.gr